ANOTHER LIGHT

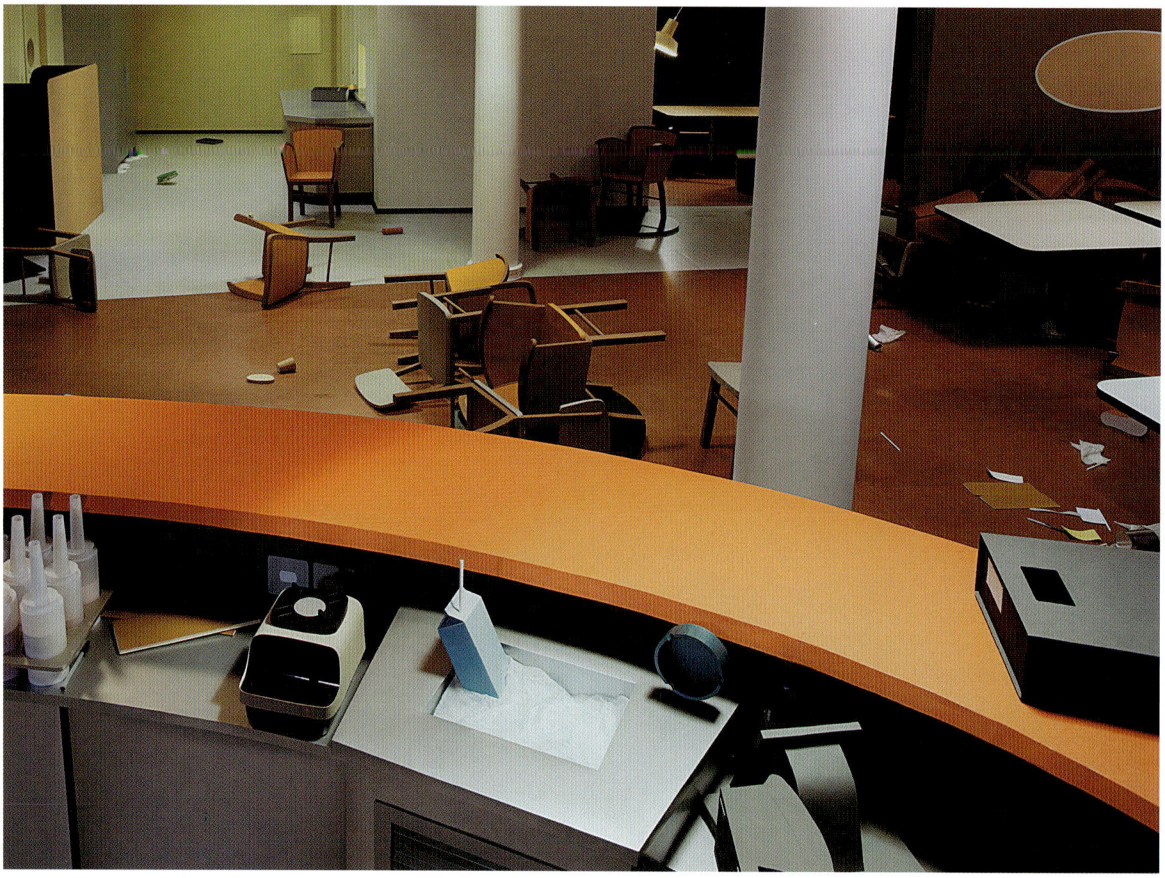

ANOTHER LIGHT

Jacques-Louis David to Thomas Demand

MICHAEL FRIED

YALE UNIVERSITY PRESS

NEW HAVEN AND LONDON

Designed by Gillian Malpass

Printed in China

Library of Congress Cataloging-in-Publication Data
Fried, Michael.
[Essays. Selections]
Another light : Jacques-Louis David to Thomas Demand / Michael Fried.
pages cm
Includes bibliographical references and index.
ISBN 978-0-300-20817-7 (hardback)
1. Art, Modern. I. Title.
N6350.F75 2014
709.03–dc23

2014013142

A catalogue record for this book is available from The British Library

Frontispiece: Thomas Demand, *Pacific Sun*, 2012, Video, 2,02 min, stereo (frame 2071)
Page vi: Gustave Caillebotte, *Paris Street; Rainy Day*, 1877 (detail of fig. 131)

To the memory of Anthony Caro

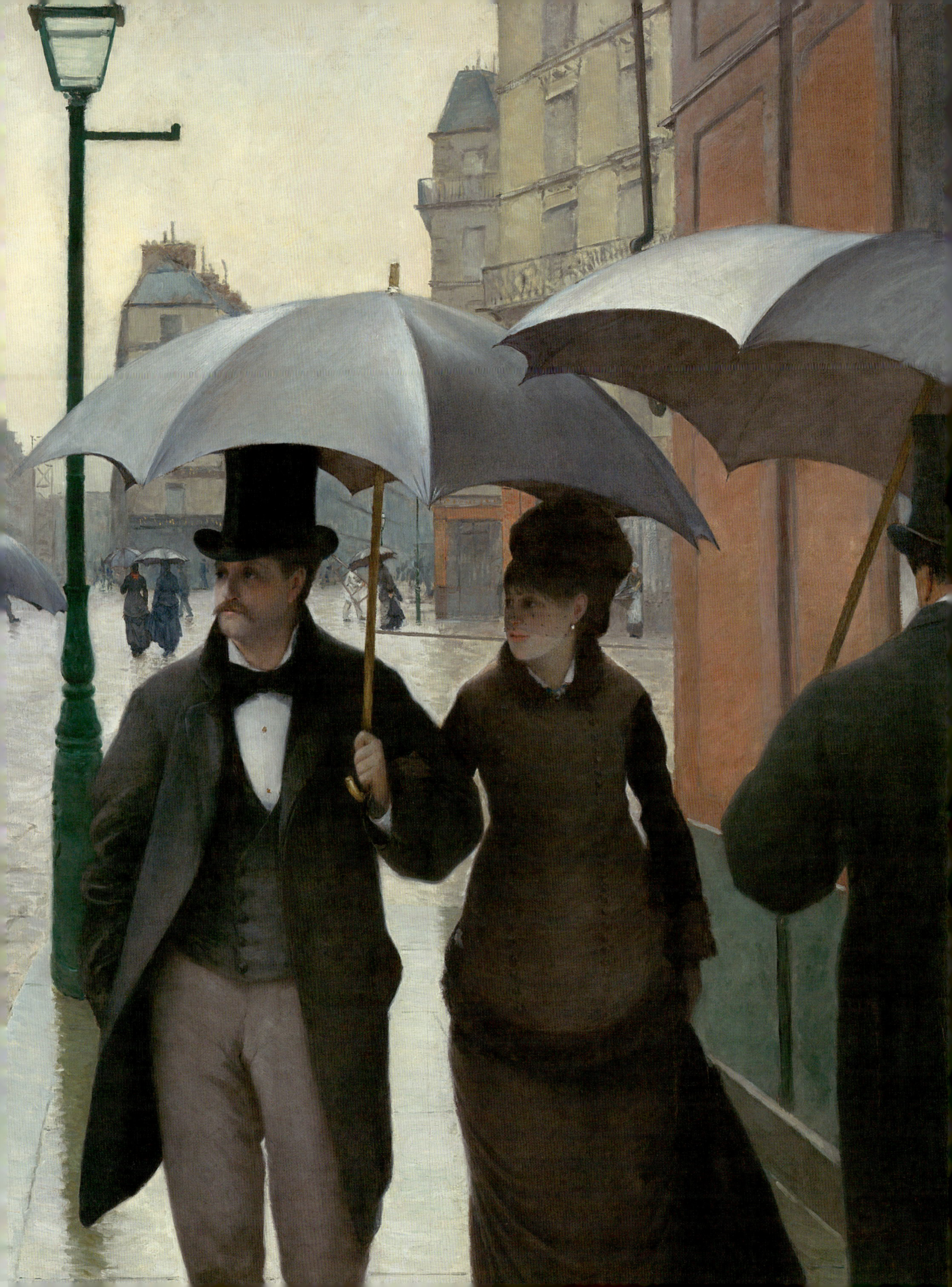

CONTENTS

The light shed by work is a beautiful light, but it only shines with real beauty if it is illuminated by yet another light.

Ludwig Wittgenstein*

* Ludwig Wittgenstein, *Culture and Value*, ed. G.H. von Wright in collaboration with Heikki Nyman, rev. ed. by Alois Pichler, trans. Peter Winch (Malden, Mass., and Oxford, 1998), p. 30e.

ACKNOWLEDGMENTS

Most of the material that usually goes into the preface of a book of this sort (circumstances of writing, first publication, and such) will be dealt with in the Introduction, which means that I have mainly to thank various friends and colleagues for their comments and support during the period when the last few essays – those on late David, Géricault, and Friedrich – were written or revised and the collection as a whole was put together. They include Jennifer Ashton, Stephen Bann, Jean-Pierre Criqui, Marc Gotlieb, Joseph Marioni, Jeremy Melius, Walter Benn Michaels, Robert Pippin, Ralph Ubl, Molly Warnock, David Wellbery, and of course my wife, Ruth Leys. I should mention also Douglas Gordon and Thomas Demand and their assistants, who were consistently helpful answering questions and providing DVDs that allowed me to watch their brilliant films *k.364: A Journey by Train* and *Pacific Sun* respectively (transmogrified to fit my computer screen) as often as I wished. My thanks, too, to Gillian Malpass, whose determination to make every book she edits as beautiful as it can be has won her the gratitude of a host of authors, myself among them.

This book is dedicated to the memory of a great sculptor and close friend, Anthony Caro.

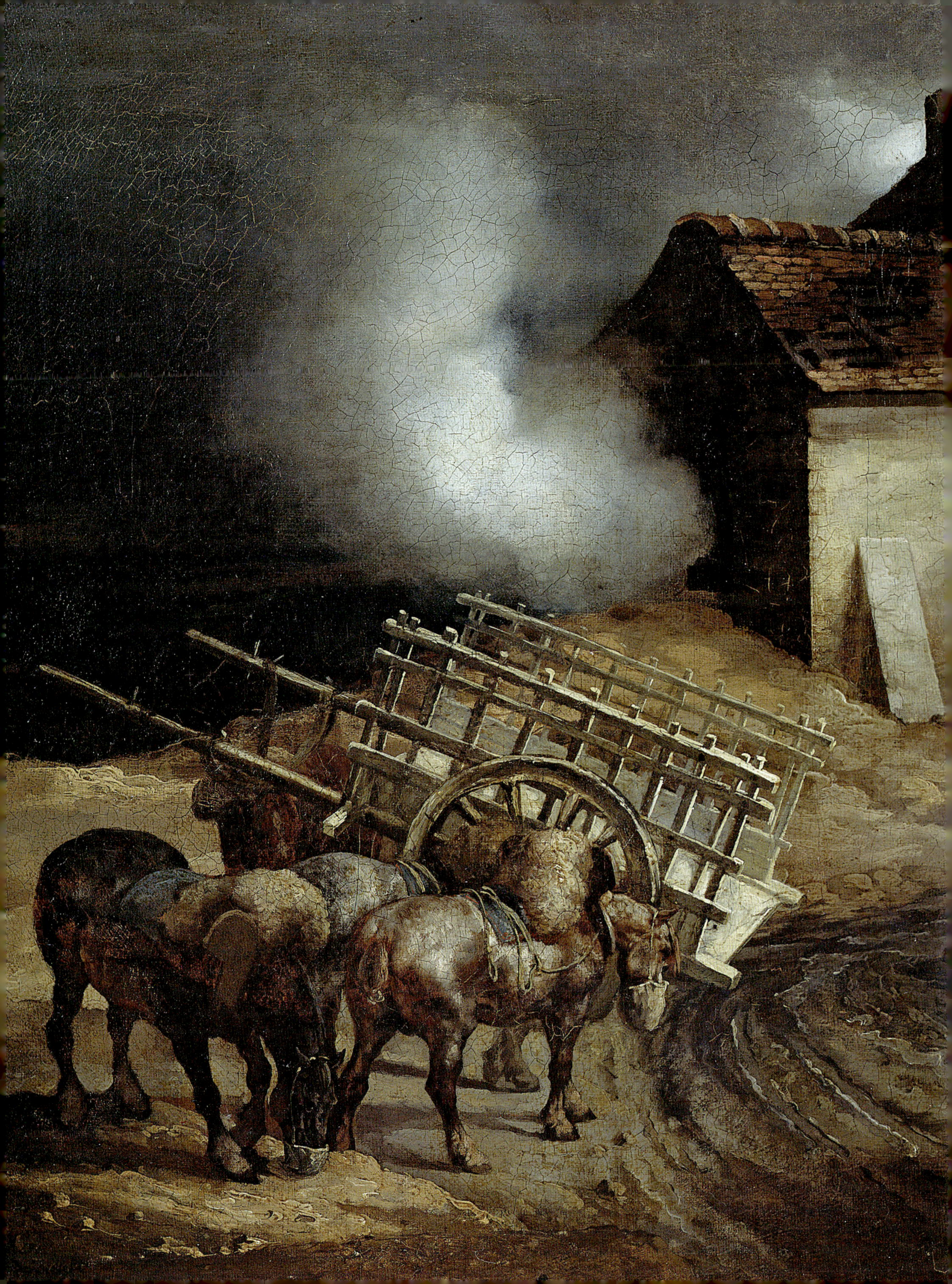

INTRODUCTION

The essays in this book were written at different times and with different ends in view. There will therefore be moments of repetition between essays, which I have muted wherever possible but by no means eliminated; in particular Géricault's strategy vis-à-vis the beholder in the *Raft of the Medusa* and *Entrance to the Adelphi Wharf* is also touched on in the essay on Friedrich, and Courbet's project of hyperbolic "merging" is summarized in both the Friedrich and Caillebotte essays. On this score I ask for the reader's tolerance.

"Caillebotte's Impressionism" first appeared in the journal *Representations* in 1999;[1] it was an attempt to come to terms with the achievement of an artist I had until then found difficult to appreciate, much less understand. "Roger Fry's 'Formalism'" belongs to the series of annual Tanner Lectures on Human Values and was delivered at the University of Michigan at the invitation of the Department of Philosophy on November 2, 2001;[2] throughout my teaching career I had often assigned writings by Fry in undergraduate and graduate seminars, and from early on had been struck by the combination in his books and essays of great critical sensitivity with, at crucial junctures, a kind of intellectual bafflement. "Roger Fry's 'Formalism'" is an attempt to make sense of that state of affairs.

"David/Manet: The 'Anacreonic' Paintings" and "Géricault's Romanticism" have more complicated origins. Both make use of (less euphemistically: cannibalize) whole paragraphs from "Approaching Courbet," the first chapter of my book *Courbet's Realism* (1990); in addition "David/Manet: The 'Anacreonic' Paintings" recycles portions of another essay, "David's Antitheatricality," which appeared in French translation in the two-volume compilation of papers delivered in the course of a memorable symposium on David that was held at the Louvre in 1989,[3] and "Géricault's Romanticism" makes similar use of an essay of the same title that was written for a Louvre symposium on that artist two years later.[4] (Both symposia were organized by the

1 *(facing page)* Théodore Géricault, *The Lime Kiln* (detail of fig. 73).

formidable Régis Michel, curator in the Cabinet des Dessins at the Louvre, to whom I remain grateful for the invitations to take part.) Behind both essays, too, lies my first stab at this material, the article "Thomas Couture and the Theatricalization of Action in Nineteenth-Century French Painting," which appeared in *Artforum* in 1970.[5] However, I always wanted to engage at greater length both with the later David and with Géricault than was possible in those lectures/essays, and at a certain moment – summer 2013 – I saw that if I sat down and did that I could put the resulting texts in a single book along with the essays on Caillebotte, Fry, and certain contemporary artists by way of illustrating the extraordinary persistence down to the present moment of the antitheatrical values first brilliantly theorized by Diderot in his writings on painting and drama of the mid-1750s and 1760s – values, as I have explained elsewhere, subsequently reformulated by me, without awareness of their provenance, in "Art and Objecthood" (1967) and other essays of around that time.[6] (I have also included a shorter essay on David not bearing directly on these matters, "David/Marat: The *Self-Portrait* of 1794," which I wrote for inclusion in the collective volume *David after David: Essays on the Later Work*, based on a symposium held at the Sterling and Francine Clark Art Institute in 2005.[7])

Both essays on contemporary figures were written in connection with exhibitions. "Douglas Gordon's *k.364: A Journey by Train*" was published in the catalogue for his exhibition at the Museum Moderne Kunst (MMK) in Frankfurt am Main in 2011,[8] and "Thomas Demand's *Pacific Sun*" in *Animations*, the catalogue of an exhibition of his films at the Des Moines Art Center and the DHC/ART gallery in Montreal in 2012.[9] In that sense the present volume extends the project of my books *Why Photography Matters as Art as Never Before* (2008) and *Four Honest Outlaws: Sala, Ray, Marioni, Gordon* (2011), in both of which I seek to show the relevance of antitheatrical issues and concerns across a wide range of recent art – not only photography but also video, sculpture, painting, and feature-length film (as in Douglas Gordon and Philippe Parreno's *Zidane: A Twenty-First Century Portrait*).

The most recent of the essays in this volume, that on the early nineteenth-century German painter Caspar David Friedrich, was composed as a lecture for a May 2013 symposium in Berlin entitled "Synergies" on the theme of Franco-German cultural relations in the nineteenth and twentieth centuries.[10] In that essay I suggest that an illuminating approach to Friedrich's art is provided by Immanuel Kant's 1786 essay "What does it mean to orient oneself in thinking?", and indeed that the famous *Rückenfigur*, or figure seen from the rear, in Friedrich's landscapes should be thought of not as a "beholder" in the Diderotian sense of the term but more as a "cognizer" as Kant would have understood the notion. I am happy with the result, though I should add that one further reason for including that essay in the present book is that it drives home the basic truth, routinely ignored by my critics, that despite my longstanding involvement with the Diderotian tradition and its aftermath, I have never believed that absorption and antitheatricality were the entire story during the late eighteenth and nineteenth centuries. (My books on Thomas Eakins and Adolph Menzel have long been there to prove the point, of course.[11])

It is not my intention to go on at length in this introduction, but one general point is worth emphasizing at the outset, and that is the concern in all these essays except the ones on David's *Self-Portrait* and Friedrich's landscapes with various crises, for so I take them to be, in the dialectical unfolding of the antitheatrical current or tradition. If we take that current or tradition as arising around the middle of the eighteenth century in France, and as receiving its first truly and, in effect, irreversibly paradigmatic pictorial statements in David's great history paintings of the 1780s – the *Belisarius Receiving Alms* (1781), *Oath of the Horatii* (1785), *Death of Socrates* (1787), and *Lictors Returning to Brutus the Bodies of His Sons* (1789) – it is striking, to say the least, that by the second half of the 1790s, when he conceived and executed the *Intervention of the Sabine Women* (exhibited 1799), that the intensely dramatic (in Diderot's sense of the term) values and effects of the earlier paintings were in some fundamental sense foreclosed to him, a state of affairs that seems only to have intensified, become more nearly unnegotiable, in the years that followed. Indeed, my focus in "David / Manet" (as the full title of the essay makes clear) is on his later, so-called "Anacreonic" paintings, in which at least one figure in every canvas faces and in effect addresses the beholder, a resolutely un- (even anti-) Diderotian manner of proceeding which nevertheless testifies to the continued pertinence of Diderotian norms as a grounding for his art. Another point I stress is the surprising resemblance between the role of facing strategies in the "Anacreonic" pictures and what takes place in Edouard Manet's epochal canvases of the early 1860s, notably the *Old Musician* (1862), *Déjeuner sur l'herbe* (1863), and *Olympia* (painted 1863, exhibited 1865), in which a radical facingness marks precisely the liquidation, though not quite the end, of the Diderotian problematic, at least in its classic form. This raises the question, which I try to address, as to why in David's case the strategy in question had zero consequences for subsequent art whereas in Manet's, in concert with other features of his work, it led to a profound rerouting of modern painting.

In "Géricault's Romanticism," I go on to consider the response of that extravagantly gifted and, I believe, profoundly antitheatrical artist to the same basic predicament, one I see as literally determining the basic parameters of his ultimately frustrated albeit marvelously resourceful and at times stupendous achievement, or perhaps I should say as determining the parameters *against which* his titanic efforts in painting, drawing, lithography, and even sculpture continually thrust themselves (I am aware of my somewhat over-the-top language in the foregoing, but if ever a modern artist merited such abandon it is Géricault, in my opinion). His romanticism, I go on to claim, consists above all in that contestation with his circumstances. The essay closes with a brief discussion of an early story by Honoré de Balzac, who I suggest may productively be thought of as continuing the Diderotian emphasis on drama and expression in another art form, prose fiction, in regard to which the issue of theatricality had an altogether different valence, and in which a certain "worldhood" that had been banished from painting could be reconstructed in other terms.

Gustave Caillebotte is another sort of figure, a painter of limited though far from insignificant gifts, whose project, I try to show, was explicitly to situate his art in relation to three distinct predecessor terms – Courbet, Manet, and the "core" Impressionists around Monet – a project that one might have thought would be doomed to failure or at any rate incoherence – how to bring together and go on from such disparate sources? – but which in the event, for a short span of years, proved extremely fecund. In particular Caillebotte succeeded in revivifying absorptive themes and motifs which Manet, one might have thought, had eliminated from the advanced painter's repertoire, if not for good at any rate for the foreseeable future, a feat that I take to suggest that the crises, more broadly the dialectic, of painting and beholder that I have been tracing for a long time now was sometimes less implacable, less all-or-nothing in its consequences than my various accounts of it might seem to imply. And in fact absorption in one form or another continued to play a role in advanced painting in France, as Todd Cronan's recent *Against Affective Formalism: Matisse, Bergson, Modernism* (2014) persuasively demonstrates.[12] (But Manet's intervention was nevertheless sufficiently decisive to make it impossible for Monet in the later 1860s to go on devising ambitious figure paintings, a claim I adumbrate in "David/Manet.") It is also true that Caillebotte's overall achievement is less than major, and that there may be a correlation between that fact and the considerable success, while it lasted, of his historically self-aware endeavor – but of course the same cannot be said of Matisse, the focus of Cronan's analyses.

As for Roger Fry, the most important English-language art critic of the first part of the twentieth century, almost everything he wrote shows plainly that he was an antitheatrical critic without knowing it (this was also true, I suggest in *Why Photography Matters*, of Roland Barthes), which is also to say that Fry was periodically led to draw a hard and fast distinction between everything to do with subject matter, literature, or illustration, crucially including considerations of drama, and what he called "form" – basically the relations among colored shapes both on the surface of the canvas and in relatively shallow illusionistic depth. Simply put, Fry's default position was that only such relations counted in the experience of art as art, which meant that he was continually led to seek to rule out – in effect to subtract – every other sort of consideration from his explanations to himself and others of why (for example) Giotto's frescoes in the Arena Chapel or one or another canvas by Cézanne, for Fry the greatest of moderns, were as supreme as art as they seemed incontestably to be. A related theme is the notion that criticism was not yet in possession of sufficiently fine-grained perceptual and intellectual procedures to actually accomplish the differentiation between drama (more broadly, subject matter) and form that he was convinced was fundamental. And still another strain is the constantly renewed impulse to absolve the artists he admired not only of the least desire to make an impression on an audience – which could only have disastrous consequences for their art – but also of the very consciousness that they were making artifacts destined to be beheld – an idea that reaches an extreme in his claim that Rembrandt's portrait of his son, Titus, is the magnificent painting that it is because the painter lost himself in contemplation of the young man (and indeed the latter's desk) rather than giving any thought to the canvas under his brush. In other words, Fry's unacknowledged antitheatricalism – part and parcel of his "formalism" – led him into quandaries he could not resolve without introducing obvious absurdities (not obvious to him, however).

More broadly, Fry's "formalist" valorization of unity was itself an antitheatrical ideal, implying a perfect closure of the work upon itself rather than to the least degree an appeal to the beholder – though of course such a conception of unity, like the notion that a great artist takes no thought for any subsequent viewership or indeed for the very work of his hands, positively implies a particular relation to the beholder, who is imagined as intuiting that the work has not been made with him or her in view (a structural contradiction, in other words). Put slightly differently, a strictly "formalist" mind-set such as Fry's inevitably undergoes its own sort of intellectual crisis, as its refusal to take subject matter seriously threatens to leave it helpless in the face of the art it most admires (as happened with Fry vis-à-vis Giotto, and with Clement Greenberg vis-à-vis representational painting generally[13]), just as its insistence that a work of art not address the viewer in any way is simply unsustainable once one thinks rigorously about the implications of such a claim. In contrast, Diderot understood with perfect lucidity that what he was arguing for was a particular set of artistic strategies rather than the accomplishment of a metaphysical impossibility: *of course* paintings, like stage dramas, were intended to be beheld – but they were not to appear to be so, in certain specific ways. Indeed, it was only by mobilizing those strategies that the painter or dramaturge could succeed in holding and moving the viewer, which was the purpose of the operation from start to finish. (The same general point holds for "Art and Objecthood," I need hardly add.) Put another way, Diderot was never tempted to *radicalize* the demand for antitheatricality, in the way for example Kant comes close to doing in the *Critique of Judgment*, where the need to suppress all signs and sense of the intentional is held to be constitutive of the judgment of the beautiful itself.[14]

The essays on Gordon's *k.364* and Demand's *Pacific Sun* have a different tenor, keyed to the artists' respective commitments to antitheatrical values and ideals in the wake of – forty-five years after – the Minimalist/Literalist intervention that ostensibly put an end to the high modernist aesthetic associated with (for example) Color Field painting and the sculpture of Anthony Caro, both championed by me in "Art and Objecthood." In that sense, Minimalism/Literalism, possibly abetted by "Art and Objecthood," which analysed the terms of the opposition with a starkness that has plausibly been seen as further precipitating the almost universal turn toward what soon came to be called Post-Modernism, instigated a late-term crisis within the antitheatrical tradition that for a long time appeared to many, including me, to be definitive. My aim in *Why Photography Matters* and *Four Honest Outlaws* was in part to demonstrate that that has turned out not to be the case (hence both books' air of triumph, or at least of palpable relief) – that on the contrary starting around 1980 and gathering force after 1990 the best and most significant "visual" art, spearheaded by the work of large-format photographers such as Jeff Wall, Jean-Marc Bustamante, Thomas Ruff, Thomas Struth, Andreas Gursky, Luc Delahaye, and Demand himself, has marked, not a return to high modernism as such (what might that mean?) but rather a reassertion, under new conditions, of values and concerns that were at its heart – values and concerns that themselves go back, dialectically, to the moment of Diderot, which was also the moment of Chardin, Greuze, Fragonard, David . . . Viewed in that perspective, *k.364* and *Pacific Sun* are also post-crisis works, which is to say that they offer further evidence of the (to me, still) surprising resilience of the stream of high-level artistic production that first sprang forth in Paris more than 250 years ago.[15]

• 1 •

DAVID / MANET: THE "ANACREONIC" PAINTINGS

I

It is now more than thirty years since the publication of my book *Absorption and Theatricality: Painting and Beholder in the Age of Diderot*, and I am going to proceed in this essay (and the ones that follow) on the assumption that a sizable portion of my readership will be familiar with the basic claim put forward in that book and in subsequent ones on Courbet and Manet – namely, that in the course of the 1750s and 1760s in France there emerged a new, *antitheatrical* conception of the art of painting. The crucial figure in the formulating of that conception was, as the title of the book suggests, Denis Diderot, both in his *Salons* and other writings on painting and in his early texts on the theory of the stage, the *Entretiens sur le Fils naturel* (1757) and *Discours sur la poésie dramatique* (1758). But the conception can also be discerned in the writings of other eighteenth-century critics, and it plays out importantly – this is what really matters – in the work of a number of significant artists from Jean-Baptiste-Siméon Chardin to Carle Van Loo, Joseph Vernet, Joseph-Marie Vien, Jean-Baptiste Greuze, Jean-Honoré Fragonard, and, the decisive figure for the establishment of modern painting in France, Jacques-Louis David. (And beyond David, in the work of artists such as Géricault, Daumier, Courbet, and, dialectically, Manet, and beyond Manet, in the art of Gustave Caillebotte, like Géricault the subject of an essay further on in this book – indeed I have argued in recent books and essays on contemporary art and photography that the issue remains alive to the present day. The essays on films by Douglas Gordon and Thomas Demand also gathered here will make that case in some detail. I shall also show its operation, so to speak behind the scenes, in Roger Fry's art criticism.) The basic idea – to remind those who already know this but also to inform those who might not – is that starting just after the middle of the eighteenth century the painter began to be called on to depict personages who would appear to the beholder to be totally engaged or (a key term in what follows) *absorbed* in what they are ostensibly doing, feeling, and thinking; only if that was the case would the beholder find himself or herself stopped and transfixed before the picture, a condition that itself emerged during these years as the sine qua non of a successful painting. By the same token, the least hint in the treatment of the personages that one or more of them were less than wholly absorbed – that instead of appearing completely caught up in what they were doing they appeared to be acting or behaving so as to make a particular impression on their audience – and both the personages and the painting as a whole would be judged *théâtral*, theatrical, the very worst of faults according to the new aesthetic. More broadly, what the rise of that aesthetic indicates is that starting shortly after the middle of the eighteenth century in France (and for the time being, only there) the very existence of the beholder – more precisely, what I have called the primordial convention that paintings (to stick with them) are made to be beheld – emerged for the first time as a fundamental problem for the art as such (I mean for its continuation at the very highest level).* Only if the presence of the beholder before the canvas could be neutralized or negated by one means or another, principally by the depiction of figures who appeared oblivious to anything but the object of their absorption, was distinguished achievement feasible.[1] And the alternative to such achievement, work that seemed theatrical, was scarcely worth consideration. (We might say that a new sort of gulf between successful and unsuccessful art opened up around this time.)

In the last pages of *Absorption and Theatricality*, I subject Jacques-Louis David's first major painting, *Belisarius Receiving Alms* (1781; fig. 2), to an extended analysis, in the course of which I try to show that various features of that work – Belisarius's blindness, the placement of the soldier gesturing in surprise, and above all the curious organization of the picture's architecture and overall composition combine to suggest a deliberate effort on the part of the painter to bring about a kind of double displacement of the beholder away from the figure of Belisarius.[2] By my reference to the picture's organization I refer, first, to its almost exaggeratedly off-center perspective structure, which I read as seeking to position the beholder over toward the painting's left-hand edge, almost directly in front of the figure of the soldier and as far as possible from that of Belisarius. (The unpersuasiveness of the ground plane as it recedes toward the vanishing point – its tendency for the leftmost rows of flagstones to appear vertical rather than horizontal – is a mark of the strain it is under to bring about this unusual

* The French word for "beholder," of course, is *spectateur*, which to my ear is translated only imperfectly by the English "spectator." In standard usage the latter connotes witnessing an event rather than the subtly different – the more narrowly focused – activity of taking in a painting.

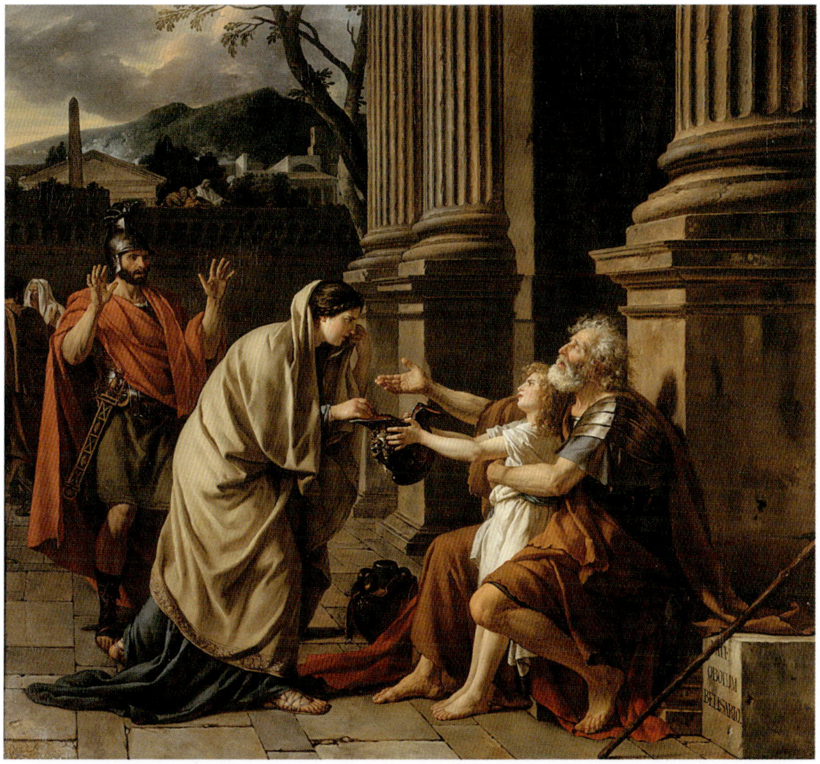

2 (*left*) Jacques-Louis David, *Belisarius Receiving Alms*, 1781. Oil on canvas. 288 × 312 cm. Lille, Palais des Beaux-Arts.

3 (*below*) Jacques-Louis David, *The Death of Socrates*, 1787. Oil on canvas. 129.5 × 196.2 cm. New York, The Metropolitan Museum of Art, Catharine Lorillard Wolfe Collecion, Wolfe Fund, 1931 (31.45).

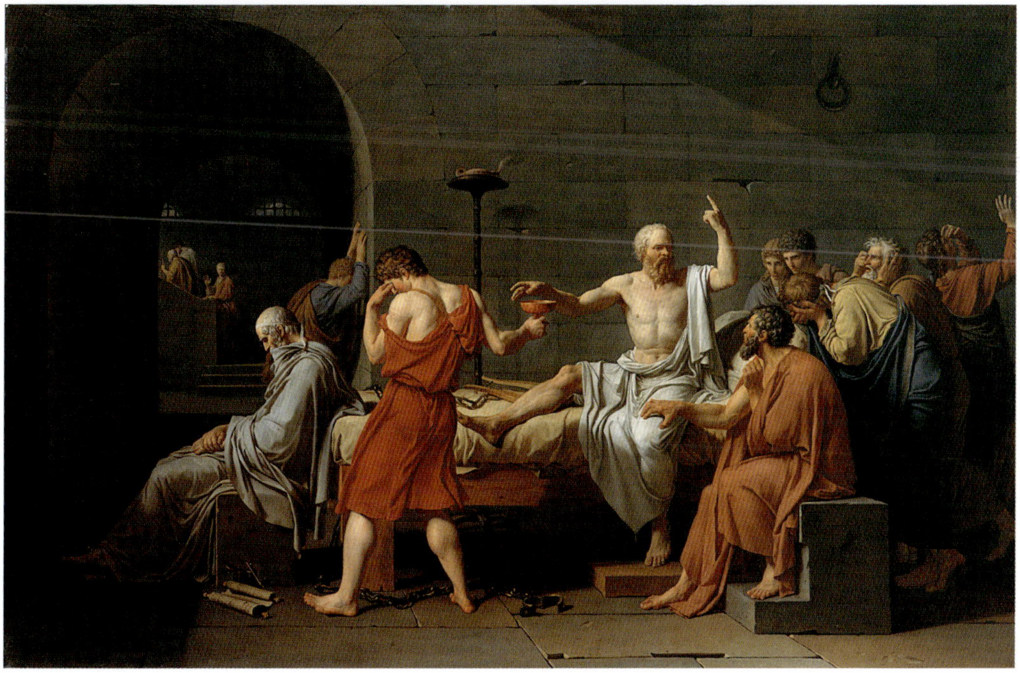

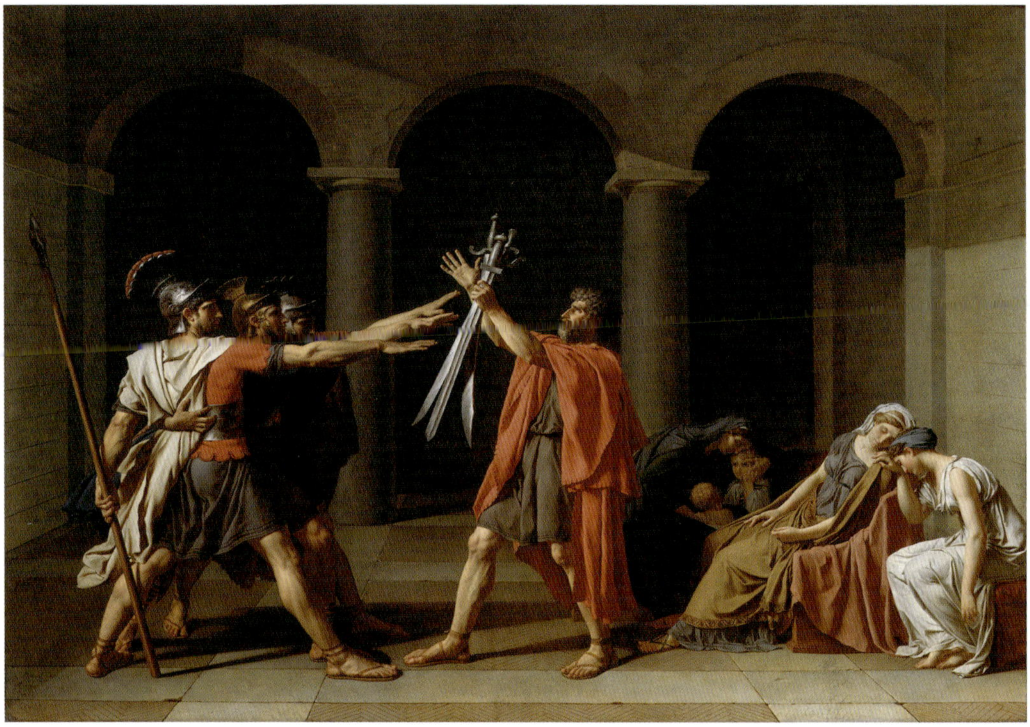

4 Jacques-Louis David, *The Oath of the Horatii*, 1784. Oil on canvas. 330 × 425 cm. Paris, Musée du Louvre.

state of affairs.[3] A comparable structure is at work far more "naturally" in the subsequent *Death of Socrates* [1787; fig. 3], the beholder being imagined in front of and looking down the strongly perspectival tunnel toward the left of the composition, at the end of which grieving visitors slowly climb a flight of stairs leading out of the prison. Indeed the third of those figures turns and gestures in farewell toward someone at the mouth of the tunnel, an action that on the one hand appears to violate the Diderotian injunction to ignore the beholder but on the other underscores the latter's separateness from the integrated group of disciples around Socrates.) And second, to the establishing in the *Belisarius* of a second plane of representation, defined by the direction in which the blind hero faces, by the main face of the arch of triumph against the base of which he sits and, most strikingly, by the plane of the masonry block on which is inscribed the traditional motto, "Date Obolum Belisario." That is, David seems to have explored the possibility of rotating the frontal plane of the representation 90 degrees clockwise along the axis of its right-hand edge, in order to isolate within his painting a

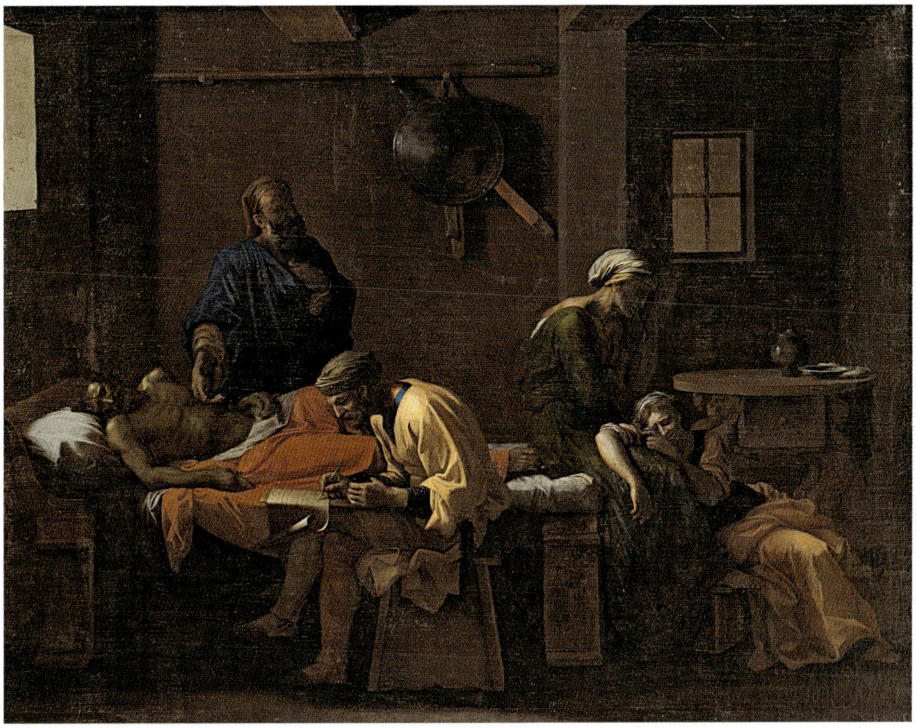

5 Nicolas Poussin, *The Testament of Eudamidas*, 1644–8. Oil on canvas. 110.5 × 138.5 cm. Copenhagen, Statens Museum for Kunst.

second, more essential *tableau*, consisting of Belisarius and his young guide, placed at right angles to the first and therefore not directly exposed to the actual beholder's gaze. Both strategies, the implied positioning of the beholder away from Belisarius and the implied rotation of the second *tableau* away from the beholder, imagine the latter to be a source of cognitive and ontological disturbance, one that must be neutralized, almost literally put out of view, if the painting is to succeed.[4]

David's next ambitious history painting, the electrifying *Oath of the Horatii* (1784; fig. 4), has been the focus of considerable discussion during the past thirty-odd years. Much of that discussion has concerned the issue of pictorial unity; specifically, it has been suggested that David sought in that canvas to challenge prevailing conceptions of unity, if not to call into question the value of pictorial unity as such. So for example Norman Bryson has described what he takes to be David's "assault on unity"[5] and Thomas Crow has argued that the very qualities of the *Horatii* that previous art historians had viewed as epitomizing its "perfect fusion of form and content" (Hugh

Honour's phrase, and now this is Crow) "exist to sustain and validate the more immediate message of discord and provocation."[6] In fact, the response of contemporary *salonniers* confirms that the *Horatii* was seen as challenging established ideas about how paintings ought to hold together. But I want to insist on the extent to which its most radical compositional feature, the stark division between the principal group of the elder Horatius and his sons swearing their oath and the secondary group of the swooning, grieving women, is based on a similar separation of male and female groups in Nicolas Poussin's *Testament of Eudamidas* (1644–8; fig. 5) – a work that Diderot particularly admired, not least as a paradigm of absorption, therefore of antitheatricality. Indeed the *Eudamidas*'s division into separate groups was viewed by Diderot as powerfully expressive of the obliviousness of the members of the two groups to everything but their own thoughts and feelings (he remarks more than once on how deeply moving he finds the figure of the grieving woman who sits with her back turned toward the dying man), while the consistency of the emotional tonality *across* that division doubtless contributed to the overall unity of effect that made the *Eudamidas* for him the very paradigm of both a stage and a pictorial *tableau*. (The key text here is his proposed pantomime of the Death of Socrates in the *Discours sur la poésie dramatique*, which I am not alone in regarding as a source for David's *Death of Socrates*.[7] In both the *Discours* and its predecessor treatise, the *Entretiens sur le fils naturel*, the *tableau* is theorized as an absorptive device or *dispositif*, operating outside the imagined consciousnesses of the dramatis personae, in contrast to the *coup de théâtre*, of which they are all aware.) I suggest that David sought in the *Horatii* to achieve a comparable thematization of absorption and unity of effect, and that his shift especially in the principal group to a far more vibrantly dramatic expressive register – from absorption in taking a dying man's pulse and transcribing his last will and testament to passionate engagement in swearing a mortal oath to fight and, if necessary, die for Rome – made the division between the groups even more salient and contrasting than in the *Eudamidas*.[8] A larger historical point is that whereas the presence of the beholder simply was not an issue for Poussin – as was noted in the Introduction, the beholder emerged as a problem for painting only in the course of the 1750s and 1760s – I take David's commitment in the *Horatii* to an exacerbated mode of pictorial drama and to a heightened, because more schematic or indeed diagrammatic, mode of compositional unity to have been essentially antitheatrical in intent.

Experience has taught me that my insistence on antitheatricality as a structure of artistic intention or, on the part of the critic, of demand and expectation rather than as a quality or effect inhering or failing to inhere (timelessly, as it were) in certain pictures is difficult to grasp, but it will, I hope, become more intelligible if we turn to a some-

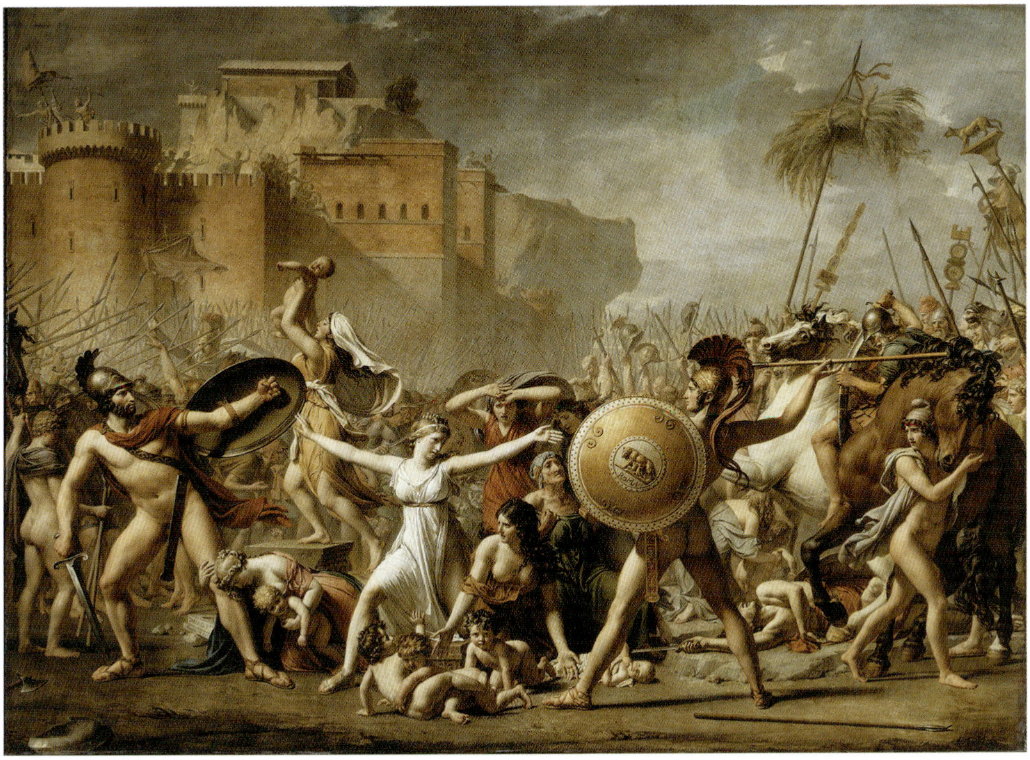

6 Jacques-Louis David, *The Intervention of the Sabine Women*, completed 1799. Oil on canvas. 385 × 522 cm. Paris, Musée du Louvre.

what later moment in David's career. The moment is the second half of the 1790s, at which time David was working on *The Intervention of the Sabine Women* in the Louvre (completed 1799; fig. 6). We know from the testimony of Etienne-Jean Delécluze, who was at that time a student in David's atelier and who later became a leading art critic, that while working on the *Sabines* David himself characterized the composition of the *Horatii* as theatrical in a pejorative sense.[9] What David seems to have meant by this was that the unprecedented dramatic intensity that made the *Horatii* so electrifying at the Salon of 1785 had come to strike him (more than ten years later) as excessive and exaggerated, which is to say as too deliberately aiming to impress. And in fact the *Sabines* marks a clear and deliberate withdrawal from the values and effects of pictorial drama as these had been brought to a new pitch of expressiveness in David's history paintings of the 1780s. In particular David plainly found it necessary to eschew the compositional strategy basic to the earlier pictures, the evocation of a single, highly specific moment of tension or crisis (a strategy that reaches its zenith and perhaps its breaking point in the *Brutus*), in favor of a less actively temporal mode of representation that might be said to depict a moment of a sort but one that has been dilated, expanded, almost to the point of no longer serving to advance the action and within which the actors themselves have been made to relax, to suspend their efforts, in a general détente. The de-dramatization of action is most apparent in the sleek-limbed figure of Romulus poised to throw his spear, but it is also at work in the crowding of the pictorial field with innumerable personages at different distances from the viewer, as well as in the atmospheric perspective that gives the painting as a whole an almost silvery tone, and it is all but made explicit in a small *livret* issued to accompany the public exhibition of the *Sabines* in 1799. There David provided a speech of more than 170 words for Hersilia, Romulus's wife, whom the painting depicts intervening between her husband and Tatius, the chief of the Sabines, to prevent further bloodshed. The effect of painting and text together might be compared to the arresting of action brought about by an aria in an opera.[10]

Now it may seem as if, for this very reason, the *Sabines* is finally more theatrical than the *Horatii*, and indeed just over ten years after its exhibition in 1799 the *Sabines* was strongly criticized by Guizot, as later by Stendhal, for its reliance on figures holding static gestures taken from the stage (the "imitation of Talma," the famous actor, was how Stendhal put it in 1824).[11] Modern commentators, among them Bryson, have essentially confirmed such a view: in the *Sabines*, Bryson writes, the "explicit surrender of the image to an audience . . . signals a regression to such outward-turning theatrical pictures as [David's earlier] *The Death of Seneca*."[12] But David's criticism of the *Horatii* reported by Delécluze suggests that the dramaturgical and stylistic innovations of the *Sabines* were largely antitheatrical in intent, as difficult as that may be to reconcile with the painting's apparent emphasis on self-display. Put slightly differently, it is as though for David in the second half of the 1790s the depiction of what would shortly come to be viewed as figures not so much acting as *posing* offered the only seemingly viable alternative to the inherent excessiveness of the dramatic. (In other words, there was no "explicit surrender" of the sort Bryson ahistorically imagines.[13])

David's withdrawal from dramatic values and effects, and in a sense from action and expression as such, is carried still further in his next and last ambitious history painting, the *Leonidas at Thermopylae* (begun ca. 1800 but not finished until 1814; fig. 7), in which the principal action, that of Leonidas seated sword in hand at the center of the composition, is explicitly atemporal and antidramatic – a purely inward act of meditation, consecration, prayer – while the numerous figures of Spartans readying themselves for the unequal combat to come are, I want to say, simply not meant to be persuasive as dramatic actors. Nor, however, does the notion of posing exactly fit the

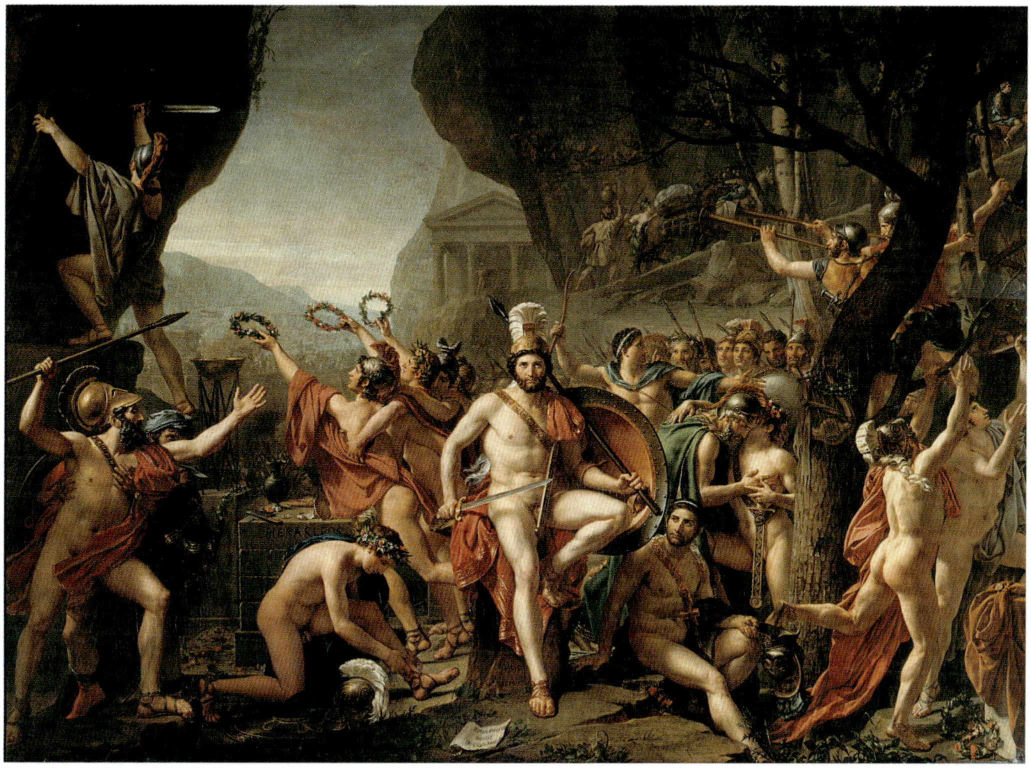

7 Jacques-Louis David, *Leonidas at Thermopylae*, completed 1814. Oil on canvas. 395 × 531 cm. Paris, Musée du Louvre.

case; rather, they are necessary to the subject even as their presence in the painting might fairly be described as nominal or notional, as if they belong to a subtly different pictorial regime, one that seeks to escape the harsh terms of the Diderotian either/or, dramatic or theatrical, by virtue of a certain "unreality."[14] Again, Delécluze's witness is invaluable. He quotes David as saying:

> I want to paint a general and his soldiers preparing for combat like true Spartans, knowing that they will not survive; some absolutely calm, others braiding flowers to attend "the banquet that they will hold in Hades" . . . I want to try to put aside those movements, those theatrical expressions, which the moderns call "painting of expression" . . . But it will be hard to establish such ideas in our time. Everyone loves *coups de théâtre*, and when one doesn't paint the violent passions, when one doesn't push expression in painting to the point of *grimace*, one risks being neither understood nor admired.[15]

David's repudiation, in terms derived from Diderot, of the taste for pictorial drama that his own painting of the 1780s had done much to promote could not be more emphatic.

All this suggests that in the course of thirty years the project of seeking to defeat the theatrical had changed its nature profoundly. The *Horatii*, the *Socrates*, and the *Brutus*, I have claimed, were quickly and widely accepted as exemplary works of major ambition largely on the strength of being seen as representing with unequalled persuasiveness personages wholly absorbed in a moment of tension or crisis in the unfolding of a heroic, tragic action. Within less than a decade, however, David moved in the *Sabines* to a far less urgently dramatic mise-en-scène, one to which the notion of absorption can scarcely be applied. (No wonder it soon came to seem an epitome of theatricality via the pose.) And by the time he came to conceive and paint the *Leonidas* he seems to have found himself compelled, throughout most of that teeming composition, to forego all but the most notional or superficial representation of action and expression, and to concentrate instead on depicting, in the figure of the Spartan general, an inward state – the term absorption once again seems appropriate – but a state that David himself described in terms so unworldly as to call into question the very possibility of its outward manifestation.[16] We see in these developments a progressive loss of conviction in action and expression as vehicles of absorption and antitheatricality and therefore as resources for ambitious painting as Diderot had theorized it. Put another way, David's history paintings from the *Belisarius* through the *Leonidas* chart the trajectory of an ever deepening pictorial and ontological crisis, certain ramifications of which I now want to discuss in some detail.

2

First, though, it is necessary to say something about another of David's projects of the early 1790s, the never completed *Tennis Court Oath*, and in particular about the large drawing in the Louvre Cabinet des Dessins in which David exploited the action of swearing an oath in order to involve a large number of figures (more than 600 deputies took part in the actual event) in a highly dramatic and, he hoped, strongly unified composition (1791; fig. 8). Philippe Bordes, in his richly informative study of that project, rightly emphasizes the importance of the fact that the central figure of Jean-Sylvain Bailly reading the oath to the assembled deputies directly faces the beholder. He writes:

> Bailly's frontality, which transfixes the beholder, is one of those *coups de théâtre* decried by Diderot; the latter maintained that illusion and persuasion could only be attained, by the actor as by the painter, in and by negating the presence of the

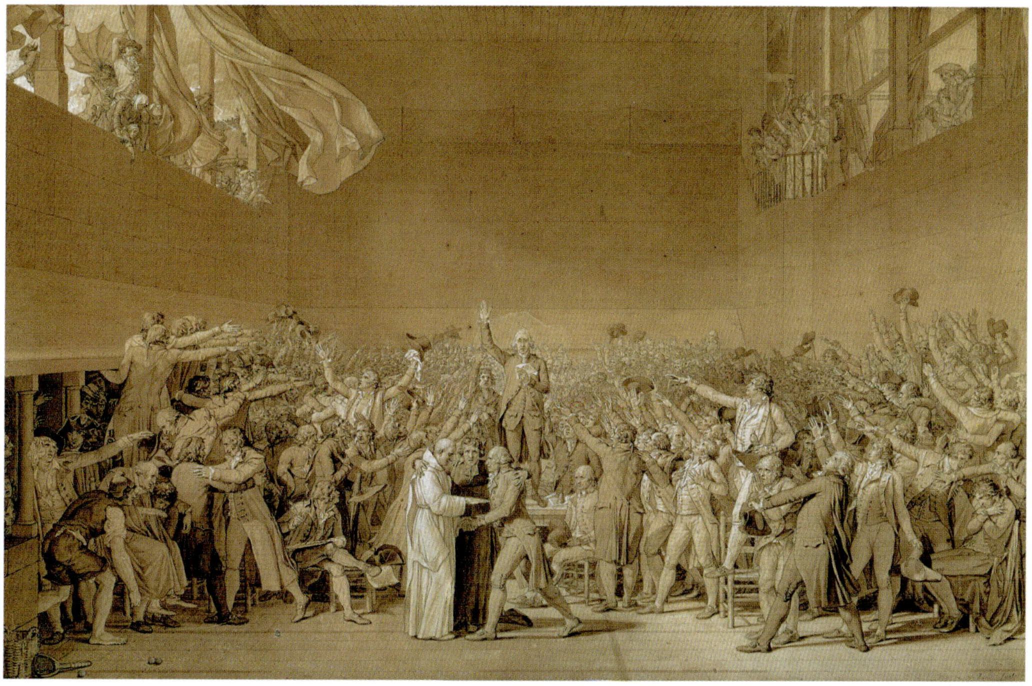

8 Jacques-Louis David, *The Tennis Court Oath*, 1791. Pen and brown ink, brown wash with white highlights on paper. 66 × 101.2 cm. Versailles, Musée National du Château (depôt du Musée du Louvre).

> beholder . . . But the beholders, and we are thinking above all of the deputies who would have had the immense canvas constantly before their eyes, could not content themselves with admiring the composition; they are called to take part physically and spiritually in the oath. Is it not precisely the new fact of a painter concretely engaged [in the political situation] which incites David to adopt a simple and direct means of communication contrary to the artistic theory of his time?[17]

(With this last phrase Bordes has in mind my reading of Diderot; thus he speaks of David's composition as producing a "theatrical effect" [59].)

Basically I agree with the gist of Bordes's analysis, though rather than seeing the figure of Bailly as breaking with Diderotian conceptions, I would want to argue that the combination of the political circumstances of the early 1790s and the political mission of David's project redefined the very issue of theatricality in such a way that it was now not only possible but imperative to directly address the beholder (the deputies, more broadly the citizen-beholder) as a means of morally if not physically absorbing them in the action of the painting. In other words, as regards David's intentions in the *Oath* there is neither a "theatrical effect" nor anything that could be called a *coup de théâtre*. (Put more strongly, there was to be no essential difference between actors and audience.) Such an interpretation emblematizes not only the resolutely antiformalist character of my approach – it is not the case that a figure who faces the beholder inevitably counts as theatrical (think of Brutus and Leonidas in this connection) – but also the level, or one level, at which the problematic of beholding I claim was at work throughout this period continually intersected with political reality, and with the political *imaginary*, which in the early 1790s was at least equally important. A similar point might be made about the *Sabines*, in which a mise-en-scène geared to dedramatization and expressive détente went hand in hand with a politics of reconciliation, or about the *Leonidas*, in which a hypostatization of purest interiority is perhaps to be understood, at least in part, as seeking refuge from the Napoleonic regime's normalizing of theatricality in and through its demand for a new kind of propagandistic painting. As Napoleon may in effect have recognized when in 1799 he criticized David for choosing to paint the defeated.[18]

3

The works to which I now want to turn (they will be the focus of this essay) are known collectively as David's "Anacreonic" paintings, on the basis of their general reliance on classical Greek subject matter of a distinctly non-tragic, indeed non-dramatic, sort – scenes of mythology, in most cases keyed to themes of love. (The reference is to the ancient Greek lyric poet Anacreon.) These belong to his later career: most were painted in Brussels, where the painter and his wife moved in January 1816 following the decree that all former deputies who had voted for the death of Louis XVI, as David had done, were to be banished from France. (David could have remained in France had he been willing to swear allegiance to the Bourbon regime but this he refused to do. He died in Brussels in 1825 at the age of 77.) For a long time the "Anacreonic" paintings received relatively little attention from scholars. The prevailing view was that the aesthetic level of his art suffered an irreversible falling off after he left Paris, and indeed the art of the preceding years, during which he was for all intents and purposes court painter to Napoleon, has also widely been perceived as of uneven quality (the *Distribution of the Eagles* [see fig. 20] being especially hard to like). More recently, however, there has taken place a sharp growth of interest in the later work, as expressed, first, in Dorothy Johnson's monographic study of 1993 and second, in Philippe Bordes's exhibition catalogue, *Jacques-Louis David: Empire to Exile* (2005) and the collection of essays mainly drawn from a symposium associated with that exhibition, *David after David: Essays on the Later Work* (2007).[19] Obviously I think that growth of interest is justified – these are important pictures by a major painter and deserve to be taken seriously both in their own right and for what they can tell us about the state of ambitious painting during the years immediately preceding the emergence of Géricault and the young Delacroix. Yet they are also deeply problematic works that continue to present a challenge to our capacity for historical and aesthetic understanding. Not surprisingly, I shall argue that the issues I have been tracing are crucial to making historical sense of what certain of these paintings place before our eyes.

The first of the "Anacreonic" paintings, *Sappho, Phaon, and Cupid* (fig. 9), today in the Hermitage, was painted in 1809, while David was still in Paris, and in some respects it remains the most fascinating of all. We know that it was painted for the Russian Count Youssapoff but there is no reason to think that the conception was not wholly David's, and it is precisely its conception that is of greatest interest to me. What is going on? Let me say up front that I think the answer is obvious, but that for various mutually reinforcing reasons scholars without exception have managed not to see it. Sappho, the famous poet of Lesbos, has been composing or improvising lyric poetry on her lyre. This has been going on for some time, with her male lover, Phaon, standing behind her. In the moment represented in the painting, Phaon has turned Sappho's head toward "this" side of the picture, which of course is where are to be found both painter and beholder, and at just that moment too the kneeling Cupid has removed Sappho's lyre from the grasp of her hands. (Until that moment, presumably, he was supporting it as she played; possibly he is still supporting it, but Phaon's gesture has moved her back from the lyre, so that her fingers seem to pluck only air.) The reason I claim that the basic scene has persisted for some time is that Phaon has been portrayed standing with his right leg crossed over his left while leaning with his right hand on the arm of the chair in which Sappho has been sitting. In other words, his stance has nothing in it of the momentary – on the contrary. Nor indeed does his gaze directly out of the painting, which gives the strong impression of having been directed for some time toward another, opposite gaze "this" side of the picture surface, one for which the entire scene has been arranged. Phaon's spear, too, with its butt end on the ground and its upper portion resting against his upper chest, bespeaks nothing if not stability.[20] And what this suggests to me – this is where description almost palpably becomes interpretation – is that Sappho and Phaon have been posing for the painter, Phaon standing and facing the latter, Sappho seated at right angles to the picture plane and accompanying herself on her lyre, or perhaps merely pretending to do so. But then something happened: perhaps Sappho became too caught up, too intensely absorbed, in her playing and singing for the good of

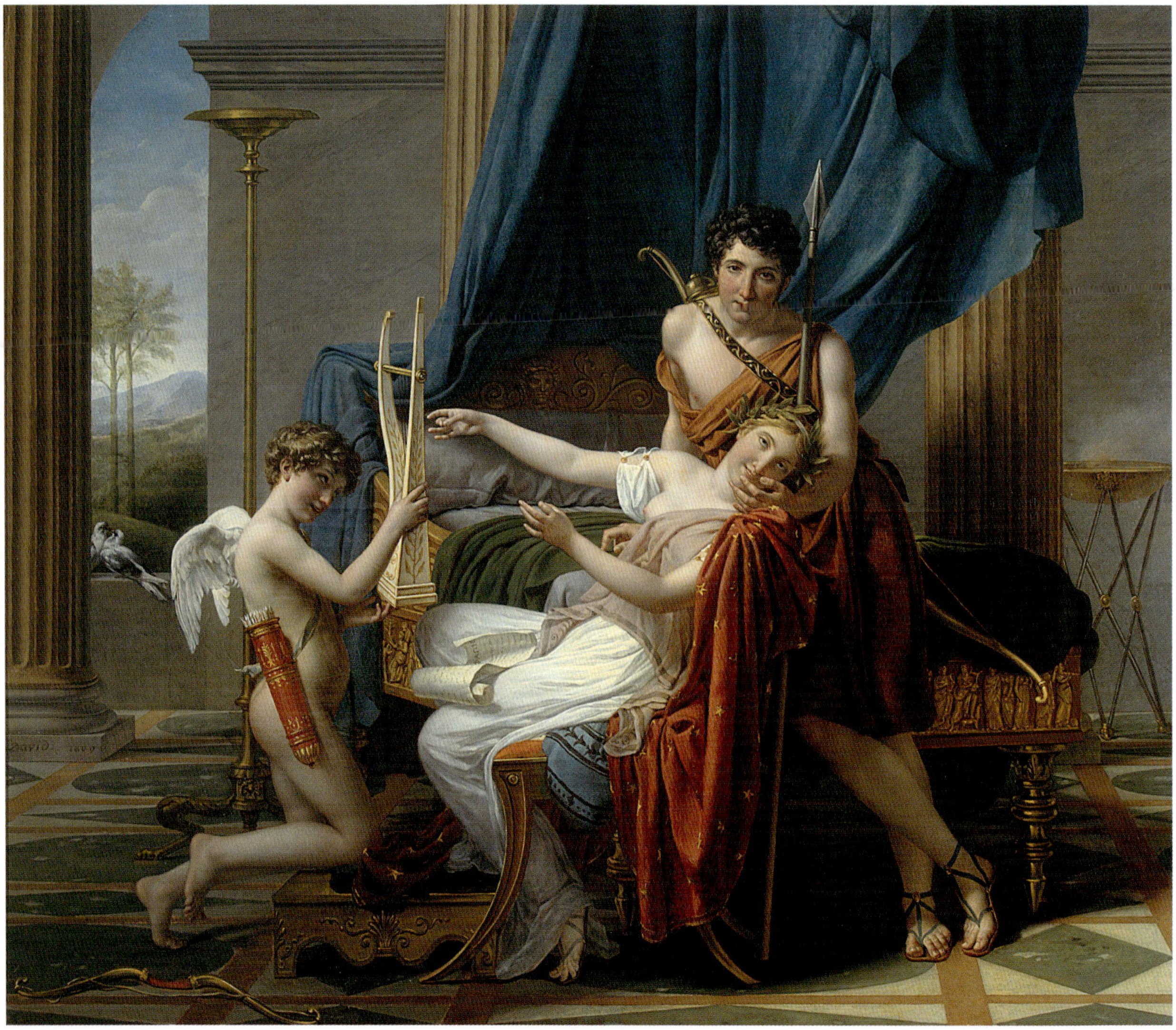

9 Jacques-Louis David, *Sappho, Phaon, and Cupid*, 1809. Oil on canvas. 225.3 × 262 cm. St. Petersburg, The State Hermitage Museum, inv. no. GE-5668.

the depiction, or perhaps there simply came a moment when she was requested to turn her gaze toward the painter (presumably *by* the painter, but of course this must remain forever an inference), a request that in the painting as we have it is now being acted on by Phaon who grasps the poet's lower face and turns it physically in the direction in question. (As if he were saying "*Chérie*, please, stop poetizing for a minute and look at David. He's been very patient.") The overall effect comes close to being photographic, all the more so in that Phaon's features convey the sense of having been based on those of an actual model. All this, I realize, amounts to a somewhat extraordinary claim, which doubtless goes some way toward explaining why the painting has not been viewed in this light by other commentators. But having spent hours within recent years standing before the actual canvas first in Williamstown and then in St. Petersburg, I see no credible alternative to the account I have just offered. (Susan Siegfried, the author of an essay in *David after David*, prefers to see in it a dream of Sappho's; this involves conflating one of Sappho's best-known poems with a poem by Ovid, and it also requires casting David's Phaon as nothing more than a figment of Sappho's erotic imagination.[21] I find this unconvincing.)

The question that now arises is what it means that David in 1808–9 conceived and executed a large painting with such an odd scenario. And the answer I want to propose is that the *Sappho, Phaon, and Cupid* marks a significant turning in David's art, the moment when, simply put, David recognized that the entire Diderotian project of somehow negating or neutralizing the beholder by virtue of the persuasive depiction of absorption and more broadly of the lateral coherence of the *tableau* (in effect closing the *tableau* to the beholder) was no longer feasible, or at any rate was no longer within the power of his art to realize; and that if he wanted to continue making works based on classical subject matter, which for him remained one of the key indices of high pictorial ambition, he had no alternative not just to relinquish but to abjure and revoke that project by emphatically turning his figures toward the viewer – in other words, by embracing the theatricality that until then he had been striving to defeat.[22] (In 1809, of course, the *Leonidas* had not been completed, but I associate that painting and its last-gasp attempt to evoke absorptive obliviousness, as regards the figure of Leonidas, with the period of its conception earlier in the decade. I should add that when I say that David "recognized" that the Diderotian project was now closed to him, I do not mean to imply that he understood this in so many words. Yet the paintings of his Brussels years leave no doubt but that a kind of recognition guided his actions from first to last.)

I find this intensely interesting simply in its own terms. What makes it even more so is that such a pictorial strategy anticipates by more than half a century the development that I have associated with Manet's breakthrough masterpieces of the first half of the 1860s, notably the *Old Musician* (1862; fig. 10), *Déjeuner sur l'herbe* (1862–3; fig. 11), and *Olympia* (painted 1863 but not exhibited until the Salon of 1865; fig. 12). More precisely, in *Manet's Modernism* and other writings my claim has been that starting around 1860 in France the Diderotian project that had got under way just over a century before had reached a new, more urgent phase of crisis.[23] Not that no painters of major ambition after that date sought to make absorptive paintings as regards both

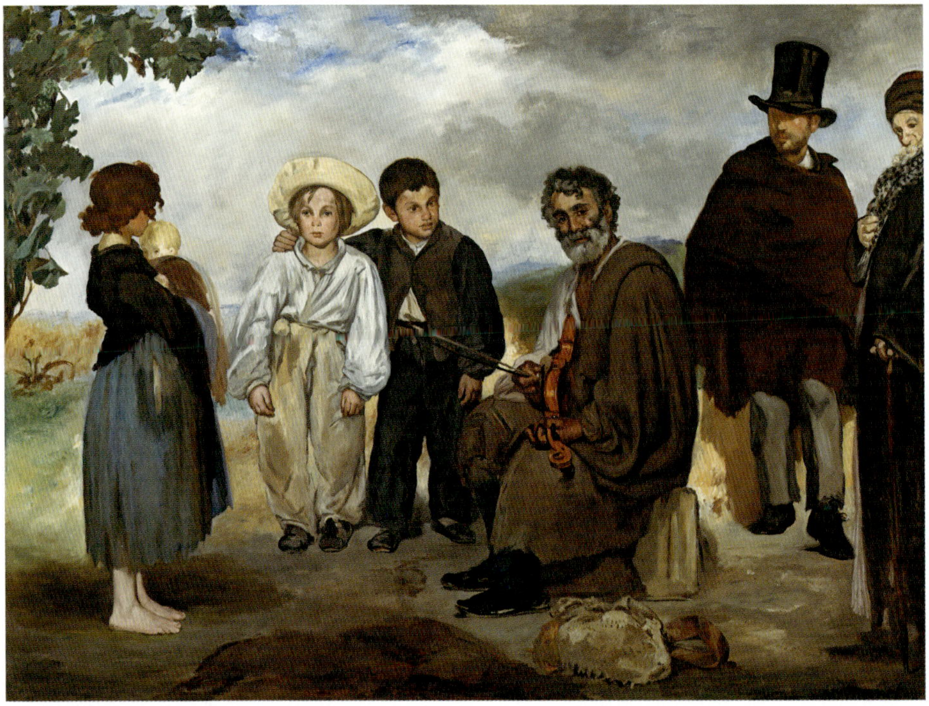

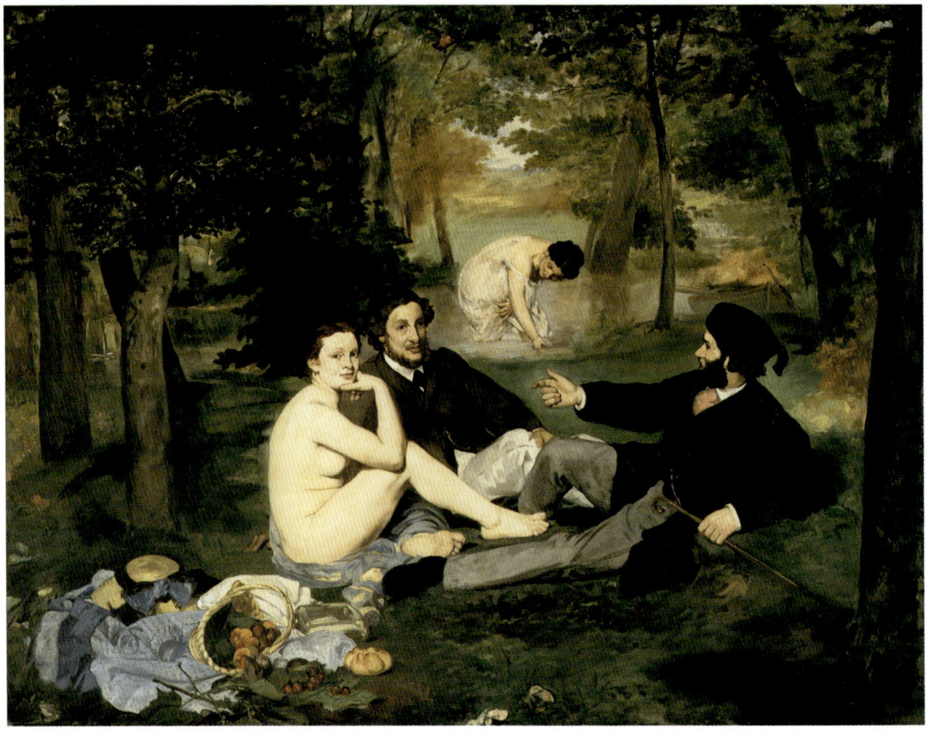

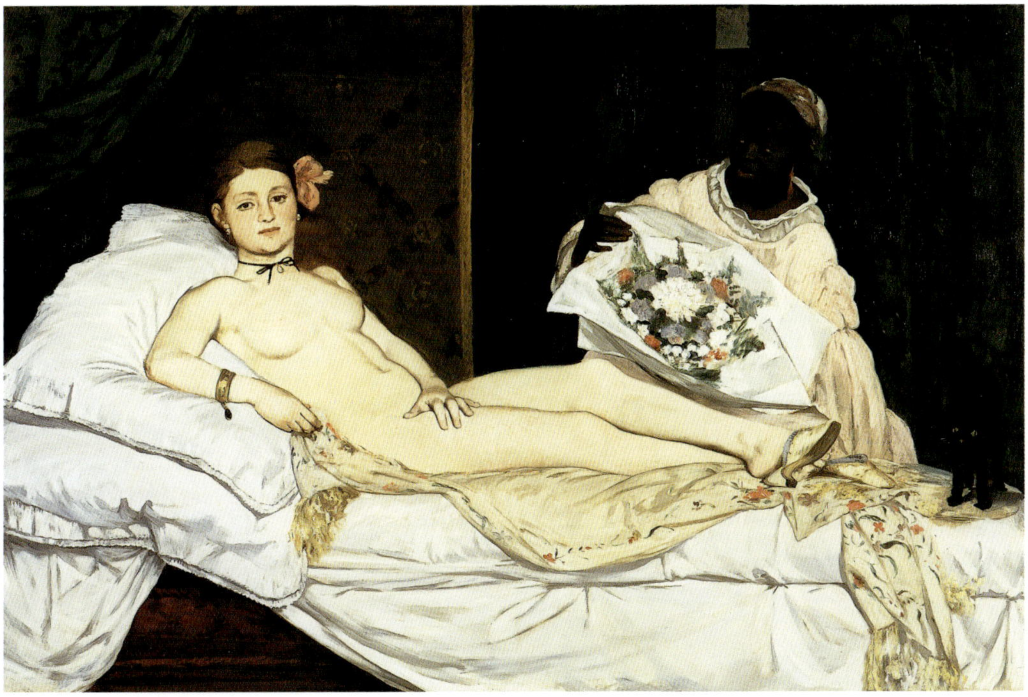

12 (*above*) Edouard Manet, *Olympia*, 1863. Exhibited Salon of 1865. Oil on canvas. 130.5 × 191 cm. Paris, Musée d'Orsay.

10 (*facing page, top*) Edouard Manet, *The Old Musician*, 1862. Oil on canvas. 187.4 × 248.2 cm. Washington, D.C., National Gallery of Art, Chester Dale Collection.

11 (*facing page, bottom*) Edouard Manet, *Le Déjeuner sur l'herbe*, 1863. Oil on canvas. 207 × 265 cm. Paris, Musée d'Orsay.

individual figures and entire compositions – far from it. (See for example the essay on Caillebotte later in this book.) But, as the key example of Jean-François Millet shows (fig. 13), by the 1850s and 1860s it was no longer possible for paintings such as his to impose themselves as truly absorptive, which is to say as antitheatrical in their overall effect, on more than a portion of the sophisticated viewing audience. At any rate, this seems to me the lesson of Millet's strongly conflictual status among the serious art critics of the day, many of whom continued to admire him on Diderotian grounds but others of whom, including writers like Baudelaire, Duranty, and Gautier (after 1861), found his peasant personages altogether false and mannered – merely pretending to plant a tree or sow potatoes or recite their prayers rather than actually doing these

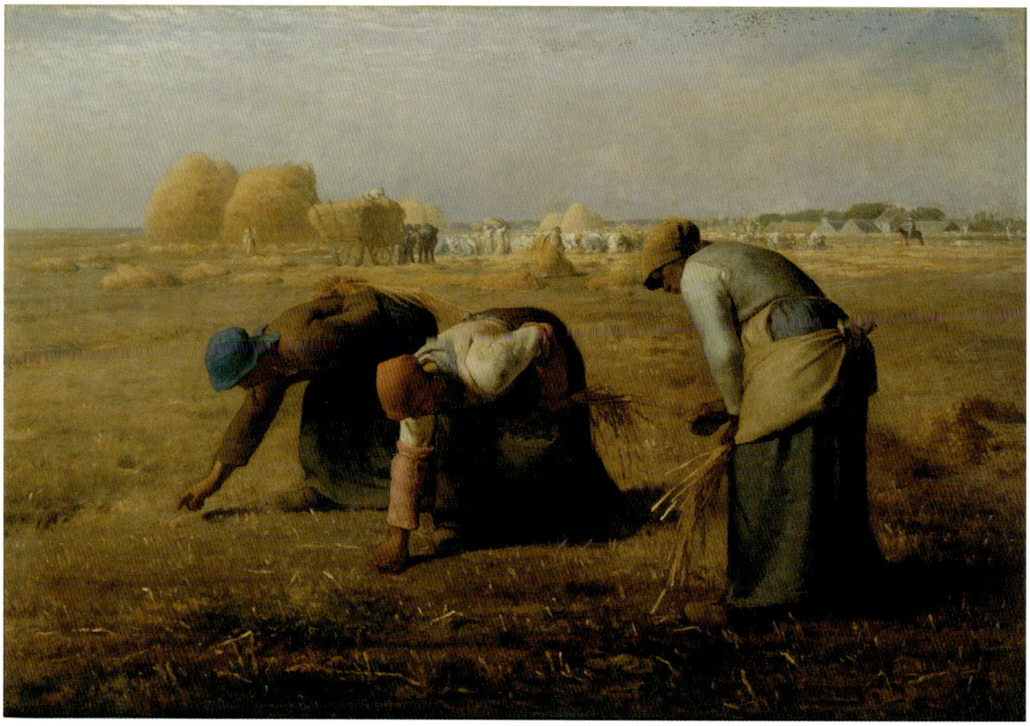

13 Jean-François Millet, *The Gleaners*, 1857. Oil on canvas. 83.5 × 11 cm. Paris, Musée d'Orsay.

things.[24] Put this way, of course, it should be clear that the task of the historian in the face of this divided body of writing is not to take sides – to decide whether Millet's peasants are or are not authentically planting a tree, and so on (remember, those figures are mere depictions, not actual peasants absorbed in what they are doing or fake peasants pretending to be so). The important point, in any case, is that the absorptive strategy as such was now likely to misfire. And the chief antitheatrical project of the previous generation, Courbet's hyperbolic attempt to paint himself all but corporeally into his paintings (a project analysed at length in my book *Courbet's Realism*), being hyperbolic, was never a pictorial option for anyone but Courbet himself, quite apart from the fact that by the 1860s the works in which that project found its fullest expression – the great Realist canvases of the late 1840s and first half of the 1850s – belonged squarely to the past.

Enter Manet – and what we find in the major paintings of the first half of the 1860s is precisely a decisive giving up of the Diderotian project in its various forms and a compensatory strategy that I have associated with two terms drawn from the criticism of his time, *facingness* and *strikingness*.[25] That is, Manet's major pictures of those years may be said to face the beholder with a new vehemence, a new power of address, keyed not just to their *mise-en-scène* but also to their handling of contrasts of light and dark, their somewhat grating – in the eyes of contemporaries – treatment of color, and certain hard to summarize aspects of their execution. (Also to their characteristic effect of abstract instantaneousness, as if the painting as a whole stamped itself out unforgettably in the very moment of beholding.) In all these respects as well as in others such as choice of subject matter, there is a considerable dissimilarity between the *Sappho, Phaon, and Cupid*, with its bright color, meticulous execution, and jewel-like details, and the *Old Musician* and related Manets of the early 1860s. And yet there is enough in common, by which I mean not simply enough of a formal accord as compositions but, more important, a deep analogy between the respective pictorial dialectics that brought them into being, to cast the differences between them in a singularly intriguing light – as if what one now would like to know (or would like to know how to begin to investigate) is by virtue of what concatenation of prior and present conditions and commitments did Manet's embrace of facingness (to name only that) have the epochal consequences that turned out to follow, whereas the same basic strategy in post-1800 David had no comparable significance. In fact the "Anacreonic" paintings led nowhere, artistically speaking. But this in turn does not mean that the *Sappho, Phaon, and Cupid*, and more broadly the "Anacreonic" paintings as a group, the chief hallmark of which is their deliberate address to the viewer, are not worth taking seriously in this connection. (Thinking about early Manet, it occurs to me that the *Surprised Nymph* [1861; fig. 14], with its female figure seated sideways but turning her head toward the viewer, makes a particularly apt comparison with the figure of Sappho.)

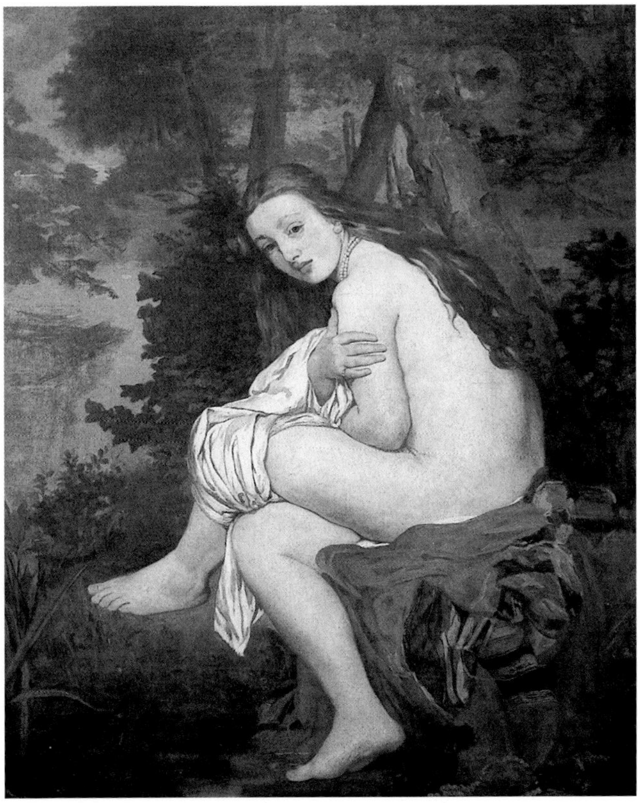

14 Edouard Manet, *Surprised Nymph*, 1861. Oil on canvas. 146 × 114 cm. Buenos Aires, Museo Nacional de Bellas Artes.

4

Here it will be useful to consider perhaps the most controversial of the "Anacreonic" paintings, *Love Leaving Psyche* or, as it is usually called, *Cupid and Psyche* (1817; fig. 15). As Dorothy Johnson and others have noted, the first critics of this canvas were scandalized by the depiction of Cupid, who has been represented disengaging himself from the sleeping Psyche while looking directly toward the beholder, a sexually frank smile on his face. Thus Kératry in 1819: "It is appalling, this empire of a base sort over idealism . . . it strangles the heart."[26] Indeed Johnson herself admits being put off by the painting on these grounds. "We are disconcerted," she writes, "by this terrible conjunction of a realistically depicted, saurian god of love, and the idealized, beautiful young woman by his side who is under the domination of this loathsome monster. The contrast between the dark, sinister, ugly [Cupid], whose cynical, leering, self-satisfied grin is directed at us, with the sensual yet vulnerable Psyche, also causes much disquiet. . . . Equally disturbing is [Cupid's] action, for he seems about to step out into our space as if he were a disquieting intruder in our world and not safely contained in a remote mythological past (that the figure is life-size contributes to this impression)" (247–8). (A detail Johnson does not mention is that although a fold of drapery conceal's Cupid's genitals, an obvious displacement occurs via the "erect" big toe of his conspicuous left foot. This is not an accident.[27]) In the pages that follow Johnson summarizes various literary sources for the subject, mainly Apuleius and La Fontaine, and concludes by suggesting that David's aim was precisely to bring about "an ironic reversal of the aubade tradition – the regret of lovers parting at dawn – to express a disturbing psychological truth that underlies the charming surface of the literary versions of the myth; he has represented Psyche as a sexual slave, captive of the leering, satiated [Cupid]" (253). A more recent commentator, Issa Lampe, writing in *David after David*, emphasizes that David had begun the painting before moving to Brussels and that in the final version the artist transformed the bedroom of Cupid and Psyche

> in the manner used for Napoleon's palaces, drawing from memory on objects that he knew from his work as the emperor's portraitist and interior designer. By dressing the scene in the *style empire*, David sets the narrative action in the historical milieu of Empire France. . . . The painting David completed in 1817 is a bawdy send-up of a traditional love story that also alludes to the Empire's demise. In it, the artist reflects on the end of an era and registers the historical disruption in the form of an unlikely – and unlovely – god.[28]

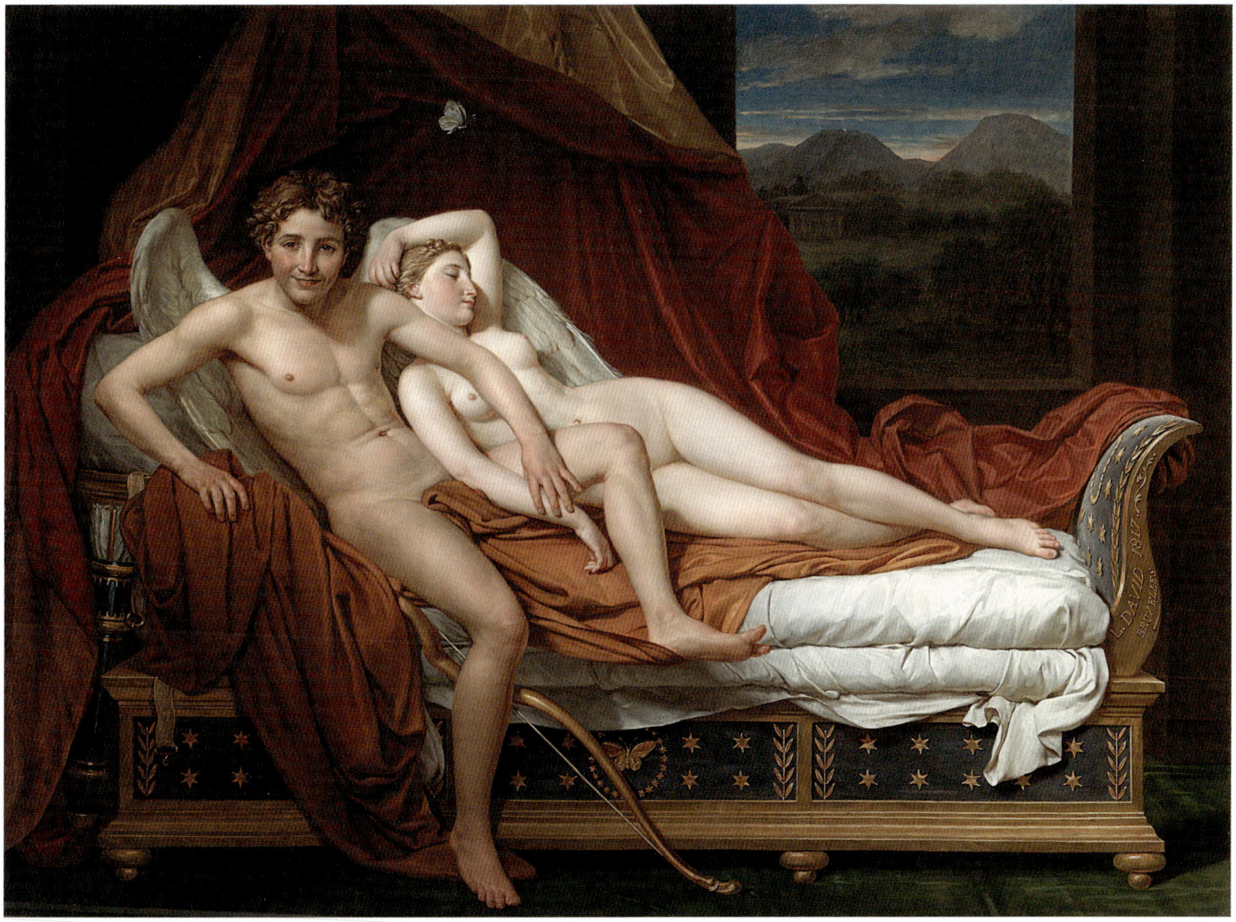

15 Jacques-Louis David, *Cupid and Psyche*, 1817. Oil on canvas. 184.2 × 241.6 cm. The Cleveland Museum of Art, Leonard C. Hanna, Jr. Fund (1962.37).

In other words, "His painting tells the story of the male god's crisis, his fall from the ideal. *Love Leaving Psyche* emerged from its metamorphosis as a memorial to Napoleon's Empire, with its divine male protagonist brought low" (120).

I am not persuaded by either of these readings, both of which in different ways deflect attention away from what I take to be the most striking feature of the painting (not that either commentator fails to note it), namely, the extraordinary daring with which the figure of Cupid has been depicted about to step from the world of the painting into the space, the world, of the beholder.[29] (Johnson sees this clearly but finds it merely disturbing – in the end it simply adds to the rebarbativeness of his portrayal. For her part, Lampe writes: "Sliding off the bed, [Cupid] seems to be falling into our space, his legs spread indecorously" [110], which does not seem quite accurate.) The result, as I understand it, is a further radicalization of the address to both painter and beholder in the *Sappho, Phaon, and Cupid*, one that aims to make all but tangible the physical presence, the corporeal reality, of the figure of Cupid, in stark contrast to the still blissfully sleeping – still utterly absorbed – but also relatively idealized figure of Psyche. In other words, my impulse is to discard the moralistic slant of the previous accounts and to stress instead the extraordinary boldness with which David made use of a classic mythological subject for his own highly unorthodox pictorial purposes – purposes, I suggest, that had essentially to do with rethinking and recasting the encounter between painting and beholder that had been at the center of his art since the early 1780s. In this connection, does it go too far to propose that the sense of extreme discomfort that the *Cupid and Psyche* evidently provoked in both early viewers and more recent commentators invites comparison with the documented responses to Manet's *Olympia* when the latter appeared before the Parisian public in the Salon of 1865? I do not think so, especially when we bear in mind that the figure of Cupid was seen and indeed continues to be seen as disturbingly realistic on the strength of his brownish skin color and distinctly non-ideal body type and facial features.[30] (E.-F. Miel in 1817: "This Amor is not at all a god, he is not even a beautiful adolescent. He is the model, an ordinary model, copied with a servile exactitude, and in which the expression of happiness is nothing more than a cynical grimace."[31] Manet faced this sort of criticism more than once.)

To be clear: nothing could be further from my purpose than to suggest that Manet had the *Cupid and Psyche* in mind when he painted the *Olympia*. (There *was* a painting by David that perhaps played a role in its conception: *Marat at His Last Breath* [1794; see fig. 28], which was on view at Martinet's, Manet's gallery, in April 1863, a time when he might well have been at work on the *Olympia*.[32] But that is another story.) My point is rather that the two canvases fairly cry out to be viewed alongside one another, so to speak. In each the genre of the female nude has been given a highly original interpretation that significantly revises the figure's traditional relation to the beholder (roughly, of being a sensuous object of the latter's gaze): in the *Olympia*, by virtue of the almost completely naked courtesan's brazen deadpan gaze and the aggressively foreshortened hand covering her sex (as many have noted, the effect is of a transfer of agency to the depicted woman), not to mention the implication that the bouquet being brought to her by her maid is the gift of the male viewer who has just entered the room; in the *Cupid and Psyche*, perhaps even more emphatically, by the actions of the naked Cupid, who seems about to call into question the very separation between real and depicted worlds (as less directly does the business with the flowers in the *Olympia*), and who in effect displaces the nude Psyche as the object of the beholder's attention. (A contrast: Cupid seems about to enter our space, the implication of the *Olympia* is that the male viewer has entered Olympia's. Is this significant, and if so, exactly how?) More broadly, both David in the *Sappho, Phaon, and Cupid* and *Cupid and Psyche* and Manet in his controversial canvases of the first half of the 1860s may be seen as instantiating a phase of overt crisis in the Diderotian tradition. But whereas in Manet's case this turned out to be profoundly productive, setting modern painting on a path that it has followed down to the present (or so I claim), in David's it was without further consequence of any sort.

The reasons behind this must be, to use a psychoanalytic notion, overdetermined. Considering David first: it is obviously pertinent that between 1816 and his death nine years later he lived in Brussels, not Paris, where the further viability of the David school was now an open question; in Brussels, it appears, he could take solace in the fact of his European reputation, even as his portrait practice during those years shows a deep involvement with Flemish pictorial tradition (and even as he berated Gros long-distance for not exerting a leadership he himself would have been taxed to achieve). It is also to the point that classical subjects of the sort he chose to paint were bound to have little interest for the most ambitious of the younger French painters (think of Géricault, who did however stop off in Brussels to pay his respects in 1820); nor were the tightness of execution of the "Anacreonic" paintings and (especially in the *Sappho*) the ornamental brilliance of the color in accord with progressive tendencies in Paris (Géricault, again, is a relevant comparison). In any case, the expressive tonality of those paintings, as exemplified by the bizarre interplay among Sappho, Phaon, and Cupid, and by the provocative and unappealing expression of the naked Cupid, scarcely seems designed to establish a new paradigm of high pictorial seriousness. (Exactly how did David expect these works to be received, one cannot help wondering. Granted, the same question might reasonably be asked of the painter of the *Déjeuner sur l'herbe*.)

As for Manet, it matters greatly that his art was viewed as realistic at a moment when the advanced painter of the previous generation, Courbet, had established realism (which Courbet spelled with a capital "R") as the most important pictorial tendency of its time – at any rate, the young painters who almost instantly responded to Manet's paintings of the first half of the 1860s, the future Impressionists, understood themselves from the first to be realists in an extended sense of the term. Not that they or anyone else at the time understood Manet's art in the Diderotian – more precisely, counter-Diderotian – register I have outlined here. Rather, Manet's significance for Monet and his contemporaries had largely to do with what Matisse later called his "simplification" of the art of painting, I mean the directness and summary brilliance with which his brushwork, more broadly his paint handling, was seen as recording his perceptions with extraordinary freshness as opposed to falsifying them in accord with stylistic conventions of one or another sort. Also contributing to the impact of his art was his elimination of continuous light/dark modeling (as in *Olympia*) while nevertheless achieving extremely refined coloristic effects – though in fact by the 1870s the future Impressionists found it necessary to "gray" their colors in the interest of pictorial unity. But Monet's coloristically bold beachscapes of the late 1860s are inconceivable without the precedent of Manet's inspired seascapes associated with the project of the *Kearsarge and Alabama* (1864), a scene of naval combat off the port of Cherbourg (which Manet may or may not have witnessed).

In my view, however, Manet's painterly innovations were themselves largely in the service of the counter-Diderotian attempt to engage the beholder in a new, more challenging, indeed positively aggressive manner. And there is something else: in the wake of Manet's embrace of facingness, which is to say following his uncompromising abandonment of the absorptive ideal (the foundational move of his artistic career), the young painters were at a loss as to how to resolve the problem of figure painting on a life-scale – what were such figures to be represented as doing, and in what relation to other figures and to the beholder? Absorption, the young painters grasped, was no longer viable as a controlling effect but facingness had Manet's stamp on it, quite apart from being almost impossible to manage, so what were they to do? Monet's ambitious figure paintings of the mid- and late 1860s, the immense, unfinished *Déjeuner sur l'herbe* (1865–6; fig. 16), the fashion-plate-like *Women in the Garden* (1866; fig. 17), and the enigmatic *Le Déjeuner* (1868–9; fig. 18), with its veiled woman in black standing to the left and its place presumably set for the artist in the right foreground (a nod to Courbet?), show in different ways that the problem was unresolvable, which I take to have been a significant factor in the young painters' collective turn to landscape as the arena of their endeavors.[33] (It is never recognized how unusual an event the Impressionist reliance on landscape was in the history of nineteenth- and early twentieth-century French painting. Of course landscape painting in France had flourished for decades. But the only truly major French painter of an earlier generation for whom landscape was primary was Jean-Baptiste-Camille Corot [I am probably slighting Théodore Rousseau and Charles-François Daubigny], while the leading French painter of the following generation, Georges Seurat, returned to the figure – also to a kind of absorption – in his most important canvases. Indeed before Seurat there was Gustave Caillebotte, a significant painter albeit not a great one, whose art is the subject of "Caillebotte's Impressionism" further on in this book.) And it was precisely within the limits of landscape as a genre, crucially including limits of picture size, that ambitious painting in

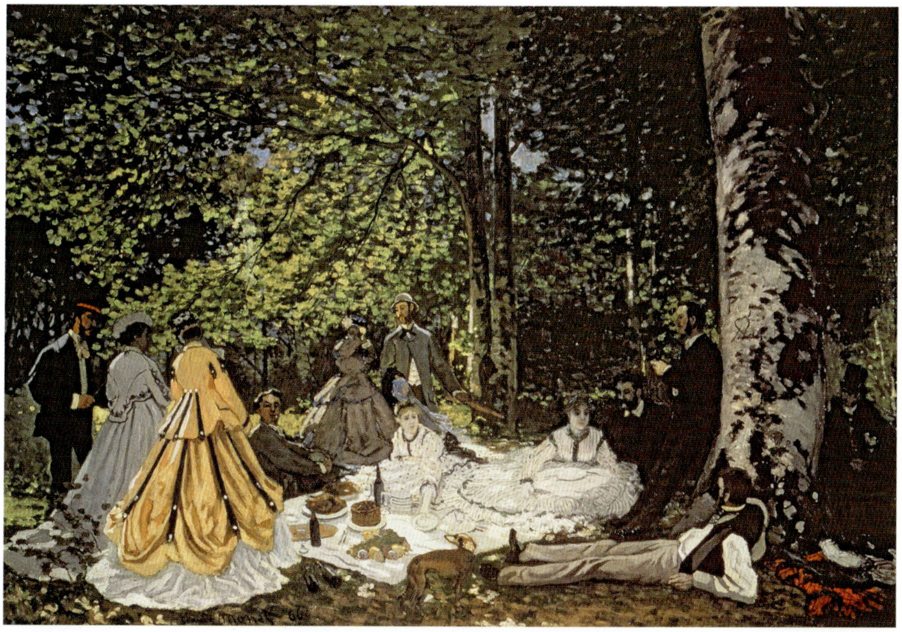

16 (*left*) Claude Monet, study for *Le Déjeuner sur l'herbe*, 1865–6. Oil on canvas. 130 × 181 cm. Moscow, Pushkin Museum.

17 (*below, left*) Claude Monet, *Women in the Garden*, 1866–7. Oil on canvas. 255 × 205 cm. Paris, Musée d'Orsay.

18 (*below, right*) Claude Monet, *Le Déjeuner*, 1868–9. Oil on canvas. 230 × 150 cm. Frankfurt am Mein, Städel Museum.

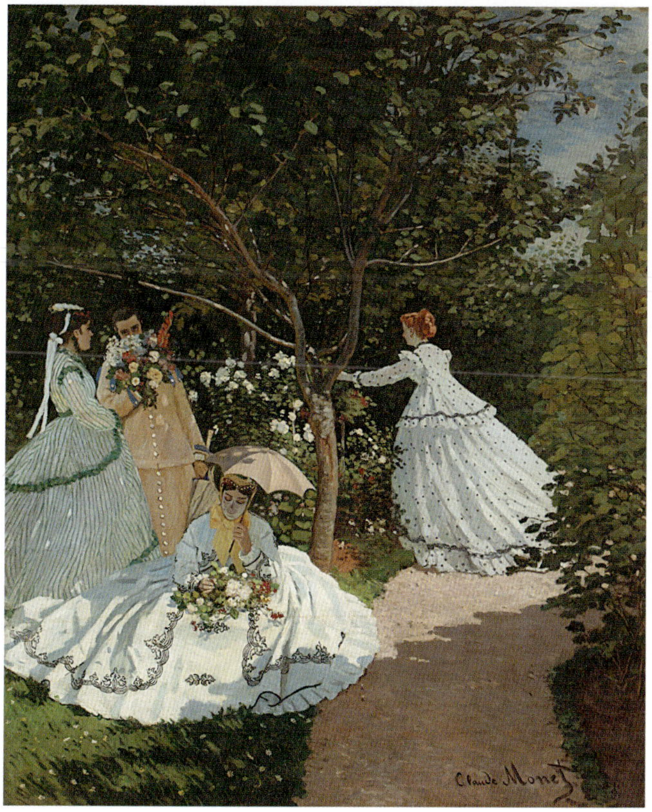

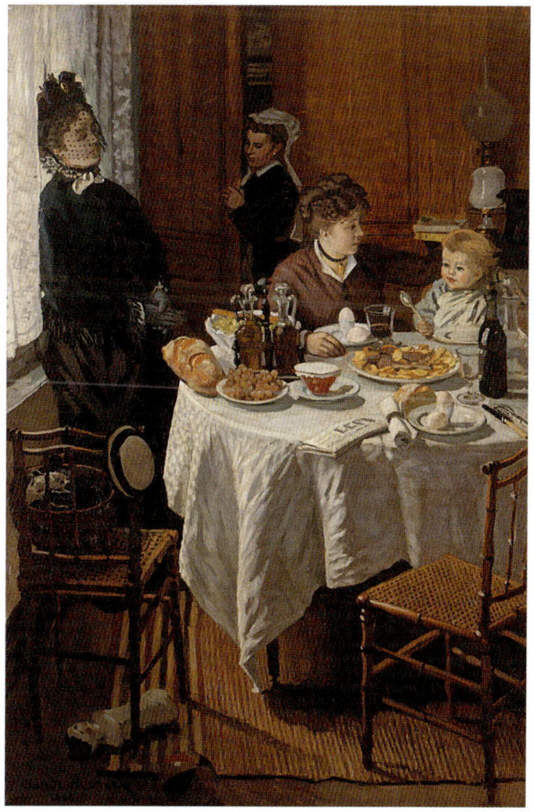

France found the means to engage with what turned out to be the decisive issue at that juncture in its evolution: the pursuit of a maximally perspicuous mode of pictorial integration down to the level of the individual brushstroke which nevertheless maintained a place for spatial illusionism, the depiction of depth – Cézanne's signature achievement in the 1880s. (This is a topic that calls for further development.) In other words, Manet's embrace of facingness played a role in motivating the Impressionists' or at least Monet's commitment to landscape, which was the enabling condition of their most important innovations. Much more might be said about these developments, which were dialectical in the fullest sense, but I hope enough has been said to flesh out somewhat the difference between 1809 or 1817 and the first half of the 1860s.

5

One final mythological, though not exactly "Anacreonic" work, the *Anger of Achilles* (1819; fig. 19), has a bearing on our topic. We are dealing with a new format, one ultimately based on that of various Caravaggios of the early 1600s, in which half-length figures are juxtaposed in a shallow space and in close proximity to the picture surface. The subject is drawn from the background to the *Iliad* and specifically, it seems, from Jean Racine's tragedy, *Iphigénie en Aulide* (1674), which Johnson tells us was performed often in Paris in the early nineteenth century (258). As Thomas Crow emphasizes though, there is no equivalent scene in the play, and Crow also cites a recently discovered letter from David to a M. Van Guffel of July 1819 in which the artist declares the subject of his painting to be as follows: "The Anger of Achilles: The painter has chosen the moment when Achilles confronts Agamemnon as he is leading his daughter Iphigenia to be sacrificed. This rage of Achilles stops the tears of Clytemnestra and gives her a brief glimmer of hope for her daughter."[34] (Iphigenia is to be sacrificed in order to propitiate the goddess Artemis, who has stilled the winds needed to carry the Greek armada to Troy.) Accordingly, going from right to left, the figures in the painting represent Agamemnon, Iphigenia, Clytemnestra, and Achilles, the last seen from behind with his helmeted head in profile. In no version of the story does Achilles actually kill the king; Johnson persuasively suggests (259) – Bordes agrees (254) – that David has tried to show Agamemnon subjugating Achilles with his gaze and the downward gesture of his right arm.

The *Anger of Achilles* marks a departure in David's art in respects other than those of format. For unlike what is to be found in any previous work by the painter, the emphasis in the Fort Worth canvas falls squarely on the particular expressivity of the

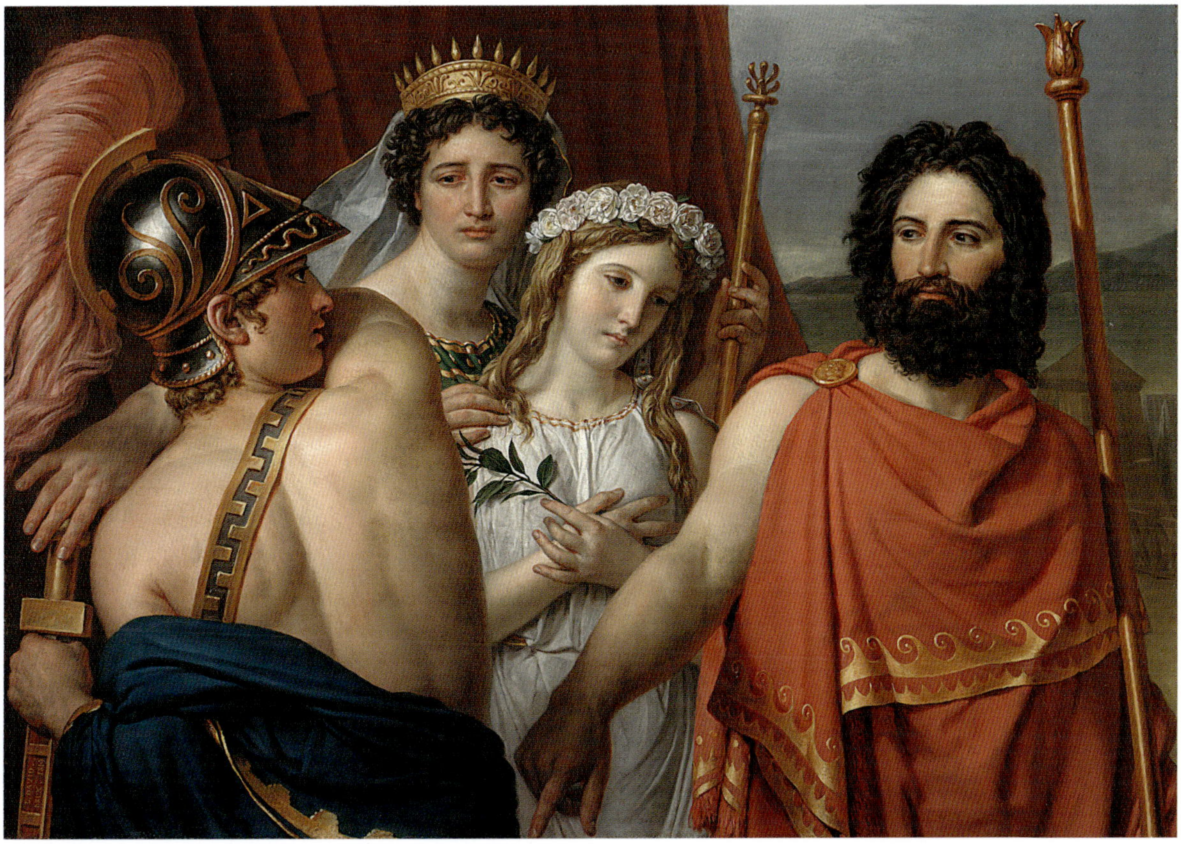

19 Jacques-Louis David, *Anger of Achilles*, 1819. Oil on canvas. 105.3 × 145 cm. Fort Worth, Kimbell Art Museum.

individual figures (Jean-Claude Lebensztejn refers aptly to "a quartet of diverging affects," which he compares to moments in contemporary operas[35]). More precisely, there is a striking contrast between the male and female figures that harks back to a not dissimilar opposition in the *Horatii* between the active but emotionally restrained men and the essentially passive but emotionally reactive women, and then a subtler pair of contrasts between the two men and the two women. Thus Agamemnon's air of command is set off against Achilles's impetuous reaching for his weapon; Iphigenia has been depicted sad, as if withdrawn into herself, evidently accepting her fate (a good daughter, in other words); while Clytemnestra, tall, wearing her crown, one hand on her daughter's shoulder, appears dignified but deeply unhappy even as she turns her gaze – hopefully, David's text suggests – on the ostensibly angry Achilles (her red eyelids show clearly that she has been weeping). In short one has the sense that for David himself the artistic success of his canvas hinged more than anything else on its ability to evoke tragic intensities of feeling, especially in the figures of the two women.[36] And yet on looking closely at the painting one comes to recognize that the figures' expressivity is curiously *external*, a matter of what might be called deliberate affective nuance, by which I do not quite mean to claim that it should be seen as false or theatrical. It is rather that one becomes aware that Iphigenia's sadness and Clytemnestra's grief have been applied to them from outside, in a manner of speaking; that instead of striking the viewer as the spontaneous overflow of feelings welling up from within their respective psyches, both women's expressions reveal themselves to be "mere" outward signs that the painter has deliberately deployed, not so much in order to produce a particular emotional effect on the beholder (who however is invited to study those signs at close range) as in an attempt to render the expressive "truth" of a potentially tragic situation (in the interests of a certain affective accuracy, one might say). Agamemnon's expression too seems more willed than spontaneous; while Achilles – it is here that the painting most palpably runs into trouble – in the first place appears almost completely facially *in*expressive (apart from the reddish flush that spreads across his cheeks, another manifestly external sign of inner feeling), and in the second has been depicted reaching with his right arm not so much across his body as across his face in a manner that lacks all physical and psychological verisimilitude. (As if David found himself driven to this extraordinarily awkward expedient by the desire to show as much as possible of Achilles's arm and hand rather than allow them to be obscured from view behind his body.) Indeed it is quite astonishing to find David, during the 1780s and for that matter the early 1790s – I am thinking of the never-finished *Tennis Court Oath* – *the* absolute master in European art of the convincing depiction of powerful bodies totally engaged in energetic action,[37] allowing such an unnatural, unpersuasive, almost boneless-seeming treatment of (admittedly an emblematic rather than a truly dramatic) action to go forth from his studio.

Let me be clear: the point of these remarks is not at all to degrade the *Anger of Achilles*, which, like the other works discussed, I take to be a painting of considerable significance. More precisely, I view this canvas as laying bare with particular clarity a development that had been visible in David's art for some time, namely, the loss of an unforced sense of lived bodily reality, as regards his figures and their worlds. Again, the considerations bearing directly or indirectly on such a development are far from obvious, but the *Distribution of the Eagles* (1810; fig. 20), with its half-stationary, half-upward-surging mass of French officers hyperbolically – and wholly unconvincingly – swearing allegiance to the Emperor, shows that the problem goes back well into the Napoleonic period, as does, in a less hysterical register, the *Leonidas* with its merely

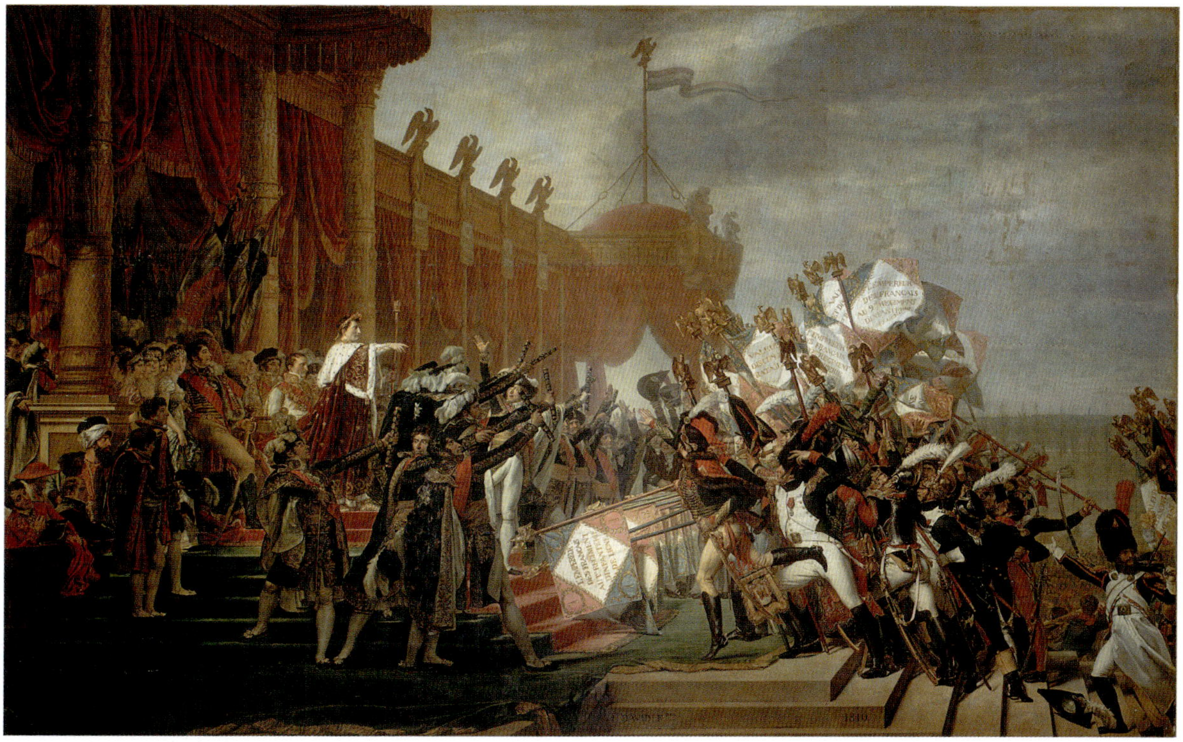

20 Jacques-Louis David, *Distribution of the Eagles*, 1810. Oil on canvas. 610 × 970 cm. Versailles, Musée National du Château.

"nominal" throng of Spartan soldiers (my point being that we are not being asked to "believe" their actions and emotions; basically they are there to set off Leonidas). Here it is tempting to consider the possible influence on David's art of the blatant theatricality of the Napoleonic regime, with its call for painting to serve propagandistic purposes (that is, to produce scenes of recent history expressly designed to be seen). But an incipient crisis of absorption is already palpable in the *Sabines* (conceived in 1796, completed in 1799), not that those years – the end of the Directory, the early rise to power of Napoleon – were themselves devoid of an emphasis on extremes of outward display.[38] Then, too, one would like to know what to make of the deeply fascinating fact that the early 1790s, the years between the Revolution of 1789 and the fall of Robespierre in 1794, saw the emergence of an extreme ideology – more precisely, an extreme politics – of personal and public antitheatricality on the part of the Jacobins, with whom David was affiliated. The particular thrust of that politics with its emphasis on perfect "transparency" and its impassioned hostility to the very idea that a person might differ inwardly from his or her outward demeanor (hence the need for continuous surveillance, hence too the paranoid suspicion that theatricality was everywhere) owed far more to Rousseau's totalizing *Lettre à M. D'Alembert sur les spectacles* than to Diderot's *Entretiens sur le Fils naturel, Discours sur la poésie dramatique,* and *Salons* (which of course theorized an aesthetic version of the inner/outer split), not that Diderot was not also part of the Revolutionary mix.[39] With what sense of continuity or discontinuity with his previous artistic commitments did David negotiate those developments and indeed play a major role in them by devising elaborate public festivals aimed at realizing the "transparent," that is, anti-spectacular, ideal?[40] (His major pictorial achievement during those years was of course the *Marat at His Last Breath,* already mentioned in connection with the *Olympia.* Note, by the way, how ingeniously the *Marat* recycles the carved block alongside Belisarius in David's first important history painting, the trompe-l'oeil incised face now turned to the beholder – think of Bailly in the *Tennis Court Oath* – in contradistinction to the lateral axis of the composition as a whole.[41]) For that matter, with what sense of artistic dislocation, if any, did he come to terms with the liquidation of the Jacobins, an event that sent him to prison and very nearly cost him his life? In any case, the subsequent evolution of French painting, culminating in Manet's canvases of the 1860s, leaves no doubt but that the absorptive aesthetic, with its fiction of obliviousness to the world "this" side of the painting, could not be sustained. And that is to say that the interaction between sheerly pictorial and extra-pictorial factors in David's career-long engagement with issues of theatricality – a distinction that would surely break down under scrutiny – is likely to resist even the most historically sensitive and informed attempts to assess their relative weight.

A further suggestion is that there exists an intimate connection between David's embrace of theatricality in the *Sappho, Phaon, and Cupid* and other "Anacreonic" paintings and the loss of all conviction of psycho-physical inwardness in those same paintings as well as, with extraordinary clarity, in the *Anger of Achilles.* That is, according to the structure of the Diderotian *tableau,* the beholder is understood as in effect walled off or say radically separated from the action taking place on the stage or in the fictive, laterally organized space of the painting. But by virtue of that strategic walling off, the beholder is also given something like free imaginative access to the depicted states of mind and feeling, even in a sense to the implied psycho-physical energetics of the dramatis personae. The immense public success of David's history paintings of the 1780s owed much to this "identificatory" dynamic. Starting in the early 1800s, however, the Diderotian strategy is abandoned and the beholder is directly addressed to the extent of feeling himself or herself the principal focus of the composition (in the *Sappho, Phaon, and Cupid,* standing in for the painter) or indeed on the verge of being

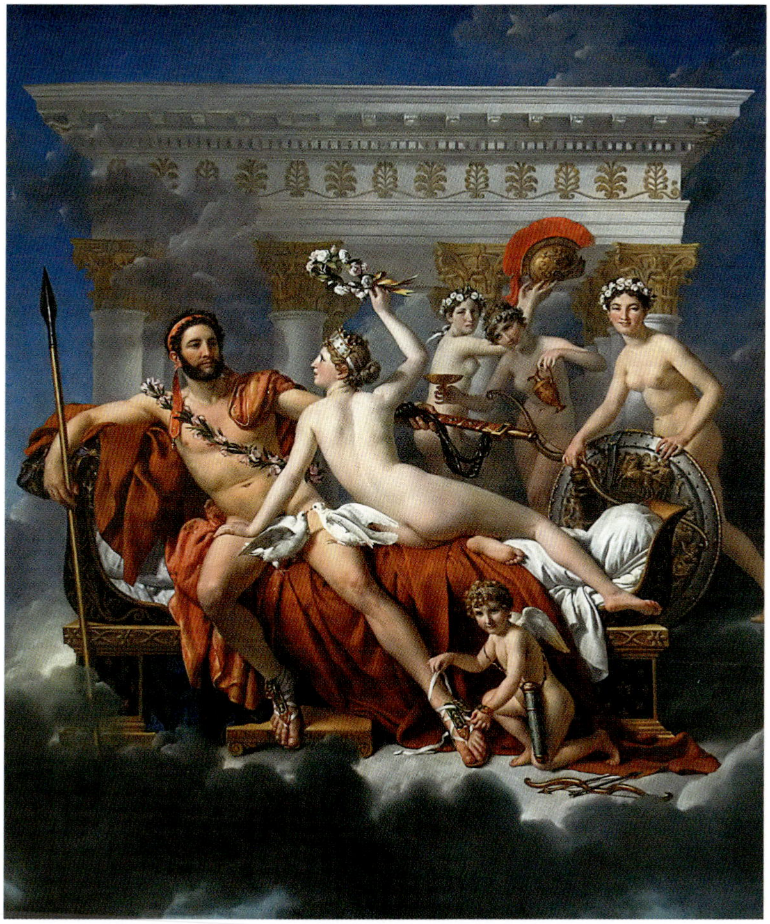

21 Jacques-Louis David, *Mars Disarmed by Venus and the Graces*, 1824. Oil on canvas. 308 × 265 cm. Brussels, Musées Royaux des Beaux-Arts de Belgique.

physically confronted by one of the figures (in the *Cupid and Psyche*). And when *that* happens, what I have just described as free imaginative access to the inner lives of the dramatis personae turns out to go by the board (in the *Anger of Achilles* the fiction of "inner lives" is definitively given up in favor of a sheerly outward "expressiveness"). In short, what I have been calling the world of the representation is now voided in favor of the world in which the painting is encountered, even as the latter is defined as one of sheerest externality, a place of mere confrontation, surfaces, theater. The singular achievement of the "Anacreonic" pictures, reaching a peak of absurdity in the large and meticulously executed *Mars Disarmed by Venus and the Graces* (1824; fig. 21), in

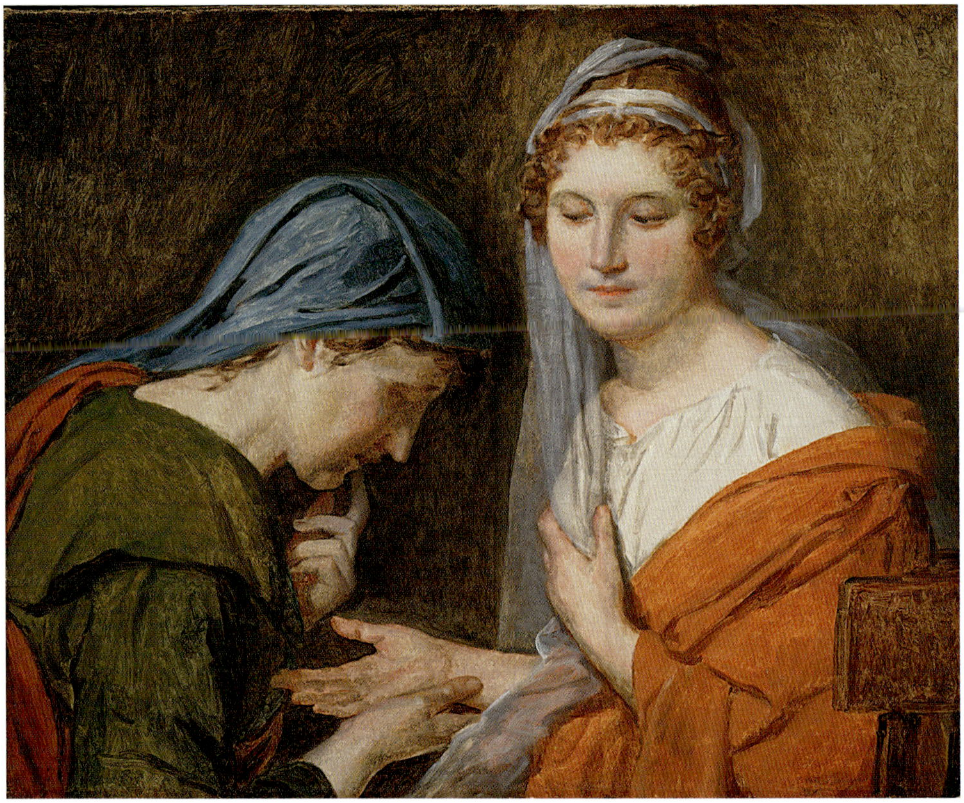

22 Jacques-Louis David, *The Fortune Teller*, 1824. Oil on canvas. 62.2 × 74.9 cm. Fine Arts Museums of San Francisco, Gift of David David-Weill.

which the heroic protagonist is being divested of the attributes of manhood – the Manet comparison at least with regard to absurdity would be the *Déjeuner sur l'herbe* – is to have pursued this logic with perfect lucidity, if also with insouciance, sexual daring, humor. Once and for all, what was David thinking?*

* One other very late work calls for comment: the seemingly unfinished or at least *ébauche*-like *Fortune Teller* (1824; fig. 22), a half-length depiction of two women, the one on the left pondering the open right palm of the "matron" on the right. What is fascinating, of course, is not only that the picture is so clearly absorptive but also that stylistically it reverts to an earlier moment in David's career (say the 1790s), two facts together suggesting that the very different dramaturgy of the "Anacreonic" paintings was in part a function of generic considerations, absorption and the earlier handling being still possible in a work of "lesser" ambition. Note too the gesture of the "matron" as she seems to draw a diaphanous violet veil so as partly to shield her face from view, though not from the beholder before the painting, a gesture that recalls the action of the woman bestowing alms in the *Belisarius* of forty-six years before.

6

A few words about David's late, so-called "aporetic" small-scale pencil drawings (figs. 23–5), which exemplify a still more extreme development. Consisting for the most part of indeterminately expressive heads in no intelligible relation to one another, some plainly absorbed and others, often seemingly troubled or haunted, gazing directly out of the sheet, these mysterious works, which David appears to have made in a semi-automatistic manner, relate only to the painter's imagination – also to his memory of previous works of his own – and thus give no purchase for the very thought of world-hood.[42] (They are without context of any kind.) In that sense they go even further along the trajectory that we have been tracing, the staring figures often giving the impression of seeking a human connection of which they despair.[43]

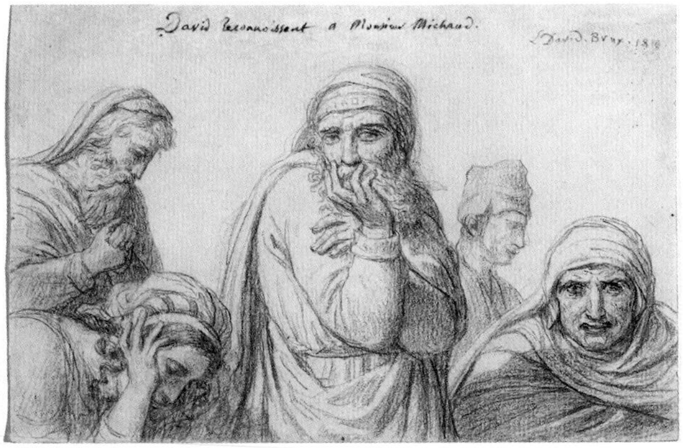

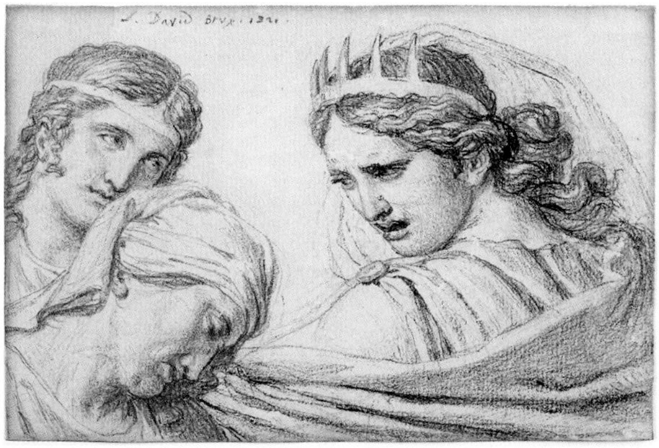

23 (*above, left*) Jacques-Louis David, *A Scene of Mourning (Composition with Five Figures)*, 1819. Black chalk on cream laid paper. 13 × 20.2 cm. Fine Arts Museums of San Francisco, Achenbach Foundation for Graphic Arts Endowment Fund.

24 (*above, right*) Jacques-Louis David, *Three Female Heads*, 1821. Pencil on paper. 13.3 × 19.6 cm. Denver Art Museum, Collection of Dr. Esmond Bradley Martin.

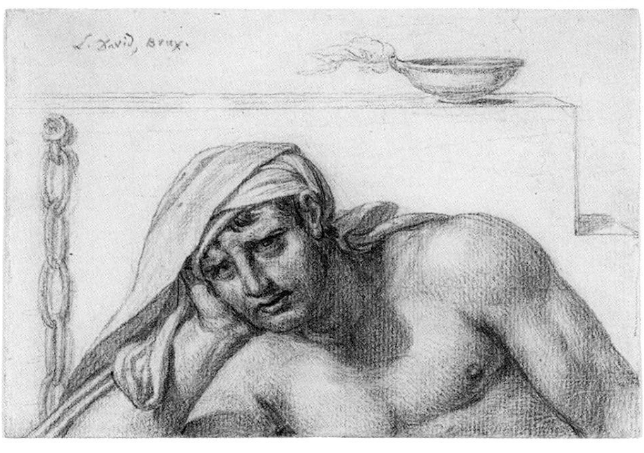

25 (*above*) Jacques-Louis David, *The Prisoner*, 1819. Black chalk on paper. 13.3 × 19.6 cm. The Cleveland Museum of Art, purchase of the J. H. Wade Fund.

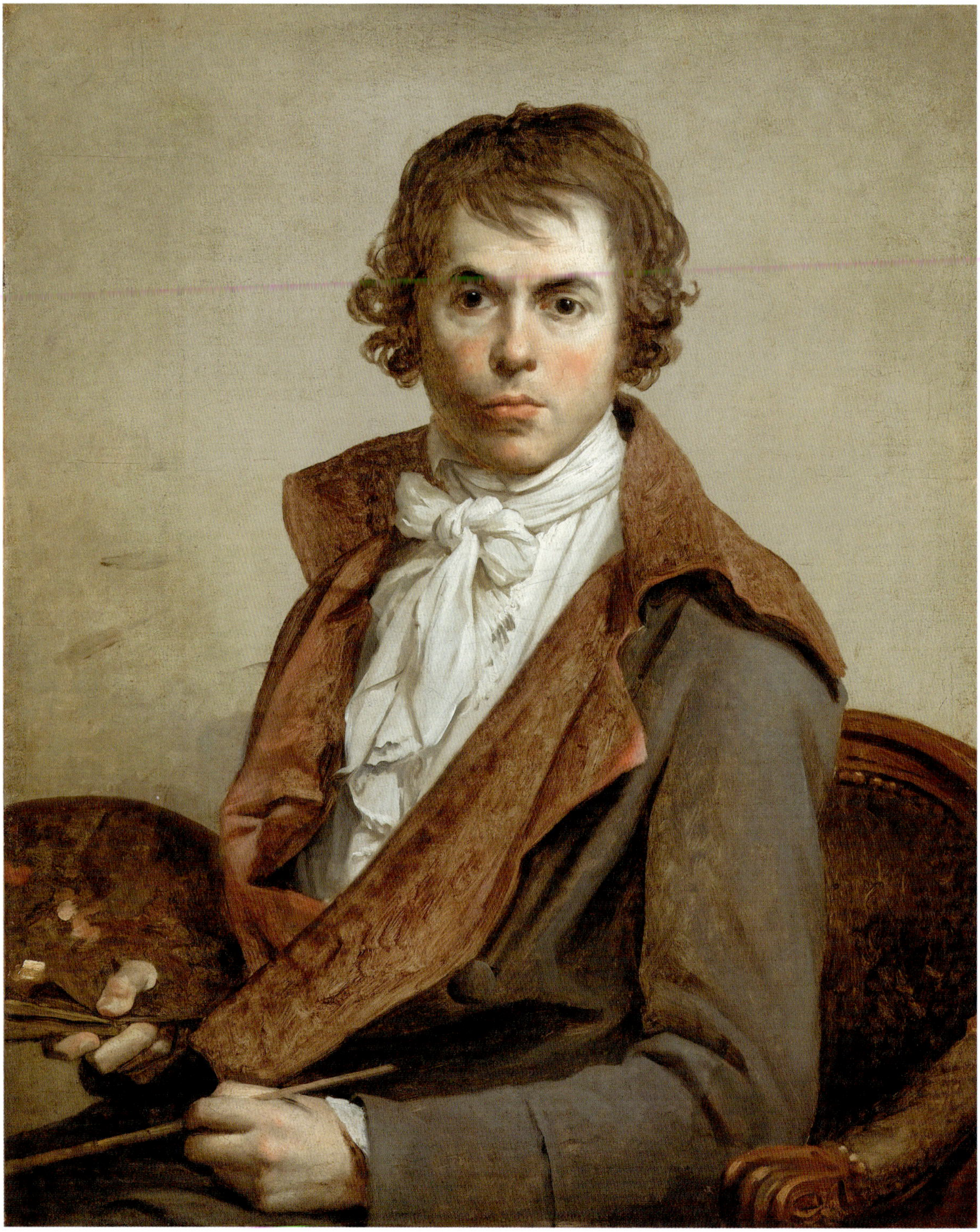

26 Jacques-Louis David, *Self-Portrait*, 1794. Oil on canvas. 81 × 64 cm. Paris, Musée du Louvre. Gift of Eugène Isabey, 1852.

• 2 •

DAVID / MARAT: THE *SELF-PORTRAIT* OF 1794

Jacques-Louis David's *Self-Portrait* (fig. 26), painted during his relatively brief imprisonment in the Hôtel des Fermes in August and early September 1794, has been the focus of serious discussion in recent years.[1] But almost nothing has been said about one of its principal, and most extraordinary, features – the fact that that the right-handed David has portrayed himself holding his brush in his left hand and his palette in his right. (Also with the disfiguring tumor inside his left cheek shifted to the right.) Now it may seem as if such silence is unsurprising. David painted his self-portrait with the aid of a mirror brought to him in prison by his pupil Pierre-Maximilien Delafontaine,[2] and his image in the mirror would itself have been reversed (in the ordinary understanding of the term[3]), so what could be more natural, it might be thought, than for him to have preserved that reversal in his painting?

What he did was anything but natural, historically speaking. Over the course of the several centuries prior to 1794 during which European painters made portraits of themselves with the aid of reflecting surfaces of one sort or another, only a handful of such self-portraits turned out mirror-reversed. (The greatest of these is doubtless Annibale Carracci's *Self-Portrait with Figures* in Milan [ca. 1585–90; fig. 27].) Rather, painters almost without exception chose (or felt compelled) to undo the reversing effects of the mirror-image in order to depict themselves as they appeared to others, that is, for right-handed painters, by far the majority, with the brush in their right hand and the palette in their left. (I am referring, of course, to that class of self-portraits in which the painter depicted himself or herself with brush and palette in hand. In self-portraits that omitted those instruments, as most did, the issue of mirror-reversal is mooted though by no means always placed in abeyance.) As Zirka Filipczak was the first to observe,[4] the situation changed dramatically around 1860, when numerous painters in Europe and the United States began to make self-portraits that were

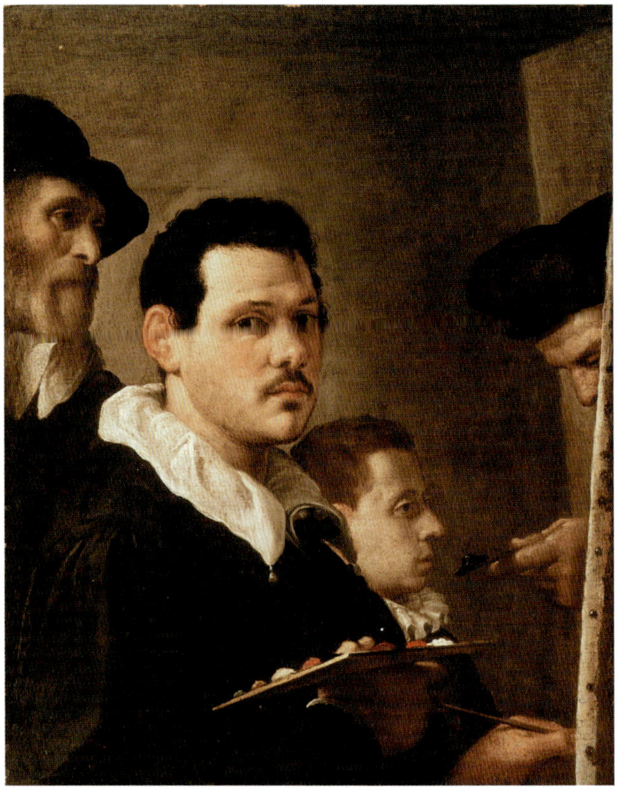

27 Annibale Carracci, *Self-Portrait with Figures*, 1590. Oil on canvas. 60 × 48 cm. Milan, Pinacoteca di Brera.

faithful to the image in the mirror – in other words, that attempted to record what the artist actually saw instead of what he or she knew to be the case. In my book *Manet's Modernism* I discuss a number of such self-portraits by Manet and other painters of his generation, notably Henri Fantin-Latour and James McNeill Whistler, and go on to contrast those works with the altogether different self-portrait strategies of their realist predecessor, Courbet (for whom the self-portrait as a genre was of fundamental importance).[5] And in a later book, *The Moment of Caravaggio* (2010), I analyze Annibale's *Self-Portrait with Figures* in connection with a larger argument to the effect that certain paintings by Caravaggio that are not explicitly mirror-reversed self-portraits may nevertheless productively be seen in those terms.[6] This is not the place to go into those and related matters; I mention them simply by way of indicating that the issue of mirror-reversal has a long and significant history in western painting, one that has almost wholly been neglected by scholars. (Let me add that the essay on Caillebotte in the present book concludes with an analysis of a mirror-reversed self-portrait that might be taken as commenting on the tradition to date [see fig. 141].)

One other point about the kind of self-portrait we are dealing with in the case of David's canvas needs to be made before we can go forward. If we provisionally take the picture as a veristic report on an actual set-up or *dispositif* and if we then ask how we are to understand the original positions of the canvas and mirror employed by David to make his painting, it soon becomes clear, first, that the mirror must have occupied the position now held by the finished painting, and second, that the canvas on which the figure of David is implicitly shown working must have been at a fairly sharp angle to that mirror – let me call it a right angle in the interest of simplicity. Not that any portion of the canvas is depicted in the finished painting, as it is, for example, in Annibale's *Self-Portrait with Figures* or for that matter in Caillebotte's *Self-Portrait at the Easel*, hence the qualifier "implicitly" in the previous sentence. Rather, the canvas must be understood as located just beyond the left-hand edge of the painting; this means in turn that the painter must have proceeded by studying his features and dress as imaged in the mirror, as indeed he is shown doing in the finished painting, and then pivoting his attention as well as his upper body ninety degrees (more or less) to the left in order to "transport" that image to the waiting canvas. Then when the painting was finished it is as if the painter took away the mirror and hung the painting in its place. I call this subgenre the "right-angle" self-portrait, and in *The Moment of Caravaggio* I show that it has played a considerable role not only in his art but also in the western pictorial tradition generally.

My claim in the present context is that David's *Self-Portrait* belongs to that subgenre, which among other things means that it is not simply or even chiefly frontal in orientation, as at first it appears to be.[7] Instead there is a strong lateral thrust to the left, in the first place because of the right-angle *dispositif* I have just described but also because of the absolutely unequivocal position of David's left forearm, hand, and brush, which parallel the picture plane and indeed come close to seeming to coincide with it if not to rest on the bottom framing edge. (The orientation of the chair is plainly a compromise between frontality and the thrust to the left.)

I now want to make a simple but far-reaching suggestion: David's *Self-Portrait* is based on, its structure and crucial aspects of its content derive from, David's great painting of the previous year, *Marat at His Last Breath* (1793; fig. 28).[8]

On taking a first glance at the two works together, the suggestion may seem unlikely, not least because the two compositions are oppositely oriented: the figure of Jean-Paul Marat "faces" to the right; the lateral direction implied by the *Self-Portrait*, once we acknowledge its right-angle structure, is to the left. But of course, as we have seen, the *Self-Portrait* is mirror-reversed, a fact that invites the viewer – in principle, so to speak – to reverse the reversal and imagine not simply a "normalized" figure of the painter

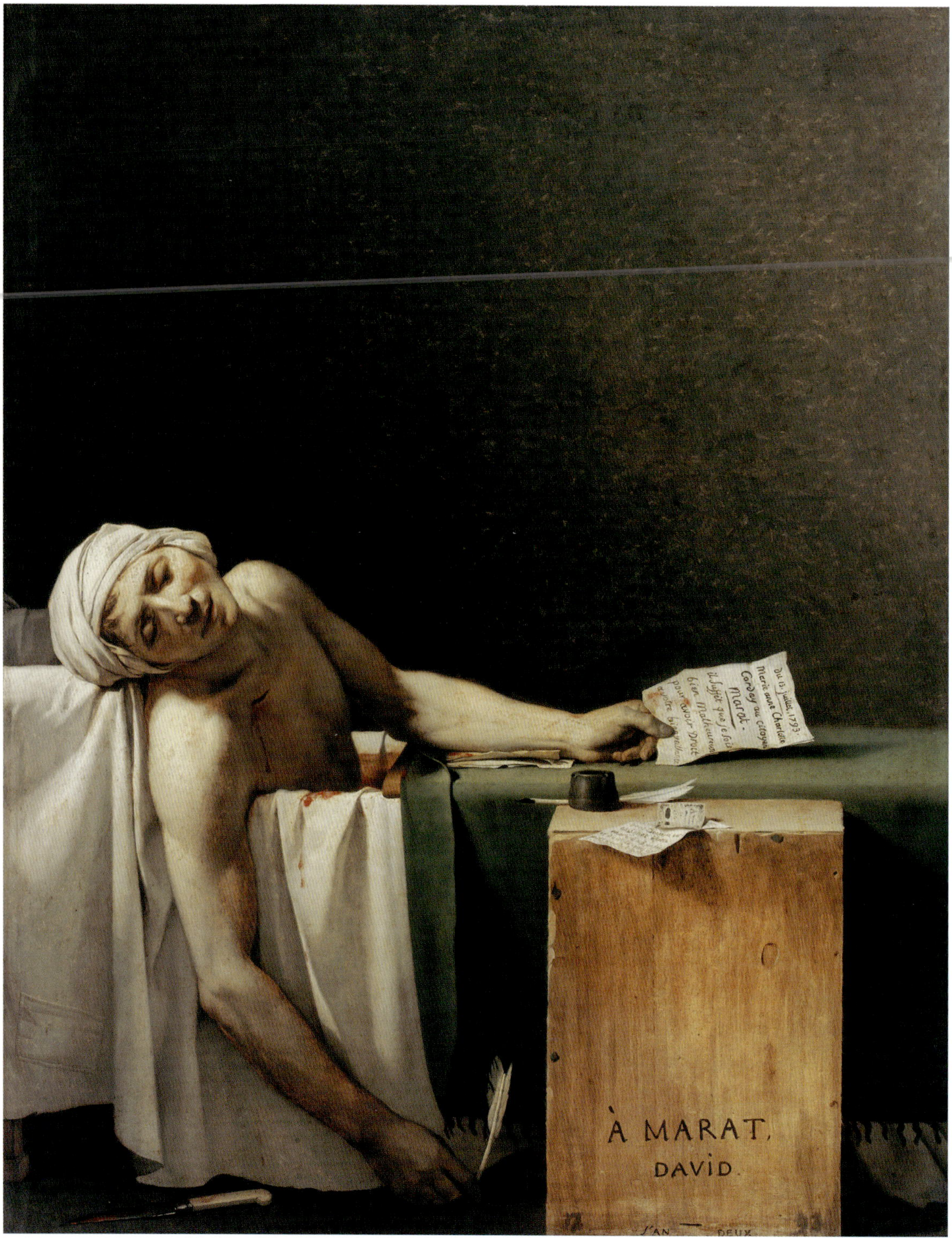

28 Jacques-Louis David, *Marat at His Last Breath*, 1793. Oil on canvas. 165 × 128.3 cm. Brussels, Musées Royaux des Beaux-Arts de Belgique.

but how the *painted image as a whole* would look the other way round. (As if one were looking at a print and being invited to imagine the original plate or block.). I say "in principle" because nothing could be clearer than that generations of viewers of the *Self-Portrait* have been unaware of the invitation, no doubt because the issue of mirror-reversal has remained below the horizon of both ordinary and art-historical consideration.[9] Here it will be helpful to introduce an "unreversed" – which is to say reversed – image of the *Self-Portrait* (fig. 29) and to ask the viewer to compare it with *Marat at His Last Breath*, at which point the suggestion that the first is based on the second gains immensely in force, or so I want to claim. Notice, to begin with, the similarities between the respective pairs of hands: in the *Self-Portrait* the painter holds a brush in his right hand and his palette in his left, while Marat still holds a pen in his right and Corday's blood-tinged note in his left. There is also a parallel, which I take to be delib-

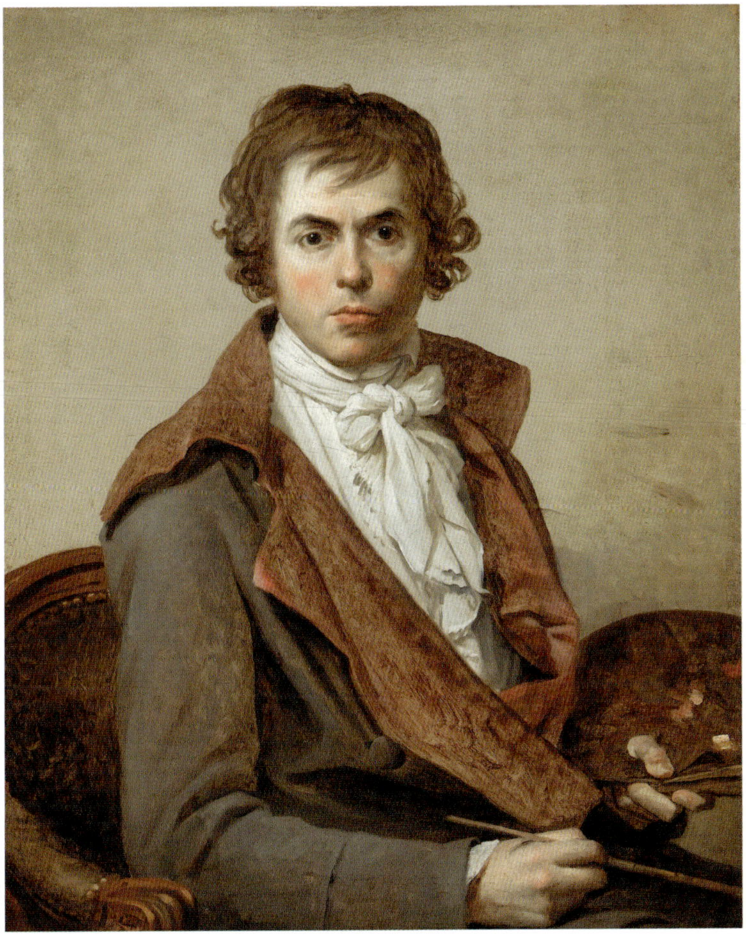

29 Jacques-Louis David, *Self-Portrait*, 1794. Reversed.

erate, between the respective positions and approximate configurations of the back of the painter's chair and that of Marat's bathtub. (Lajer-Burcharth has commented on the oddness of the position of the armchair and of David's relation to it.[10]) In the same structural vein, (the depicted) David's left arm and hand holding a paintbrush improbably describe a right angle (upper arm versus forearm) that comes close to coinciding with the picture plane. This seems to allude to the wooden block, the near face of which (bearing the inscription "À MARAT / DAVID" made with such a brush) appears to coincide perfectly with the picture plane in *Marat at His Last Breath*. And then there is a looser analogy, which nevertheless does not seem fanciful once one grants the basic connection between the two works, between David's white linen cravat and the linen cloth or bandage in which Marat's head has been wrapped.

Finally, perhaps most tellingly, there is the strange lack of finish and the disturbing color of the wide, wine-red lapel of David's *houppelande*, a kind of coat associated, Lajer-Burcharth has noted, with the revolutionaries.[11] But the fundamental discussion of the coat and its pictorial treatment is in T. J. Clark's superb essay on the self-portrait, "Gross David with the Swoln Cheek," in which he writes:

> Four things at least contribute to [the lapel's] power. Its being so large: its going on and on across David's chest and lap till it ends abruptly in an edge drawn at right angles to one of the fingers holding the palette. Its being unfinished: that is, marked so openly with the painter's brush, whose traces are so broad and animate in places, notably halfway down, that they look like nothing so much as fingerprints. Its having such an evocative color, which most writers call crimson, but which might as well be that of dried or drying blood. . . . And above all, its having the look of being the *inside* of something, turned or folded out, exposed to a view by a new Doctor Tulp. (291; emphasis in original)

Clark continues:

> A lot depends at this point on how hard and fast we take the analogy to be between the body and the clothes that it wears. Some kind or degree of analogy there is. The lapel is simply too strange an object to stay safely inside the circuit of possible reference: it is too long, too wide, too regular, too stiff with what seems to color it, too translucent or anyway too insubstantial (stiff with matter but also strangely impalpable). These qualities seem to be metaphorical. Could we not say that what we are looking at in the lapel is a kind of imagining of one's flesh as if it no longer belonged to you, as it would look if it were put on display? (292)

This could not be bettered, and it takes only a small additional step to connect Clark's description of the fleshliness of the lapel with David's previous rendering of Marat's naked and fatally wounded body, a rendering that includes the masterly use of transparent shadows in the area of Marat's chest, neck and upper arms (to spell this out, I am suggesting that such shadows in *Marat at His Last Breath* are one implied reference of the unfinish of the lapel in the *Self-Portrait*).[12] I might add that the more I study the comparison between the two works the more I am inclined to see the fall of the broad lapel onto (the depicted) David's left shoulder and upper back as all but miming the collapse of Marat's head and upper body.

Another focus of Clark's discussion is the painter's hands and the instruments they hold:

> One hand is intent on keeping hold of a palette and paints which look liable to slip out of the realm of reference altogether into that of nightmare. Perhaps the slippage has already happened: the bits and pieces of the hand seem as much extruded by the palette as getting a grip on it, and the configuration they become part of is only half legible (and wholly uncanny). The other hand is the opposite – clenched and close to us, coming out of its sleeve as abruptly as Jack in the box, a bit wooden like the knuckles on the chairarm, and hanging on to its brush like grim death. (295)

As for the palette, Clark astutely says, "Some care seems to me to have been taken to make the palette a poor candidate for the Truth of anything" (299). And after stressing the palette's quasi-physiognomic character, in a flight of imagination he characterizes it as "[David's] brain, decomposing between his fingers. His thumb through the hole in the palette . . . is his premonition of the guillotine" (301).[13] The point is not whether one subscribes to Clark's metaphors in their entirety. What matters is his sense that the palette is also *something else* – I want to say that it is also the blood-tinged note from Corday – as well as his intuition that both hands in David's *Self-portrait* are acting in excess of any visible cause and moreover are doing so in a way that is essentially deathly. Finally, I cannot help thinking that David's tumor, which the *Self-Portrait* places in shadow but does not seek to eliminate, was for him analogous to Marat's skin disease, which *Marat at His Last Breath* depicts in a similarly restrained fashion.

Let me assume that by this point the reader is persuaded of the basic connection between the two works. For such a reader it no longer suffices to be told by Philippe Bordes that by virtue of depicting the painter holding the tools of his profession, "the image of the artist at forty-two, after two years in the demanding role of a politician, emblematizes his determination to become once again a full-time painter."[14] It is not just that the prison *Self-Portrait* implies no such distinction between politician and painter, rather it effectively counters it by deliberately superimposing David's image of himself on his previous image of the dead or dying *ami du peuple*, as Marat styled himself in his eponymous newspaper. Nor will Lajer-Burcharth be found convincing when she suggests that what she calls

> David's hesitant commitment to the pictorial sign . . . an economy of disjunction on the level of form . . . has to be seen as an effect of David's troubled negotation with his own body as a material site of political meaning. The houppelande, and the palette that "did not take," had something to do with the way the Revolution drenched the body and its accoutrements with political meaning, turning them into signs difficult for David to handle under the circumstances . . . (41)

For Lajer-Burchharth, all this belongs to an unconscious stratum of conflictual forces: ultimately she wishes to argue that it is "the aesthetic and subjective pressure under which David found himself in the Hôtel des Fermes that manifests itself here as the shadow of the unrepresentable" (47), a depressingly conventional formulation, for all the sophistication of what has gone before. But once it is recognized that David must have intended his *Self-Portrait* to be readable (again, in principle) as alluding intimately to *Marat at His Last Breath*, the "economy of disjunction" Lajer-Burcharth describes takes on an altogether different valence.

The question that now arises is this: what are we to make of David's determination at that precarious time and in that disheartening place to portray himself as very nearly a second Marat? Nothing seems clearer than that it must be viewed as a sign of his continuing admiration for the *ami du peuple*, indeed of a sense of identification with Marat's status, at least until 9 Thermidor, as the greatest of the revolutionary martyrs. But how is this to be reconciled with the threat of the guillotine hanging over David himself? The overthrow of Robespierre and the Jacobins had taken place on July 27, and Robespierre, Saint-Just, and nearly a hundred others of their party had been executed within a few days. In late August and early September David could only have felt that he faced the extreme risk of a similar fate. And indeed it seems to have been during those weeks, more or less, that he drafted the so-called "Speech of David, Representative of the People, in Response to the Calumnies Launched against Him," a fourteen-page handwritten manuscript of a speech that he expected to deliver in his defense at the National Convention.[15] (At issue was the precise extent of David's guilt for the excesses of the Jacobin Terror and related events.) So how are we to understand his deliberate and ingenious exploiting of the resources of the self-portrait to suggest an identification with Marat at a moment, we might think, when the least continuing association with the abhorred Jacobins could have been fatal to his chances of survival?

The answer, it turns out, has to with the continuing albeit ultimately short-lived cult of Marat, which in August and early September 1794 was still a living force. Marat was murdered on July 13, 1793 and a public display of his embalmed body, organized by David, followed two days later. On November 25 the National Convention voted to transport his ashes to the Panthéon. (David himself had called for this when he presented *Marat at His Last Breath* to the National Convention roughly ten days before.[16]) Gracchus Babeuf, the radical journalist and future leader of a failed *coup d'état*, renewed the call on September 14, 1794, and Marat's ashes were in fact conveyed to the Panthéon on September 21 (even as the disgraced Mirabeau's were removed). The most useful summary of these developments is by Jean-Claude Bonnet in *La Naissance du Panthéon*:

> If the cult of the martyr had its high points and low points, it survived for a certain period, in a muted way, with such success that the pantheonization finally took place on 21 September 1794. Thus the Friend of the People seemed, for a time, to be the only one to retain some degree of influence after the shipwreck. "The apotheosis of a Marat? Is that believable? Especially after 9 Thermidor!" as Mercier rightly exclaimed. And this fact still remains a partial enigma for us. No doubt there is in it an illustration of the uncertainties and contradictions of the thermidorian Republic at its beginnings. The patheonization of Marat appears in effect as an out of focus event that is absolutely typical of the period. It was undoubtedly accepted as both a guarantee of revolutionary continuity and a symbolic revenge against Robespierre. Did this last not constantly manifest his annoyance at the senseless deification of Marat and postpone the pantheonization of the Friend of the People? To this idolatrous faith whose initiative amounted almost exclusively to the *sans culottes* and whose unpredictable effects he always dreaded, he always opposed those, more philosophical, of Reason and the Supreme Being. In this way Marat could appear, under the circumstances, to be the victim of Robespierre after having been that of Charlotte Corday.[17]

So exceptional and unstable a situation could not last. "Artificially maintained by a handful of the faithful," Bonnet goes on to write, "devotion to the Friend came to an end in February 1795: the gilded youth gave the signal of the destruction of his bust in the Théâtre Feydeau on the 2nd of that month, then the Convention overturned the declaration of pantheonization on the 8th, the Carrousel monument was destroyed on the 10th, and the remains removed from the Panthéon on the 26th."[18] After which plaster busts of the *ami du peuple* were destroyed all over France. In Bonnet's ironic prose: "Thus the Friend of the People disappeared, in fireworks without seriousness which were no doubt less than he would have dreamed of, but which were so many firecrackers rather appropriate to his explosive inspiration."[19] By then, too, the portraits of Lepelletier de Saint-Fargeau and Marat that had been hanging in the

National Convention had been removed from their places of honor and returned to the artist.[20]

There we have it. David painted his *Self-Portrait* at a moment when the cult of Marat was on the verge of enjoying its last public success, the transport of the martyr's ashes to the Panthéon. It was a moment when a distinction could be drawn between Marat and Robespierre (and was so drawn, by Babeuf among others) – and in fact it is Robespierre whom David singles out for blame in his draft "Speech" of late August 1794.[21] The reference to *Marat at his Last Breath* in the *Self-Portrait* was therefore not immediately full of risk for David himself, who probably intended the association as perpetuating his own image not only as a painter but also, at least as importantly, as a revolutionary martyr in the style of Marat, should events turn out badly in the weeks and months to follow. (This fits with what seems to have been his resolve to begin the portrait immediately following his imprisonment: there might well have been no time to lose, in which case it would have been both his pictorial and his political testament.) Clark's suggestion that "what we are looking at in the lapel is a kind of imagining of one's flesh as if it no longer belonged to you, as it would look if it were put on display" thus comes close to capturing the truth of David's intentions. The flesh in question is not just David's but also Marat's – say David/Marat's. By February 1795 the situation had changed fundamentally – Marat was now an extremely dangerous reference – and it is not surprising that David subsequently gave, in effect entrusted, the *Self-Portrait* to his former student Jean-Baptiste Isabey, preferring not to have so potentially self-incriminating a work in his possession.[22] (Unfortunately we know nothing about when or under what circumstances the gift was made.)

One last point concerns David's much less famous but marvelously intense *Self-Portrait* of 1791 (fig. 30), since the late nineteenth century in the collection of self-portraits in the Uffizi.[23] Like the prison *Self-Portrait*, it is manifestly mirror-reversed, as is shown by the position of the tumor inside the painter's right cheek instead of the left. (For David, avoiding the issue of mirror-reversal by eliding his hands was not an option – the tumor was bound to force the issue one way or the other.) And here, too, we seem to be in the presence of a right-angle *dispositif*: although the head of the painter faces us directly (as in the *Self-Portrait* of 1794), his torso is turned even more strongly to the left (our left, which is also to say to the actual painter's left) than in the later work and his left arm (the reflection of the actual painter's right arm) is shown in the act of crossing his body in the direction of the implied canvas just off-picture to the left. This is not quite to say that he is shown in the act of painting: the arm's body-crossing action, what we see of it, remains ambiguous in its significance, though it is just possible that the arm and (elided) hand holding a brush are to be understood

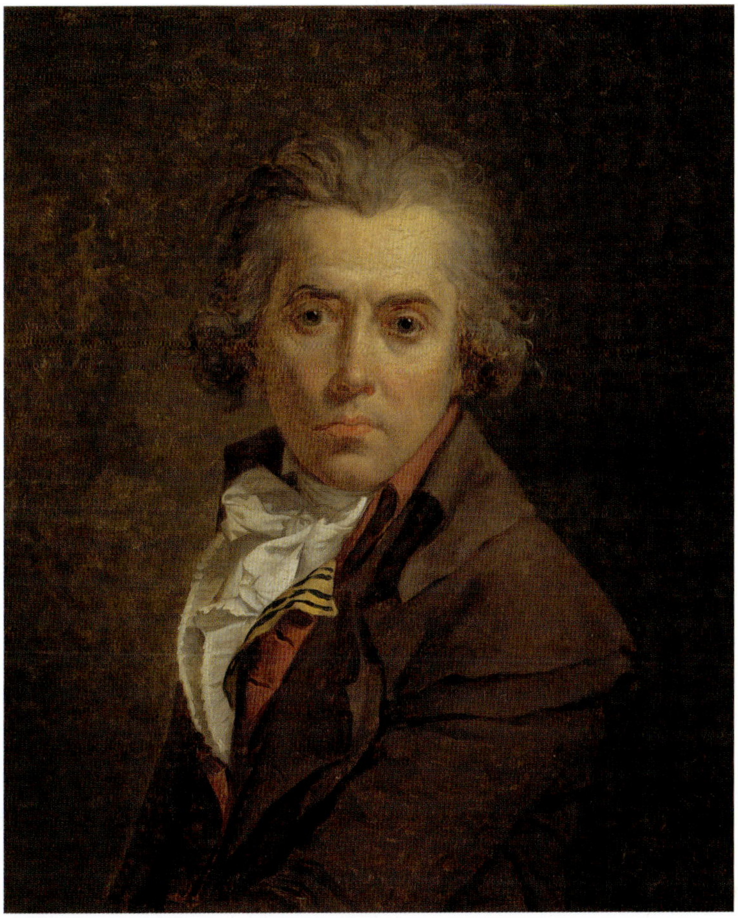

30 Jacques-Louis David, *Self-Portrait*, 1791. Oil on canvas. 64 × 53 cm. Florence, Galleria degli Uffizi.

as reaching toward a palette gripped in the other hand – but this is conjectural. What the 1791 canvas does make clear, however, is that when David in the Hôtel des Fermes, under the shadow of the guillotine, began to envision a new and perhaps valedictory self-portrait, the strategy of openly acknowledging mirror-reversal – historically a rarity, as I have said – was already in his armory. The further, altogether brilliant stroke was to use that strategy in concert with the right-angle arrangement at once to enable and to mask an intimate connection between the prison *Self-Portrait* and *Marat at His Last Breath*. To mask but not to deny – though after February 1795 it doubtless would have greatly relieved David to know that the connection would remain undetectable to posterity for as long as it has.[24]

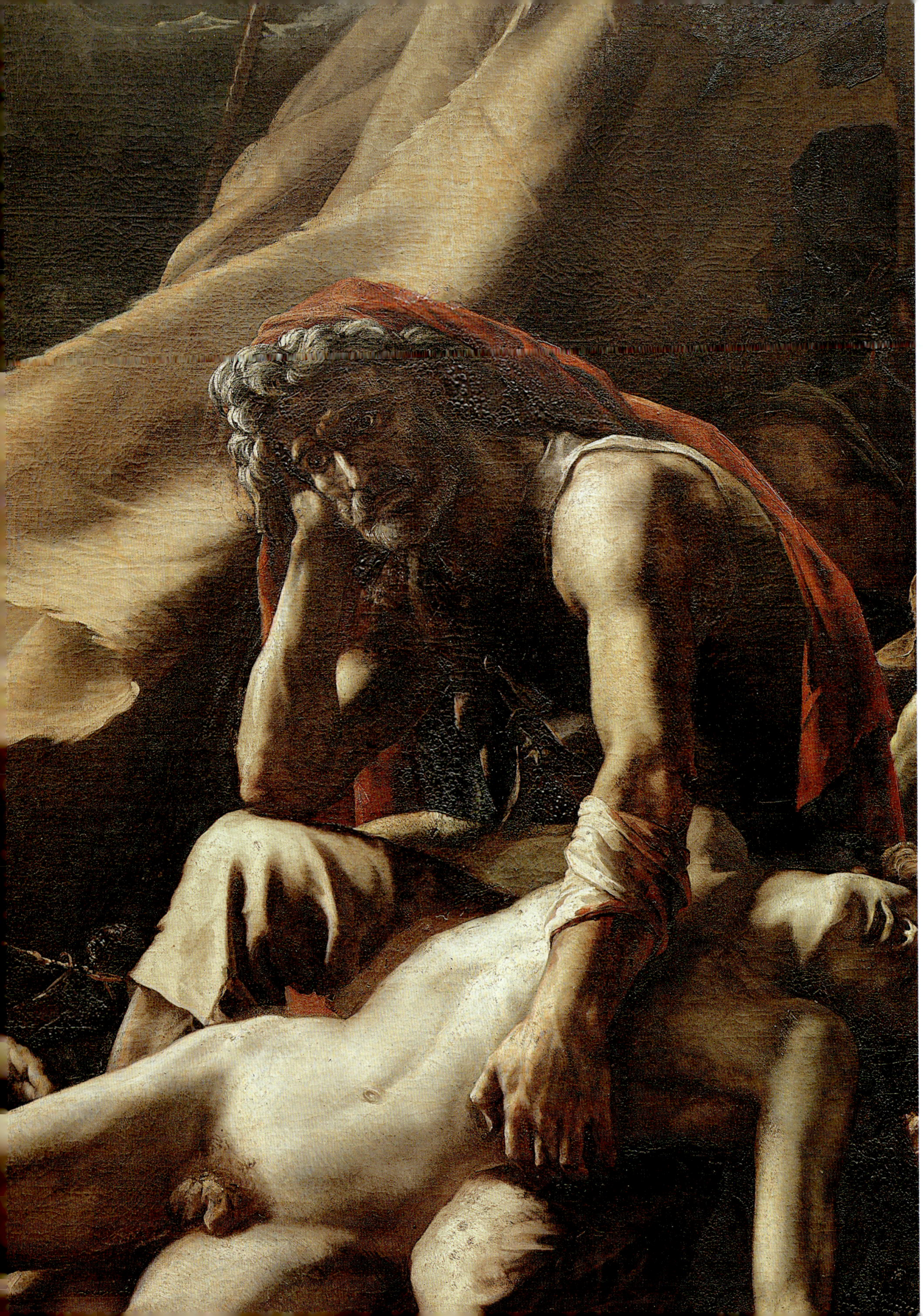

• 3 •

GÉRICAULT'S ROMANTICISM

I

Historiographically speaking, we know as much about the life and career of Théodore Géricault as we are ever likely to.[1] Maybe some scholar will get lucky and a few additional biographical facts will emerge about his year – more or less – in Italy or his year – slightly over, comprising a short stay and a longer one – in London, both largely blanks in his chronology. And in the course of time new drawings and a few more oil paintings are bound to come to light. But even then, the essential picture will not be altered. Born in Rouen in 1791, to a family of means that included one of the Revolutionary regicides, Géricault seems to have been passionate about two things, painting and horses (also women, especially one woman, his maternal uncle's young wife, Alexandrine-Modeste Caruel, with whom he had a disastrous affair). As a young aspirant, he studied briefly with Carle Vernet and somewhat longer with Pierre-Narcisse Guérin, noted for highly concentrated and stagey scenes based on classical subjects (Phaedra and Hippolytus, Andromache and Pyrrhus, Clytemnestra and Agamemnon), though Géricault is often aptly described as largely self-taught. He made his Salon debut in 1812 with a *tour de force* of astonishingly vigorous brushwork and intensely glowing color featuring a magnificent rearing horse, the *Charging Chasseur* (see fig. 38), which is said to have attracted admiring notice from David himself ("Where does he come from? I don't know this touch," he is supposed to have said[2]), and two years later exhibited another single-figure military painting of comparable size, of another warrior, this time on foot, with a splendid horse accompanying him, the *Wounded Cuirassier* – on the whole a less successful but still extremely imposing work (Géricault was then just 23). During these years too he made numerous smaller paintings based on military themes as well as countless studies of horses, his perennial obsession.

In 1816 he journeyed to Rome – stopping at Florence and visiting Naples as well – where he stayed roughly a year, studying Michelangelo, Raphael, and, it also seems,

31 (*facing page*) Théodore Géricault, *The Raft of the "Medusa"* (detail of fig. 49).

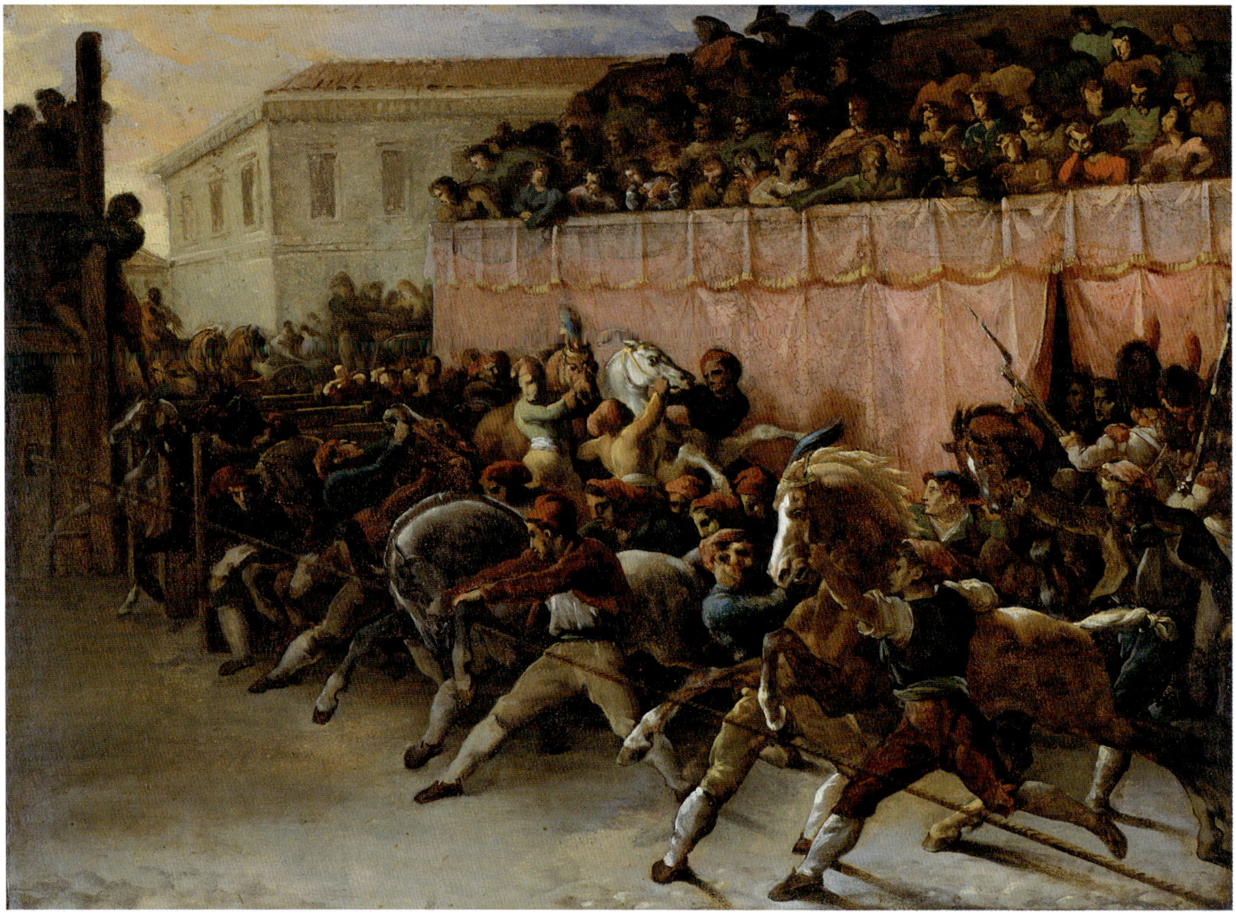

32 Théodore Géricault, *Start of the Race of the Barberi Horses*, 1817. Oil on paper mounted on canvas. 44.9 × 59.5 cm. Baltimore, Walters Art Museum.

Roman equestrian sculpture, producing a host of small works on classical themes (among them a Michelangelesque *Leda and the Swan*), and laboring on an ambitious project based on an annual Roman event, the race of the riderless Barberi horses down the Corso, from the Piazza del Popolo to the present Piazza Vittorio Emmanuele. In the end, the project was abandoned (he is said to have ordered a canvas thirty feet wide [nearly ten meters]), but not before he had made scores of drawings and twenty small paintings (five of which have since been lost), mainly depicting the start of the race as muscular grooms struggle to bring the horses to the starting line and to keep them from bolting prematurely once they are there. Two of those paintings in particular, one from early on and the other from near the end of his efforts, in Baltimore (1816; fig. 32) and the Louvre (1817; see fig. 46), give a vivid idea of the interplay between men and horses that evidently attracted Géricault to the theme.

Back in Paris, Géricault resumed his affair with Alexandrine-Modeste, and soon enough a son was born, precipitating a family scandal the secret of which emerged only in 1976. He also made a gripping small painting based, it seems, on a Roman subject, the *Cattle Market* at the Fogg Art Museum at Harvard (1817; see fig. 47), an oil on paper that held me spellbound virtually every day during my graduate student and junior faculty years. But the major project of the post-Roman period was of course the monumental *Raft of the "Medusa"* (1819; see figs. 31, 49, 51), a work based on recent history, the shipwreck of a French frigate off the coast of Senegal and then the abandonment of a makeshift raft bearing 147 men (and one woman) from the ship, all owing to the incompetence of the captain. The incident was politically charged, the captain, a returned émigré, being a recent appointment under the Bourbon regime; Géricault himself has been associated with the Liberal circle centered in the studio of his close friend, the painter Horace Vernet (son of Carle), which like his own studio was on the rue des Martyrs below the village of Montmartre.[3] Probably during the fifteen-month-long campaign on the *Raft* (1818–19), much of which was conducted in a larger studio in the faubourg du Roule, Géricault also painted a series of severed heads and limbs, the "models" for which were taken from a nearby hospital (1818; see figs. 42, 43); these remain among the most intense and original canvases of the first decades of the nineteenth century. Eventually he produced the stupendous picture that today hangs in the Louvre. In the Salon of 1819, however, it was at best a moderate success, in part because Géricault, who was allowed to determine its placement, made the mistake of having it hung too high, greatly diminishing its effect.[4] Partway through the exhibition it was lowered, which helped considerably. When awards were distributed Géricault received a gold medal, and an offer was made to buy the *Raft* by the state, but he seems to have been disappointed by the offer, despite the fact that he must have known that the subject could only have been regarded as a provocation. In the wake of these events he is said to have been seriously depressed, though as so often we know much less about this than we would like. In any case, there was to be no subsequent submission by him to the Salon.

In April 1820 Géricault traveled to London to exhibit the *Raft* at the Egyptian Hall on Piccadilly; the exhibition ran from June to December 1820 and was a financial triumph. As already mentioned, facts about his London adventure are scarce, though we do know that he was recognized as a significant figure by the British art establishment, that he enjoyed at least one gratifying "conquest," and that he produced a series of magnificent lithographs, taking advantage (he wrote a friend) of the British taste for

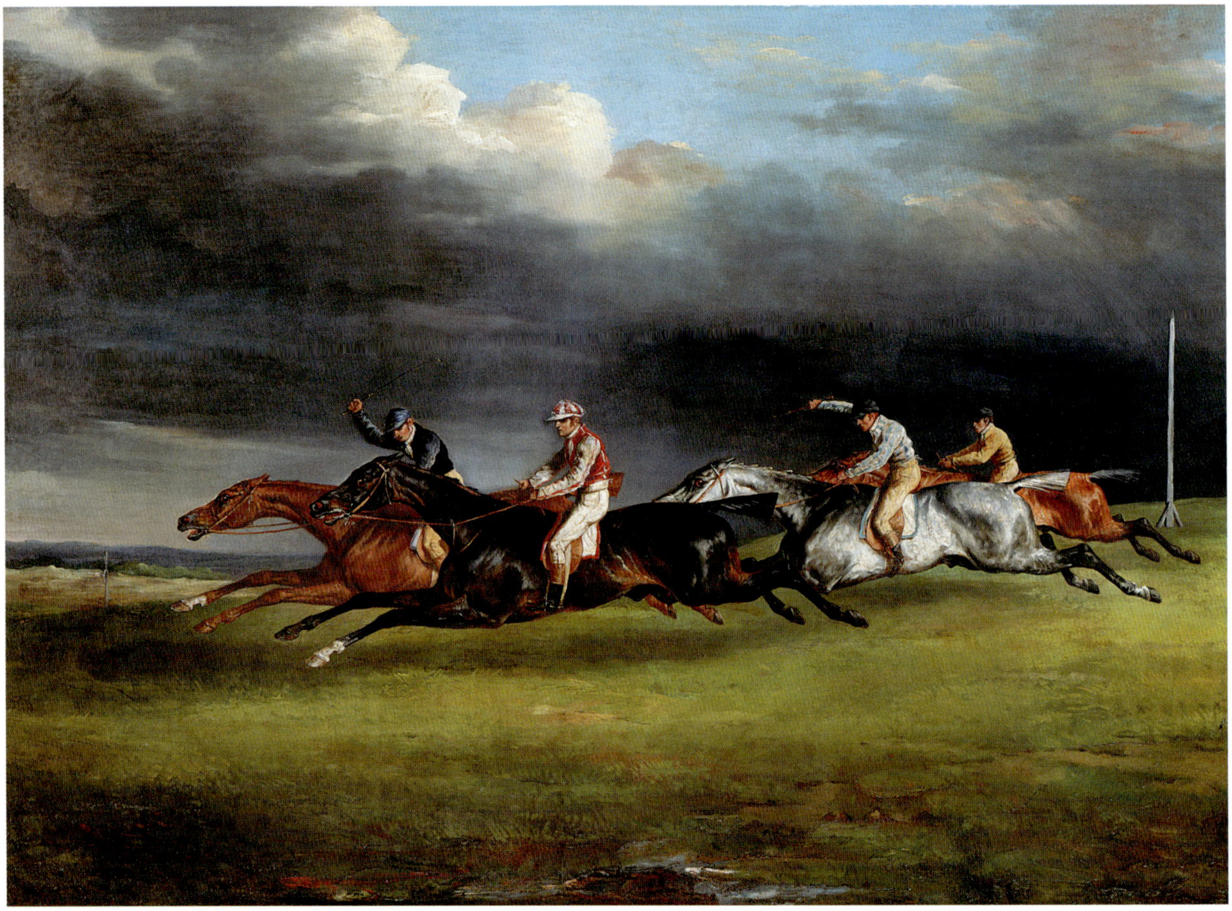

33 Théodore Géricault, *Epsom Derby*, 1821. Oil on canvas. 92 × 122.5 cm. Paris, Musée du Louvre.

that relatively new medium.[5] The outstanding painting to come out of his London stay is the haunting *Epsom Derby* (1821; fig. 33), which makes something new and unforgettable – an image of time-consciousness unlike any other in pictorial art – out of the all-four-legs-outstretched schema of traditional British racing prints. One additional meaningful fact is that in November 1820, on their way back to Paris, Géricault and Horace Vernet stopped in Brussels to pay their respects to David. The older artist was deeply gratified by this, as he made clear in letters to no less than four of his former students.

In December 1821 Géricault returned for good to Paris, and probably some time after that painted a series of "Portraits of the Insane" (1821–2; see figs. 74–6) – supposedly there were ten, of which five survive – about which once again we know nothing certain (not even whether originally there were indeed ten). Possibly, they were done at the suggestion of the celebrated psychiatrist Jean-Etienne-Dominique Esquirol, a reformer in the treatment of the mentally disturbed and a pioneer in the study of what he called "monomania." But this is speculation. Géricault also made several series of lithographs largely based on images of horses, as well as a number of smaller paintings in oil, including the unforgettable *Lime Kiln* (1822; see fig. 73) about which I shall have more to say. In the spring of 1822 he suffered the first of several horseback accidents that gravely wounded his spine; infection followed, eating away at the spine itself; he spent much of 1823 in bed in great pain, stoically enduring terrible operations, attended by devoted friends who watched in horror as their handsome, muscular, athletic friend wasted away before their eyes. He died on January 26, 1824, in his thirty-third year. His death mask is skeletal.

Géricault himself felt that he had failed to make good on his immense talents. "If I had only made five *tableaux*," his assistant Antoine Montfort reports he said toward the end, "but I've done nothing."[6] This is much too harsh – Géricault accomplished more than enough to secure his position as one of the great painters, draftsmen, print makers, and indeed sculptors of the nineteenth century – but not completely unreasonable. By *tableaux* he would have meant ambitious, large-size, fully realized paintings, capable of commanding attention at the Salon, and this he rightly understood he had failed to do. (The *Raft*, Montfort adds, no longer satisfied him.) More broadly, Géricault was prodigiously gifted – in fact one could defend the view that no painter or draftsman in all of modern art was more richly endowed.[7] And yet in the end his achievement, for all its range, originality, overwhelming vitality, and moments of exceptional grandeur – also, I shall suggest, its philosophical profundity – was, one cannot help feeling, nothing like what it might have been under other circumstances. But what circumstances, exactly, does one have in mind? This question among others will concern me in what follows.

2

In the last pages of his informative book, *Géricault in Italy* (1997), the art historian Wheelock Whitney writes, "The whole of Géricault's brief, brilliant career can be viewed as an intense and ultimately fruitless quest for satisfactory subject matter." This is an interesting claim, though the terms in which it is phrased are far too limited. "[Géricault's] dilemma," Whitney goes on to say, "resulted in large measure from the times in which he lived, a period of transition and uncertainty in the history of art. He found himself torn between the conventional values of his early academic training, with its reverence for the antique and the great masters, and his own distinctly naturalist tendencies, his precocious thirst for the real . . ."[8] Such an account issues naturally from Whitney's survey of the Riderless Horses project, which on the one hand was based on an actual event and on the other continually veered toward a kind of classicism, with heroic male nudes (or near-nudes) struggling with magnificent horses in "timeless" settings: thus the culminating canvas in the Louvre (1817; see fig. 46) places men and horses before ancient temple architecture, though the principal figure wears green tights that end mid-calf – a concession to actuality. (But he is barefoot and his upper body is bare, while the figure at the left wears a short tunic that is unabashedly classical in inspiration.) Nor was the Riderless Horses project unique in this regard: at some point in 1818, shortly before or after embarking on the *Raft*, Géricault made a series of ink-and-wash drawings based on a sensational murder that had recently taken place, the so-called Fualdès affair, and in these too the participants and victim are depicted both clothed and naked (in one they wear "transparent" tunics). The further implication of Whitney's remarks seems to be that Géricault could neither break free of his classical training nor – presumably because the time was not yet ripe – move directly into a forthright realism.

No doubt I am putting more pressure on a few sentences than they were meant to bear. My point, in any case, is that Whitney is on to something important but also that far more than considerations of subject matter or indeed "style" (in the sense of classicizing tendencies versus an incipient realism) must be kept in mind if we are to grasp the true nature of Géricault's difficulties. One way of framing the issue is to glance ahead at the first ambitious paintings by Géricault's junior by seven years, Eugène Delacroix, who not only knew and admired Géricault but actually posed for one of the figures in the foreground of the *Raft*. (Looking back roughly thirty-five years later Delacroix reports that after seeing the not yet completed *Raft* he was so excited that he ran like a madman all the way home.[9]) In the *Barque of Dante* (fig. 34), for example, exhibited in the Salon of 1822 – Delacroix was then just twenty-four – there is, as has always been recognized, a canny reference to the *Raft* of three years before, both in the depiction of a "marine" theme and in the extremity of the subject, with five figures of the damned threatening to swamp the barque and two others grappling fiercely in the boiling Styx. But in the first place the *Barque* is much smaller and more concentrated than the *Raft*; in the second, the subject is entirely literary and imaginative, without the least reference to actuality. Beyond that, Delacroix has succeeded in shifting the emphasis strongly toward "aesthetic" or say "stylistic" considerations in and through the marriage of vigorous brushwork and extraordinary colorism, reminiscent in some

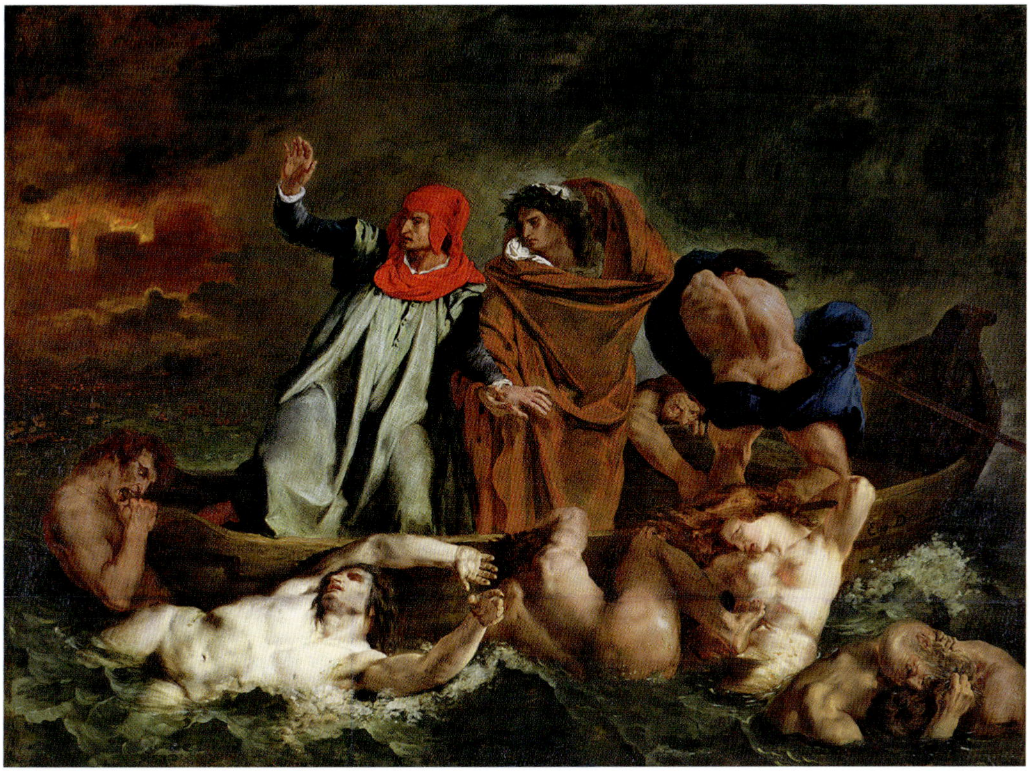

34 Eugène Delacroix, *The Barque of Dante*, 1822. Oil on canvas. 189 × 241.5 cm. Paris, Musée du Louvre.

respects of the *Charging Chasseur* but even more "Rubensian" in its freedom from strictly descriptive concerns (the famous drops of water, consisting of separate touches of red and green, are an emblem of this). In the same "aesthetic" spirit, the painting declares its independence from the laws of verisimilitude, as in its treatment of the barque itself, an implausible vessel for any purpose much less for navigating the waters of Hell (such a declaration would reach its *ne plus ultra* in the extravagant *Death of Sardanapalus* of 1827), and the hyper-expressive physiognomies and extreme behavior of several of the damned either struggling with each other or assaulting the bark. Finally, most important from my point of view, the two protagonists, Dante and Virgil, although looking off to the viewer's left, have been depicted from the front (in fact the entire composition faces the beholder without reservations of any kind), which is to say that Delacroix felt under no obligation to seek to comply with the antitheatrical animus of the Diderotian *tableau* – indeed I would say that the deepest originality of the *Barque*, and more broadly of Delacroix's career-launching canvases of the 1820s, is the way in which, from the very first, he brilliantly contrived not to resolve or even to confront but rather to circumvent the entire Diderotian problematic, as if the latter were simply no longer an issue for ambitious painting.[10] Something of the sort also holds for the seemingly antithetical art of Delacroix's arch-rival, the older Jean-Auguste-Dominique Ingres, in that throughout his production too what I have just called imaginative and "aesthetic" considerations, in his case keyed to the genres of the nude and the portrait, an ornamental, Raphaelesque mastery of line, a highly original taste for large areas of decorative color, an "orientalist" fascination with minutely wrought, glittering metallic objects such as women's jewelry, and an adamant refusal of stylistic consistency, take precedence over dramaturgical concerns, which seem almost incidental in comparison.[11]

All this is given particular significance by the fact that by 1822 or indeed 1827 (the year of the *Sardanapalus*) the Diderotian problematic had by no means run its course. On the contrary, as mentioned in "David / Manet,", the persuasive representation of absorption subsequently emerged as the central aim of Millet's peasant pictures of the 1850s and 60s, even as sophisticated contemporaries, as exemplified by art critics such as Baudelaire, Gautier, and Duranty, were sharply divided as to the success of his efforts.[12] And in *Courbet's Realism* I have presented Courbet's art, starting with his earliest self-portraits of the 1840s and including all his Realist canvases of the late 1840s and 1850s from the *After Dinner at Ornans* to the magnificent *Painter's Studio* of 1855, as consistently antitheatrical in intent, based on a hyperbolic project of seeking to paint himself all but corporeally into the painting being realized at the end of his brush, my thought being that if this could be brought about – though of course it could not – at least one beholder, the painter-beholder, would no longer be present before the painting. (In that quite limited albeit ontologically charged sense the painting would escape being beheld.) And, as is rehearsed in the first essay in this book, I understand Manet's breakthrough paintings of the 1860s as signaling the ultimate "failure" of Courbet's project as well as a momentous crisis for the Diderotian undertaking generally, the supreme fiction or metaphysical illusion that the beholder does not exist having become no longer tenable – hence the turn to facingness, strikingness, and in other respects too the radical acknowledgment that paintings are indeed made to be beheld.

• • •

3

What of Géricault? To begin with, how are we to understand his situation with regard to the Diderotian critique of theatricality? More particularly, in the light of the claims and arguments put forward in "David/Manet," what relation if any exists between the abrupt and total abandonment of the antitheatrical project in David's figure paintings from the *Sappho, Phaon, and Cupid* to the *Mars Disarmed by Venus and the Graces* (exhibited in Paris the year of Géricault's death) and, for example, the *Raft of the "Medusa"*?

What makes the latter question tricky to answer is the fact that the outpouring of large-scale, formally and stylistically inventive Napoleonic painting that dominated French culture during the first decade of the nineteenth century appears on the face of it to have nothing to do with David's resort to "Anacreonic" subject matter and concomitant counter-Diderotian "turning" toward the beholder. But this is only partly true. Take, for example, Antoine-Jean Gros's celebrated canvases, *Bonaparte Visiting the Plague-Stricken at Jaffa* (1804; fig. 35) and *Napoleon Visiting the Battlefield of Eylau the Morning after the Battle* (1808; fig. 36), both of which, I want to say, reveal an unqualified acceptance of action and expression as *already* wholly theatrical – an acceptance of the theatrical as not merely pervasive but normative, a universal condition of action and expression rather than an inferior and in principle overcomeable modality of these.[13] Simply put, in Gros's Napoleonic canvases, as in Napoleonic painting generally, action and expression were intended to be beheld by viewers inside and outside the representation. Questions about the relation of inner meaning to outward manifestation are thus rendered moot (the notion of absorption seems no longer to have any purchase), or at any rate they are continually displaced in ways that make them impossible to resolve (although one might think to say of Napoleon in the *Jaffa* that he appears absorbed not in touching the sick man's plague sore but rather in being seen to do so, the painting's political effectiveness would not have been compromised by such a reading, which in any case seems artificial, importing a distinction where one does not apply). Understood in this way, the rise of Napoleon and the call for propagandistic painting not only mobilized a younger generation of painters – Géricault's immediate predecessors – but also placed in abeyance, effectively suspended, the entire Diderotian project. That David himself was less than comfortable with this development is suggested by his spectacularly unpersuasive *Distribution of the Eagles* (1810; see fig. 20); fortunately for him, the immense *Coronation of Napoleon* (1805–7) gave him a static, group-portrait-like subject he could treat in a straightforward yet richly painterly manner, without having to deal with physical movement or ostensible displays of emotion.

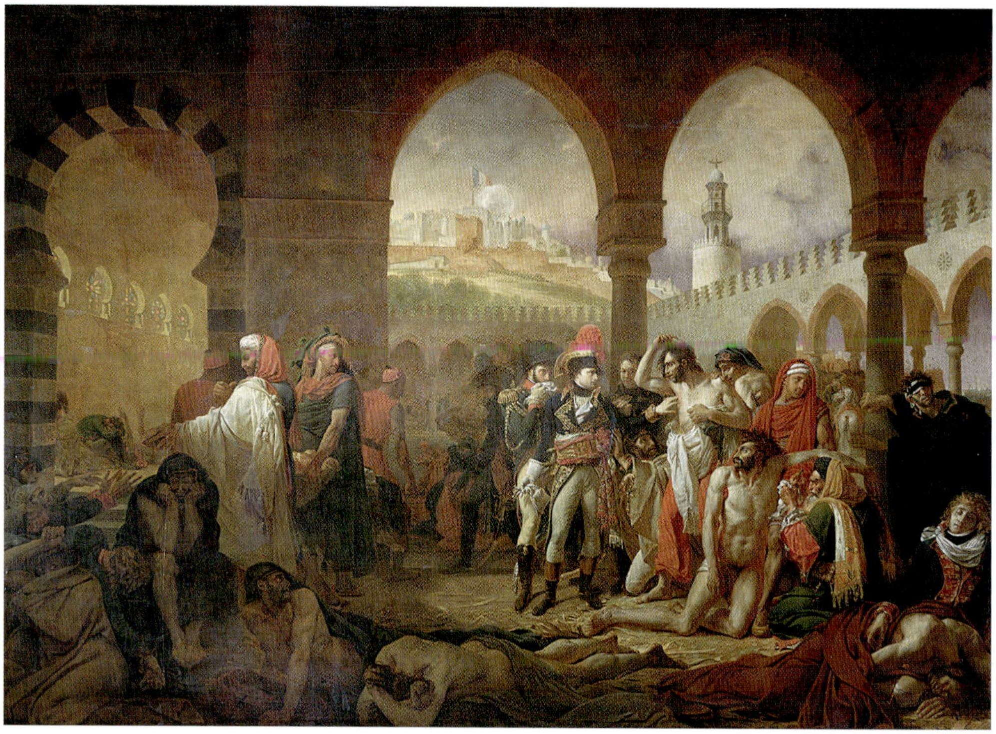

35 Antoine-Jean Gros, *Bonaparte Visiting the Plague-Stricken at Jaffa*, 1804. Oil on canvas. 523 × 715 cm. Paris, Musée du Louvre.

36 Antoine-Jean Gros, *Napoleon Visiting the Battlefield of Eylau the Morning after the Battle*, 1808. Oil on canvas. 521 × 784 cm. Paris, Musée du Louvre.

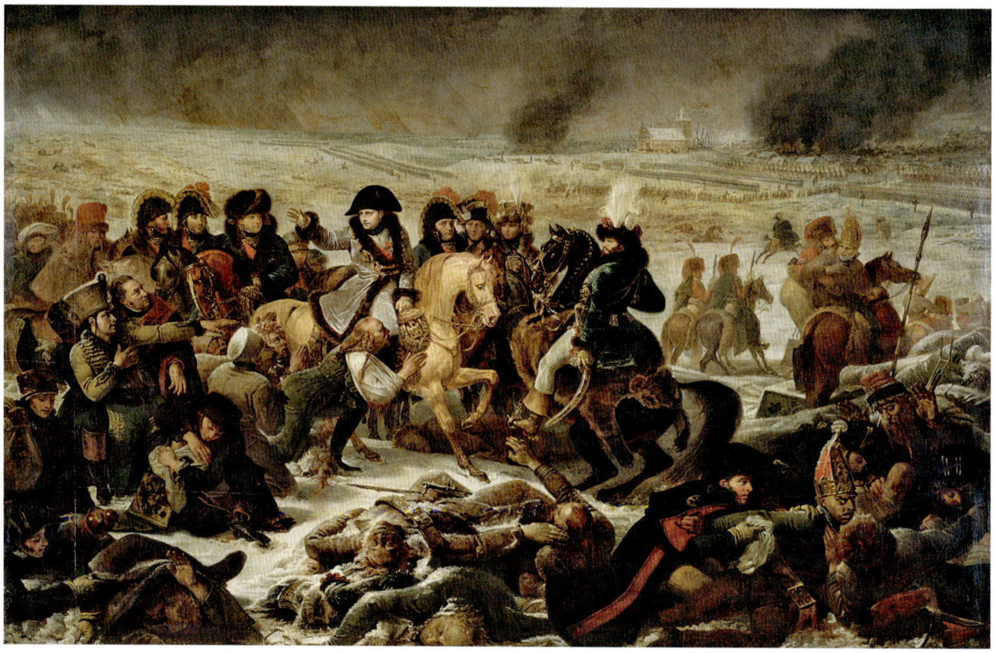

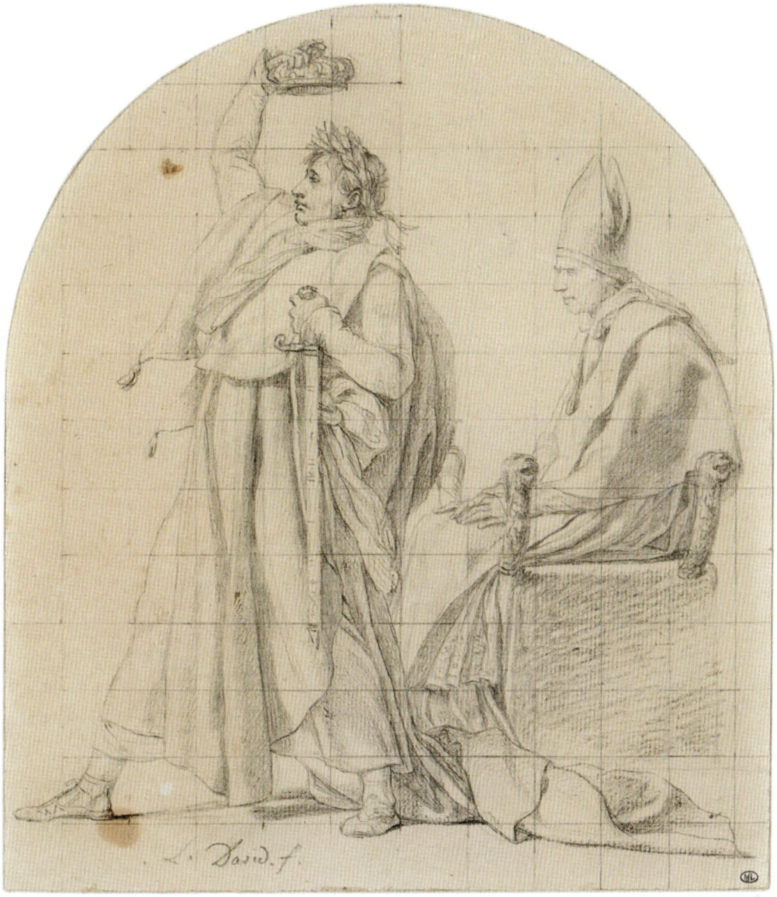

37 Jacques-Louis David, *Napoleon Crowning Himself*, ca. 1804–7. Pencil on paper. 29.2 × 25.2 cm. Paris, Musée du Louvre.

(Nothing could be less to the point than what any of the 150 men and women in the *Coronation* might be thinking or feeling. All this notwithstanding, however, David's original conception of a Horatii-like Napoleon crowning himself [1804–7; fig. 37] – a notion he was forced to abandon – bears witness to the persistence of a desire for dramatic force that by 1806 was all but completely foreclosed to him.) Indeed it well may be that an apprehension of the pervasive "default-setting" theatricality of Napoleonic culture, at least as it applied to ambitious painting, contributed to his decision to seek an alternative pictorial aesthetic, one that featured a special class of classical subject matter (the "Anacreontic") and at the same time positively embraced theatricality but on his own, proto-Manet-like terms.

4

Once more, what of Géricault? My basic claim is this: reaching early maturity during the last years of the Empire, Géricault from the first was drawn to values of action and expression such as had inspired David's history paintings of the 1780s – of painting as drama in the Diderotian sense of the term – under conditions that made the actualization of those values very nearly impossible. Not that he was critical of Gros and other Napoleonic painters. On the contrary, he admired Gros enormously, and of course the stylistic resources that the young Géricault deployed with astonishing panache – the painterliness and colorism that make the *Charging Chasseur* so dazzling to the eye – owe far more to the painter of the *Jaffa* and the *Eylau* than they do to David. But what sets Géricault apart from Gros or any other artist of the Napoleonic generation (also from his teacher Guérin) is the overriding ambition, manifest in every stroke of his brush, to reclaim for painting certain powers that it was on the verge of losing (more strongly, that it had in effect already lost) – above all the power of representing dramatic and expressive action of a Diderotian stamp, action that not only was not primarily intended to be beheld but would on the contrary be so directed toward, so caught up in the accomplishment of its impassioned purpose as to refute the very possibility that the beholder had been taken into account. And what in my view largely determined the course of Géricault's baffled and in the end tragically frustrated and incomplete career was an inherent tension or contradiction between that radically antitheatrical ambition and what had become the extreme difficulty, the near-impossibility, of realizing such an ambition in large-scale, multifigure, narratively coherent *tableaux* that would in effect undo or reverse the retreat from action and expression that I have traced in the *Sabines* and *Leonidas* and beyond them in the "Anacreonic" works. (Considerations of subject matter are relevant but far from being the whole story.) One might even say – I want to say – that precisely the ambition and the near-impossibility together form the core of Géricault's romanticism, as if he intuited in the theatrical an ever-present existential threat not only to his art but also to his humanity, not that from our vantage point the two are separable other than in principle. It is that "existential" aspect of Géricault's artistic vision that sets him largely apart from other French Romantics, and indeed establishes a sort of commonality between his art and that of poets and writers such as Hölderlin, Leopardi, Kleist, Lermontov. (And leaping ahead in time, a special affinity, Stephen Crane.[14])

For example, Géricault from the outset seems to have found it all but impossible to organize entire paintings around manifestly dramatic situations, as though the least hint of dramatic staging, of *mise-en-scène*, was felt by him to be irremediably tainted by theatricality. In David's *Horatii*, as we have seen, the vibrant figure group of the three brothers swearing their mortal oath becomes fully meaningful only in the context of the larger scene, the total composition, of which they are a part – and beyond that composition, in the context of the still larger narrative or rather web of narratives that constitutes the painting's imaginative frame. (Also, I have suggested, in relation to Poussin's *Eudamidas* and ultimately to Diderot's reflections on the latter in the *Discours* and various writings on painting.) In contrast, we have in the *Charging Chasseur* (fig. 38) a single figure mounted on a fiery horse, and although it is clear that they are to be understood as in the midst of a battle, the fact remains that they have been portrayed in a manner that isolates them from their surroundings (Régis Michel speaks aptly of a structure of "synecdoche"[15]), or at least does not make the meaning of their actions dependent either on those surroundings or on a framing *récit* in any way. In this connection Michel emphasizes the importance of the fact that the *chasseur*, a Lieutenant Dieudonné who would not survive the Russian campaign (the painting was presented in the Salon *livret* as a portrait), pivots in the saddle and that his expression with its deflected gaze is one of absorption in thought (as the historian Jules Michelet had earlier remarked).[16] So that the burden of violent action and passionate expression mostly falls on the horse, which is shown simultaneously rearing (if we look at his front legs) and striding diagonally into the picture space (if we focus on his rear legs), a physically impossible feat which we do not quite register as such, perhaps because it combines the equine and the human and so perfectly embodies the conjunction, almost the fusion, of horse and rider that the painting dramatizes. (Is it merely fanciful to compare the action of the horse with that of the nearest of three oath-swearing brothers in the *Horatii*? As we shall see, Géricault seems to have been imaginatively possessed by that figure throughout his career.) Moreover, the horse's position within the painting confers primary importance on his massive haunches, which here as elsewhere in Géricault's oeuvre are felt to be the seat of power, including sexual power, for horse and man alike (more on this further on). All this is to say nothing of the horse's magnificent head with its flaring mane, an emblem of extreme if unspecific emotion that assumes even greater authority than would otherwise be the case by virtue of its presentation in profile. (The privileging of profile views is of course a basic tenet of Davidian Neoclassicism. All in all, it is easy to see why David would have been stopped in his tracks in the Salon of 1812. Let me add that Géricault's inimitable touch is nowhere more evident than in the horse's streaming, one might almost say "erect" tail.)

The relative isolation as well as intensification of apparently self-sufficient dramatic and expressive motifs are characteristic of Géricault's art. To take an extreme example,

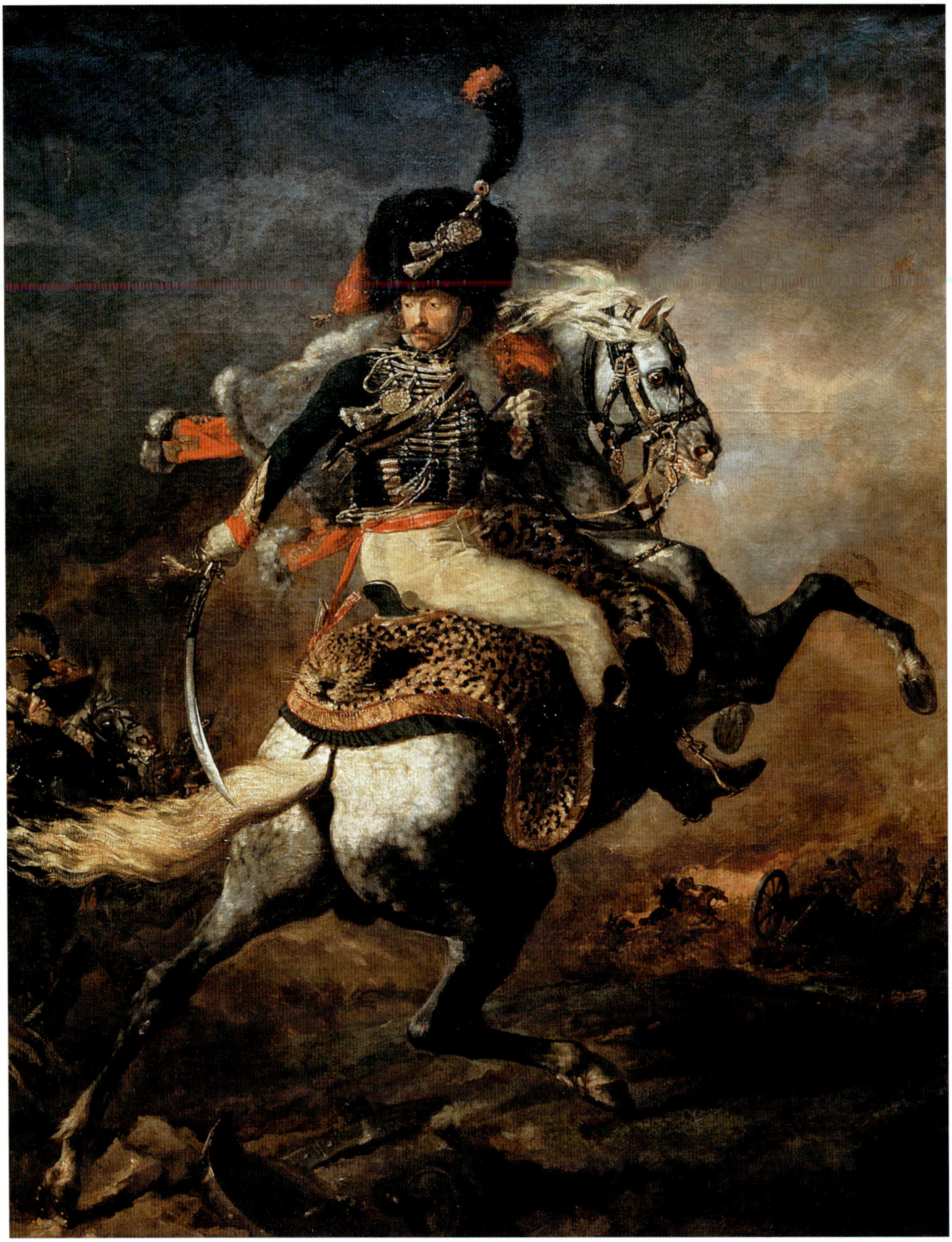

38 Théodore Géricault, *Charging Chasseur*, 1812. Oil on canvas. 349 × 266 cm. Paris, Musée du Louvre.

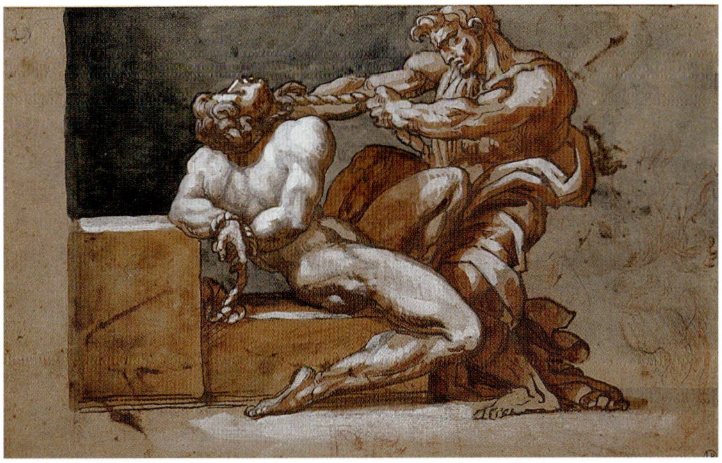

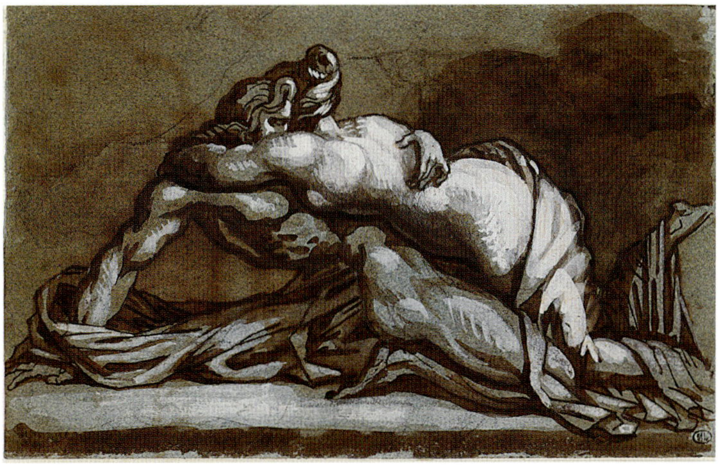

39 (*top*) Théodore Géricault, *Executioner Strangling a Prisoner*, ca. 1815. Watercolor and gouache on paper. 11.6 × 23.9 cm. Bayonne, Musée Bonnat.

40 (*above*) Théodore Géricault, *The Embrace*, ca. 1815. Pencil, ink, and gouache on blue paper. 13.5 × 21.3 cm. Paris, Musée du Louvre, Département des Arts Graphiques.

in the Michelangelesque wash drawing in Bayonne, *Executioner Strangling a Prisoner* (ca. 1815; fig. 39), the straining, grotesquely muscled figures cannot be identified with any literary or historical subject but instead seem virtual personifications of titanic physical effort countered by heroic, tragic suffering, if not of the principle of opposition, of dramatic conflict, itself. The effect is compounded by stark contrasts of light and dark that at once evoke the tormented physicality of the antagonists' bodies and impart a lurid atmosphere to the otherwise minimal scene. In a related drawing in the Louvre, the *Embrace* (ca. 1815; fig. 40), a male and a female figure are depicted in the act of coitus; the kneeling man rocks far back on his haunches as an equally powerful-seeming woman violently embraces him, presumably impaled on his sex.[17] It is an image to make one gasp, but what I want to stress is less its overt sexual content, however one understands that, than the sense it conveys of almost superhuman opposing (or should one say mutually attracting?) forces simultaneously cancelling each other out and maintaining each other in a perpetual state of the highest imaginable tension – no sexual climax at the end of this encounter, in other words – the result being that, as in the *Executioner Strangling a Prisoner*, the very issue of theatricality seems as if outstripped, made inoperative, by the sheer extremity of the proceedings. Moreover, the character of the drawing in these and similar pre-Rome images – their tendency to geometricize and abbreviate the forms they enclose – suggests an equally fierce struggle between contour and matter, as if that too provided an arena in which theatricality could be exceeded and thereby undone (as Géricault remarked, he would have liked to draw with "a steel wire" ["un fil de fer"][18]). Viewed in this light, Géricault's problem was not only how to keep such insensate dramatic energies within the realm of the pictorial but more precisely how to make paintings of recognizably major ambition on the basis of a predilection for pictorial drama that found its ideal expression in implosively condensed scenes of hyperbolic opposition.*

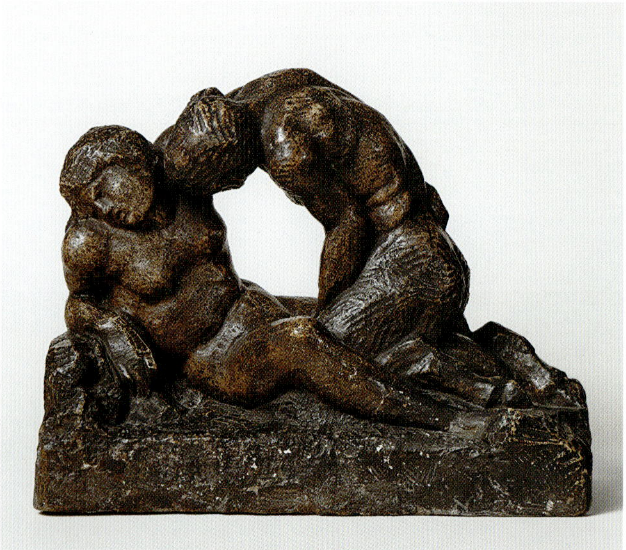

41 Théodore Géricault, *Nymph and Satyr*, 1820. Stone, colored brown. 28 × 36 cm. Rouen, Musée des Beaux-Arts.

No wonder Géricault in his career completed just one large-scale multifigure composition and that some of his most mem-

* In this connection something should be said about several surviving sculptures by Géricault, above all the sublime *Nymph and Satyr* (1820; fig. 41) in Rouen, a small *tour de force* of carving in stone. I suppose what most grips me is not simply the utter mastery of what Roger Fry will call "form" but the palpable emotion, a kind of postcoital sadness – even though the sexual act is yet to take place; though it occurs to me that the satyr might just be seen as withdrawing – that radiates from the two figures with tragic force.

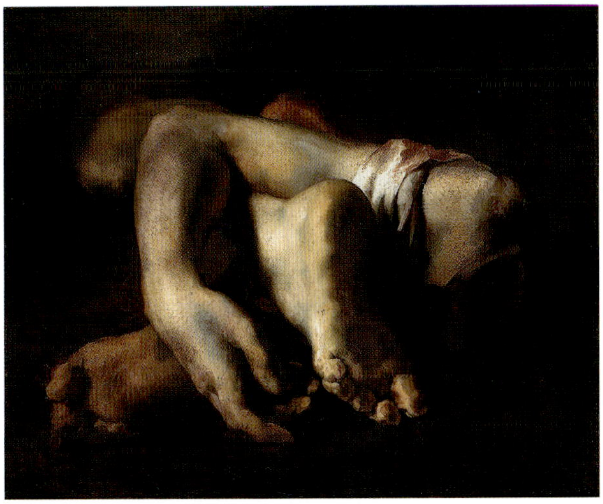

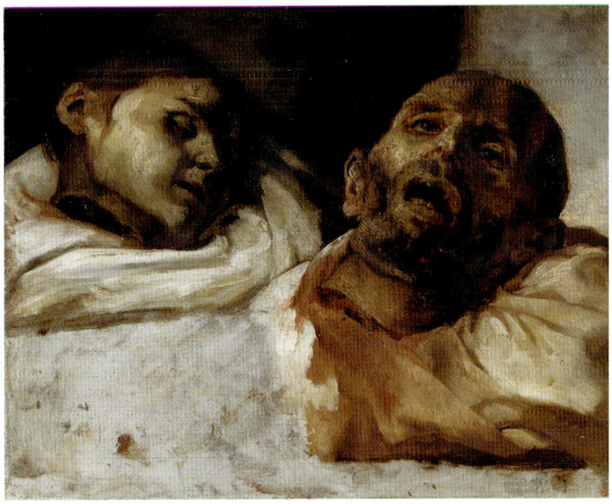

42 (*above left*) Théodore Géricault, *Study of Severed Limbs*, 1818. Oil on canvas. 52 × 64 cm. Montpellier, Musée Fabre.

43 (*above right*) Théodore Géricault, *Study of Two Severed Heads*, 1818. Oil on canvas. 50 × 61 cm. Stockholm, Nationalmuseum.

orable and unprecedented works are ones in which opposition and contrast structure virtually every aspect of the image. In the Montpellier *Study of Severed Limbs* (1818; fig. 42), for example, one of a number of studies of severed heads and limbs painted in connection with the project of the *Raft*, death-dealing violence of the sort depicted in the *Executioner Strangling a Prisoner* is manifest only through its effects but is far more horrific for that; the dramatic chiaroscuro of the earlier work is made the vehicle of a pathos-charged realism; and the juxtaposition of an arm cut through at the shoulder and two legs severed around the knee involves by inadvertent synecdoche the fatal dénouements of countless history paintings and of the narratives on which they are based (not least David's *Brutus*). This last impression is all the more indelible in that the Montpellier canvas suggests sexual difference – the contrast of male and female – without in any way stating it, though in other works of the same moment, notably the Stockholm *Study of Two Severed Heads* (1818; fig. 43), both male–female opposition and the intimation of an erotic scenario, hence of sexual violence, come piercingly to the fore. (The autobiographical implications of all this scarcely need elaborating.)

• • •

5

In fact one way of framing the entire Riderless Horses undertaking is as an attempt to find an other than strongly conflictual – in that sense other than Davidian – basis for an ambitious *tableau*.[19] That is, on the one hand the subject seems to involve a continual struggle between the unruly horses and the strapping grooms seeking to control them, and indeed in many of the drawings and paintings (of the fifteen that survive) this is what one finds, the energetic oil on paper in Lille (1817; fig. 44) being a particularly impressive example. On the other, numerous works also convey a sense of at least partial harmony or accord between men and horses, a kind of parallelism of the sort more than

44 Théodore Géricault, *Start of the Race of the Barberi Horses*, 1817. Oil on paper mounted on canvas. 45 × 60 cm. Lille, Palais des Beaux-Arts.

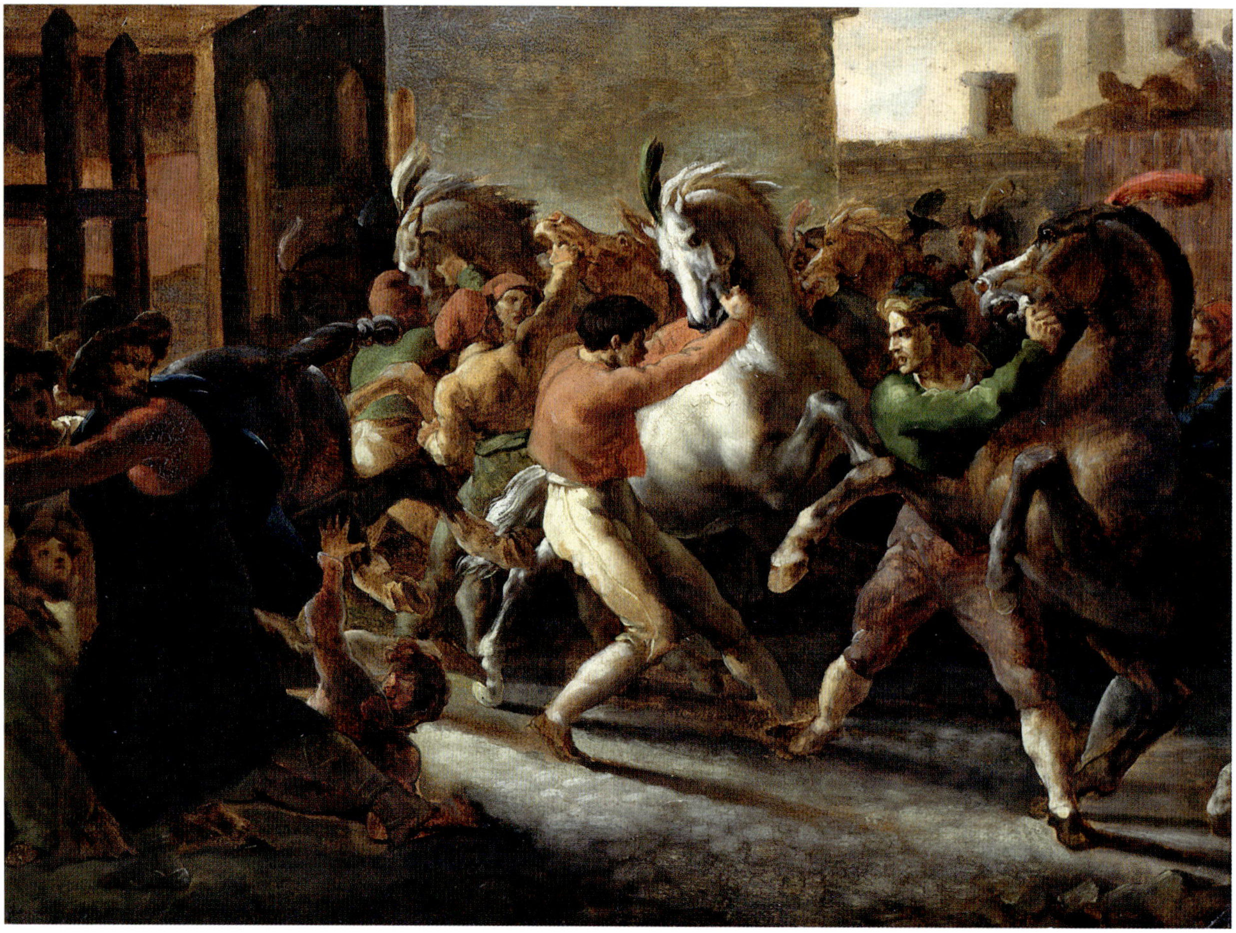

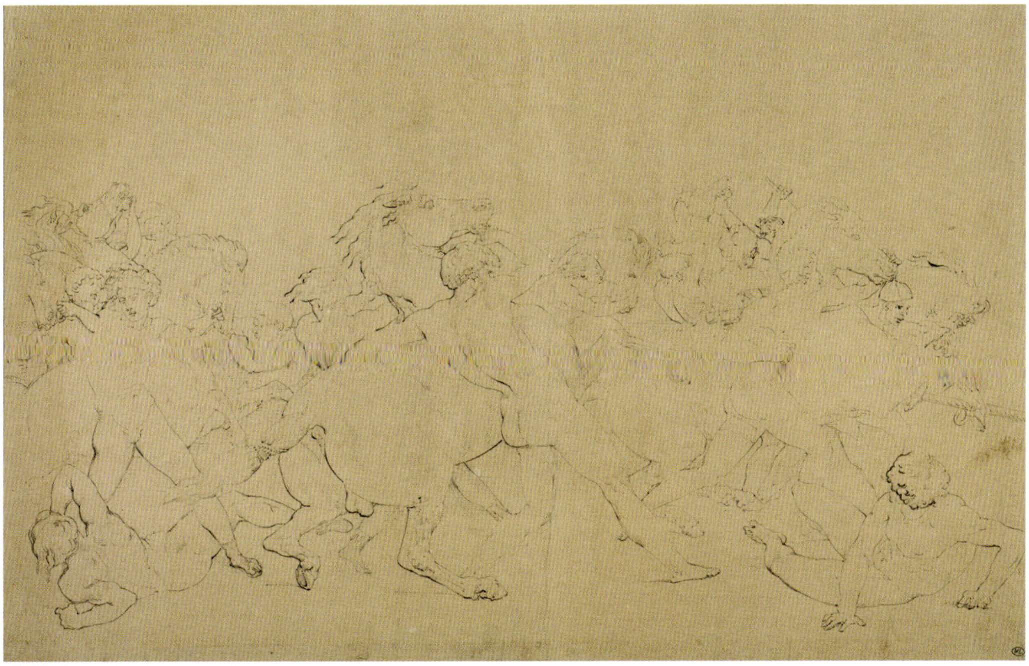

45 Théodore Géricault, *Start of the Race of the Barberi Horses*, 1817. Pen and ink and pencil on paper. 29.5 × 46 cm. Paris, Musée du Louvre, Département des Arts Graphiques.

hinted at in the *Charging Chasseur* as well as numerous other pre-Rome works in Géricault's oeuvre, and as the project advanced this became at least equally important. I shall have more to say about Géricault and horses before I am done, but it is as if in Rome he realized that his profound, virtually identificatory feeling for the latter held out the possibility of a new sort of large-scale *tableau*, one that would be unidirectional (from left to right in its final versions), not a clash of opposing vectors, and in which the total absorption in vigorous muscular effort on the part of the grooms would be not so much contrasted with as complemented by the magnificent, inherently untheatrical physicality of the straining animals. An outline drawing in the Louvre (1817; fig. 45) perhaps represents such a conception at its most developed, while *Start of the Race of the Barberi Horses,* also in the Louvre (1817; fig. 46), which draws back from the horizontal expansiveness of the latter, is usually considered the culminating work in the series. I have already mentioned its classical setting, which effectively removes it from its popular source, the annual race; now I want to focus attention on the marvelous pairing of the man in green tights and the (slightly too compressed) brown and white horse he is controlling, with particular emphasis, first, on the unmistakable sense of

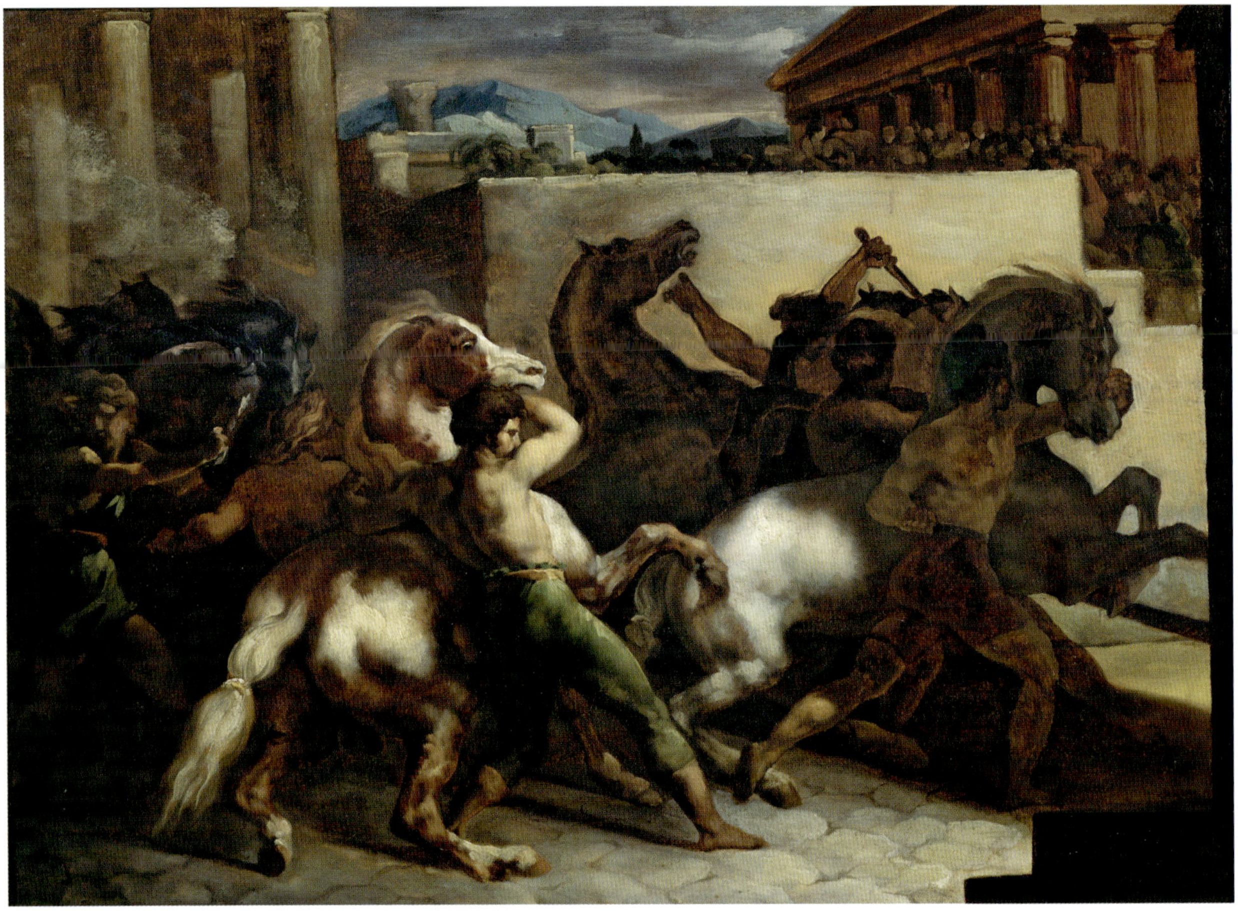

46 Théodore Géricault, *Start of the Race of the Barberi Horses*, 1817. Oil on paper mounted on canvas. 45 × 60 cm. Paris, Musée du Louvre.

physical rapport between man and animal (again, the parallelism between their haunches could not be more evident), and second, on the moving juxaposition of the former's absorbed, downward-looking profile (partly obscured by his right shoulder) and the febrile, straining, almost frightened-seeming head of the partly rearing horse, the effect once more being one not so much of simple contrast as of a single compound subjectivity, with neither man nor horse primary. (Note, by the way, the continued "presence" of the nearest of the three Horatii. I should mention, too, that according to Géricault's friend Dedreux-Dorcy the artist's legs were much like those of the man in tights.[20]) It may be that it was at this stage that Géricault abandoned the notion of treating the subject on a monumental scale, exactly why we shall never know. Perhaps the question of whether he was depicting an actual event or a timeless scene, with its attendant uncertainties as to costume and setting, proved unresolvable; perhaps in the end the (in itself brilliant) notion of a unidirectional composition involving separate groupings of life-size men and horses seemed to him not sufficiently dramatic to provide the basis for an effective *tableau*; or perhaps after months of strenuous effort and reflection he had reached the end of his interest in the subject. (Whitney's book illustrates pretty much all the paintings and drawings associated with the project.) One sign of trouble in the Louvre picture is the strange dark architectural element or group of elements that in effect closes the composition at the extreme right, as if otherwise the painting's energies threatened to dissipate there, to stray beyond the right-hand framing edge. Or perhaps the point of those elements is to acknowledge that the work in question is only a vestige of the larger, laterally more extensive composition that various drawings show he had been contemplating. In any case, the large canvas went unused and in late September 1817 he left Rome for Siena, Florence, and, by the first half of November, Paris.

That compositional considerations of the sort just outlined were in fact at stake in the Riderless Horses project is suggested by an oil on paper made shortly after Géricault's return, the gripping and enigmatic *Cattle Market* (1817; fig. 47) in the Fogg Museum, which Whitney acutely notes (86) amounts to an adaptation – also a transformation – of David's *Sabines* (see fig. 6) then on view along with the *Leonidas* in the large Cluny studio that remained open to the public during these years. (We know from Montfort that Géricault visited the studio and came back in a state of enthusiasm.[21]) No doubt in Géricault's mind the *Cattle Market* involved an act of homage to the older master. But in another sense it is also a critique, the "posing" figures of Romulus and Tatius facing off against one another – already viewed by critics as theatrical in the pejorative sense of the term[22] – having been replaced by powerfully muscular, indisputably engaged personages all of whose attention is directed toward the struggling, pathos-charged bulls whom they are in the act of subduing, beating, and, not quite yet, killing. The setting, Whitney notes, appears to be outside the walls of Rome (at any rate, the landscape seems plainly Italian), and in fact two of the three butchers, if that is what they are, are essentially naked. Furthermore, again as Whitney remarks, the diverse groups of women and children in the *Sabines* – instruments of peace-making, as the Salon *livret* makes clear – have been replaced by the dense mass of terrified and struggling cattle, a substitution that has the seemingly paradoxical result of giving far greater expressive weight to the responses of two of the bulls – the ones being grasped by the horns – than is the case with respect to any of the figures in the *Sabines*. In fact the only "brutes" on view are the butcher at the left and perhaps the dogs. (A closely related work from the Roman

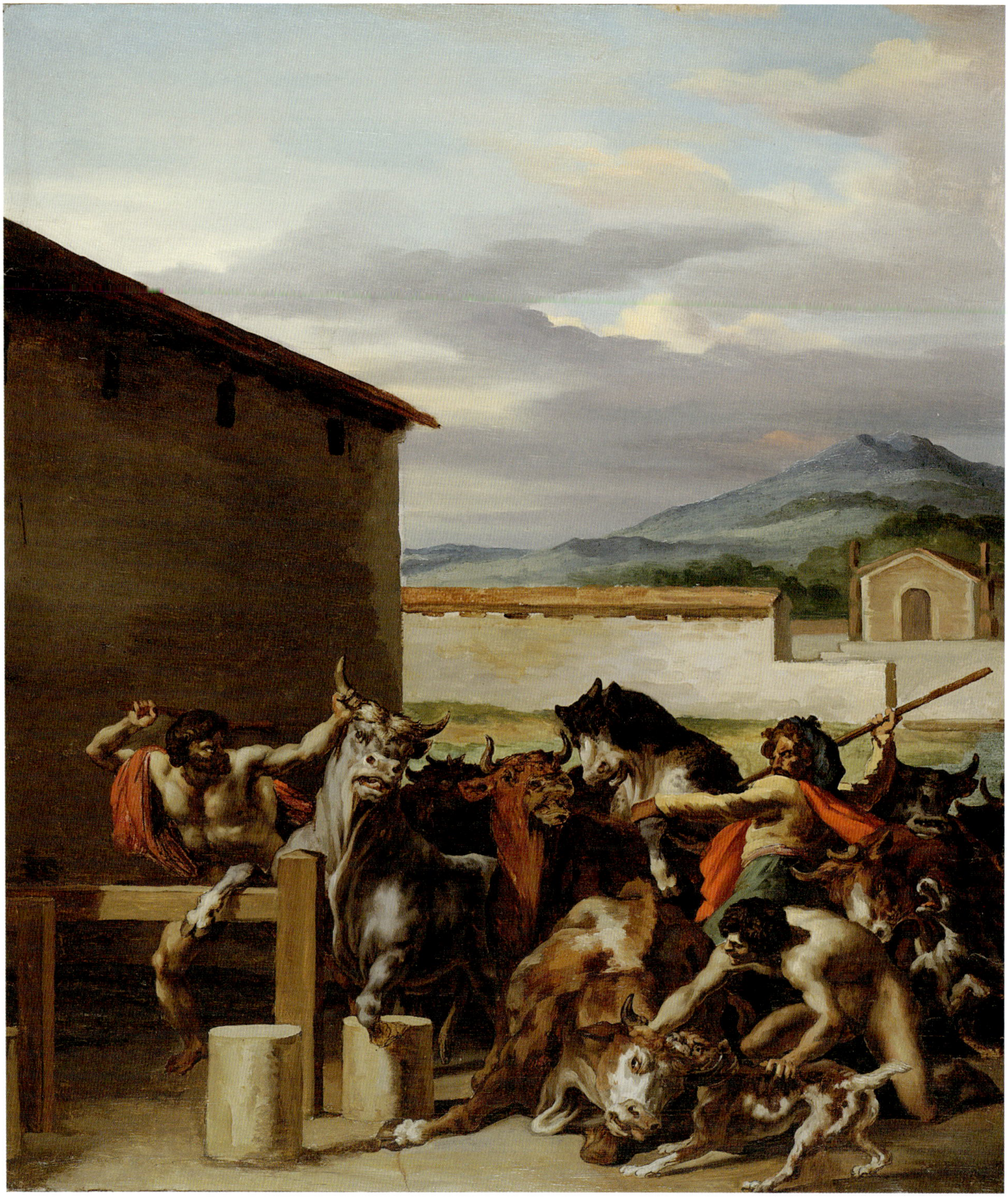

47 Théodore Géricault, *Cattle Market*, 1817. Oil on paper mounted on canvas. 59.5 × 50 cm. Cambridge, Mass., Harvard Art Museums/Fogg Museum, Bequest of Grenville L. Winthrop, 1943.242.

year is the astonishing drawing called *Ancient Sacrifice* [1817; fig. 48], one of the most complex, brutal, and moving images in all Gericault's oeuvre. Also, despite the complexity, one of the most urgently communicative: there is something uncanny and electrifying in the hoisted-up, seemingly helpless bull's gaze directly out of the drawing. The men, in contrast, seem mere killing machines.)

From the point of view of execution, too, the *Cattle Market* is a marvel: the oil pigment has been applied confidently but not exactly thickly, the treatment of the men and animals is at once sculptural and full of textural nuance, the interplay of light and dark is combined with a feeling for strong local color (one of Géricault's perennial strengths), and the landscape and sky – it is near dusk – are masterly in their breadth and illumination. The touch everywhere is beyond praise. At the same time, a point of special interest for the present essay, the composition as such feels, in the end, almost painfully divided, the men and animals forming a compact frieze without meaningful connection to the empty middle ground or the mountain and sky beyond it. True, the dark wall receding at left is a brilliant makeshift, taking the eye back at least some of the

48 Théodore Géricault, *Ancient Sacrifice*, 1817. Ink and gouache on oiled paper. 28.5 × 42.2 cm. Paris, Musée du Louvre, Département des Arts Graphiques.

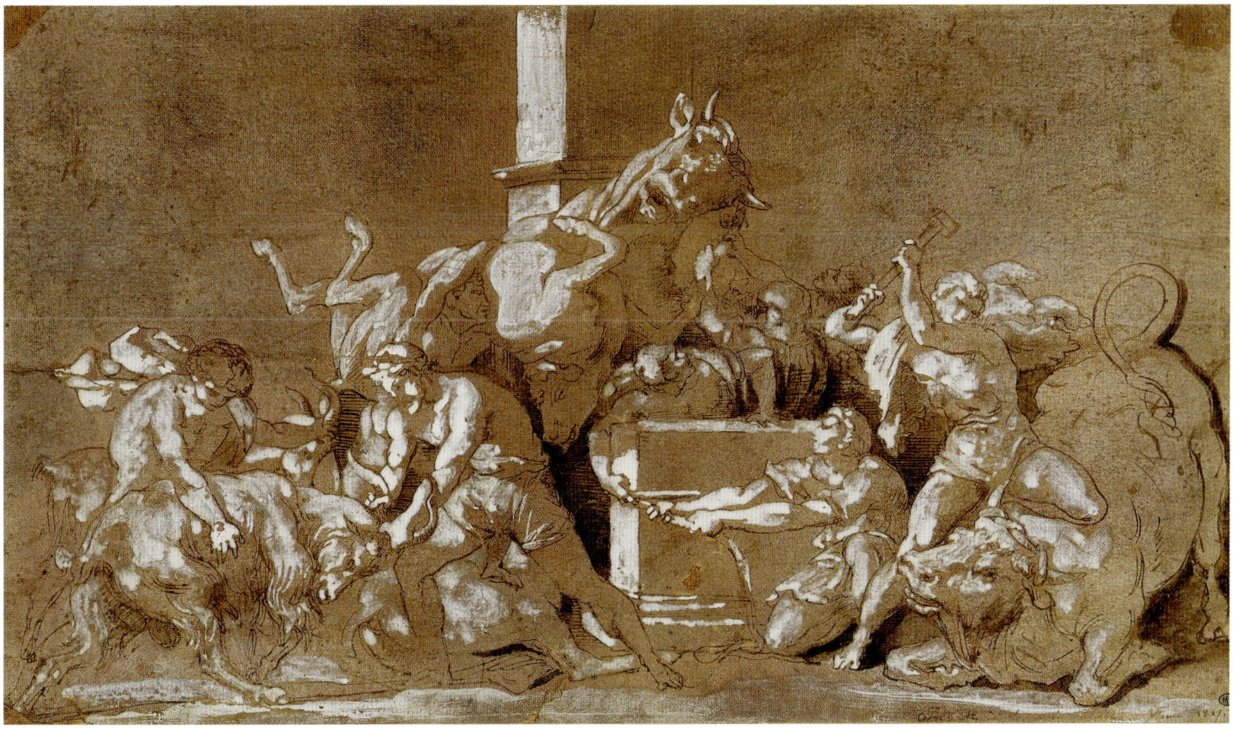

way and providing a vibrant coloristic foil for the man and beast silhouetted against it. But the laterally disposed walls and the building seen end-on in the middle distance appear virtually to enact a structural severing or blocking of the principal action from its larger context, which gives the total scene with its suggestion of imminent sunset an added poignance but as much as concedes that the Davidian solution will be without further usefulness.

6

Appropriately, it is Géricault's one grandly large-scale multifigure painting, the *Raft of the "Medusa"* (1819; fig. 49), that most powerfully exemplifies his antagonism to the theatrical – put more strongly, his adherence, whether he was aware of it or not, to the values, though not the strategies, advocated by Diderot in his writings of the 1750s and 60s.[23] The subject of the *Raft*, as already mentioned, was based on an actual event, the shipwreck of the French frigate *Medusa* off Cap Blanc in West Africa and the atrocious sufferings of almost 150 officers and passengers on a makeshift raft that was supposed to be towed by lifeboats but was shamefully abandoned to its fate. And the specific phase of the subject that Géricault, after much deliberation, chose to represent took place when, after two weeks on the open sea, the last survivors, now just fifteen men, discerned a ship (the British brig *Argus*, which had been part of the initial expedition) on the far horizon and mounted a desperate collective effort to attract its attention. In fact the *Argus* failed to spot the frantically signaling men and sailed out of sight; but later the same day, having changed direction, it bore down on the raft and rescued its occupants. (Géricault considered but rejected depicting the actual rescue.) The subject finally selected thus implies an exceedingly drawn-out "moment" – at that distance the minuscule brig would have appeared to be moving with extreme slowness – and yet, unlike the dilated, deliberately suspensive "moment" of the *Sabines*, one that could hardly have been more racking, physically and psychologically. It is worth emphasizing that the strategy of singling out an absorptive "moment" in a definite narrative ties Géricault to the Davidian (and Diderotian) paradigm; significantly, Delacroix would soon break with this, nowhere more perspicuously than in the *Scenes from the Massacre at Scio* (1824; fig. 50), whose internal structure might be likened to a gathering of stanzas in a poem, each devoted to a particular cluster of motifs, with only a thematic connection among them. (Another declaration of his "aesthetic" approach.) The genius of Géricault's choice of "moment," in other words, is that it justifies, indeed motivates, a sustained collective effort of truly colossal proportions, one however that feels

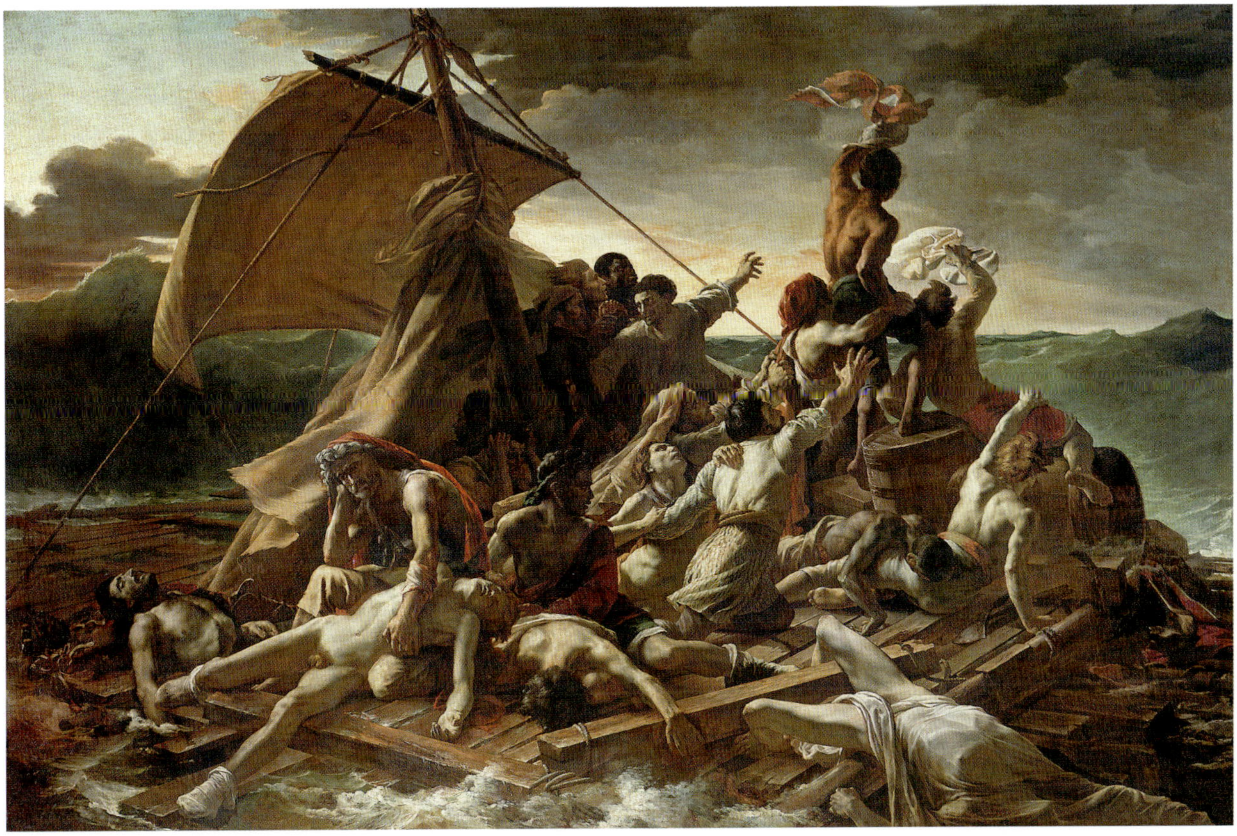

49 Théodore Géricault, *The Raft of the "Medusa,"* 1819. Oil on canvas. 491 × 716 cm. Paris, Musée du Louvre.

entirely plausible – for all the artful construction of the pyramid of bodies culminating in the two men waving bolts of cloth – within the overall logic of the composition.

Moreover, the total absorption (for such it appears to be) of the straining, climbing, waving *naufragés* in their efforts to draw attention to the raft is underscored not only by the desperateness of their situation and the presumed feebleness of their physical condition (as has often been remarked, however, they look far too strong for what they are supposed to have gone through), but also by the fact that they have been depicted largely from the rear (the faces of four of the most active figures are turned away from us), which further emphasizes their ostensible obliviousness to our presence. This in itself was a major compositional innovation, a radical alternative to the lateral mode of organization basic to the Diderotian *tableau* as well as to David's history paintings of the 1780s and, as we have just seen, to Géricault's Riderless Horses project and *Cattle Market*. (And to the art of Poussin and other classical seventeenth-century masters.)

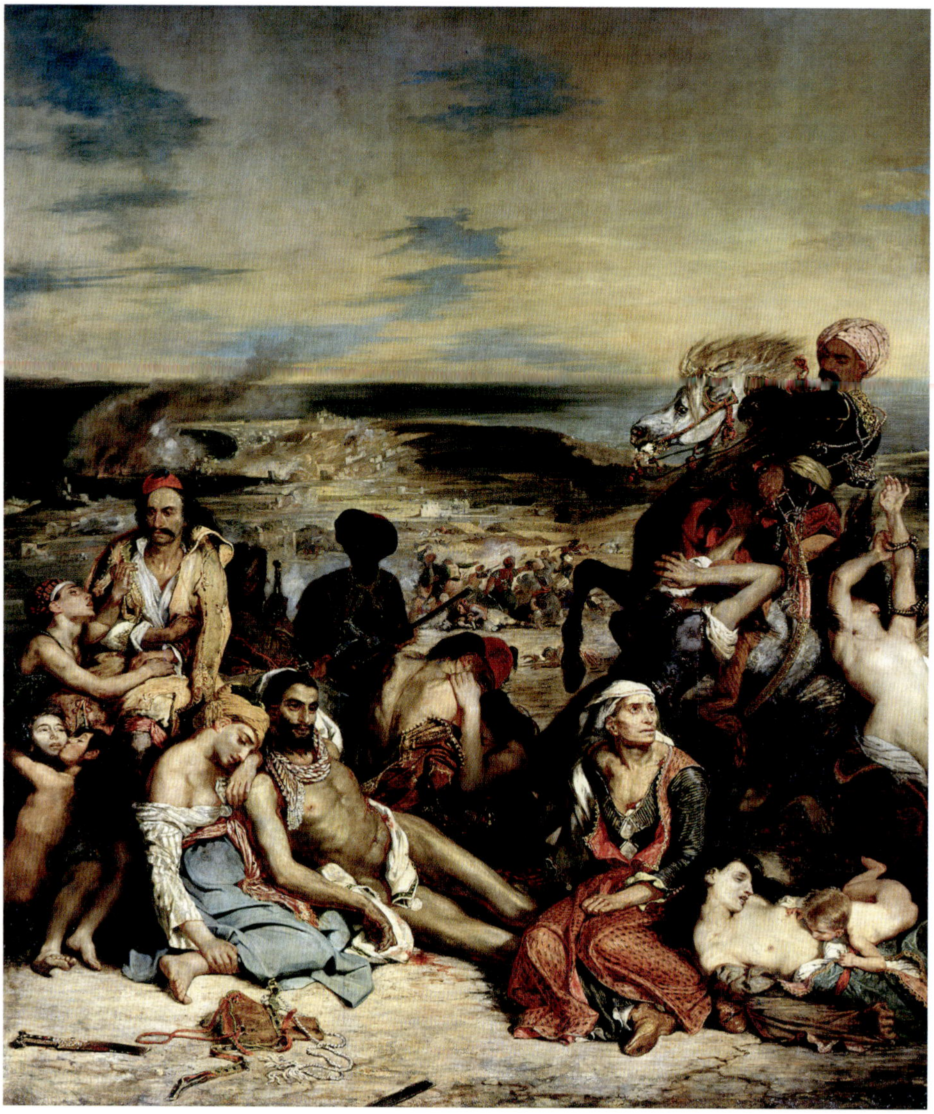

50 Eugène Delacroix, *Scenes from the Massacre at Scio*, 1824. Oil on canvas. 419 × 354 cm. Paris, Musée du Louvre.

Not only that: one way of describing the "moment" represented in the *Raft* might be to say that the figures of the victims – all those in the right-hand half of the composition, at any rate – are striving to be beheld by a potential source of vision, the *Argus*, located at the farthest limit of illusionistic space, a source that, if it could be activated, would rescue them at last *from being beheld by us* – as if our presence before the painting were the ultimate cause of their plight, or, less luridly, as if the primordial convention that paintings are made to be beheld, or perhaps the progressive coming to the fore of that convention, threatened to make theatrical even their sufferings. (I advanced the core of this argument in print for the first time in the opening chapter of my book *Courbet's Realism* in 1990. My impression is that almost no one then found it believable; such an account of Géricault's intentions was simply too far removed from the norms of disciplinary consensus. How things stand now I do not presume to say – probably much the same. For myself, I am more convinced than ever that the composition of the *Raft* amounts to the strongest imaginable proof of the centrality of the issue of beholding to Géricault's art and career.)

In this regard one feature of Géricault's composition deserves particular emphasis – the minuteness of the brig on the horizon (fig. 51), or rather the enormous, distinctly unclassical disparity in scale between the brig and the colossal figures on the raft. On the one hand, a great deal – almost everything – depended on the ability of the painting's viewers to notice the *Argus* and so grasp the meaning of the actions of the straining *naufragés*. On the other, Géricault's desire to render those actions as desperate and as extreme as could be imagined also compelled him to make the brig so minuscule and far-removed as to be very nearly imperceptible at even a moderate distance from the canvas. There can be little doubt that when the *Raft* was first exhibited at the Salon of 1819, many viewers failed to realize that the *Argus* was there: not only is this implicit in certain descriptions of the painting by contemporary critics, the *Argus* is significantly missing from the engraving of the *Raft* that accompanied C. P. Landon's account of the Salon.[24] Presumably, the situation was improved when the painting was lowered; as Delacroix remarked in a letter, "[O]ne is on the same footing with it, so to speak. So much so that one believes one already has a foot in the water. It has to be seen close up in order to feel all its merit."[25]

A related point: the need to view the *Raft* from up close also reflects the conditions of its execution – the physical circumstances of Géricault himself at work on the painting. And this suggests that the dominant orientation of the men on the raft (facing into the picture) as well as the actions of the uppermost personages tirelessly waving scraps of cloth are also finally to be referred back to the orientation and actions of the painter: as if Géricault not only identified imaginatively with the sufferings of the shipwrecked men but also, in and by the act of painting, identified physically with their efforts to make themselves seen by the *Argus* and so bring about their eventual rescue. Such a reading of the *Raft* goes in the direction of what I have argued is the meaning of Courbet's Realism as exemplified in works such as *After Dinner at Ornans*, the *Stonebreakers*, and the *Wheat Sifters*, to mention just three of his major works.[26] In those

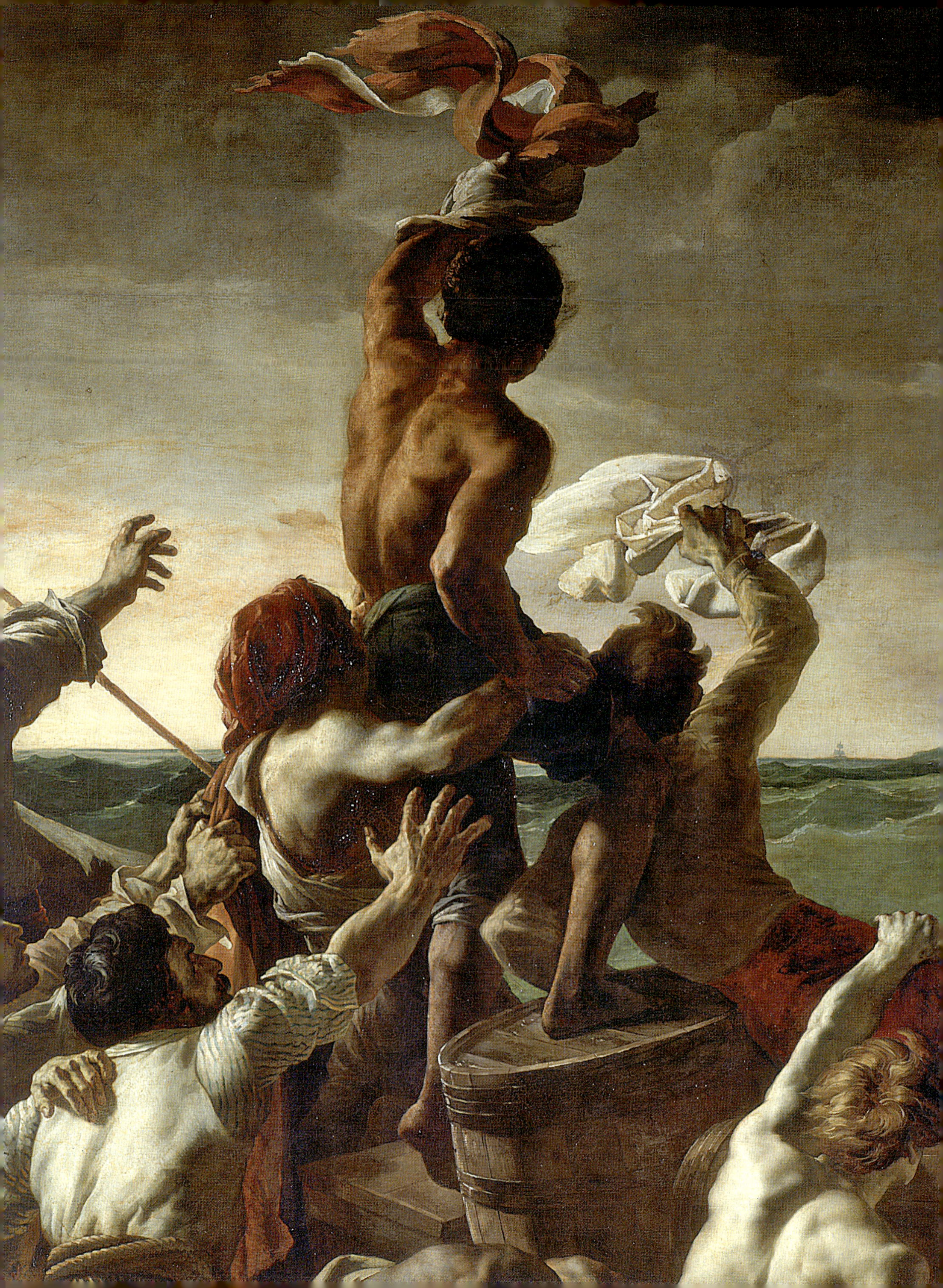

paintings the dominant orientation of personages (at least of the central personage) is to a greater or lesser degree congruent with that of the painter (or painter-beholder, as I call him); the actions they depict may be read as figuring the act of painting; and the ultimate intention I attribute to the painter-beholder is that of seeking to transport himself quasi-corporeally into the picture on which he is working and by so doing to remove himself as a potentially theatricalizing presence from in front of it. But although in this sense the *Raft* may perhaps be said to contain the germ of Courbet's later "solution" to the problem of theatricality, it resolutely refuses the basic condition of that "solution," namely the restriction of the painter's effective field of action to a single beholder, the painter himself.

Finally, it might be noted that the uppermost figure in the *Raft* bears a certain formal resemblance to the Spartan at the upper left engraving Simonides's lines into the rock wall in the *Leonidas* (see fig. 7), which Montfort tells us Géricault saw and admired while at work on the *Raft*.[27] Interestingly, as Eitner shows, it was only very late in the process of determining the final composition that Géricault introduced the uppermost figure, whose "torso stands out against the sky high above the horizon, [as] the cloth unfurling in the wind from his uplifted arm gives the scene a splendid climax."[28] And is there not also an affinity of sorts between the three Spartan warriors with their arms around each other raising wreaths toward the carving figure in the *Leonidas* and the *naufragés* reaching upwards as if in support of the men waving their scraps of cloth in the *Raft*? Granted the two paintings could not be more disparate stylistically, expressively, imaginatively, corporeally. But might this not have been precisely Géricault's point, even as the connection with David's last major history painting would have had something positive in it for him as well? (The connection would amount to a much more monumental version of Géricault's adaptation of the composition of the *Sabines* in his *Cattle Market* of 1817.)

All this leaves unmentioned two other obviously important figures, the older bearded man seated to the left of the mast with his head supported by his right arm and hand and the naked and presumably lifeless young man sprawled between his legs (the pair are often misleadingly described as a father and son; fig. 31). In effect the older man faces us, though he does not do so directly – his body is slightly angled to the left (his right) – and his gaze seems inward (this was already true of the *chasseur* pivoting in his saddle); the impression conveyed is that rescue, if that is on offer, has come too late, that the worst has already happened – and indeed the actual events that transpired on the raft (starvation, extreme thirst, combat, murder, cannibalism, bouts of madness) could not have been more dire. Art-historically speaking, the older man's sources are clear: David's *The Lictors Returning to Brutus the Bodies of His Sons* (1789; fig. 52) and

51 *(facing page)* Théodore Géricault, *The Raft of the "Medusa"* (detail of fig. 49).

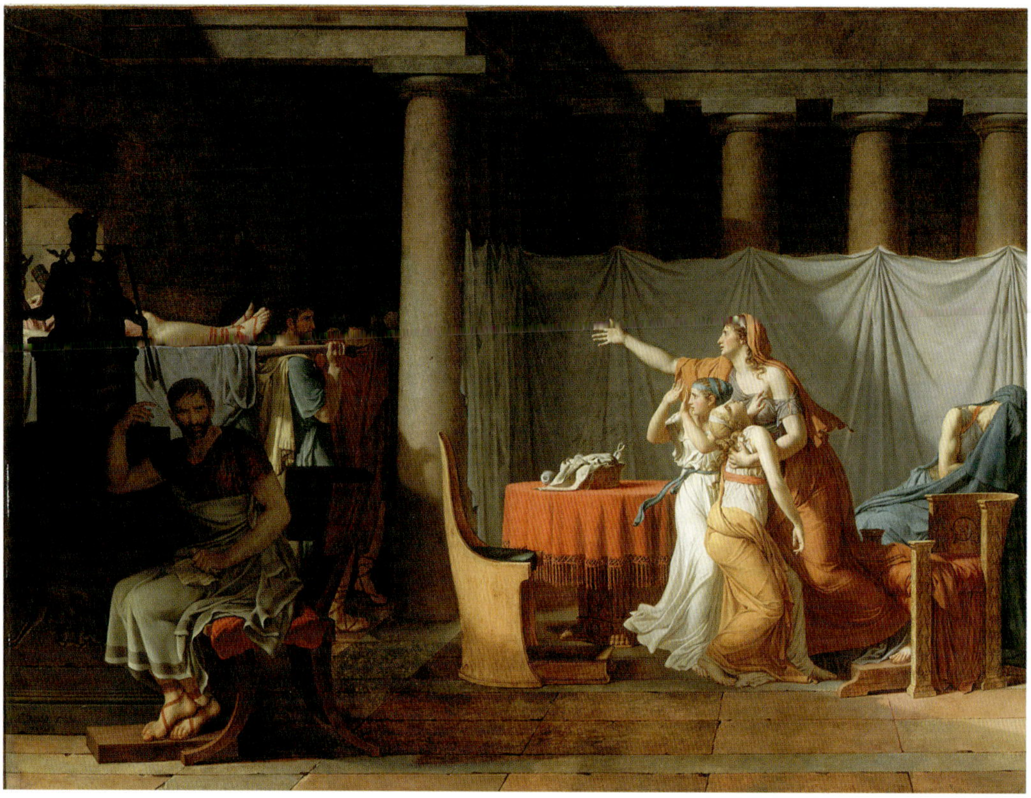

52 Jacques-Louis David, *The Lictors Returning to Brutus the Bodies of His Sons*, 1789. Oil on canvas. 323 × 422 cm. Paris, Musée du Louvre.

Géricault's teacher Guérin's *The Return of Marcus Sextus* (1799; fig. 53).[29] To begin with the *Brutus*: the "father of his country," seated facing outward in the shadowy left foreground of the large canvas that today hangs alongside the *Horatii* in the Louvre, struggles to contain his emotions as the lictors return the headless bodies of his sons to the family home (because they had been found plotting against the Republic, Brutus had obeyed the laws and ordered them killed).[30] The basic organization of the canvas is lateral with a vengeance – sightlines leap across the picture space to tremendous effect – but the figure of Brutus is clearly intended to compound the sense of obliviousness to being beheld by virtue of the fact that although he occupies the extreme left foreground and faces outward he is entirely consumed by his own tormented thoughts. (There is also the hint that he has just been jolted from those thoughts by the outcry of the women of the household as they see the lictors arrive.) Guérin's Marcus Sextus, another stricken, outward-facing figure, in this case having just returned to Rome from

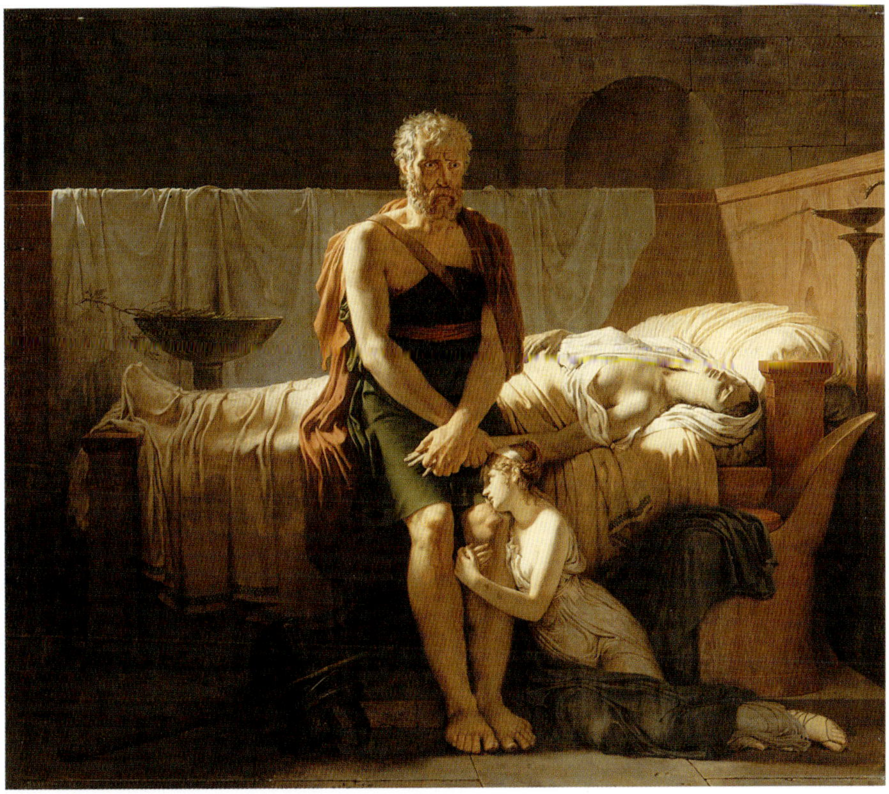

53 Pierre-Narcisse Guérin, *The Return of Marcus Sextus*, 1799. Oil on canvas. 217 × 243 cm. Paris, Musée du Louvre.

exile only to find that his wife had died, is in turn plainly based on the figure of Brutus. In other words, while the large-scale organization of the *Raft* goes beyond anything in the *Brutus*, the tragic figure of the older man wrapped up in his thoughts unmistakably acknowledges that precedent.[31] Also Davidian in its way is the non-communication between the pair of the old man and dead youth and the men straining to be seen; as Michel notes, the two groups turn their backs to one another,[32] a formulation that recalls, once again, the basic structure of the *Eudamidas* and its variants in the *Horatii* and the *Socrates*, here inflected away from the lateral axis. (Also in the *Brutus*, with its empty chair turning its back on the anguished protagonist.) Pure Géricault, however, is the beautiful, realistic lifeless ephebe with his extended left arm and partly open left hand in magisterial foreshortening, a figure that went on to inspire French painters for generations to come.[33]

7

Earlier I said that Géricault's art from the outset is marked by the ambition to reclaim for painting the capacity to depict dramatic action and expression in a manner consistent with, though also going on from, David's history paintings of the 1780s, but that the evolution of French painting in the 1790s and after, as manifested in the art both of David himself and of the Napoleonic painters (Gros and others), was such as to make the realization of that ambition all but impossible – "all but" being in the nature of an understatement. Now I want to enlarge on this by suggesting that what more than anything else enabled or indeed drove Géricault to thrust himself with such resolve against the limits of his situation was nothing other than an extraordinarily acute sense of his own embodied physicality, about which we can of course know nothing first-hand but which on the evidence especially of the profusion of drawings that have come down to us must have been altogether out of the ordinary, issuing in often rapidly sketched images of immense muscular effort, struggles but also moments of deep accord between men and animals, sexual relations (including sexual combat), and various forms of unbridled violence. (The sheer kinetic quality of many of the drawings bears further witness to his transcendent physical gifts.) In an essay of 1994, Norman Bryson analyses what he called the construction of "masculinity" in Géricault's art, emphasizing, on psychoanalytic grounds, its necessarily divided character, which the pervasive muscularity, to the point virtually of caricature, of many of the artist's male personages at once expresses and masks.[34] And in "Le Nom de Géricault" introducing two volumes of essays based on the Louvre colloquium of 1991 (published in 1996), Régis Michel seconds Bryson's point, finding in the "super-virility" of many of Géricault's figures evidence of a "fixation," understood, again in Freudian terms, as a "defense reaction against the anguish of castration," and further claiming that although the artist knew very well that the handful of men left alive on the raft at the end of their ordeal were anything but robust, his unconscious "*could not renounce* that stubborn postulate of his libidinal economy, the cult of virility" – hence the often remarked conflict in the final painting between historical fact and artistic representation (23–4; Michel's emphasis).

Such a line of argument is fine so long as it takes nothing away, as indeed it need not, from the basic fact of Géricault's commitment to a bodily energetics as extreme as any in the history of art. And now I want to make a further suggestion: that one way, a productive way, of recasting Géricault's predicament – of explicating what I have called his romanticism – is to think of him as seeking to find a place for that commitment – for the direct expression of the instinctual but also the ardently imagined and passionately willed life of the physically highly developed male body – within the parameters and possibilities of the art of painting as he conceived it; which is also to say – thinking of my discussion of the later David – as seeking to represent a *world* in which that commitment and all that went with it might be exercised freely, in a manner (this is the crucial point) that emphatically did not seem merely destined to be beheld. In later David, as we have seen, worldhood as such becomes increasingly problematic, increasingly a matter of what following Diderot I have called theater, and as this comes about embodiment itself loses its "inwardness" and turns into mere appearance, until, in the *Anger of Achilles*, that most "outward" of paintings, all sense of lived bodily reality – in the contemporaneous terminology of the French philosopher Maine de Biran, all hint of any "sensation of effort" – almost palpably goes by the board.[35] (The late "aporetic" drawings are in their way still more extreme, but to what extent they bear directly on our topic is an open question.) It is as though from the very first Géricault sought to reverse this state of affairs by force, *to make a world for the body by way of the body*, to the extent that such a project can even be imagined. How difficult it was for Géricault himself to imagine is shown by his predilection for summarily visualized scenes of warfare, in which a generalized destructiveness provides the framework for not quite believable but nevertheless gripping images of superhuman effort and exertion. (Let three works, *Mameluke Unhorsed by a Charge of Grenadiers* [ca. 1818], *Cavalry Battle* [ca. 1818], both drawings on bistre-colored paper with wash and gouache, and *Horse Artillery of the Guard in Action* [ca. 1818], a lithograph with watercolor, stand for many in this connection [figs. 54–6].) Even more extreme are the elaborated drawings of the mutiny on the raft, above all the version at the Fogg Museum at Harvard (1818; fig. 57), another work I came to know intimately – to sit in awe of in the Fogg Museum Drawing Room – during my graduate student years.*

I am aware, of course, that to speak of world and worldhood in this manner, although prepared for in crucial respects by my discussion of late David, has no precedent in accounts of Géricault's life and career. Or for that matter in art-historical writing generally. But several sets of (necessarily brief) observations will perhaps go at least some of the way toward justifying my choice of concepts.

* In neither this essay nor "David / Marat" do I make more than incidental use of the critical and art-historical literature of the nineteenth century by way of showing the extent to which considerations of drama and theatricality (and of course antitheatricality) played a role in the art writing of the period. But here for example are some remarks on Géricault by Ernest Chesneau, a leading French critic of the 1860s and 1870s, from his book *La Peinture française au XIXe siècle: Les chefs d'école* (Paris, 1862): "Apt to experience all the violent and unmeasurable emotions, the artist was equally apt in rendering them. He sought and he succeeded in specifying the violence of his emotion with a skill the secret of which seems lost today. The

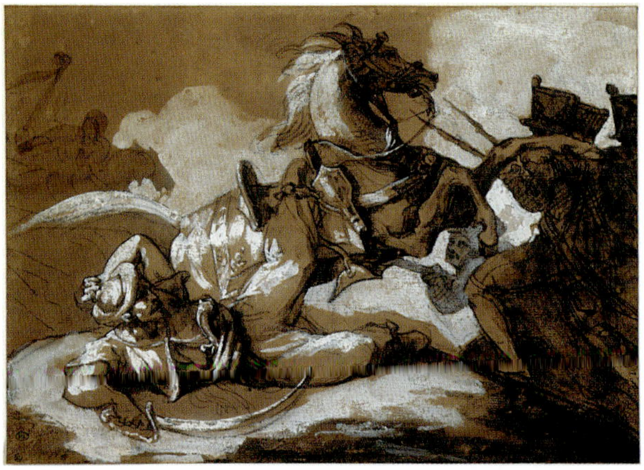

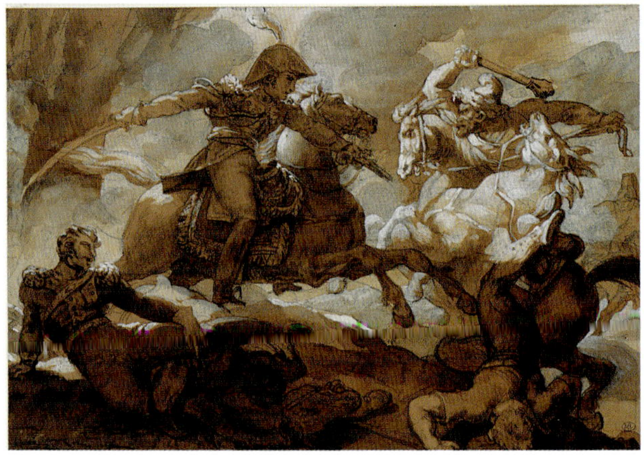

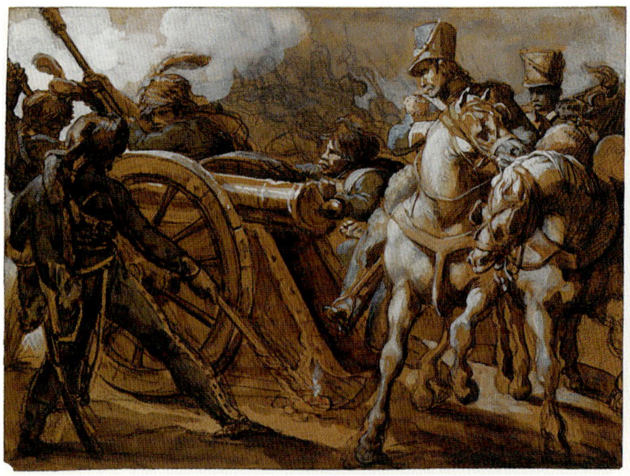

54 (*above left*) Théodore Géricault, *Mameluke Unhorsed by a Charge of Grenadiers*, ca. 1818. Pencil, ink, and gouache on beige paper. 20.6 × 28.2 cm. Paris, Musée du Louvre, Département des Arts Graphiques.

55 (*above right*) Théodore Géricault, *Cavalry Battle*, ca. 1818. Pencil, ink, and gouache on beige paper. 19 × 27 cm. Paris, Musée du Louvre, Département des Arts Graphiques.

56 (*left*) Théodore Géricault, *Artillery of the Guard in Action*, ca. 1818. Black chalk, wash, and gouache on bistre paper. 21 × 28.3 cm. Paris, Musée du Louvre, Département des Arts Graphiques.

(1) Géricault's preoccupation with animals, especially horses, has an obvious basis in his often reckless passion for riding.[36] But much more than this seems to have been at stake: in the first place, as has already emerged, a vision of powerful and straining horses as in some elemental sense complementing, one might say amplifying, the (male) human form. There are several aspects to this, none more compelling than the accord

figures that animate his paintings are not there so that one can watch their suffering; they have no care for the public, they do not know that the public exists; they are there only because they suffer, and in order to suffer. Very few masters, even among the greatest, have known how to avoid the restraints of [theatrical] mise-en-scène" (176; translation mine). (The emphasis on suffering shows that Chesneau is thinking chiefly of the *Raft*.) Several pages later he adds that had Géricault lived longer he would have been the "David of romanticism" (183), and shortly after that he characterizes him as "the painter of human drama" (185). Of course, the same pro-drama, anti-theatricality mind-set that led Chesneau to admire Géricault put him at a disadvantage in front of early Manet (see Fried, *MM*, 283–4, 565 n. 45).

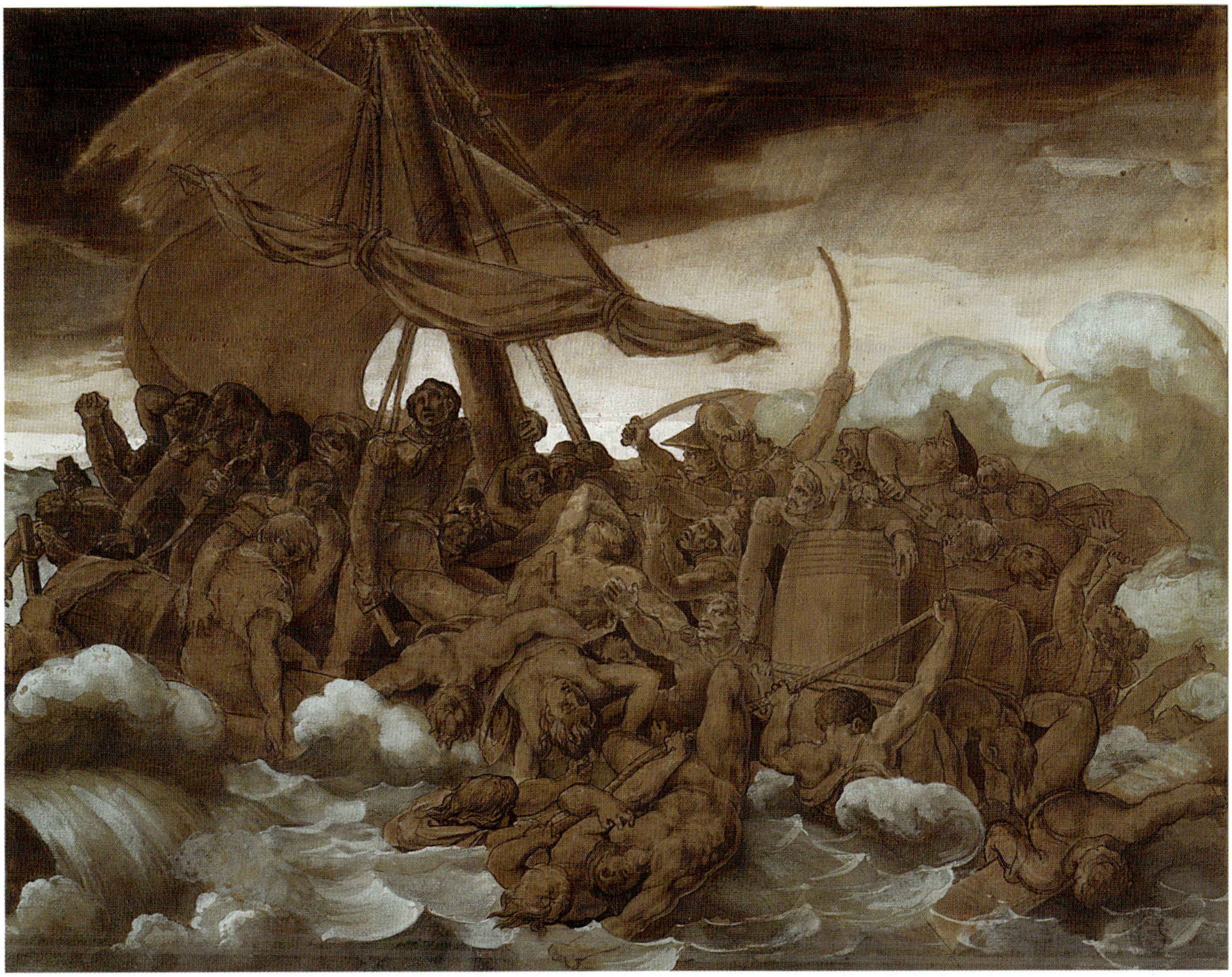

57 Théodore Géricault, *Mutiny on the Raft*, 1818. Black chalk, black crayon, white chalk, brown and blue-green watercolor, and white gouache on brown modern laid paper. 40.5 × 51 cm. Cambridge, Mass., Harvard Art Museums/Fogg Museum, Bequest of Grenville L. Winthrop, 1943.824.

already noted between horses' and men's respective haunches, the former lending something of their immense power to the latter, not to mention casually exposing male sexual organs in a way that inevitably colors our perception of the men as well.[37] (One has the impresssion that Géricault thinks of men's haunches as the seat of masculine force, which is true only for certain actions; in drawing after drawing they are *clenched* in a way that does not appear to be strictly accurate but nevertheless conveys an impression of tremendous force, the ink drawing *Man Throwing a Bull* in the Louvre [1817; fig. 58] being a particularly vivid case in point.) Then there is the febrile,

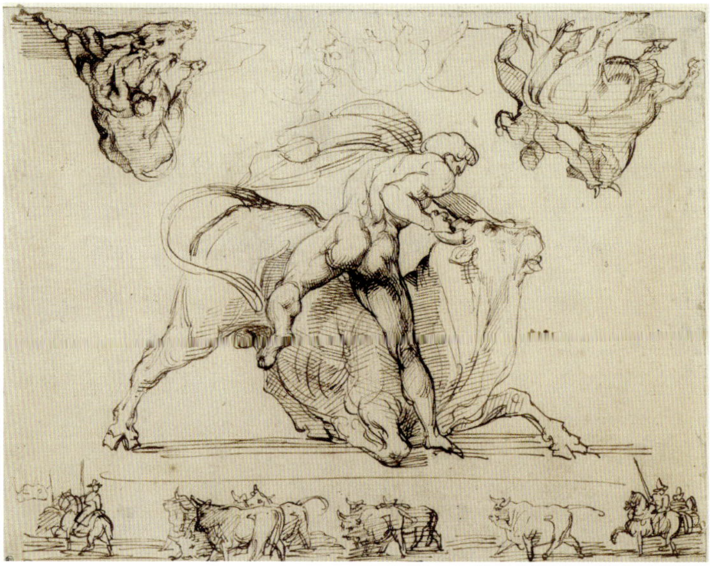

58 Théodore Géricault, *Man Throwing a Bull*, 1817. Ink on paper. 24 × 30 cm. Paris, Musée du Louvre, Département des Arts Graphiques.

"feminine" expressiveness of the horses' heads in scenes of violence and excitement, such as the *Charging Chasseur* and many of the Riderless Horses drawings and paintings (the most prominent horse in the Baltimore *Start of the Race of the Barberi Horses* [see fig. 32] being a singularly affecting instance of this); especially when placed in close conjunction with the more impassive and contained heads of the companion men (as in the *Chasseur* and the Louvre *Start of the Race of the Barberi Horses* [see fig. 45]), the effect, as already suggested, is of a psychic doubleness or, better, *completeness* unlike anything in Davidian painting, with its consistent emphasis on male/female differentiation. (We touch here on a feature of Géricault's art fundamentally different from the flawed "masculinity" evoked by Bryson.)[38]

But there is something else I have in mind, which more directly concerns the issue of worldhood and which can perhaps best be broached by way of Martin Heidegger's contentious but suggestive three-part distinction: "The stone is worldless; the animal is poor in world; man is world-forming." The crucial discussion of these propositions is found in *The Fundamental Concepts of Metaphysics*,[39] where Heidegger is careful to specify that "poor in world" involves a notion not of hierarchy but rather of a kind of "deprivation," in comparison with "man" whose essence gives him a fullness of "access to beings" that animals are said to lack (192–3). Needless to say, this hardly resolves all the problems such a formulation raises, not that Heidegger thinks it does – his discussion of animals is characteristically circuitous and difficult (one section of chapter four is titled "Being open in captivation as a not-having of world in having that which disinhibits" [268]), much too circuitous and difficult for me to try to summarize it here. Rather, my suggestion – a historical-ontological rather than a metaphysical one – is that an intuition of something like "world-poverty" or "world-deprivation" – I am in effect hijacking Heidegger's language for my own simpler purposes – can be said to attend Géricault's images of horses, especially in the many superb lithographs, where it is felt to be in keeping with, even so to speak to compensate for, the unavailability of world that I have suggested marks his art generally. Put slightly differently, it is as though the men – and occasional women and children – in Géricault's lithographs inhabit the restricted albeit profoundly imagined and, as already remarked, inherently untheatrical world of the horses, not the other way round. (Heidegger would not be comfortable with this, though he does write at one point, "No animal can become depraved in the same way as man" [194]. And he speaks of animals as "absorbed" in their condition [238–40]. But he also states that as far as household animals are concerned, "we enable them to move within our world" [210] – whereas with respect to horses and Géricault I am suggesting rather the reverse.[40])

So for example in the strongly mooded *Les Boueux* (1822; fig. 59) a trio of yoked and blinkered draft horses on a cobbled urban street wait patiently for a laborer, much less clearly defined than they, to finish shoveling waste into a wooden cart, which they will then pull to its next destination. But even in the tonally quite different *Flemish Farrier* (1821; fig. 60) with its muscular Horatii-like blacksmith attaching a horseshoe to a large, piebald horse's rear left hoof, the impression conveyed is less of the horse being under the protection of the man than of the latter being given purpose and meaning by his relation to the horse – indeed the copious white smoke presumably rising from an unseen forge seems the very image of the blacksmith's "subjectivity," here explicitly presented as a product of his task. (Note too the man in a smock leaning back against a post and looking off toward the right, the small boy reaching up toward the horse's muzzle, and a further figure, a youth, laboring in the shadows: it is as if the horse unknowingly but effectively provides the basis for a fragile, impermanent, unselfconscious community.)

In still another register, the wonderful *Flemish Horses* (1822; fig. 61) in the French series "Suite de douze petites pièces," depicts two splendid animals, one white or gray, the other dark, the former possibly male (his thick tail blocks a view of his sex), the latter probably female (no genitals are visible), fitting their rounded, substantial bodies into a rhythmic relation that could serve as an ideal image of friendship or marriage;

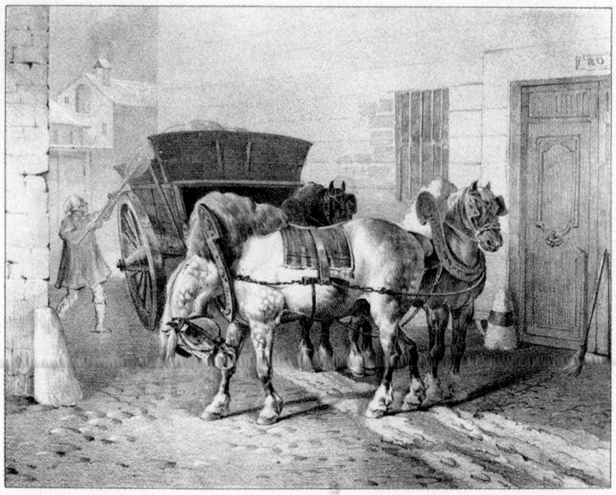

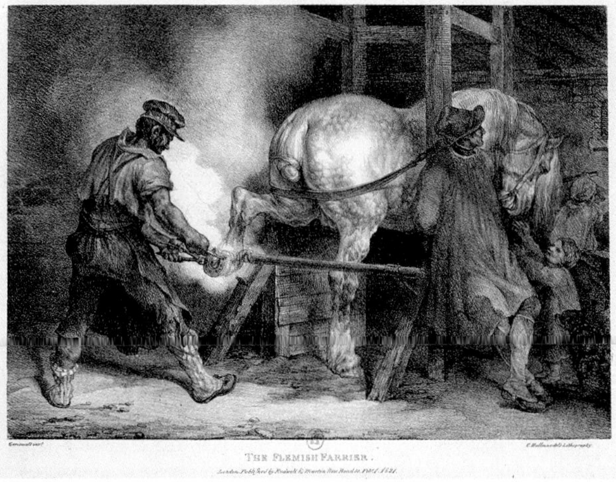

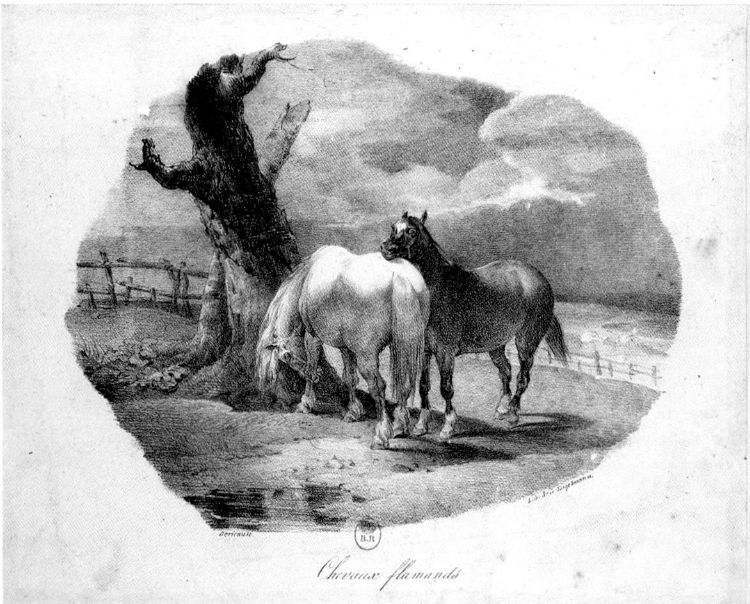

59 (*above, left*) Théodore Géricault, *Les Boueux*, 1822. Lithograph. 19.5 × 24.6 cm. Paris, Bibliothèque Nationale, Département des Estampes et de la Photographie.

60 (*above, right*) Théodore Géricault, *The Flemish Farrier*, 1821. Lithograph. 22.7 × 31.5 cm. Paris, Bibliothèque Nationale, Département des Estampes et de la Photographie.

61 (*left*) Théodore Géricault, *Flemish Horses*, 1822. Lithograph. 17.1 × 21.4 cm. Paris, Bibliothèque Nationale, Département des Estampes et de la Photographie.

the harmony between them is as moving as any male/female pairing in Poussin (the obvious comparison). The hour seems to be late – is there a hint of moonlight? – and next to the horses are two trees, the smaller of which is stunted, dead (we are not shown enough of the larger one to know whether it is in leaf or not). Here as elsewhere in Géricault's images of horses the strength of a certain ineffable mood – in this case tender if not entirely reassuring – is as impressive as his mastery of equine physique and physiognomy.

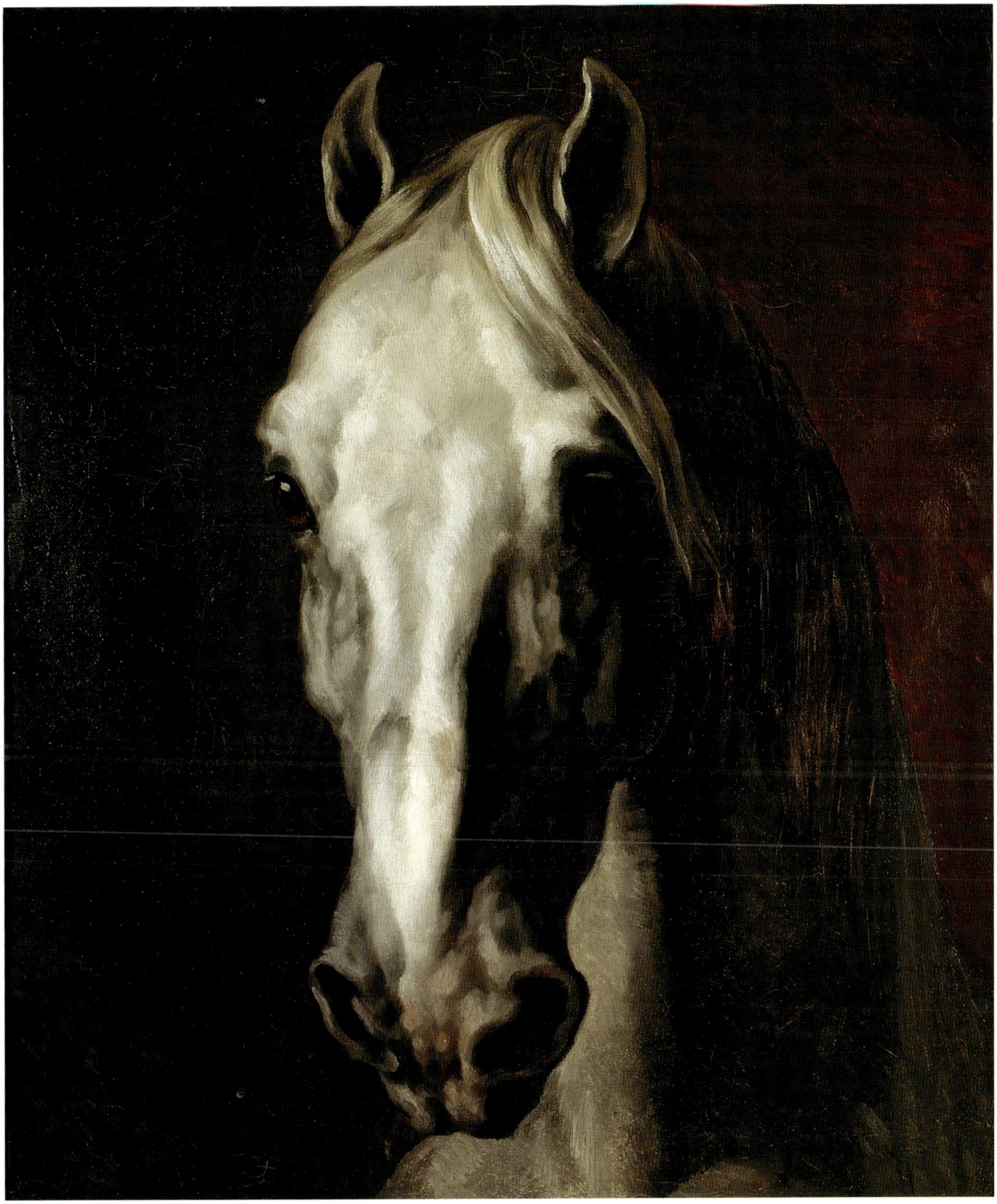

62 Théodore Géricault, *Head of a White Horse*, ca. 1810–12. Oil on canvas. 65 × 54 cm. Paris, Musée du Louvre.

But beyond question the most compelling instance of the general phenomenon I am trying to evoke is the large *Head of a White Horse* in the Louvre (of uncertain date: the consensus places it before the Italian trip but I find that hard to believe; fig. 62[41]), a work that goes a long way toward envisioning the replacement of persons by horses – as if in this strangely compelling canvas Géricault explores to what extent a magnificent horse's head, seen at close range and almost exactly from the front, might not just be adaptable to the schema of the human portrait but might exceed and revise, not to say improve, that schema as if from within. Thus *Head of a White Horse* minimizes the horse's "gaze" (the eyes are too much to the side) and elides the mouth and chin while emphasizing the magnificent forehead, the long and exquisitely sculpted "bridge" of the nose, and the flaring, rose-tinged nostrils; the result is a shift away from confrontation, not to say aggression towards sensitivity, attentiveness, receptivity. That there is no way of knowing whether the subject of the portrait is male or female is also to the point. (I do not say that the extraordinary animal in Géricault's painting is imagined as "world-forming" – but almost. In any case, to stand for a length of time in contemplation of the *Head of a White Horse* is positively chastening.)

Much more could be said about specific works if there were space to do so; I shall simply add that the "vignette" format of many of the French lithographs, such as the "Flemish Horses," perfectly expresses the notion of a deprived or reduced – but not fragmentary; rather, intact, even concentrated – world in visual terms.[42]

(2) The London lithographs raise another possibility – that "world-poverty" or "world-deprivation" in Géricault might be understood, at least up to a point, in social and political terms. Significantly, David once again is the presiding genius of three of the most memorable of the London images. Thus *The Piper* (1821; fig. 63) with its blind musician in profile harks back to the *Belisarius* (and beyond that to Jean-Baptiste Chardin's *Blind Man* of 1753, one of the last of his genre inventions). *Pity the Sorrows of a Poor Old Man* (1821; fig. 64) recycles the "father" in the *Raft*, which is also to say that it returns to the *Brutus*-invention of the oblivious facing figure, in this case a surprisingly robust-seeming beggar whose averted gaze is hidden under the brim of his hat (there is also something of the "son" in the *Raft* in his sprawling legs and half-open right hand). A dusky street scene recedes to the right, and immediately to the old man's left (his right) a woman serving in a bakery is seen through a partly open window on whose sloping ledge several loaves or rolls are practically within the old man's reach. The quiet drama of the scene (is there a suggestion in it, too, of the *Belisarius*?) concerns the relation of the loaves or rolls or indeed of the woman to the old man – are we to imagine that she is on the verge of slipping him a gift of food? Or

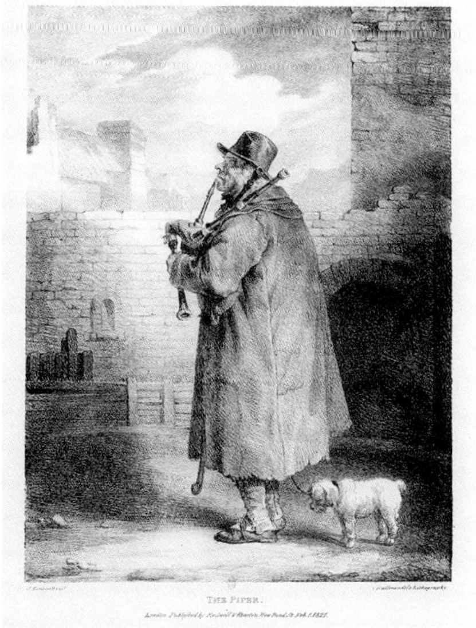

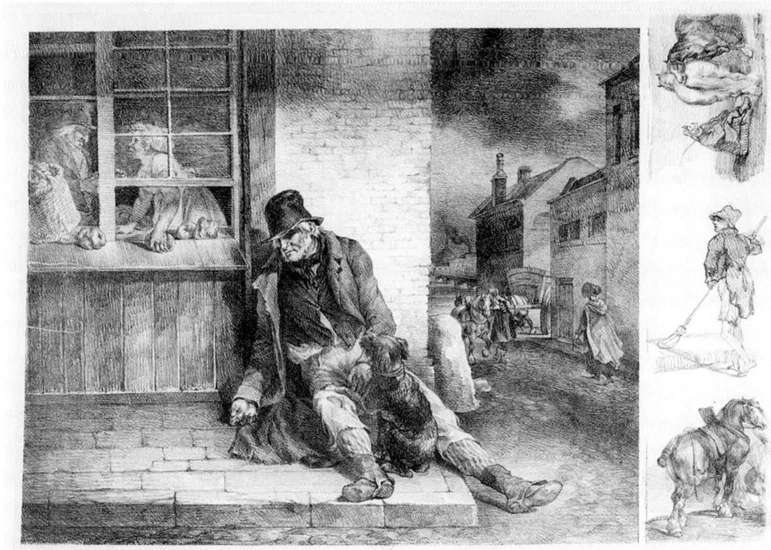

63 (*above, left*) Théodore Géricault, *The Piper*, 1821. Lithograph. 31.5 × 23.3 cm. Paris, Bibliothèque Nationale, Département des Estampes et de la Photographie.

64 (*above, right*) Théodore Géricault, *Pity the Sorrows of a Poor Old Man*, 1821. Lithograph. 31.7 × 37.6 cm. Paris, Bibliothèque Nationale, Département des Estampes et de la Photographie.

is the point that she is oblivious to his existence? The latter seems more likely, but our attention keeps being drawn to the partly open window and to her hand holding a roll that just might be intended for the old man – to what extent Géricault intended the viewer to be thus in doubt is impossible to say. Note too the affecting dogs in both lithographs, no "poorer in world" than are their owners.

Then there is the stunning, somber lithograph, *A Paraleytic* [sic] *Woman* (1821; fig. 65), which is rigorously Davidian in its layout, with the back-to-back pair of the older woman and her brutish servant providing still another variant of the *Eudamidas* motif of the *Horatii*, *Socrates*, and *Brutus*. I take the deep structure of the *Paraleytic Woman* to express a certain dread of looking, though here as often dread goes with fascination – at any rate, I take the young woman's haunted, backward stare across the empty middle of the composition (compare the *Brutus*) as expressing a mixture of fear of contagion-through-looking and something like guilt for what she sees: as if for Géricault in 1820–21 vision as such were essentially two-way, at once a source of vulnerability or fatal chink in the body's armor and a channel of (potentially malign) power, and as if

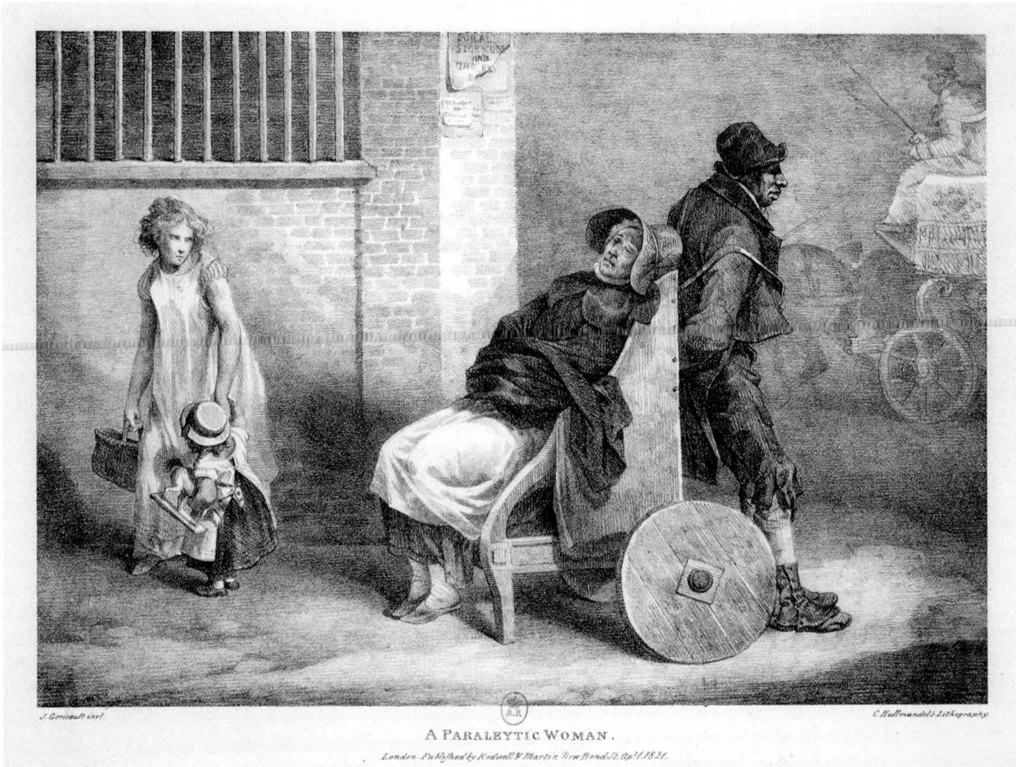

65 (*above*) and 66 (*below*) Theodore Géricault, *A Paraleytic* [sic] *Woman*, 1821. Lithograph. 22.2 × 31.5 cm. Paris, Bibliothèque Nationale, Département des Estampes et de la Photographie.

the effects of seeing were therefore incalculable, contradictory, out of control. All this may seem to go pretty far, but consider the implications of the tattered handbill attached to the brickwork at the upper center of the image (fig. 66). It reads in English: "FOR ALL SICKNESS AND THE E . . . E . . ." – which leads me to propose that the disfigured words are "EVIL EYE." If this is right, it amounts to a further thematization of the *topos* of the evil eye – the disfiguring gaze – just as the literal disfiguring, the tearing almost to unreadability, of the handbill itself, may be seen as epitomizing, even allegorizing, the disfiguring power of one such gaze: the viewer's own (compare my reading of the *Raft*).

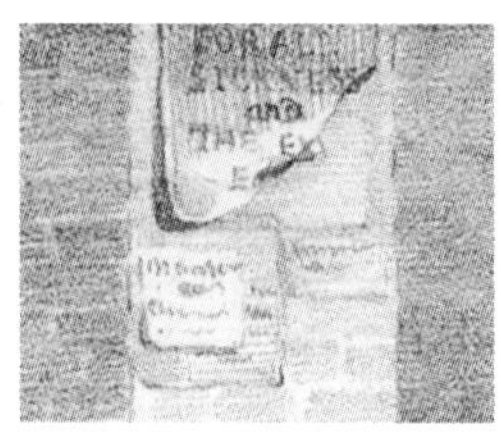

(In a related work apparently made shortly after Géricault's arrival in London, the large and harrowing wash drawing *Public Hanging in London* [1820; fig. 67],

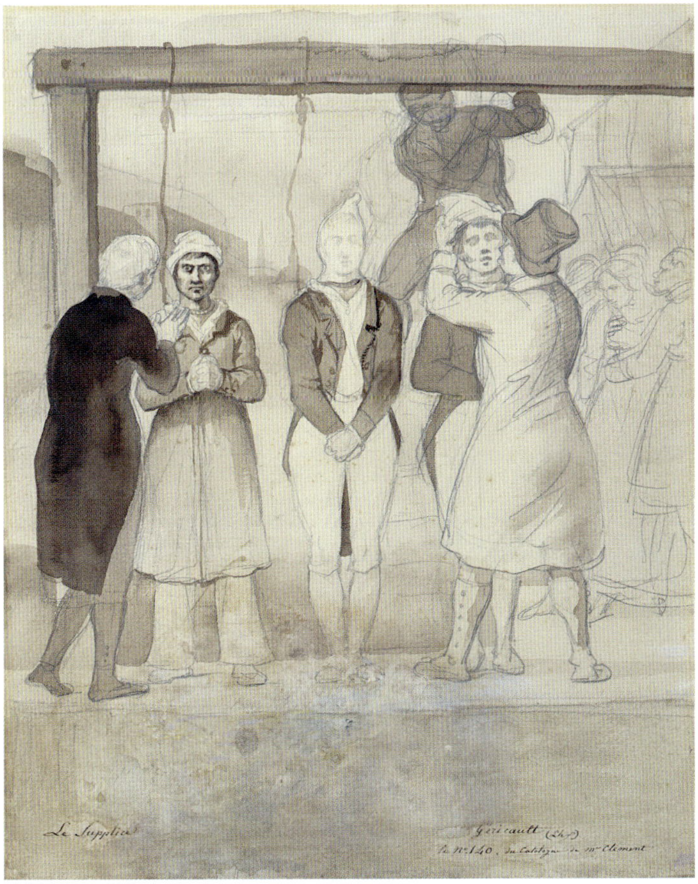

67 Théodore Géricault, *Public Hanging in London*, 1820. Watercolor and pencil on paper. 40.8 × 32.2 cm. Rouen, Musée des Beaux-Arts.

probably depicting the execution of the so-called Cato Street conspirators, a realism that has no equal in its age and has often been viewed as simply breaking with current artistic norms turns out to be grounded in issues of absorption and beholding *in extremis*. Thus the prisoner standing with clasped hands at the left, whose face and in particular whose staring eyes are the focal point of the image, appears so terrified at the prospect of execution as to be capable of seeing nothing, a condition literalized in the figure of the hooded man at his left. Should one be looking on or not? Is there a price to be paid for one's inability (mine anyway) to avert one's fascinated gaze? And what about the artist – where exactly is he in all this? Here too the *Brutus* motif may well be reflected in Géricault's treatment of his theme and point of view.)

(3) In perhaps the greatest of the London lithographs, the quietly monumental *Entrance to the Adelphi Wharf* (1821; fig. 68), three draft horses accompanied by two drovers with long, flexible whips walk slowly and directly away from the viewer into the low, deeply shadowed, indeed perfectly black brick tunnel of the Wharf. Light falls diagonally across both the cobbled ground and the tunnel face; Géricault's mastery of the still relatively new medium is evident in his treatment of a range of textures, including the gleaming coats of the horses, the overgarment of the man nearest us, and

68 Théodore Géricault, *Entrance to the Adelphi Wharf*, 1821. Lithograph. 25.3 × 31 cm. Paris, Bibliothèque Nationale, Département des Estampes et de la Photographie.

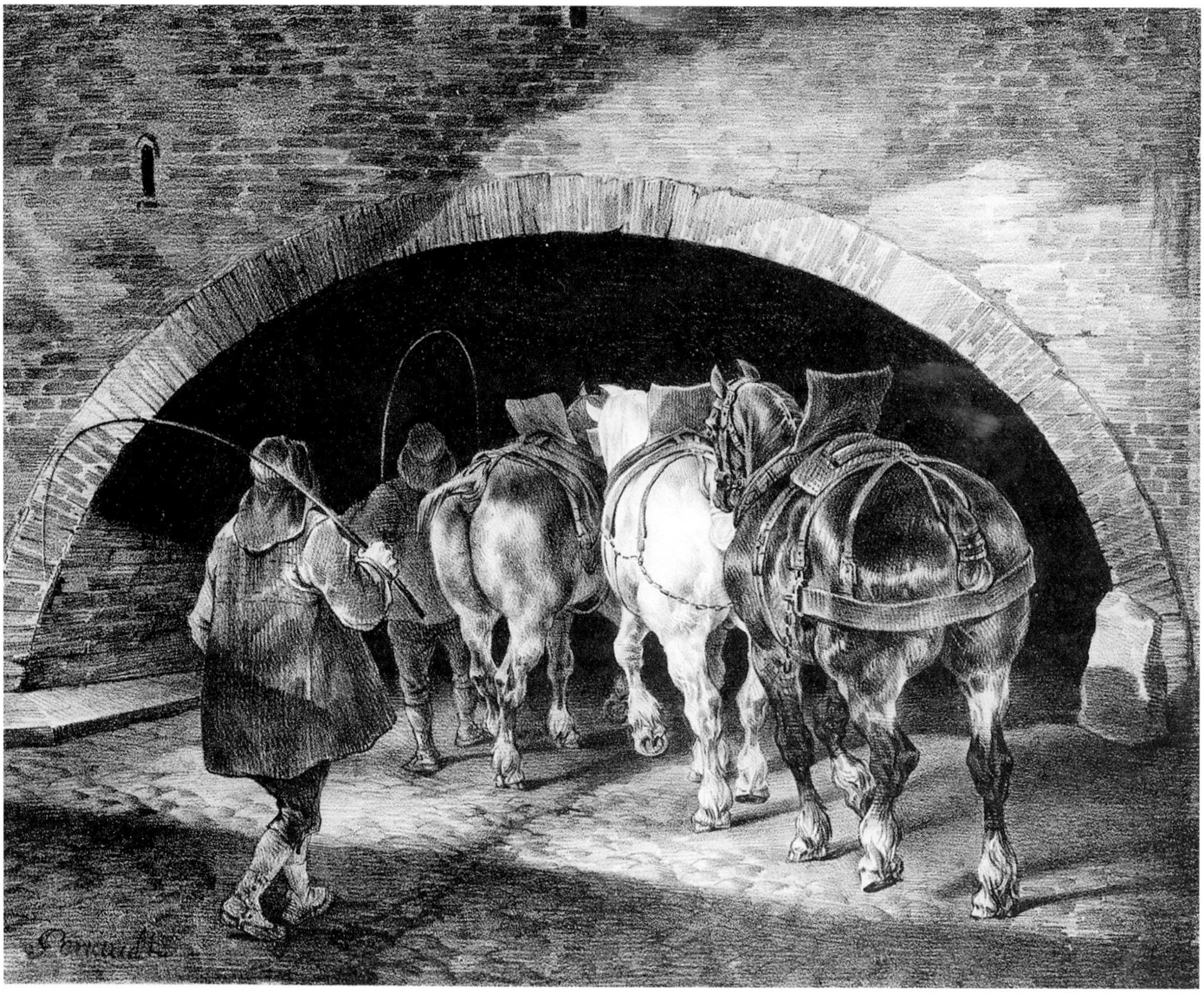

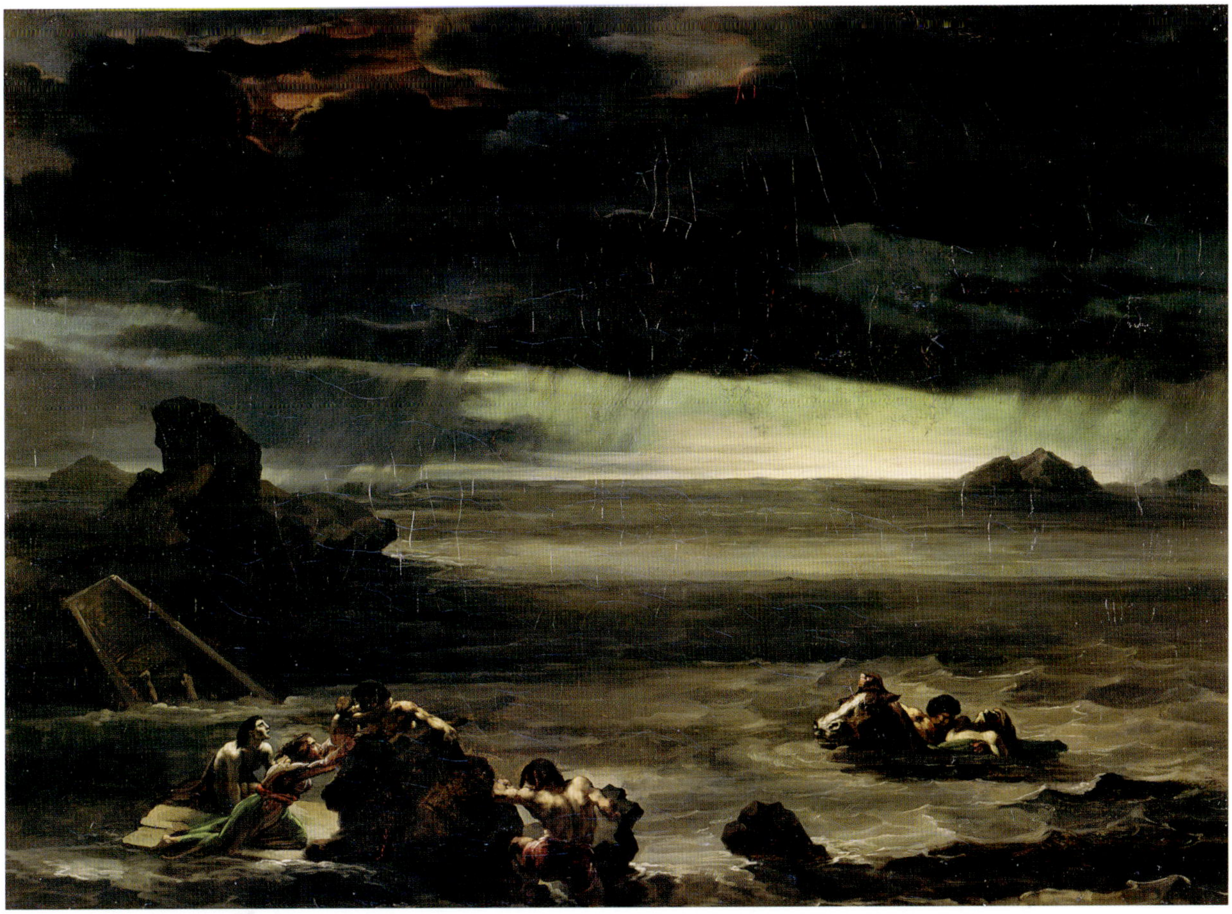

69 Théodore Géricault, *Scene of a Deluge*, ca. 1815–18. Oil on canvas. 97 × 130 cm. Paris, Musée du Louvre.

the worn brickwork. In an obvious sense, the structure of the *Adelphi Wharf* amounts to a radicalization of that of the *Raft* – horses and men not only turned away but actually retreating from our gaze. (Into blackness. Or nothingness. Without repeal. Also without drama: whatever world remained to Géricault is receding at a steady pace.)

Some years before, it is unclear exactly when, Géricault painted a devastating *Deluge* (ca. 1815–18; fig. 69), explicitly an image of the end of the world – of his world, which comes to the same thing. (It is hard to say whether the woman handing a small child to a male figure clinging to a rock at the left or the swimming horse and horseman rescuing a figure who may or may not be a woman to the right strikes a more personal note.) And a further suggestion: that the three similarly stylized large landscapes with figures, obviously meant to be part of a single decorative scheme, painted during the summer

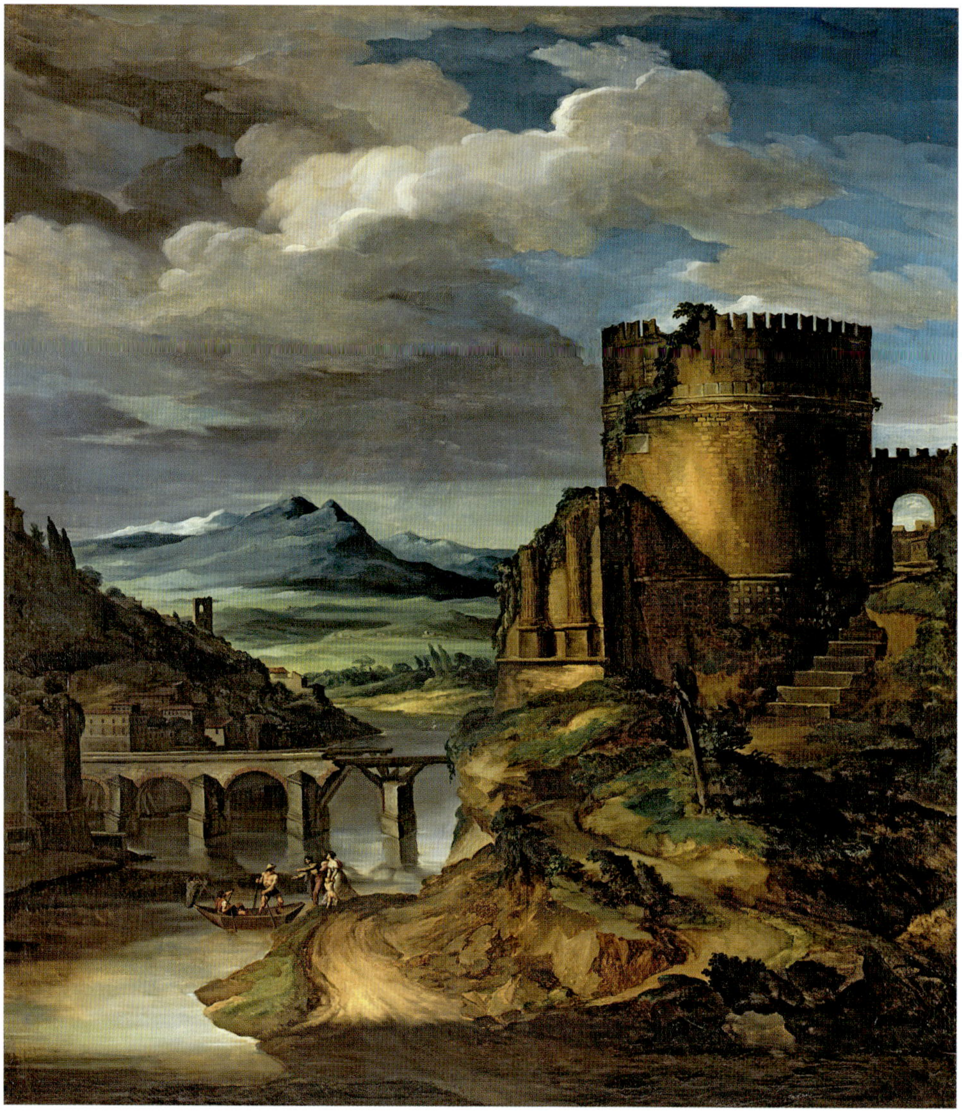

70 Théodore Géricault, *Landscape with a Roman Tomb*, 1818. Oil on canvas. 250 × 219 cm. Paris, Musée du Petit Palais.

and early fall of 1818 – *Landscape with a Roman Tomb* (Paris, Petit Palais; fig. 70), *Landscape with Fishermen* (Munich, Neue Pinakothek), and *Landscape with an Aqueduct* (New York, Metropolitan Museum of Art) – seem less like depictions of a credible world (even making allowance for their ostensible purpose) than something like painted screens beyond which there is to be imagined . . . nothing at all.[43]

And of course the *Raft* itself, with its implied dismissal of the very possibility of rescue, can be, should be, seen in this light.* Another sort of image of the end of the world is found in the large drawings for an earlier moment in the *Raft* narrative, the *Mutiny* (see fig. 57), which in addition to being a scene of almost unimaginable violence is largely based on Michelangelo's *Last Judgment*, as conveyed by Rubens's so-called *Little Last Judgment*, an etching. Then there are two late paintings that seem to bear on the topic: *Le Haquet* in Providence, Rhode Island (date uncertain but probably 1821–3; fig. 72), a scene of glacial stasis, two horses and their two-wheeled dray loaded with barrels in the absence of humans and framed by an architectural ensemble, a rounded arch with buildings closing off the space beyond, that speaks of nothing but blockage and frustration (the only note of "hope," a small one, is the dog); and one of Géricault's defining canvases, *The Lime Kiln* (1822; fig. 73), almost devoid of human presence and with four unattended yoked and burdened horses feeding in the left foreground. The point of view is curiously elevated, as if to stress the fact of separation, and from within the nearer of the two buildings in the

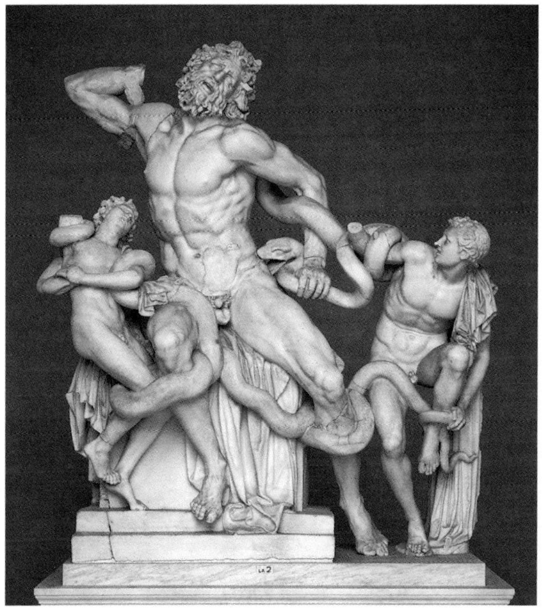

71 *Laocoön*, Roman copy, perhaps after Agesander, Athenodorus, and Polydorus of Rhodes. First century CE. Marble. H. 208 cm. Vatican State, Museo Pio Clementino, Vatican Museums.

* All the more so in that (again, to my eye) the *Raft* almost fantasmatically evokes the famous Hellenistic statue, a copy of a Greek original, of *Laocoön and His Sons* (fig. 71), brought by Napoleon in 1799 to Paris where Géricault would have had ample opportunity to study it before its return to Italy in 1816. What makes this especially intriguing is that the statue has often been seen as distinguishing between the two sons, the younger one on the beholder's left dead or dying, the older one on the beholder's right in the act of escaping from the serpent's coils. Translated into the terms of the *Raft*, the younger son would be the dead young man, which is perfectly straightforward, while the older one would be the pyramid of *naufragés* straining to be beheld – in other words, no longer looking toward the father's face but away from him toward the far horizon where the *Argus* sails on by – a radical, ultimately *less hopeful*, variation on the sculpture. These brief remarks are indebted to Allen Grossman's magnificent essay, "The Passion of Laocoön," which defies summary but which I have found invaluable for thinking about the *Raft* (*True-Love: Essays on Poetry and Valuing* [Chicago and London, 2009], 71–125). (The theme of world-destruction figures prominently in that essay.) See also Thomas Crow, "Géricault: The Heroic Single Figure," in *Géricault* 1996, where it is suggested that "[t]he chain of mingled bodies, uniting the races of Europe and Africa, becomes the equivalent of one single body in a state of transformation" (1: 53); the suggestion is elaborated in Crow, *Emulation*, 291–2.

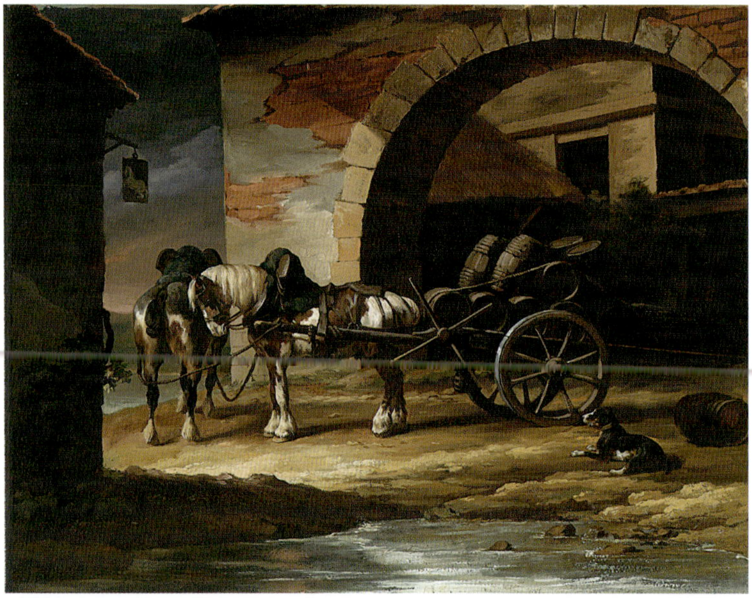

72 (*left*) Théodore Géricault, *Le Haquet*, 1821–3. Oil on canvas. 60 × 73 cm. Providence, Museum of Art, Rhode Island School of Design, Works of Art Reserve Fund, 43.539.

73 (*below*) Théodore Géricault, *The Lime Kiln*, 1822. Oil on canvas. 50 × 61 cm. Paris, Musée du Louvre.

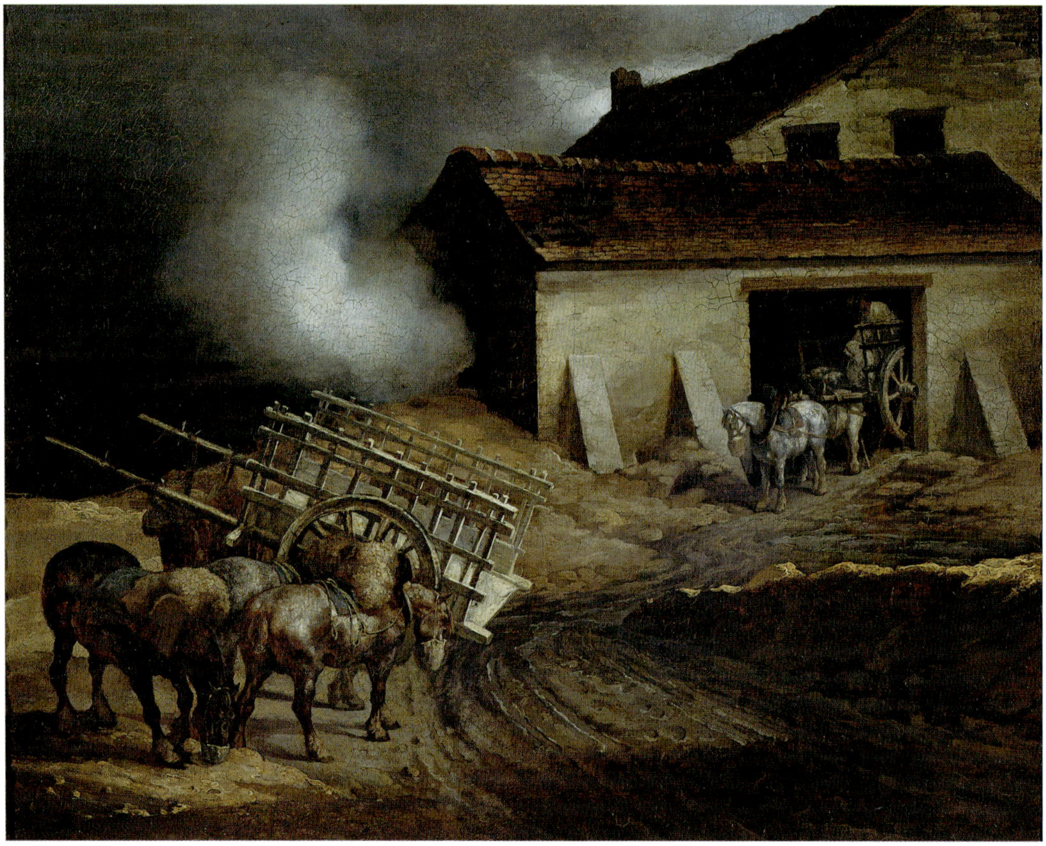

middle distance a cloud of white smoke issues and rises, in this case, Michel specifies, from the burning of gypsum to make plaster ("Mythe de l'oeuvre," 220). The hour seems late, the scene as a whole is deeply shadowed, though gleams of light fall on the horses, on the floor of a wagon, on the ridge of earth in the right foreground. The interior spaces, viewed through a broad doorway and two cut-off windows, are black; the horses and wagon partly within and partly just outside the doorway seem oddly far away. The dense smoke, once again, conveys a sense of subjectivity but a subjectivity that has become unmoored, orphaned, cut loose from the world, or from all but the last remnants of the world. The painter's touch is masterly but subdued; this is tragic painting, tragic *lyric* painting, a canvas to put alongside the second stanza of Hölderlin's "Hälfte des Lebens" . . . And yet the horses have been fed, they are not wholly beyond the realm of care. (Logically the horses can have been fed only by persons such as those loading the wagon in the doorway. But the impression conveyed is of a small society for all intents and purposes on its own.)

(4) Not quite forty years after Géricault's death, five "Portraits of the Insane" were discovered by chance in Baden-Baden; as mentioned earlier we know nothing solid about them, including exactly when they were painted (1821–2 seems a reasonable guess; figs. 74–6).[44] Tradition holds that the portraits are of *monomanes*, monomaniacs, that is, persons wholly absorbed in one or another delusion or obsession but otherwise normal. (Géricault's sitters – three men, two women – are said to be monomaniacs of theft, the stealing of children, gambling, envy, and delusions of military grandeur.) All five paintings are incontestably among the most compelling portraits ever made, masterpieces at once of hyperacute objective observation and of unimpeded sympathetic identification (but how can this be?). Each facial expression is utterly individual in its suggestion of mental disturbance but without the least hint of exaggeration, much less of caricature. The gazes are oblique, not so much vacant as haunted-seeming (each in its own way), and one has the sense that this or rather the absorption or distraction that the gazes signify allowed the painter to scrutinize each sitter with a closeness and an intensity – also, as I have said, a sympathy – that ordinary interaction between social peers would have made inconceivable. The brushwork is vigorous but impasto has mostly been eschewed in an attempt to record the actual texture and condition of the sitters' skin – again, scarcely a feature of conventional portraiture even at its most distinguished. And as Michel remarks, attention also is paid to the individual subjects' dress (also to their *tenue* or bearing), which he rightly sees as conferring on them a dignity that implicitly argues for their humane treatment ("Mythe de l'oeuvre," 244). To all this I will simply add that one way of characterizing their general condition

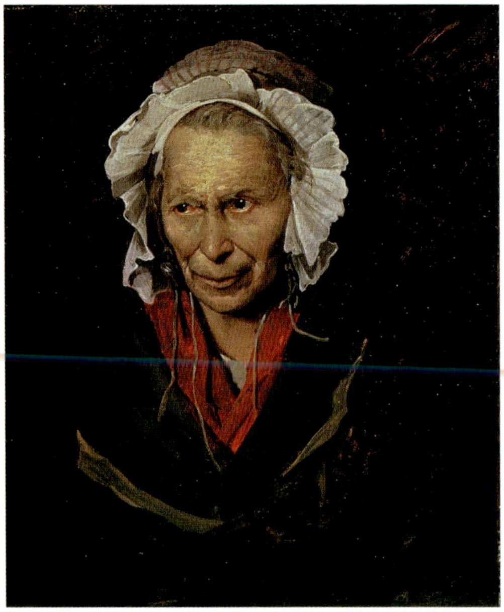

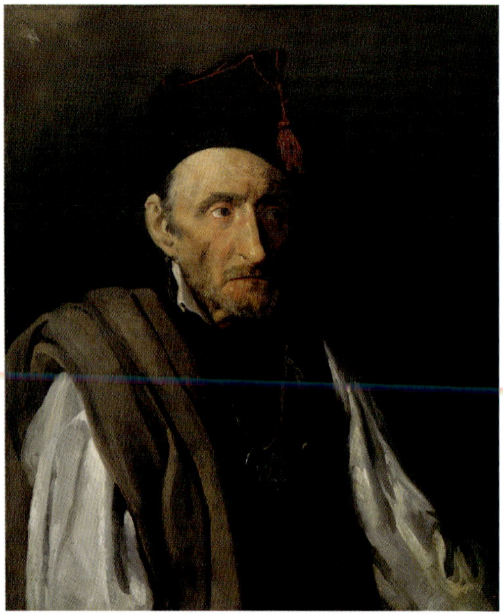

74 (*above, left*) Théodore Géricault, *Monomaniac of Envy*, 1821–2. Oil on canvas. 72 × 58 cm. Lyon, Musée des Beaux-Arts.

75 (*above, right*) Théodore Géricault, *Monomaniac of Military Command*, 1821–2. Oil on canvas. 81 × 65 cm. Winterthur, Collection Oskar Reinhart am Römerholz.

as portrayed by Géricault might well be as self-evidently "poor in world," if not indeed as very nearly worldless – a basis, perhaps, for the rapport between painter and sitter that can be felt in every touch of the brush.[45]

(5) As Géricault's condition worsened, his world, in the ordinary sense of the term, was constricted to a single room, a bed of pain. Still, he did what he could, and among the results is the Louvre's superlative drawing with watercolor of his left hand (1824; fig. 77).

8

I am painfully conscious of not having had the space to discuss numerous works – paintings, drawings, lithographs, sculptures – that would further support my argument (and which in any case I would have relished evoking), but I hope that at least the

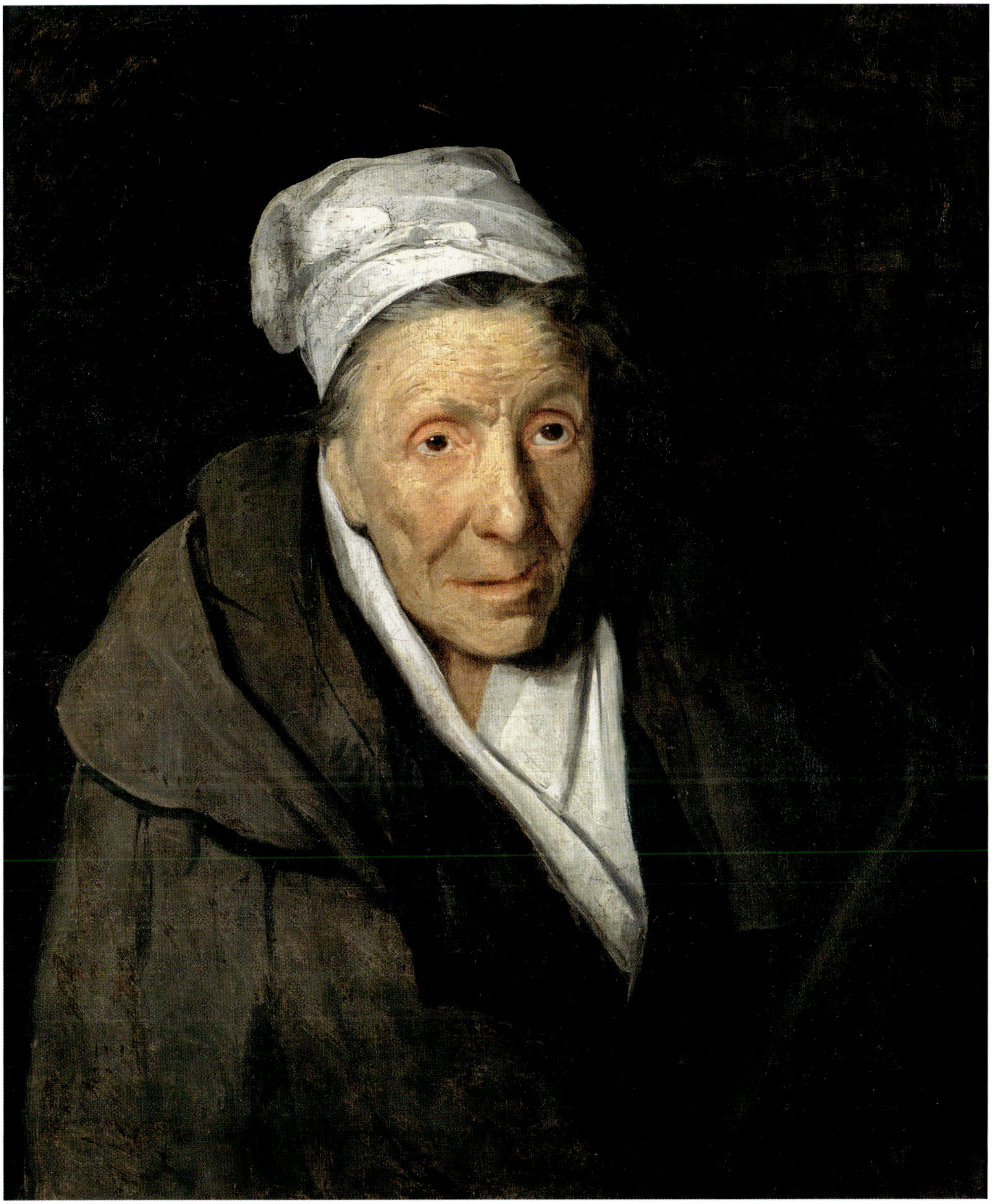

76 Théodore Géricault, *Monomaniac of Gambling*, 1821–2 Oil on canvas. 77 × 64 cm. Paris, Musée du Louvre.

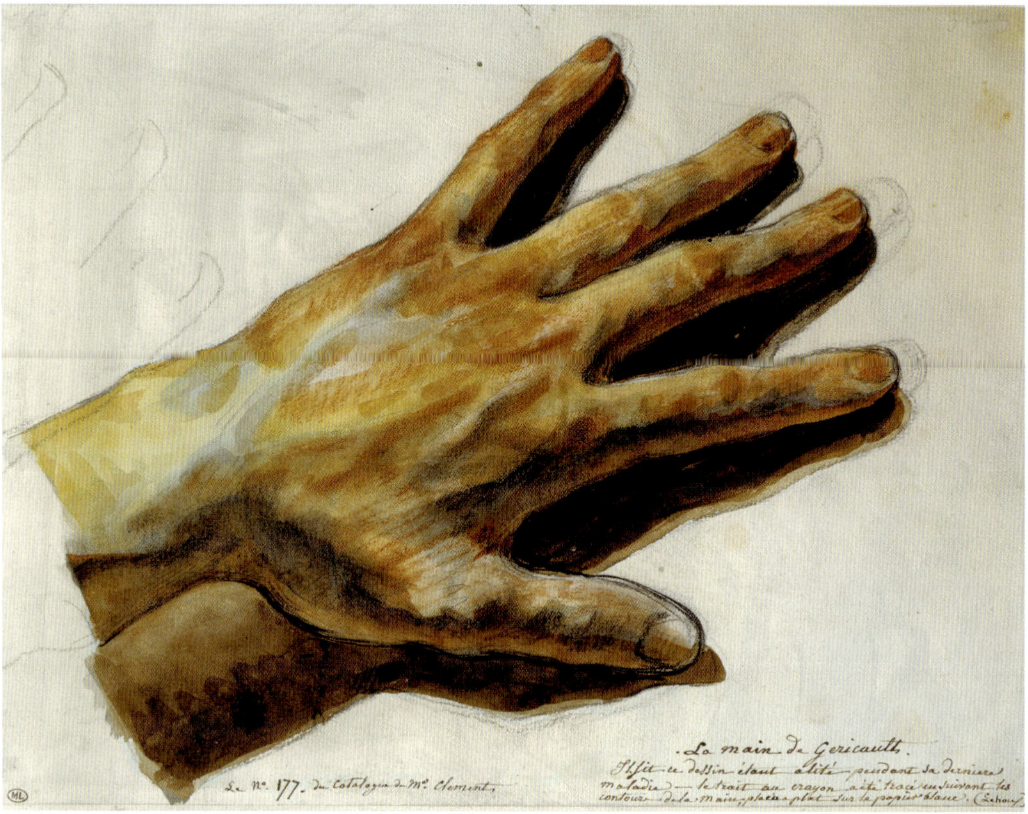

77 Théodore Géricault, *Study of Artist's Left Hand*, 1824. Pencil and watercolor or sanguine wash on paper. 22.5 × 29.5 cm. Paris, Musée du Louvre, Département des Arts Graphiques.

outlines of what I have been trying to suggest are by now clear. In this final section I want to leave Géricault behind and leap ahead . . . to Honoré de Balzac (b. 1799), specifically, to his early story "Le Colonel Chabert."[46] On the following grounds: what we have been tracking in the present essay and its predecessor, "David/Manet," is the progressive exclusion from ambitious painting in France between the 1790s and the 1820s of the very possibility of dramatic action and expression. In later David this exclusion is as it were embraced in works of surprising originality and strangeness. In Géricault it is fought, resisted, every inch of the way, with the artistic consequences – immense but also tragic – that I have tried to evoke. With Delacroix, Géricault's younger successor and a "romantic" artist of a different stamp, the Diderotian project is replaced by what might be described as the transposition of dramatic values and effects into an explicitly "aesthetic" or "poetic" register, so that Baudelaire will later say of

Delacroix that he has the merit of being "supremely literary."[47] And then all at once in the early 1830s dramatic action and expression, based on themes of violent opposition and involving antagonists depicted in intensely corporeal terms, positively surge to the fore in early Balzac, who understands perfectly well that this is what is happening – see for example the repeated invocation of the notion of drama (*drame*) in "Le Colonel Chabert" or indeed the first pages of *Le Père Goriot*, the decisive early novel. (From the latter: "These boarders [at Madame Vauquer's] hinted at dramas past or present; not the dramas performed in the glare of the footlights, against painted backcloths, but living, wordless dramas, icy dramas to stir and sear the heart, dramas without end."[48]) Put slightly differently, it is as if in Balzac the Diderotian ideal is given new life, with two vital differences or indeed advantages: first, literally nothing in the realm of human action or desire or sheer will is inherently too excessive to be dramatically credible (hence the understandable invocation by modern commentators of the notion of melodrama to characterize his narratives[49]); and second, a related point, the problematic of theatricality such as was developed by Diderot in response to the theater and painting of his time has only limited application to prose fiction, the dynamics of reading stories and novels being fundamentally different from that of beholding stage plays and paintings (needless to say, I am simplifying a complex topic, which deserves further treatment). The result is a new representational freedom with regard to the issues I have been tracing, personified, in a certain sense, in the superhuman Vautrin (real name Jacques Collin, also known as the Abbé Carlos Herrera), who among other powers enjoys an almost total mastery of his appearance to others – along with an almost total ocular ability to see through others' pretenses and disguises.[50]

What of worldhood, which I have been suggesting is something like a necessary condition for the accomplishment of Diderotian aims? The answer seems to be this: it is only in the relatively new medium of "realistic" prose fiction that it becomes possible to portray the economic and political reality of the time – more precisely, of the immediately preceding period, the Bourbon Restoration (Balzac's favored field of operation) – and by so doing to depict, almost stone by stone to construct, a social world in which action and expression of the most passionate and determined sort turn out to have pride of place. Not that the Restoration as a period was other than theatrical in the broadest sense of the notion. Recent historians have shown that even the widespread resistance to the Bourbon regime resorted to theatrical means – specifically to repeated performances of Molière's *Tartuffe*, understood as laying bare the hypocrisy of contemporary Jesuits, themselves involved in another kind of theater, the so-called "missions" to the interior of France – to make its political point.[51] But it was also then that a new phase in the emergence of early capitalism took shape, wealth, not glory as under Napoleon, becoming the decisive factor. (Is this oversimple? No doubt. Is it basically true? Yes.) And this meant that the artistic reconstruction of worldhood could only be accomplished in political and economic terms – just as the depiction of Géricault-intensity conflict turned out to involve the sustained and often tortuous efforts of characters like Vautrin or Rastignac (each "a weapon charged with willpower to the muzzle," in Baudelaire's memorable phrase[52]) to overcome their limited beginnings and achieve a position of mastery with respect to the moneyed and class forces arrayed against them – a project altogether beyond the representational capabilities of even the most resourceful and ambitious painting. (Toward the end of his life Géricault made several drawings toward possible paintings on the slave trade and the freeing of the prisoners of the Inquisition by French troops; the compositions, tentative as they are, show the limit of his imagination in this regard.) A partial exception should perhaps be made for the "lesser" art of political caricature as practiced by the young Honoré Daumier in 1834–5, but then came the anti-caricature laws of September 1835, which in effect put an end to his first exceptionally creative period. Through no fault of his, the *caricatures de moeurs* that followed are of lesser quality and significance.[53]

In other words, I am claiming to see in Balzac starting in the early 1830s what might be called the rebirth of drama through prose fiction, to paraphrase a later thinker. And of all Balzac's early texts, the one that bears most closely on the concerns of the present essay is "Le Colonel Chabert," a long short story (sometimes, however, called a "roman") published for the first time in *L'Artiste* in 1832.

The narrative, most of which is set in 1819, begins in the Paris office of M. Derville, a young and ambitious lawyer who will go on to figure importantly in the *Comédie humaine*. It is lunchtime and a team of his clerks is present; looking out the window one spots a ghastly-looking wreck of a man in an aged "carrick," an overcoat that had long since gone out of style, who has come there before; he arrives and asks to see Derville but is told to return at 1 A.M., when Derville typically begins to plan the day's battles, if he wishes to speak with him. (The youngest clerk in particular treats the visitor with disrespect.) This the old man does, and in the course of a conversation with Derville reveals that he is Colonel Hyacinthe Chabert, the supposedly dead hero of the Battle of Eylau (1807), one of the bloodiest in Napoleon's career. Briefly, Chabert played a leading role in the decisive cavalry charge against the Russians, but returning to the French lines was struck from his horse by a saber-blow that opened his skull and then was ridden over by 1500 horses; left for dead, he was buried in a mass grave, but in fact was still alive and with the aid of a severed arm ("of a Hercules," he tells Derville) managed by dint of fierce exertion to dig himself partly out. He was rescued by a German couple and eventually was taken to a hospital, where under the care of a sympathetic doctor he made a difficult recovery; there were relapses, and in Stuttgart he was interned in a madhouse for two years because he insisted that he was Chabert, the famous hero who was known to be dead; finally he gave up the claim and was released. At first in the company of a fellow soldier and then alone, he painfully made his way back to Paris, arriving, he tells Derville, with the Cossacks in 1815 – a horribly scarred, bald, toothless, prematurely aged, impecunious, and psychologically shattered remnant of his former handsome and heroic self.

Now, Chabert in 1799 had married a beautiful prostitute, Rose Chapotel, picked up in the gardens of the Palais Royal. When his death was announced she was free to remarry, which after Napoleon's fall she did to a returned émigré, the Count Ferraud. Chabert himself had been made a Count of the Empire by Napoleon, which also meant that he had left his wife a rich woman; as the Countess Ferraud in the first years of the Restoration she worked closely with a factotum named Delbecq to increase her funds vastly (Delbecq plays an important role in what follows). Understandably, the news that Chabert was still alive was unwelcome, and in fact she ignored letters from him and made sure that he was not received when once he tried to call on her at home. Derville decides to take Chabert's part, and having secured proof of his identity confronts the Countess and threatens to expose her, brilliantly intuiting (the brilliance of course is all Balzac's) that the Countess herself lived in terror of being abandoned by Ferraud, to whom under the Bourbon regime she brought nothing by way of social connections. (Once shed of her, we are told, he could aspire to marry an only daughter of a peer of France; the Restoration world involved the coming together of hereditary rank and considerable fortunes; by 1819 the importance of the former was on the increase; the Countess's hope is to make so much money through Delbecq's machinations that Ferraud would never leave her.) Derville hopes to persuade her to sign a document attesting that Chabert is still alive; in return Chabert would legally pursue the dissolution of their marriage; and she would grant him an annual bequest of 24,000 francs, considerably less than what in fact ought to have been coming to him. The crucial scene takes place in Derville's office, where Chabert, having semi-miraculously recovered his physical well-being, is waiting in an adjoining room. The plan was for him not to reveal himself, but when he hears the Countess protest that the sum in question is too large, he bursts in angrily and denounces her, at which point she leaves in haste.

Chabert, too, departs, but the Countess, a consummate actress, intercepts him and without difficulty carries him off to her country house in Groslay, where she succeeds in persuading him that while she loves her new husband and the two children she has had by him, she still has strong feelings for Chabert, who in turn gallantly proposes to disappear from her life, becoming "dead" once more. (Significantly, from my point of view, the tipping point occurs when the two young children approach their mother and naïvely ask why she is crying, creating a Greuze-like "sudden and delicious painting" [128].) Sensing that she has won, the countess sends for Delbecq, who draws up a statement for Chabert to sign, effectively declaring himself to be a fraud; this goes too far; Chabert angrily refuses and takes a long, solitary walk that ends up at a pavilion in the grounds, where he comes upon the Countess and Delbecq in conversation. Neither is aware that he is there, and their cynical exchange reveals to him that he has been duped, that his former wife has no feelings for him whatsoever and would be glad to see him committed to an asylum. The scales fall from his eyes; he declares that he feels nothing for her but contempt but that she has nothing more to fear from him; the new world of Restoration society is beyond enduring and he disappears. (Balzac writes, "The colonel had known the countess of the Empire, he now saw a countess of the Restoration" [125], and the difference proves crushing. As Chabert said to Derville earlier, "I was buried under corpses, but now I am buried under the living, under legal acts, under facts, under the entire society, which wants me to return to under the ground" [80].) Six months later, not having heard from Chabert, Derville writes to the Countess, whom he also represents, asking to be reimbursed for various modest expenses incurred on Chabert's behalf but receives a frosty letter of refusal from the Count. And some time after that, in a courtroom, he comes across Chabert himself, arrested for vagrancy under the name Hyacinthe; when the latter learns that Derville has not been paid, he sends a note to the Countess, no doubt threatening to make public his identity, and the lawyer is quickly recompensed.

The story is over except for a further dénouement that takes place in 1840 (changed in a later edition from the initial 1830). Derville and Godeschal, his former clerk and now his successsor, are walking together outside of Paris, when, approaching the grounds of the asylum Bicêtre, Derville recognizes Chabert, now obviously an inmate, sitting on a milestone. Two days later, returning to Paris, they come on him again, sitting on the stump of a tree and tracing lines in the sand with a staff. Derville greats him as Chabert but the old man refuses the name ("Not Chabert! not Chabert!" [138]), saying that he is not a name but simply number 164, seventh room – his official designation. The two men give him money for tobacco; he calls them "Brave troopers," mimes the firing of a musket as he cries "vive Napoléon," and "describes in the air with his cane an imaginary arabesque" (139). (A delusion of military grandeur? Or something more?) The story ends with Derville making a short speech that includes the famous remark that there are three men, all dressed in black, perhaps to mark their mourning for all the virtues – the Priest, the Doctor, and the Man of Justice – who are capable of estimating correctly the world in which they live, and that of these the most unhappy is the lawyer, because his professsion exposes him the most to human depravity. From now on he will live in the country with his wife. His closing words: "Paris horrifies me" (141).

There is no evidence that Balzac in 1832 had Géricault in mind, though he could not have lived through the first years of the Restoration without being aware of the scandal of the *Medusa* and probably of the lesser scandal of the *Raft*, and in fact Géricault is mentioned a number of times in the *Comédie humaine*.[54] Moreover, a year before, in 1831, Balzac had published in *L'Artiste* the story "Le Chef-d'oeuvre inconnu," arguably the greatest work of prose fiction ever on the subject of painting. (He had also published "Sarrasine," another story about the arts, which happens to feature a painting by David's teacher, Joseph-Marie Vien.) So painting was by no means foreign to his concerns. Be this as it may, there is to my mind something keenly suggestive in the fact that in "Le Colonel Chabert," one of his earliest "mature" fictions, he chose to tell the story of a heroic commander of cavalry under Napoleon – a character who might have stepped (more likely, ridden) out of one of Géricault's battle scenes – who "dies" at Eylau (the subject of one of Gros's two masterpieces, admired by Géricault) but then after much suffering survives into the Restoration (the crucial year being 1819, the year of the *Raft*), which he soon concludes is not a world for him – hence his decision to "die" to that world by retreating to the Hospice de la Vieillesse at Bicêtre, where Derville discovers him and brings the story to an end. It is as though Balzac at this critical juncture in his career found himself compelled to demonstrate, to spell out almost didactically, that the heroic values of the previous period had no purchase in the new era, and that whatever place there turned out to be in his writing for action, expression, and passion – in short for "drame"[55] – and place for these there was in abundance – required to be constructed on a different basis, in keeping with the new and from an earlier perspective grossly amoral social realities he saw emerging around him. That in the end Chabert – who helped save the Empire at Eylau, who after the battle dug himself out of a mass grave with the aid of a severed limb, who with the awakening of hope recovers something of his former exceptional physicality, who at Groslay in the clutches of his scheming wife is moved against his own advantage by a "painting of a family," and who having been disabused of his illusions then willingly accepts a status not unlike that of one of Géricault's monomaniacs – is described drawing in the sand with his staff – he also waves the staff in the air, as if it were a paintbrush, limning "an imaginary arabesque"[56] – only makes the absence of any reference to the painter of the *Raft* all the more striking. In any case, Balzac's brilliant, searing story provides a fitting epilogue to Géricault's inspired but ultimately doomed endeavor.[57]

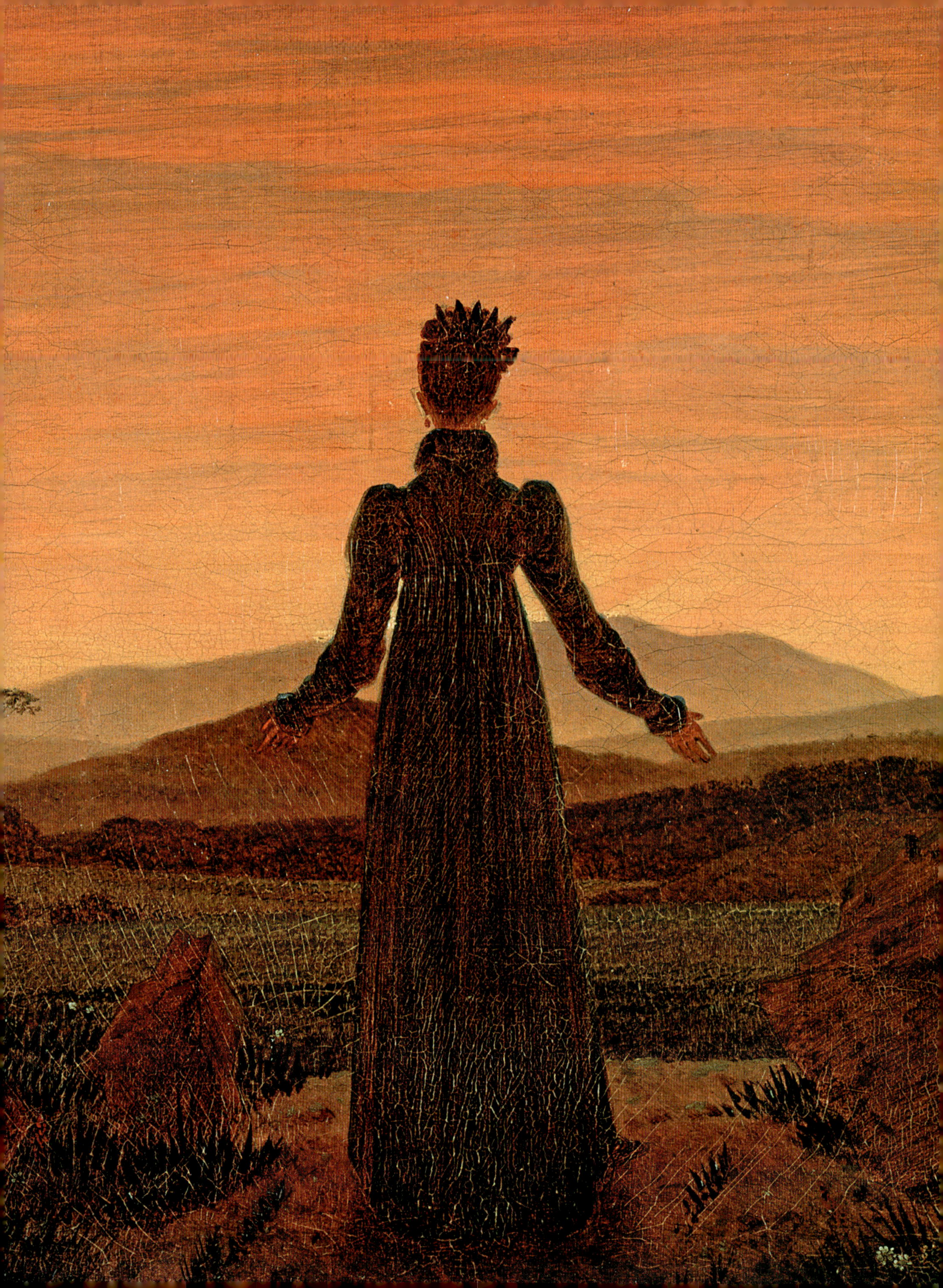

· 4 ·

ORIENTATION IN PAINTING: CASPAR DAVID FRIEDRICH

Let me begin by singling out for extended consideration what is beyond question the most famous motif in Friedrich's art, the human figure, man or woman, depicted from the rear – the so-called *Rückenfigur*. As countless scholars have stressed, such figures are by no means wholly new in Western painting. But no artist before (or indeed since) Friedrich has made of them one of the defining features of his art, as for example in the *Woman before the Rising Sun* (ca. 1818) in Essen; or the *Woman at the Window* (1822) in Berlin; or the *Chalk Cliffs of Rügen* (1818–19) in Winterthur; or the *Wanderer above the Sea of Fog* (ca. 1818) in Hamburg; or *Neubrandenburg* (1817–18) in Greifswald; or *Sisters* (1820) in St. Petersburg; or *A Man and a Woman Contemplating the Moon* (1830–35) in Berlin (see figs. 86, 87, 90, 98, 99, 104). It is safe to say that no one who has ever written about Friedrich's art has failed to remark on his *Rückenfiguren*, and it is probably also the case that no commentator has ever failed to recognize in them a kind of surrogate for the viewer, or perhaps I should say for the viewing subject, as well as for the painter – though as Joseph Koerner, the author of by far the best English-language book on the artist, adds, "the event they dramatize is never the actual labour of making [of the painting, he means], but rather the originary act of experience itself. Appearing alone," he continues, "in symmetrical pairs or in groups contemplating a sublime view, they dominate the natural scene with their presence, defining landscape as primarily the encounter of subject with world."[1] I think this last claim is largely correct though, as we shall see, there is a great deal more that must be said about the nature of that encounter; Koerner would agree, but my sense of what remains to be said differs somewhat from his.

The occasion for which this essay was originally composed was a symposium on exchanges between German and French culture in the nineteenth century.[2] Accordingly, before actually turning to Friedrich I conducted a brief survey of figures seen

78 (*facing page*) Caspar David Friedrich, *Woman before the Rising Sun* (detail of fig. 86).

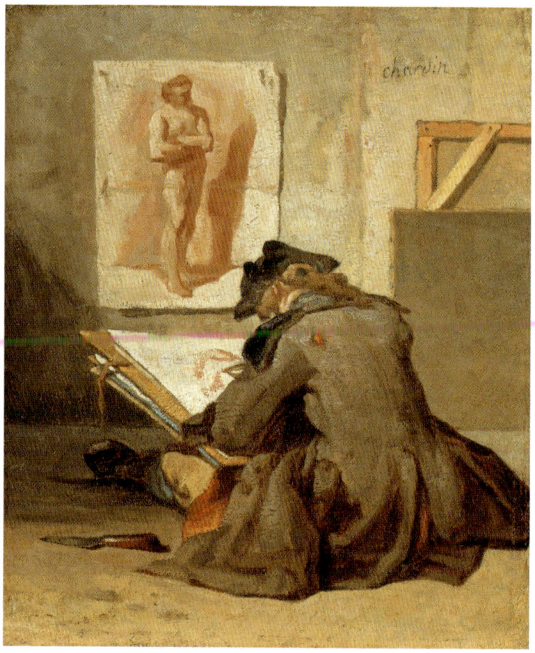

79 Jean-Baptiste-Siméon Chardin, *Young Student Drawing*, Salon of 1738. Oil on wood. 19.5 × 17.5 cm. Stockholm, Nationalmuseum.

from the rear – *Rückenfiguren*, in a manner of speaking – in French painting of the eighteenth and nineteenth centuries. For it is a significant fact, one that has never fully been appreciated, that French painters too made creative use of such figures, though never, it should at once be granted, with the particular emphasis – the singular allure – that the motif invariably assumes in Friedrich's canvases. So for example in Jean-Baptiste-Siméon Chardin's *Young Student Drawing* of around 1735–6 (fig. 79) the protagonist, a young man in a coat and hat, sits on the floor of a studio copying a red crayon drawing of a standing man that has been tacked to the wall before him. He does not face directly away from the viewer, rather his body is angled somewhat into space so that we see much of his left side as well as not quite half of the drawing on which he is working, but his face is wholly lost to view as are his hands, though (brilliantly) we are shown just the tip of his pencil as it makes contact with the paper. What gives this small picture the quality of a *tour de force* (what makes it a Chardin) is the strength of the impression it nevertheless conveys that the young draftsman is totally engaged or, as I tend to say, absorbed in what he is doing. Even the small tear near the left shoulder of the young man's coat can be understood in this light, as a sign of his obliviousness to everything but the act of drawing.[3]

Or consider the supreme pictorial masterpiece of French Romanticism, Géricault's *Raft of the "Medusa"* (1819; see fig. 49). Here, too, none of the figures faces directly away from us as is often the case in Friedrich, and indeed the bearded male figure at the left who holds the almost naked body of a (presumably dead) young man across his thigh appears to face toward "this" side of the canvas, but in the first place it becomes clear that his state of mind is to be understood as wholly enclosed within itself (and therefore the matter of which way he faces becomes somewhat beside the point), and in the second the rest of the figures in the painting take part in a collective movement away from the viewer, culminating in the actions of the pyramid of surprisingly muscular *naufragés* toward the right waving lengths of cloth in a desperate attempt to attract the attention of a distant ship, the English brig *Argus*, which even when one stands before the enormous painting itself is barely visible on the horizon. Another work by Géricault, the masterly lithograph *Entrance to the Adelphi Wharf* (1821; see fig. 68), drawn by him in London, deploys the same compositional structure in an even starker form, the three magnificent draft-horses with gleaming coats being conducted by two drovers directly away from the viewer into the blackness of a broad, low brickwork tunnel with a curved arch. Granted, nothing could be more foreign to the hushed, religious mood of Friedrich's landscapes than the monumental, tragic *Raft* or for that matter the quotidian-seeming *Adelphi Wharf*. But if that is the case, and I do not question that it is, how are we to understand the different uses that the two artists evidently made of the same or at least a similar motif, the figure or figures seen from the rear?[4]

Another nineteenth-century French painter who must be seen in this light is the great Realist, Gustave Courbet, about whom I have written at length.[5] Let me set aside his fascinating self-portraits, which in fact are relevant to our topic even though only one or two minor ones show the sitter from behind, and move directly to the first of his Realist canvases, the *After Dinner at Ornans* (1848–9; fig. 80), with its central figure, Courbet's friend Auguste Marlet, seated in a wooden chair facing into the picture (with his head turned toward Alphonse Promayet, another friend, playing the violin) and lighting his pipe from a burning brand. The second of the Realist works, the brilliantly laconic *Stonebreakers* (1849; fig. 81), destroyed in the Second World War, appears to depict its protagonists in profile, but then one realizes that the young man's face is turned away from us (indeed his body too is subtly turned away) and that the older man's face is mostly hidden by the brim of his hat and the shadow it casts, which is to say that at least as regards their faces both figures are nearly as inaccessible to our gaze as they would be were they depicted from the rear. In any case, an ambitious painting of a few years later, the *Wheat Sifters* (1854; fig. 82), returns to the central-figure-in-the-foreground-depicted-from-the-rear structure of the *After Dinner*, a structure I relate, in my book *Courbet's Realism*, to the orientation of the painter or, as I also say,

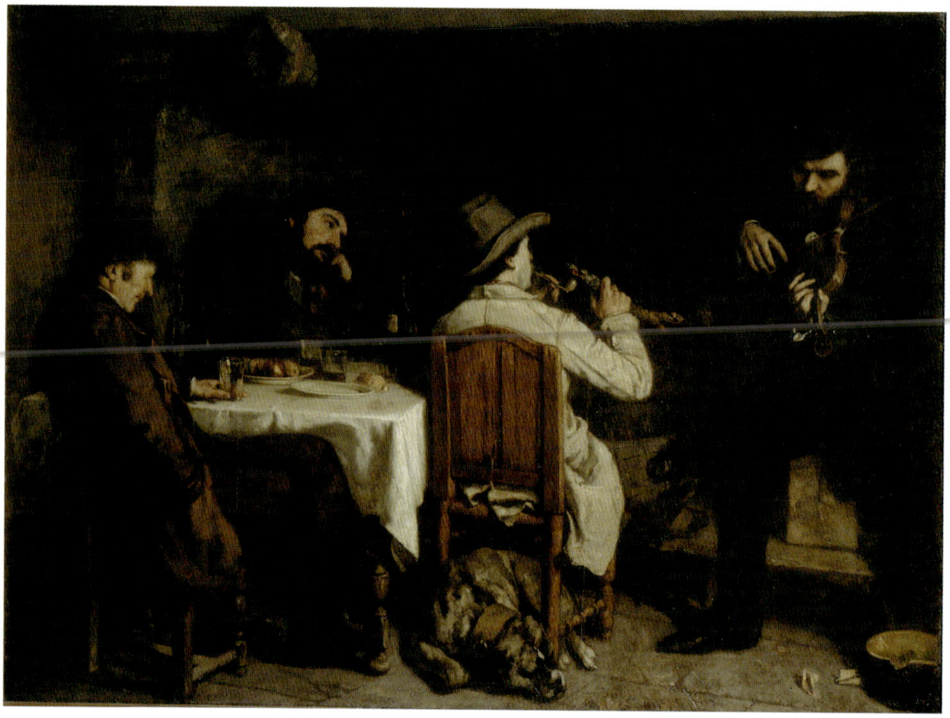

80 Gustave Courbet, *After Dinner at Ornans*, 1848–9. Oil on canvas. 195 × 257 cm. Lille, Palais des Beaux-Arts.

81 Gustave Courbet, *The Stonebreakers*, 1849. 159 × 259 cm. Oil on canvas. Formerly Dresden, Staatliche Gemäldegalerie.

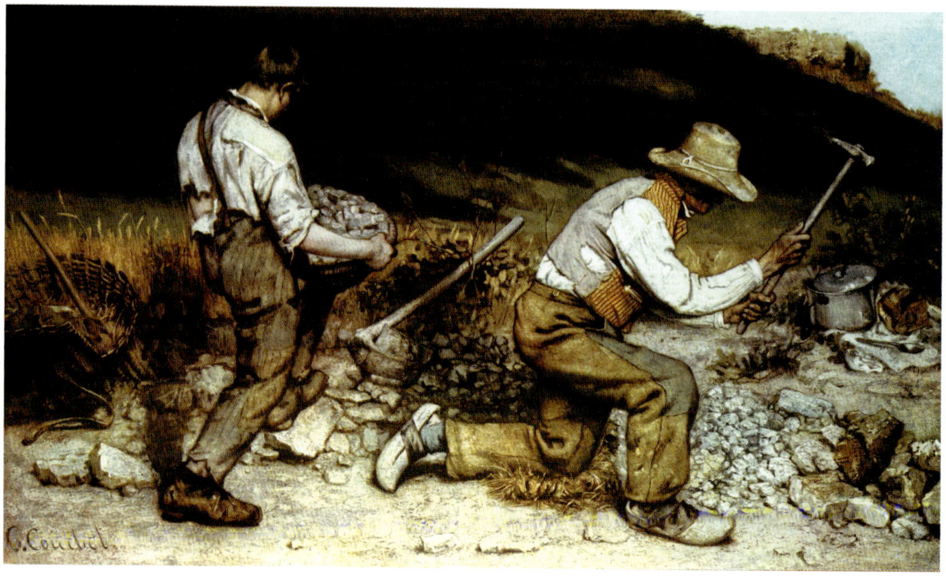

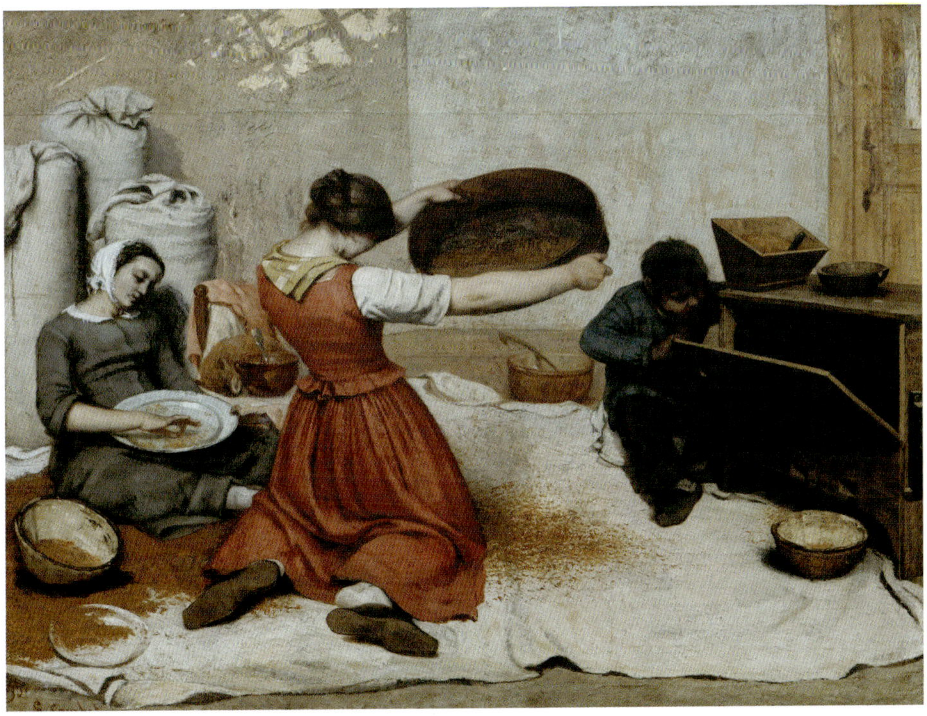

82 Gustave Courbet, *The Wheat Sifters*, 1854. Oil on canvas. 131 × 167 cm. Nantes, Musée des Beaux-Arts.

the painter-beholder at work on the painting – an orientation that also matches that of the beholder *tout court*, whom I imagine occupying the painter's place once the picture is done.

One further work by Courbet is to the point in this connection, *The Source* (1868; fig. 83), which depicts a naked woman seated on a rock ledge in a woodland setting with her elevated right hand gripping a branch and her left hand held palm-up under a smallish waterfall. In *Courbet's Realism* I argue that *The Source* in effect recapitulates the central group from Courbet's *Painter's Studio [Atelier du peintre]* (1855; fig. 84), which bears the subtitle *Real Allegory, Determining [i.e. Summarizing] a Phase of Seven Years in My Artistic Life* (his Realist years, in other words). In the central group, beyond all doubt, the seated painter and standing nude have been visually "rhymed" with one another, most palpably in the relation between his left shoulder and her hip and buttock; another, exquisite "rhyme" relates the tilt of her head and the angle of her hairline to the trees growing out from the hillside in the painting on the painter's easel, thereby binding the woman not only to the painter but to the canvas on which he is working;

83 Gustave Courbet, *The Source*, 1868. Oil on canvas. 128 × 97 cm. Paris, Musée d'Orsay.

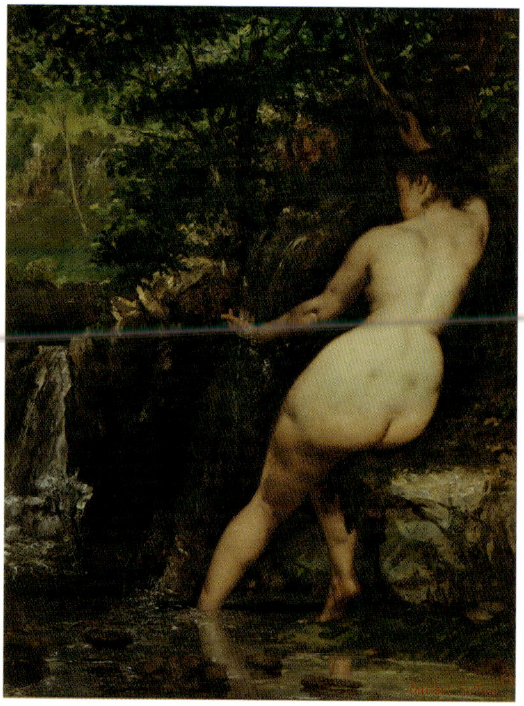

84 (*facing page*) Gustave Courbet, *The Painter's Studio* (detail), 1855. Oil on canvas. 361 × 598 cm. Paris, Musée d'Orsay.

while the waterfall in the extreme foreground of the canvas continues beyond ("this" side of) the depicted picture surface in the fall of the white sheet the woman presses to her breast and then her discarded dress on the studio floor, not to mention the playful white cat, a minor rapid. Seen in this light, the *Source* combines the figures of seated painter and standing nude in a single seated female figure while depicting her hands engaged in actions that have a close parallel to the painter's in the *Studio*. The waterfall in the *Source* also has its prototype (prototypes, really) in the central group, and there is even a sense in which the reflection in the forest pool may be seen as analogous to the painted landscape on the easel. More might be said about these relations, but the larger point is that all the works by Courbet we have just briefly looked at epitomize what I take to have been his hyperbolic attempt throughout his career to paint himself all but corporeally into the painting being realized on his easel, an attempt that I further suggest should be understood in terms of a fundamental project to undo his status as the first beholder of his own paintings. Thus Marlet in the *After Dinner* is seated in exactly the position that Courbet's friend Francis Wey describes the painter as occupying while working on the painting; the young and the older man in the *Stonebreakers* may be understood as versions of the painter's left (or palette) hand and right (or brush) hand

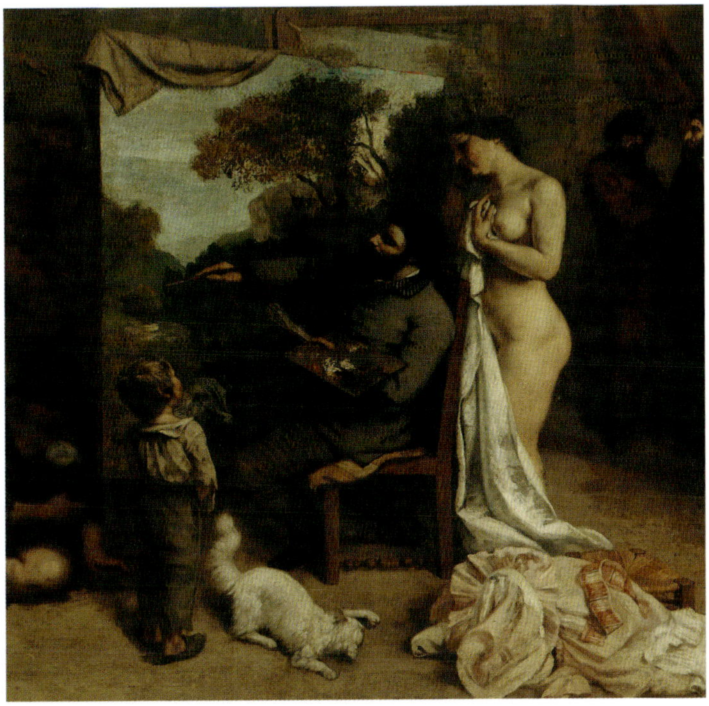

respectively; while the kneeling wheat sifter in Nantes can also be seen as a surrogate for the painter at work on his painting (indeed the fall of sifted grain onto the white ground-cloth can itself be seen as a figure for the act of applying paint to canvas, just as the fact that the ground-cloth already "subsumes" the kneeling woman may be taken as a further indication of the pursuit of quasi-immersion in the painting itself).

More broadly, all the works, not just the Courbets, we have just surveyed engage with a single overarching problem, first theorized by Diderot in the 1750s and 60s: how to make paintings that, by one means or another, manage somehow to establish the supreme fiction or ontological illusion that they were not made to be beheld. One solution to that problem, already at work in the art of Chardin, was to depict figures who appeared so deeply absorbed in what they were doing, thinking, and feeling that they also struck the beholder – for whom of course the painting in question had in effect been made and presented – as wholly unaware of being observed. In Chardin's *Young Student Drawing*, the protagonist's seeming absorption in his task is underscored by the fact we see mainly his back; in Géricault's *Raft* and *Adelphi Wharf*, the artist has found it necessary to depict figures and animals that not only are turned away from the beholder but that strive actively to move into the space of the representation (in the

Raft, in a collective attempt to be beheld by a ship at the farthest pole from where we are, in the perhaps even more fatalistic *Adelphi Wharf* into a blackness that defeats beholding in its own right); and in Courbet's *After Dinner*, *Stonebreakers*, *Wheat Sifters*, and *The Source* (also in a sense in the central group of the *Painter's Studio*) the project of escaping or defeating beholding has become even more dire, the painter now finding it imperative to seek to undo his own spectatordom, indeed his own separateness from the work of art gradually coming into being under the actions of his brush.*

Returning now to Friedrich: in my book *Absorption and Theatricality*, in which I first began to develop the account of eighteenth- and nineteenth-century French painting I have just summarized, I wrote in a footnote:

> One might go on to contrast this new sort of beholder (or new "subject") [i.e. the beholder theorized by Diderot in his writings on the stage and on painting] with the profoundly different conception of the self, as in some sense *brought before* itself in the activity of representation (*Vorstellung*), which emerges as a central theme in the writings of late eighteenth-century and early nineteenth-century German philosophers, Fichte in particular. This would be worth doing if only because such a conception of the self may be held to be posited by the art of Caspar David Friedrich and other Northern painters of the period; indeed it provides a key to the interpretation of some of the most salient (and un-French) features of that art, e.g., the predilection for symmetrical compositions, the use of foreground figures depicted from the rear cognizing [note the verb: cognizing, not beholding] a landscape or similar scene, the minimizing of surface qualities in favor of effects of transparency, and so on. (104; emphasis in original)[6]

In the remainder of this essay I want to pick up one thread in those remarks, not by trying to say more about Fichte or other post-Kantian philosophers in this connection, and even less by commenting on artists other than Friedrich, but in the first place by emphasizing a point I have already underlined in passing but which seems to me to be fundamental, namely, that the *Rückenfiguren* in Friedrich's paintings should not be thought of as beholders or spectators in the Diderotian (more broadly, the French) construction of the terms. Rather, I think of those figures as something like "cognizers," meaning by that deliberately odd-sounding notion to implicate the range of issues first

* The next essay in this book, "Caillebotte's Impressionism," opens with along discussion of still another French painting featuring a protagonist shown from the rear, Gustave Caillebotte's *Young Man at His Window* (1875; see fig. 117). One strand of my analysis concerns the relation of that painting to the abovementioned works by Courbet.

introduced by Kant in the *Critique of Pure Reason* when he set out to determine the basis of a human being's capacity to experience the sensible world. Needless to say, this is an enormous topic, one that lies well beyond the modest scope of this essay. Instead I want to turn to a short text by Kant of 1786, "What does it mean to orient oneself in thinking?," his contribution to the so-called Spinoza controversy triggered by F. H. Jacobi's claim, initially in letters to Moses Mendelssohn, that the recently deceased Gotthold Ephraim Lessing had been a secret Spinozist. The details of the controversy need not concern us. But the third and fourth paragraphs of Kant's essay are another matter:

> In the proper meaning of the word [Kant writes], to *orient* oneself means to use a given direction (when we divide the horizon into four of them) in order to find the others – literally, to find the *sunrise*. Now if I see the sun in the sky and know it is now midday, then I know how to find south, west, north, and east. For this, however, I also need the feeling of a difference in my own subject, namely, the difference between my right and left hands. I call this a *feeling* because these two sides outwardly display no designatable difference in intuition. If I did not have this faculty of distinguishing, without the need of any difference in the objects, between moving from left to right and right to left and moving in the opposite direction and thereby determining *a priori* a difference in the position of the objects, then in describing a circle I would not know whether west was right or left of the southernmost point of the horizon, or whether I should complete the circle by moving north and east and thus back to the south. Thus even with all the objective data of the sky, I orient myself *geographically* only through a *subjective* ground of differentiation; and if all the constellations, though keeping the same shape and position relative to one another, were one day by a miracle to be reversed in their direction, so that what was east now became west, no human eye would notice the slightest alteration on the next bright starlit night, and even the astronomer – if he pays attention only to what he sees and not at the same time to what he feels – would inevitably become *disoriented*. But in fact the faculty of making distinctions through the feeling of right and left comes naturally to his aid – it is a faculty implanted by nature but made habitual through frequent practice. If only he fixes his eye on the Pole Star, he will be able not only to notice the alteration which has taken place, but in spite of it he will also be able to *orient* himself.
>
> Now I can extend this geographical concept of the procedure of orienting oneself, and understand by it orienting oneself in any given space in general, hence orienting oneself merely *mathematically*. In the dark I orient myself in a room that is familiar

> to me if I can take hold of even one single object whose position I remember. But it is plain that nothing helps me here except the faculty for determining position according to a *subjective* ground of differentiation; for I do not see at all the objects whose place I am to find; and if someone as a joke had moved all the objects around so that what was previously on the right was now on the left, I would be quite unable to find anything in a room whose walls were otherwise wholly identical. But I can soon orient myself through the mere feeling of a difference between my two sides, the right and the left. That is just what happens if I am to walk and take the correct turns on streets otherwise familiar to me when I cannot right now distinguish any of the houses.[7]

Kant goes on, as he says, to

> extend this concept even further, since it could be taken as consisting in the faculty of orienting myself not merely in space, i.e. mathematically, but in *thinking* in general, i.e. *logically*. By analogy, one can easily guess that it will be a concern of pure reason to guide its use when it wants to leave familiar objects (of experience) behind, extending itself beyond all the bounds of experience and finding no object of intuition at all, but merely space for intuition . . . (5; emphasis in original)

I do not propose to follow him there: the analogy leads him to assume the existence of God on the basis of "the feeling of a need that is inherent in reason itself," and indeed it was that above all that Kant was after from the first. What interests me, however, is his stunning account of persons as (if I may so put it) primordially oriented with respect to the felt difference between right and left, a difference that I want to claim can be sensed at work everywhere in Friedrich's art. And of course what makes that difference palpable – this is a further claim, closely tied to the first – is a feature of his art even more prominent than the occurrence of *Rückenfiguren*: I mean his almost invariable reliance in paintings both with and without human figures on a centralized mode of composition, a structure that imposes an obvious sort of bilateral symmetry on the representational field as a whole while at the same time setting the stage for the viewer's registration of departures from symmetry both large and small.

Take for example the nearly incandescent *Woman before the Rising Sun* (1818; fig. 86).[8] I shall refrain from pointing out its closeness to Kant's notion of orientation as literally seeking "to find the sunrise" – I take that to be a coincidence, in that Friedrich certainly did not have Kant's words in mind. But in fact a surprising number of Friedrich's paintings are oriented toward the east, starting with the spectral *Riesenbirge in Moonlight* [1810; fig. 85], with its risen moon above the central peak seemingly

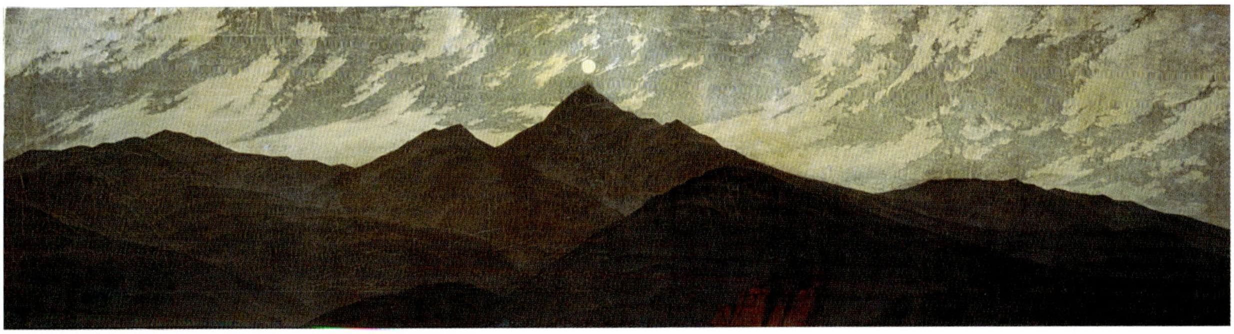

85 Caspar David Friedrich, *The Riesenbirge in Moonlight*, 1810. Oil on canvas. 47.5 × 167 cm. Weimar, Klassik Stiftung Weimar, Bestand Museen

almost nailed into the canvas. In any case, the woman in the Essen picture, depicted from the rear and wearing a long, *altdeutsch*-style dress with a high waist, long sleeves, and a slightly fluffed collar and shoulders, stands on a path leading into a country landscape with fields and trees and then ranges of low hills and distant mountains. The woman is centered but the path itself seems to wind toward the right; just off the path to the woman's left there appear to be two brown rocks of different sizes and to her right, similarly placed, a single rock larger than either of the others. (We should be a bit surprised, or at least struck, by the presence of the rocks, which hardly seem to belong naturally to the painting's scenery. As will emerge, they are characteristic of this artist's procedures.) She holds her open hands apart, as if greeting the sunrise – some have said as if in spontaneous prayer – but the gesture is not quite perfectly symmetrical: her left arm remains closer to her body than her right, a difference that is felt all the more strongly, once one notices it, for the fact that her right arm and hand are silhouetted against the illuminated low mountain at the horizon. As for her head, it is perhaps turned extremely slightly to the left; at any rate, only her left ear is seen to bear an earring while six small ornaments on a decorative comb protrude above the crown of her hair (which the comb holds in place), inflected very slightly to the right. Beyond the woman the countryside itself takes part in the play of right–left difference, the two trees in the left middle distance bending left and right in counterpoint to the woman's gesture (the tree to the left being larger and denser than the one to the right, again in felt relation to the woman's arms and hands). (Not that that relation is simple to describe; the point is rather that the more one "opens" oneself to the painting, the more aware one becomes of these and other intimate accords.) All this is to say nothing of the delicate interplay among the hills and mountains as they recede toward the horizon, or

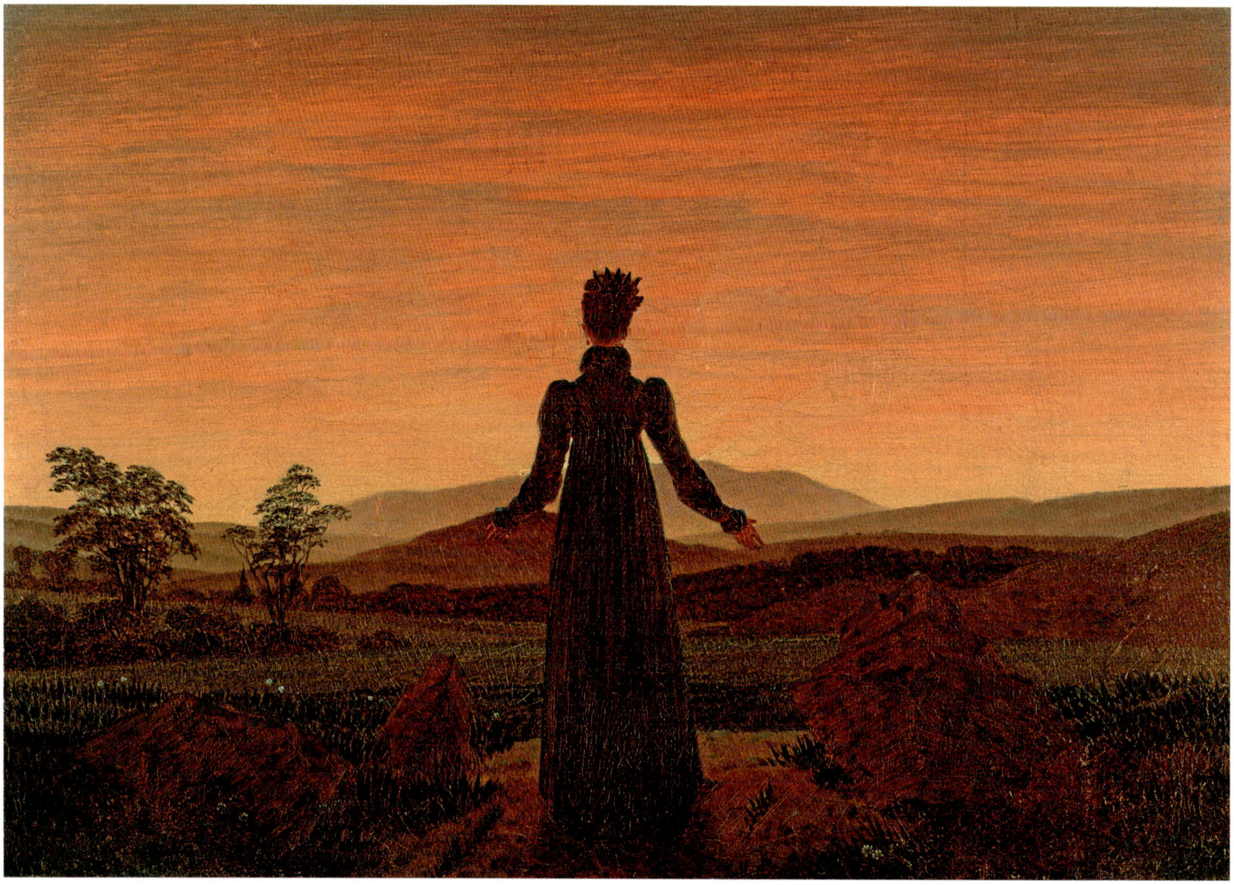

86 Caspar David Friedrich, *Woman before the Rising Sun*, 1818. Oil on canvas. 22 × 30 cm. Essen, Museum Folkwang.

indeed of the fact that the rays of the sun springing as if from her body are themselves asymmetrical with respect to right and left. I don't pretend to be the first commentator on Friedrich to observe such subtleties. But to the best of my knowledge I am the first to suggest that they are crucial not just with respect to the painting's formal structure (that is, its composition) but also, more important, to its essential meaning, which I take to be a virtual allegory of subjective orientation, in Kant's sense of the term, with respect to the experience of sensuous reality – in the first place the woman's and in the second, of course, our own.

A closely related painting, *Woman at the Window* (1822; fig. 87), depicts a woman, thought to be the artist's wife, Caroline, standing at an open lower window in his studio in Dresden; the studio looked directly out onto the Elbe, as is indicated by sailboat masts, one close by, the other farther away, that we see beyond her to the right. As in *Woman before the Rising Sun* the protagonist has been portrayed wholly from the rear; she wears a long greenish dress and, like the woman in the earlier painting, her hair is gathered on the top of her head. (Her hands are out of sight.) But what particularly distinguishes *Woman at the Window* is its altogether more complex treatment of the theme of centering, by which I mean the calculated interplay between several factors: first, the position of the woman on the central vertical axis of the canvas; second, the reinforcement of that centering by the extremely thin mullions between the panes of the upper window that cross each other at ninety degrees in the upper portion of the picture; and third, the slightly off-center perspective implied by the dark grooves between the floorboards and the fact that we see part of the alcove wall to the woman's right but almost none of the one to her left (in other words, the painting posits a perspectival "point of view" somewhat to the left of the middle of the canvas). William Vaughan in his 2004 book on the artist helpfully diagrams the perspective structure to this effect.[9] But Vaughan perhaps underestimates the extent to which the centering of the woman and in particular the right-angle "cross-hairs" in the upper window far outweigh considerations of "point of view" in one's actual experience of the work; certainly it is in relation to the former that one registers the woman's slight but unmistakable lean to the left, the leftward placement of her head and upper body within the rectangular opening in the lower window, and, equally telling, the two sail-less masts-plus-rigging beyond her head and to the right, the smaller and more distant of the two just to the right of her ear and in almost a direct line from the vertical division in the upper window. The lower window has been swung open to her right as well, and on the ledge beneath the window further to the right two small brownish bottles (and a smaller third one?) stand on a cloth or low pad alongside each other. As in *Woman before the Rising Sun*, I take these obviously deliberate departures from strict bilateral symmetry, including the indications of "point of view," to be crucial not just to the painting's formal structure but also, again more importantly, to the subtle play of forces anchored in the felt difference between right and left that for me constitute the core of the painting's meaning. In fact I would go farther and suggest that we might see the upper window and its "cross-hair"-like mullions as a brilliant figure for consciousness as such, which on the one hand is always absolutely centered in the cognizing subject but which on the other is incapable by itself of providing the orientation on the basis of which, according to Kant, the very possibility of experience depends – consciousness *in advance* of cognition, in a manner of speaking.[10] (The upper section of the nearer of the two masts and rigging, not to mention the angled wisps of cloud in the otherwise featureless sky, may be taken as suggesting that the task of orientation is already under way. As does, for the

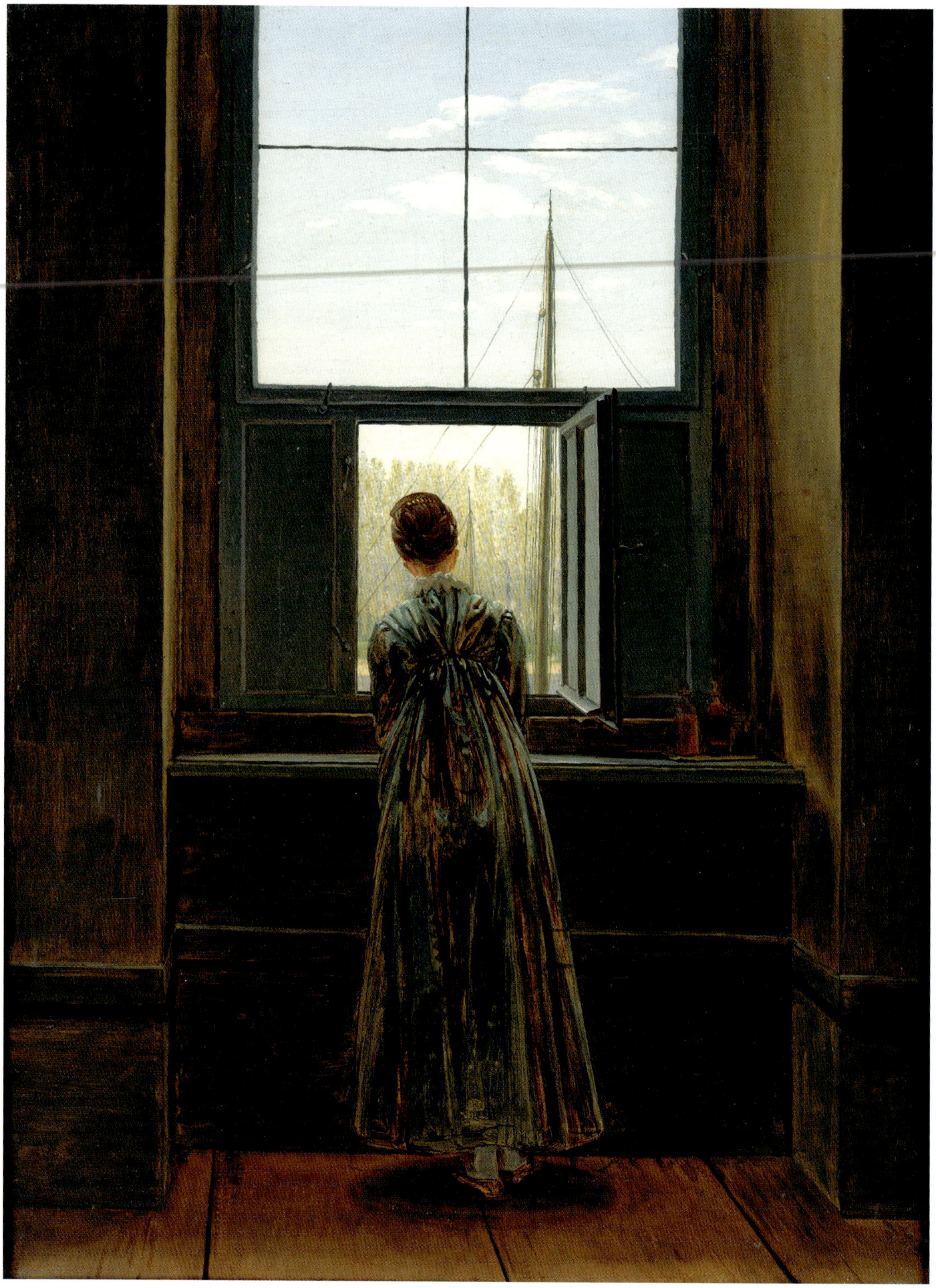

87 Caspar David Friedrich, *Woman at the Window*, 1822. Oil on canvas. 44 × 37 cm. Berlin, Nationalgalerie, Staatliche Museen zu Berlin.

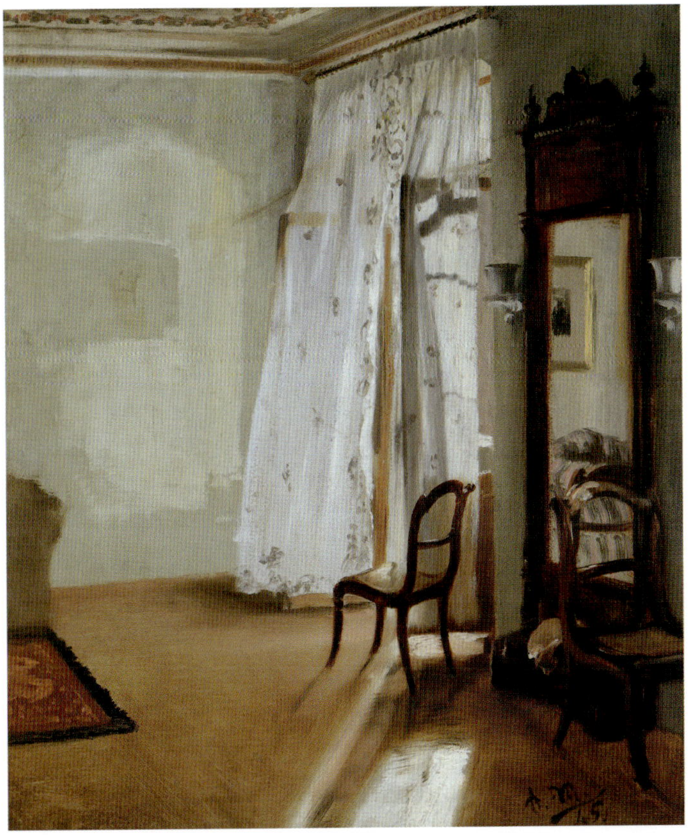

88 Adolph Menzel, *The Balcony Room*, 1845. Oil on board. 58 × 47 cm. Berlin, Nationalgalerie, Staatliche Museen zu Berlin.

viewer, not the woman, the seeming "transparence" – not the right word but it is hard to know how else to describe the lack of opacity of the paintstrokes – of the treatment of the woman's dress, "transparence" here and elsewhere in Friedrich's art, with its glaze-like handling of the oil medium, betokening the saturating or irradiating of reality by subjective cognition. Nothing like this can be found in French painting of the period.) This, too, of course, is an allegorical reading, one that finds in the *Woman at the Window* perhaps the aptest term of comparison in Friedrich's art with Adolf Menzel's extraordinary *Balcony Room* (1845; fig. 88) of twenty years later. I discuss the *Balcony Room* in detail in my book *Menzel's Realism*; here I will simply say that throughout Menzel's paintings and drawings the orientational issues at work in Friedrich's corpus are given a much more active, comprehensively bodily development.[11]

The third major *Rückenfigur*, and by far the most dramatic, in Friedrich's art is found in *The Wanderer above the Sea of Fog* (1818; fig. 90), a work that has drawn extensive commentary over the years. As in the case of the *Woman before the Rising Sun* and *Woman at the Window*, the impressive figure in question occupies the central axis of the painting, in this case mounted on a pile of rocks which we sense instinctively to be the top of a crag as he gazes out over, precisely, a sea of fog or mist. Above the latter, here and there, thrust other crags (to the left) and, farther away, a bluff with trees (to the right). To the wanderer's left, almost as if springing from his head, a conical mountain rises while to his right, somewhat nearer as regards apparent distance though farther away on the surface of the canvas, a strange, distinctly non-conical rock formation echoes his form or at least his uprightness. As for the wanderer himself, he wears trousers and a short coat, his blonde hair (the color of Friedrich's) blows in the wind, and he steadies himself with a long staff gripped in his right hand (which we do not quite see). His footing seems secure but it is also uneven, the left foot resting higher than the right; similarly his left arm is contiguous with his body whereas his right arm, the one holding the staff, is bent outward at the elbow. In these and other ways the painting is at once strongly symmetrical (in overall statement) and richly asymmetrical (on closer looking); in the terms of my argument, it offers still another allegory of orientation, the wanderer exemplifying more fully than either of the women the play of asymmetry – of difference between right and left – in his own quasi-heroic person even as what can be seen of the largely shrouded mountain landscape spells out the same theme in discontinuous segments.

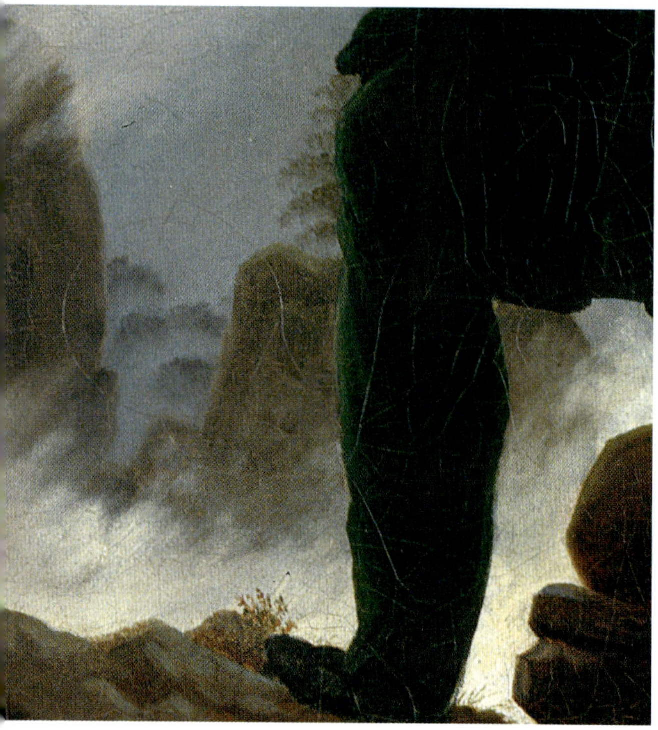

Two further, seemingly incidental details are worth commenting on: the wanderer's left foot steps on a tiny plant, which it partly crushes; and just beyond his bent left knee one discerns the tips of branches of a tree growing on a crag largely obscured from view by the rest of the wanderer's left leg (fig. 89). I take the point of these, which the viewer registers only at close range and after serious inspection of the picture, as effecting a subtle dis-identification between viewer and wanderer, or perhaps I should say a partial dis-identification, the wanderer's role as surrogate being too strongly implied to be entirely undermined. (Much the

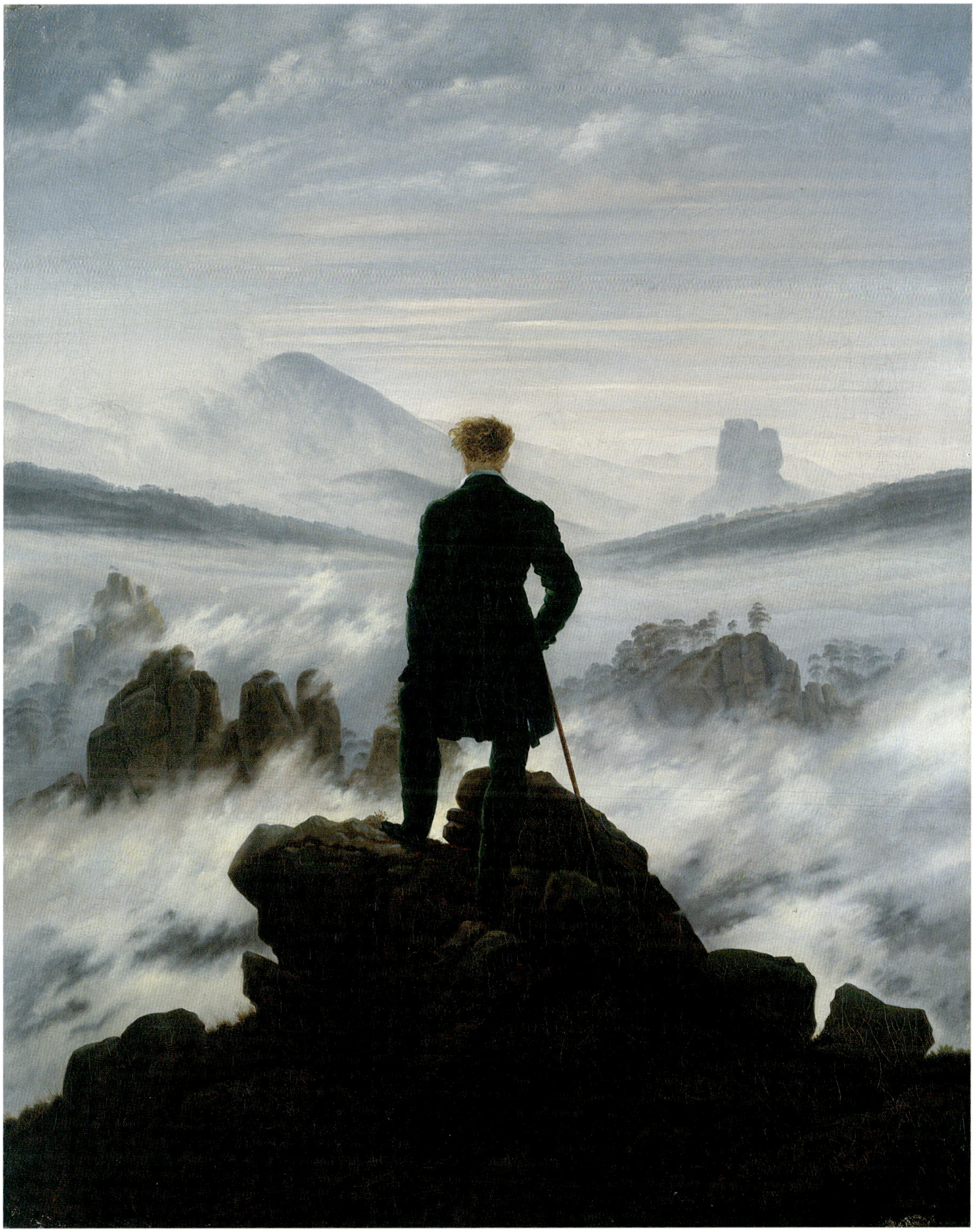

89 (*facing page*) and 90 Caspar David Friedrich, *The Wanderer above the Sea of Fog*, 1818. Oil on canvas. 74.8 × 94.8 cm. Hamburg, Kunsthalle.

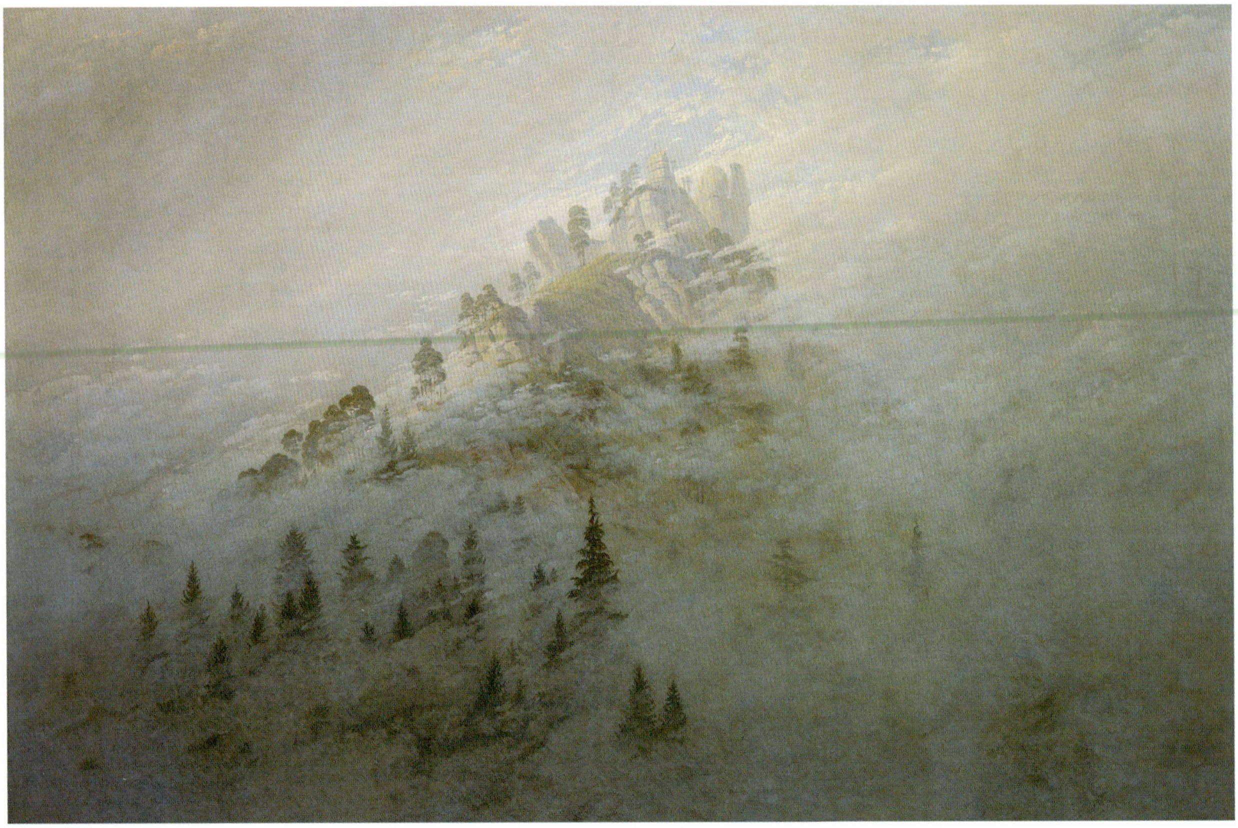

91 and 92 (*facing page*) Caspar David Friedrich, *Morning Mist in the Mountains*, 1808. Oil on canvas. 71 × 104 cm. Rodolstadt, Thüringer Landesmseum Heidecksburg.

same might be said about the function of the off-center perspective of the floor boards in the *Woman at the Window*[12] or indeed the studded comb in the hair of the *Woman before the Rising Sun.*) In other words, the viewer is in the end meant to understand himself or herself as placed before a painting, not, even in imagination, before an actual landscape. And something else: returning to the theme of right versus left, there is the fact that the wanderer's hair blows toward the left (the same direction toward which the crag he stands on thrusts) while the mist directly beyond him suggests movement toward the right; further away, however, the thinner mist partly obscuring the conical mountain seems to rise toward the upper left, even as the clouds toward the top of the canvas intimate a rightward drift. In all these respects the *Wanderer above the Sea of Fog* deserves its status as the most commanding of Friedrich's paintings based on figures viewed from behind.

Not, though, that *Rückenfiguren* are necessary for the sort of readings I have been advancing to take hold – on the contrary. A strikingly original early instance of this is *Morning Mist in the Mountains* (1808; fig. 91), which depicts a rocky conical peak studded with trees (evergreens, others) and partly covered with dense mist. The peak is almost perfectly aligned with the picture's central vertical axis – actually it is slightly to the right, the axis being more nearly indicated by the most prominent of the fir trees in the foreground – and the right half of it considerably more obscured by mist than the left. In other words, one's response to the painting involves, first, the perception of a simple, centered form and second, the recognition of a surprisingly acute contrast between the right- and left-hand halves of the pictorial field. (The treatment of the mist and of various fir trees glimpsable through it is a technical *tour de force*.) On closer looking one becomes aware as well of the leftward lean of most of the rocky formations in the upper portion of the peak, as well as of three improbable-seeming upright formations at or near its crest. Finally, looking closer still, one discerns rising from the smallest and topmost of those formations a tiny cross (fig. 92), which in the present context functions less as a religious symbol (though of course it is that) than as a minute "cross-hair" – as if what one discovers, barely, at the peak's highest point is still another token of centered consciousness, a sine qua non of orientation.

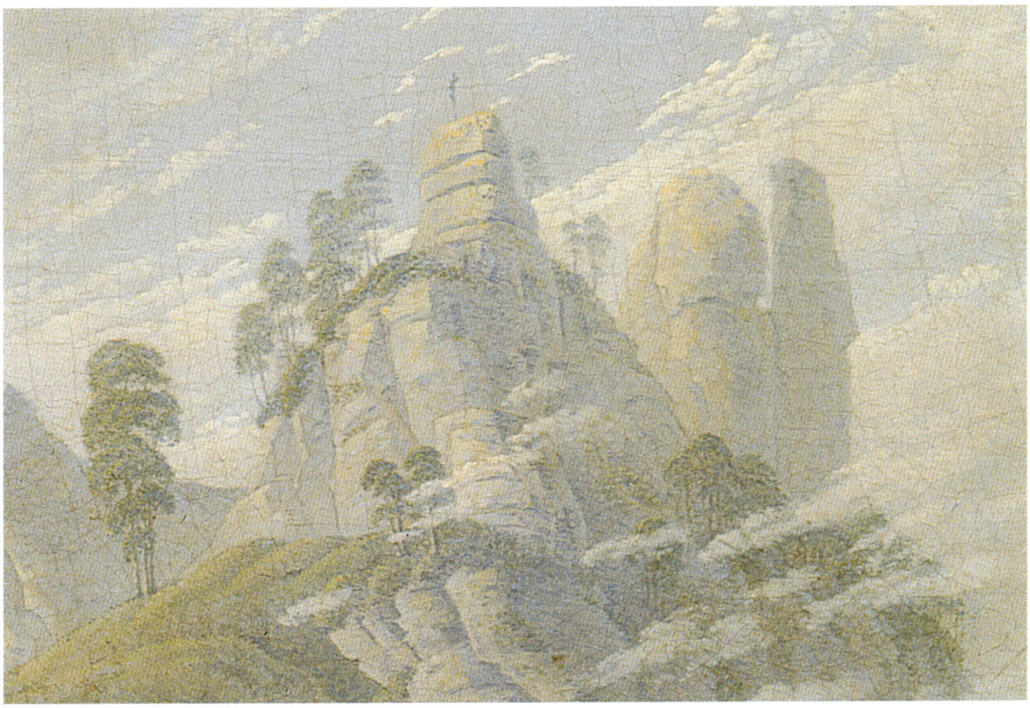

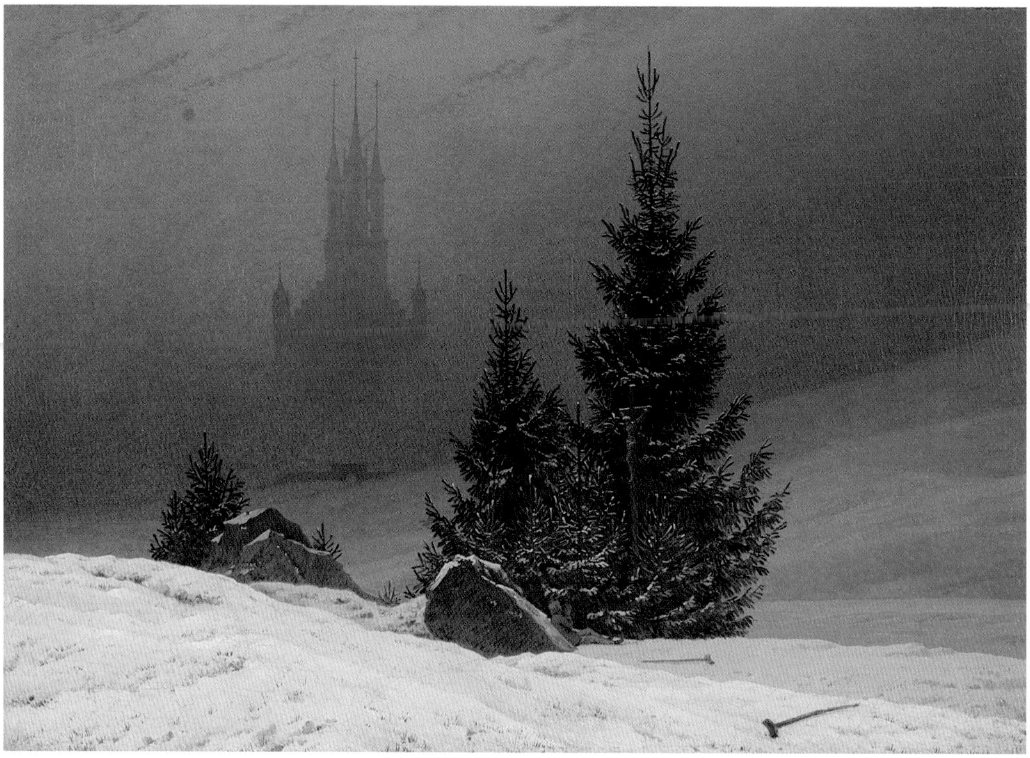

93 Caspar David Friedrich, *Winter Landscape with a Church*, 1811. Oil on canvas. 32.5 × 45 cm. London, National Gallery.

So, too, in the early *Winter Landscape with a Church* (1811; fig. 93) – not one of Friedrich's strongest canvases but characteristic in its mode of construction – the interplay among the various rocks, the fir trees, and the (somewhat apparitional) triple-spired Gothic church partly obscured by mist in the left middle distance makes itself felt in relation to a central axis suggested by the nearest rock and the smaller of two main trees. One then becomes aware of the pair of crutches discarded on the snow in the right foreground, the nearer one the left crutch (from the direction of its fall), the farther one the right crutch (ditto), and of a man, possibly a "portrait" of the artist, reclining back against the central rock and, with hands clasped in prayer, looking up toward an elevated cross that bears a sculpted image of Christ. There can thus be no question as to the painting's religious content. But does this by itself invalidate the kind of considerations I have been stressing? I do not think so; rather I take *Winter Landscape with a Church* to suggest that the issue of orientation not only is compatible with religious, that is, Christian meaning but even that it undergirds the latter in the precise sense that the very uprightness, or say heavenwardness, of the trees, the spires, and the crucifix are for the viewer if not for the figure in the painting (but why not for him as well?) *in the first place* a matter of subjective experience, a point further emphasized by what I take to be the delayed perception of a smaller tree, relatively bare of branches so that it is the upright trunk that draws the eye, to the left of the crucifix and then of two still smaller ones to the left of that (in effect I am suggesting that one's attention is drawn away from the crucifix back toward the central axis of the picture). (The feeling of uprightness goes unmentioned in Kant's text but is implicit from the first.) The crutches, with their implied coding of left then right, and their further intimation of the effort that is sometimes involved in maintaining uprightness, are also pertinent here. And of course – to state the obvious – a cross is a religious symbol based on the double thematization of verticality or uprightness and the difference between right and left, a difference, moreover, that is not without significance in Christian doctrine. I am not saying that this explains Friedrich's frequent depiction of crosses but it does perhaps throw light on their suitability for his art. Finally, in the sky to the left of the church spires a moon, easy to miss, floats in the dusk.

Or to take a far more complex and to my mind more rewarding canvas, in *Morning in the Mountains* (1822–3; fig. 94) the central axis is marked by a deep cleft or ravine (another of Friedrich's basic structures), at the lowest point of which we glimpse traces of mist; in the right foreground two hillsides, one earthy, the other grassy, slope downward (the second, grassy hillside may in fact be two, it is difficult to tell); a path winds across both (or at least across the nearest and farthest of the hillsides); and on the nearer grassy slope, relatively low down, we glimpse sheep and goats peacefully grazing despite the steepness of their footing. Then come two strange, cone-like peaks, the one on the right slightly higher than the other and partly obscured by the farther hillsides; while on top of the one on the left sit two tiny figures (shepherds, one holds a staff or crook) looking into the distance. Beyond the peaks a yellow-green ridge slopes gently from right to left, and beyond that rise successive ranges of hills and mountains, partly covered with mist. At the horizon, a gentle peak – actually a pair of peaks, the one on the right slightly higher than that on the left – marks, more or less, the central axis of the canvas, or at least it seems to do so until one's gaze returns to the ravine at the bottom of the canvas, which lies slightly to their right: in fact the "true" central axis lies somewhere to the right of both, in close proximity to two small trees that on inspection one discovers growing atop the far ravine wall (as it happens, Friedrich-style, bending slightly to the left). All this is to say nothing of the leftmost portion of the scene, with its evocation of trees growing from an even steeper slope than the ones to the right. The result is one of the subtlest treatments of matters of orientation in Friedrich's oeuvre, the

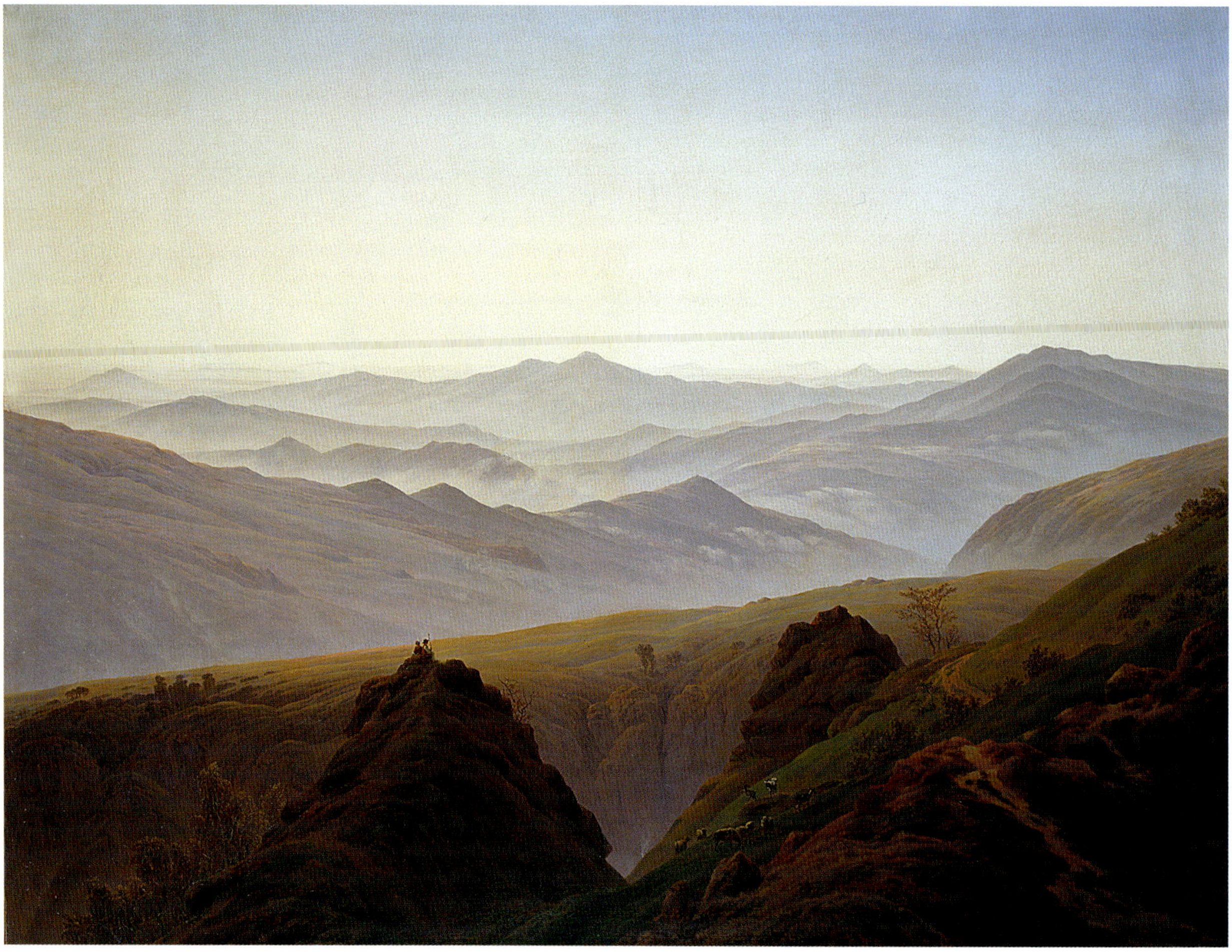

94 Caspar David Friedrich, *Morning in the Mountains*, 1822–3. Oil on canvas. 135 × 170 cm. St. Petersburg, The State Hermitage Museum, inv. no. GE-9773.

viewer being compelled inwardly to "find" or say "situate" himself or herself again and again in relation to one or another portion of the canvas.[13]

The unlikely paired peaks in *Morning in the Mountains* introduce another characteristic motif, that of pairing as such, which of course introduces difference between right and left as an explicit theme. So for example in *Bohemian Landscape* (ca. 1808; fig. 95) the two trees in the center foreground, the one on the right somewhat more robust than that on the left, both bending toward each other even as the lower portion of the one on the right seems to reach towards the right, are in counterpoint with two peaks in the middle and far distance (the farther, taller one on the central axis of the picture), as

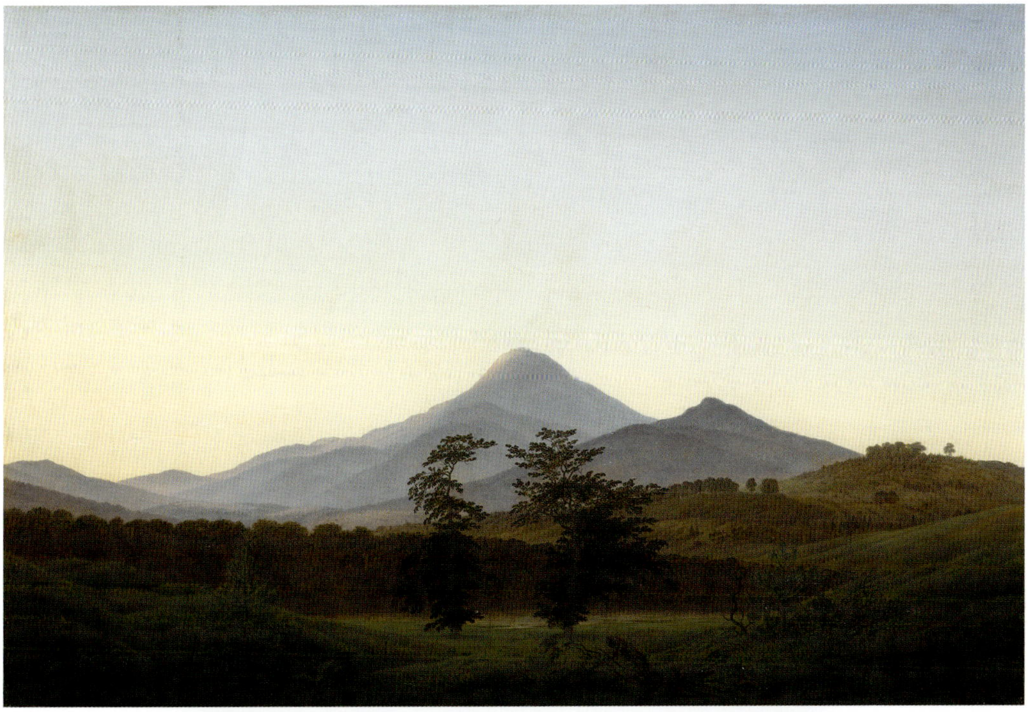

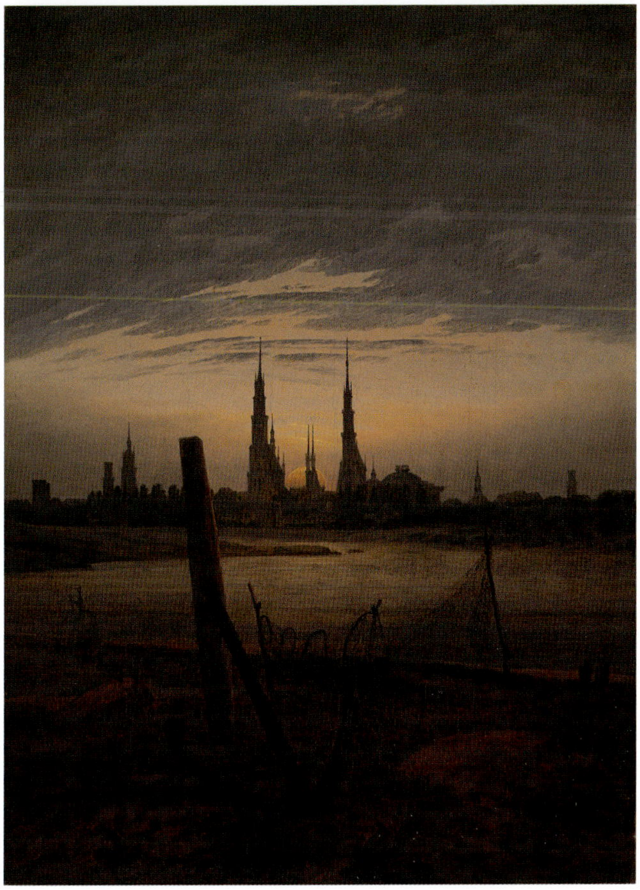

95 (*above*) Caspar David Friedich, *Bohemian Landscape*, ca. 1808. Oil on canvas. 70 × 104.5 cm. Stuttgart, Staatsgalerie.

96 (*left*) Caspar David Friedrich, *City by Moonlight*, 1817. Oil on canvas. 45 × 32 cm. Winterthur, Museum Oskar Reinhart am Stadtgarten.

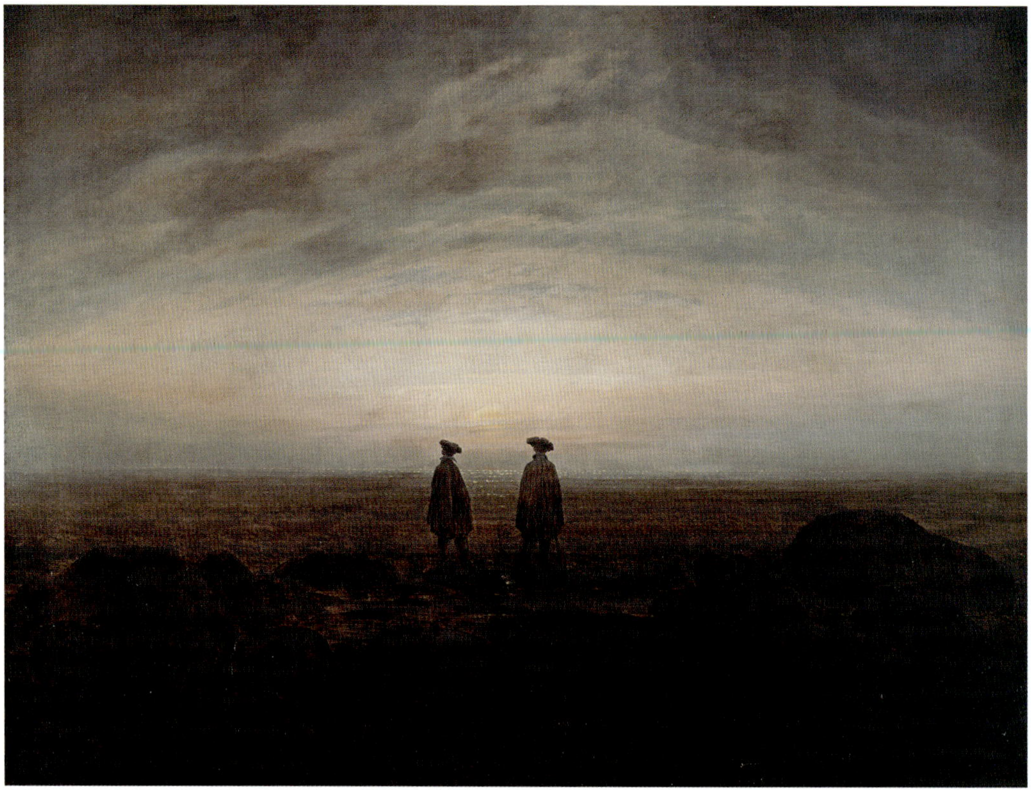

97 Caspar David Friedrich, *Two Men by the Sea at Moonrise*, 1817. Oil on canvas. 51 × 66 cm. Berlin, Nationalgalerie, Staatliche Museen zu Berlin.

well as with the smaller fir trees in the foreground (and the hill to the right, and so on and so forth); once again my suggestion is that all these relationships, as well as others that have not been mentioned, are keyed to the viewer's sense of right–left difference, also to that of his or her uprightness, as well as, of course, to the further intuition of relative distance. Much the same might be said about *City by Moonlight* (ca. 1817; fig. 96), with its paired identical church spires and, halfway between them, another, lower pair of spires, this time in counterpoint both with other structures to the right and left and, more tellingly, with the prominent left-tilting wooden post and leaning anchor in the near foreground (note too the slender posts supporting a drying net and, near the right-hand edge of the canvas, the two low posts near the shoreline). Sometimes, too, the pairing is of figures, as in *Two Men by the Sea at Moonrise* (1817; fig. 97), with its twinned but subtly differentiated *Rückenfiguren* in *altdeutsch* costumes standing on rocks surrounded by water and gazing toward the east; the ravishing *Neubrandenburg in the*

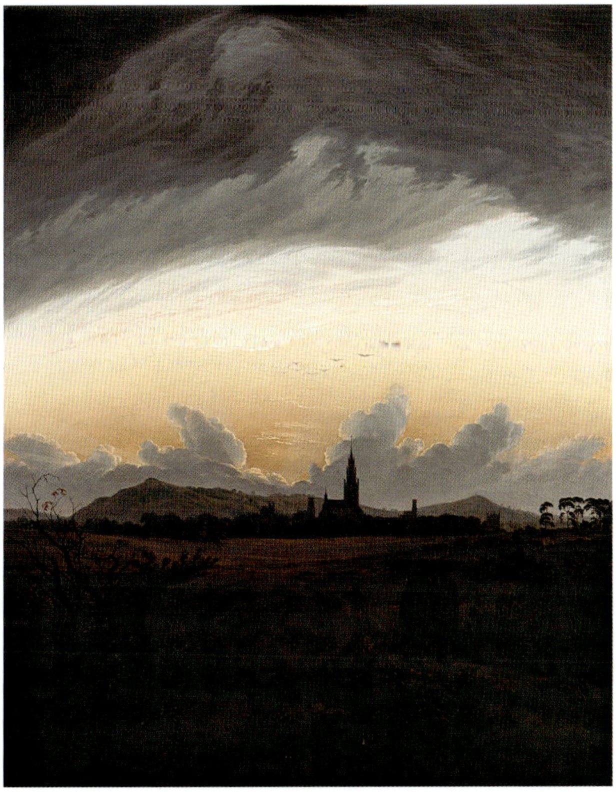

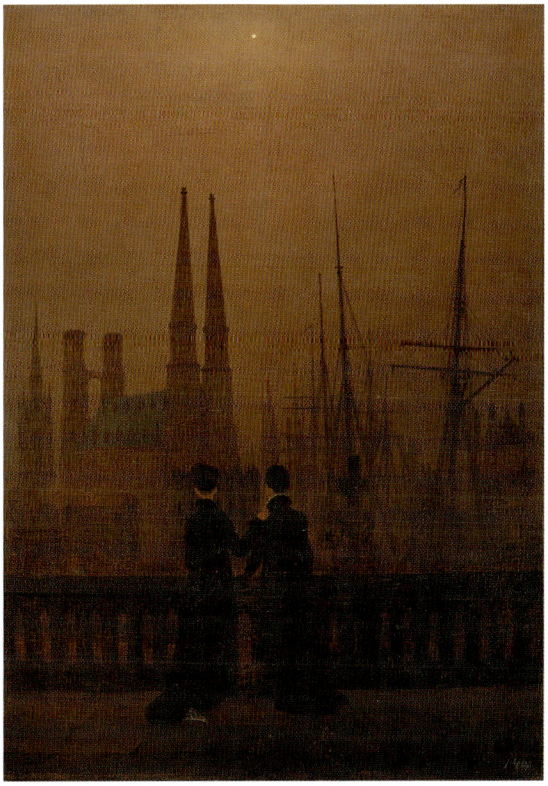

98 *(above, left)* Caspar David Friedrich, *Neubrandenburg in the Morning Mist*, 1816–17. Oil on canvas. 92 × 71.5 cm. Greifswald, Pommersches Landesmuseum.

99 *(above, right)* Caspar David Friedrich, *Sisters* (or *The Harbor at Night*), 1818–20. Oil on canvas. 74 × 52 cm. St. Petersburg, State Hermitage Museum.

Morning Mist (1816–17; fig. 98) with its similarly clothed halted travelers in the right foreground gazing at the town from beyond its outskirts as fingers of illuminated cloud reach right and left above a silhouetted steeple (the picture's central axis being marked by a smaller structure to the steeple's left); and the haunting *Sisters* (1818–20; fig. 99), with its two women (supposedly Caroline and a sister-in-law, the first with her hand on the shoulder of the other) standing on a balcony looking out on a nocturnal harbor scene with the moon behind clouds, twinned church towers to the left, and two tall, oppositely tilted masts to the right. In these and other canvases, the motif of pairing, while thematizing right and left, has the immediate dis-identificatory consequence of enhancing the viewer's sense of his or her own singleness, a crucial aspect, needless to say, of the sense of orientation generally. At the same time (a point not mentioned until now) the close resemblance between the members of the pairs suggests a certain intersubjective relation between the two – as if orientation in Friedrich's paintings is not solipsistic but rather incipiently social.

To enlarge briefly on the essential point of the affinity between Kant's remarks and Friedrich's paintings as I understand it: the felt difference between right and left is also, by its very nature, an experience of oneself as a subjective center, a fact reflected in Friedrich's commitment to the central axis – to uprightness – in picture after picture. One might think of that centeredness and uprightness as a kind of universality but not the universality of what the world might be imagined to look like if cognition were not grounded in subjective feeling as Kant suggests (that is, if it were wholly objective, without reference to the experiencing subject);[14] by the same token, the subjectivity in question is not *mere* subjectivity, a kind of unanchored and essentially formless responsiveness to visual or say sensuous stimuli in all their multifariousness and profusion. (We might think of that as a Lockean or perhaps Berkeleyan picture of experience.) And this is why not just the centeredness of so many of the paintings but the continual emphasis on and play with asymmetry and off-centeredness, is crucial: because it requires us to see and feel simultaneously, which is one interpretation of what Friedrich meant when he famously wrote that "a picture should not be invented [*erfunden*] but felt [*empfunden*]."[15]

More precisely, it requires us to feel, in that sense to acknowledge, what is otherwise automatic and can therefore escape notice: the proto-empathic bodily basis of our orientation to the world, which is also to say of our cognition of reality. Thus the wanderer above the sea of mist evokes in the viewer a consciousness of his or her more stable footing, while in *Morning in the Mountains* the animals comfortably grazing on their steep hillside invite the thought that remaining upright on so sharp a slope might well be beyond one. (One might wonder, too, exactly how – by dint of what effort – the two shepherds seated atop the conical peak on the left physically assumed their lofty perch.) By the same token, the magnificent blasted but still blossoming oak tree at the heart of *The Lone Tree* (1822; fig. 100) rises along the central vertical axis of the pictorial field but its very rootedness in the landscape is registered by the viewer as different in kind from his or her own groundedness before the painting – an effect reinforced somewhat differently by the elevated point of view, which would locate the viewer as if on a hill (but is such a formation credible as regards the image as a whole? – I think not). Even more forcefully, the strangely convexly configured *The Great Enclosure* (1831; fig. 101) offers an elevated, not to say airborne view of a well-known feature of Dresden's environs, a view that just possibly, one imagines, might be that of a low-flying bird – a suggestion I mean at least half-seriously. In any case, a distinctly human dimension or say axis is

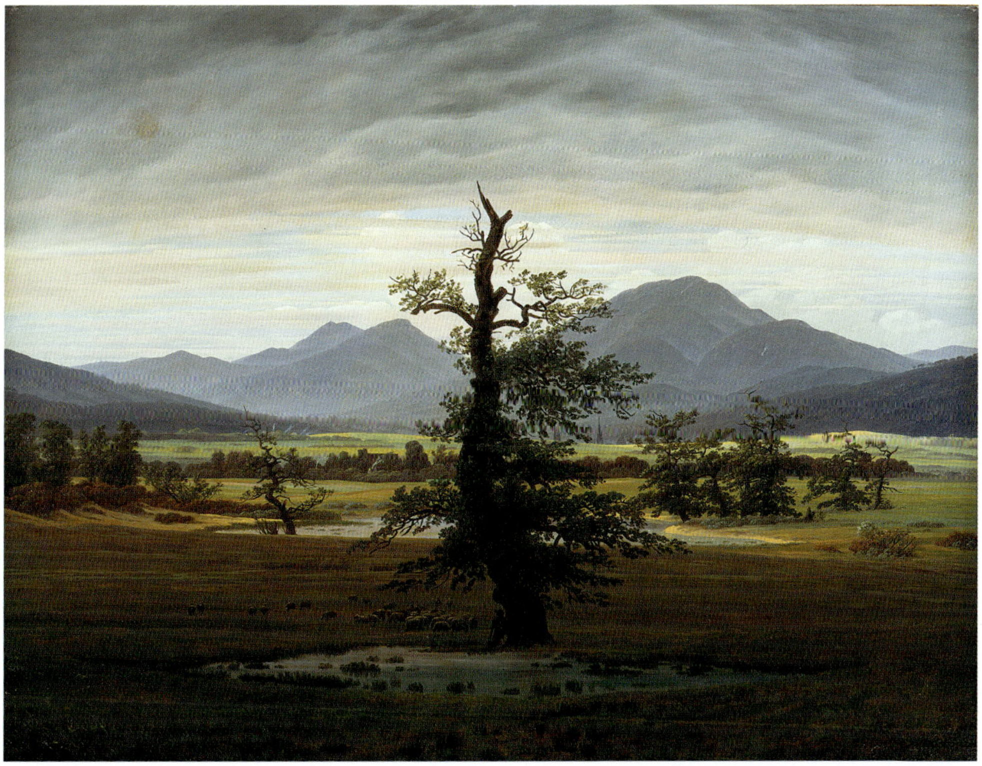

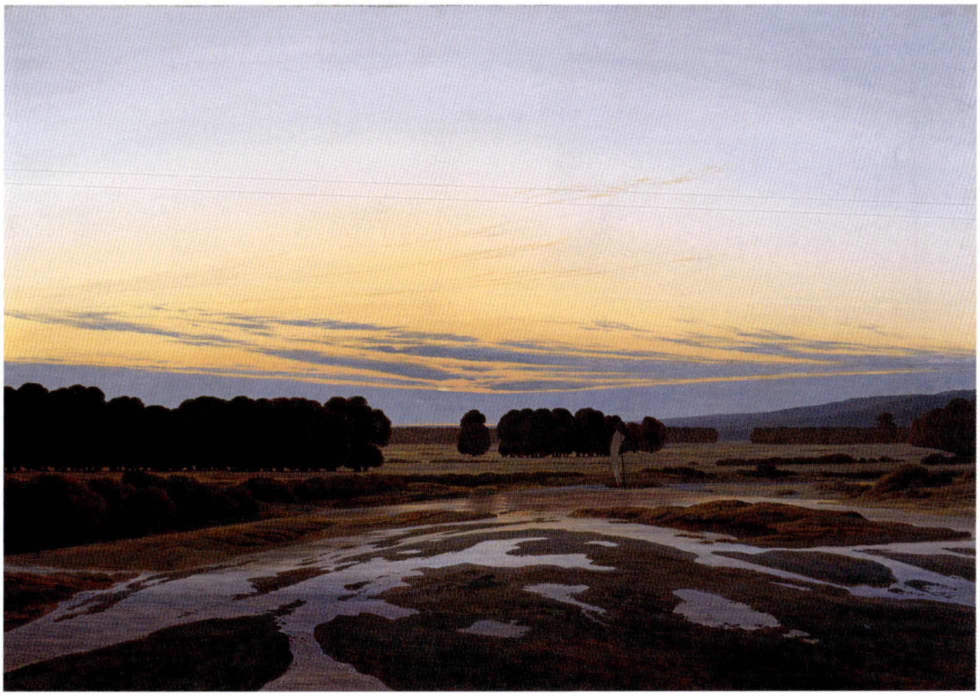

100 (*top*) Caspar David Friedrich, *The Lone Tree*, 1822. Oil on canvas. 55 × 71 cm. Berlin, Nationalgalerie, Staatliche Museen zu Berlin.

101 (*above*) Caspar David Friedrich, *The Great Enclosure*, 1831. Oil on canvas. 73.5 × 103 cm. Dresden, Galerie Neue Meister, Staatliche Kunstsammlungen.

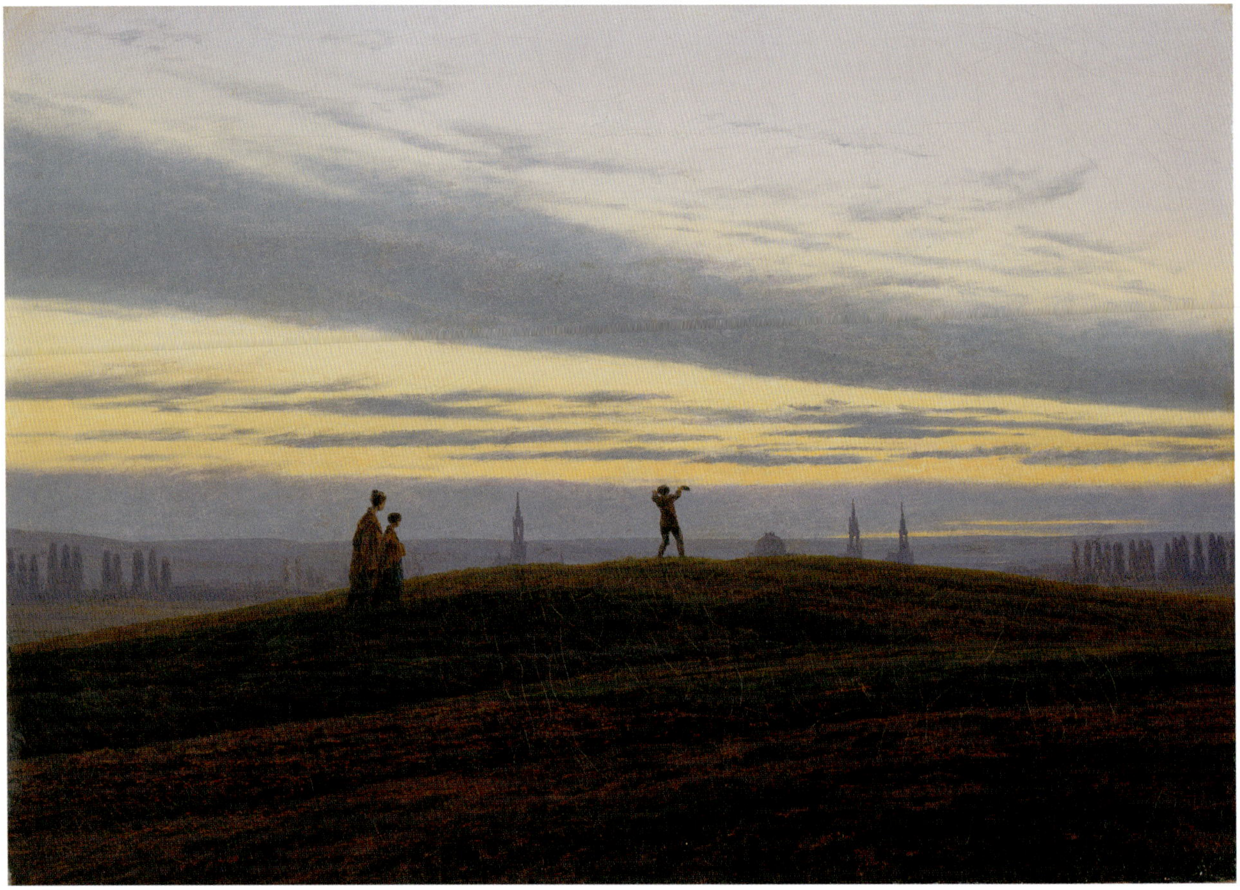

102 Caspar David Friedrich, *The Evening Star*, ca. 1830. Oil on canvas. 33 × 45.2 cm. Frankfurt am Mein, Frankfurter Goethe-Museum.

indicated by the small sailboat moving from right to left, an axis that receives its fullest development in Friedrich's art in the touching and beautifully cadenced *Evening Star* (ca. 1830; fig. 102), in which a young boy – the artist's son? – seen from the rear on a slight rise at the center of the composition excitedly salutes the (hard to discern) evening star with raised arms and his hat doffed, as a woman and a younger girl walk slowly toward him from the left. Beyond the figures lies a gently undulating horizon and in counterpoint with them, framed by stands of trees (at the left and right), three spires and a dome indicate a town otherwise hidden by the rise.

Another deservedly much admired painting, *In the Boat* (1818–20; fig. 103), by virtue of placing the slanting mainmast in the near foreground almost disconcertingly evokes

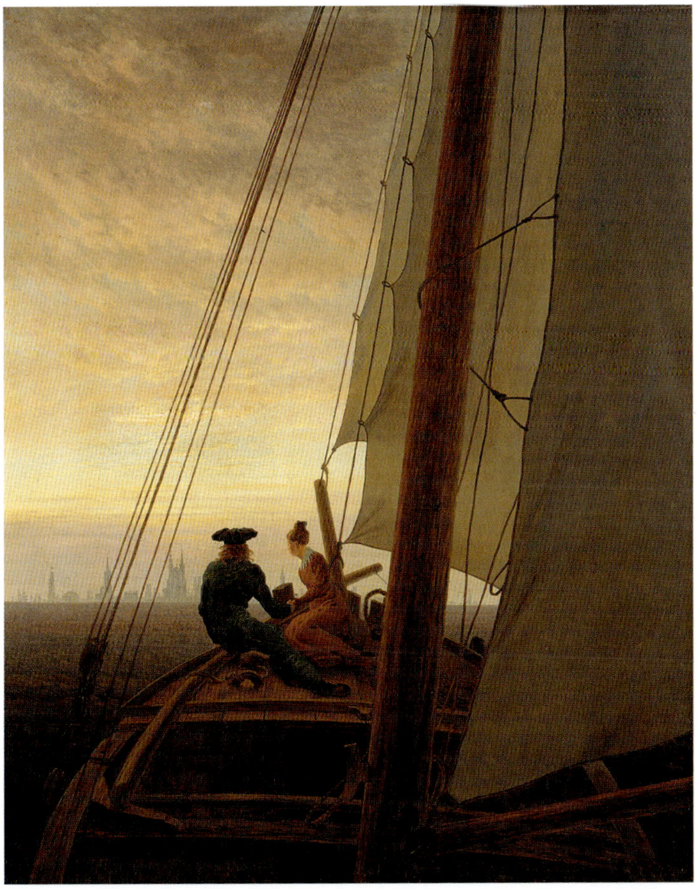

103 Caspar David Friedrich, *In the Boat*, 1818–20. Oil on canvas. 71 × 56 cm. St. Petersburg, The State Hermitage Museum, inv. no, GE-9773.

the port-to-starboard list of a sailboat in the grip of a breeze, hence also the norm of uprightness from which the mast has departed; that the man and woman toward the bow are half-sitting, half-reclining on the fo'c'sle seems appropriate to their situation, though one is also struck by the perfect uprightness of the man's head and the near-perfect horizontal "crown" of his hat. (The faint city spires and towers at the horizon also quietly declare the otherwise unstated vertical norm.) No end of symbolic interpretations have been lavished on this canvas, but by now the relevance of *In the Boat* to the issue of orientation should be self-evident. Or to glance cursorily at one of Friedrich's most intriguing pictures, *The Chalk Cliffs of Rügen* (1818–19; fig. 104), the relation of the three foreground personages – *Rückenfiguren* of a sort – to the abyssal vista beyond

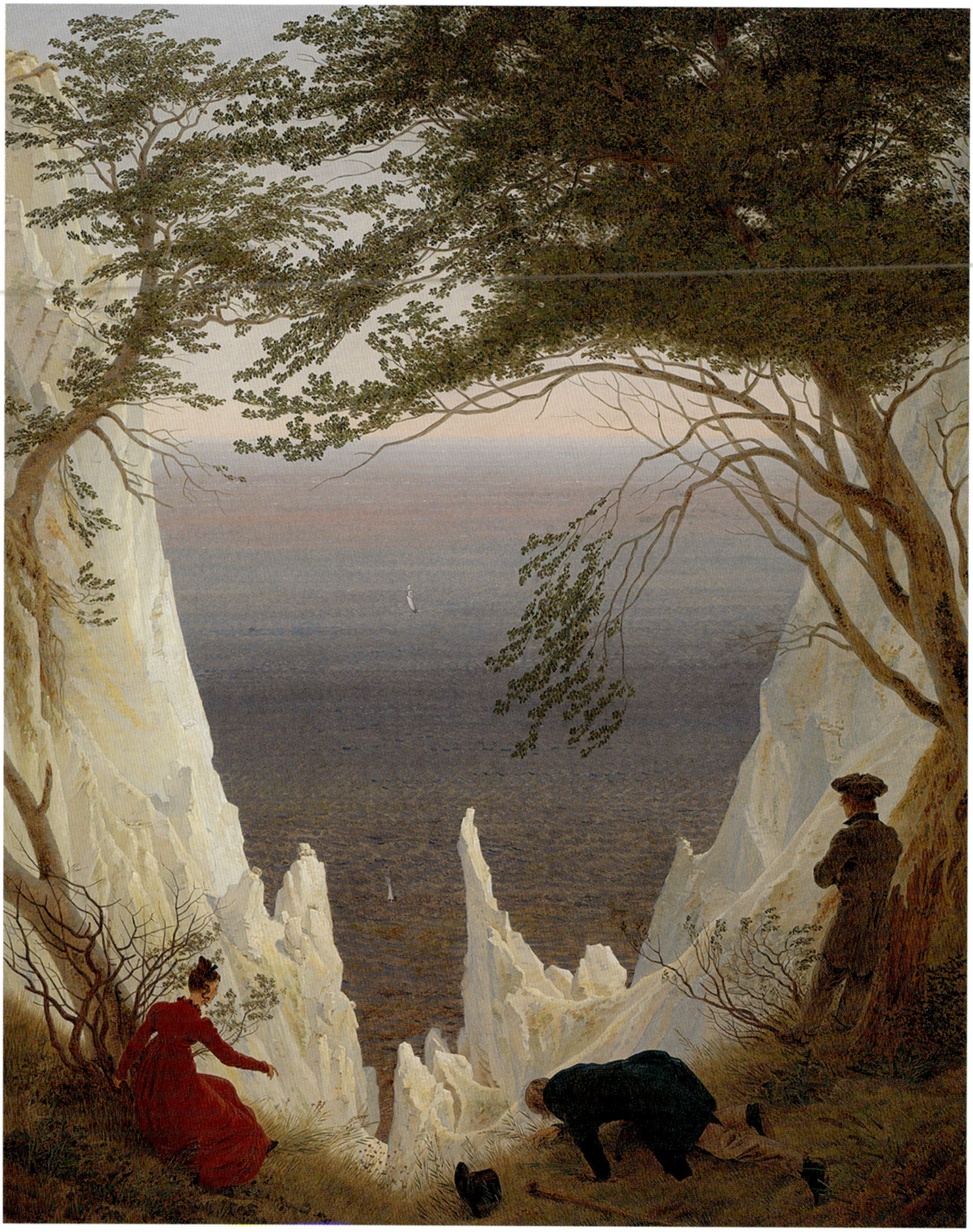

104 Caspar David Friedrich, *The Chalk Cliffs of Rügen*, 1818–19. Oil on canvas. 90.5 × 71 cm. Winterthur, Museum Oskar Reinhart am Stadtgarten.

them (the woman in red seated and pointing, one man on all fours looking plungingly down, a second man with feet firmly planted leaning back against a tree) is for me less an evocation of the *frissons* of the "sublime," though surely it is that too, than a further exploration of the bodily basis of our experience of the world. (The woman has been identified with Caroline and the man on all fours, plausibly, I think, with the artist.) In Werner Hofmann's discussion of the *Chalk Cliffs* he remarks that the woman appears to have her eyes closed.[16] I am dubious – I think she is simply looking down – but it is true, as Hofmann remarks, that Friedrich also wrote, "Close your bodily eyes so as to first see your painting with your spiritual eye"[17] – and of course with one's eyes closed or, as Kant suggests, in a dark room, with merely visual stimulation momentarily in abeyance, the sense of right–left difference – more broadly, of bodiliness – is if anything enhanced. Finally, three mutually contrasting works: *Dolmen in Autumn* (ca. 1820; fig. 105), in which a heavy "blocking" boulder supported by smaller rocks (in that sense curiously "elevated" despite its weight) occupies the middle portion of the pictorial field as a violent storm gusts from left to right (but in the sky also from right to left), the difference between right and left playing out forcefully in other ways as well; *Oak in Snow* (1829; fig. 106), a portrait of a grossly asymmetrical, indeed almost comically anthropomorphic cut back but still thriving tree in a winter landscape, with an even more anthropomorphic-seeming cluster of broken branches lying at its base (the analogue for these last in Menzel would be the fallen manikin in the superb small gouache *Crown Prince Frederick Pays a Visit to the Painter Pesne on His Scaffold at Rheinsberg* [1861; fig. 107]);[18] and the modest-sized, entirely peaceful *Thicket of Firs in the Snow* (ca. 1828; fig. 108) with its tall central fir tree standing amid roughly a dozen others of various sizes and distances from the central axis (and from the viewer). More than any other work we have considered, the *Thicket of Firs* with its repeated, deeply invested motif amounts virtually to a "musical" variation on the themes we have been tracing.

One more major canvas calls for detailed commentary: the large and magnificent *The Watzmann* (1824–5; fig. 109), which depicts a famous mountain in the Bavarian Alps. The basic structure is, once again, centralized, with the main snow-covered peak somewhat to the right of the central vertical axis of the canvas, other smaller peaks to the left and right of the main one, and the rounded, darker, lesser cliff in the middle distance closest of all to that axis. The upward thrust of all the mountains is unmistakable, and naturally my suggestion is that our sense of that thrust is crucially a function of our own uprightness before the canvas, or to put this slightly differently, that Friedrich's painting seeks to make one aware of the mountains' vertical longings largely in those terms. But what continually compels one's attention (the feature to which one's gaze continually returns) is the distinctive, oddly stratified, leftward-leaning outcrop to

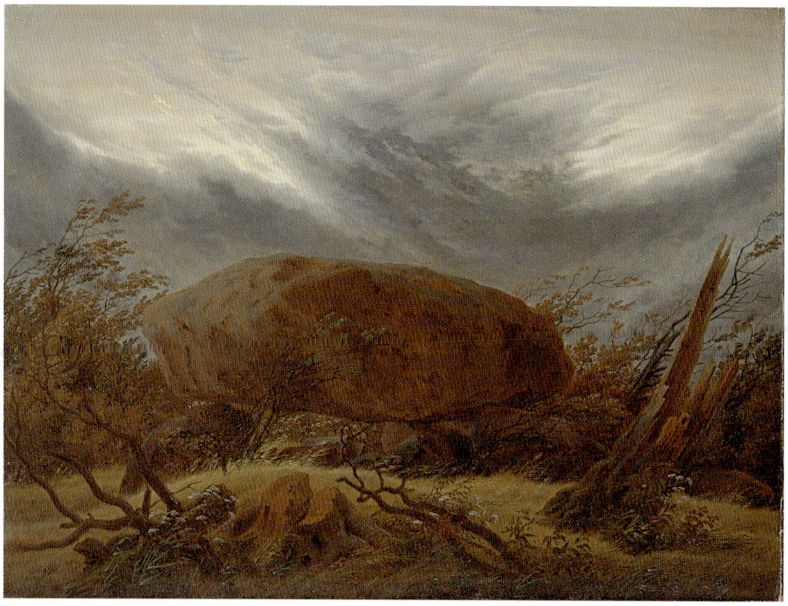

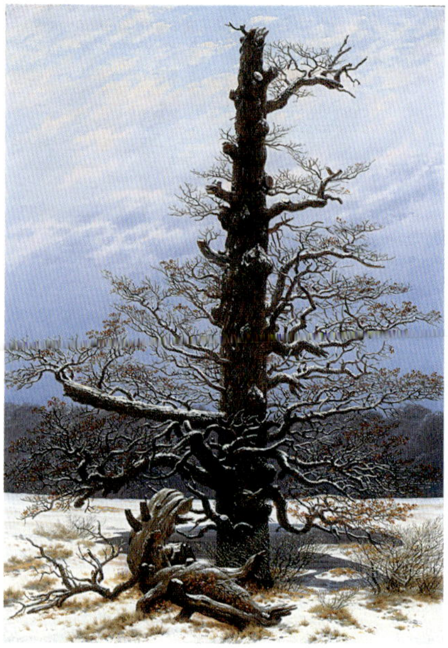

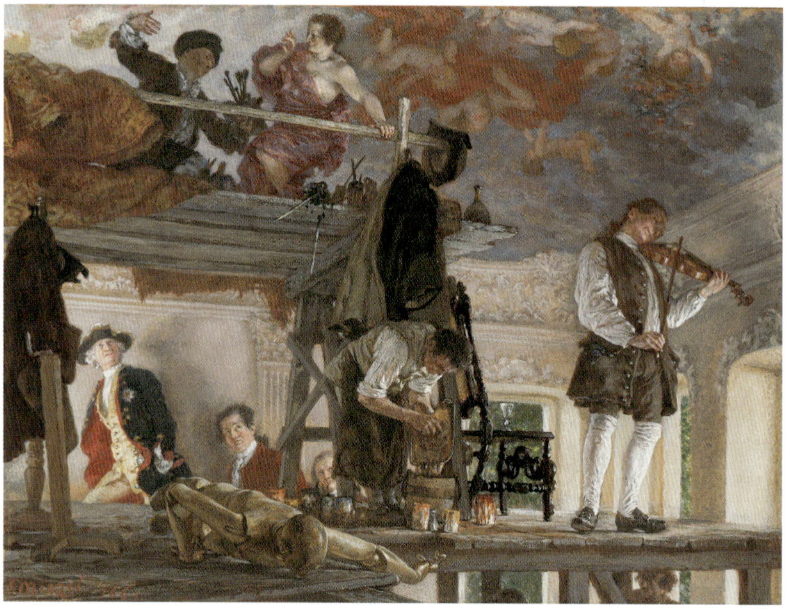

105 (*above, left*) Caspar David Friedrich, *Dolmen in Autumn*, ca. 1820. Oil on canvas. 55 × 71 cm. Dresden, Galerie Neue Meister, Staatliche Kunstsammlungen.

106 (*above, right*) Caspar David Friedrich, *Oak in Snow*, 1829. Oil on canvas. 71 × 48 cm. Berlin, Nationalgalerie, Staatliche Museen zu Berlin.

107 (*left*) Adolph Menzel, *Crown Prince Frederick Pays a Visit to the Painter Pesne on His Scaffold at Rheinsberg*, 1861. Gouache on paper, board backing. 24 × 32 cm. Berlin, Nationalgalerie, Staatliche Museen zu Berlin.

the left of center foreground, an actual granite formation known as the Erdbeerkopf, which however comes not from the neighborhood of the Watzmann but from the Harz Mountains in northern Germany, where Friedrich had encountered and drawn it almost fifteen years before. (Friedrich never saw the Watzmann itself.) According to one

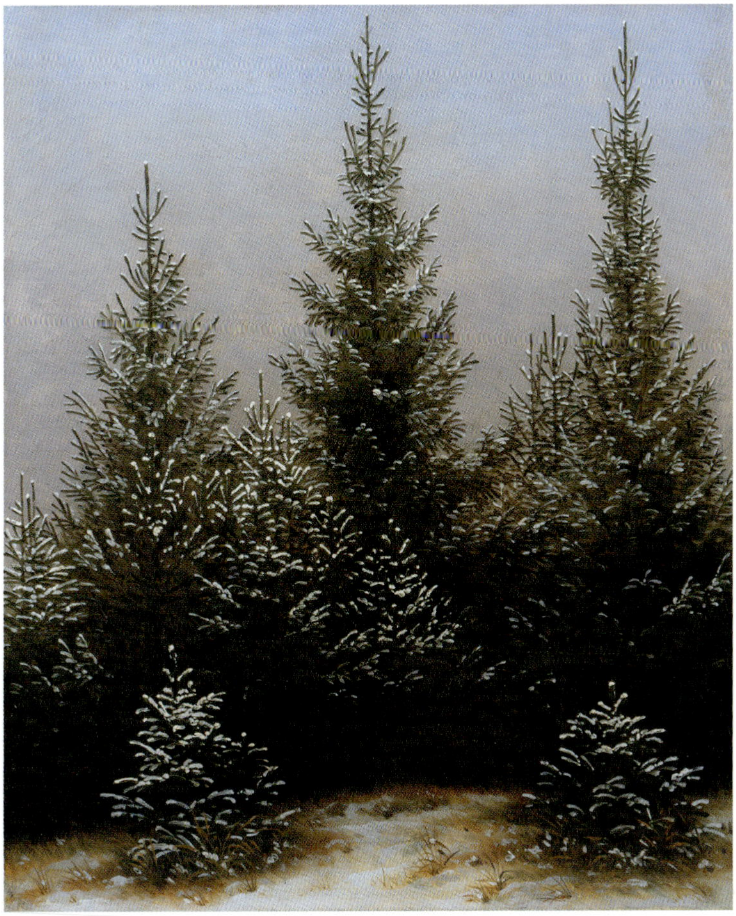

108 Caspar David Friedrich, *Thicket of Firs in the Snow*, ca. 1828. Oil on canvas. 31.3 × 25.4 cm. Munich, Bayerische Staatsgemäldesammlungen, Neue Pinakothek.

interpretation, this surprising inconsistency is to be understood in terms of the artist's alleged interest in a contemporary geological theory that focused on the role of granite in mountain formation, an interest which is taken to justify the inclusion of the Erdbeerkopf in the present canvas,[19] but not surprisingly I find such an explanation less than fully persuasive. Instead I want to emphasize (what else?) the orientational significance of the Erdbeerkopf, by which I mean the felt salience of its leftward lean even as it rests on or grows out from a hillside that slopes from upper left toward lower right, and even as its various strata tilt downward to the right as well. Indeed the viewer can only be uncertain whether the strata represent separate slabs of stone, with the

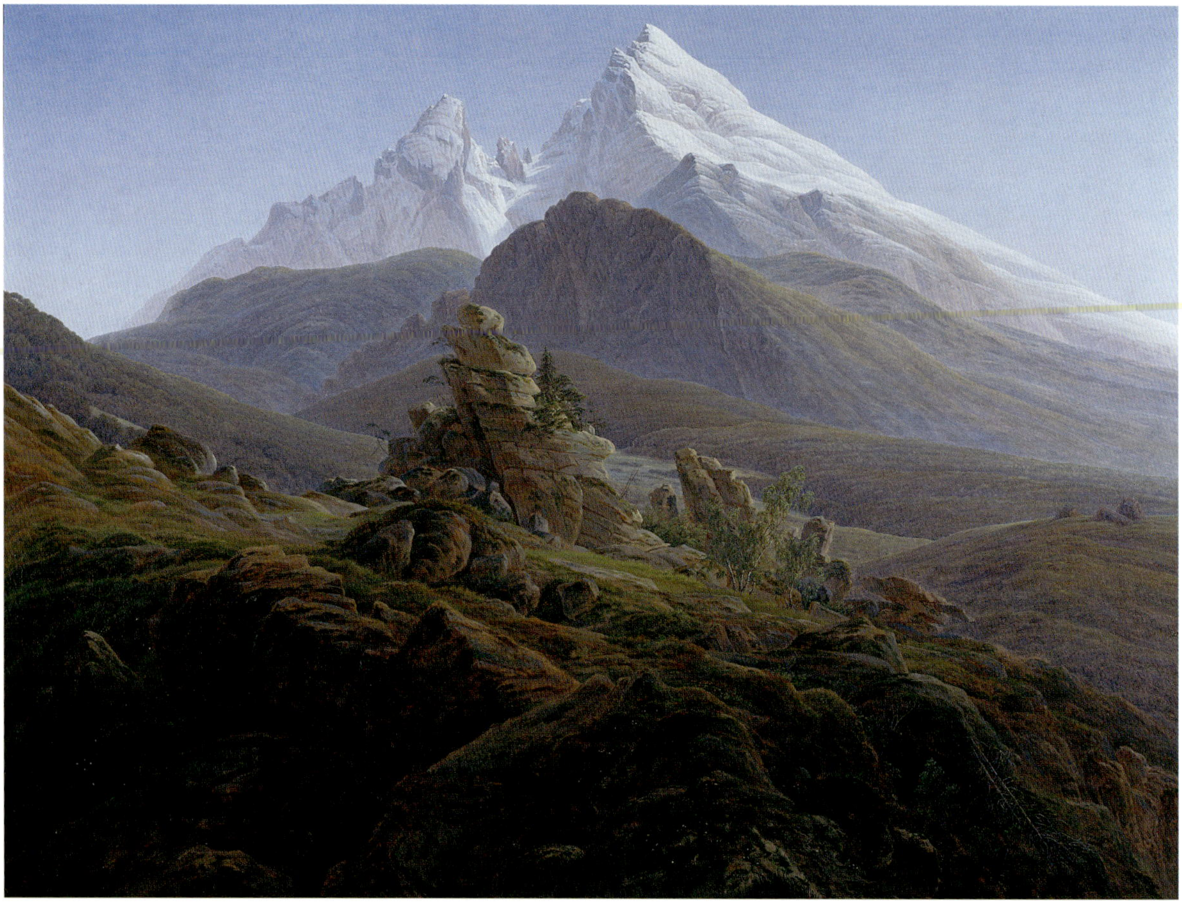

109 Caspar David Friedrich, *The Watzmann*, 1824–5. Oil on canvas. 135 × 170 cm. Berlin, Nationalgalerie, Staatliche Museen zu Berlin.

smallest one at the top seemingly balanced against the likelihood of toppling down. Note too the small fir or pine tree that grows upward from a shelf-like lower stratum, thereby introducing a distinct if also precisely calibrated vertical upthrust in intimate relation with the outcropping as a whole (an upthrust, moreover, that comes very close to the central vertical axis of the canvas). (In fact the fir or pine tree seems to slant very slightly to the left.) Plus there is the smaller, also leftward-leaning outcrop further back and to the right, the rightward-springing bush partly in "front" of that, as well as the entire richly articulated rocky foreground that provides no sure footing for the viewer and thus makes one all the more aware of the need for such – and of course one does have such footing "this" side of the picture surface. (Note in particular the large rock

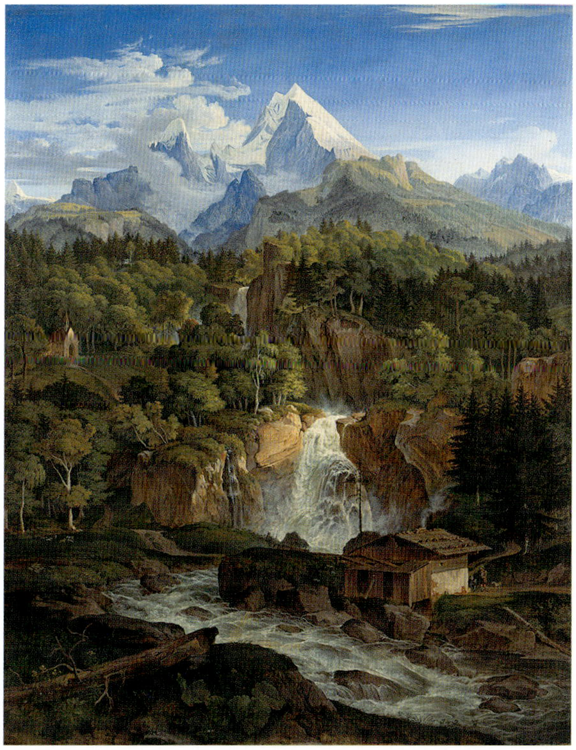

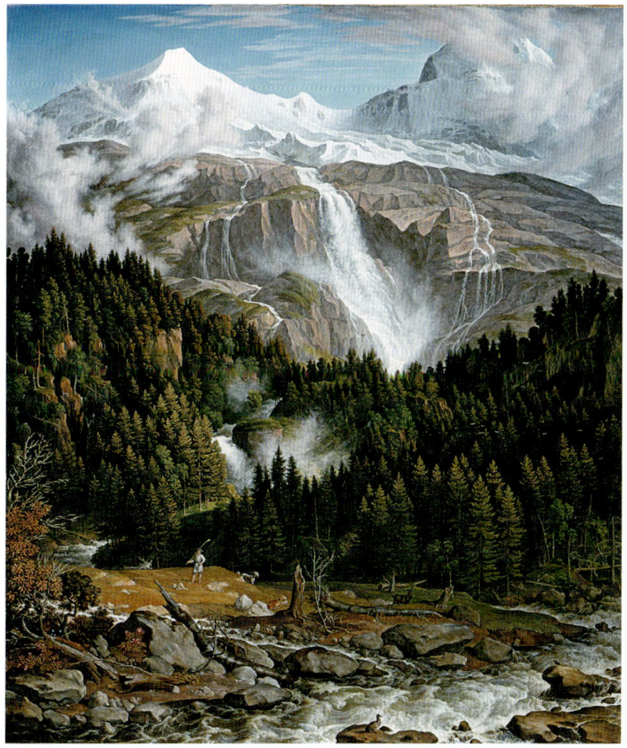

110 (*above, left*) Adrien Ludwig Richter, *The Watzmann*, 1824. Oil on canvas. 121 × 93.5 cm. Munich, Bayerische Staatsgemäldesammlungen, Neue Pinakothek.

111 (*above, right*) Joseph Anton Koch, *The Schmadribach Waterfall*, 1822. Oil on canvas. 131.8 × 110 cm. Munich, Bayerische Staatsgemäldesammlungen, Neue Pinakothek.

in the immediate center foreground, which in effect "mimics" the soaring peaks in the distance.)

I have just referred yet again to the "viewer" but in a fundamental sense Friedrich's canvas is not a "view" of a mountain scene at all (the same might be said of the other landscapes we have considered). Nor does the "viewer" occupy what we normally understand as a "point of view" relative to the scene as a whole, with its implication that the very structure of the latter is a function of the taking up of a particular ocular position *vis-à-vis* the world of appearances – as if were the "viewer" to move just a bit toward the right or left, the composition as we have it would fall apart, lose coherence, become artistically meaningless. Whereas in keeping with the Kantian argument I am associating with Friedrich's oeuvre, it would in principle be replaced by another such

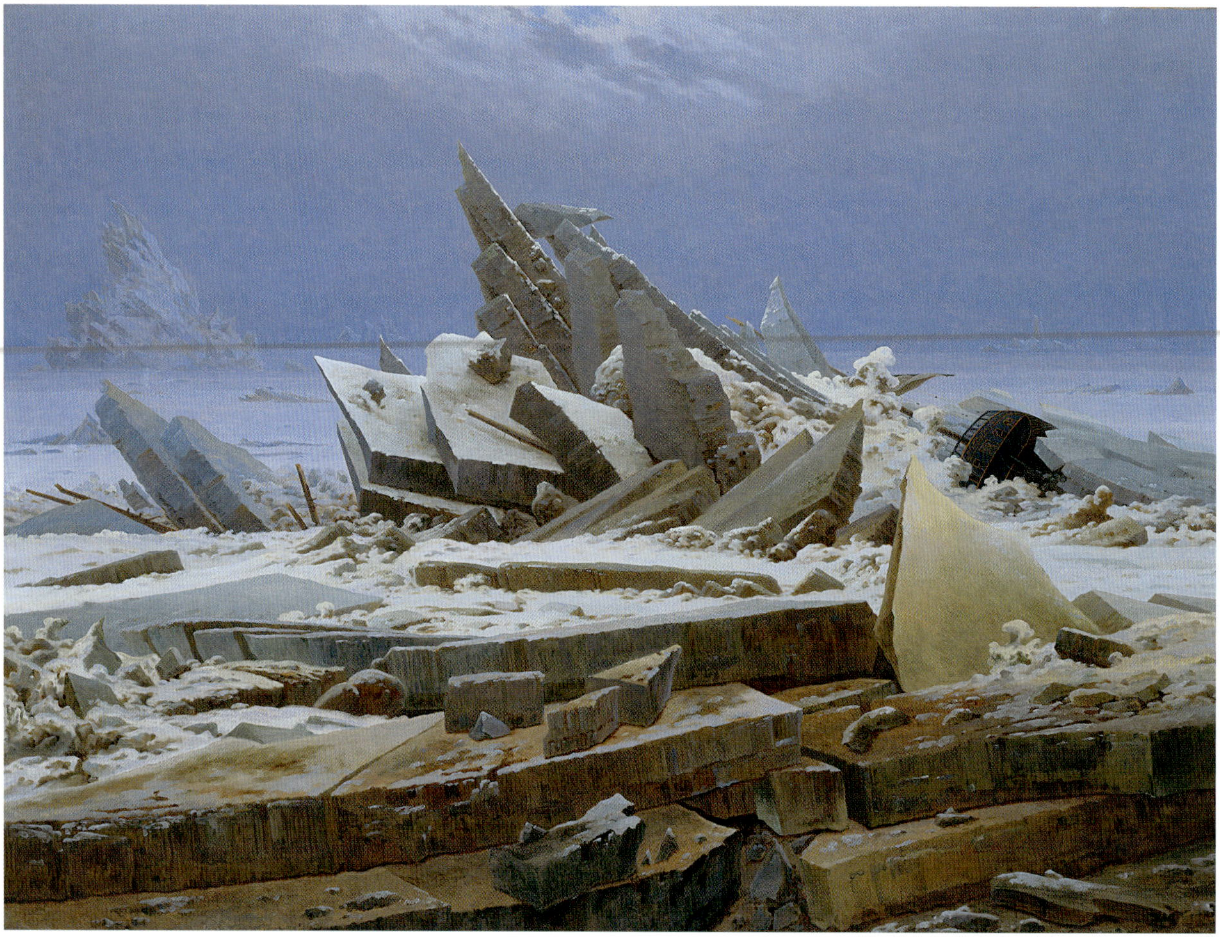

112 Caspar David Friedrich, *Arctic Shipwreck*, ca. 1823–4. Oil on canvas. 96.7 × 126.9 cm. Hamburg, Kunsthalle.

scene which, even if less spellbinding than the first, would nevertheless be structured by the same *a priori* considerations, *a priori* being Kant's term in the passage from "What does it mean to orient oneself in thinking?" that I began my approach to Friedrich by citing. What replaces "point of view," in other words, is the truth of orientation – more broadly, I would like to say, of "cognizing" – which as Kant insists begins in bodily feeling.[20] There is perhaps no painting by Friedrich that makes this point more transcendentally, across every bit of its surface, than *The Watzmann*. (In the Louvre "De l'Allemagne" exhibition mentioned in note 8, *The Watzmann* was hung in close proximity to two comparably sized mountain landscapes by distinguished and successful contemporaries, Adrian Ludwig Richter's *The Watzmann* [1824; fig. 110] and

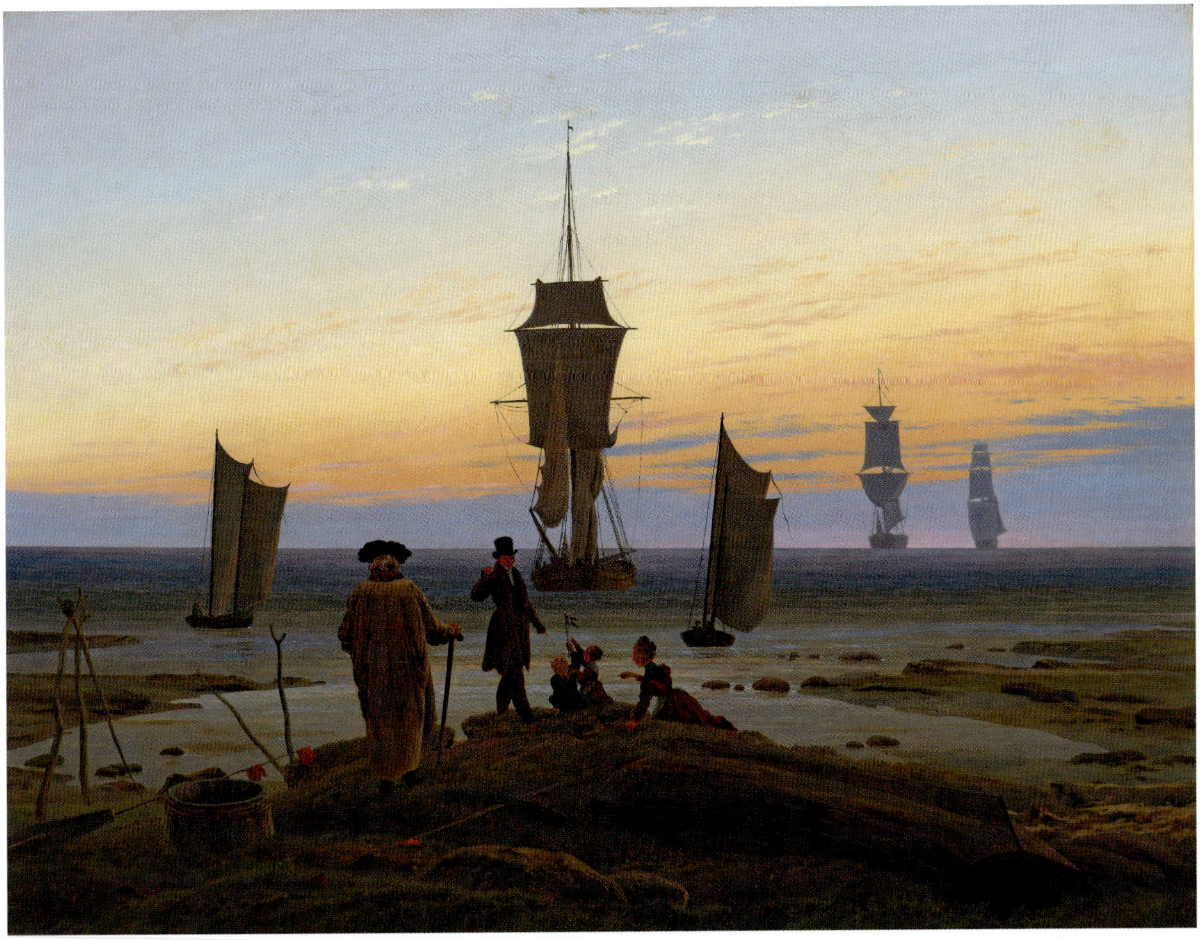

113 Caspar David Friedrich, *The Three Ages of Man*, 1834–5. Oil on canvas. 72.5 × 94 cm. Leipzig, Museum der bildenden Künste.

Joseph Anton Koch's *The Schmadribach Waterfall* [1822; fig. 111]. The contrast between the almost vibratory liveness and so to speak the ontological translucence of the entire pictorial field in Friedrich's canvas and the compositional fixity and material opacity of Richter's and Koch's paintings could not have been more instructive.)[21]

For a while I thought of bringing this essays to an end with a few remarks about Friedrich's masterly and chilling *Arctic Shipwreck* (ca. 1823–4; fig. 112), in which the sense of orientation is placed under greater duress than any other in his oeuvre, I mean by the jagged, angled, piled up slabs of ice that seem ready to contest the very possibility of taking an upright bearing. (But notice the smallish, more or less horizontal chunk of ice that is supported from below high up in the main ice mass; more than any other element in the composition, it, or rather the way it is supported, connotes the operation of the law of gravity, hence at a remove the norm of uprightness. It also happens to come closer than any other to declaring, almost literally pointing to, the central axis of the painting.) Another strong candidate for closure is the intensely poetic *Three Ages of Man* (1834–5; fig. 113), with its proximate *Rückenfigur*, doubtless the ailing Friedrich himself, walking haltingly toward the shoreline, tall sailing ship approaching the shore on the painting's central axis, and tiny Swedish flag (which Friedrich was born under) – again, on that axis – with its yellow cross on a blue field – a national symbol, of course, but also, I want to suggest, a final, unexpected orientational "cross-hair" (fig. 114). (In the hand of a child, with all that that implies.) After further reflection, however, I want to conclude with Friedrich's last ambitious canvas, *Moonlight on the Sea* (1835–6; fig. 115) in Hamburg, with its magnificent banks of inky clouds, moon in the east at the very top center of the canvas, dark rocky shoreline with two beached dinghies in the left

114 Caspar David Friedrich, *The Three Ages of Man*, (detail of fig. 113).

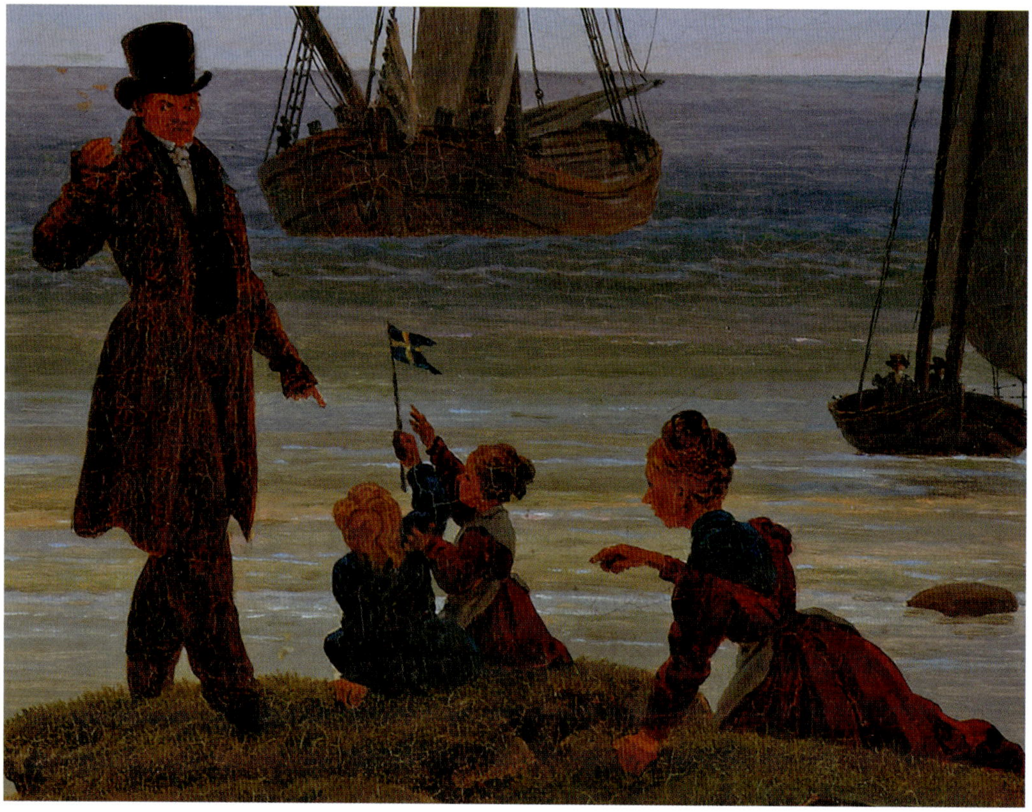

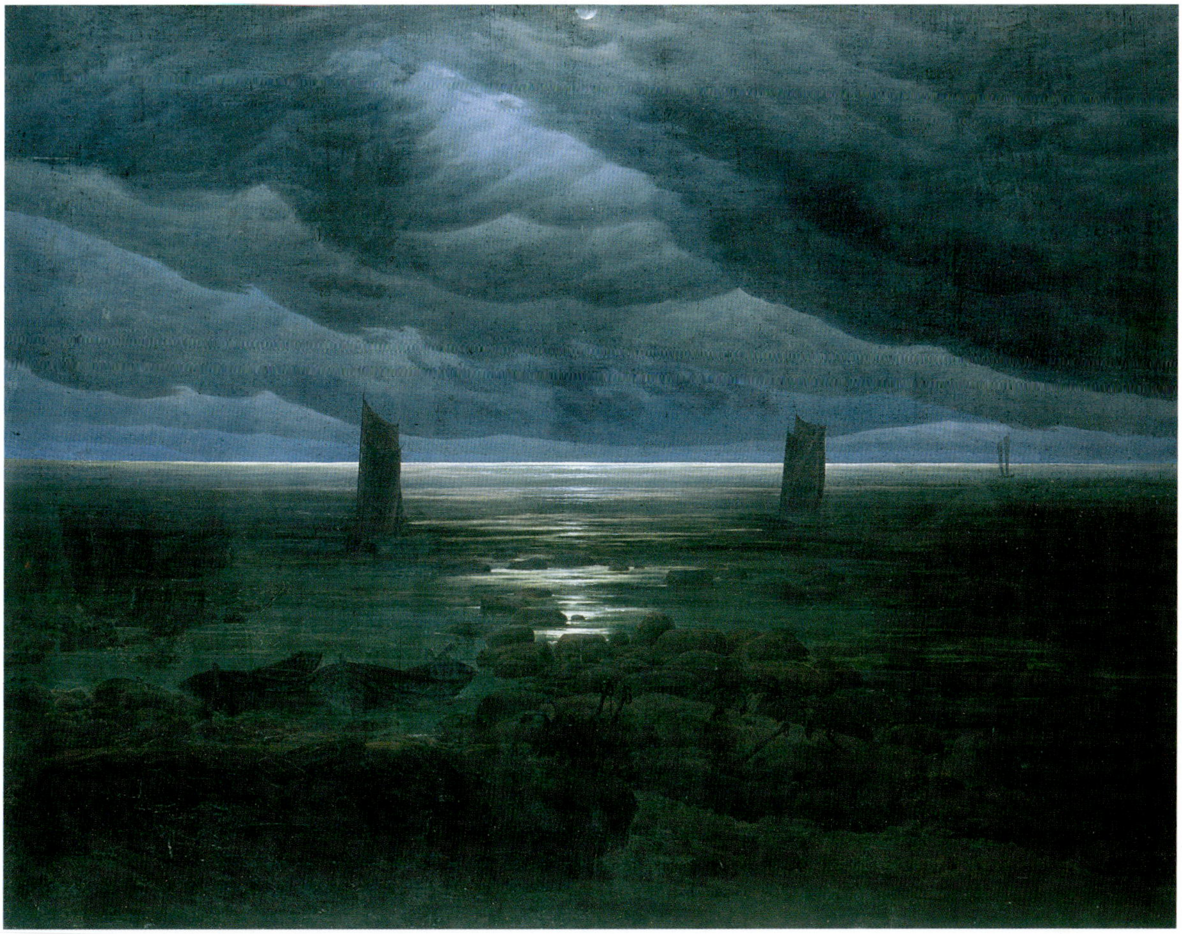

115 Caspar David Friedrich, *Moonlight on the Sea*, 1835–6. Oil on canvas. 134 × 169.2 cm. Hamburg, Kunsthalle.

foreground, and two boats under sail in the middle distance, the one on the right just slightly farther from the central axis defined by the moon's broken reflection in the water than the one on the left, the one on the left just a bit nearer to us than the one on the right. (The fineness of those discriminations is what matters here. There is also a third boat further away toward the right.) As always in Friedrich, the path to symbolic interpretation has been left wide open: no doubt death beckons in those inky depths, and just possibly the promise of life beyond death in that thin line of silver light that marks the horizon. But while earthly life lasts, orientation reigns and gives meaning to experience.[22]

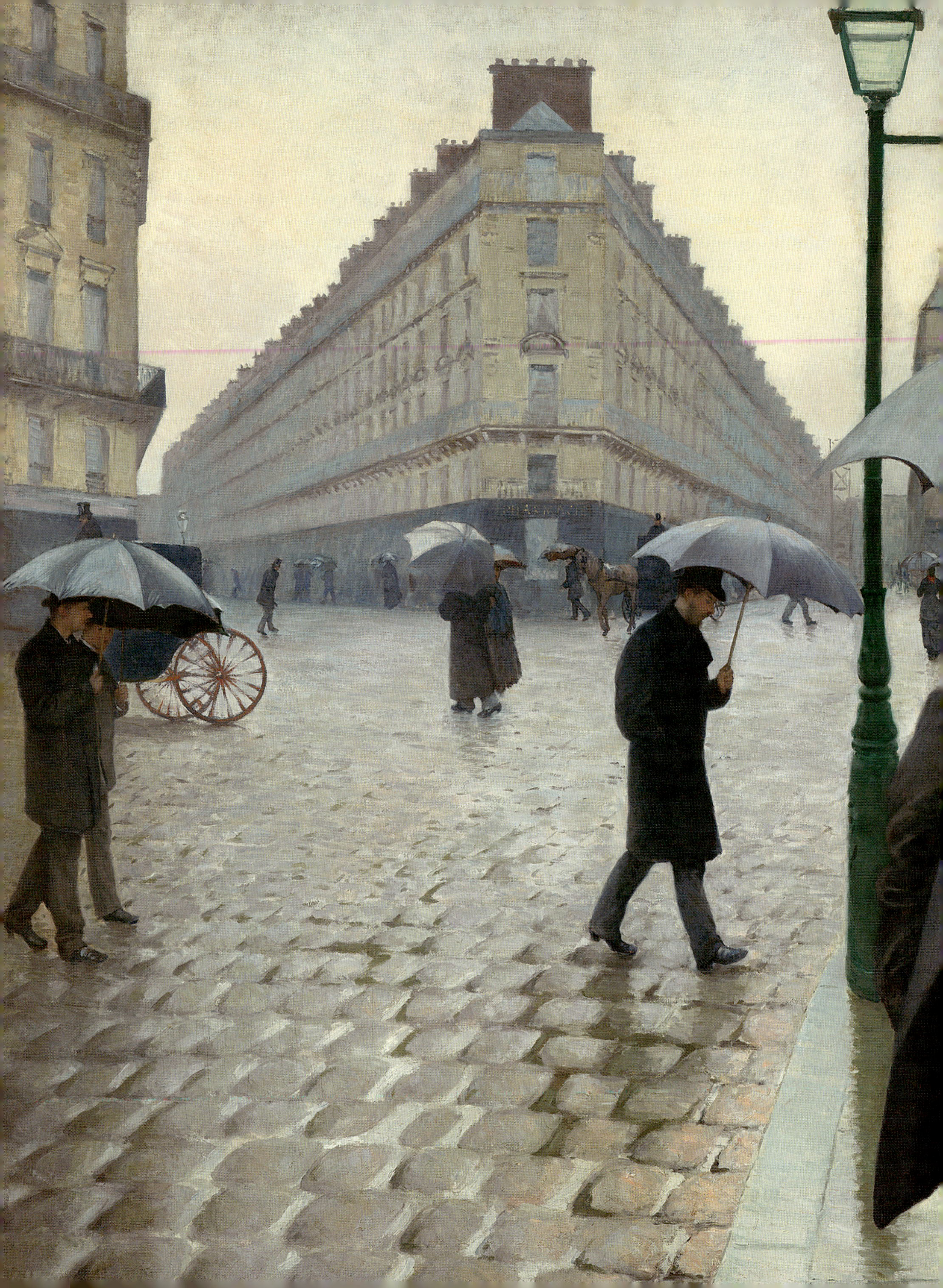

• 5 •

CAILLEBOTTE'S IMPRESSIONISM

To start with the bedrock facts, Gustave Caillebotte was born to a well-off bourgeois family in Paris in 1848 and died at the early age of forty-six in 1894.[1] His art and career are closely connected with those of the Impressionists: he began to show his work at the second Impressionist exhibition of 1876 and quickly became a moving force behind subsequent exhibitions, specifically those of 1877, 1879, 1880, and 1882. He also used his wealth to build a superb collection of recent art, which he left to the French state on his death; today it forms the core of the Impressionist holdings of the Musée d'Orsay. In his own time his work was much commented on. More precisely, his paintings in the Impressionist exhibitions were often singled out for praise, and he was much admired by one of the key art critics of the late 1870s and early 1880s, Joris-Karl Huysmans. Relatively soon, however, his work fell into obscurity, and it was not until the major retrospective exhibition of 1976–7, organized by the late Kirk Varnedoe and others, that the importance as well as aspects of the seriousness of his achievement began to be recognized. (The Varnedoe catalogue, an exemplary piece of work, remains the most useful and insightful text on Caillebotte's art.[2]) Since then interest in Caillebotte has grown exponentially, as is dramatized by the prominence given to the large and compelling painting Varnedoe calls his masterpiece, *Paris Street; Rainy Day* (1877; see fig. 131), in the main Impressionist room in Chicago's Art Institute. I shall have more to say about that canvas further on. But at the outset I want to call attention to one of its most conspicuous features, the paving stones glistening in the rain. Later I shall suggest that some measure of Caillebotte's interest in the scene depicted in *Paris Street* concerned that glistening, that reflective dazzle, itself.

My personal relation to Caillebotte's art is slightly checkered. I admit to resisting the late 1970s vogue for his painting on the grounds that the "revisionist" claims that were then often made on his behalf seemed exaggerated.[3] But in 1994–5 I saw the second, definitive retrospective exhibition of his art that was held in Paris and Chicago (I caught

116 (*facing page*) Gustave Caillebotte, *Paris Street; Rainy Day*, 1877 (detail of fig. 131).

it in both places), and I became converted. For the most part I did not change my mind about the sheerly artistic level of his achievement; Caillebotte as a painter, a paint-handler, is not in the same league as Corot, Courbet, Manet, Monet, Pissarro, Cézanne, or Seurat. But I became aware as I had not previously been of the deep seriousness and considerable originality of his overarching project, and it is those qualities, along with the meaning of that project, that I shall try to convey in this essay.

A bit more should be said about Caillebotte himself before turning to his paintings. I have noted that Caillebotte was born in 1848, which means that he was not quite a member of the Impressionist generation by right of birth. Claude Monet, point man for the movement, was born in 1840; Edouard Manet, the central figure in the previous generation, was born in 1832; Gustave Courbet, Manet's Realist predecessor and in decisive respects the instigator of the modern movement as a whole, was born in 1819; and the leading painter of the Neoimpressionist generation, Georges Seurat, was born in 1859, eleven years after Caillebotte. So there is no clear-cut way of locating Caillebotte generationally, other than to point to that slight but significant divergence in age between him and the "core" Impressionists around Monet. Another basic fact is that Caillebotte made almost all the paintings that are of interest to us today in a short span of years, between 1875 and 1882. (A sizable number of his key works belong to 1875–6.) Modern commentators have rightly insisted that he did not cease painting altogether in 1882, but from then until his death he painted relatively little, and almost without exception the works he produced seem not just minor but unambitious. In other words, painting ceased being the main focus of his life (he became a serious gardener and successfully took up sailboat racing and boat design), with the result that we are confronted in Caillebotte with the unusual case of a short, pictorially ambitious career not cut off by death or illness, one that reached a natural terminus or perhaps dead end. This was surely a factor in the eclipse of his reputation within his own lifetime. But it is also a matter that the interpreter of his work must seek to understand.

I

With these remarks in place, I begin by looking at one of the two major canvases Caillebotte exhibited in the second Impressionist exhibition in 1876, *Young Man at His Window*, painted in 1875 (fig. 117). As has often been observed, the picture is based on a characteristically Impressionist motif, a view of city streets, here the juncture of the rue de Miromesnil and the rue de Lisbonne, with the boulevard Malesherbes beyond it. (The young man looking out is René Caillebotte, the painter's younger brother who was to die of a sudden illness in 1876. The family lived in a spacious apartment at 77, rue de Miromesnil in the eighth *arrondissement*, then as now an excellent address.) Or rather I should say that the picture is based on the bringing together of the Impressionist motif of the view of city streets with another, not obviously Impressionist motif, the figure seen from the rear. The zone of suture between the two is the window, and commentators have been quick to note the accords between this painting and various passages in Edmond Duranty's famous pamphlet of 1876, *La Nouvelle Peinture* (*The New Painting*), a defense of the group of artists who exhibited that year at the Durand-Ruel Gallery (that is, the Impressionists). "With a back," Duranty wrote, "we want a temperament, an age, a social condition to reveal themselves. . . . Hands held in pockets can be eloquent." And:

> From within, it is by way of the window that we communicate with the outside; the window is another frame that incessantly accompanies us, during the time we pass indoors, and that time is considerable. The frame of the window, according to whether we are far from it or near it, and whether we are seated or standing, crops the exterior spectacle in the most unexpected and changeable manner, producing eternal variety, the impromptu that is one of the great flavors of reality.[4]

(Duranty also attached special importance to the sense of connectedness between persons and their milieux, in particular their apartments.[5]) Not that Caillebotte followed Duranty in these respects; on the contrary, Duranty is rightly thought to have based his remarks on actual paintings, notably ones by Degas and Caillebotte. At the same time, it is often said or implied that Duranty in 1876 was Degas's spokesman, with Caillebotte along for the ride, so to speak. But the truth is more complex: Degas's and Caillebotte's paintings were seen by Duranty as at once realizing and giving a new inflection to certain values that he had always held (more on that too shortly), and *The New Painting*, without mentioning their names, registers that fact. At any rate, the *Young Man at His Window* was plainly a central work for Duranty, as it must be for us.

In his catalogue entry on the painting Varnedoe notes what he calls "a psychological or emotive dimension [in Caillebotte's treatment of the window] that would seem to have more to do with the heritage of Romanticism, and most especially German Romanticism" (*GC*, 89). Varnedoe has in mind works like Caspar David Friedrich's *Woman at the Window* (see fig. 87) and, although he goes on to emphasize various differences between Friedrich's and Caillebotte's pictures, the comparison itself is beside the point. The relevant term of comparison for Caillebotte's young man seen from the rear is, instead, any of a number of figures in paintings by the French Realist painter Gustave Courbet. For example, in Courbet's *After Dinner at Ornans* (1848–9;

see fig. 80), the first of his Realist masterpieces, the figure of his friend Marlet has been depicted seated in the center foreground and lighting a pipe, with his back (and the back of his chair) turned toward the viewer and his face all but completely turned away. Similarly, in a painting of roughly twenty years later, *The Source* (1868; fig. 83), a nude seated on a rock in the middle of a wood with her back mostly turned toward the viewer and her face yielding only the hint of a *profil perdu* holds her left hand palm upward under a small cascade while with her right hand she lightly grips a branch above her head. Now, in my trilogy of books on the evolution of French painting between the middle of the eighteenth century and the advent of Manet and his generation in the 1860s, I argue that Courbet was one of two culminating figures, the other being Manet, in an antitheatrical current or tradition that lay at the heart of French painting during that period.[6] At the core of that current or tradition (putting this as succinctly as possible) was the demand, first advanced by Diderot in his writings of the 1750s and 1760s on the theater and painting, that a picture somehow establish the metaphysical illusion that the beholder does not exist, that there is no one present before the canvas. In the work of a succession of major figures from Greuze to Millet, this was to be done by closing the representation to the beholder, above all by depicting figures wholly engrossed or absorbed in actions or states of mind and who therefore were felt to be unaware of being beheld. By the 1840s and 1850s, however, the resort to absorption increasingly fell short of producing the desired effect; the figures in question tended more and more to be perceived not as truly given over to what they were doing, thinking, or feeling but as merely wishing to appear so, which far from persuading the beholder that he or she had been forgotten positively confirmed the suspicion of theatricality that the absorptive strategy originally had been mobilized to defeat.

In Courbet's art of the 1840s and after, the issue of theatricality is differently engaged: by a strategy of the all but literally corporeal merger on the part of the painter – identified now as the painting's first beholder, or painter-beholder – with the painting before him, the painting being realized under his brush. At least with respect to *that* beholder the painting would ideally escape beholding completely; there would be no one before it looking on because the beholder who had been there was now incorporated or disseminated in the work itself. One early sign of that endeavor was Courbet's reliance throughout the 1840s on the genre of the self-portrait. In the present context, though, what I want to stress is that another crucial operator of Courbet's strategy of quasi-merger is the prominence in his art of figures depicted *from the rear*, figures who by virtue of their bodily orientation are to be seen as congruent with that of painter-beholder at work on his canvas and whose actions may often be understood as displaced or metaphorical versions of the two-handed act of painting a picture. So for

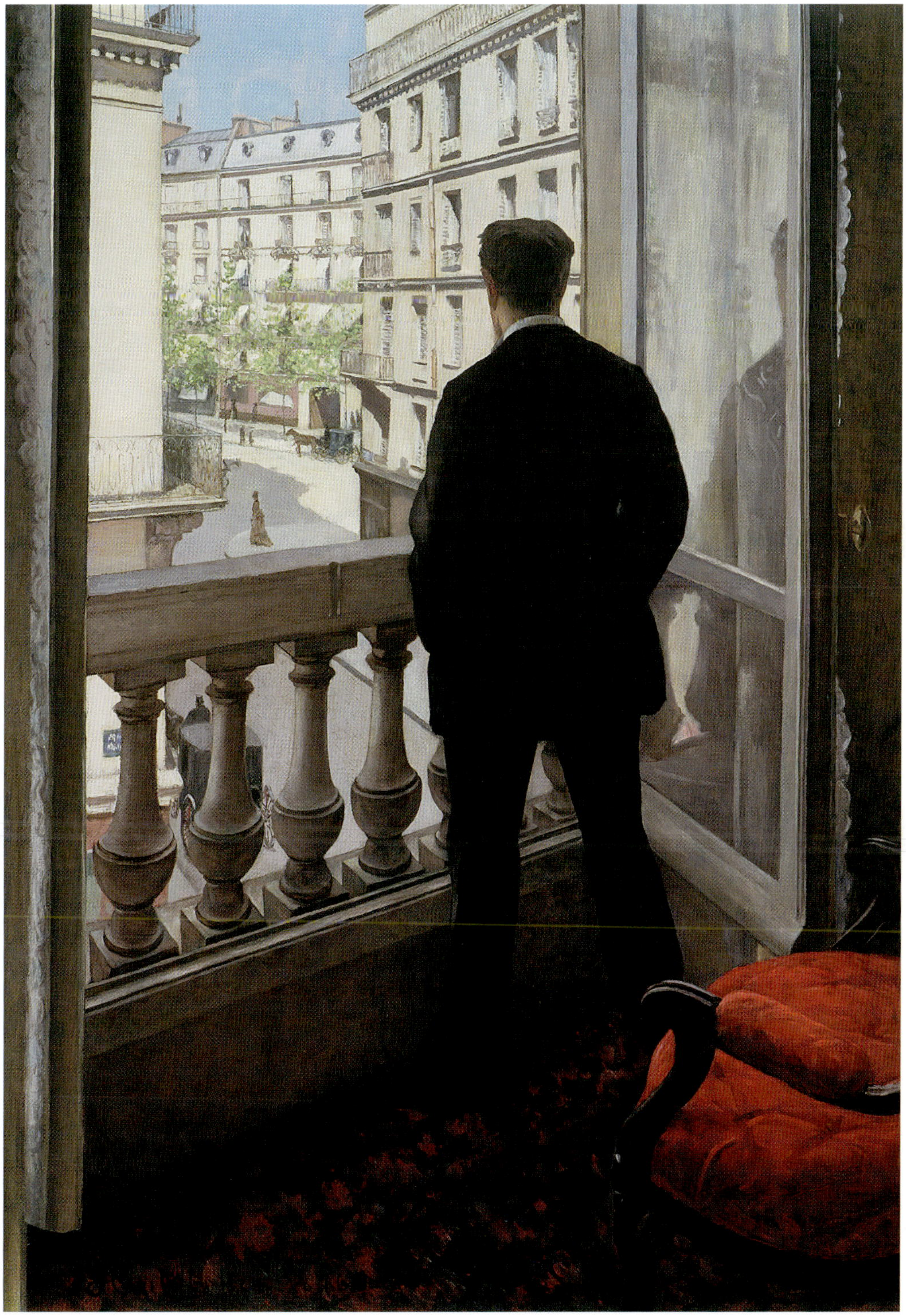

117 Gustave Caillebotte, *Young Man at His Window*, 1875. Oil on canvas. 117 × 82 cm. Private collection.

example in the *Source* the woman's open left hand under the stream of water may be taken as a version of the painter-beholder's left hand holding his palette while her right hand gripping the branch may be likened to his right hand wielding a brush. This is to say more than that the woman is a surrogate for the painter-beholder, though that is surely true. It is also to stress the importance to Courbet's art of an ideal of something like physical continuity between painter-beholder and painting, between the act (or acts) of painting and the worked canvas; in Stephen Melville's words the ideal is one of a kind of "prolongation" of the act of painting within the painting itself.[7]

If we now look closely at Caillebotte's picture, several differences as well as similarities come into view. In the first place, the young man is not doing anything or at least is not performing an action in the manner of Marlet in the *After Dinner* or the woman in the *Source*. So there is no question of his representing the act of painting or of being a surrogate for the painter in a strong, Courbet-like sense of the term. For all the young man's seeming passivity, however, the beholder is made acutely aware of his *embodiedness*, by which I mean the beholder registers empathically not only the young man's stance (legs somewhat spread and firmly planted, knees straight but with the suggestion of bounce or spring, hands in pockets, pelvis thrust forward, shoulders ever so slightly hunched) but also the imagined thrust and counterthrust of internal and external forces determining that stance (including the interplay between the young man's trunk and limbs and the parameters of his well-cut suit). And that evocation of embodiedness or corporeality is an effect Caillebotte shares with Courbet, despite the differences between them.

Second, there is no hint in the *Young Man at His Window* of anything like merger or continuity or prolongation between painter-beholder and painting. Not only does the young man stand farther from the picture plane than the woman in the *Source*; more important, the carpeted floor falls steeply away (plunging perspectives of this sort are a recurrent feature of Caillebotte's art), separating us from the young man as if by a chasm; finally, at the lower right of the painting a wooden armchair with reddish-orange padding looms between us and him, further marking our mutual separation while at the same time confirming, even enhancing, the prior suggestion of embodiedness: the chair with its generously cushioned seat and curving arms seems made for the young man's body (they are in silent dialogue, not unlike that between the young man and his reflection in the open window). Altogether, it is by no means clear exactly how we are to understand our relation as viewers to the young man (that is to say, it is not clear what relation to the beholder the painting's structure posits); a partial identification with the young man is probably inevitable, if only because of the seeming proximity of the window towards the left and the brightness and vividness of the street scene beyond, but because the painting also stresses the young man's apartness from the viewer and manages with impressive economy to characterize him "physiognomically" (although we do not see his face we register the oddly flattened shape of his head and a hint of the style of his whiskers), our ultimate implied position is not the same as his. And yet we are not invited – so I want to claim – to imagine ourselves standing back and detachedly observing him (and the scene through the window) from a point of view that we feel to be distinctly our own.

This becomes clearer, I think, if we consider the relation of the young man to the street scene beyond the open window and stone balustrade. What Caillebotte's young man presumably is doing is looking (maybe looking and thinking, maybe looking and daydreaming, but in any case looking), and that too is an Impressionist motif in a double sense: because Impressionist paintings often depict figures looking and because from the outset Impressionism as a movement was understood by both its admirers and its detractors as placing new (some said exclusive) emphasis on visual or ocular experience.[8] This is in contrast to Courbet's focus on bodily experience even to the extent of minimizing or denying vision (think of all the figures with eyes shut in Courbet's paintings, including a few self-portraits). And what I want to suggest is that a version of that contrast has been made central to Caillebotte's *Young Man at His Window*, in the stark juxtaposition of the shadowy apartment interior and strongly physical depiction of the young man with the whited tones of the sun-filled streets several stories below. Indeed aspects of that contrast may be found in certain features of the street scene itself – specifically, in the compelling suggestion of *movement* conveyed by the rendering of the woman in a brown dress walking from right to left, by the treatment of the horse and carriage traveling up the boulevard Malesherbes, and (perhaps most tellingly) by the indication of no more than the head and forequarters of a white or gray horse, no doubt pulling a carriage and moving from left to right, emerging into view from behind the metal balustrade across the way just beyond the woman in brown (fig. 118). I have stressed the notion of movement because I want to underscore the extent to which the scene as a whole is not perceived as an instantaneous gestalt. That is, although the woman, horse and carriage, and truncated horse are all necessarily captured at a single "moment" in their respective paths, the dominant impression, verging on illusion, is one of temporal dilation, of a protracted moment within which something like perceptible movement almost does take place. I want to suggest, first, that that impression of temporal dilation and virtual movement belongs to a bodily register, as opposed to the ideal instantaneousness of the Impressionist *coup d'oeil*, which the street scene nevertheless invokes. And second, that our perception of the scene through the open window is in the end associated simply and wholly *neither* with the

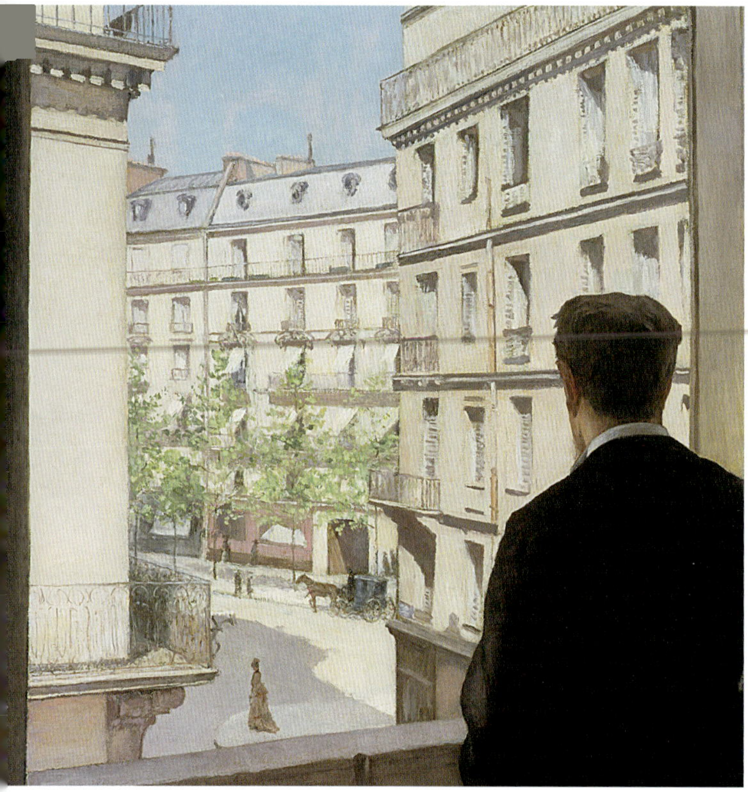

118 Gustave Caillebotte, *Young Man at His Window* (detail of fig. 117).

point of view of the young man, as if we are meant to forget our separateness from him in our involvement with the scene, *nor* with a distinct point of view that includes him and the scene, as if the relative positions of the young man and woman, carriage, and horses were strictly a function of our situatedness further back in the apartment. All this is to say that the *Young Man at His Window* at once raises the question of its relation to the beholder in an especially pointed way and leaves the question unresolved, hovering in the air, between two alternatives neither of which exactly fits the case.[9]

Finally, although we cannot see the young man's face, his stance and demeanor are such that we do not doubt that he is deeply absorbed in his contemplation of the scene below. Absorption, of course, plays a central role in my account of the issues at stake in French eighteenth- and nineteenth-century painting; here I need only add that in Manet's revolutionary cavases of the first half of the 1860s – where the primordial convention that paintings are made to be beheld is thematized with a new explicitness, not to say vehemence – a number of motifs which, treated differently, could have been made to serve the ends of absorption were on the contrary treated in a way that voided or "flattened" them, that positively denied their absorptive potential, to the consternation of Manet's viewers for a long time to come. (The relevant comparison is with Manet's *Balcony* [1868–9; fig. 119], a work that Caillebotte not only knew but bought for his collection.) Much more is said about Manet's negation of absorption in *Manet's Modernism*,[10] but here I want simply to point out, first, that Caillebotte throughout his career was an intensely absorptive painter, and second, that Caillebotte's exploitation of absorption must be seen as returning to, as deliberately resuming, a tradition (to stay with that term) which Manet's paintings of the 1860s and after may be said, if not to have liquidated, at any rate to have radically called into question.[11] Alternatively it might be argued that Caillebotte unthinkingly continued an absorptive tradition that despite

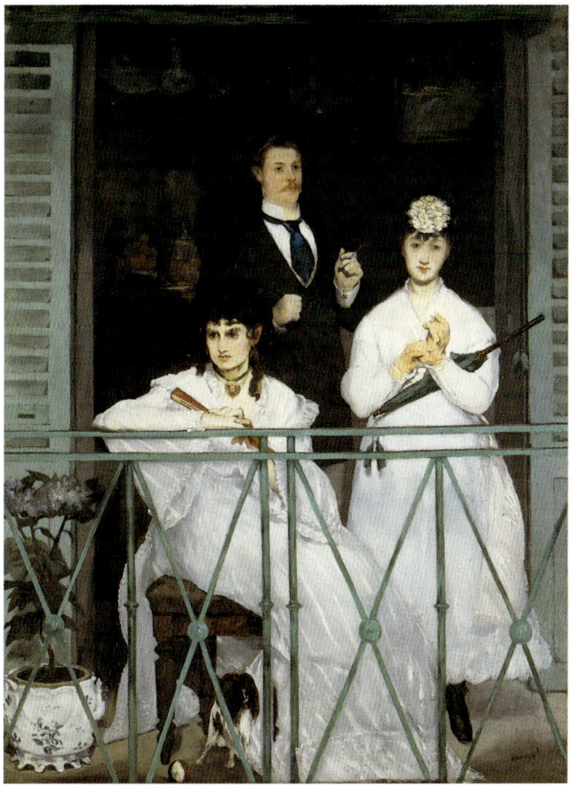

119 Edouard Manet, *The Balcony*, 1868–9. Oil on canvas. 169 × 125 cm. Paris, Musée d'Orsay.

Manet's intervention was never simply abandoned. But I credit Caillebotte with a degree of historical awareness that leads me to favor the first account. In any event, Caillebotte's art raises in a particularly acute form the issue of the meaning of Manet's paintings of the 1860s and early 70s for the advanced painters that followed immediately in his wake (in 1875, when *Young Man at His Window* was painted, Manet was forty-three years old and a vital force on the contemporary scene). I will add that Duranty, the author of *La Nouvelle Peinture*, was from first to last an absorptive critic, which is why Caillebotte and for that matter Degas appealed to him so powerfully.[12] (It also explains his lack of enthusiasm for Manet.) This is equally true of Huysmans, who, like many critics of the time, like Duranty in fact, reserved his most fervent admiration for paintings in which an absorptive thematics gave rise to an effect of more than ordinary realism. "That supreme quality of art, life, shines forth from this canvas with a truly incredible intensity," Huysmans wrote of Caillebotte's *Interior, Woman at the Window* (1880; fig. 120), a work whose affiliation with the canvas we have been looking at is obvious.[13] The *Interior* is particularly fascinating in that the woman viewed from behind

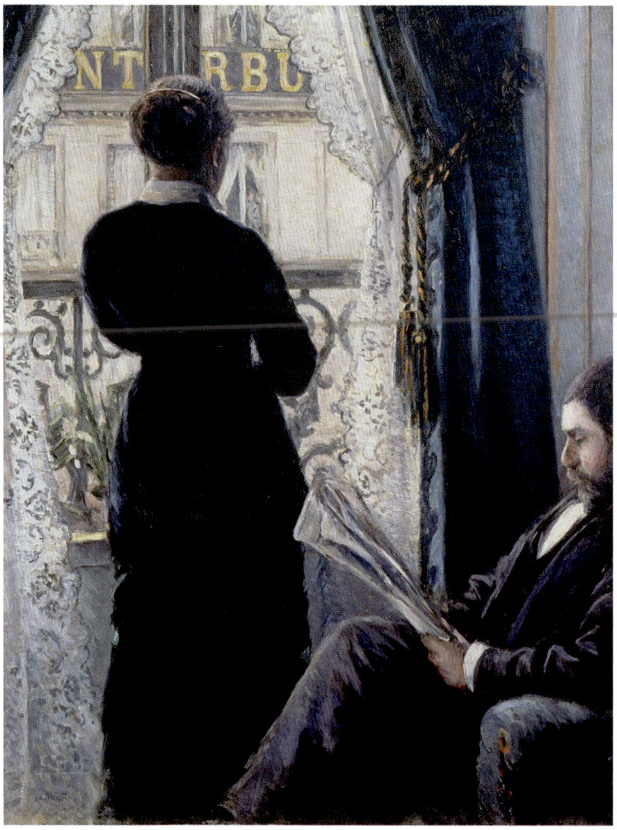

120 Gustave Caillebotte, *Interior, Woman at the Window*, 1880. Oil on canvas. 116 × 89 cm. Private collection.

is shown looking toward a building on the other side of the street that bears on a slightly higher level a large sign with letters of gold (we are shown the letters "NT" and then, after a gap, "RBU"). I see that facing and eye-catching element[14] as an affirmation of Manet's stress on what in *Manet's Modernism* I call "facingness," just as I see the bearded man seated in an armchair and reading a newspaper as a further thematization of absorption. (The whole of Huysmans's commentary on the *Interior*, with its emphasis on the physical reality of the woman, the man's obliviousness to her, and the gold letters of the sign on the building across the street, is pertinent to our discussion.)

The other major picture that Caillebotte exhibited in 1876, the *Floor-Scrapers* (1875; fig. 121), also invites comparison with Courbet's art, specifically with his famous painting of men at work, the *Stonebreakers* (1849; fig. 81).[15] In the *Floor-Scrapers*, however, the workers are not depicted from the rear or from the side with faces turned away or

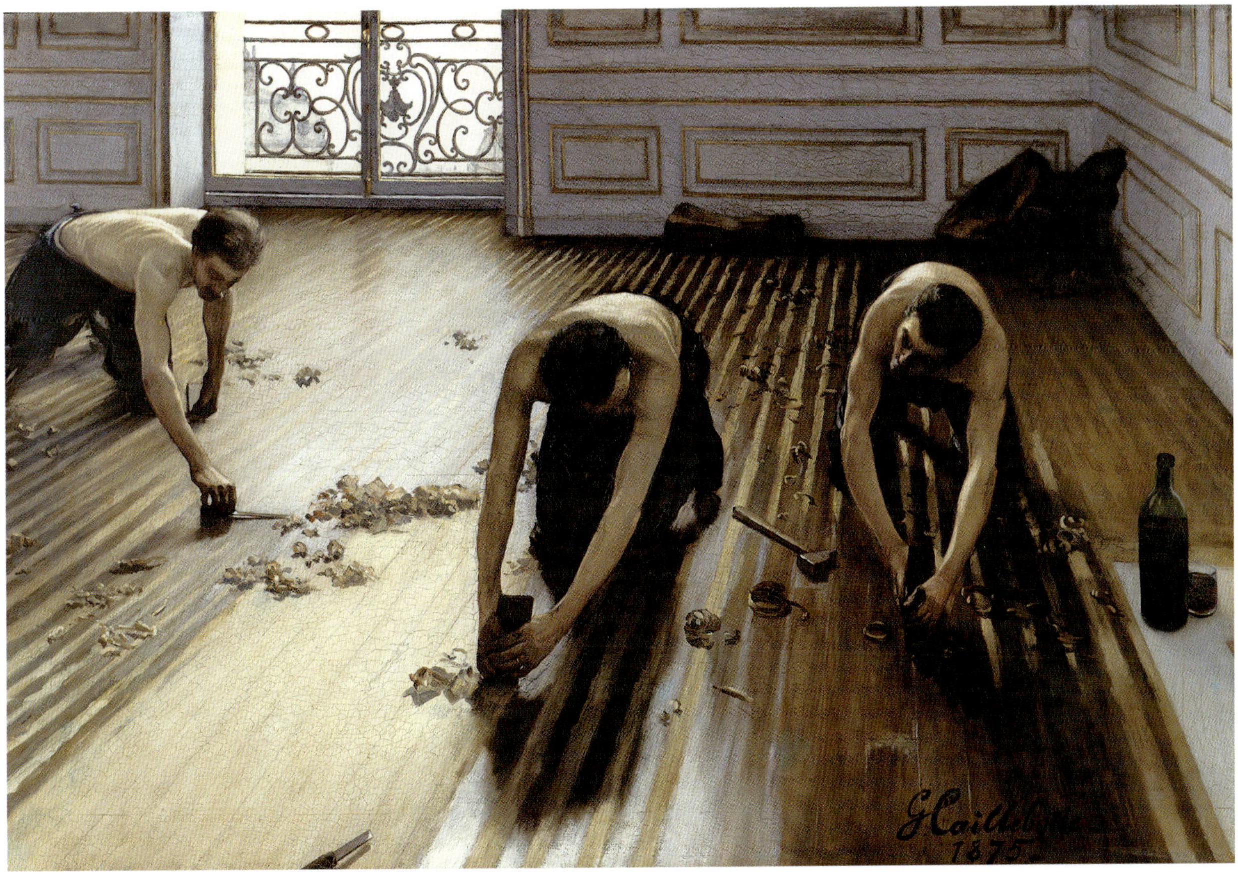

121 Gustave Caillebotte, *The Floor-Scrapers*, 1875. Oil on canvas. 102 × 146 cm. Paris, Musée d'Orsay.

otherwise withheld from view, as in the *Stonebreakers*, but instead are presented more or less frontally, reaching and thrusting bodily toward the foreground of the picture. Or so it appears at first glance. In fact, the actions of the central worker are more complex than this implies: looking at him closely, and considering his actions in relation both to the patch of lighter floor to his right (our left) and to the pile of wood-shavings at the back end of that patch, we see that he is drawing his tool toward him, which would mean that even as he "faces" us and has reached toward us he is in the act of moving away. This is not true of the worker at the right, however, who although slightly farther back seems to be moving toward us. The verbal communication that appears to be taking place between the two men (the worker on the right glancing toward and seemingly saying something to the one in the middle) would therefore mark their approaching one another in the course of their labors.[16] Crucially, however, the nature

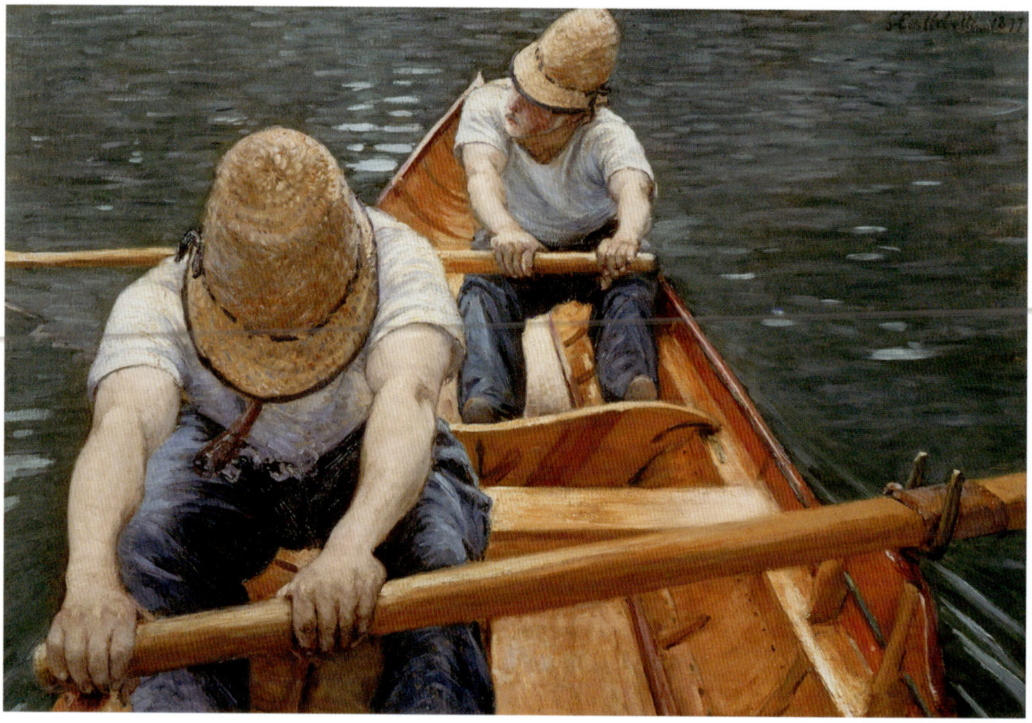

122 Gustave Caillebotte, *Oarsmen*, 1877. Oil on canvas. 81 × 116 cm. Private collection.

of all three workers' labors together with the unusual perspective of the ground plane largely obscures their faces (the light falling on their backs contributes to this as well), and even more powerfully than in the *Young Man at His Window* we intuit their *un*Manet-like absorption in their repetitive and demanding physical tasks. Put slightly differently, there is in the floor-scrapers' bodily orientation a kind of *forcing* of the issue of absorption – although the figures "face" and reach towards us, they appear wholly immersed in the world of their labors, as if in simultaneous affirmation of and dialectical response to Manet's liquidation of absorption in the interests of facingness.[17] This type of structure recurs in Caillebotte's oeuvre, nowhere more conspicuously than in his *Oarsmen* (1877; fig. 122). In that picture Caillebotte has artfully and, I think, altogether knowingly invested figures whose bodies face the viewer and who (especially the nearest rower) are extremely close to the picture plane with the quality of absorption, and moreover has found in the dynamics of rowing (which involve the sort of double arm movements just attributed to the actions of the middle floor-scraper) a means of propelling those figures into the space of the painting in a Courbet-like manner, or rather with a sense of vectoredness that goes well beyond anything in Courbet. Note too how,

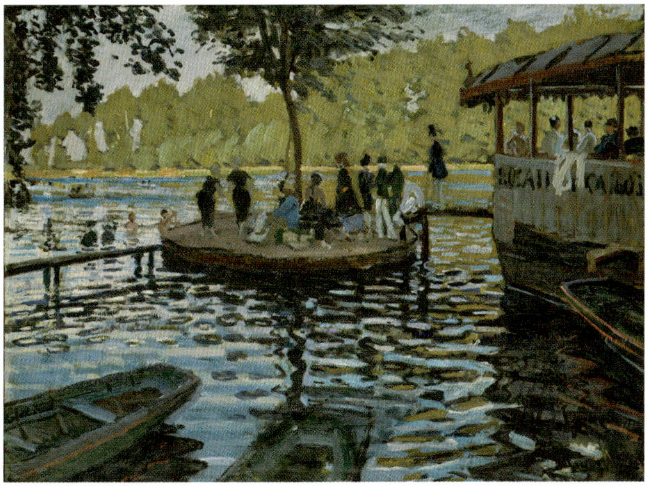

123 Claude Monet, *La Grenouillère*, 1869. Oil on canvas. 74.6 × 99.7 cm. New York, The Metropolitan Museum of Art, H. O. Havemeyer Collection, Bequest of Mrs. H. O. Havemeyer, 1929 (29.100.112).

despite the orientation of their bodies the two rowers' faces are effectively obscured, much like those of the stonebreakers in Courbet's canvas. It may be that the rather mechanical execution of the *Oarsmen* is related to the extent to which it represents an almost diagrammatic solution to the problem of reconciling Courbet and Manet in a single compositional structure.[18]

Two other features of the *Floor-Scrapers* deserve particular emphasis. The first, often commented on and briefly mentioned above, is the distinctive perspective structure that makes the floor seem to fall away beneath our feet (we saw a less dramatic version of this in the floor-plane of the *Young Man at His Window*).[19] The second feature, which has been noted but never thought to call for interpretation, is the bright, diffuse reflection of daylight entering the room through the window at the left rear from the wetted floor. I want to focus for a moment on that reflection, which I take to be one of the signature effects or tropes of Caillebotte's art. (As in the gleaming wet paving stones in *Paris Street; Rainy Day* or, in a different register, the partial reflection in the open window of the protagonist of the *Young Man at His Window*.) Simply put, I see the reflected daylight in the *Floor-Scrapers* and other works by Caillebotte not only as deriving from but also as alluding to one of the most sensational Impressionist or more accurately proto-Impressionist discoveries, the evocation of broken or diffuse reflections, of optical glisten or dazzle, as for example in Monet's *La Grenouillère* (1869; fig.

123) or similar pictures of bodies of water by him, Pissarro, and Sisley.[20] More strongly, I take Caillebotte's obsession with reflections and dazzle to be *the* marker or signal in his work of an overarching though also only partial allegiance to the ocular priorities of Impressionism, meaning by the latter the art of the "core" or landscape Impressionists around and including Monet. (Caillebotte being essentially a figure painter, this is tantamount to a desire to bridge the potential division between the landscapists and the figure painters within the larger group.[21]) But if that is the case, how are we to understand the relation of those reflections and dazzle, in the *Floor-Scrapers* as well as in other works by Caillebotte, to the plunging perspective construction that there as elsewhere largely governs our sense of relation as beholders to the representation as a whole? Observe, in this connection, how in the *Floor-Scrapers* the perspective structure and the reflection are, if not at odds, at least plainly disjunct from one another; the lines of the floorboards recede precipitously toward a vanishing point just slightly above the canvas and considerably to the right of center (it sits almost directly over the right shoulder of the rightmost of the three workmen), while the daylight flooding the room from the window at the rear left seems to obey another set of laws entirely or at any rate to spill across the receding floorboard lines without regard for their ever-accelerating recession. (The dazzle floods toward us, the floorboards race away.) This leads me to suggest that in the *Floor-Scrapers* and similar works a violently receding perspective structure produces effects of dislocation and spatial vertigo that belong to a bodily register, in opposition to the ocular register of the reflections or dazzle. But the opposition is not absolute, not only because the ocular as such is a bodily register (as Merleau-Ponty indefatigably reminds us[22]), but also because in the *Floor-Scrapers* the dazzle like the perspective recession is scenically dislocating. More precisely, it threatens to dematerialize the ground plane, though in other respects the dazzle itself (here and throughout Caillebotte's art) is a quintessentially material or say materialist effect, a point brought out with near-hallucinatory force by its juxtaposition with the brilliantly rendered, almost trompe-l'oeil wood-shavings that in terms of the represented scene are nothing other than a material *excess* over and beyond the horizontal surface of the floor. (They are also a corporeal motif in that as *coils* of wood they may be seen as palpably expressing or "containing" the bodily labor that produced them.[23])

One more association with Courbet is worth noting: the similarity between Courbet's characteristic and notoriously large signature – for example, the one in the *Stonebreakers* (fig. 124) – and Caillebotte's signature at the lower right of the *Floor-Scrapers* (fig. 125). Obviously it is the merest coincidence that the two men shared the same first name and that their surnames began with the letter "C." But it is not at all a coincidence that Caillebotte signed his painting in a manner that deliberately recalls the master of

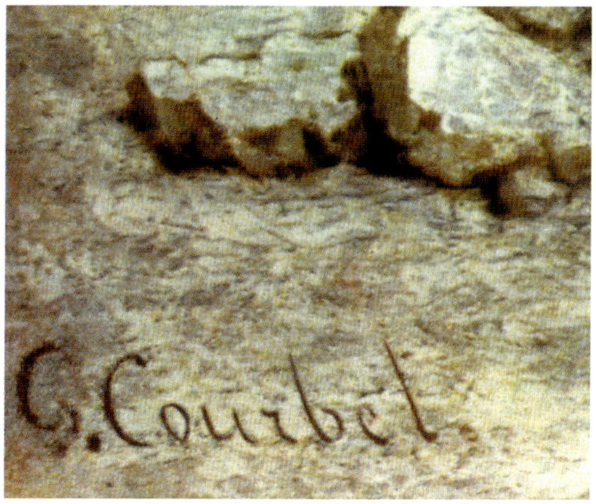

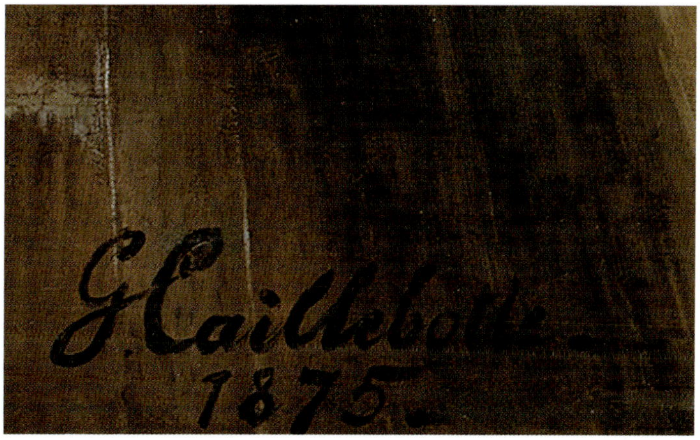

124 (*above, left*) Gustave Courbet, *Stonebreakers*, 1849 (detail of fig. 81).

125 (*above, right*) Gustave Caillebotte, *The Floor-Scrapers*, 1875 (detail of fig. 121).

Ornans by virtue both of the use of the first initial ("G. Courbet"/"G. Caillebotte") and of the striking orthographic similarity between the two signatures, the main difference being that Caillebotte replaced the backward lean of Courbet's printlike signature with the more scriptive forward lean of his own. I shall have more to say about the implications of this highly charged reference to Courbet further on.[24]

2

At this juncture I want to accelerate my analysis by putting forward five large generalizations about Caillebotte's project as I have come to understand it, the last of which will involve a detailed discussion of the political resonance of several of his paintings. Following that I shall look briefly at a further sequence of works by way of bringing this essay to a close. The generalizations are as follows:

(1) Whatever else it may have involved, Caillebotte's project was an attempt to return to – more accurately, to recover – a certain realism of the body, the most forceful modern French expression of which was the art of Courbet, while remaining faithful to key premises of the ocular realism associated with Impressionism and also while taking account of the epochal if profoundly ambiguous fact of Manet's intervention.[25] The three elements in Caillebotte's attempted synthesis – Courbet, Manet, Impressionism –

represent distinct, successive, not obviously compatible moments or phases in the dialectic of recent painting; the effort to be faithful to them all would therefore have put Caillebotte's art under enormous strain, a recognition that makes the brevity of his career as an ambitious painter seem less surprising. But the concentration and purposiveness that we discover in his most impressive canvases must surely have been inseparable from the magnitude of that effort.

(2) Closely related to the project just summarized but not identical with it, Caillebotte's art imagines a *material or materialist* Impressionism, perhaps in opposition to what from an early date were recognized to be Impressionism's *idealist* propensities, that is, its tendency as a matter of practice to define the "impression" as an internal, necessarily subjective "event" rather than strictly as the objective record of an external object or scene.[26] The key text in this regard is the critic Jules-Antoine Castagnary's largely positive article on the first Impressionist exhibition of 1874, in which however he expressed reservations about what he saw as the young painters' commitment to rendering "not the landscape but the sensation [that is, the impression] produced by the landscape. . . . In this way, they leave reality behind and fully enter idealism."[27] Insofar as it was within his power, Caillebotte was determined not to let this happen. (More on his materialism below.)

(3) I have already said that Caillebotte throughout his career favored absorptive subjects of the sort that had been the staple of the Diderotian tradition from Greuze through Millet. (Manet's cogenerationists Legros and Fantin-Latour were also strongly absorptive painters, as indeed was Courbet, though the latter fact was often missed by commentators brought up short by other aspects of his art.) In fact Caillebotte favored particularly intense and, where possible, bodily versions of such subjects, as in the *Floor-Scrapers*, the *Oarsmen*, or, a late and inadvertently almost comic work, *Portrait of a Man Writing in His Study* (1885; fig. 126), which comes across as an evocation not just of absorption in writing but also of the bodily condition of nearsightedness to the extent that it scarcely seems a portrait at all. But the portraits by Caillebotte that are farthest from that canvas, portraits in which the sitter gazes frontally out of the painting, more often than not are marked by an awkwardness of *mise-en-scène* and even a harshness of color and execution that suggest that the painter was uncomfortable when for whatever reason he found himself compelled to portray a personage not absorbed in the world of the representation. (The feeling of self-assurance conveyed by Caillebotte's *Self-Portrait at the Easel* [see fig. 141], in which the depicted painter presumably gazes straight ahead at his own reflection in a mirror, only proves my point [see the detailed

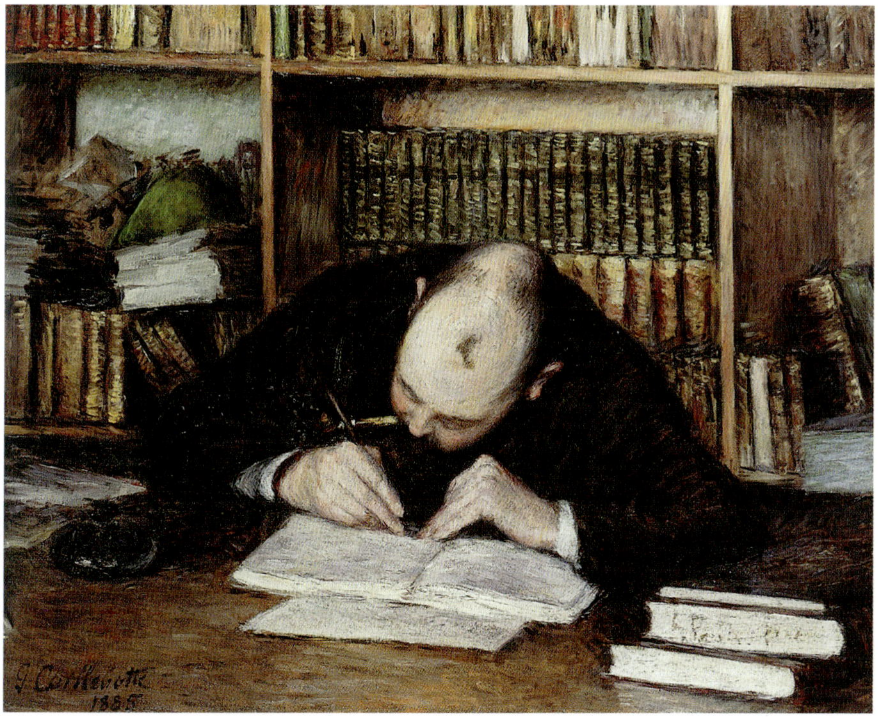

126 Gustave Caillebotte, *Portrait of Man Writing in His Study*, 1885. Oil on canvas. 65 × 82 cm. Private collection.

discussion of that painting in the last part of this essay].) There is thus an important sense in which Caillebotte's commitment to absorption, like his concern with a Courbet-like realism of the body, was backward-looking or at least at odds with the attitude of the most advanced painting of his day. It is significant, for example, that – as I remarked in "David/Manet" earlier – Monet in the late 1860s found himself compelled to give up figure painting for landscape largely because he could not resolve the problem of the appropriate states of mind of his personages, whom he evidently wished to appear unaware of the beholder but whom he drew back from depicting as absorbed in the traditional manner. (*Women in the Garden* [1867; see fig. 17] shows his quandary at its most acute.[28]) This in turn suggests that it was Caillebotte's embrace of absorption that allowed him, for a time, to practice figure painting in an ambitious spirit while remaining more or less faithful to Impressionism as a movement. But we should not be surprised to find that absorption's dependence on effects of inwardness and closure – on a metaphorics of "depth" – was in tension with Impressionism's emphasis on surface liveliness and what as early as 1874 was called decorative unity.

(4) Because of their divided, multiple commitments, Caillebotte's paintings posit a complex, often seemingly conflictual relation to the beholder. We have seen instances of this in the *Young Man at His Window* and the *Floor-Scrapers* (also in the *Oarsmen*), and various observations by Varnedoe and Galassi bear on the topic,[29] but perhaps no picture in Caillebotte's oeuvre is more revealing in this regard than *The Pont de l'Europe (Variant)* in the Kimbell Art Museum in Fort Worth (1876–7; fig. 127), which seems at once to thematize absorbed beholding and to give the actual beholder as good as nothing to look at. The depicted scene takes place on the bridge itself; the principal figure, a *bon bourgeois* in an overcoat and top hat, pauses with his back partly turned toward us and his face mostly turned away as he looks past the massive iron trellis towards the Gare St.-Lazare, which we glimpse in the right background through an opening in the bridge. A second man, also seen from the rear, in a bright blue workman's smock and bowler hat (a combination, the recent exhibition catalogue suggests, indicating that he is a *petit bourgeois*, probably "both a laborer and a businessman, possibly a shopkeeper" [*UI*, 107]), leans on the iron rail to the left of the standing man and apparently gazes down at the tracks below. And a third man, also in overcoat and top hat, walks briskly out of the picture space at the extreme left, his face and body cropped down the middle by the left-hand framing edge. In this case the refusal to show all three men's faces is a source of frustration for the viewer, as are, if my experience is a guide, the painting's overall gray and blue tonality and just slightly blurred or out-of-focus facture, which come close to neutralizing the distinctions of costume and social class that the painter was at pains to record (and that, as we shall see, are sharply described in the Geneva *Pont de l'Europe* and the *House-Painters*). Moreover, the large crossing girders that dominate the right-hand half of the composition invite being read as cancelling vision itself, or at least as equating the entire scene with an act of deliberate negation (I am mainly thinking of the girders that cross very near the right-hand framing edge, but there is also the smaller crossing that takes place just to the right of the head of the standing *bourgeois*).[30] Indeed the unconvincing, because too upright, perspective recession of the two pairs of diverging tracks that we glimpse through holes in the iron railing toward the right is a further sign of a vexed relation to vision, as if the difference in social class between the two gazing figures and perhaps also a related difference between the respective *degrees* of their absorption – the central figure seeming merely to pause and look as opposed to gaze intently as does the *petit bourgeois* – precluded a coherent, natural-seeming treatment of the vista open before them (compare the political reading of the Geneva *Pont de l'Europe* to be developed shortly [see fig. 129]).[31] Also contributing to an effect of standoff is the tension between the painting's thematics of absorption or say of (perhaps momentarily) captivated viewing, with its suggestion of

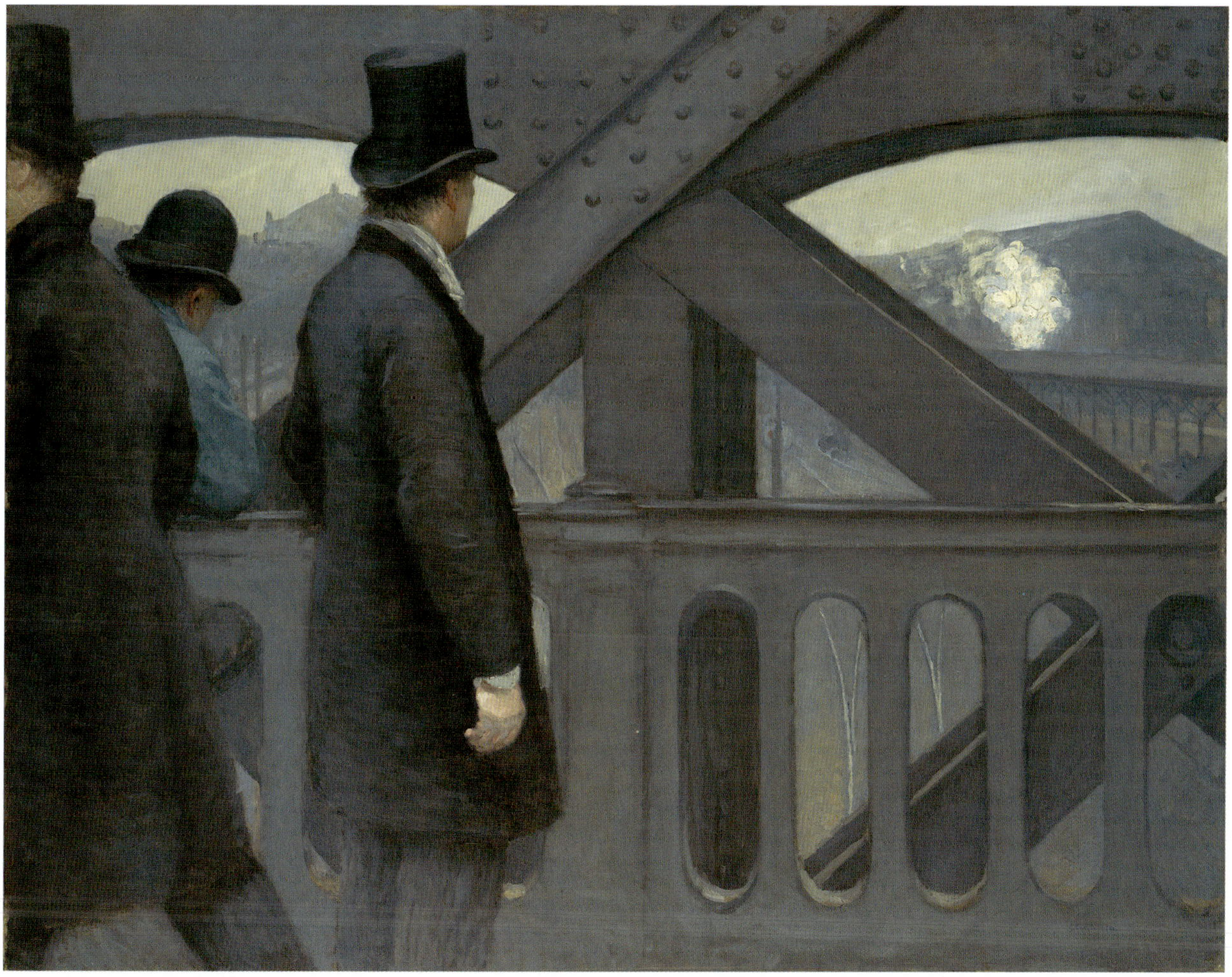

127 Gustave Caillebotte, *The Pont de l'Europe (Variant)*, 1876–7. Oil on canvas. 105.7 × 130.8 cm. Fort Worth, Kimbell Art Museum.

a "beyond" that the viewer is led at least to imagine, and the uncharacteristically brushy and quasi-monochromatic handling of the picture surface that enforces a more distanced or "aesthetic" stance towards the painting as a whole.[32] The larger issue at stake in all this is the fate of ambitious figure painting – also of absorption – in the wake of Manet's momentous but in his own time scarcely intelligible liquidation of the Diderotian enterprise, his acknowledgment, mobilizing every technical, formal, and thematic resource at his command, of the ineluctable truth (I earlier called it the primordial convention) that paintings *are* made to be beheld. (In *Manet's Modernism* I argue that

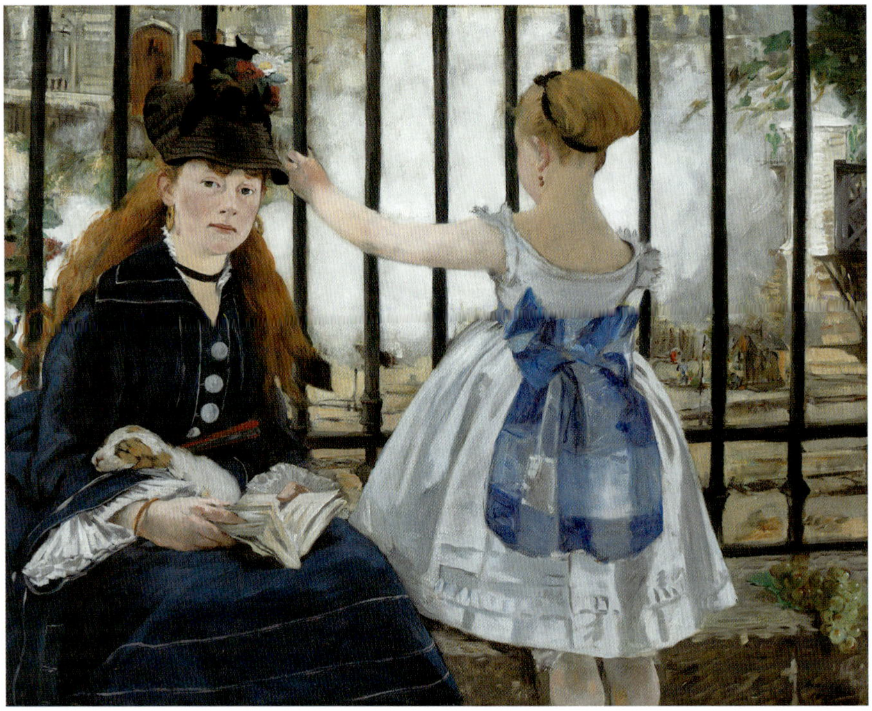

128 Edouard Manet, *Gare St.-Lazare*, 1873. Oil on canvas. 113 × 132.7 cm. Washington, D.C., National Gallery of Art. Gift of Horace Havemeyer in memory of his mother, Louisine W. Havemeyer, 1956.10.1.

the effect of that liquidation is something other than theatricality *tout court.*[33]) In the Fort Worth picture a similar acknowledgment is conveyed by its sheer resistance to vision – not just to visual penetration but, to a large extent, to visual pleasure and interest – a *tour de force* of self-denial that distinguishes Caillebotte's canvas from a work it otherwise partly resembles, Manet's *Gare St.-Lazare* (1873; fig. 128). In the latter, of course, the young girl looking away from us through iron railings at a cloud of steam from a passing train is accompanied by a seated woman, the mature Victorine Meurent, whose gaze confronts our own. For all the conflictedness of Caillebotte's art, a *strikingly* oppositional structure of that sort was simply out of bounds, as was the vibrant, energizing contrast in Manet's picture between the dark railings and the white steam.[34]

(5) I agree with some of Caillebotte's recent commentators that there is a specific politics to several of his paintings. I have noted a version of that politics in the *Floor-Scrapers*, where it finds expression not simply in the Courbet-like depiction of urban

laborers at work in a bourgeois apartment but also, no less tellingly, in the obviously intended similarity between Caillebotte's and Courbet's signatures. In 1875 Courbet was in exile in Switzerland, having been condemned by the French courts to outrageous penalties for allegedly having been responsible for the toppling during the Commune of the Vendôme Column celebrating Napoleon's victories.[35] Caillebotte's double reference to Courbet's art, by way of subject matter and signature, can only have been intended as a declaration of political as well as artistic allegiance, if not as a deliberate provocation, at a moment when moderate Republicanism was in the ascendant but when a significant faction within the government, headed by the monarchist president, Marshal MacMahon, was anything but devotedly Republican in orientation.[36] Caillebotte's gesture appears to have gone unnoticed, and no doubt would have been regarded as quixotic had it been understood.

Two other works by Caillebotte have been recognized as being of particular relevance in this connection. The more important of the two, *The Pont de l'Europe* in Geneva (1876; fig. 129), is interestingly and, up to a point, insightfully discussed by Julia Sagraves in an essay entitled "The Street" in the 1994 catalogue. Briefly, she associates that painting with what she calls the moderate Republican agenda for the streets of Paris. "Perhaps even more so than the imperial government before it," she writes,

> the coalition of men who worked together during the 1870s to establish a Republican government were anxious to wipe away the memories of revolution and to diffuse both the imperial and the revolutionary associations of the Paris street. Thus, the stabilization of the republic in the years between 1876 and 1879 was accompanied by a national, and overtly Republican, reclamation of the street [*UI*, 91].

What was partly at stake in this, she explains, was the notion of a reconciliation of social classes (92); accordingly she sees Caillebotte's *Pont de l'Europe* as implicitly promoting such a notion via the relationship between the *bon bourgeois flâneur* in black overcoat and top hat who is depicted walking toward us and the worker in a blue smock leaning on the iron railing of the bridge, "a relationship . . . reinforced by the gaze that the *flâneur* appears to cast in the direction of the leaning worker" (97).[37] If, as seems likely, the figure of the *flâneur* is a self-portrait, Sagraves adds, the "distinctly emphasized, albeit tense" relationship between the *flâneur* and worker "at whom he seems to stare" is given added significance. By analogy with what she takes to be Caillebotte's apparent identification with the figures of house-painters in a picture we shall examine in a moment, "it may also be possible to consider *The Pont de l'Europe* as an image that addresses Caillebotte's own dual social identification" as a worker, that is, a painter, and as a *bon bourgeois* (97).

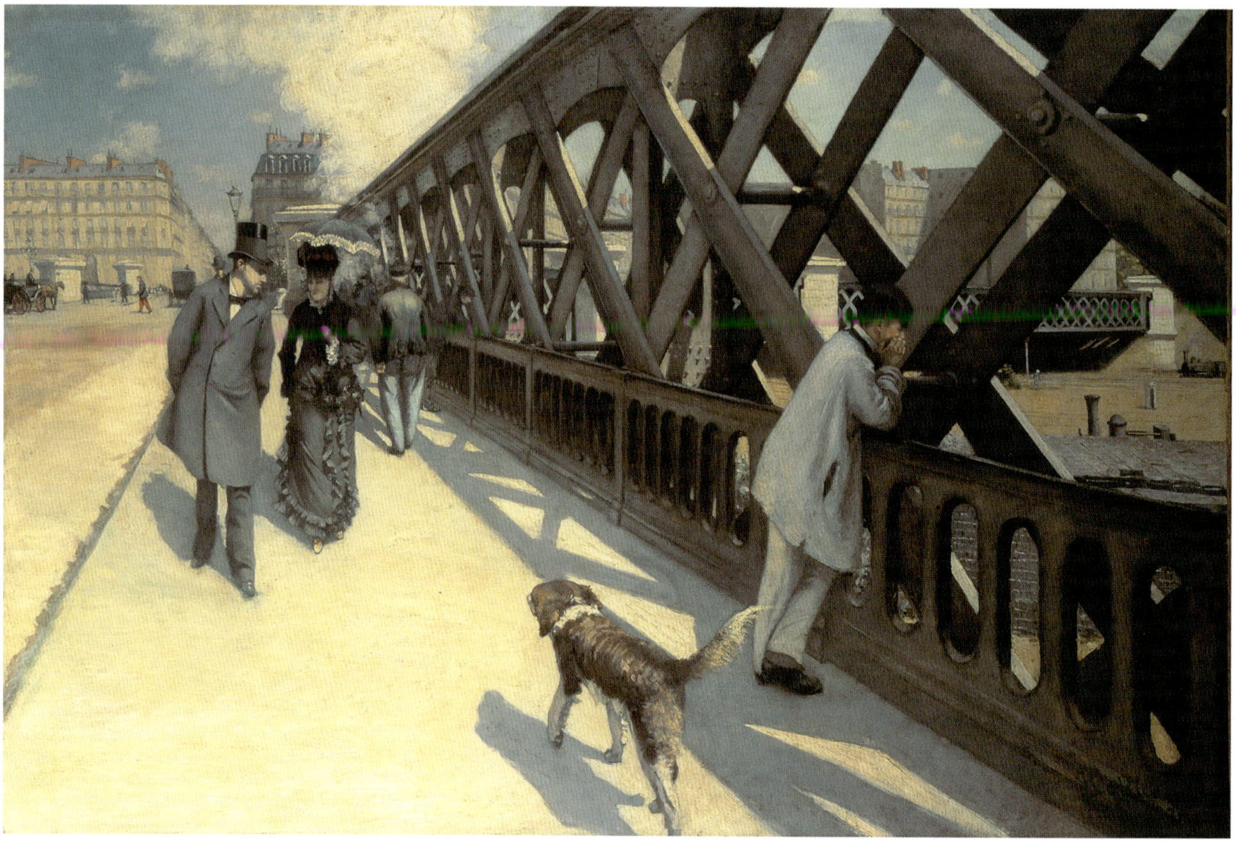

129 Gustave Caillebotte, *The Pont de l'Europe*, 1876. Oil on canvas. 125 × 180 cm. Geneva, Musée du Petit Palais.

The locale itself, Sagraves stresses, was one where different social classes came into daily contact; although the site had been the scene of heavy fighting during the Commune, the painting presents a "roomy, airy expanse of sidewalk that allows pedestrians ample passing distance, permitting them to share its space comfortably with dissimilar social types, and even a dog" (97, slightly recast).[38] In short the *Pont de l'Europe* is read by Sagraves as a determinedly pacific and antihierarchical image, "the compositional leveling underlining the social leveling suggested by its subject" (97). As for the elegantly dressed woman in black and carrying an umbrella to ward off the sun, Sagraves characterizes her relationship to the *flâneur* as unclear, which it surely is. But whereas she sees the *flâneur* as distracted by the woman while the latter in turn glances suggestively toward him (Sagraves also says that "the gaze that this artist-*flâneur* directs towards the worker . . . is indeterminately shared with" the woman [97]), closer scrutiny reveals that he has overtaken her and is looking with interest to his left (note the forward and sideways lean of his upper body) while she may well be looking not at the *flâneur* but at someone or something else entirely beyond the picture edge to her right. Here I arrive at a further and pivotal disagreement with Sagraves, which is that I read the *flâneur*'s look as directed not, as she believes, *at* the absorbed worker but rather in the *same slightly downward direction* as that of the worker, which is to say in the direction of an off-canvas scene (perhaps the Gare St.-Lazare itself, perhaps simply the gleaming tracks) which is the object of both their contemplations but which we cannot see.[39] The political meaning of the painting would therefore reside not in any supposed homology between compositional and social leveling, and even less in any supposed reference to the social space-sharing that took place on the Pont de l'Europe itself, but rather, simultaneously, in the assertion, at that historical moment, of unnegotiable difference between the two men and the social classes they exemplify *and* in the intimation of a common or rather a converging aim or destination, one that remains at a distance from the present reality and cannot actually be represented but can only be imagined, wished for, fantasized. It follows that the figure of the woman, however we are to understand the precise social connotations of her dress and demeanor, is a kind of feint or lure; the direction of her glance, toward our left, throws into relief the impossible but, I suggest, passionately desired communion between the men.[40] Understood in this light, the *Pont de l'Europe* is indeed a Republican work, but one that honors the terrible wounds left by the bloody repression of the Commune not quite five years before and that therefore portrays the contemporary situation as disallowing the very inter-class identification and leveling that the painting implicitly posits as a social and political ideal. Put slightly differently, the imaginary politics of the *Pont de l'Europe*, like that of the *Floor-Scrapers* with its allusions to Courbet, may be more *radically* Republican than Sagraves's intelligent but at times insufficiently nuanced commentary suggests.[41]

One last point: the implication that the two men's lines of sight converge and meet somewhere off-picture distinguishes the Geneva canvas from its Fort Worth variant, in which the *petit bourgeois* and *bon bourgeois* appear to be looking in somewhat different directions. On the other hand, the difference in the Geneva picture between the *flâneur*'s mobile, fleeting, though definitely interested look and the worker's prolonged absorption in the off-picture scene is analogous to the difference in the Fort Worth variant between the halted *bourgeois*'s seemingly momentary act of attention and the temporally extended gazing of the *petit bourgeois*. In both cases, the difference between modes of seeing occurs across class lines.[42] But perhaps the deeper, quasi-allegorical meaning of that difference is that the enterprise of painting as Caillebotte understood it required *both* mobile looking and prolonged gazing, and that by personifying the first by the

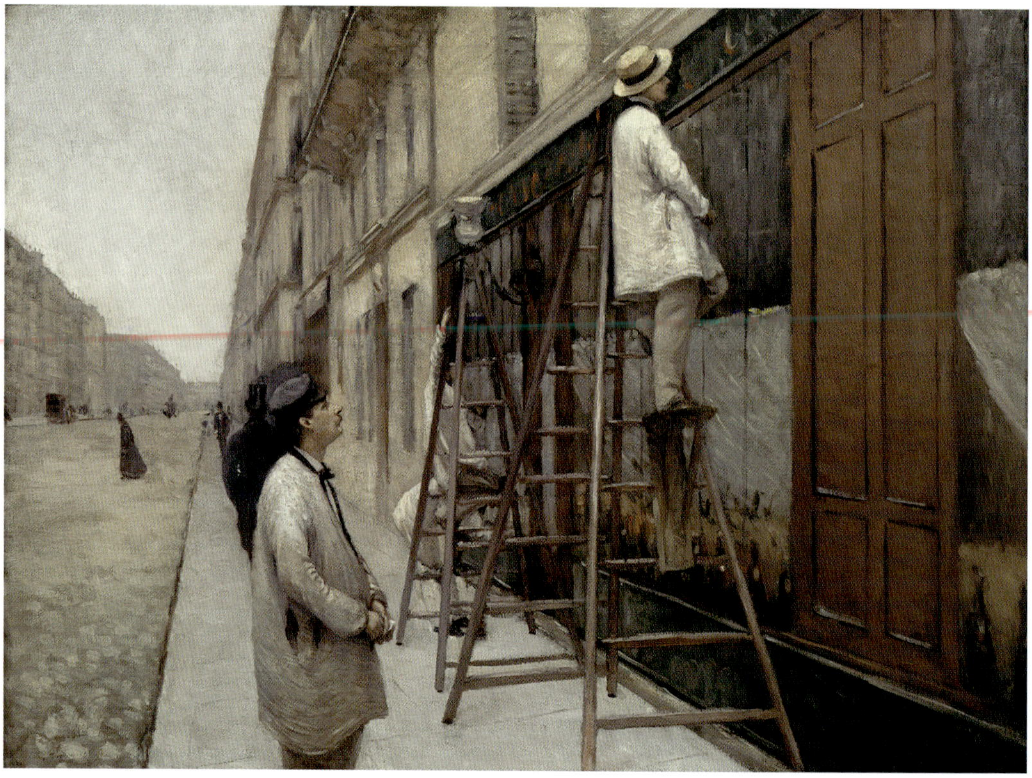

130 Gustave Caillebotte, *The House-Painters*, 1877. Oil on canvas. 87 × 116 cm. Private collection.

flâneur and the second by the worker and *petit bourgeois*, he associated painting itself with the social leveling or unification that, I have been claiming, was still only an ideal.

In a valuable discussion of another canvas of the mid-1870s, *The House-Painters* (1877; fig. 130), Sagraves calls attention to the pejorative association on the part of hostile critics between Impressionism and house-painting. This leads her to wonder whether Caillebotte might have been "responding to this criticism by underscoring the inadvertent truth of the association," that is, whether "he was indeed identifying the Independents with house-painters – working painters – in the sense that his métier and that of his Impressionist colleagues could be related to the work of the *petit bourgeois* artisan, and insofar as the project of both was to *paint* the city." "If so," she adds, "*House-Painters* underscores the social democracy many believed to be at the heart of the post-war Republican project" (93–4).[43] Again, I would qualify her remarks by questioning the aptness of the notion of identification. For one thing, the stance and action of the nearest and most prominent of the house-painters – standing with hands clasped and looking up contemplatively at the decorative work that has just been done – implies an analogy between that figure and the *viewer* of the painting and by extension of the Impressionist exhibition as a whole. More important, as in the case of the *Pont de l'Europe*, I see the *House-Painters* as asserting, not minimizing, the sharpness of the class difference between the white-smocked workers with their characteristic physiognomies and body language and the top-hatted *bon bourgeois* who is shown walking directly away from the viewer toward the picture's vanishing point and whom the artist has juxtaposed with, indeed partly screened by, the principal house-painter. The inter-class analogy that the painting implies is thus cast in an ironic light that pointedly disables the very identification it seems to propose.[44]

One other painting, *Paris Street; Rainy Day* (1877; fig. 131), is interpreted by Sagraves in political terms, but here I find myself in flat disagreement with her claims. Simply put, she finds in Caillebotte's picture "of Haussmannian Paris after a rainfall an analogous portrait of the modern city just beginning to recover after the hard times – the rainy weather – of 1870–71" (95, slightly recast). I am not persuaded by the analogy, and I am even more skeptical of Sagraves's insistence on the listlessness and spiritlessness of most of its inhabitants and on the negative social import of the scene as a whole. She goes on to write:

> Critics in 1877 often complained that, in Caillebotte's painting of a rainy day, there is no rain [see the excerpts from reviews quoted in *NP*, 209]. Nevertheless the strollers continue to hold open their umbrellas, apparently unaware or unsure of whether the rain has stopped. This cold and damp Paris street appears to be an uncertain, even inhospitable, unwelcoming space, its over-insistent regularity and cleanliness almost psychologically disturbing. It is a space where umbrellas may indeed continue to be necessary for protection, even when there is no longer any rain. In addition to offering cover from the weather, an umbrella was considered at the time as a kind of "defensive arm," requiring a wide passing distance between oneself and one's fellow pedestrians. Umbrellas impose social separation, carving out private from public space. Certainly, the notable presence of steel-framed umbrellas in *Paris Street* reinforces the modernity of the image, dating this portrait of Haussmannian Paris clearly to the postwar decade. But they also intensify the unsociability of Caillebotte's chosen urban space: few figures appear to communicate or to engage another's gaze, and even the two principal figures [the man and woman in the near right foreground] seem deliberately to avoid eye contact with the viewer and with his or her pictorial surrogate, the passerby cut off at the right. (96)[45]

None of this seems right, for the following reasons:

In *Manet's Modernism* I argue that Duranty's *The New Painting* must be understood in the context of his writings of the 1860s and specifically in that of an important but neglected essay published in 1867, "Those Who Will Be the Painters." This leads to the claim that his lifelong advocacy of realism was grounded in a Diderotian commitment to effects of absorption (and hostility toward theatricality), and more broadly that there exists a continuity of concerns between *The New Painting* and "the entire absorptive problematic of the 1860s" which I develop at length earlier in the same chapter. Among those concerns is what I call "a theory of the cloister," according to which the isolation from the world (that is, from beholders) of the cloistral milieu promoted absorptive activities such as meditation and prayer that in turn lent themselves to a an antitheatrical mode of realistic representation (see *MM*, 251–61). Thus for example Dubosc de Pesquidoux, writing in 1863, remarks on how in works by Jules Breton, François Bonvin, Théodule Ribot, and others "the monks, priests, nuns, and choirboys that these artists put before us have a marvelous reality and life," and Duranty in the essay mentioned above praises Alphonse Legros's *Ex-Voto* of 1861 by saying "The accent of a particular world was completely expressed," a statement I gloss by emphasizing that the world in question was a world *apart* and by stressing that "what gave it its apartness, and in a sense its worldlikeness, was the absorption of the kneeling women and in particular their seeming obliviousness to everything but their devotions" (*MM*, 253). The notion of obliviousness or *oubli de soi* is crucial; not only is that state the necessary concomitant of absorption (its outward face, so to speak), it is also, pictorially speaking, the infallible *sign* of absorption, which is to say that according to Duranty's (and other critics') absorptive realist aesthetic, as well as in the painting to which it responded so positively, a certain mutual isolation from one another of persons or small groups of persons – each enclosed in his or her own absorptive lifeworld (to lift a term from early twentieth-century phenomenology) – is positively required. In *The New Painting*, with its insistence on the need for the contemporary painter to leave the studio and go out into the modern urban universe, the theory of the cloister is, as I put it, elaborated "into a theory of the *apartment*, or rather of the relation between the modern urban individual and the particular social spaces – interiors and streets – in which he or she was not just to be found but to be found imprinted, habituated, distracted, absorbed."[46]

Not surprisingly, therefore, where Sagraves sees in *Paris Street; Rainy Day* an image of a conspicuously unsociable urban space within which umbrella-bearing monads avoid all communication with each other, I find a strongly absorptive painting in which the motif of carrying an umbrella to protect oneself from the rain becomes an ingenious device for thematizing a newly mobile and, up to a point, permeable mode of

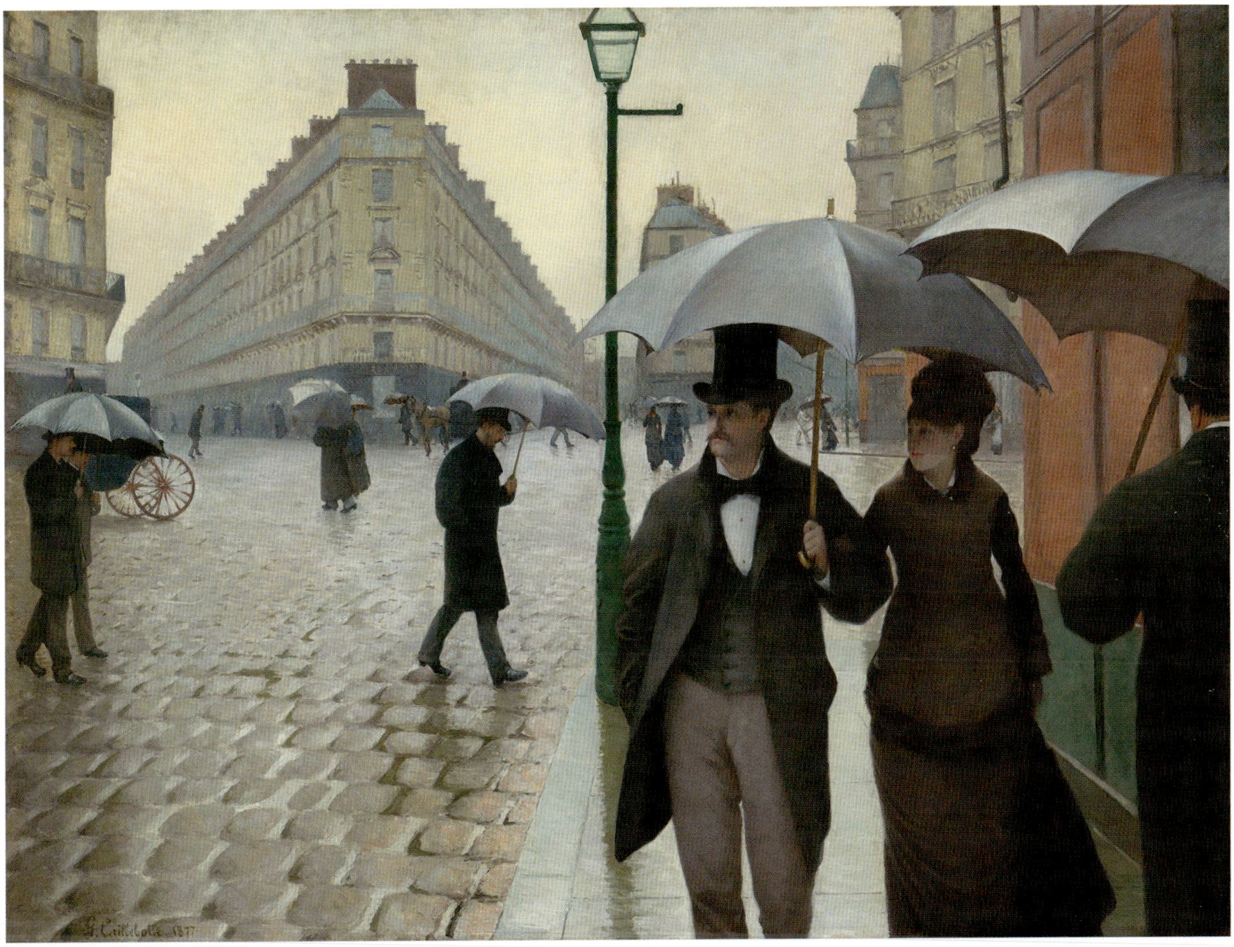

131 Gustave Caillebotte, *Paris Street; Rainy Day*, 1877. Oil on canvas. 212.2 × 276.2 cm. The Art Institute of Chicago, Charles H. and Mary F. S. Worcester Collection, 1964.336.

absorptive closure, one that also allows for the sharing or merging of individual life-worlds, as in the four pairs of figures who perhaps should be seen as the painting's true *leitmotif*: the two men at the extreme left, the two figures in long coats to their left (our right), the two women walking into the distance immediately to the right of the lamp-post, and most prominently the fashionable couple in the right foreground who share a single umbrella and look attentively to their right – their matched gazes seemingly in perfect synchrony – as if at a storefront, person, or other source of interest across the street. Indeed to describe the foreground couple as deliberately and, Sagraves implies, unsociably avoiding eye contact with the viewer, seems to me off-key. The absorptive logic of the composition would have ruled out eye contact from the start, just as the desire to affirm Manet's insistence on facingness would have conduced to having the couple walk directly toward us.[47] (There is no more reason to see the couple's presumed states of mind as alienated or unsociable than there would be to see the rowers in the *Oarsmen* in those terms.) More broadly, Sagraves's distinction between private and public space corresponds neither to Caillebotte's practice nor to Duranty's arguments.[48] All this is not to deny that absorption or its equivalent (for example, attention or distraction) in an urban setting *could* have been thematized in such a way as to evoke a mood of alienation and social fragmentation. But if we approach *Paris Street; Rainy Day* with an understanding of the consistently absorptive basis of Caillebotte's art, as well as with an awareness of the pictorial and critical tradition to which he looked back, we will be unlikely to conclude that that is what is going on.[49] Instead we will see that it offers a new and positive solution to the depiction of absorption in the modern city, and will recognize the sheer dignity of the picture's evenness and openness of color, the muted intensity of its pictorial animation, the absolute rightness of its treatment of movement and gesture. And of course we will discern in the almost magical motif of the glistening paving stones a sign of the painter's allegiance to Impressionism.

"Pay attention in the street toward evening, when the weather is bad, to show how much grace and sweetness can be seen in the faces of the men and women," Leonardo da Vinci wrote in his notebooks.[50] Especially as regards the figure of the foreground woman, whose delicately lidded eyes we glimpse through a fine-meshed, dotted black veil, whose softly parted lips intimate that she may be about to speak, and whose subdued but glowing complexion under her companion's umbrella is set off by her black costume and luminous pearl(?) earring,[51] Leonardo's words evoke an aspect of Caillebotte's intentions that an emphasis on alienation automatically occludes. (This is not to say that the latter was familiar with Leonardo's moving remarks – moving because they seem to imply emotional distance from the men and women he observed with close appreciation – but merely that the remarks bear suggestively on this most poetic of Caillebotte's creations.)

3

A brief look at various works in different genres will help flesh out the broader claims I have just advanced. First, Caillebotte's *Luncheon* (1876; fig. 132), which depicts his mother seated at the far end of a round table and being served by a butler as his brother René intently cuts a piece of meat, forms the latest term in a chronological sequence of

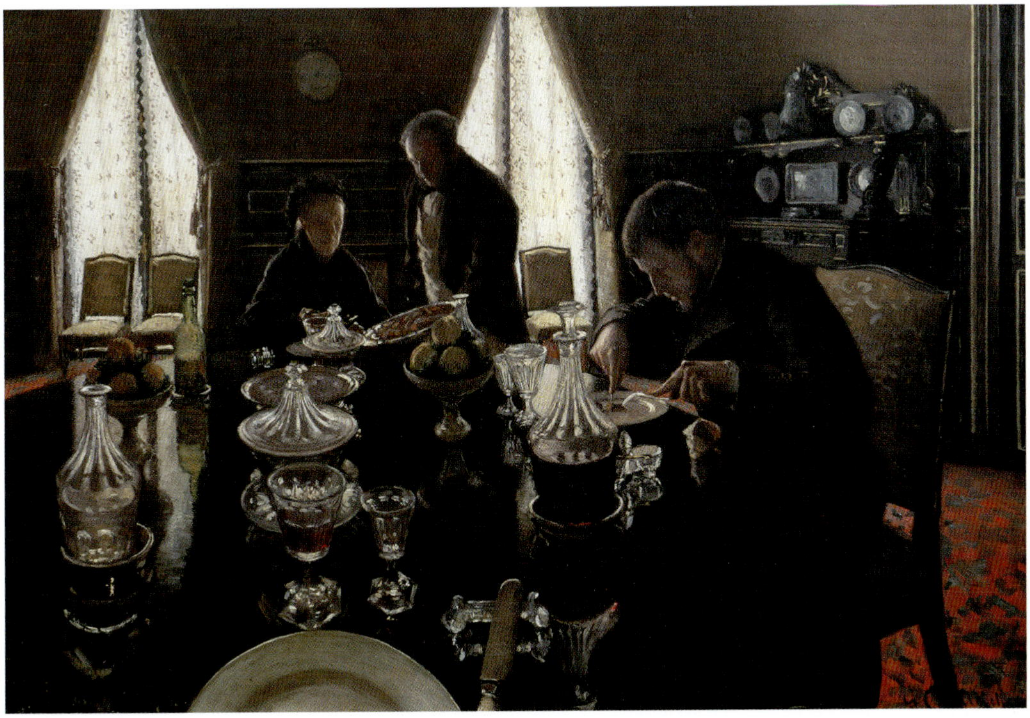

132 Gustave Caillebotte, *The Luncheon*, 1876. Oil on canvas. 52 × 75 cm. Private collection.

133 (*below, left*) Alphonse Legros, *Le Souper*, ca. 1860. Etching. 12.3 × 17.6 cm. Paris, Bibliothèque Nationale, Département des Estampes et de la Photographie.

134 (*below, right*) Edouard Manet, *The Luncheon in the Studio*, 1868. Oil on canvas. 118 × 153 cm. Munich, Bayerische Staatsgemäldesammlungen, Neue Pinakothek.

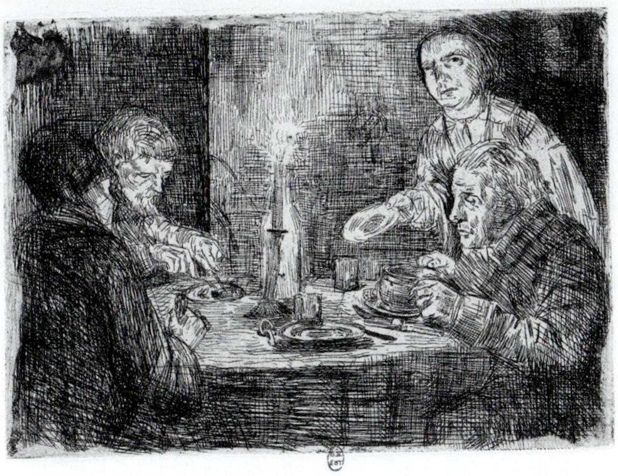

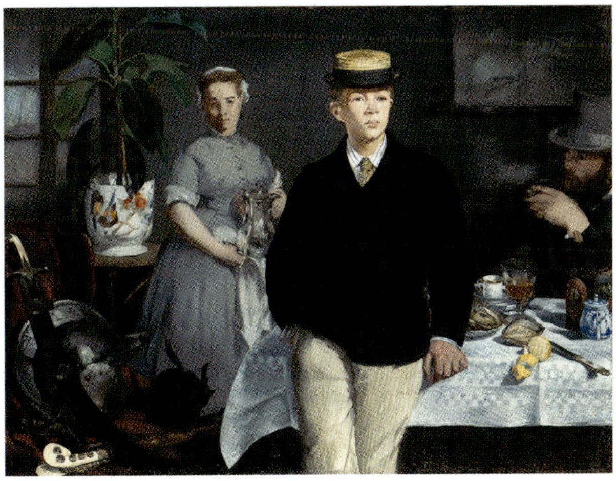

realist depictions of persons seated at table for a meal: Courbet's *After Dinner at Ornans* (fig. 80), Legros's little etching *Le Souper* (ca. 1860; fig. 133), and Monet's *Déjeuner* (1868; fig. 1.17). (Manet's *Luncheon in the Studio* [1868; fig. 134] *refuses* that arrangement in almost emblematic way. By now it should be clear that I see Caillebotte as an intertextual painter par excellence, one who worked with a latecomer's knowledge of the entire modern realist tradition vividly present to his mind.) I suggested earlier that the figure of Marlet lighting his pipe in the center foreground of Courbet's *After Dinner* was a surrogate for the painter; similarly, in both Legros's etching and Monet's canvas empty places at the nearest parts of the table appear to have been laid for the artists themselves (see *MM*, 392–3; Monet's *Déjeuner* is cited and briefly discussed by Varnedoe in *GC*, 93). Caillebotte's *Luncheon* drives home that suggestion by corporealizing it; the beholder looks almost directly down on the place setting in the immediate foreground, as would be the case if he or she were seated at the table, though of course the painting transposes the image of the setting from the horizontal plane of the actual table to the vertical plane of the canvas. More broadly, the treatment of the spatial recession of the large round table appears to obey the laws of a "lived perspective" (Merleau-Ponty's phrase, used in a slightly different context[52]) according to which we are made to feel we look down at the portion of the table nearest us, then progressively raise our eyes (or rather our heads) to take in ever more distant stretches of the scene, until by the time we reach the far end of the table where Mme Caillebotte is being served we have adopted a normative, straight-on point of view like that of traditional one-point perspective or the objective of a camera. But in fact the division of the table into distinct but continuous spatial zones keyed to various angles of embodied vision brings out the fundamental difference between Caillebotte's corporeal realism and the photographic realism it has sometimes been held to resemble.[53] At the same time, the reflective surface of the table is a further reference to Impressionism, while the absorbed figures serving, being served, and cutting food in the shadowy dining room evoke a mood of inwardness or "cloistering" that is in tension with the suggestion of openness to the world of the painter, and by implication of the viewer, at the bottom of the canvas.[54]

Or consider an altogether different sort of picture, *The Yerres, Effect of Rain* (1875; fig. 135).[55] We are shown a fairly close-up view across the greenish surface of the riverbank in the Yerres park (the family's country property at the time); the near bank runs diagonally from right to left almost beneath our feet; by the far bank a skiff has been moored and just beyond we see a stand of youngish trees and then an open field; but what most arrests our attention in this appealing but ordinary-seeming canvas is the juxtaposition in the surface of the water of gleaming reflections of the trees and sky

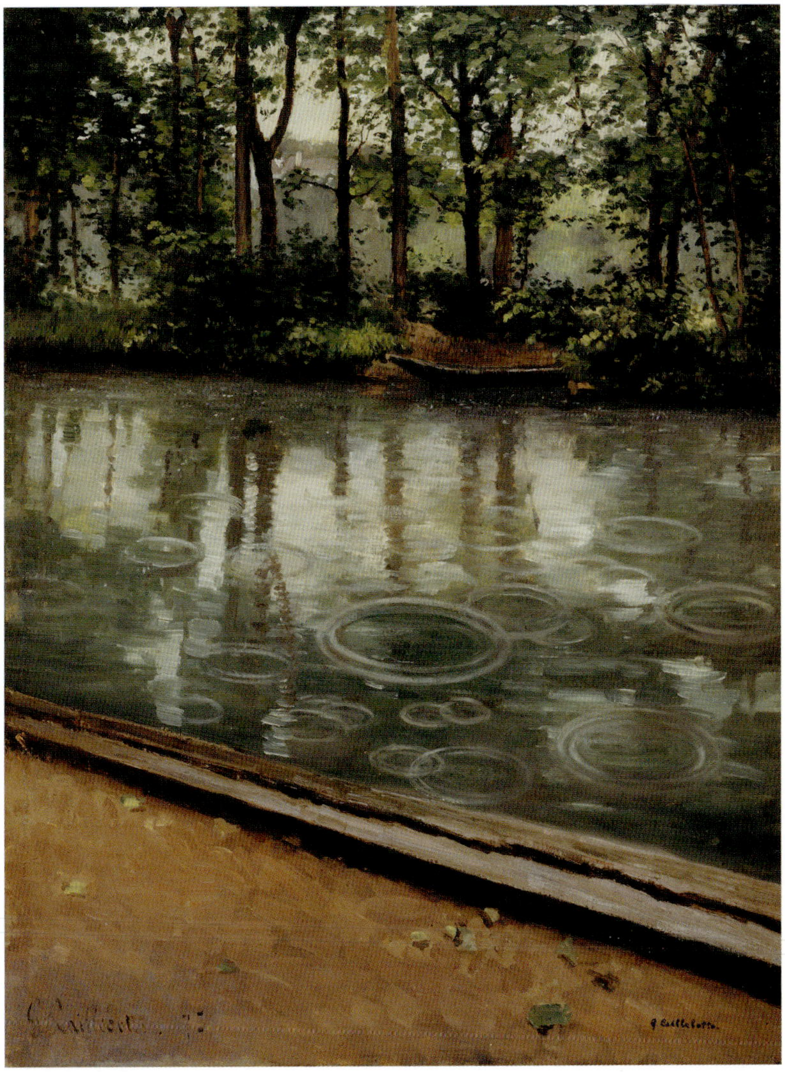

135 Gustave Caillebotte, *The Yerres, Effect of Rain*, 1875. Oil on canvas. 80.3 × 59 cm. Bloomington, Indiana University Art Museum. Gift of Mrs. Nicholas H. Noyes, 71.40.2.

with a host of concentric circles of different sizes that appear to have been caused by drops of rain. I have proposed more than once that Caillebotte's interest in reflections and dazzle signals his allegiance to Impressionism, and in my discussion of the *Floor-Scrapers* I observed that the diffuse light reflecting off the water-soaked boards was a materialist motif even as it threatened to dematerialize the floor-plane itself (also that the nearly trompe-l'oeil wood-shavings more than compensated for that threat). Now I want to suggest that the outward-radiating concentric circles marking the fall of raindrops in *The Yerres, Effect of Rain* may be read as evoking a strictly physical, strictly material Impressionism: as if what Caillebotte discovered in that otherwise unremarkable motif was a means of representing the impacting of impressions from the outside on a sensitive or rather a responsive skin or membrane – a skin or membrane which, in this canvas, must be understood as disconnected from all subjective registering of those impressions, all inner experience, in short all "ideality." Note, too, the implication of temporal duration, not instantaneousness, in the sheer expansiveness of the concentric circles; the motif itself, as well as the widely varying diameters of individual "bunches" of circles (the smaller "bunches" having been initiated by more recently fallen raindrops), and indeed the partial overlapping of "bunches" as dilating circles cross one another's circumferences, so insistently evoke the passage of time that the viewer's experience of the painting manifestly involves a protracted, absorbed, and embodied act of contemplation. It is essential, by the way, that we are not shown raindrops actually striking the water, that is, making tiny splashes; that would be to thematize the *instant* of impact and thereby utterly to break the absorptive mood Caillebotte has summoned and sustained. This is also the reason that there are no raindrops visible in *Paris Street; Rainy Day*, a feature of that work which troubled critics at the time and that Sagraves notes in perplexity. What makes the absence of raindrops in *Paris Street* especially disturbing is that nothing in that picture corresponds to the concentric circles in *The Yerres, Effect of Rain*, which at least indicate the previous existence of the absent raindrops.[56] By the same token, the implied impact of the undepicted raindrops on the open umbrellas in *Paris Street* anticipates the materialist thematics of the Yerres picture.) In any case, I know of nothing quite like *The Yerres, Effect of Rain* – of its low-key materialist lyricism – in all nineteenth-century painting.[57]

In still another vein – Caillebotte, for all the brevity of his productive years, covered a lot of ground – there is the remarkable *Nude on a Couch* (ca. 1880; fig. 136). A naked slender young woman with blonde hair piled on her head lies back on a sofa and, without looking out of the picture, folds her raised left arm across her shadowy upper face and with the extended fingers of her right hand plays with the nipple of her left breast. It cannot be long since she undressed; her boots in the foreground suggest she stood facing the sofa when she took them off, her skirt and blouse or shift lie across one of the pillows toward the right, and her naked waist still bears the impress of a belt or elastic (as Varnedoe observes).[58] Below the waist Caillebotte has frankly depicted the woman's pubic hair, a feature that alone sets this nude apart from the works it tacitly recognizes as its precedents, Manet's *Olympia* and Courbet's *Woman with a Parrot*.

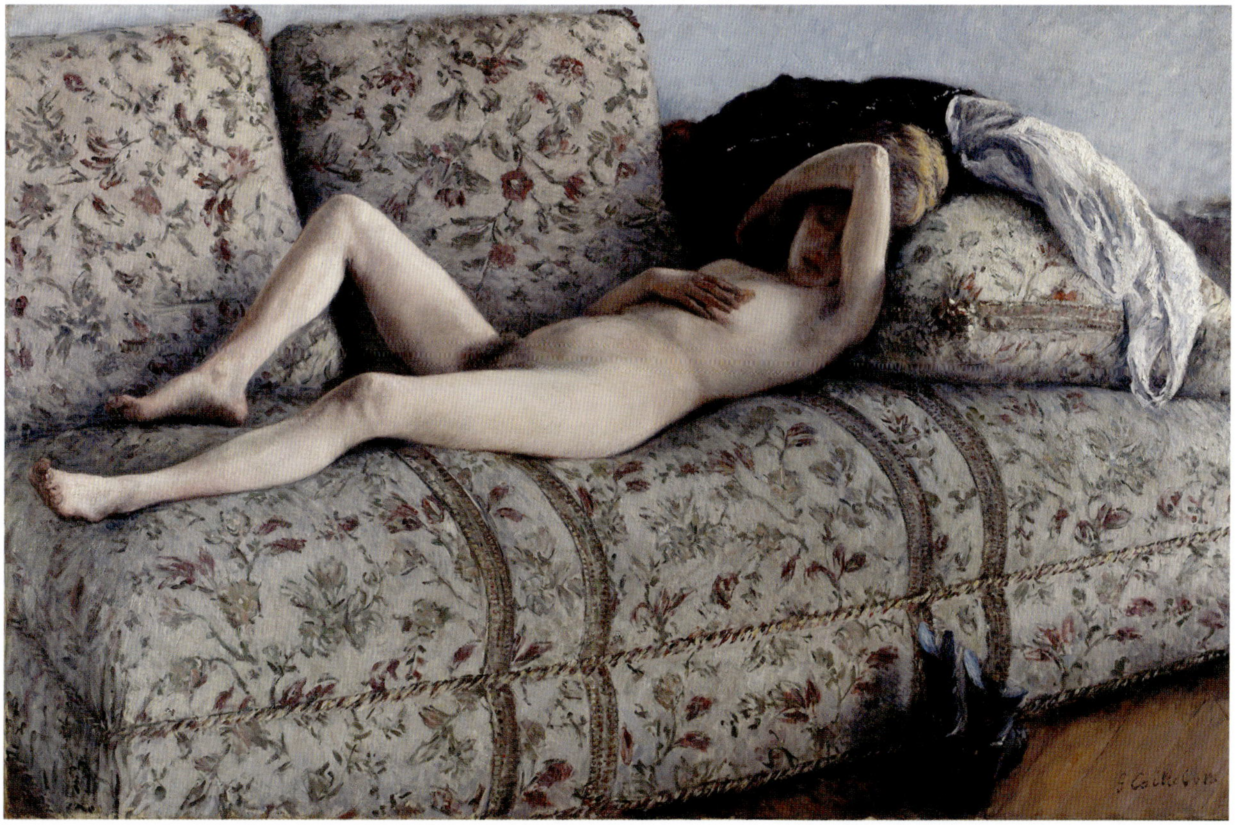

136 Gustave Caillebotte, *Nude on a Couch*, ca. 1880. Oil on canvas. 129.5 × 195.5 cm. Minnesota, Minneapolis Institute of Arts, The John R. Van Derlip Fund.

As for her state of mind, both Varnedoe and Groom suggest that the woman may be feeling shame (Groom says guilt), perhaps after sex, though she at once concedes that "the painting [may impart] a different mood, one of equanimity between the model and the artist, who may well be the absent lover" (*UI*, 214). Groom also claims that the painting is "discomforting since the subject challenges our experience of spectatorship and activates our own anxieties about sexuality and looking." In any case, both Groom and Varnedoe seem uncertain about the painting's precise subject, though both note that the woman touches her breast in an autoerotic gesture. But this does not go far enough; the woman is deliberately arousing herself, and the tension visible in her feet and toes implies that she is in fact aroused. And this is to say that the painting attempts to render accessible or say intuitable, to an audience traditionally figured as male (but the basic situation would be no different if it were figured otherwise), a particular

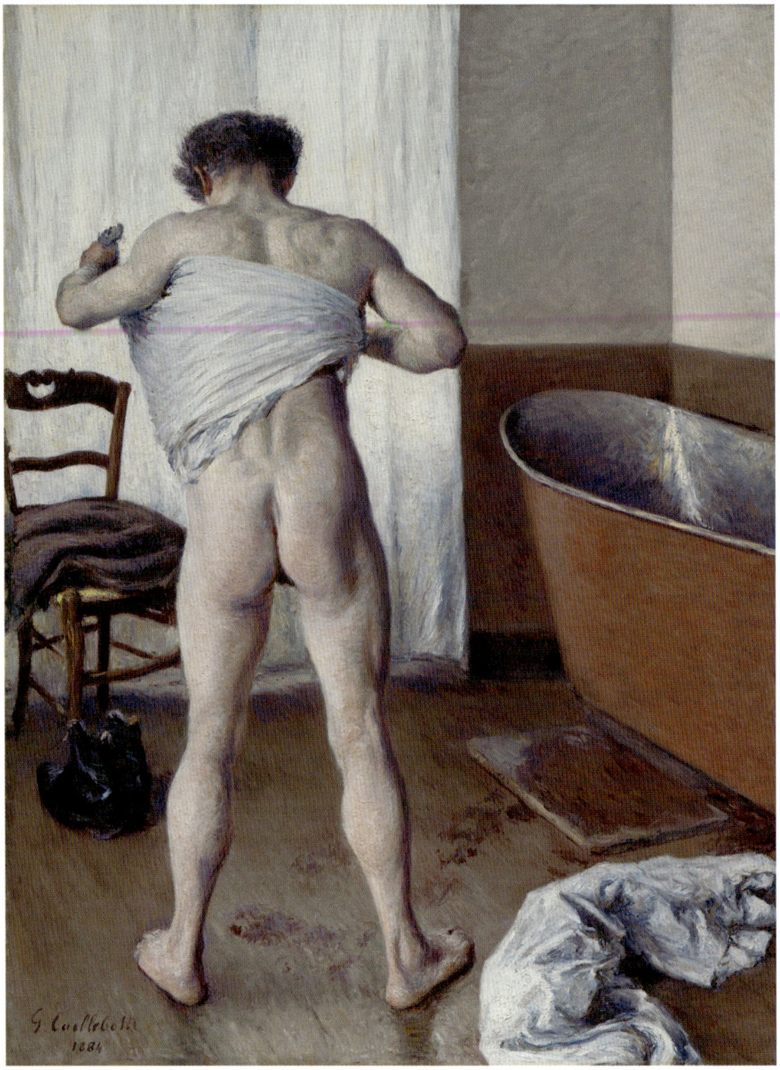

137 Gustave Caillebotte, *Man at His Bath*, 1884. Oil on canvas. 144.8 × 195.5 cm. Boston, Museum of Fine Arts.

absorbed bodily state – female autoeroticism or autoaffection – which despite the unprecedented display of female nakedness is effectively private, withdrawn, closed.

Something not dissimilar takes place in a related work, almost a pendant, the *Man at his Bath* (1884; fig. 137). There Caillebotte has depicted a naked man seen from the back who has just climbed out of the bathtub to the right (note the material "impressions" of his wet feet on the bathroom floor) and now dries himself vigorously with a white towel. This painting too is unusually frank (we are given an unmistakable glimpse of the man's genitals between his legs), but again the emphasis is not on sexual explicitness as such but rather on a kind of autoaffection as the man's action is directed toward himself, though more acutely even than in the *Nude on a Couch* the viewer is made aware of the extent to which Caillebotte's phenomenological aspirations, or at least his efforts to represent bodily sensation, were in the end unrealizable. It is as though for the *Man at his Bath* to succeed in the terms that the painting proposes, the viewer would have to be able to feel, not merely see, the man's fists clenching the towel ends, the effort and motion of pulling the towel back and forth across his body, and – something that can not be seen at all – the chafing sensation of the towel against his not yet dry skin. Not only is that impossible; the strain imposed by the painter's desire to accomplish the impossible is apparent in the man's bizarrely small left forearm and hand. (It might be argued that what I am reading as a foredoomed or hyperbolic attempt in *Man at His Bath* and perhaps also *Nude on a Couch* to make the viewer feel the respective protagonists' sensations is on the side of "idealism," in the sense given to the term by Castagnary in 1874 [see note 27]. Inasmuch as nothing like that attempt can be discerned in Caillebotte's earlier figure paintings, it may be that another factor in his withdrawal from ambitious painting in the early 1880s was the dissonance between an emergent desire to represent sensations – a desire that could be realized only within strict limits – and his unwavering commitment to a materialist epistemology.[59])

Two more pairs of works will bring us within reach of the end of this essay. The first comprises two still lifes (for want of a better word), *Calf in a Butcher's Shop* (ca. 1882; fig. 138) and a *Calf's Head and Ox Tongue* (1882; fig. 139). There is in both an obvious conflict between the brutely corporeal subject matter and the highly stylized, even confected character of the finished works, but I take that conflict to be intentional (the *Calf in a Butcher's Shop*, with its gutted, splayed, and amputated carcass decorated with a wreath of flowers and, in its lower belly, a single rose, alludes to the contemporary art of window display or *étalage*),[60] which further suggests that insofar as both pictures carry the disparity between subject and technique to a barely tenable extreme they may express the frame of mind of a painter who understood himself to be nearly at the end of his project. The *Calf's Head and Ox Tongue* is especially interesting for its relation to the metaphorics of silence that is sometimes held to be implicit in still life as a genre.[61] In Caillebotte's oddly poignant canvas, an entire purplish red naked tongue with its fleshly roots – the organ of speech, of articulation – has been hung from a metal hook, as if indeed to align the work with a thematics of silence while registering a vigorous protest on behalf of the body: in this case an animal's body, but the protest is no less felt for that. In fact the artist's point would seem to be that the viewer cannot *not* make the

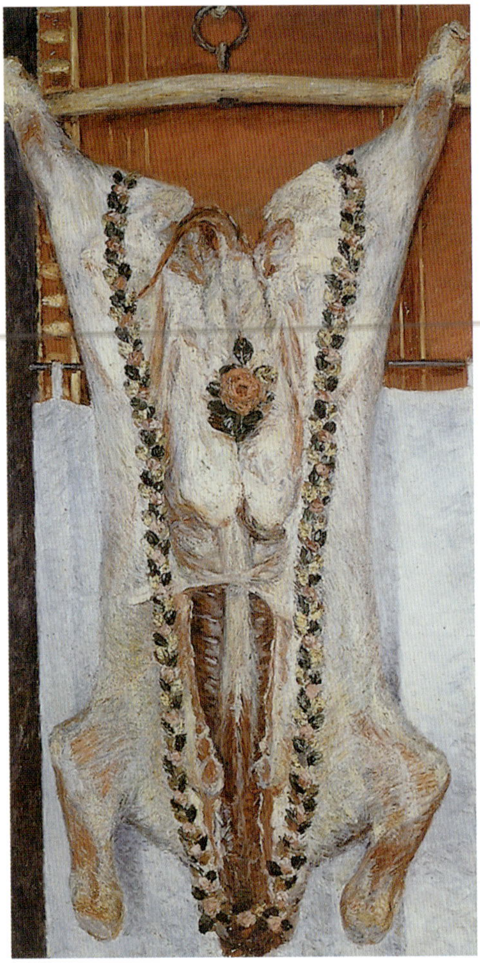

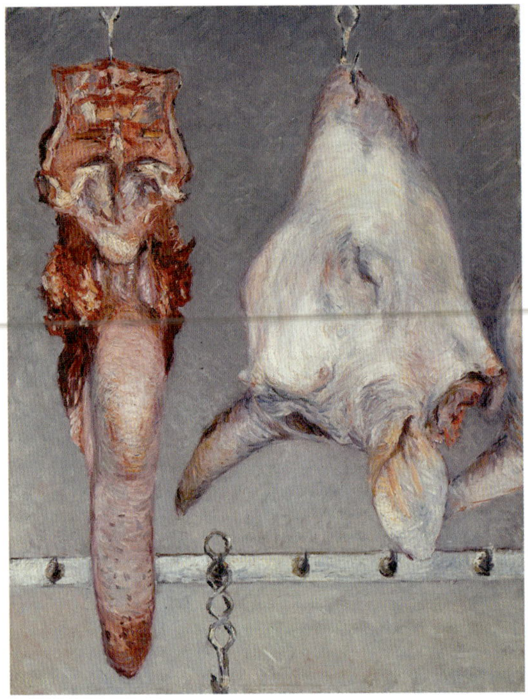

139 (*above*) Gustave Caillebotte, *Calf's Head and Ox Tongue*, ca. 1882. Oil on canvas. 73 × 54 cm. The Art Institute of Chicago, Major Acquisitions Centennial Endowment, 1999.561.

connection with his or her own body. Is that too a political point? I see no reason not to think of it as such.

The second pair comprises two late landscapes that even more emphatically than the butcher-shop still lifes indicate that Caillebotte's project had no future, *Laundry Drying along the Seine, Petit Gennevilliers* (1892; fig. 140) and probably a study for that work, *Laundry Drying, Petit Gennevilliers* (1892; fig. 141). By 1892 Caillebotte had been retired from serious painting for roughly a decade, and the works in question do nothing to qualify that assessment; technically they are proficient but nothing more, their subject matter, laundry drying in sunlight, was by then an Impressionist cliché, and neither picture shows the least response to the momentous innovations that had taken place in advanced painting during the later 1880s and early 1890s (by 1892 Seurat and Van

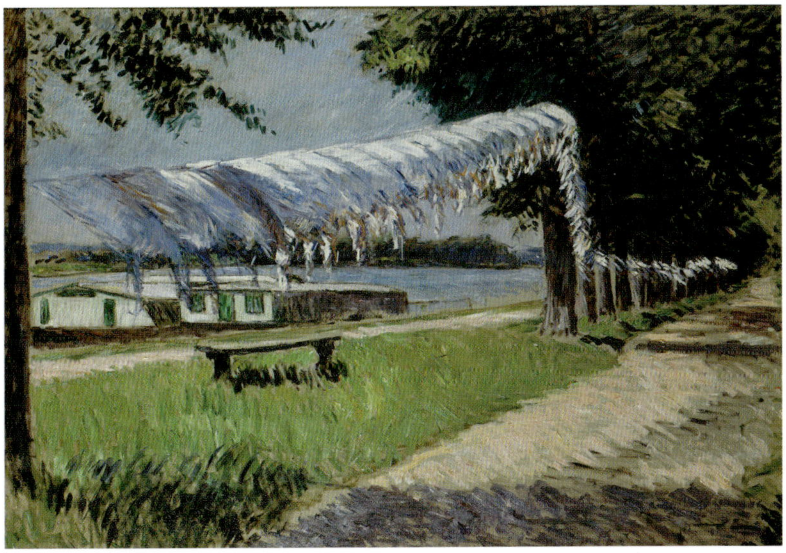

140 Gustave Caillebotte, *Laundry Drying along the Seine, Petit Gennevilliers*, 1892. Oil on canvas. 106 × 150 cm. Cologne, Wallraf-Richartz Museum.

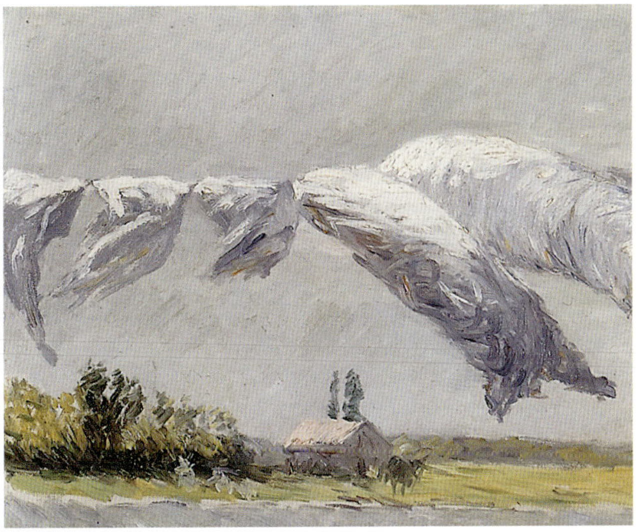

141 (*left*) Gustave Caillebotte, *Laundry Drying, Petit Gennevilliers*, 1892. Oil on canvas. 54 × 65 cm. Private collection.

138 (*facing page, left*) Gustave Caillebotte, *Calf in a Butcher's Shop*, ca. 1882. Oil on canvas. 144 × 74 cm. Private collection.

Gogh had come and gone). But especially in the smaller and simpler of the two canvases there is for me something intensely characteristic in the way that Caillebotte has depicted five or six pieces of white linen of different sizes not just drenched in sunlight (the cliché) but, more important, blowing and flapping in a strong wind (all him). (The small *Laundry Drying* is as surprisingly full of sound as the *Calf's Head and Ox Tongue* is painfully silent.) In effect, Caillebotte's long-standing desire at once to express his fidelity to Impressionism and to go beyond the optical assumptions of the

Impressionist aesthetic in the direction of embodiedness and materiality is here carried to a vivid if artistically modest climax. But the terms of that climax involve not just a tension but an incompatibility between the uncontrollably mobile and noisily aural (also temporally protracted) motif of the thrashing laundry and the flat, unmoving, silent surface of the painting – as if Caillebotte's desire to expand the parameters of Impressionism could go no further without shaking or rending or otherwise destabilizing the picture surface itself, which at that moment was not even remotely imaginable as an artistic strategy. I find it suggestive, though, that the mid-1890s in France saw the birth of the movies. The "action" of these paintings, like the action and structure of other works we have considered, is in crucial respects cinematic.[62]

4

I want to close by looking at the most complex and demanding of Caillebotte's self-portraits, *Self-Portrait at the Easel* (1879–80; fig. 143). In an essay originally written for a colloquium on and around the writings of Jacques Derrida and later expanded into a chapter in *Manet's Modernism*, I call attention to the prominence in the art of Manet and others in his generation, notably Fantin-Latour and Whistler, of self-portraits that are conspicuously mirror-reversed – that depict right-handed painters and draftsmen wielding a brush or pencil in their left hands (*MM*, 365–98). (Fantin-Latour's *Self-Portrait* drawing of around 1860 [fig. 142] is representative of those works. A rare earlier example is David's *Self-Portrait* of 1794 [see fig. 26], the subject of the second essay in this book; others, notably including Annibale Carracci's *Self-Portrait with Figures* [ca. 1585–90; see fig. 27], are analysed in *The Moment of Caravaggio*.[63]) I associate that development with the advent of a new, essentially ocular mode of realism, by which I mean a new commitment to painting exactly what was seen – in these instances in a mirror – instead of

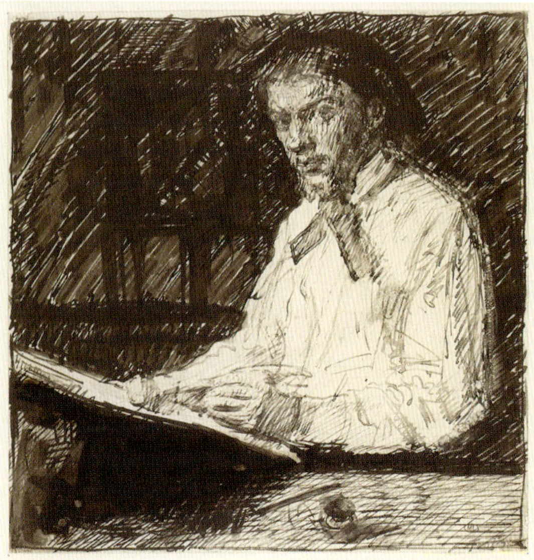

142 Henri Fantin-Latour, *Self-Portrait*, ca. 1860. Pen, brush, and ink accentuated by gum Arabic, scraped; face reworked with graphite. 21.7 × 20.7 cm. Paris, Musée du Louvre, Musée d'Orsay Collection.

correcting the reversed mirror-image so as to produce a normative representation, as in fact had been done, with only a few exceptions, since the Renaissance. In that connection I contrast the mirror-reversed self-portraits not only with their traditional predecessors but also with Courbet's decidedly non-traditional self-portraits, in which the artist in his pursuit of quasi-corporeal merger with the painting on which he was working sought to bring about a relation of congruence of left and right between the painted image and the painter-beholder. (It is just such a relation of congruence, mediated by the facing-into-the-picture orientation of key figures, that we find in the works by Courbet cited in this essay. This is obviously true of the *Source*, but it also holds for *After Dinner* and *Stonebreakers*. Taking Marlet in *After Dinner* as a surrogate for the painter, his right hand holding the burning brand matches up with the painter's right hand holding a brush, while in *Stonebreakers* the young and older laborers may be read respectively as representations of the painter-beholder's left hand gripping a palette and right hand wielding a brush.) And I go on to suggest that the artists of the generation of 1863 not only pioneered the new, ocular ideal but also, simultaneously, took steps to register their bodies' actual orientation in the act of painting; so for example Fantin in his drawing has shaded vigorously with diagonal hatching running from upper right to lower left, a direction keyed to and indicative of of the artist's actual right-handedness. In other words, I attribute to Fantin and his generation the project of seeking to *combine* ocular and corporeal modes of realism, which is what I have been claiming for Caillebotte in this essay, and I further suggest that with the advent of Impressionism advanced painting moved into the realm of the ocular in force, which is what gives Caillebotte's attempt to bring together both modes a significantly different – more deliberate or systematic – emphasis than we find in the work of the earlier artists.[64]

Viewed in this context, Caillebotte's *Self-Portrait at the Easel* emerges as probably the most highly elaborated and self-conscious of all mirror-reversed self-portraits of the later nineteenth century. To begin with, it reiterates Caillebotte's basic allegiance to Impressionism via the device of mirror-reversal, which it proceeds to underscore by also reversing the composition of the painting on the wall behind the painter, Auguste Renoir's *Ball at the Moulin de la Galette* (1876). (The reversal of the Renoir establishes beyond a doubt, as if for a viewership ignorant of the facts of Caillebotte's handedness, that his image as well is mirror-reversed.) At the same time, the *Self-Portrait at the Easel* finds a number of original ways of thematizing embodiment. Perhaps most obviously, the unusual fullness of the depiction of the room in which the task of painting is being carried out directs the viewer's attention to the presumed facts of the actual painter's situatedness, by which I mean both his physical presence "this" side of the picture-surface and the implication that what he saw in the mirror was not just his own reversed

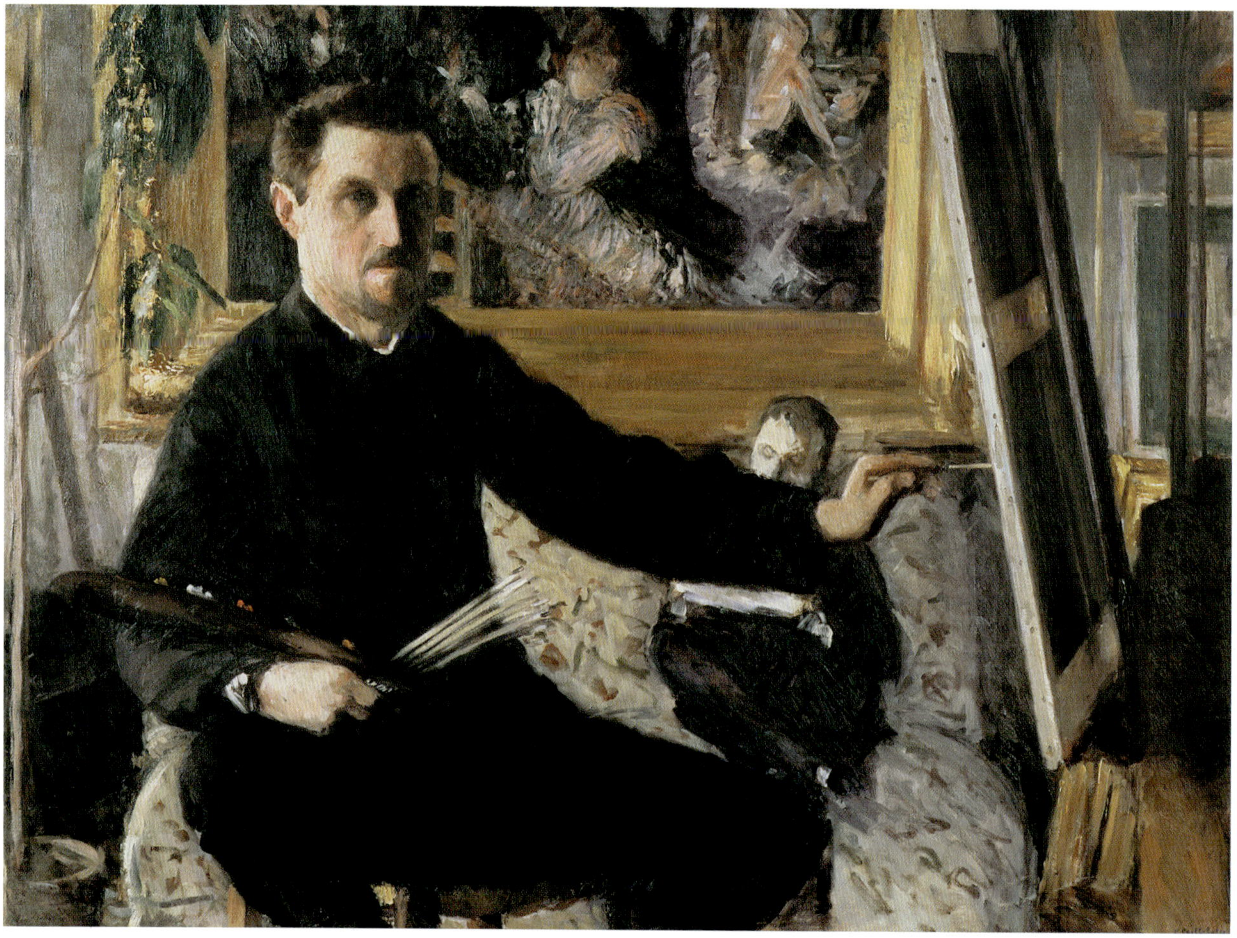

143 Gustave Caillebotte, *Self-Portrait at the Easel*, 1879–80. Oil on canvas. 90 × 115 cm. Private collection.

facing image but also a generous segment of the world behind his back. (We might say that this painting, like other works by Caillebotte we have considered, makes a point of the truth that human beings have faces *and* backs.[65]) Another factor promoting an awareness of embodiment is the self-contradictory or aporetic character of the depicted painter's actions. On the one hand, Caillebotte has portrayed himself looking directly out of the painting, presumably at a large mirror reflecting the scene we are shown. On the other, he has portrayed his right (in the picture his left) arm and hand extended in the act of depositing a brushstroke on a canvas that rests tilted forward on an easel near the right-hand edge of the composition and which the implied narrative suggests is the depicted "original" of the actual canvas. And what is paradoxical or self-contradictory

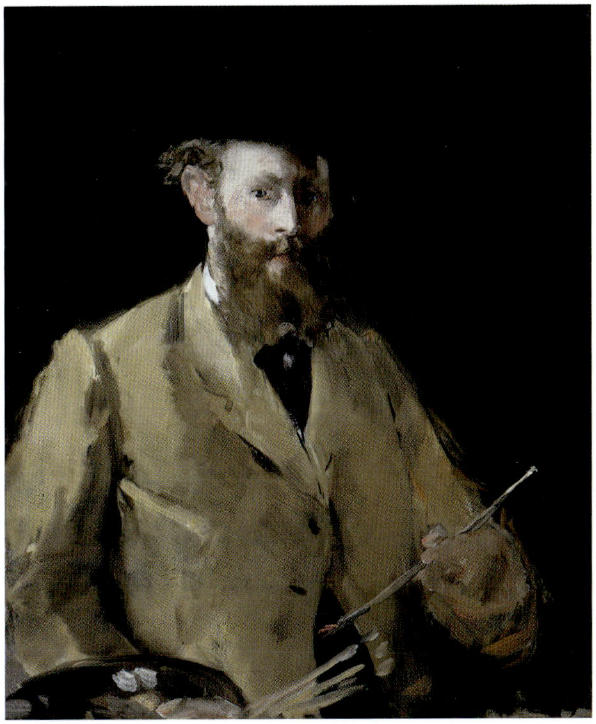

144 Edouard Manet, *Self-Portrait with a Palette*, 1878–9. Oil on canvas. 83 × 67 cm. Private collection.

is that the actual painter would not and in a strong sense could not have made the brushstroke the painting depicts without looking *away* from the mirror and *toward* the canvas where the stroke was to be applied. (I note in passing that Caillebotte's picture goes further than any other "right-angle" mirror-reversed self-portrait of which I am aware in showing just what was involved physically for the painter in pivoting back and forth between the mirror reflecting his image and, set at ninety degrees to the mirror, the canvas on which he was working.) In other mirror-reversed self-portraits, such as the Fantin drawings discussed in *Manet's Sources*, we are made to feel that the depicted artist's gaze, for all its probing intensity, rests only momentarily on his image in the mirror and that in another moment it will return to the sheet of paper across which his pencil or pen is moving or just above which it is poised. (And that a moment after that it will return to the image in the mirror, and so on indefinitely until the drawing is completed – hence the impression of ongoingness or duration that the drawings also convey.) Alternatively, the great example being Manet's *Self-Portrait with a Palette* (1878–9; fig. 144), the blurriness and speed of execution of the depicted painter's left hand holding a brush suggests a hyperbolic attempt by the actual painter's right hand to capture its reflection on the fly, so to speak.[66] In contrast, Caillebotte's self-portrait stresses the fixity or at least the deliberateness both of the painter's outward gaze and of his gesture of applying paint to canvas, a stress that gives his self-portrayal the feeling of an image of a painter *posing* to be painted or indeed to be photographed. And this intimation of a Manet-like quasi-theatricality (as in the figure paintings of the 1860s, not the *Self-Portrait with a Palette*), this pointed disruption of the mirror-reversed self-portrait's conventional implication that it faithfully represents the production of the work in question, all but forces the viewer to try to imagine as if corporeally – and, it goes without saying, on insufficient evidence – exactly how the painting was made. Indeed it may have been above all the intrusion of such quasi-theatricality that required the supplement of the roughly brushed-in man seated on the sofa beneath the Renoir and absorbed in reading a newspaper or journal, even as the partial eclipsing of that figure and his reading matter by the depicted painter's extended left arm has the effect not only of calling attention to the studiedness of the painter's action but also of subtly emphasizing just how little is required in order that absorption yield its characteristic effect.

Some final thoughts concern the depicted canvas, which in the *Self-Portrait at the Easel* is given much more prominence than is usually the case in right-angle mirror-reversed self-portraits. Because we are shown almost the entire canvas (only the topmost edge is cut off by the top of the painting), and also because it has been represented (in extreme foreshortening) from behind, the question of its relation to the actual painting is raised in particularly acute form, and this too is not a question that can be answered. Put slightly differently, to the extent that Caillebotte has disrupted the conventional fiction of the self-portrait's production, there is no reason to assume that the canvas on the easel *is* the "original" of the *Self-Portrait at the Easel*, and the fact that the depicted canvas plays so conspicuous a role in the latter only aggravates our uncertainty. (We are led to wonder, for example, whether the canvas on the easel is large enough to be the work before us.) There is also a sense in which the depiction of the canvas from the back and side invites comparison with the artist's propensity for depicting *persons* from the back, which in turn promotes an awareness of the basic bodily analogy between paintings and persons that undergirds the evolution of painting in France throughout the period we have been discussing. Even more arresting is the canvas's decidedly forward tilt, which for a viewer today inevitably introduces an added dissonance between the depicted and actual canvases as regards their respective orientations. Not that we know how Caillebotte intended to hang his self-portrait when it was done, if indeed he had any definite intention along those lines; among the works on the wall behind the depicted painter, the Renoir gives the impression of being hung more or less flush with the wall, as does the framed and matted print or drawing to its right, but immediately above the latter work, in the upper right-hand corner of Caillebotte's canvas, a picture in a gold frame is shown hanging with a conspicuous downward tilt. What seems clear, in any case, is that Caillebotte knowingly highlighted the depicted painting's physical orientation in a way that forces us to consider its relation both to the *Self-Portrait at the Easel* (of which it may or may not be the "original") and to its own later conditions of exhibition. All this goes pretty far, but the further significance of the forward tilt of the depicted canvas is that its purpose can only be *to minimize the reflection of daylight* from the wet picture surface as seen by the depicted painter.[67] In other words, we have here still another version of the Impressionist trope of reflective glistening or dazzle (supplementing the dazzle-less reflection of the scene as a whole), one that unlike the others we have examined is not actually visible to us, but precisely for that reason is able to identify that glistening or dazzle with the materiality of paint. This is a last, knock-down instance of what it means to think of Caillebotte as practicing a materialist as well as a corporeal Impressionism.[68]

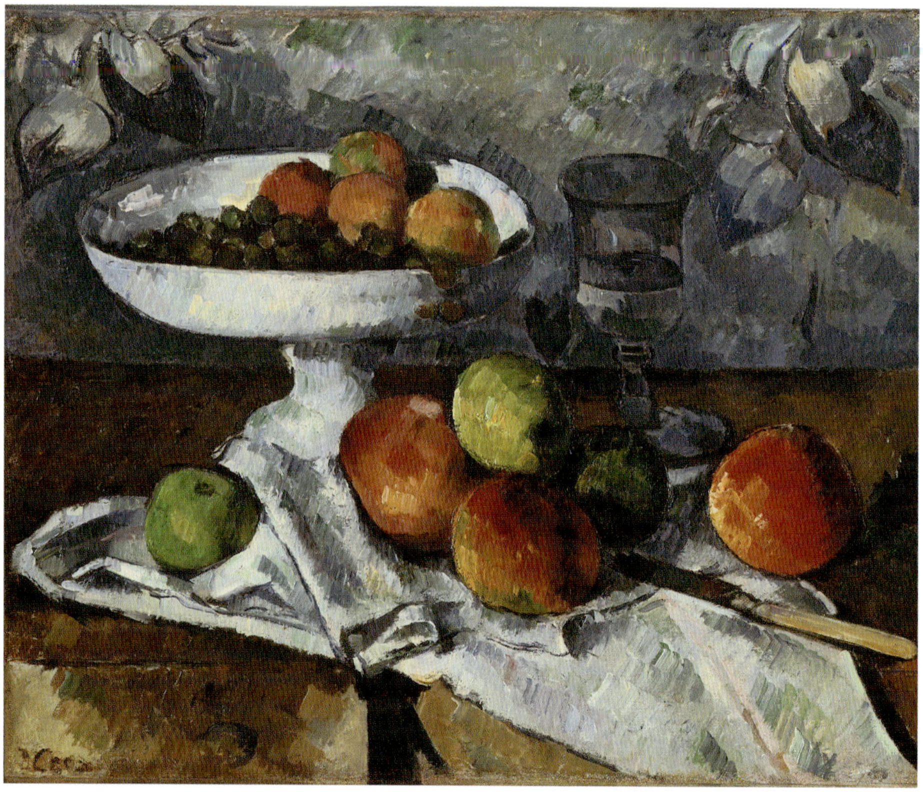

145 Cézanne, *Still Life with Fruit Dish*, 1879-80. Oil on canvas. 46.4 × 54.6 cm. New York, Museum of Modern Art. Fractional gift of Mr. and Mrs. David Rockefeller.

• 6 •

ROGER FRY'S "FORMALISM"

I want to begin my consideration of Roger Fry's art criticism by looking again at a familiar crux – his 1901 article on Giotto, or rather that article together with the notorious footnote which he later attached to it when the article was reprinted in *Vision and Design* (1920).[1] Throughout his article Fry stresses Giotto's tradition-inaugurating mastery of an essentially dramatic mode of pictorial representation. For example, referring to the mosaic of the *Navicella* designed by Giotto for St. Peter's in Rome (ca. 1300; fig. 146), a work that is less than a shadow of its original self, Fry writes: "We can, however, still recognize the astonishing dramatic force of the conception and the unique power which Giotto possessed of giving a vivid presentation of a particular event, accompanied by the most circumstantial details, and at the same time suggesting to the imagination a symbolical interpretation of universal and abstract significance" (*V*, 130). (The symbolical interpretation Fry has in mind concerns the three-part contrast among the drifting ship and its distraught crew, the despairing Peter, "who has here the character of an emissary and intermediary, and the impassive and unapproachable figure of Christ himself" [ibid.]). The best-preserved portion of Giotto's achievement, of course, are the frescoes in the Arena Chapel in Padua, nearly every one of which, Fry asserts, "is an entirely original discovery of new possibilities in the relation of forms to one another" (*V*, 136) and at the same time is a masterpiece of dramatic narration. Among the particular subjects Fry comments on are the *Christ Appearing to Mary Magdalen*, to which he returns in a late essay, and the Joachim and Anna cycle, culminating in the scene of *Meeting of Joachim and Anna at the Gate of Jerusalem* (ca. 1305; fig. 147), in which, we are told, "Giotto has touched a chord of feeling at least as profound as can be reached by the most consummate master of the art of words" (*V*, 138). Fry then writes:

> It is true that in speaking of these one is led inevitably to talk of elements in the work which modern criticism is apt to regard as lying outside the domain of pictorial art.

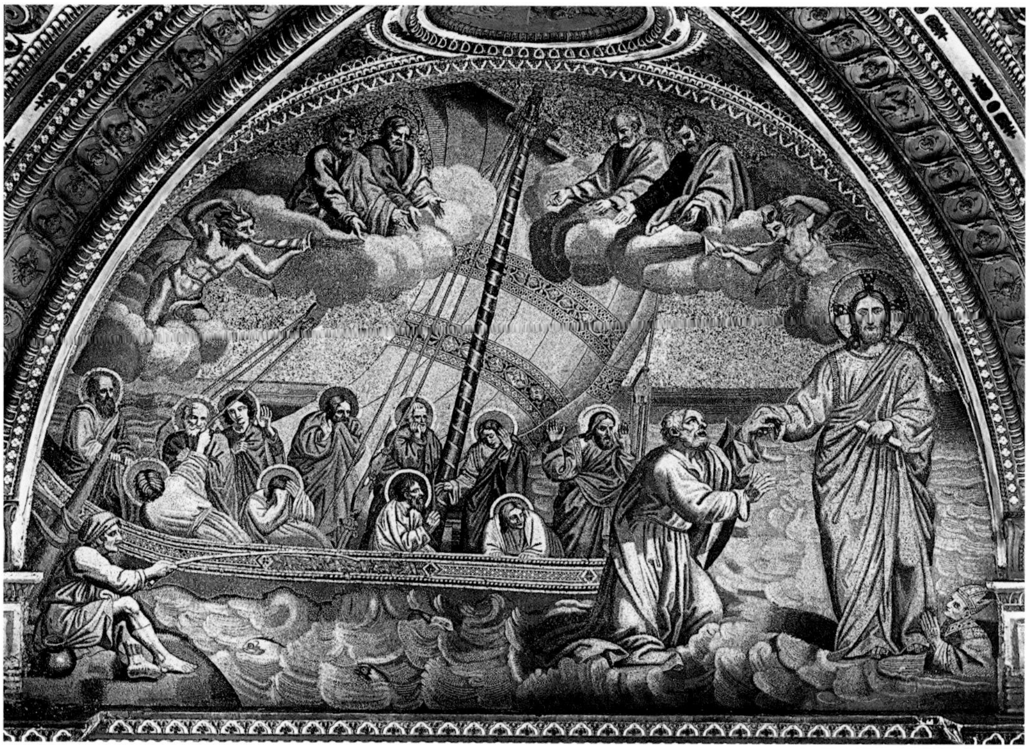

146 Giotto, *Navicella*, ca. 1300. Mosaic, heavily restored. Rome, Vatican State, St. Peter's Basilica.

It is customary to dismiss all that concerns the dramatic presentation of the subject as literature or illustration, which is to be sharply distinguished from the qualities of design. But can this clear distinction be drawn in fact? The imaginings of a playwright, a dramatic poet, and a dramatic painter have much in common, but they are never at any point identical. Let us suppose a story to be treated by all three: to each, as he dwells on the legend, the imagination will present a succession of images, but those images, even at their first formation, will be quite different in each case, they will be conditioned and coloured by the art which the creator practises, by his past observation of nature with a view to presentment in that particular art. The painter, like Giotto, therefore, actually imagines in terms of figures capable of pictorial presentment, he does not merely translate a poetically dramatic vision into pictorial terms. And to be able to do this implies a constant observation of natural forms with a bias towards the discovery of pictorial beauty. To be able, then, to conceive just the appropriate pose of a hand to express the right idea of character and emotion in a

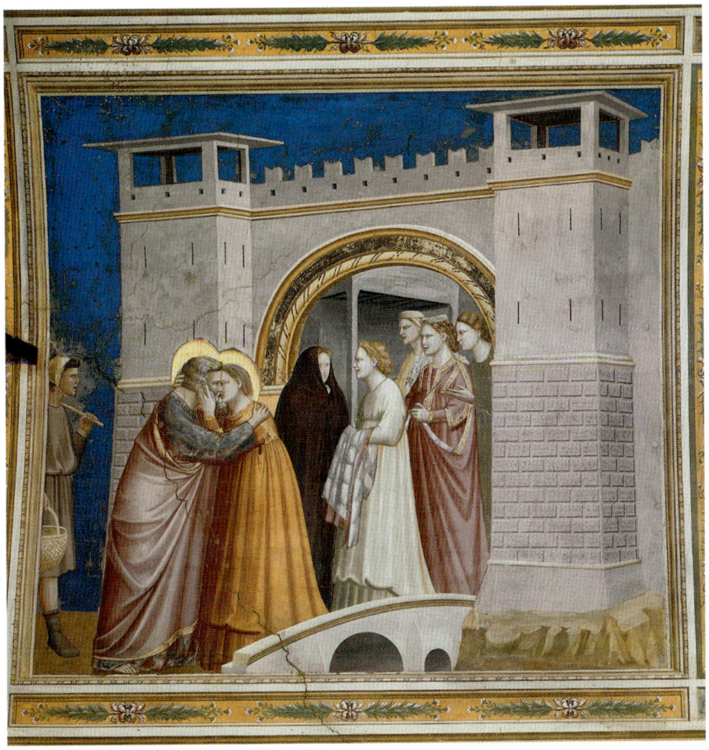

147 Giotto, *Meeting of Joachim and Anna at the Gates of Jerusalem*, ca. 1305. Fresco. Padua, Arena Chapel.

picture, is surely as much a matter of a painter's vision as to appreciate the relative "values" of a tree and cloud so as to convey the mood proper to a particular landscape. (*V*, 138–9)

(Earlier in the article Fry had remarked that "it is impossible to find in [Giotto's] work a case where the gestures of the hands are not explicit indications of a particular emotion" [*V*, 125].)

I take his reference to modern criticism to indicate two writers above all, the French painter and critic-theorist Maurice Denis, whose 1907 article on Cézanne Fry was later to translate and whose landmark essay "Définition du néo-traditionnisme," in which a rigorously "formalist" pictorial aesthetics was first explicitly stated, appeared in 1890, and Bernard Berenson, who in *The Florentine Painters of the Renaissance* of 1896 cautioned against "the error of judging a picture by its dramatic presentation of a situation."[2] In any case, there is an obvious tension between the passage I have just cited and the footnote Fry added at the beginning of the "Giotto" article almost twenty years later:

> The following, from the *Monthly Review*, 1901, is, perhaps more than any other article here reprinted, at variance with the more recent expressions of my aesthetic ideas. It will be seen that great emphasis is laid on Giotto's expression of the dramatic idea in his pictures. I still think this is perfectly true so far as it goes, nor do I doubt that an artist like Giotto did envisage such an expression. I should be inclined to disagree wherever in this article there appears the assumption not only that the dramatic idea may have inspired the artist to the creation of his form, but that the value of the form for us is bound up with recognition of the dramatic idea. It now seems to me possible by a more searching analysis of our experience in front of a work of art to disentangle our reaction to pure form from our reaction to its implied associated ideas. (*V*, 109).

I think it is fair to say that Fry held this position, more or less, for the remainder of his life, though he never quite stopped wondering whether there might not be rare instances in which dramatic expression and the expression of properly "aesthetic" emotion through relations of pure form actually fused and became one (along with Giotto, it was mainly Rembrandt who kept that possibility alive for him). For the most part, however, Fry maintained that the two kinds of expression are essentially distinct, a view he continually put to the test of introspective analyses of his actual feelings before particular works.[3] This is the core of his own so-called "formalist" aesthetics (not an epithet that Fry himself employed), the conviction that all persons capable of experiencing aesthetic emotion in front of paintings (to speak only of the latter) are responding when they do so to relations of pure form – roughly, of ideated volumes in relation both to one another and to the surface and shape of the canvas – rather than to whatever dramatic expressiveness the work in question may be held to possess.

Fry's position on these matters seems dated, to say the least: it would surely be impossible to find anyone today who shares his belief that the task of an artist is essentially to communicate aesthetic emotion, or that what he means by pure form or relations of pure form actually exist.* Let me quickly say that I have no wish to challenge

* This essay was written before the rise of what has come to be called affect theory, which broadly speaking holds that works of art trigger affects – strong feelings and emotions of one sort or another – directly in the subject (indeed in the subject's body), bypassing not just consciousness but also cognition as such. Gilles Deleuze's *Francis Bacon: The Logic of Sensation* (orig. 1981; English trans. 2003) remains the classic study in this vein but the pickup on it in the English-speaking world has been widespread. See, by way of (to my mind devastating) rebuttal, Todd Cronan, *Against Affective Formalism: Matisse, Bergson, Modernism* (Minneapolis,

this negative consensus, though perhaps I ought to add that despite the prima facie unpersuasiveness of Fry's aesthetic theories I consider him a writer on art of immense subtlety and interest (I assume that this too is a widely shared opinion). Instead I propose to take the discussion of his thought in a new direction by underscoring the fact that, in his writings from the Giotto article onward, the counter to form, form's "other," is not primarily subject matter, content, illustration, literariness, or representation as such – though at times he speaks of all of these in this connection – but *drama*, that is, *dramatic expression*. In the case of Giotto, the problem Fry encountered was the apparently perfect synchrony of form and drama, which led him in 1901 to conflate the two to an extent he wished in 1920 to call into question. But other artists presented different problems. Take El Greco, whose spectacular canvas *The Agony in the Garden*, now thought to be a studio copy of the original in the Toledo (Ohio) Museum of Art (late sixteenth century; fig. 148), entered London's National Gallery in 1919.[4] In Fry's article on the *Agony* in *Vision and Design* he notes both its "melodramatic apparatus," by which he means the " 'horrid' rocks, the veiled moon, the ecstatic gestures," and in general the pushing of expression to its limit, and "the extraordinary emphasis and amplitude of the rhythm, which thus gathers up into a few sweeping diagonals the whole complex of the vision" and thus "affects one like an irresistible melody, and makes that organisation of all the parts into a single whole, which is generally so difficult for the uninitiated, an easy matter for once" (*V*, 166). (Fry was impressed by the public enthusiasm for the *Agony*.) He goes on to observe:

> El Greco, indeed, puts the problem of form and content in a curious way. The artist, whose concern is ultimately and, I believe, exclusively with form, will no doubt be so carried away by the intensity and completeness of the design, that *he will never even notice* the melodramatic and sentimental content which shocks or delights the ordinary man. It is none the less an interesting question, though it is rather one of artists' psychology than of aesthetics, to inquire in what way these two things, the melodramatic expression of a high-pitched religiosity and a peculiarly intense feeling for plastic unity and rhythmic amplitude, were combined in El Greco's work; even to ask whether there can have been any causal connection between them in the workings of El Greco's spirit. (ibid.; emphasis added)

2013); idem, "The Aesthetic Politics of Affect," a review of *The Affect Theory Reader*, ed. Melissa Gregg and Gregory J. Seigworth, nonsite.org issue #5; and Ruth Leys, "The Turn to Affect: A Critique," *Critical Inquiry* 37 (Spring 2011): 434–72. More broadly, see Leys, *From Guilt to Shame: Auschwitz and After* (Princeton and Oxford, 2007).

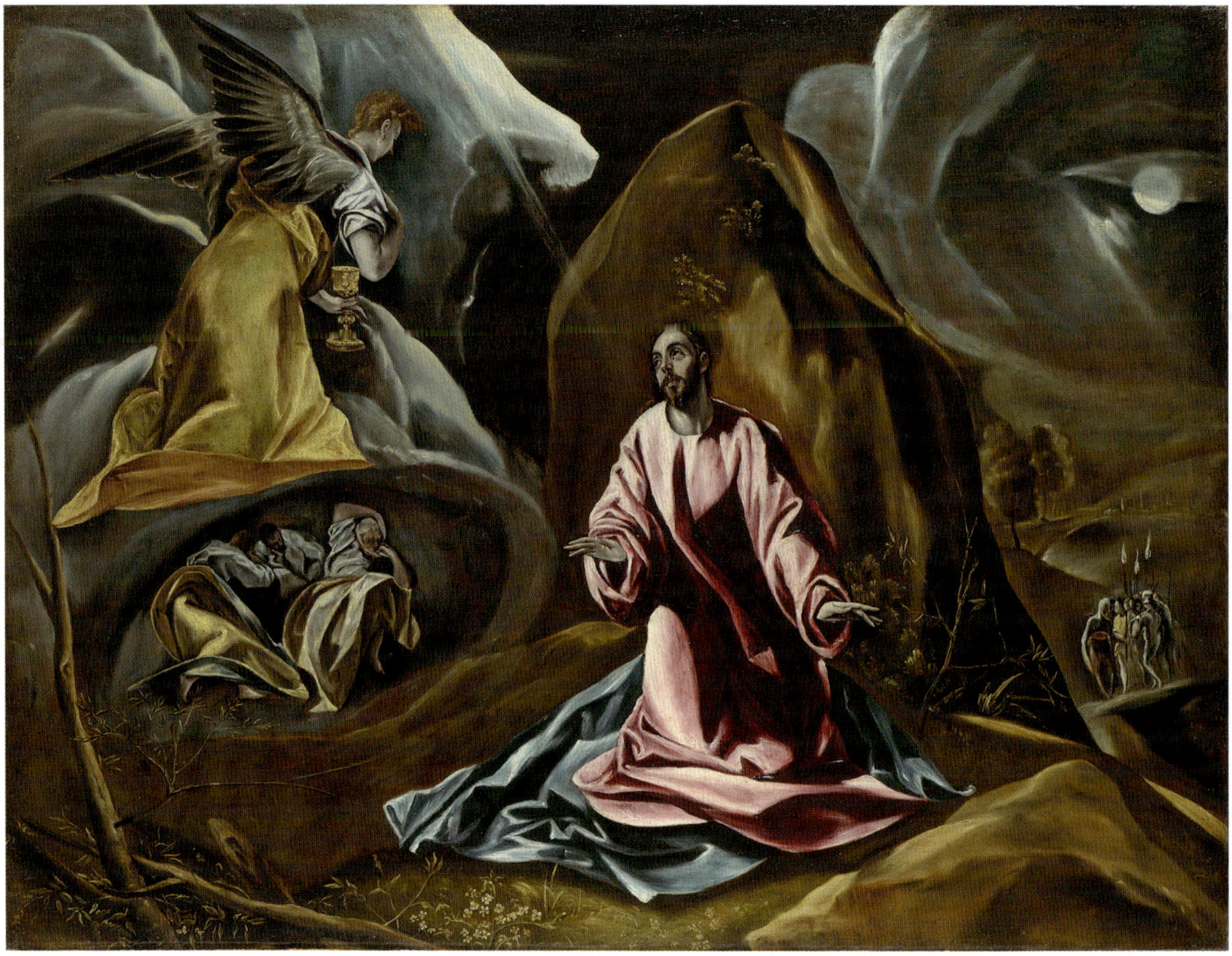

148 Studio of El Greco, *The Agony in the Garden*, late 16th century. Oil on canvas. 102 × 131 cm. London, National Gallery.

A page or so later, Fry contrasts El Greco with the leading Baroque sculptor Bernini, whose sculptures he finds equally excessive and rhetorical but whom he sees as "express[ing] great inventions in a horribly impure technical language" based on a desire to make the crowd, "including his Popes, gape with astonishment" (*V*, 168). El Greco, however, was out of touch with any public, and moreover "was a singularly pure artist, he expressed his idea with perfect sincerity, with complete indifference to what effect the right expression might have on the public" (ibid.). Such courage and purity bring El Greco close, Fry suggests, to the stance of the modern artist, which also accounts for the fact that whereas nearly everyone is revolted by Bernini's sentimental sugariness, "very few artists of today have ever realised for a moment how unsympathetic to them is the literary content of an El Greco. They simply fail to notice what his pictures are about in the illustrative sense" (*V*, 169).

This seems somewhat unlikely, but what I wish to emphasize is, first, Fry's claim that in El Greco's picture dramatic and formal considerations are fundamentally at odds (melodrama being a dramatic notion), and second, the related view that although the *Agony in the Garden* is formally extreme, the impulse behind that extremeness had only to do with the complete realization of an artistic idea and not at all with exerting an effect on an audience (which is why the form cannot be considered melodramatic in turn).[5] In contrast, Bernini's sculptures are also formally extreme but their extremeness is compromised, made artistically null and void, by his desire for public acclaim.

The next stage in Fry's exploration of these ideas takes place in the essay that brings *Vision and Design* to a close, "Retrospect," despite its brevity perhaps the most important of his mainly aesthetic texts. There Fry briefly discusses his early career as a connoisseur of Italian Renaissance paintings, summarizes his growing interest in modern French paintings that led to the organization of several influential exhibitions at the Grafton Galleries in 1910, 1911, and 1912 (also to his coining the term Post-Impressionism), acknowledges the influence on his thinking of Tolstoy's *What is Art?* with its insistence that the end of art is not beauty but emotional communication between human beings, and – rejecting Tolstoy's moralism – proceeds to ask: of what kind of emotions is art the expression? His answer, inspired partly by Clive Bell's *Art* (1914) and by his own further reflection on modern French painting (Cézanne being the central figure), is that he has come to conclude with Bell that "the artist [is concerned] with the expression of a special and unique kind of emotion, the aesthetic emotion" (*V*, 231); and that this has led to what he describes as "an attempt to isolate the purely aesthetic feeling from the whole complex of feelings which may and generally do accompany the aesthetic feeling when we regard a work of art" (*V*, 232).

Fry turns to a particularly challenging example, Raphael's *Transfiguration* (1517–20; fig. 149), a work he says "a hundred years ago was perhaps the most admired picture in the world, and twenty years ago was one of the most neglected" (ibid.). He notes that the painting depicts two events in the Gospel story of Christ that occurred simultaneously at different places, Christ's Transfiguration and the unsuccessful attempt by his disciples in His absence to heal the lunatic boy. The composition thus falls into two halves, one above the other, which also happen to contrast pictorially with one another in obvious respects. In a characteristic thought-experiment, Fry imagines a Christian spectator wholly familiar with the dramatic story the picture tells, and further imagines that such a spectator is also a student of human nature who will therefore be struck by

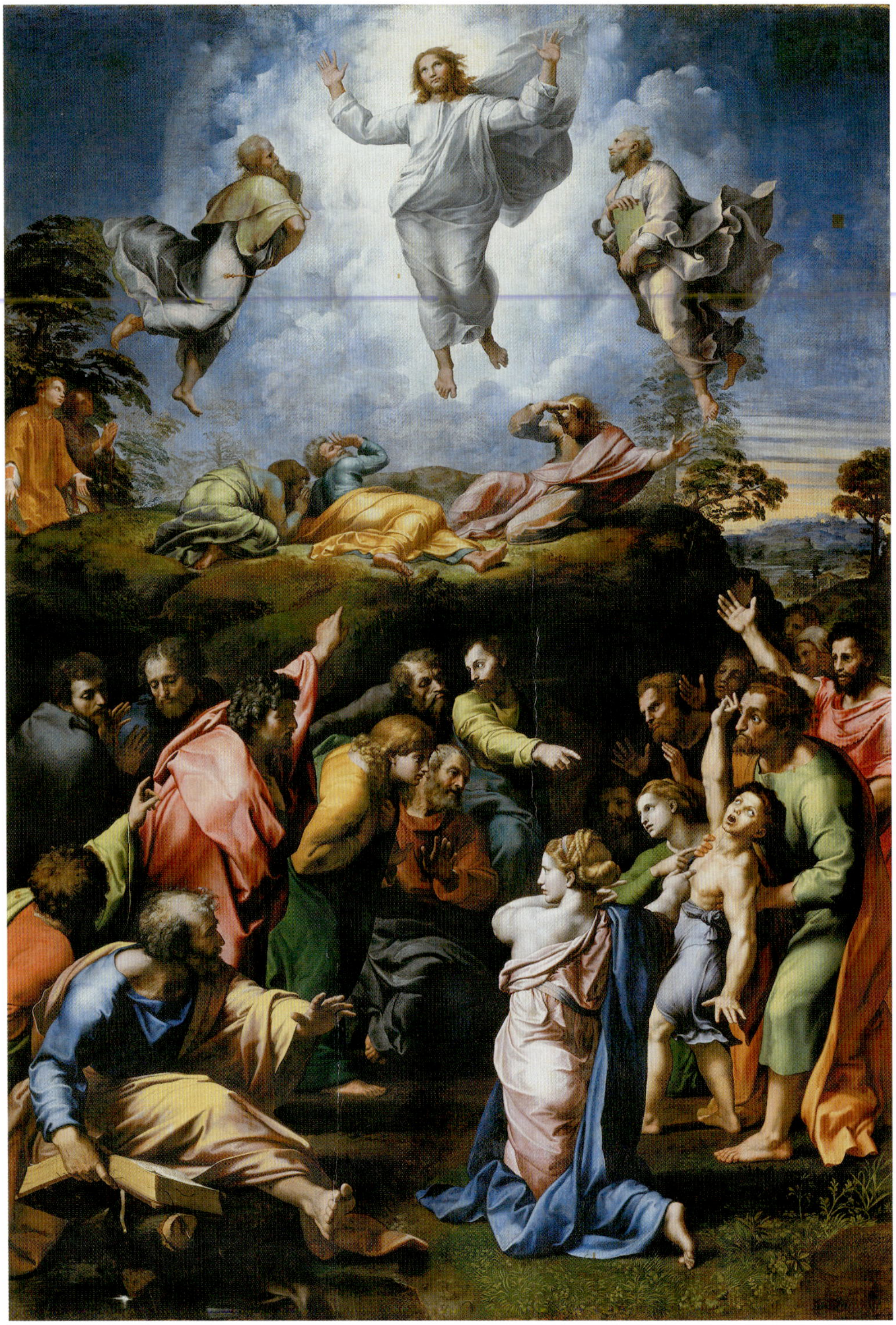

149 Raphael, *The Transfiguration*, 1517–20. Oil on wood. 405 × 278 cm. Rome, Pinacoteca Vaticana.

the incongruity between the usual notion that Christ's disciples were simple peasants and fishermen and the sight of "a number of noble, dignified, and academic gentlemen in improbable garments and purely theatrical poses" (*V*, 233).[6] Fry then posits a different sort of spectator, one highly endowed with a special sensibility to form and either ignorant of or indifferent to the Gospel story. Such a spectator, Fry contends, will at once be struck by "the extraordinary power of coordination of many complex masses in a single inevitable whole, by the delicate equilibrium of many directions of line." That is, he will "at once feel that the apparent division into two parts is only apparent, that they are co-ordinated by a quite peculiar power of grasping the possible correlations," but his emotions will have nothing to do with the factors previously mentioned (the Gospel story), "since in this case we have supposed our spectator to have no clue to them" (ibid.).

Fry concedes that a spectator entirely preoccupied with considerations of form is extremely rare, and

> that owing to our difficulty in recognising the nature of our own feelings we are liable to have our aesthetic reaction interfered with by our reaction to the dramatic overtones and implications. I have chosen this picture of the Transfiguration precisely because its history is a striking example of this fact. In Goethe's time rhetorical gesture was no bar to the appreciation of aesthetic unity [Fry had earlier quoted Goethe's remarks on the mutually complementary character of the painting's upper and lower halves]. Later on in the nineteenth century, when the study of the Primitives had revealed to us the charm of dramatic sincerity and naturalness, these gesticulating figures appeared so false and unsympathetic that even people of aesthetic sensibility were unable to disregard them, and their dislike of the picture as illustration actually obliterated or prevented the purely aesthetic approval which they would probably otherwise have experienced. It seems to me that this attempt to isolate the elusive element of the pure aesthetic reaction from the compounds in which it occurs has been the most important advance of modern times in practical aesthetic. (*V*, 234–5)

And two paragraphs later Fry cites his Giotto article of 1901, in which the current of feeling associated with the dramatic idea and that stemming from his experience of pure form ran so together in his mind that he regarded them as being completely fused. Now, however, he would say that the fusion was only apparent and was due to his imperfect analysis of his mental state (*V*, 235, paraphrase).

Again, my concern is not with Fry's claims about the nature of strictly aesthetic experience so much as with his identification of considerations of drama as the antithesis to those of form, glossed as "the spatial relations of plastic volumes" (*V*, 234), and especially with his characterization of Raphael's *Transfiguration* as a work in which the "rhetorical insincerity" (ibid.) of the gestures and expressions of the figures in the lower half of the composition is so egregious as effectively to destroy one's appreciation of the painting unless it is somehow ignored or otherwise put out of mind (think back to Fry's contemporary artist in front of El Greco's *Agony in the Garden* being so caught up in contemplating the form of the work that he "takes no notice" of the melodrama of the *mise-en-scène*).

All this leads me to advance a thesis that will not surprise anyone familiar with my work on eighteenth- and nineteenth-century French painting (or who has read the essays on David, Géricault, and Caillebotte in this book): namely, that Fry was in crucial respects an *antitheatrical* critic, one whose most habitual and determining thoughts and feelings about painting (and art in general) belong to the tradition of antitheatrical pictorial practice and critical reflection that goes back at least to the middle of the eighteenth century in France and that found its major theoretician and founding art critic at the outset in Diderot, a figure whom Fry, for reasons we shall come to, failed to recognize as a precursor. In *Absorption and Theatricality*, I argue that for Diderot the central task of the painter was somehow to negate, neutralize or otherwise put out of play the presence of the beholder[7] – to establish what I called the supreme fiction or ontological illusion that the beholder did not exist, or at least that he or she had effectively been ignored – obliviated is another term I used – by the maker of the painting. This was chiefly to be accomplished in two mutually reinforcing ways: by depicting personages who appeared to be wholly absorbed or engrossed in their actions, feelings, and states of mind, and therefore wholly unaware of anything other than the objects of their absorption; and furthermore by relating those personages to one another and to all the other elements in the picture in so dramatically perspicuous and persuasive a manner as to give rise in the beholder to the conviction of an immediately graspable unity, the effect of unity implying the perfect closure of the composition within the borders of the painting.[8] (The dramaturgical and theoretical instrument binding both strategies together was the *tableau*.) The result was a new, all-or-nothing conception of the pictorial enterprise. In Diderot's writings on painting and the stage, two notions, drama and theater, which until that moment had been more or less interchangeable, emerged for the first time as antitheses: the first or positive term, drama, signified the entire participation of the personages in the world of the representation; the second or negative term, theater, indicated an open or surreptitious address to an audience as if to solicit its applause. To the extent that a painting succeeded as drama, it was free of even the merest taint of theatricality; conversely, the least suggestion that the personages in the painting were not wholly caught up in what they were doing and feeling but on the contrary were aware of being beheld irremediably sapped the work in question of dramatic credibility. In the passages from Fry we have just examined, this corresponds to the distinction between the powerfully dramatic art of Giotto and the rhetorical or theatrical treatment of gesture and expression in Raphael's *Transfiguration*. Where Fry differs from Diderot, of course, is in his insistence, first, that drama in Giotto needed to be distinguished from his mastery of form, and second, that the "aesthetic" viewer will not be repulsed by Raphael's treatment of gesture and expression, as the previous generation was (and as Diderot and subsequent critics in his lineage had been repulsed by what they saw as the failure of absorption for one reason or another), but on the contrary will find a way to ignore or look past it in order to perceive the deeper formal unity that in Fry's view makes the *Transfiguration* absolutely remarkable.

This may make it seem that Fry entertained a more nuanced view of the painting–beholder relationship than his great predecessor – but the impression, if such it is, is misleading. By the time Fry arrived on the art-critical scene – roughly forty years after Manet's decisive interventions of the early 1860s – the issue of theatricality was no longer quite the urgent topic that it previously had been; exactly how it plays out in relation to Van Gogh or Cézanne or early Matisse and Picasso is an open question.[9] Nevertheless, antitheatrical values had been largely assimilated in some of the most interesting recent criticism and theory, and Fry seems to have accepted such values as fundamental – to have made them his own – without ever pausing to inquire as to their exact provenance.[10]

Among other things, this meant that he felt no inhibition in applying antitheatrical criteria not just within the modern French tradition but across the entire expanse of painting, sculpture, and related arts of all eras and cultures; his commentaries in *Vision and Design* on El Greco, Raphael, and Bernini are cases in point, as is, to cite an almost comic instance of his willingness to range far afield, his general reservation, in the article "Some Aspects of Chinese Art," about the makers of Chinese ritual bronzes of 500 BCE to the effect that "you can never quite catch the artist unprepared for you, never see him so completely absorbed in his idea that he does not know you are looking over his shoulder" (*T*, 93). Perhaps even more egregiously, he was put off by what he earlier characterized as "the assertive and self-conscious calligraphy of the Japanese."[11] But in the right context he could be acute, as when in the second of his articles on the Post-Impressionists he writes of Gauguin, "I do not always feel sure of the inner compulsion towards the particular form he uses. I cannot shake off an occasional hint of self-consciousness, of the desire to impress and impose; in fact, of a certain rhetorical element" (*R*, 92).

It is possible to understand Fry's insistence on the separateness of dramatic and aesthetic considerations as in part a response to the fact that so much of the supposedly great art of the past, in particular so much of the art of the foremost Italian painters of the High Renaissance, when assessed from what may loosely be called a Diderotian point of view, now appeared rhetorical or theatrical, so that if the claim for its greatness were to be renewed and sustained a fresh basis for that claim would have to be found. For Fry, this involved an appeal to qualities of form or design, which being closed in on themselves, in that sense wholly internal to the work in question, rather than addressed to a beholder, provided an antitheatrical "core" that far outweighed in significance all other aspects of the work. (Of certain works, that is.) By the same token, if all paintings of figures in action were like the Arena Chapel frescoes, in which drama and form appeared perfectly consonant with one another, the idea of a fundamental separation between the two might never have occurred to Fry, or if it did occur to him it would not have had remotely the same force. Among major painters the discrepancy between considerations of dramaturgy on the one hand and of form on the other was perhaps most consistently acute in the case of Poussin, whose art fascinated Fry for just that reason.[12] In contrast, it was, I suggest, above all the masterly evocation of utter absorption in Michelangelo's *Jeremiah* (1512; fig. 150) that led Fry, in his 1909 "An Essay in Aesthetics," to cite that figure as one in which the "emotional elements [of form] are combined with the presentation of natural appearances" to produce "powerful sentiments of reverence and awe" (*V*, 25).

In this connection it is worth noting that Fry came to see much High Renaissance painting as theatrical in the pejorative sense of the term several years *before* his discovery of the primacy of form, a development the origins of which are usually associated with his first encounter with two canvases by Cézanne in January 1906.[13] The crucial text is a 1903 review of the English translation of Heinrich Wölfflin's *The Art of the Italian Renaissance*. Of the figures in Andrea del Sarto's sacred conversations Fry remarks:

> One feels . . . that they are arranged entirely with a view to the effect to be produced on the spectator, and that even when they do not turn round and look anxiously at him, they are none the less preoccupied with his presence. And what is true of Del Sarto is true in varying degrees of most of the masters of the grand style. The dramatic ideal of mediaeval art, the presentment of definite personalities acting freely and unconsciously under the impulse of a strong emotional situation, gives place in the art of the High Renaissance to an essentially theatrical idea in which the scenic effect is calculated for the spectator. He no longer, as with Giotto and Masaccio, and

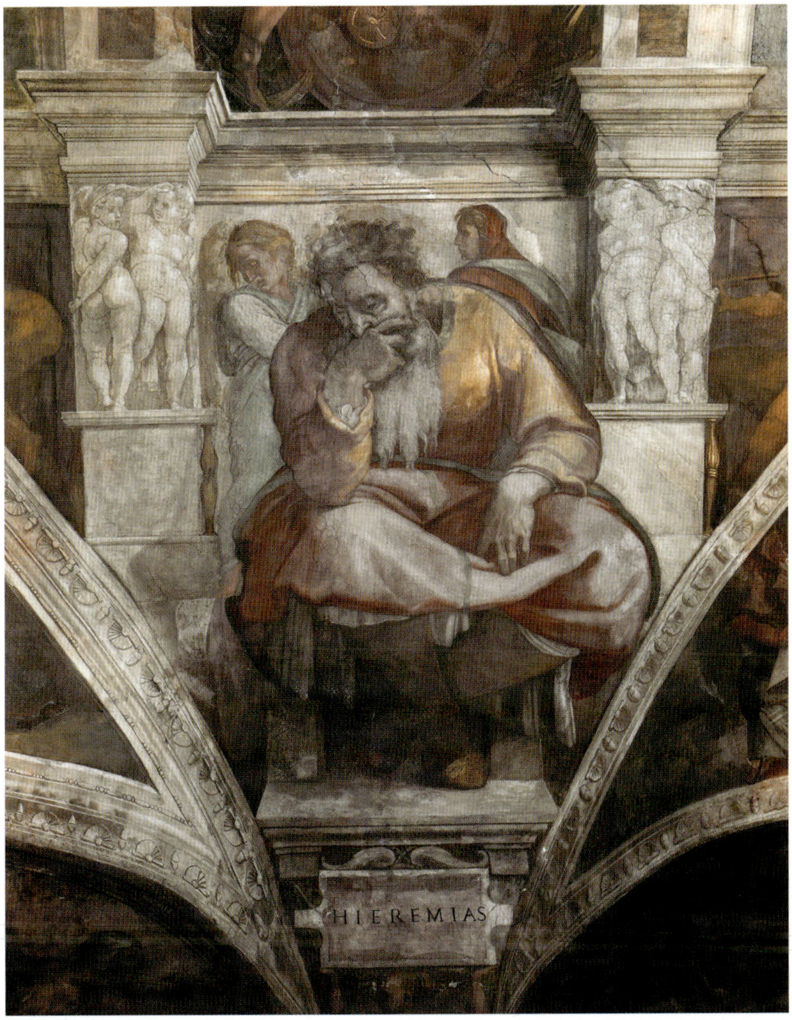

150 Michelangelo, *Jeremiah*, 1512. Fresco. Rome, Vatican State, Sistine Chapel.

with Leonardo, is the unseen spectator of a great and all-absorbing event; his coming is anticipated, and before the curtain rises all the actors have taken their allotted places. Even in Raphael's cartoons something of this will be felt, some sense that the poses are over-explicit, "rhetorical rather than truly dramatic." [Fry gives no reference for this phrase.] Michaelangelo, most people will feel, just escapes this, for though his figures sometimes display unnecessary movements in order to accomplish the simplest things, they always have an air of self-absorption in some ends of

> infinitely greater moment than the situation itself can explain. Certainly they never seem to become conscious of the spectator's presence; they miss being truly dramatic only because the internal drama of their own existence weighs too heavily upon them.[14]

Further on, Fry contrasts Raphael's *Transfiguration* with a painting of the same subject by Giovanni Bellini at Naples, which he prefers. "The miraculous, it is true, is absent [from Bellini's painting]," he writes, "but the superhuman is made startlingly evident by the almost ominous gravity of movement of these three mysterious forms, transfigured, indeed, but by no *coup de théâtre*, whereas Raphael's miraculous performance is just a theatrical presentment."[15] By the time Fry came to write "Retrospect," his view of Raphael's dramaturgy had not changed but the discovery of Raphael's *Transfiguration*'s profound formal unity fundamentally altered his judgment of its artistic merit.

As for Fry's conception of pictorial unity, perhaps the most revealing discussion of the topic occurs in a letter of November 23, 1920 to Marie Mauron, the wife of the French writer and aesthetician Charles Mauron, in which Fry discusses his own landscape painting in terms of a pursuit of wholeness, "a unity where all the parts [are] bound to each other inevitably." He continues:

> One can call such moments inspiration, and the whole thing is to preserve this moment of vision when one is aware of the necessity of everything. As one works one is always being side-tracked by the cold observation of unnecessary facts that bother one and that have nothing to do with the essential unity. Therefore the whole effort should be bent towards this question of unity and necessity. This perception of unity and necessity is very like the perception and comprehension of a natural law when one recognises that many different phenomena are governed by a single principle.[16]

More than a century and half earlier, Diderot had called for the elimination of all incident that did not contribute directly and indispensably to the dramatic treatment of the subject, insisted that all the elements in a painting be subordinated to the central compositional idea, and put forward a causal, in that sense machinelike, notion of the relations among those elements, all of which were to be understood as combining together in a single powerful effect.[17] Above all a painting had to induce in the viewer a conviction of the absolute necessity of the various relationships it comprised, the experience of that conviction being a subjective criterion of artistic success as well as implying that the relationships in question are as they are owing to the play of forces internal to the work rather than because of a desire to appeal to the beholder. Needless to say, the conviction of unity and necessity I have just invoked is itself the product of an attempt to affect the beholder *in a certain way*.

I do not claim that Fry could only have derived his ideas about unity from Diderot's writings; on the contrary, the issue of pictorial unity had been central first to the Italian and then to the French traditions for centuries, and Diderot's dramatic and causal (dramatic *because* causal) inflection of the issue had been assimilated by subsequent French art critics to an extent that makes any ascription of direct influence beside the point. Moreover, Fry would have disavowed an affinity with Diderot if only because of the prominence of dramatic concerns in the latter's writings on painting. From Fry's perspective, this gave Diderot's criticism a literary cast that he deplored. "Diderot's celebrated critiques of the Salons of his day are almost entirely devoted to the psychological aspects of illustration," Fry writes in "Some Questions in Aesthetics." "No wonder that for him Greuze was the greatest of painters" (*T*, 55). For Diderot, too, chiaroscuro, contrast of light and dark, was a major resource of painting (and a major vehicle of pictorial unity) mainly because it lent itself to the production of dramatic effects. Not surprisingly, Fry distrusted chiaroscuro, which he saw both as serving melodramatic ends and as tending to obscure contours and hence relations of forms while dissolving the picture surface in an illusion of indeterminate depth[18] (but there was always Rembrandt to give him pause). Finally, Diderot stressed the instantaneousness with which the effect of unity was to be achieved,[19] an emphasis often lacking in Fry, who mostly admired artists who "[allow] the motif to unfold itself gradually to the apprehension" (*R*, 348).[20] (The idea of instantaneousness returns in force in the criticism of Clement Greenberg.[21]) So there are differences of inflection between Diderot's and Fry's ideas about pictorial unity. Nevertheless, I want to suggest that Fry's conception of painting, including its emphasis on unity, belongs in its essence to the intellectual tradition keyed to considerations of drama and antitheatricality set going by Diderot's writings of the 1750s and 60s. (The writings on the stage would have been especially important early on, inasmuch as the *Salons* did not begin to be published until after Diderot's death in 1784.) Again, Fry would have dismissed such a suggestion, not only for the reasons I have summarized but also because, in his view, "it is only by representation of persons or events that any dramatic element can enter into a picture,"[22] an assumption that effectively excludes the possibility of dramatic relations among forms. But this forecloses the issue much too abruptly, and in the remainder of this essay I shall seek to bring out even more than has already been done the Diderotian tenor of Fry's thought.

Take, to begin with, one of Fry's most characteristic and recurrent phrases – "almost unconscious" (and its variants). Again and again Fry will say of some admired feature of a work of art under discussion that it came about as the result of an unconscious or (more frequently) almost unconscious choice or decision on the part of the artist.

This is a major feature of Fry's discussions of Cézanne, for example.[23] To cite one characteristic statement: "[Cézanne's work] has that supreme spontaneity as though he had almost made himself the passive, half-conscious instrument of some directing power."[24] Or another: "What [Cézanne] did seems to have been done almost unconsciously. Working along the lines of Impressionist investigation with unexampled fervour and intensity, he seems, as it were, to have touched a hidden spring whereby the whole structure of Impressionist design broke down, and a new world of significant and expressive form became apparent."[25] My point is that unconsciousness lines up with antitheatricality, not having a thought for an audience; more precisely, under the Diderotian paradigm unconsciousness in the mode of *oubli de soi*, self-forgetting, is the infallible sign of a personage's complete absorption. Fry's harping on the *artist's* unconsciousness (or half-unconsciousness or almost-unconsciousness) thus amounts to both a displacement and a radicalization of Diderot: to the extent that an artist is imagined as having been unaware of doing a particular thing, it cannot be claimed that he or she did it in order to make a particular impression on the viewer.[26]

Moreover, the issue of unconsciousness in Fry goes far beyond Cézanne. So for example (and there are many examples) Fry in "On Some Modern Drawings" insists on a particular psychological fact: "namely, that perfect rhythmic continuity and coherence is only attainable by human beings when their activity is at least partially unconscious. To fix the attention on any gesture is to deprive it fatally of that specific quality of rhythmic unity" (*T*, 266–7). Matisse was for Fry the exemplar of rhythmic unity understood in those terms, though in 1918 he was delighted to find certain younger British artists conceiving of a drawing "as the almost unconscious overflow of a vivid aesthetic experience rather than as a performance before an imagined public."[27] Walter Sickert, an artist (and writer on art) about whom Fry's feelings were often ambivalent, is praised for "the exquisite choice, none the less perfect that it seems to be half-unconscious, of the few tones of violet-grey, dull maroon, orange, and green, out of which he builds his colour schemes."[28] In the same vein, a drawing by Sickert is admired because its "synthesis is the result of an unconscious and impromptu gesture."[29] Vanessa Bell is praised for recognizing that " 'handling' and quality of paint are only really beautiful when they come unconsciously in the process of trying to express an idea."[30] Manet is held to have had "a deep, perhaps unconscious concern for the picture surface."[31] And in a late essay Fry speculates that Rembrandt "attained to design by an indirect method. It was, one guesses, an almost unconscious habit rather than a deliberate and conscious aim."[32] All these are instances of a larger principle. "It is one of the curiosities of the psychology of the artist," we read in "The Jacquemart-André Collection" (1914), "that he is generally trying very hard to do some-

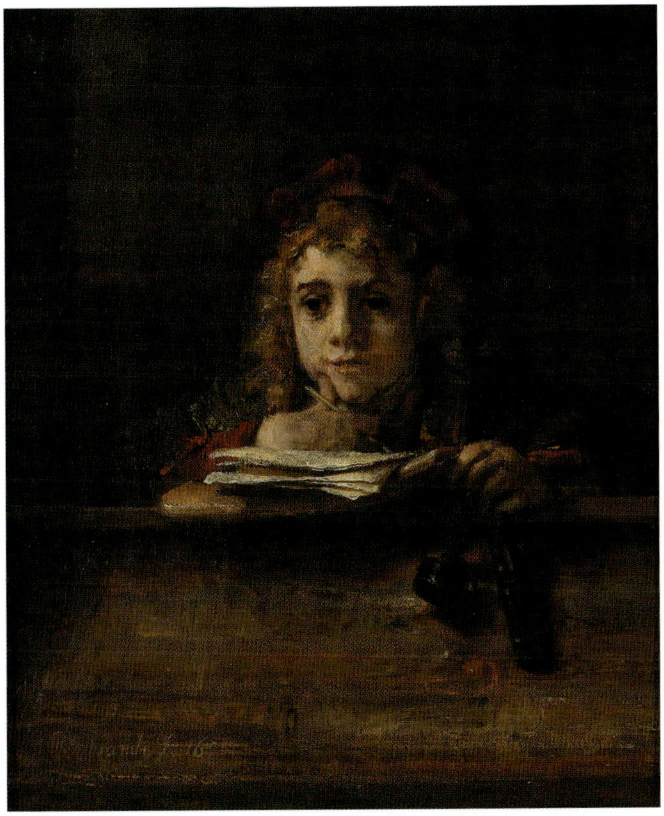

151 Rembrandt van Rijn, *A Schoolboy at His Desk (Titus at His Desk)*, 1655. Oil on canvas. 77 × 63 cm. Rotterdam, Museum Boijmans Van Beuningen.

thing which has nothing to do with what he actually accomplishes; that the fundamental quality of his work seems to come out unconsciously as a by-product of his conscious activity" (*V*, 153). This is said as a preamble to a discussion of Paolo Uccello, in whose art the conscious pursuit of elaborate perspectival constructions turned out to facilitate an unconscious mastery of form,[33] but Fry stands behind it in all its generality.

Or consider the following excerpts from Fry's analysis in "Some Questions in Aesthetics" of Rembrandt's *A Schoolboy at His Desk* (1655; fig. 151). The topic Fry is pursuing is the nature of realism, which on the face of it would seem to present difficulties for his argument by virtue of its apparent concern with the depiction of reality at the expense of considerations of form. But Fry finds precisely in what he takes to have been Rembrandt's entire engrossment in the scene before him the psychological or say spiritual precondition for his creating harmonious plastic unities out of the data of experience. "The boy was at his lessons," Fry writes of the imagined original scene. "Puzzled and bored by them, he looked up from his task; his thoughts wandered, and he sat there day-dreaming, with his cheek propped on his thumb." Then: "Rembrandt painted this scene with complete realism, without a thought of anything but the vision before him. . . . If one looks carefully in the original at the passage where the thumb indents the cheek one can see why such works occur at very rare intervals. If for a moment Rembrandt had thought about his picture he was undone; nothing but complete absorption in his vision could sustain the unconscious certainty and freedom of the gesture. Each touch, then, had to be an inspiration or the rhythm would have broken down" (*T*, 53–4). Fry goes on to discuss the painting of the desk, in itself "a plain flat board of wood, but one that has been scratched, battered and rubbed by schoolboys' rough usage." He continues:

> Realism, in a sense, could go no further than this, but it is handled with such a vivid sense of its density and resistance, it is situated so absolutely in the picture space and plays so emphatically its part in the whole plastic scheme, it reveals so intimately the mysterious play of light upon matter that it becomes the vehicle of a strangely exalted spiritual state, the medium through which we share Rembrandt's deep contemplative mood. It is miraculous that matter can take so exactly the impress of spirit as this pigment does. And that being so, the fact that it is extraordinarily like a schoolboy's desk falls into utter insignificance beside what it is in and for itself. (*T*, 54).[34]

Similarly, Fry observed a few pages earlier of Courbet's *Blonde endormie*,

> However "realistic" this is we are not tempted ever to refer to what lies outside the picture. This plastic unity holds us entirely within its own limits because at every point it gives us an exhilarated and surprised satisfaction. Everything here is so transmuted into plastic terms and finds therein so clear a justification that we are not impelled to go beyond them or to fill them out, as it were, by thinking of the model who posed more than half a century ago to M. Courbet in Paris, or of any other woman whatever. (*T*, 49)[35]

It is worth pausing a moment to gloss these remarks:

(1) Fry writes on the assumption that Rembrandt's painting depicts an original scene – an actual schoolboy sitting at a desk and lost in a daydream. But is that likely, given the apparent obliviousness of the boy in the painting to the immediate presence of the painter? My claim, however, is not simply that Fry's mini-narrative of the picture's genesis is unpersuasive. It is rather that that mini-narrative allows Fry to specify Rem-

brandt's state of mind, and that this is important because he believes, following Tolstoy (also Maurice Denis), that a work of art is essentially an act of communication of emotion (or a mental state) from the artist to the viewer, from which it follows that by specifying the mode of the artist's activity the critic is able to determine the expressive or, his word, spiritual content of the picture. In this instance the artist's state of mind is understood as wholly absorbed in what Fry calls his "vision," hence as oblivious to everything else including, Fry imagines, the canvas on which he is working.

(2) The subject of Rembrandt's picture is manifestly absorptive, in a vein that was later mined by Chardin and indeed by Greuze.[36] In subsequent essays Fry singles out Rembrandt's *David Harping before Saul* (no longer given to the master), in which Fry especially admires "the astonishing invention of [Saul's] unconscious seizing the curtain to wipe his tears,"[37] and *Bathsheba*, two equally absorptive canvases. And Courbet's *Blonde endormie* is asleep, sleep being an absorptive motif *par excellence*, as was first argued in *Absorption and Theatricality*. Fry's strong preference for paintings with absorptive themes and motifs is evident throughout his career (as when he singles out Michelangelo's *Jeremiah* in "An Essay in Aesthetics"), though naturally he is repulsed by works that exploit an ostensibly absorptive framework for what he considers artistically illicit purposes (Luke Fildes's *The Doctor* in Tate, London, to be glanced at shortly, is an instance of this). But at no point in his career was Fry in the least aware that his admiration for paintings of absorptive subjects could be understood in those terms; like numerous other critics in the Diderotian tradition down to the present moment, he found himself moved and impressed by such paintings without ever recognizing that it was the treatment of absorption that largely determined his response. And had it been explained to him that that was so, he would have rejected the explanation because from where he stood what I have been calling absorption merely concerned considerations of drama or illustration and not at all those of form.

(3) Fry imagines the finished painting to be wholly autonomous with respect to the real world to the extent of not even suggesting comparison with it, despite being a ne plus ultra of realism – or rather, this is what being a ne plus ultra of realism turns out to mean. So for example the fact that the desk in Rembrandt's canvas bears an extraordinary resemblance to the original desk becomes utterly insignificant in the light of the spiritual intensity of the depiction (reflecting the intensity of Rembrandt's purely contemplative mood); similarly, the viewer of Courbet's canvas is said to be so deeply satisfied by the plastic unity of the whole that it never occurs to him or her to "go beyond" that unity by thinking of the woman whom Fry assumes modelled for Courbet

when he made his painting. Again, Fry's claims are improbably extreme, but what should be underscored are the rhetorical lengths he is prepared to go to secure the fiction of the painting's hermetic closure *vis-à-vis* the outside world. I think of this as a radicalization of Diderot's conception of the autonomous, hence antitheatrical *tableau* (it never occurred to Diderot to deny comparison with external reality, on the contrary in his remarks on Chardin he explicitly courted it[38]), as if for Fry mere reference to reality – to a "beyond" or "outside" of any sort – undermined a painting's unity and hence disqualified it artistically.[39]

Fry's preference for Seurat over Van Gogh is explained on these grounds: although the impassioned Van Gogh was a master of design and color, his "whole nature impelled him to regard even the most indifferent object, a pair of boots or a chair, as charged with dramatic significance" (*T*, 245), a stance toward the world that inevitably limited his achievement (after recovering from the first shock of encountering Van Gogh's work "we look in vain for further revelations"; ibid., 248).[40] Seurat, in contrast, in a painting like the *Young Woman Powdering Herself* (1888–9; fig. 152), took off from "the gimcrack finery of the period," but "for all [the painting's] reality nothing of the original theme, of the thing seen, remains untransformed, all has been assimilated and remade by the idea. And perhaps this complete transmutation of the theme by the idea is the test of great art. It means that in proportion as a picture attains to this independent reality and inherent significance the element of illustration drops out and becomes irrelevant" (*T*, 257–8). Not surprisingly, although Fry devotes a longish paragraph to a discussion of the function of Seurat's painted frames (*T*, 259), the general topic of framing, with its implicit problematization of the distinction so important to Fry between what lies within and outside a painting, goes unexamined in his texts.[41]

(4) As we have seen, Fry praises Rembrandt for being so absorbed in his vision of the schoolboy at his desk that he never thought about his picture but instead handed over its making to his unconscious. Similarly, Corot's *Seated Woman with Bare Breasts* is said in "Some Questions in Aesthetics" to evince "an almost reckless indifference to all else but the artist's fascinated response" to his model (in *T*, 52),[42] while in *Characteristics of French Art* Fry remarks apropos of the same picture that "Corot was not thinking at all about making a work of art, it was not even a proper '*académie*' or nude study, he was much too moved by his thrilled contemplation of the actual appearance to care whether the result was a work of art or not" (*C*, 96)[43] In the same spirit he remarks of Vanessa Bell:

> One feels before her works that every touch is the outcome of her complete absorption in her general theme. So complete is this devotion to the idea that she

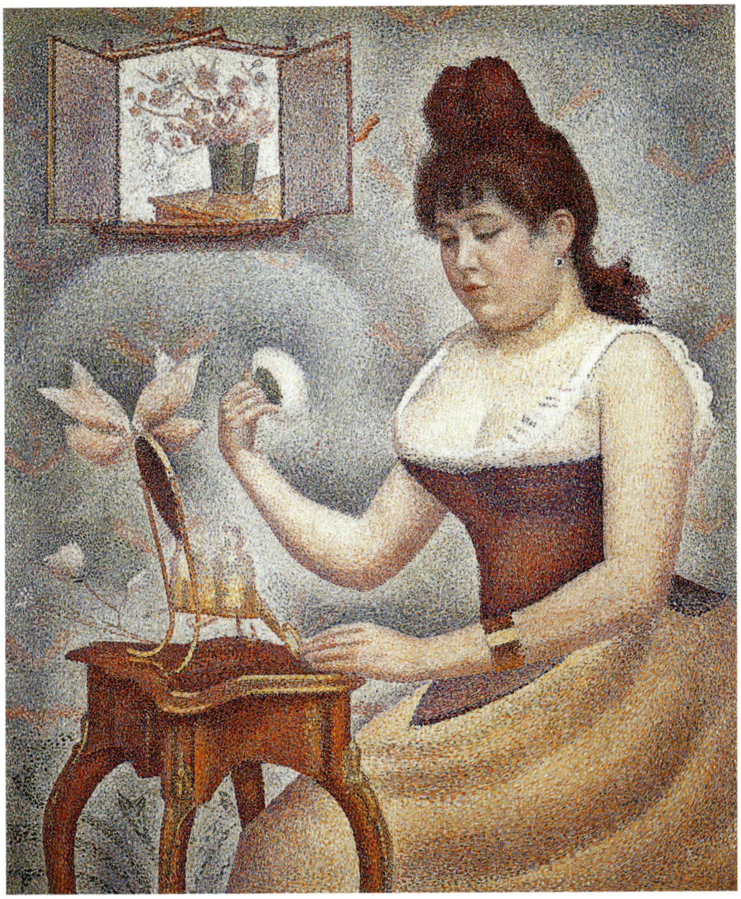

152 Georges Seurat, *Young Woman Powdering Herself*, 1888–9. Oil on canvas. 96.5 × 79.5 cm. London, Courtauld Institute Galleries.

> seems to forget her canvas and her *métier*. In fact, she is a very pure artist, uncontaminated with the pride of the craftsman. How much harm, by the by, the honest craftsman has done to art since William Morris invented the fiction of his supposed humility! (*R*, 348).

(A related topic concerns Fry's ambivalent regard for the sheer painterliness – the pictorial craftsmanship – of the work of Sickert and his students.[44]) More broadly, Fry in "On Some Modern Drawings" argues that there are two ways by which to arrive at rhythmic drawing, the first calligraphic, calling for the artist to suspend his attention to the gestures he is making, the second when the artist "becomes so concentrated upon the interpretation of a contour as to be unconscious of what goes on between his hand

and the paper. The ideal of such a situation is that he should actually never look at the paper" (*T*, 268).

A different sort of statement bearing on this topic is found in the late text "Henri-Matisse" (1935). "The artist himself has a double nature and a double allegiance," Fry writes. "He longs on the one hand to realise his vision, on the other to be a maker; he longs to tell of his experience and also to create an object, an idol, a precious thing. And almost always the vision and the precious thing, – the *objet d'art*, – are at variance. His vision and his craft pull different ways and his orbit is determined by their relative powers and proximities" (*R*, 401). The struggle to reconcile the two longings is a basic theme of Fry's summary account of the history of European painting. As Fry tells it, the struggle largely takes the form of a tension between representation on the one hand and design on the other; Matisse's distinction, in Fry's view, is that "in the entire history of European art no one has ever played so many delightful, unexpected, exhilarating variations upon the theme of the dual nature of painting as he has" (*R*, 406). But there is also in Fry's characterization of the contrary longings, especially when read in the light of the other remarks just cited, the suggestion of a hierarchy according to which realizing one's vision far outweighs considerations of craft, the making of a "precious thing, the *objet d'art*," though naturally both elements must be present if the result of the artist's labors is to be a painting. It is almost as though Fry invites us to imagine that an artist might somehow realize (and communicate) his or her absorbed vision *and yet not produce an object, an artifact, for others to see and admire*; if that were possible, and of course it is not, it would place the viewer in the same position as that of "pure" artists like Rembrandt, Corot, and Bell for whom the work in progress, in Fry's hyperbolic account of their states of mind as they painted, virtually did not exist. This is perhaps the most extreme expression of Fry's hyperbolic antitheatricalism: to produce an actual work, an *objet d'art*, is to make something that inescapably is there to be beheld; whereas to share certain artists' absorbed visions is to enter into communion with states of mind that not only care not at all for potential viewers but have lost sight of the work of art itself. (The title *Vision and Design* takes on a new inflection in this light.)

One book of Fry's in particular makes fascinating reading within the framework I have been developing – *Characteristics of French Art* (1933). Fry begins by noting that the French possess "a peculiar alertness of observation and nimbleness of mind," along with an interest "in life as it is and in people as they happen to be" (*C*, 6). This seems unexceptionable, but when Fry a page or so later turns to specific examples of French art his thought acquires an edge. The first work he discusses is a thirteenth-century sculpture of a boy musician from the façade of a house at Rheims (fig. 153). "[W]hat is striking here is the certainty with which the artist has grasped the central character of the figure," Fry writes.

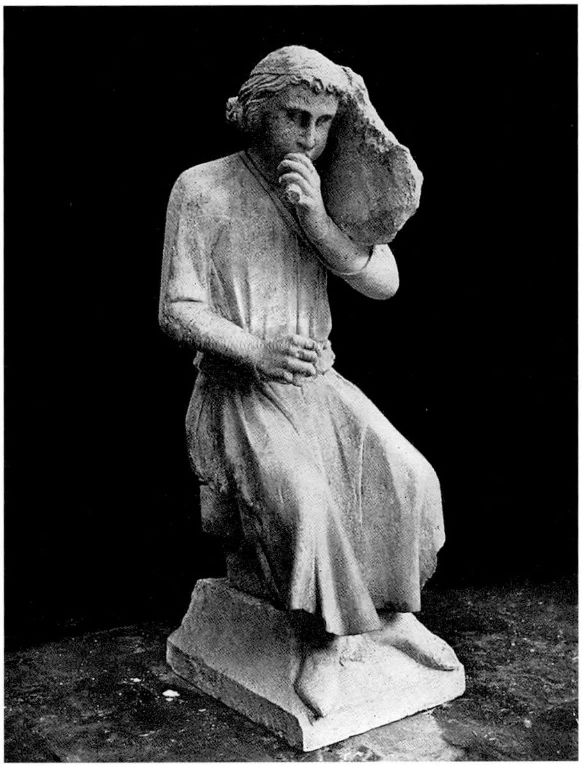

153 *Boy Musician*, thirteenth century, Rheims. From Roger Fry, *Characteristics of French Art*.

> In the movement of the head and the expression of the face he has made us vividly aware not only of the character of the boy but of his state of mind. In his intentness on the music which he is playing he is scarcely aware of the outer world – his face has that vague unseeing regard which comes from a withdrawal from the outside, from concentration on what is passing within the mind. (*C*, 8)

A few pages later Fry describes another representative sculpture, a Burgundian Madonna and Child of the fifteenth century (fig. 154). "[T]his is essentially a snapshot," Fry says,

> the artist must have seen this very thing happen, must have been so struck by its odd, unexpected significance and by the opportunity it gave for an entirely new and beautiful plastic harmony that he was able to carry it through without losing anything of its momentary quality and its intimate intensity of expression. He has watched some young mother – one fancies her sitting, as they so often do, in the street, just outside her door. Something attracts her attention, and she looks round one way while the child struggles away from her in the opposite direction. She holds him firmly but so

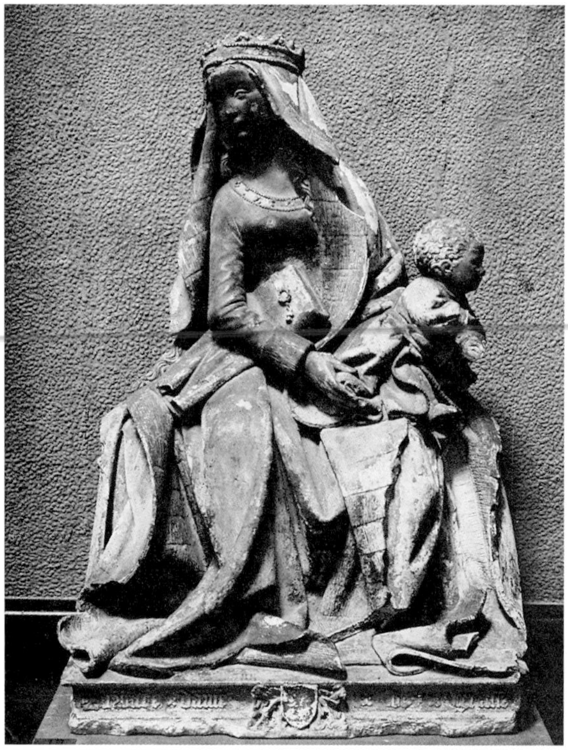

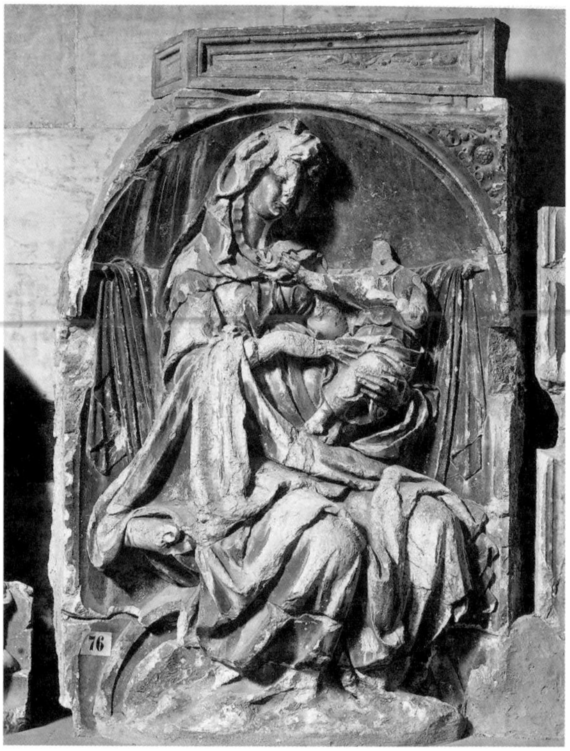

154 (*above, left*) *Madonna and Child*, fifteenth century, Burgundy. Toulouse, Musée des Augustins. From Roger Fry, *Characteristics of French Art*.

155 (*above, right*) Jacopo della Quercia, *Madonna and Child*, early fifteenth century. Preserved in Palazzo Pubblico di Siena. From Roger Fry, *Characteristics of French Art*.

> easily that she seems scarcely conscious of what he is doing as she becomes absorbed in a tender, slightly melancholy reverie. (*C*, 10)

Fry then contrasts the Burgundian sculpture with an Italian version of the theme by Jacopo della Quercia, in which he finds no hint of a momentary actual event (early 15th century; fig. 155). Not that della Quercia would have neglected to study nature deeply; but his primary concern, Fry suggests, was to achieve "a simple and grand rhythmic motive" while at the same time expressing the tenderness and grace appropriate to the subject. The result is "an intenser plastic unity" than the Burgundian sculpture possesses; more broadly, "the Italian imagination worked at a higher emotional pitch [and] with a greater momentum towards a preconceived end" (*C*, 11). But if the comparison with della Quercia gives the honors of form to the Italians, the victory is less significant than it seems for the simple reason that by the seventeenth century the transcendent

achievements of the Italian Renaissance in the realm of design were a thing of the past. The problem, in part, was consciousness itself. "In the full Renaissance," Fry had written twenty years earlier (referring, I think, to what we would call the High Renaissance), "this idea of design became the object of conscious and deliberate study, and the decadence of Italian art came about, not through indifference to the claims of artistic expression, but through a too purely intellectual and conscious study of them."[45] In practice that meant that the value of unity was carried down to the present by painting in France. And what from my point of view is almost startling (and yet, at this stage in our argument, not altogether surprising) about the two French sculptures Fry begins his book by discussing is that both emerge in his account as quintessentially absorptive, in two by now familiar complementary modes: the first in and through intensity of effort, the second in and through a kind of distraction, which leaves the gesture of restraining the child to operate unconsciously, automatistically – in short the pair corresponds approximately to the two modes of losing sight of the page in "On Some Modern Drawings."

Put more strongly, the entire book is written under the twin signs of absorption and antitheatricality, but without the writer being at all aware that this is so, and *a fortiori* without his recognizing that both absorption and antitheatricality became pressing issues for painting in France starting around the middle of the eighteenth century and continuing or rather dialectically evolving at least until the advent of Manet and his generation. (In fact they continued to play a role beyond Manet, but in significantly modified terms; see in this connection "Caillebotte's Impressionism" in this book.) This is not said in derogation of Fry: the very force and coherence as well as the continual productiveness of the French antitheatrical tradition seem largely to have depended on its invisibility as such to the artists and critics who took part in it. But Fry does offer the exemplary spectacle of a major critical intelligence who spent almost his entire viewing and writing life in the grip of certain fundamental assumptions and attitudes that continually inform his judgments and determine his preferences but that he was never able to bring into focus in their own right. And because he could not do this, he remained in the dark about their historicity (his negative attitude toward Diderot, the ultimate source of his most deeply held values, is only the most striking instance of that obliviousness[46]), which is also to say that he never suspected that there might be a problem in applying those assumptions and attitudes as universal criteria to all the art that came his way.

This last is a large topic, but a portion of its complexities may be glimpsed when it is recalled that in "David/Manet" in this book I claim that David's intentions in the *Sabines* were essentially antitheatrical, even as his withdrawal from what had come to seem to him the too-overt drama of the *Horatii* meant that the *Sabines* soon came to be seen as theatrical in the sense of figures posing (rather than overacting). It follows that, with respect to works belonging to the French antitheatrical tradition, Fry treats as an absolute quality (theatricality, antitheatricality) inhering permanently and unchangingly in a given picture what historically speaking is best thought of as a structure of intention on the part of the artist, one that will be perceived differently by different cohorts of spectators with the passage of time, or indeed, as in the case just mentioned, by the artist himself. As for works by artists before or simply outside that tradition (for example, Andrea del Sarto, Raphael, El Greco, Bernini, Poussin, Caravaggio, and Turner, not to mention makers of Chinese ritual bronzes and Japanese calligraphers), it seems altogether unlikely (to put it mildly) that the concept of theatricality in the pejorative sense of the term can be made to apply to them in any consistent or illuminating way.

It would be instructive to examine a series of passages in *Characteristics of French Art*, each dealing with a different painter from the perspective of an unexamined antitheatricalism, but by this stage in my argument that should not be necessary.[47] Instead I want to conclude by focusing in turn on three rather disparate items.

The first is a passage in Fry's *Cézanne: A Study of His Development*. The topic is still life, and Fry has just remarked on Goya's ability to give "even to the still life, a kind of dramatic significance."[48] Then:

> Cézanne at one time might well have had similar aims [Fry had earlier stressed the young Cézanne's taste for pictorial melodrama], but by the period which we are considering he had definitely abandoned them. He eagerly accepts the most ordinary situations, the arrangements of objects which result from everyday life. But though he had no dramatic purpose, though it would be absurd to speak of the drama of his fruit dishes, his baskets of vegetables, his apples spilt upon the kitchen table, none the less these scenes in his hands leave upon us the impression of grave events. If the words tragic, menacing, noble or lyrical seem out of place before Cézanne's still-lifes, one feels none the less that the emotions they arouse are curiously analogous to these states of mind. It is not from lack of emotion that these pictures are not dramatic, lyric, etc., but rather by reason of a process of elimination and concentration. They are, so to speak, dramas deprived of all dramatic incident. One may wonder whether painting has ever aroused graver, more powerful, more massive emotions than those to which we are compelled by some of Cézanne's masterpieces in this genre.[49]

I find this extraordinary. Throughout his career as a critic (after the Giotto essay, I mean), Fry has been insisting that drama has nothing whatever to do with form. Cézanne was for Fry the supreme modern master of form, and yet it suddenly turns out

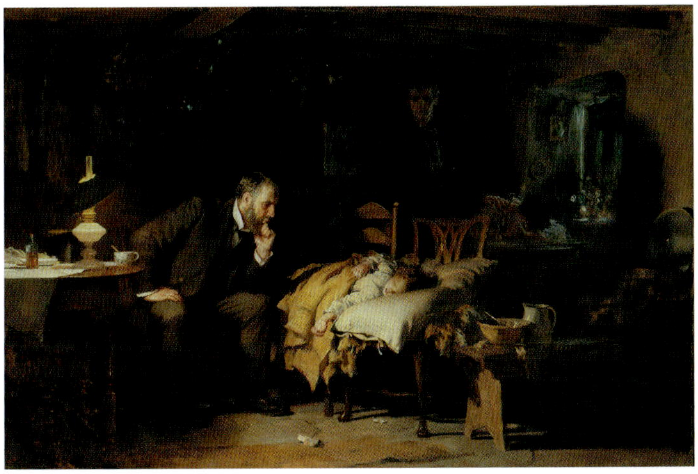

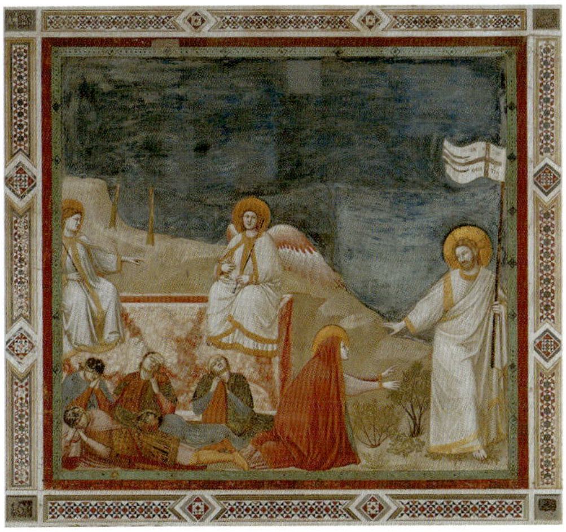

156 (*above, left*) Luke Fildes, *The Doctor*, exhibited 1891. Oil on canvas. 166.4 × 241.9 cm. London, Tate Gallery.

157 (*above, right*) Giotto, *Christ Appearing to Mary Magdalen*, ca. 1305. Fresco. Padua, Arena Chapel.

that his finest paintings, the still lifes, are – not dramatic exactly, in a tangled sentence Fry seems explicitly to state that they are not – but "dramas deprived of all dramatic incident." This would seem to identify form at its most purged and concentrated with drama, period. Diderot would agree.

The second item is the first of six radio broadcasts of 1929, "The Meaning of Pictures; I – Telling a Story," which turns on a highly charged comparison between two sharply different works: Luke Fildes's *The Doctor* (1891; fig. 156) in the Tate, which depicts a doctor caring for a sick child as dawn breaks following an all-night vigil, and Giotto's *Christ Appearing to Mary Magdalen* in the Arena Chapel (ca. 1305; fig. 157). Naturally, Fry abhors Fildes's canvas. After praising its ingenuity, he writes: "[A]ll the same there is something profoundly wrong. For all the mass of details which are correctly described for us there is something false about the whole thing: the dice are loaded: these people are too noble, they would not be like that unless we were looking on" – an antitheatrical complaint if there ever was one. And another point: "We feel here," Fry says, "an invitation to identify oneself with the doctor; we feel that we, too, are capable of this devotion, and we get a certain moral satisfaction which we have done nothing to earn. I suspect that a great deal of the attraction of sentimental art and sentimental stories comes from an indulgence in this fictitious sense of one's moral worth" (*R*, 398).

In contrast, the Giotto makes no such factitious appeal to our emotions. On the contrary, we feel that the sleeping soldiers "are shut out completely from the dramatic situation." As for the angels, we are struck by "the awful indifference and serenity with which they watch the scene." Near the right-hand edge of the scene Mary Magdalen reaches out her arms to embrace Christ, who however "slides away from her touch." The entire design produces an effect "of loneliness, isolation and mystery" that accords well with the hour of dawn when it is supposed to have taken place. Plus the Giotto is devoid of the accessory details that clutter *The Doctor*. "We are dealing," Fry writes, "only with the fundamental psychological facts of the story, the great oppositions and contrasts of the situation, and we see that such a bleak, abstract treatment, shows us the fundamental drama with incredible force" (*R*, 399). And something more:

> For all its dramatic intensity we are not asked to come so close to the action as we are by Luke Fildes. We watch it taking place in a world which is somewhat removed from the actual world, a world which we cannot enter into – wherein we shall never be actors. We cannot identify ourselves with these people; the scene remains there for our contemplation rather than for any immediate personal contact. (*R*, 399–400)

Once again Fry does not consider the possibility that the very features of the scene he singles out for praise all but allegorize the distance and detachment he seeks: the sleeping soldiers, oblivious to the dramatic situation; the angels, surrogate beholders, whose awful indifference and serenity the actual beholder can only aspire to match; the loneliness and isolation of the overall mood; and especially the central event, the risen Christ evading the Magdalen's touch as he exits the picture, his gesture of denial insisting on separation, distance, an uncrossable gulf between worlds.[50] Moreover, throughout the discussion of *Jesus Appearing to the Magdalen* there is not a single mention of form or design (granted, these are not Fry's topic), only evocations of the dramatic force and concentration of Giotto's stupendous invention.[51] As in the passage from *Cézanne*, all this suggests an unexpected closeness to Diderot, an ascetic and disidentificatory analogue to his conception of the *tableau*, which itself may be characterized precisely in terms of separation, distance, a gulf between worlds.[52]

The last item I want to consider is a letter Fry wrote several months before he died to the woman he lived with, Helen Anrep. The letter was composed in Paris in March 1934 (Fry would die in September), and it mainly concerns a day he had spent in Milan looking at paintings in the Brera and other museums. He mentions portraits by Antonello and Tintoretto in the Castello Sforzesco, and then begins a new paragraph as follows:

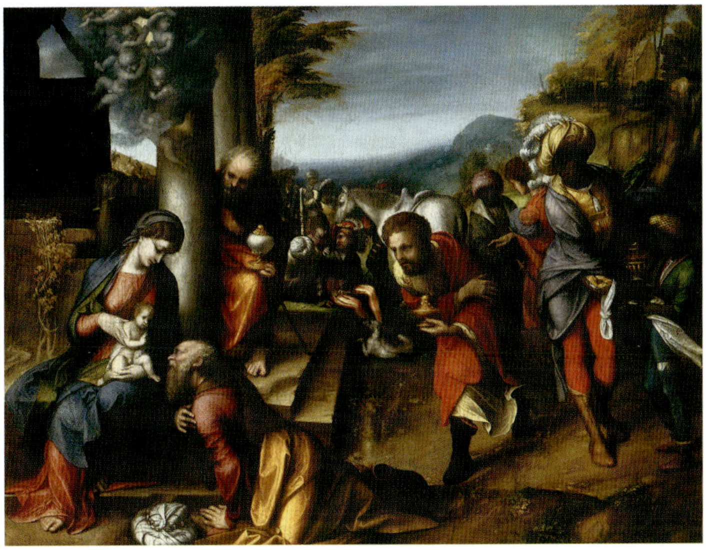

158 Antonio da Correggio, *Adoration of the Magi*, 1516–17. Oil on canvas. 84 × 108 cm. Milan, Pinacoteca di Brera.

> And Correggio. There's something we've both missed in his psychology, I because I've looked too purely at form, you because you're put off by his form, but there's an *Adoration of the Magi* [1516–17; fig. 158], a rather nasty picture in some ways but with such a rare piece of imagination in the Virgin, who's almost hiding from all these grandees behind a pillar and entirely absorbed in her baby and so incredibly tenderly human. I see I'm in danger of getting shockingly "literary" under your influence. But I see that the pictures that "count" most *generally* have some quite new and personal conception of the situation.[53] (emphasis in original)

Is this not revealing? Fry the inveterate museum-goer, once again being moved by an absorptive motif (the Virgin hiding from visitors, absorbed in her baby), and once again unable to think of it other than as a "literary" device, yet struggling, not solely to please his correspondent, to find a way to take it seriously – and not quite succeeding. The quotation marks around "count" and the italicization of "generally" bespeak the failure of his effort, the unclarity of the thought they strain too hard to qualify. Fitting, therefore, that the letter ends in a bilingual flourish that shows how little Fry's basic values evolved in the course of his long critical career. The last sentence reads: "I send you a few cards – the innocent crank Scaletti [not of interest to us] and the terribly *'averti'* [hyper-aware] Dosso who's much too conscious and anxious to *épater* [amaze]."[54]

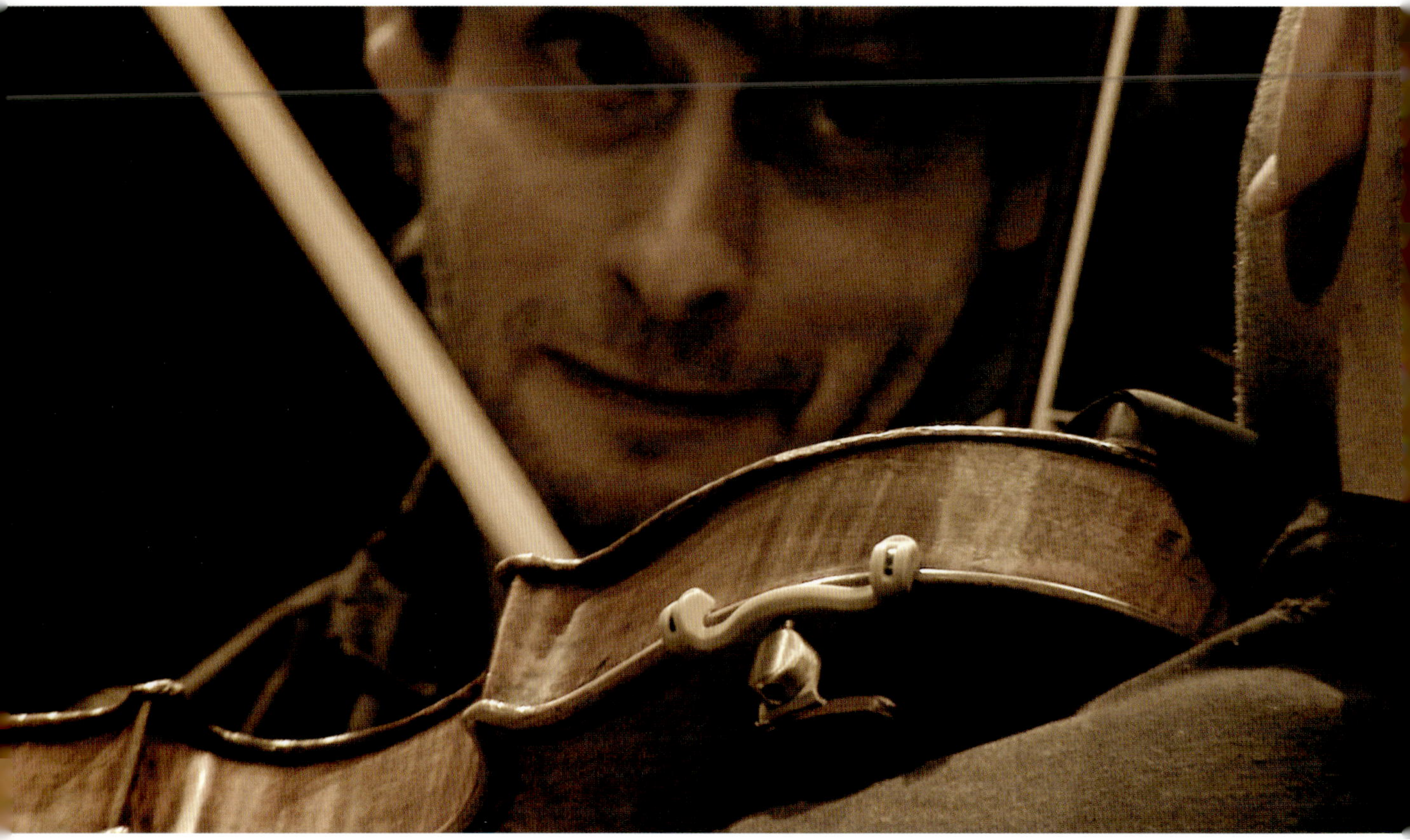

· 7 ·

DOUGLAS GORDON'S *k.364: A JOURNEY BY TRAIN*

Here are the broad outlines of Gordon's 2011 film, *k.364: A Journey by Train*: two Israeli musicians from Polish Jewish families, the violist Avri Levitan and the violinist Roi Shiloah (hereafter, Avri and Roi), both in their late thirties, take a train journey from Berlin to Warsaw via Poznan.[1] In Poznan they rehearse the piece that gives Gordon's movie its title, Mozart's "Sinfonia Concertante in E Flat Major" for violin, viola, and orchestra with the Amadeus chamber orchestra, based in that city and conducted by Agnieszka Duczmal. (Mozart composed it in 1780, when he was twenty-four, but we are not told that, or anything else about the piece.) In Warsaw at the Philharmonic concert hall Avri and Roi perform it with the orchestra from first note to last; when the performance is over the movie is almost at its end. In the course of the train ride Avri and Roi talk about several subjects, including, unsurprisingly, the Holocaust. A related topic concerns a swimming pool in Poznan, which was originally a synagogue; *k.364* opens with shots taken in the water and we return to the pool at two other moments as well. The duration of the film is 68 minutes and 10 seconds.

There is also a back-story that has to do with Gordon's companion, the Israeli singer Ruth Rosenfeld (hereafter, Ruth), whom he met in 2007 in Manchester, England when she took part in a ten-soprano piece based on *Madame Butterfly* arranged by Gordon's friend, the artist Anri Sala. (They now have a young daughter, Lili.) Before living with Ruth, classical music was pretty much a closed book to Gordon; since their connection that has changed, and whatever else it may be, *k.364* is testimony to that fact. It also turned out that Ruth had earlier been married to Avri, whom she introduced to Gordon shortly after they became a couple. Gordon: "After four or five seconds of strange hostility, we became very close friends."[2] This eventually led to his accompanying Ruth and three Israeli friends on a train ride to Poznan to hear Avri and a violinist named Guy Braunstein perform the "Sinfonia Concertante." Gordon was

159 (*facing page*) and 160–79 (*following pages*) *k.364: A Journey by Train*. Directed by Douglas Gordon. Produced by Lost but Found Film / Lovestreams Productions / Agnés b. Productions. Distributed by Lost but Found Film UK, 2010.

moved, both by the music and by the journey, and he decided to make a film based on both; Braunstein, however, was not available, so Avri suggested Roi, whom he had known since they were children. When Gordon met Roi and saw the two musicians together, this seemed an excellent idea, for reasons that will become clear as we proceed.

I first saw Gordon's film in Berlin in not quite finished form in December 2010; even in its tentative state it was compelling. Since then I have watched it countless times on DVD, and I have not the slightest doubt that it is a work of great power and subtlety. My job now is to try briefly to explain why. I will do this under five headings.

I ANTITHEATRICALITY

According to a synopsis published by the Gagosian Gallery, *k.364* is "an exercise in portraiture, following on from Douglas Gordon and Philippe Parreno's *Zidane: A 21st Century Portrait*"; well yes, all right, though there is far more to the film than that, and to say as the synopsis also does that it "is a portrait of a piece of music" also falls somewhat short of capturing the truly large scope of Gordon's ambitions, as I read them, anyway. But there can be no doubt as to the connection with *Zidane*, which in my book *Why Photography Matters as Art as Never Before* I discuss in terms of an almost Diderotian investigation into the possibilities of sustaining absorption under modern conditions of maximum publicity.[3] For Diderot writing in the 1760s, the problem of portraiture consisted in the seemingly inescapable fact that the sitter was understood as having presented himself or herself to be beheld (and, of course, painted), this under a pictorial regime – so I claim – that called for the creation of the ontological illusion that the figure or figures in a painting were so absorbed in what they were doing, feeling, or thinking that they were without the least awareness of the very existence of anything else – certainly of anyone looking at them, which by extension also meant the beholder standing before the canvas. Not surprisingly, Diderot's favorite portrait of himself depicted him resting his chin and cheek in his hand and lost in thought. Roughly 250 years later, the Zidane project amounts to a sustained study of the famous footballer – filmed with his consent by no less than seventeen movie cameras in the course of a regular Spanish league match – as he apparently remains (for the most part) absorbed in the action on the field, even as subtitles representing his thoughts or speech declare that at times he is aware of everything taking place in the stands, someone talking to a neighbor, or shifting in his seat, or coughing, even, he imagines, the ticking of a watch. As he also "says": "One is never alone." (Whereas according to the classic Diderotian paradigm the impression of aloneness was precisely the point.) The work that results is deeply fascinating and also strongly resistant to any simple interpretation of the basic issue of remaining "oneself" under the pressures of modern spectacle culture, pressures that the film brilliantly hyperbolizes as if in a dual effort to celebrate Zinedine Zidane's capacity for intactness and to discover the least fraying or weakening of that capacity as the game proceeds.

In *k.364* we are dealing not with one but two protagonists, Avri and Roi, and the basic situation involves another sort of performance, before another sort of audience, much smaller and more restricted – in a concert hall, not a sports stadium, and with no suggestion of an outside audience in the tens of millions, as in *Zidane*. But the more confined conditions hardly mean that the problem of theatricality is not potentially acute – if anything, the opposite is true: everyone, probably, has had the experience of attending a concert in which the gestures and expressions of soloist and/or conductor, readable even at a distance, have struck him or her as unbearable – certainly I have. Plus there is at least one earlier work by Gordon, *Feature Film* (1999), that can be understood as addressing the problem in its own ingenious way.[4] Briefly, the American conductor James Conlon is shown leading an orchestra that we never see in a performance of Bernard Herrmann's soundtrack for Hitchcock's *Vertigo* (the limit of Gordon's "serious" musical tastes before he came under Ruth's influence); the absence of the orchestra – also of a visible audience – only enhances one's sense of the theatricality of the handsome Conlon's soulful expressions and sweeping hand gestures, as if he were conducting the piece for himself alone, or perhaps not actually conducting it, only pretending to do so. Moreover, the filming of his performance, at extremely close range and with three cameras, two static and one mobile, is such as show us only his face and hands, seemingly compounding the problem. At the same time – crucially, as I see it – the extremely active cropping and editing that followed, montaging short, discontinuous bits into a flowing whole, has the effect of displacing attention away from face and hands as such (as vehicles of "feeling") toward what I will call the film as a film (the film as an aesthetic entity in its own right). In other words, the theatricality which shot by shot is milked for all it is worth is at the same time continuously redeemed or transcended by the extraordinary, almost balletic editorial skill with which those shots have been joined to one another for the duration of the movie (the film's power to bring this about is doubled when, as in Gordon's 2006 exhibition in Edinburgh, it is projected on two facing screens with the image-streams mirroring each other).

The result is impressive but of course it also works somewhat "against" the music, as does the implied reference to the unshown movie, which Gordon likes to think of as present in the viewer/listener's awareness throughout *Feature Film*. Not only is this not a fault, however, it positively befits a work in which the music itself is – how shall I put

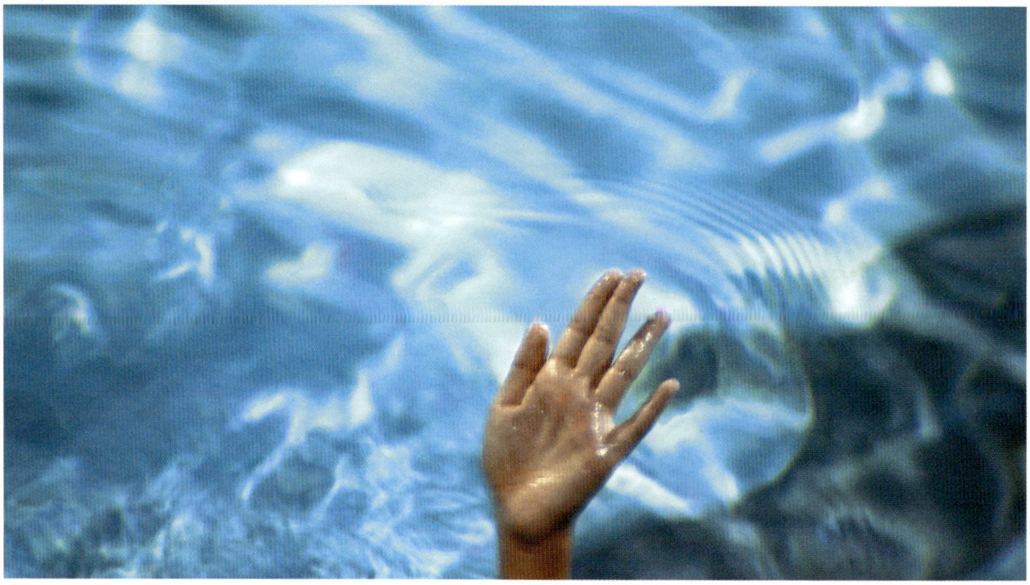

160

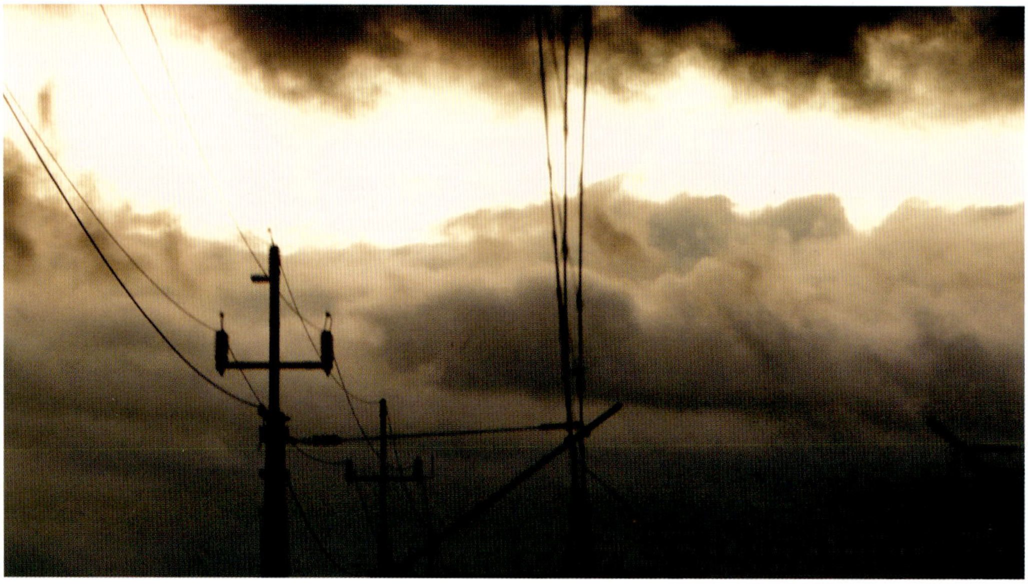

162

it? – not quite immortal. Less judgmentally, it is music that does not aim at formal and expressive autonomy but rather shapes itself to the narrative and other needs of Hitchcock's movie, including the need for intervals of silence. Mozart's "Sinfonia Concertante" presents a different problem both because of the sheer quality and

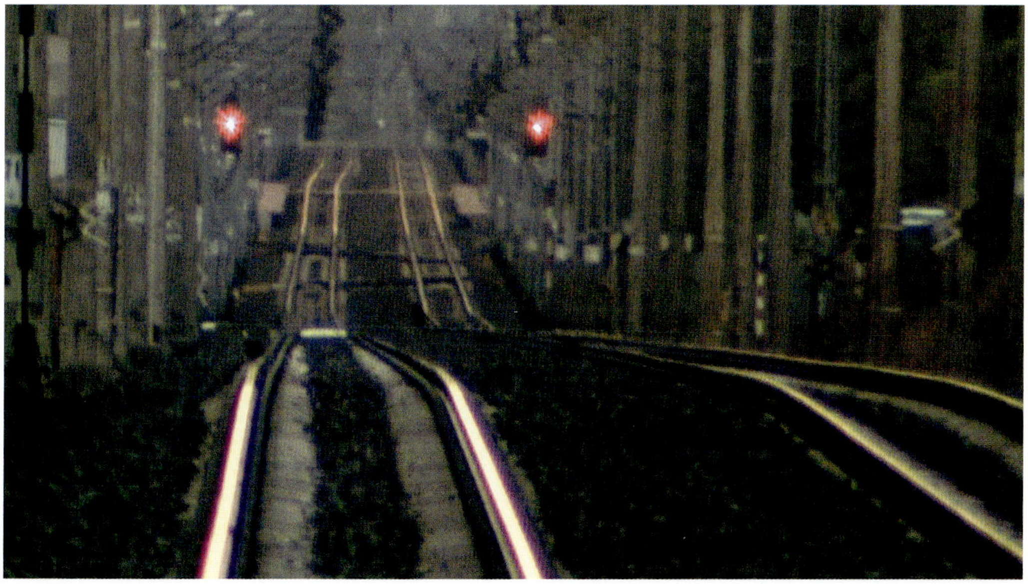

161

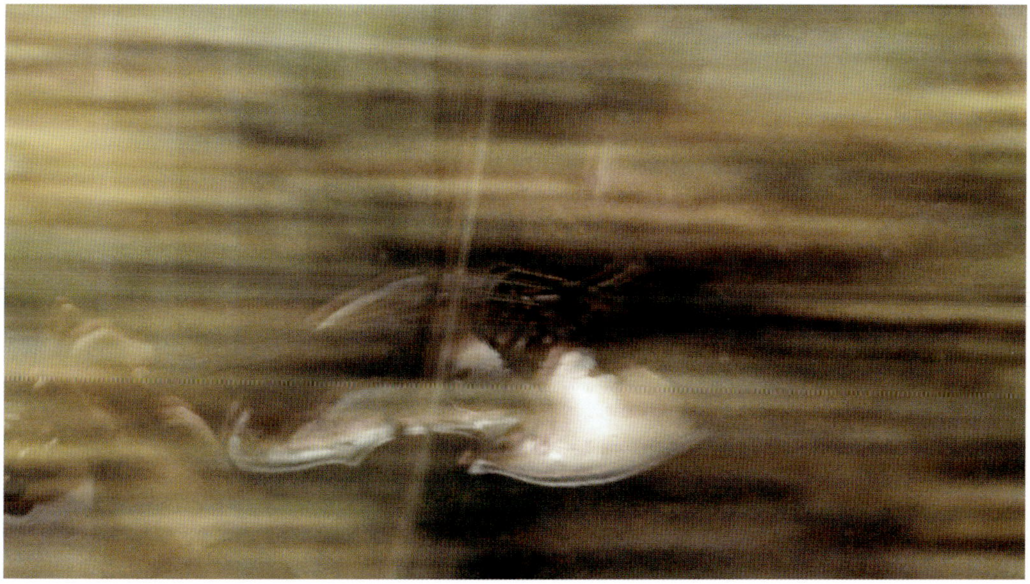

163

expressiveness of the music and because Gordon is committed to a view first stated by Avri several minutes into the film when he remarks that music is not what is on the paper; paper is nothing, paper is . . . paper with little black dots on it. Rather: "Music exists only when it is in the air, when the sound is in the room, when somebody is performing it." (Later, at a crucial juncture – just before we enter the concert hall in Warsaw – Gordon puts on the screen the words "music exists only when it reaches your ears," thus signing off on Avri's sentiment.) Simply put, *k.364* is a portrait of a musical performance, and its twin tasks are to depict that performance in such a manner that the music comes through in all its beauty and power and at the same time to divest the performance of the least trace of theatricality, which turns out to mean the least trace of a *primary* relation to the audience that has been gathered to experience it – and beyond that, I shall suggest, to the audience for the film. Actually, the two tasks are linked in that the first can be accomplished only by means of the second, one implication of the film perhaps being that even a performance as admirable as the one it ostensibly records stands in need of such an operation of divestiture.

Various features of *k.364* contribute to this end, none more importantly than the choice of music, or rather the fact that the piece in question involves two soloists, not just one. As the viewer/listener quickly comes to realize, the film positively feasts on the relationship between Avri and Roi, which is clearly extremely close and also full of nuance. For example, Avri explains that he first became aware of Roi when he himself was six and Roi was seven and already, one gathers, something of a legend in Israel. Later they went to the same high school and played together in an Israeli army string quartet. But none of this would matter in relation to the film apart from their respective *looks*. To begin with Roi, his face compares with Zidane's sheerly as an object of cinematic fascination (which is saying a lot); like Zidane's, too, there is something bird-like in his mien; but whereas Zidane with his shaven head and lean, hawklike features conveys an overwhelming impression of predatory maleness, Roi's face, set off by a shock of thick brown hair divided in the middle and falling across his forehead, seems almost childlike (bird-childlike), with a beaky nose, large nostrils, deep eye-sockets, gray-blue eyes with delicate lids and long eyelashes, and – his most striking feature – a large mouth with thinnish flexible lips that seem, until one gets used to them, impossibly purple in color. Avri in contrast has a shaven head, blunt, "masculine" features, dark eyes with thick dark eyebrows, and an expressive mouth; strong as his looks are, they are less remarkable in themselves than Avri's but the two faces together, neither one exactly clean-shaven, make an unsurpassably cinematogenic combination, as Gordon, lucky man, must instantly have realized. (More on this shortly.)

Gordon's luck did not stop there: the train arrives at Poznan, we see a warmly dressed Avri and Roi on the platform (virtually our only sighting of them other than in close-ups, about which more further on) – it appears they are expecting to be met – and then the scene shifts abruptly to the rehearsal and the wholly unexpected introduction of a third protagonist, a woman, the conductor Agnieszka Duczmal. And she too is marvelous to look at, especially in relation to the two soloists: think Iris Murdoch's Slavic sister – thick fairish hair in bangs, like Murdoch – intense, studious (she wears rimless glasses), not tall, in her early sixties, with a wonderful smile that lights up the screen whenever it flashes. Workmanlike hands, the right one holding a wandlike baton. (I can not quite see my way clear to calling her Agnieszka.) So that suddenly there are three not two terms to the constantly rebalancing equation, with the latest to be added perhaps the most dynamic of all. From now on, in both the rehearsal and the performance, paying attention to the music on the part of the viewer/listener involves paying equally close attention to the interaction among the three main characters, who (we soon realize) constitute what might be called the world or perhaps better the "society" of the performance for the purposes of the film. That is, in the Philharmonic hall in Warsaw we are given only the most cursory glimpse of the audience for the concert followed by a longer scan, still lasting only seconds, of the orchestra as a whole. Instead, the film's focus, Gordon's focus, is entirely and consistently on the two soloists and the conductor, whom we see from different angles of vision but always and only at close range (as in *Feature Film*; the camera work is brilliant, the editing superb), focusing mainly on their faces but also on their hands, with the result that we have no sense whatever of their location in the hall or their relation to the audience or indeed to the orchestra – in short their actual circumstances have been effectively suspended, neutralized, detheatricalized. (We do see from time to time the rather impassive bespectacled head of a seated male cellist.) Moreover, from the first notes of the actual performance the screen divides in two down the middle, which of course impels the viewer/listener to pay even closer attention to what is offered to be seen, with the further twist that there is no anticipating, as the different camera positions come into play, and are played with in turn in the process of editing, who will turn up on the left-hand and who on the right-hand screen or for how long. Sometimes the same soloist, often Roi, appears on both screens, at other times both soloists are on one screen or the other or both, and we are also given fleeting views of Agnieszka Duczmal, usually in conjunction with one or both of the others. (The use of telephoto lenses has the effect of compressing the space between them.) Toward the very end, though, it is mainly Roi on the right as the left-hand screen is largely blurred; we sense Avri's presence there until he is replaced by the moving blurred lights of the train journey, and then, briefly, by an earlier shot of his resting features reflected in a train window . . . as if in anticipation of the return journey to Berlin that is soon to come. All this while the piece is rushing toward its close. The fleetingness of the moment could not be more strongly marked.

Finally, when the short and thrilling third movement (the last) comes to an end, the soloists turn toward the unseen audience, but there is no applause, only a "loud"

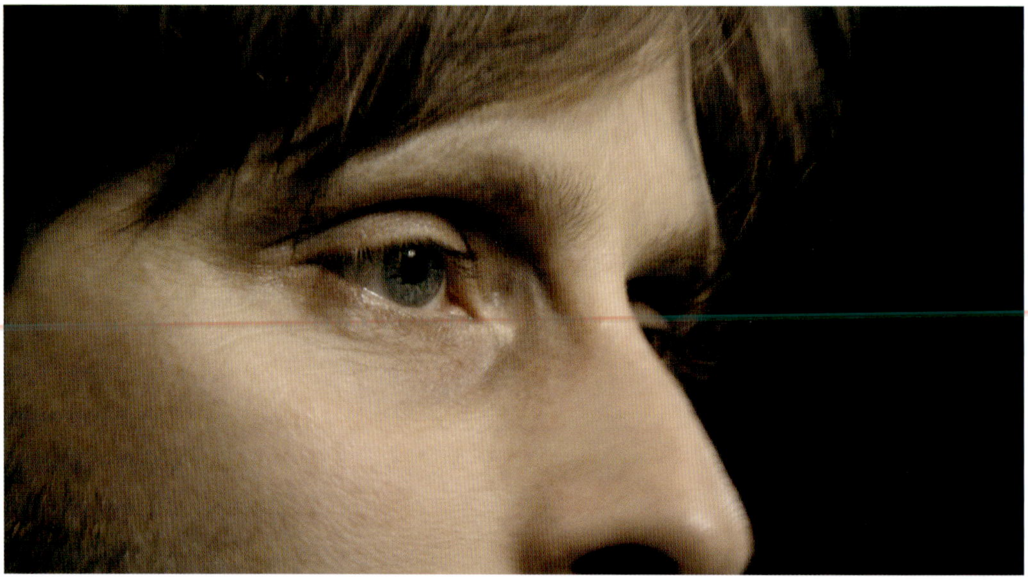

164

166

silence (I mean Gordon has cut out the applause that undoubtedly resounded), and then triumphantly take their bows, but these are shown on the split screens from opposite points of view so that what one mainly sees is Avri (on the right) and Roi (on the left) bowing as if *to each other* – there was obviously no means of including Agnieszka

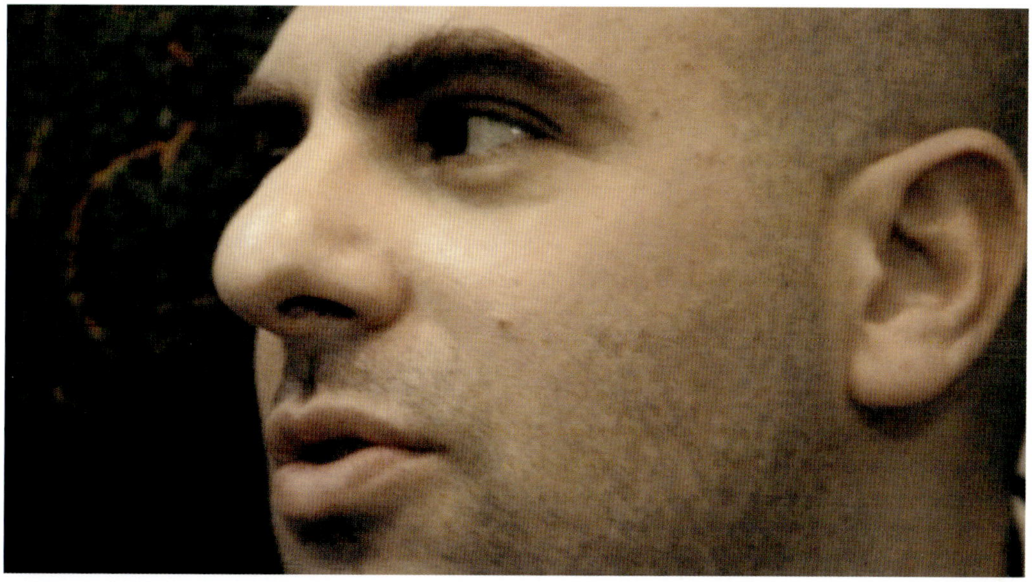

165

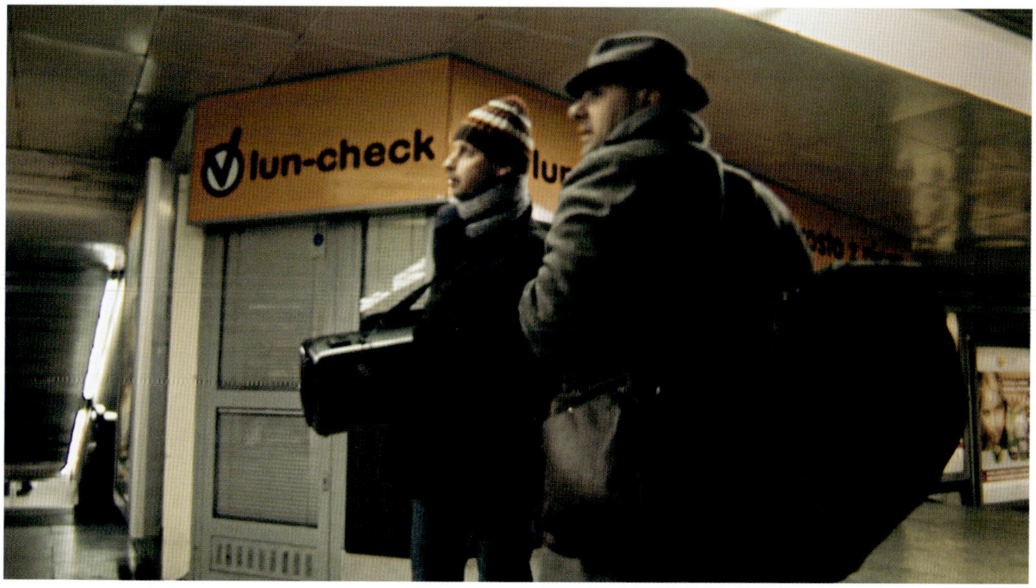

167

Duczmal in this – an inspired stroke that almost comically clinches the bracketing of the audience and more broadly of the literal situation that the film has been seeking to bring about almost from the first.

2 PRESENTNESS

Another framing context for *k.364* has to do with the bringing together of imagetrack and soundtrack in recent video and short artists' films. Gordon's *Feature Film* is an early, and I think influential, case in point, but equally relevant to my argument is Anri Sala's *Long Sorrow* (2005), a remarkable video (really, a short film edited digitally) that features the American free jazz saxophonist Jemeel Moondoc improvising on his instrument while standing on a small platform outside a window on the eighteenth story of a large apartment complex in Berlin.[5] The video begins inside a seemingly bare apartment with a slow traveling shot *en avant* toward a mysterious object that appears to rest on the sill of a partly open window or rather just outside it; throughout the shot we hear Moondoc's saxophone but only when we have come quite close to the object do we realize that it is the head of a black man with dreadlocks (also with flowers in his hair); and it is only after that that the scene shifts to outside and the basic situation becomes clear. More precisely, it becomes clear to a limited extent: for example, we never see more than the mouthpiece of Moondoc's instrument, and most of the time he is filmed at extremely close range such that we rarely are shown his entire face (this is done telescopically but the effect is of the camera coming uncomfortably near, as if to penetrate his "wall" of safety and break his concentration, if at all possible). As in *Feature Film*, which Sala surely knew, the close-ups are discontinuous and the editing extremely active, promoting a sense of the utter precariousness of the situation and in particular of the special effort which Moondoc appears to be making to convert that situation into improvised music. And this in turn makes one all the more aware of the unguaranteed, instant-by-instant bringing together, the almost physical joining, of the imagetrack and the soundtrack so as to produce an effect that I think of as one of *presentness* – according to my 1967 essay "Art and Objecthood" a high modernist ideal but here achieved, if one agrees that it is achieved, by decidedly non-high modernist means.[6]

Simply put, Gordon in *k.364* shares that ideal just as he shares Sala's passion for music but instead of seeking to realize it via jazz improvisation, his project (as we have seen) relies on the performance of a classical work, the "Sinfonia Concertante," which has a definite beginning, middle, and end, in short a predetermined form – indeed every note is predetermined though of course there is some slight room for "interpretation." And instead of focusing on a single protagonist, Gordon has undertaken to deal with a collective effort. Yet Gordon's aim, if I am right, is to achieve an equivalent effect of presentness from first note to last. How was this to be done?

What exactly, though, is the problem? Is it not at least conceivable that a piece of music of the artistic distinction of the "Sinfonia Concertante" simply evokes or achieves what I am calling presentness if it is performed adequately? – that presentness is a fundamental quality of the best compositions in what has come to be called the classical style? One source of difficulty here is that the concept itself has no track record in discussions of music, with one exception, which I want briefly to introduce: Stanley Cavell's speculations about presentness in relation to Shakespeare and specifically Shakespearean dramatic poetry in his early essay, "The Avoidance of Love: A Reading of *King Lear*" (1969). "It is not uncommon to find Shakespeare's plays compared to music," Cavell writes, then continues:

> but in the instances I have seen, this comparison rests upon more or less superficial features of music, for example, on its balance of themes, its recurrences, shifts of mood, climaxes – in a word, on its theatrical properties. But music is, or was, dramatic in a more fundamental sense, or it became so when it no longer expanded festivals or enabled dancing or accompanied songs, but achieved its own dramatic autonomy, worked out its progress in its own terms. Perhaps this begins with Monteverdi (born three years after Shakespeare), but in any case it is secured only with the establishment of tonality and has its climax in the development of sonata form. The essence of the quality I have in mind has to do with the notion of *development*: not, as in early sonata forms, merely with an isolated section in which fragments of earlier material are recolored and reassembled, but with the process, preeminent in late Beethoven and Brahms, in which the earlier is metamorphosed into new stabilities, culminating in a work like the *Hammerklavier* Sonata, in which *all* later material can be said to be "contained" in the rising and falling interval of a third in the opening two bars. The question I wish to raise here is: How is music made this way to be perceived? *What* are we to perceive in order to understand and respond to what is said? Obviously not, in the example alluded to, merely or primarily the rising and falling thirds. I will say that the quality we are to perceive is one of *directed motion*, controlled by relations of keys, by rate of alteration, and by length and articulation of phrases. We do not know where this motion can stop and we do not understand why it has begun here, so we do not know where we stand nor why we are there. The drama consists in following this out and in finding out what it takes to follow this out.[7]

As he also writes:

> The perception or attitude demanded in following this drama [in *Lear* or the music in question] is one which demands a continuous attention to what is happening at each here and now, as if everything of significance is happening at this moment, while each thing that happens turns a leaf of time. I think of it as an experience of *continuous presentness*. Its demands are as rigorous as those of any spiritual exercise – to let

> the past go and to let the future take its time; so that we not allow the past to determine the meaning of what is now happening (something else may have come of it) and that we not anticipate what will come of what has come. Not that anything is possible (though it is) but that we do not know what is, and is not, next. (322; emphasis in original)

(Cavell also speaks of drama such as *Lear* as finding it necessary to defeat theatricality, a notion, along with that of presentness, which he relates to "Art and Objecthood" [333 n. 16]. Cavell and I could not have been closer intellectually during those years.)

Now, Mozart's "Sinfonia Concertante" is not a piece that exhibits development in the full Cavellian sense; there is a long way to go, not so much in years (not quite 40) as in musical evolution, before we reach the "Hammerklavier." But remember, Gordon's project ultimately involved making a film, not a piece of music, that would be marked by presentness; put another way, he had to find a piece of music that would lend itself to certain filmic operations as regards both image and sound – and in my view he succeeded brilliantly. Moreover, precisely by so doing, he in effect reinterpreted or re-presented the "Sinfonia Concertante" in a way that aligns it, as we watch and listen, with something like an ideal of "continous presentness" – an ideal Gordon expresses by the words "no past – no future" which appear as a visual text immediately following the statement about music existing only when it reaches the ear. (The two notions are complementary.) As he also remarks in a conversation with the British composer Michael Berkeley, "I suppose one of the great things I've begun to discover, the more I listen to music, is that it hovers somewhere between the past and the future, and that kind of indefinable present is very much where I want the artwork to go."[8] One such art work, of course, is *k.364*.

Indeed if one bears in mind the notion of directed motion, the fact that the entire film is based not simply on a performance but also on a train journey turns out to be appropriate to say the least. The film proper begins – following no less than fifteen rapid alternations between shots in the swimming pool in Poznan and the opening titles – with shots of receding tracks and overhead wires, the latter viewed against a stormy sky as night comes on, and colored lights in and out of focus – that is, with a visual cluster associated with a journey on a fixed path, literally on rails – and here it may even be relevant that we are shown two parallel sets of tracks, one for each of the soloists, so to speak (I do not suggest that this was consciously intended from the first). At the same time, the deliberate blurring and then sharpening of focus, at work even during the opening moments at the pool, and for that matter the repeated alternation between pool and titles that opens the film, signal in the plainest possible way that a highly refined artistic intelligence is in charge, that we are in its grip, that however predetermined the journey may be (from Berlin to Poznan to Warsaw, from first note to last of the "Sinfonia Concertante"), the film-maker's intentions reign supreme throughout. Or at least that they are intended to do so. (Deliberate blurring – going out of and back into focus – will be a major element in *k.364*'s visual rhetoric all the way.)

Not that the journey is without detours. On the contrary, Gordon has also designed a film in which certain challenges to directedness not only have been welcomed but have been made part of the proceedings. This is the structural significance of the fact that the first conversation in the carriage is about the Holocaust, as Avri comments on the trees rushing by outside and explains that it is impossible for people like himself and Roi not to think of Jewish prisoners working in those woods in the cold of winter. Roi then briefly tells the story of his family being given ten minutes to leave their home in Pułtusk; they fled to Russia, spent time in work camps, and eventually made their way to Israel, where he was born. For him, it seems, visiting Poland is no special matter; indeed the food and certain words strike chords from his childhood; but his mother has refused ever to return (likewise *her* mother), and as he tells an unseen and unheard interlocutor (presumably Gordon), the greatest compliment anyone can give her is to be surprised that she was not born in Israel. There will be more to say about this conversation later on, but for the moment I want simply to note the risk, deliberately courted by Gordon, of the stupendous and tragic event of the Holocaust overwhelming or say kidnapping the performance of the "Sinfonia Concertante" and therefore also the film. (Indeed the mere conjunction of Israeli offspring of survivors with images of tracks and a train traveling east from Germany would suffice to raise the thought of the Holocaust even in the absence of conversation.)

In an important sense, the pursuit of presentness throughout *k.364* is a matter of the relation of shot to shot, close-up to close-up, montaged bit to montaged bit, including intervals of darkness, all these in relation to the montaging and sometimes the overlaying of sound, both snatches of playing – mainly the "Sinfornia Concertante" (only the soloists) but also, in Warsaw, as the camera enters the Philharmonic building and makes its out-of-focus way toward the concert hall, an orchestral air marked "andante religioso" from Grieg's "Holberg Suite" – and the sound of the train wheels crossing the points of the tracks (also, at key moments, announcements in German and Polish), though as I have said once the concert begins – roughly halfway through the film – we hear the entire piece from beginning to end. If all such relations are "right," if the camera work and the dialogue and the editing and the sound mixing all come off as Gordon means them to, then just conceivably the film will succeed in its exalted aim – but it is impossible to demonstrate that this is in fact the case. However, two brief sequences are worth noting in this context – I mean the stretch of less than a minute during the

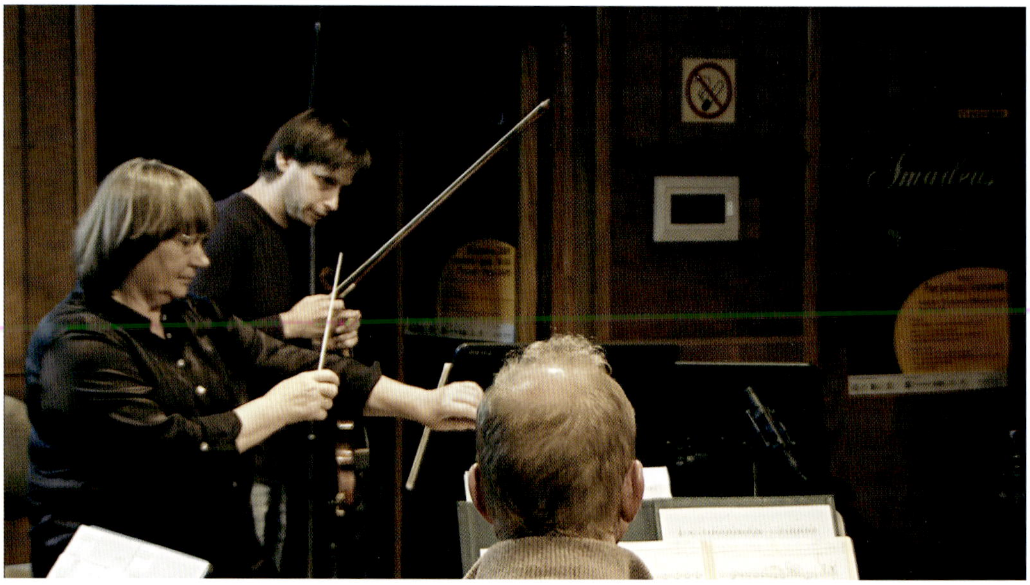

168

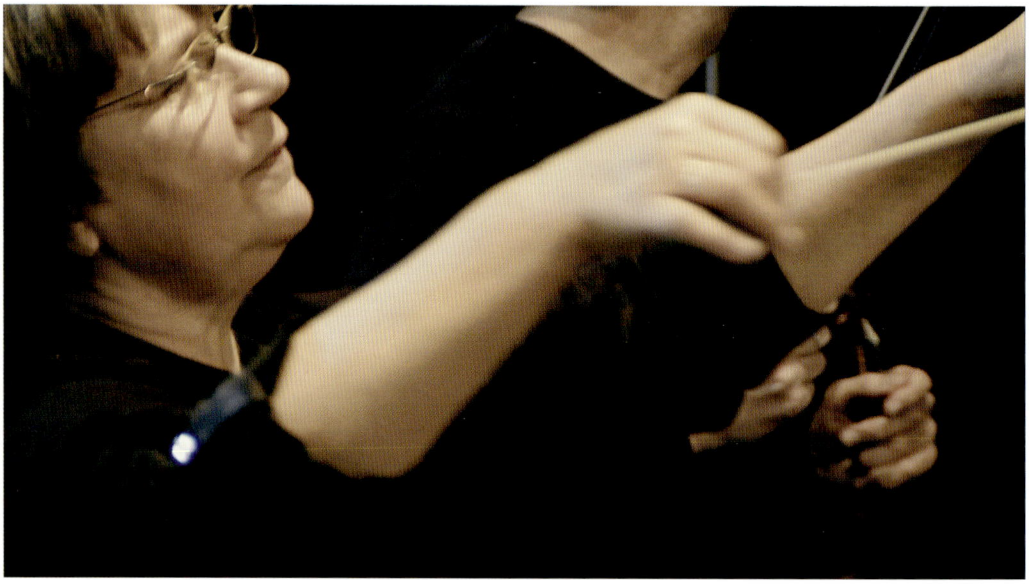

170

playing of the second movement in Warsaw followed by an even shorter stretch toward the end of that movement when suddenly we are shown on the left-hand split screen not one or another close-up view of Avri or Roi or Agnieszka Duczmal as they actually, punctually "are" at that moment in the performance but rather Avri (to begin with) at that previous, electrifying but also somewhat comic moment during the rehearsal in

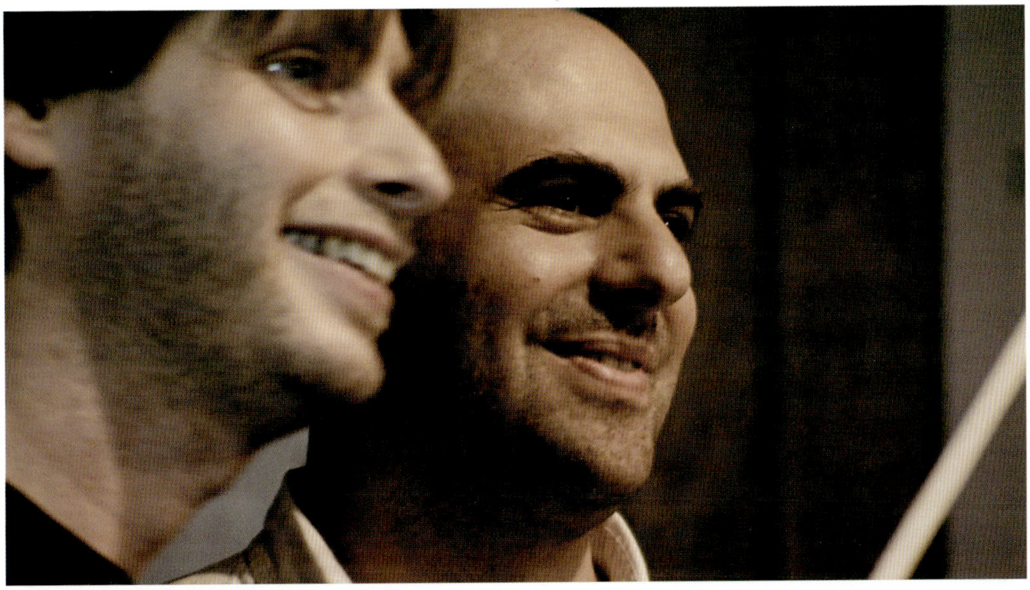

169

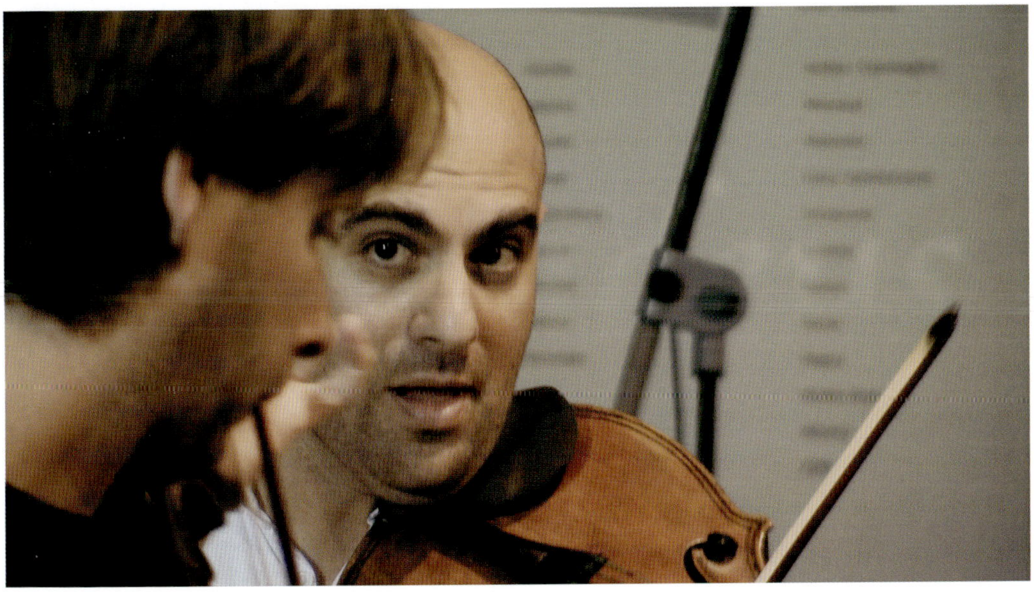

171

Poznan when he broke off playing to make a point about how to accent a musical phrase or series of phrases with respect to the beat (in English, German, and Polish, with asides in Hebrew to Roi; also in a kind of verbal mime – "ta-*ti*, ta-*ti*, ta, ta, ta"). (Actually, the first interpolation also shows Avri bent over the score and gesticulating as we never actually saw him do during the rehearsal.) In other words, the rehearsal is visually made "part" of the performance, but without the least announcement that this is taking place; indeed it is easy to miss one or the other interpolation, at least the first time through the film, as the music continues without interruption to the end of the movement: the key is that both players wear black for the performance but that Ari wore a white shirt in rehearsal. Once noticed, this has the triple effect of recalling to the film's audience the earlier effort, not only at the rehearsal but by implication during countless hours of instruction and practicing and indeed other performances beginning in childhood on the part of everyone concerned, that went into the performance in Warsaw (a related implication, of an entire tradition or culture, is carried by the wall of framed photographs of famous musicians that we glimpse on our way to the concert hall); of asserting in the strongest possible terms that "presentness" ("no past – no future") in this context does not mean literally forgetting or denying what has gone before (not merely the hours in question or previous European musical culture but also the Holocaust, for example) but rather of finding the proper means of acknowledging them; and of making it absolutely clear that even as this tremendous piece of music moves toward its close it "belongs" not only to Mozart – who is never mentioned; the drag toward the past might simply be too great – and the musicians but also to the film-maker, whose devotion both to the "Sinfonia Concertante" and to the musicians is by this stage in the film beyond question. The last point is underscored by the fact that starting part-way through the second movement we notice on the left-hand split screen at some distance from the players what appears to be a camera on a tripod – also an operator standing behind it – which presumably is filming the imagetrack on the right-hand split screen. Gordon's willingness to acknowledge the camera is a familiar modernist trope, but it is no less effective for that.

3 CLOSE-UPS, FACES, EXPRESSIVENESS

In the end, nothing matters more to the effectiveness of *k.364* as a work of art – besides the music itself, but even to say that is not quite right – than the many close-ups of the two performers, which is to say, the presentation in the film of their remarkably expressive faces (also, as mentioned, their extraordinarily competent and, as it happens, highly photogenic hands).[9] Needless to say, it is difficult to know how to treat this topic analytically. One place to begin is with the obvious contrast in this regard between the two players, Roi's face all "feminine" sensitivity, Avri's, as mentioned earlier, distinctively "masculine," not that I want to make too much of this (though nothing could be physiognomically more phallic than the back of Avri's shaven head); but in the course of the conversations during the train ride one receives the definite impression, first, of

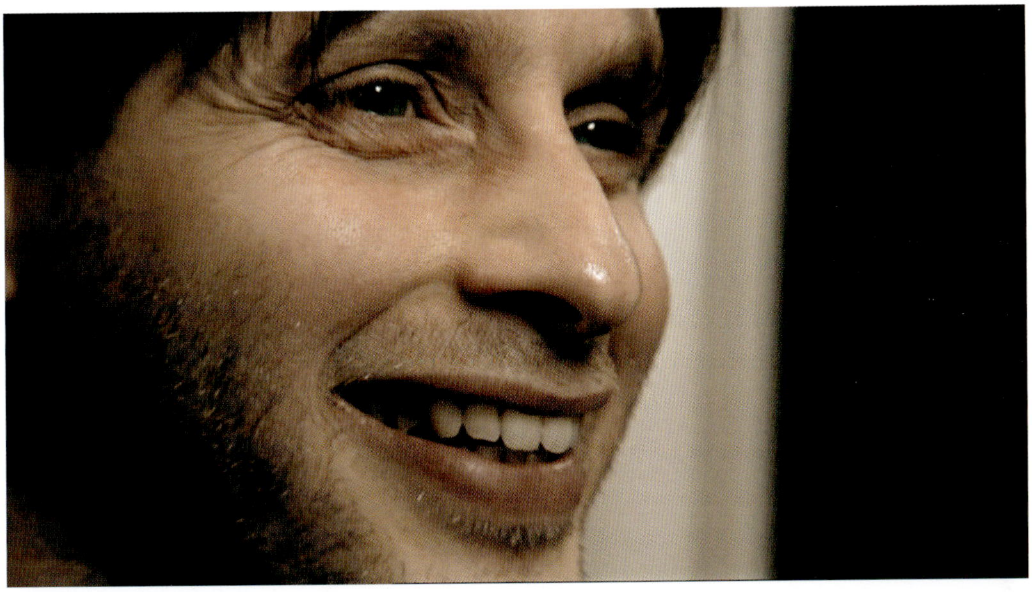

172

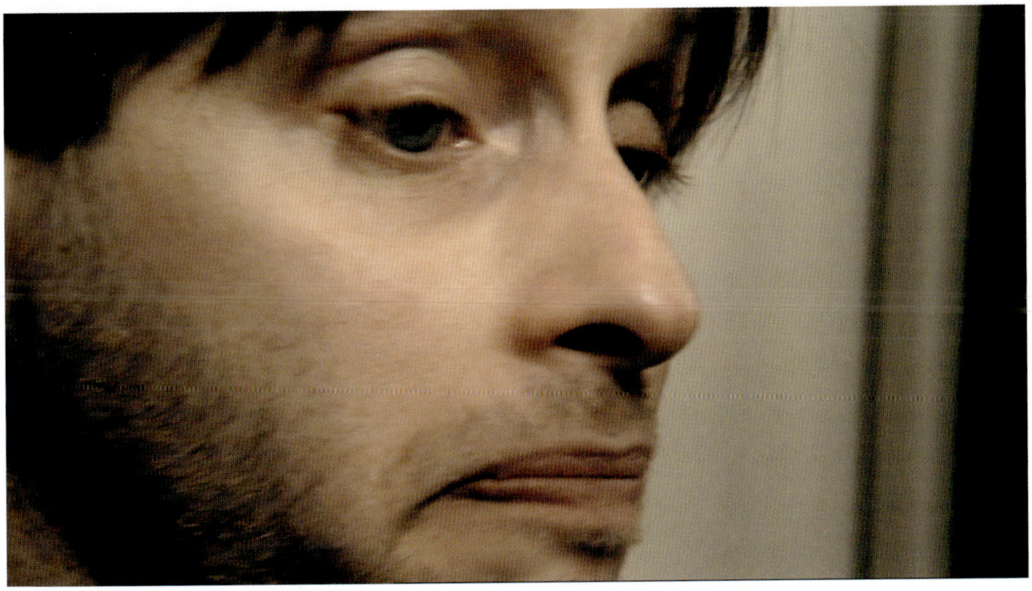

173

Avri's high regard for Roi and second, of Roi's extreme, virtually anticipatory responsiveness to Avri's stories about them both. Thus while Avri recounts the incident when as members of an Israeli army quartet Roi in effect refused an order to have his long hair cut and Avri explained to the officer who had issued the order that Roi had permission to keep his long on the grounds that he would lose all power ("Kraft") if he

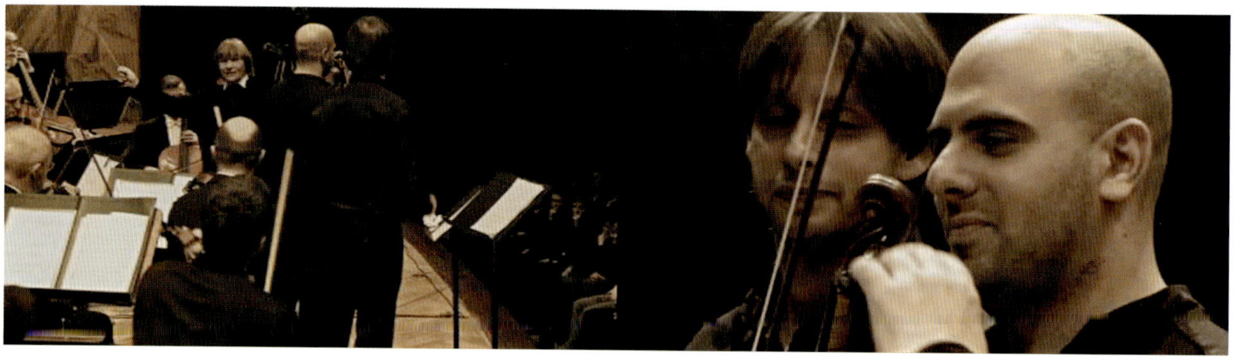

174

were shorn – we are never told whether the permission was real or not – the camera stays trained on Roi's face at extremely close range, sometimes showing only the eyes and nose or indeed the mouth, to which he has raised a forefinger, so that we are made aware of something like Roi's hanging on Avri's words (almost as if anxious about how the story would come out, though it must have been told between them hundreds of times) and then, well before the narrative reaches its climax, Roi's bursting into laughter in a manner that seems not quite hysterical, that would be to go too far, but as if full of some "excessive" and not quite specifiable emotion suddenly welling up out of nowhere. Followed immediately by Roi's face seeming to go almost blank, as if the flood of emotion had been cut off just as suddenly.

There is also, just a few moments later, an extraordinary sequence during which Roi is filmed at close range as his head lolls about, eyes shut, while on the sound track he recounts the story of how he came into possession of his violin because of a chance meeting with a collector of violins in a small town in Argentina (briefly, it had once belonged to a convicted murderer and had not been played for fifty or sixty years before he acquired it). It is at first impossible to know for sure exactly what we are seeing: in fact he appears to be playing the violin but the focus is blurred and the entire sequence is shot in deep chiaroscuro, and in any case his expressions have something ineffably sad about them, as if he were in pain, or dreaming of something tragic (we have an impulse to wake him). The sequence lasts just two minutes but together with what has gone before it suffices to persuade the viewer, or perhaps I should say this viewer, that Roi's face is as intensely expressive, charged with affect, and liable to abrupt and drastic changes of mood, as any in the history of film. (A large claim, I realize; perhaps I should say as any male actor's face, to qualify it; even this is probably overdone; but still.) Avri's face too is expressive albeit in a less singular, febrile, minutely responsive register. In particular the expressions that cross his face while he plays certain passages

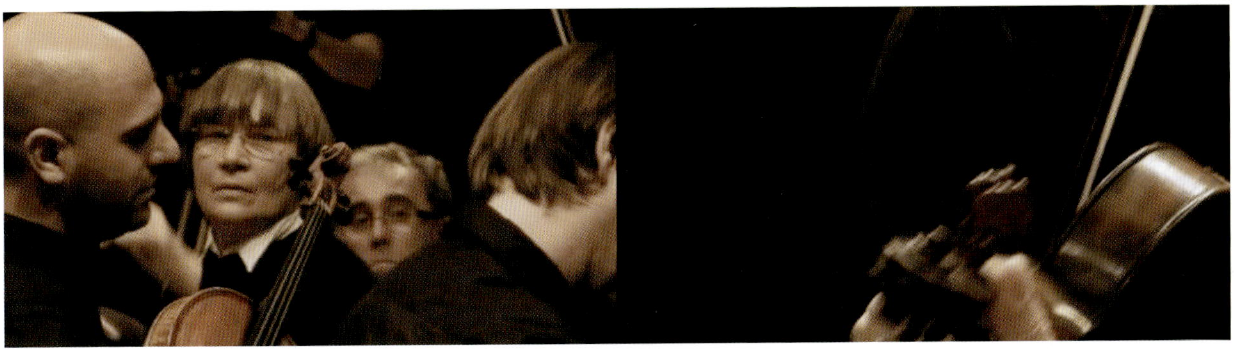

175

of the "Sinfonia Concertante" – eyebrows raised, brow furrowed, mouth open, tongue just visible between his teeth – perfectly express both the delicacy of the task at hand and the tremendous pleasure he appears to be taking in bringing it off. Nothing of the sort seems to mark Roi's expressions as he plays; rather there is something positively exalted, ascetic, one might almost say withdrawn, yet also rapturous, about the way in which his absorption in certain passages leads him to do something strange with his mouth (it remains closed but as if his jaws separate and the skin between nose and mouth becomes stretched downward), making him look even more bird-childlike than before. (Unlike Avri, however, Roi rocks forward and back continually, and toward the end of the film we are briefly shown what must be his foot in its black shoe beating time. He also, often, seems to be holding his violin unusually high.) But of course what really matters in the film, and what there is no way of describing even remotely adequately, is the continually changing contrast between the two men's respective expressions as they perform, not to mention the moments when their glances meet (Roi in particular looks almost beseechingly at Avri at crucial instants when they are playing together without the orchestra) – and not to mention also the further contrast with the very different range of expressions of Agnieszka Duczmal as, head bobbing, she vigorously conducts the orchestra and from time to time glances encouragingly, more than once with fantastic sweetness, toward her soloists. I will only add that nothing in the film is more suspense-filled than the shots of Avri and Roi waiting to make their first entrance; one of the remarkable features of the "Sinfonia Concertante" is how protracted a build-up there seems to be – roughly two minutes and ten seconds but it feels longer – before first the violin and immediately thereafter the viola are released into flight. When this finally occurs we too are more than ready to take off with them.

I could go on adducing further moments in the film but the essential point is simple: Gordon has made a film about a musical performance in which the close-range (often

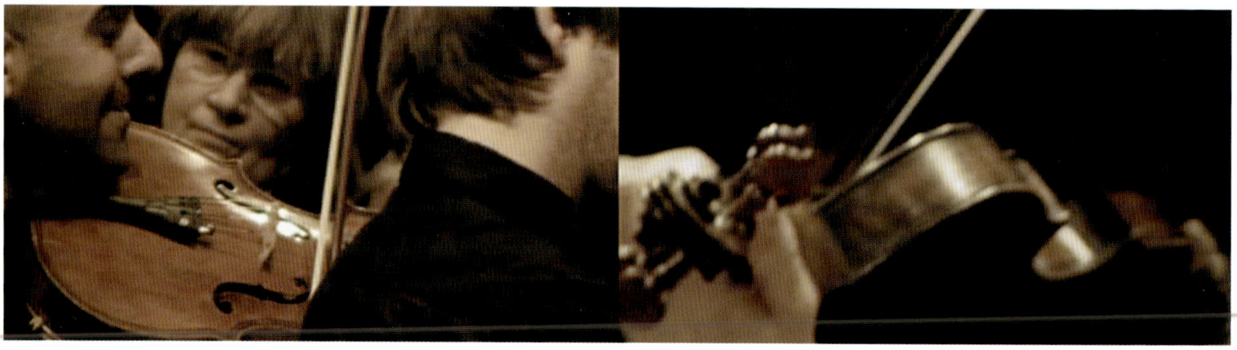

176

extremely close-range, much nearer than a standard movie close-up) concentration on the facial expressions as well as the hands of the two performers and, to a lesser extent but nevertheless importantly, on the face and actions of the conductor has the effect – this is my claim, my only warrant for which is my own experience though it is also true that I have tested it on select others, who do not disagree – of intensifying, also, surprisingly, of clarifying the expressiveness of the music itself. And of course the piece of music in question is famously expressive in its own right; thus Charles Rosen in *The Classical Style* singles out the second movement as one of the three great "expressions of grief and despair" among Mozart's concerto movements[10] (Gordon in a conversation with Ben Luke remarks that that movement "allegedly is a requiem in disguise for Mozart's mother, but it's always been a little tenuous"[11]). Apropos of that movement Rosen describes "the two soloists play[ing] antiphonically, each phrase seeming to outdo the previous one in depth of expression" (215), which seems exactly right; and of a particular moment in the first movement Rosen notes an "almost painfully expressive orchestral climax . . . [which] is picked up again by the solo instruments" (217). ("Almost painfully expressive" perfectly captures my response to the piece as a whole. Also to Roi's face much of the time.) He also notes that Mozart himself played the viola and loved its sound, which in this work is "translated into the language of the full orchestra" (215). (A thought: Avri and Roi seem virtual personifications of their instruments.) What is remarkable, if I am right, is that a musical masterpiece of this order turns out not only not to be traduced or vulgarized even a little bit by being made the basis of a film, one feels instead that it is enhanced, as if precisely a certain moment-to-moment quality – a certain presentness – is brought to the fore by the interplay between performance and filming-plus-editing, soundtrack and imagetrack. How can this be?

Again, it is not at all clear what might count as an answer to such a question. But I find hints that intrigue me in certain detached thoughts of Ludwig Wittgenstein, for

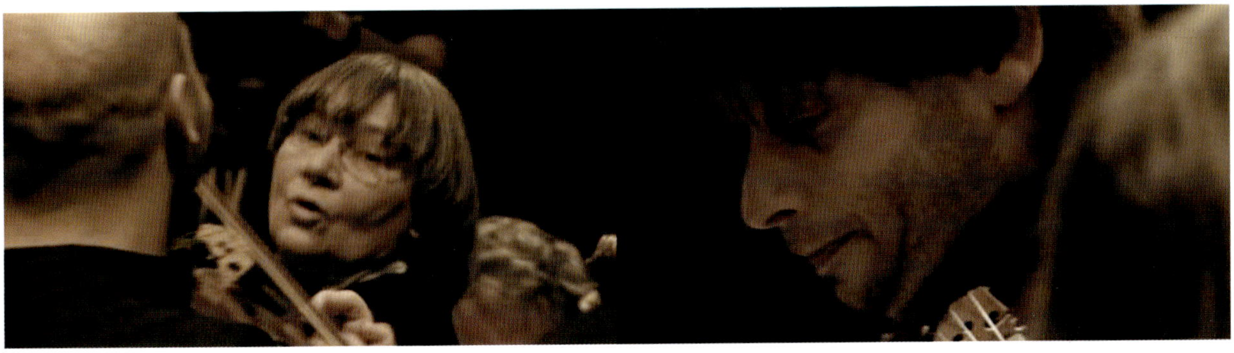

177

whom of course music was second only to philosophy among his intellectual passions (if it makes sense in his case to rank the two at all). For example, in the posthumously edited volume *Culture and Value*, a series of notebook passages from 1946 focus on the topic of expression. The first three sentences from an entry of September 22 are very nearly enough in themselves for my purposes. They read:

> What does it consist in: following a musical phrase with understanding? Observing a face with a feeling for its expression? Drinking in the expression on the face?[12]

Indeed they almost seem designed to serve as a commentary on *k.364* – I mean not just the leap, which Wittgenstein treats as natural, from following a musical phrase with understanding to observing a face with a feeling for its expression, but the further formulation (the further leap), "Drinking in the expression on the face" (the German is *eintrinken*), which is precisely what Gordon's film enables or rather compels the viewer/listener to do throughout the performance in Warsaw, indeed throughout the film: as if drinking in the expressions on Roi's face during the train journey to Poznan were already, by the logic of the film, equivalent to following or understanding or indeed drinking in the music – and of course the journey itself is by no means devoid of music, including snatches of the "Sinfonia Concertante." Put slightly differently, it is as if Wittgenstein's brief remarks infallibly locate an important but hitherto unarticulated connection between music and faces precisely as regards the concept of expression or say expressiveness. (Also as regards the concept of "drinking in," about which one would be happy to hear more.)

Wittgenstein's further thought is that the right answer to the question "What does it consist in?" in this context is *not* one that appeals to some distinct "inner" experience on the part of the listener or viewer (the "drinker-in," we might say). He goes on immediately to write:

> Think of the demeanour of someone who draws the face with understanding for its expression. Think of the sketcher's face [and?] his movements; – what shows that every stroke he makes is dictated by the face, that nothing in his sketch is arbitrary, that he is a *delicate* instrument?
>
> Is that really an *experience*? I mean: can we say that this expresses an experience? (58e; emphasis in original)

The implication of his questions is that we cannot, at least on the basis of *that* idea of an "experience." Not that Wittgenstein would deny that the draftsman is experiencing *something* as he draws; his point seems to be that whatever the draftsman may be experiencing is irrelevant to the matter at hand: our conviction as to what he is doing is grounded in, or directed toward, what is before our eyes. And what is before our eyes is not the basis for some further *inference*. As he writes:

> Once again: what does it consist in, following a musical phrase with understanding, or playing it with understanding? Don't look inside yourself. Ask yourself rather, what makes you say that's what *someone else* is doing. And *what* prompts you to say *he* has a particular experience? Indeed, do we ever actually say that? Wouldn't I be more likely to say of someone else that he's having a whole host of experiences?
>
> I would perhaps say: "He is experiencing the theme intensely"; but ask yourself, what the expression of this is? (58e; emphasis in original)

In the light of the above we might venture to say that the genius of *k.364* in this regard is that it presents us with the moment-to-moment connection between music and faces, both at a pitch of maximum expressiveness, and that it does so in a way that never for an instant tempts us to imagine that we might go beyond or behind what is before our eyes and what reaches our ears. (One more sentence from Wittgenstein that could have been written with *k.364* in mind: "A theme has no less a facial expression than a face." [59e][13])

4 HOLOCAUST MEMORIES

The Holocaust comes up early in *k.364*, as early as the opening credits in which we are shown close-up shots from the swimming pool in Poznan that we are subsequently told was originally a synagogue (as a surviving window attests). Almost immediately Avri talks about the winter trees rushing past the train window and how it is impossible for himself or Roi or others like them not to think of what took place there almost seventy years ago; after which Roi talks about his mother's and grandmother's refusal to return to Poland. In view of the fact that the two musicians are Israelis, the topic seems inescapable. The question, however, is to what extent the thought of the Holocaust has been made integral to the film.

I have already suggested that it bears a relation to concerns of directedness and presentness, not so much as promoting these but rather as challenging them, confronting them with a difficult task. Now as briefly as possible I want to suggest one set of terms in which I see that challenge as having been met, or at least risen to. The crucial moment in this regard is the beginning of the rehearsal in Poznan, when we first lay eyes on Agnieszka Duczmal, whose immense human attractiveness seems to me undeniable and who is also – the thought is inescapable – old enough to be the two musicians' mother. Once she makes her appearance (how different, how much less gripping the film would be if the conductor had been a man!), the distinction between "feminine" and "masculine" that I have associated with Roi and Avri respectively goes into abeyance; instead one instinctively sees them as two sons, two Jewish sons, and Agnieszka Duczmal as their Polish Gentile mother, shepherding them through the "Sinfonia Concertante" or at any rate energetically and committedly supporting their playing, and also, as mentioned, flashing encouraging looks some of which seem full of spontaneous affection. In sum, on a fantasmatic level the film "replaces" the original mother who refuses to return to Poland (with good reason, no one could doubt that) with an imaginary mother who in effect "adopts" the two sons for the duration of the performance. (In the grip of this fantasy the bespectacled cello player takes on a somewhat detached "paternal" aura.) I do not suggest that this was part of Gordon's intentions, or even that he would consider signing off on it as a partial interpretation of his brilliant film. But it helps explain the surprising force of the protracted moment during the closing titles when the typically Polish names of the various members of the orchestra go up on the screen – not all at once but in groups of three or four at a time, until the screen is filled (the effect is as of the players themselves taking belated bows in their places) – as if to acknowledge in some special way not only the orchestra members' participation in the "extreme occasion" (Edward Said[14]) of the performance despite figuring barely at all in the actual film but also the cultural-historical fact of their nationality, with no further guidance from the film-maker as to what to make of that fact. (Another "event" reserved for the closing titles: the appearance for the first and only time of "Wolfgang Amadeus Mozart." The composer, too, gets his last-seconds bow.) Nor am I suggesting that the subliminal "adoption" motif I have no doubt too crudely sketched represents a happy solution to anything; Gordon himself has spoken of *k.364* as "ultimately bleak,"[15] which is perfectly compatible with my proposal. The synagogue-turned-swimming pool in particular seems to weigh on his mind. But it

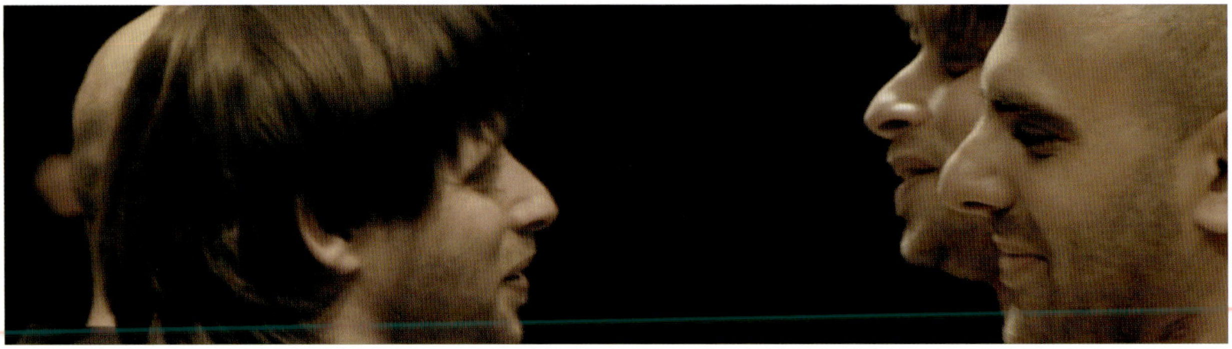

178

would represent an answer of sorts to the question as to how the Holocaust theme relates to the other, more strictly aesthetic issues that I have tried to show structure Gordon's film.

5 THE ARTIST'S VOICE

I am aware of having left uncommented on certain other features of *k.364*, such as Gordon's characteristically poetic use of reflections of the two musicians in the train windows (it is positively disorienting to see them bowing with their left arms), or the relation of his choice of a piece of music featuring two performers on similar though not quite identical instruments to his lifelong fascination with doubles of all sorts (the reflections in the train windows are obviously relevant to this, too). Even the concentration at times on the musician's hands, active and at rest, has precedents in his earlier work. And I have not mentioned, because I do not quite know what to make of them, the shots of the Polish synchronized swimming team practicing in the pool in Poznan; perhaps they are the one "ironic" note in an otherwise deeply unironic film. In closing, though, I want to say just a bit about several moments when, without warning, we hear Gordon's own Glaswegian voice saying first: "I'm not swimming." Then: "She told me she was always in another place when she was swimming. Because where we are is not where it seems to be." Then: "I'm not swimming, I'm floating." (Actually what he says is "floatin'.") And finally, just as the camera begins its climb to the concert hall in Warsaw: "I feel like I'm in the wrong place at the right time."

Naturally, no definitive reading of these detached statements is possible, but we can at least say that the allusions to swimming return us to the pool or rather to the painful historical nexus the pool represents. The unnamed "she" turns out not in fact to be

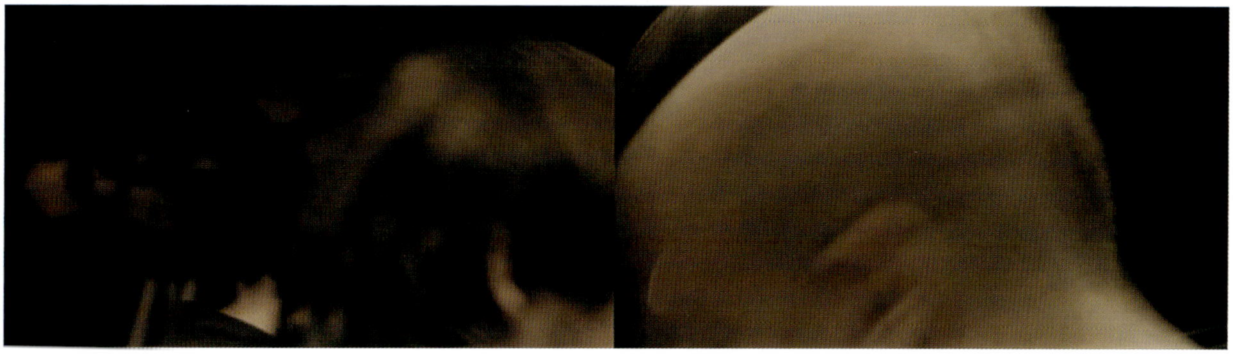

179

Gordon's mother (I asked) but in the context of the film it is hard to escape the thought that it might well be. Put another way, it is a statement that one might think to associate with Roi's mother, as he earlier presented her, even though the voice is plainly Gordon's. In either case it supports the notion of a maternal motif at work in the film as a whole. (Another thought: water imagery is traditionally associated with the theme of rebirth, which is not so far from that of adoption. Do I mean to suggest that Gordon specifically intended the swimming pool sequences and swimming references to be taken in that light? Again, no. But in the first place they are not in the film by accident, and in the second they resonate, so it seems to me, with other considerations that we have touched on; the question, to which this proposes an answer, is how. In any case, there are moments away from the pool that have an almost underwater feel: the stretch during the train ride when we see Roi playing with eyes shut as the soundtrack records his story of acquiring his violin; and, partly owing to the blurring, the climb to the concert hall.) "I'm not swimming, I'm floating" further evokes the film's ultimately unresolvable relation to the history that troubles it even as it also evokes the image-track's often oneiric visual texture. As for "I feel like I'm in the wrong place at the right time," that too expresses a troubled intuition of historical dislocation but the last phrase, "at the right time," is nothing if not hopeful. In art as in life, one settles for what one can get.[16]

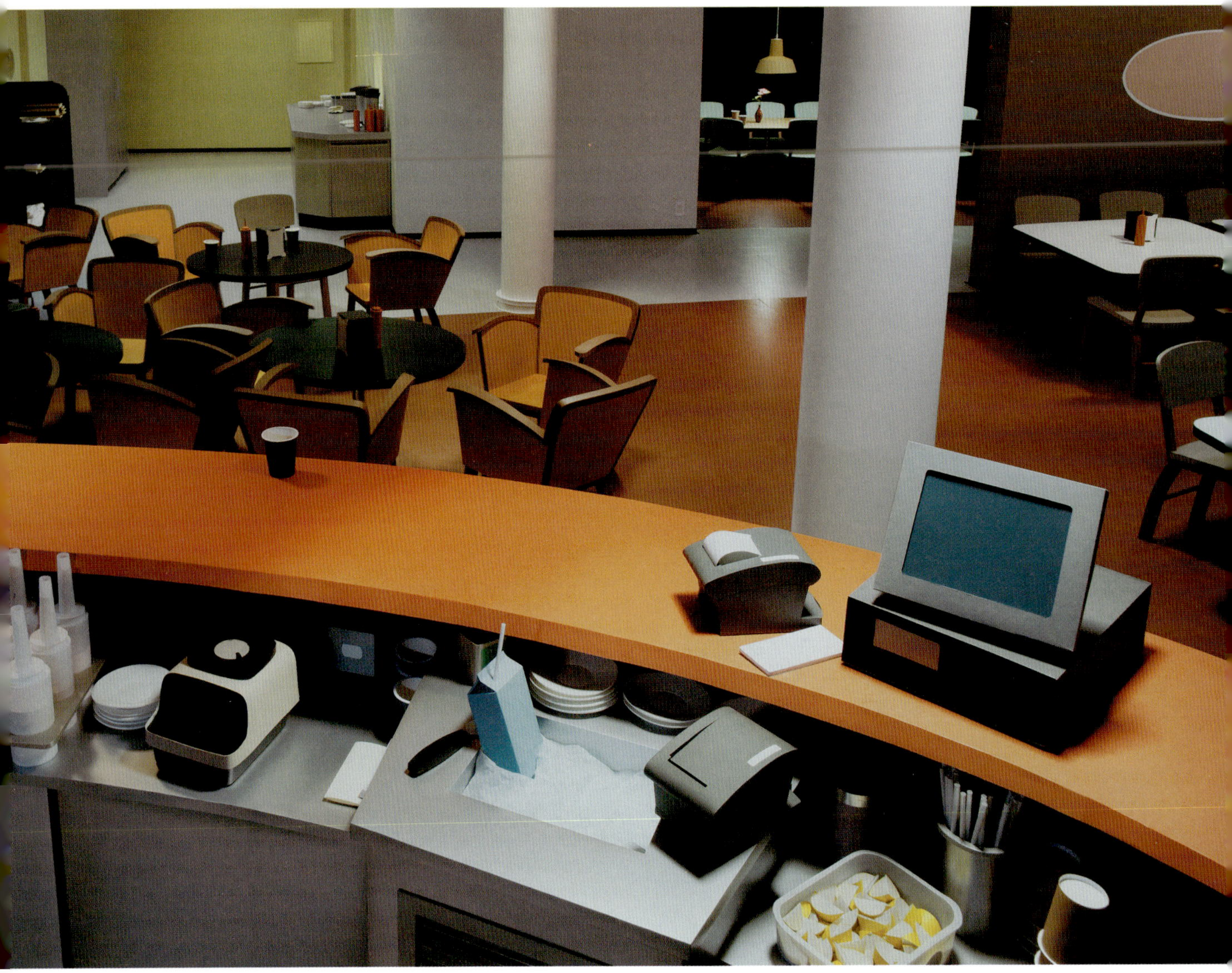

180 Thomas Demand, *Pacific Sun*, 2012, Video, 2,02 min, stereo (frame 141).

• 8 •

THOMAS DEMAND'S *PACIFIC SUN*

Once for each thing, only once. Once and no more.
    And we, too,
only once. Never again. But to have been
once, even though only once:
this having been *earthly* seems lasting, beyond repeal.

Rilke, "The Ninth Elegy"[1]

On July 30, 2008 the *Pacific Sun*, a cruise ship carrying more than 1,700 passengers, was rocked by heavy seas during a severe storm about 400 miles off the coast of New Zealand. The swells reached heights of seven meters (22 feet) and the wind measured more than 50 knots per hour. The worst of the buffeting was fairly brief, and was captured by an internal closed-circuit television camera in the ship's bar. Soon copies of the video were posted on YouTube, where they have been watched by more than a million viewers.[2] When Thomas Demand moved from Berlin to Los Angeles in late September 2010, for the first six months as a visiting artist at the Getty Research Institute, one of the projects he had in mind was to make his most ambitious film to date, based on the *Pacific Sun* footage. To this end he rented a studio and set to work.

The film Demand eventually produced lasts something over two minutes and two seconds – roughly the duration of the violent buffeting just referred to. The medium is stop–motion: that is, the film comprises 2,944 frames,[3] each of which was photographed individually – as a "still" – with only minute and precise changes in the disposition of objects from frame to frame. As for the objects and the setting, Demand proceeded as he has always done: by making (with the help of assistants, who did the bulk of the actual fabrication) full-scale cardboard and paper models based for the most part, but not exclusively or slavishly, on items in the original video – chairs (with arms and without), tables of various shapes and sizes, a bookcase, a large upright piano-like credenza, a refrigerator, a television-type screen on the bar, a small printer also on the bar, a flowerpot containing a small plant, a yellow plastic mop-trolley with mop (the last two make only brief, hectic appearances), a metal pail, metal coffee dispensers, a hanging lamp, a small vase with a flower in it, cups, plastic ketchup bottles, napkin dispensers, ashtrays, a milk container with a straw, crushed ice, lemon slices (onto which the bar printer falls), a woman's sandal, what appear to be pencils or straws and pieces of paper – no doubt the list is incomplete. According to Demand, no less than 55 chairs had to be constructed, a number that includes replacements for ones damaged in the course of shooting. This in itself was a considerable task, not only because constructing the model chairs required skill and patience but also because, before the job of construction could begin, Demand himself had to devise the correct protocol for his helpers: one of his singular abilities, not that we are meant to think about it, is that of figuring out how to translate ordinary objects of various kinds (and sometimes not at all ordinary ones, such as space vehicle trainers) into paper and cardboard equivalents.

So much was familiar territory. But where the project broke new ground for Demand was the problem it posed of replicating, more or less, the infinitely varied and complex movements of the individual objects as the giant waves struck the *Pacific Sun*. At this point the artist summoned a dozen professional animators, who ended up working long hours for three and a half months on what Demand calls the film's "choreography."[4] (It is hard to imagine this being feasible anywhere but in Los Angeles.) Their labors involved, in the first place, analysing, frame by frame, the movements of the objects in the original video; together with Demand, they then plotted – established a shot-by-shot script for – the precise position and orientation of each of the hundreds of fabricated objects; finally, once that was done, each of those objects, large and small, had to be shifted into the required position for each of the 2,944 shots. (Falling objects, such as the small white dishes that spill from the nearby counter partway through the film, had to be supported seemingly in mid-fall by stands and rigs, invisibly placed. This is also true of toppling chairs and the like. It was also necessary to make adjustments to his camera so that the entire space from near to far would be in sharp focus.) Most often the changes of position and orientation were extremely slight, a matter of a few fractions of an inch; what is daunting to contemplate, however, is having had to concentrate on each item individually – one 24th of a second at a time, so to speak – when the overall impression sought by the artist and his team was precisely that of unbridled chaos or disorder as more objects than the viewer could possibly track slide and topple first this way and then that, crashing into one another and sometimes even coming apart as they do so, or if they are small simply falling onto the floor, until the unseen waves subside and something like normalcy reigns once more.

Once the shots were assembled to make the film, the question that remained concerned the soundtrack. Initially, at a March 2012 showing at the Getty Research Institute,[5] Demand used music composed expressly for the film by Carter Burwell, but then decided that music of any sort was not right and replaced it with a track devised with the help of David Cunningham that evokes rather than "reproduces" the sounds of tables, chairs, and other objects sliding across the floor, banging into one another and falling over, and so on. (More on the soundtrack below.)

I

Demand, of course, is best known as a photographer. By now his standard mode of operation is familiar to anyone who follows contemporary art: he starts out from an image usually taken from the media, often of a place or situation where something criminal or suspicious or otherwise untoward has happened (recent photographs are based on Whitney Houston's last meal and the control room at the Fukushima nuclear reactor plant); reproduces at full scale in paper and cardboard the scene and the objects it contains; photographs with a large-format camera the construction that results; and then allows the construction to collapse or simply destroys it. The mostly large, life-scale in feeling photographs that issue from this procedure are then laminated behind Plexiglass and mounted on aluminum so as to allow them to be exhibited without a frame. I discuss Demand's photographs at length in *Why Photography Matters as Art as Never Before*,[6] where I stress the fact – as others had before me – that the brilliantly constructed objects in his images, while appearing plausible at first glance, quickly reveal themselves as the mere constructions they are by virtue of their overall immaculateness as well as of certain slight imperfections, strategic omissions, and other characteristic features. So for example in the exemplary *Poll* (2001; fig. 181), which ostensibly depicts the Emergency Operations Center in West Palm Beach, Florida, where in 2000 a manual recount of 425,000 ballots took place (until cut off by a decision of the U.S. Supreme Court) in the final showdown between George W. Bush and Al Gore, all the ballots we see are pristine, the telephones are without numbers or letters on their faces, the sticky notes are blank, there seems to be no place for workers to sit or stand, and in general the scene ultimately conveys a sense of unreality, or rather of no reality other than that of the construction itself.

The question is why Demand chose to go this route – why he took up and continues to practice this elaborate, labor-intensive way of making photographs, so different from the approaches of his somewhat older Düsseldorf-trained contemporaries, Thomas

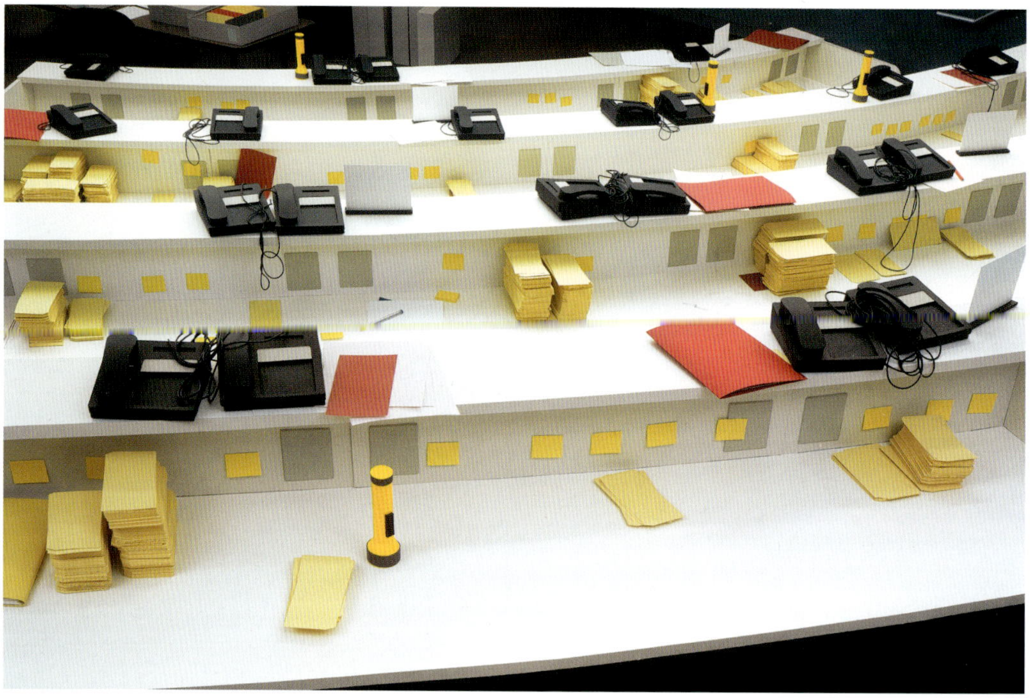

181 Thomas Demand, *Poll*, 2001. Chromogenic process with diasec. 180 × 260 cm.

Ruff, Thomas Struth, Andreas Gursky, Candida Höfer, and others. In this connection I remark in *Why Photography Matters* that I am not persuaded by arguments that hold that the point of Demand's art is to lead the viewer to reflect on the place of media and mediatic images in contemporary life; I do not believe that so vague and banal an aim could begin to motivate so complex and technically demanding a project (no pun intended). Rather, the answer I propose is that Demand's photographs function as what I call allegories of intention, by which I mean that they seek to replace original scenes marked by evidentiary traces and marks of human activity – more precisely, to replace mediatic images of such scenes – with counter-images "of *sheer artistic intention*, as though the very bizarreness of the fact that the places and objects in the photographs, despite their initial appearance of quotidian 'reality,' have all been constructed by the artist throws into relief the determining force – also the inscrutability, one might say the opacity – of the intentions behind them" (271; emphasis in original). What makes *Poll* exemplary, in this connection, is that the volunteers at the Emergency Operations Center were taxed with the responsibility of examining hundreds of thousands of ballots in order to detect the intentions of those who marked them. In the final photograph, however, all trace of such intentions have been eliminated in favor of the very different indications of the construction of the paper and cardboard not-quite-simulacra of the original objects.

It is worth stressing that the role of photography in this operation is crucial, indispensable: as actual things in the world, occupying real, three-dimensional space, Demand's constructions would be no more "saturated" with his intentions (to use a well-chosen verb of Régis Durand's[7]) than would be any other made thing, art or non-art, with the intentions of its maker or makers; in other words, they would be ontologically on a par with the larger real-world context in which they were encountered. Whereas by photographing the objects and situations he constructs, Demand effectively replaces the real-world context with a merely depicted one, every detail and aspect of which, including lighting and point of view, is *exactly* what he intends it to be. (It is all too easy to underestimate the importance of lighting for Demand's art.) This, by the way, is why it matters that the photographs are understood to be rigorously indexical, that is, devoid of digital manipulation: only then can the viewer "trust" the image accurately to record the artist's intentions as embodied in the objects of his making and indeed in their presentation. So that one might say that in the teeth of what was soon to become the all but universal digitalization of the photographic universe, Demand found his way to a project that positively requires – in that sense motivates – the retention of indexicality. (One more small turn of the dialectic.)

2

Another way of framing Demand's enterprise is to say that the intervention of photography turned out to enable him to realize hitherto unimagined *sculptural* ambitions. It is often noted that Demand began as a sculptor, making constructions roughly of the sort I have described, and that over time, starting in the early 1990s, he realized, first, that he wanted to photograph what he had made, and then, having done so, that the photographs mattered to him more than the constructions themselves (though he has also insisted in interviews that the point of the operation has never been to produce the photographs as such). An excerpt from the 25-year-old Charles Baudelaire's *Salon of 1846*, specifically from the section entitled "Why Sculpture is Tiresome," is relevant to the topic:

> Sculpture has several disadvantages, which are a necessary consequence of its means and materials. Though as brutal and positive as nature herself, it has at the same time a certain vagueness and ambiguity, because it exhibits too many surfaces at once. It

> is in vain that that the sculptor forces himself to take up a unique point of view; the spectator who moves around the figure can choose a hundred different points of view, except for the right one, and it often happens that a chance trick of the light, an effect of the lamp, may discover a beauty which is not at all the one the artist had in mind – and this is a humiliating thing for him. A picture, however, is only what it wants to be; there is no other way of looking at it than on its own terms. Painting has but one point of view; it is exclusive and despotic, and therefore the painter's expression is much more forceful.[8]

In a sense, Baudelaire's remarks, with their clear-sighted focus on the issue of intention, amount to an uncompromisingly modernist insight. And with their emphasis on considerations both of point of view and of lighting they anticipate by 150 years Demand's sculptural/photographic practice – a striking fact that speaks to the overall coherence of the modernist enterprise in the so-called visual arts.

This is pretty much how I characterized Demand's project in *Why Photography Matters*. But in the years since, I have come increasingly to be struck by the thematizing of intention in some of the most ambitious art of our time. To take a particularly impressive example, in Charles Ray's sculpture *Hinoki* (2007), a 32-foot long fallen oak log that Ray had come across in the California wine country has been reproduced, more or less, by expert Japanese artisans in cypress wood (or *hinoki*).[9] The task of carving took more than five years; in the end, the entire surface of the sculpture, outside and inside (the log was hollow), bears intensively, even when viewed at a distance, the diverse marks of the various carving and gouging tools used to shape the cypress blocks that had been joined together to make the basic form. And those marks are perceived by the viewer as, above all, intentional – more strongly, as so many carriers of intention – in the first place, at the origin of the entire project, the relatively undefined intention of the artist who discovered and rescued the original log, and in the second, more perspicuously, the multiple sharp-focus intentions of the individual members of the team of elite artisans who labored for years over the sculpture-to-be, in effect channeling and multiplying the artist's will – itself a work in progress – into the ravishing final product. Other works by Ray such as *Untitled (Tractor)* (2003–05) might be cited in this connection,[10] but what I want to insist on is simply that a new emphasis on intention (or intentionality) has emerged as a basic concern of some of the most important art being made in our time, with Demand's photographs in the vanguard of this development.[11]

No doubt there is more than one reason why this has happened. But a major factor surely has been a corrective reaction, not premeditated, perhaps not always recognized as such by the artists themselves, against the Minimalist/Literalist and, more broadly, the Post-Modernist advocacy of an aesthetic of indeterminacy, an aesthetic that gave primacy to the viewing or reading subject's experience of the works in question rather than to the internal relations that make those works what they are (or, more simply, to the works themselves). Essentially, such an aesthetic conceives of the subject as constituting the work or text in and by his/her experiencing of it; put another way, the work is in effect replaced by the experience, which in the case of "visual" art is of the larger situation in which the encounter takes place. This of course is a target of criticism in my 1967 essay "Art and Objecthood," where I draw the strongest possible contrast in this regard between modernist painting and sculpture as exemplified by the work of Louis, Noland, Olitski, Stella, David Smith, and Caro and the Minimalist/Literalist work of Judd, Morris, Andre, and Tony Smith, the last of whose account of a night drive with several students on the unfinished New Jersey Turnpike leads finally to the claim, "There is no way you can frame it, you just have to experience it" – understood by him as a liberating insight tantamount to the end of art.[12] In fact, the concept of intention is not mobilized as such in "Art and Objecthood," but as various commentators, starting with Walter Benn Michaels,[13] have recognized, it is implicit in my fundamental opposition between the two contending approaches. As I have said elsewhere,[14] contemporary art during the following decades overwhelmingly pursued the "theatrical" path blazed by Minimalism/Literalism, but with the emergence of tableau-scale, destined-for-the-wall art photography around 1980 (such as the work of Jeff Wall, Jean-Marc Bustamante, and Thomas Ruff) the first signs of a reaction against such a tendency were there to be seen (though not yet by me – I remained in the dark for years to come). At some point in the early or mid-1990s, it is hard to say exactly when, the counter-tendency – a dialectical return not to modernism itself but to certain of its basic values – began to gather force, to the extent that I would now want to claim that the most vital and important artists at work today – including the photographers treated in *Why Photography Matters* as well as the four artists featured in my recent book *Four Honest Outlaws: Sala, Ray, Marioni, Gordon* – are firmly in the "reaction" or anti-indeterminacy camp.

3

One major issue in regard to which the arguments of "Art and Objecthood" have been superseded by events is that of duration or temporality. Simply put, in that essay I associate the recent modernist art I admire with what I call *presentness*, a quality I found it impossible exactly to define but which in any case I understood to be at the farthest pole from an emphasis on duration. Whereas the experience valorized by Minimalism/Literalism took place in time, it was, I wrote, "as though the experience of [modernist painting and sculpture] *has no* duration – not because one in fact experiences a picture by Noland or Olitski or a sculpture by David Smith or Caro in no time at all, but because *at every moment the work itself is wholly manifest*. . . . It is this continuous and entire *presentness*, amounting, as it were, to the perpetual creation of itself, that one experiences as a kind of *instantaneousness*, as though if only one were infinitely more acute, a single infinitely brief instant would be long enough to see everything, to experience the work in all its depth and fullness, to be forever convinced by it" (167; emphasis in original). It was this intuition that led me to add to my essay the following epigraph from Perry Miller's masterly study of the eighteenth-century American Puritan divine, Jonathan Edwards:

> Edwards's journals frequently explored and tested a meditation he seldom allowed to reach print; if all the world were annihilated, he wrote . . . and a new world were freshly created, though it were to exist in every particular in the same manner as this world, it would not be the same. Therefore, because there is continuity, which is time, "it is certain with me that the world exists anew every moment; that the existence of things every moment ceases and is every moment renewed." The abiding assurance is that "we every moment see the same proof of a God as we should have seen if we had seen Him create the world at first." (148)

In an important book, *From Modernism to Postmodernism: American Poetry and Theory in the Twentieth Century* (2006), Jennifer Ashton argues convincingly that the entire point of this and similar statements by Edwards is that the world is sustained from moment to moment by divine intention, not, as a materialist world view would have it, by ongoing relations of causality (for Edwards the world is not "a seamless fabric of cause and effect" [173])[15] – which is to say that having written my essay I placed the issue of intention at the head of it, even if, as was certainly the case, I did not quite know that that was what I was doing at the time.

Put slightly differently, although I found in the Miller passage on Edwards an analogy to the issue of presentness that was central to my thinking about the clash between High Modernism and Minimalism/Literalism, I could not then imagine the possibility that something like Edwards's vision of the logic of creation, or rather a secular version of that vision, might turn out to be at the core of a work of art that itself engaged directly with temporal issues – that worked positively with duration rather than seeking to circumvent it through one or another version of instantaneousness. But is not that exactly true of *Pacific Sun*? For consider: the CCTV video that inspired Demand to undertake his ambitious project depicts roughly two minutes' worth of multifarious effects following mechanically from external causes – the seven strong mid-ocean swells or waves that struck the cruise ship, knocked passengers and crew off their feet, and sent them along with innumerable pieces of furniture and a host of small objects of various sorts skidding across the restaurant floor, where in many cases they collided with one another in unpredictable but once again mechanically determined ways. By the same token, the basic thrust of Demand's and the animators' procedures, from the design and fabrication of every single object in the film to the precise reproduction of the movements of the objects in space and time and then the taking of 2,944 photographs of the successive ensembles, was to *transform causality into intention* – to replace the one by the other – frame by frame, one 24th of a second by one 24th of a second, for the roughly two minutes called for by the duration of the original events. Indeed it is that quasi-magical operation that foregrounds intentionality in this medium, the stop–motion film, much as the remaking of a scene of vote-counting – of determining voters' intentions – in *Poll* foregrounds it there.

4

More broadly, some of the most ambitious artists today, Gordon and Sala prominent among them, have pursued a diverse series of investigations having to do with movement and duration, in that regard breaking the conceptual frame of my now 45-year-old essay while nevertheless (I have argued) being firmly on the side of determinacy and antitheatricality. This is not the place for even a summary discussion of individual works by those artists, though I should add that Sala's eight minutes and nineteen seconds-long video *Mixed Behaviour* (2003), with its disc jockey mixing music to accompany and then, apparently, to exert control over New Year's Eve fireworks in Tirana, Albania, ingeniously performs a version of the causality-to-intention transformation.[16] (Other videos by Sala – *Long Sorrow* [2005] and *After Three Minutes* [2004] – have been seen by me as exemplifying a pursuit of presentness by durational means.[17] As has Gordon's *k.364*, of course.) Demand's earlier films – *Tunnel* (1999), *Escalator* (2000), *Recorder* (2002), *Yard* (2002), *Trick* (2004), *Camera* (2007), and *Rain* (2008) – also belong to this larger development. But *Pacific Sun* brings those concerns to an altogether new pitch of intricacy and refinement. Let me close this essay, then, with a series of observations about that film, in no particular order:

(1) It matters greatly that the CCTV camera was fixed to the bar so that it did not move relative to the rest of the room. What this meant is that in the original video –

therefore also in *Pacific Sun* – we never actually see the room tilt under the impact of the swells. Instead we see the effects of that tilt – the crew member just in front of the bar suddenly disappearing below it, followed by the movement of chairs, tables, and other objects elsewhere in the room, the lurching and falling (and disappearing and reappearing) of crew members and passengers farther back in space, and countless similar occurrences. Not surprisingly, it takes a moment or two for the viewer to grasp exactly what is going on: the initial rush of events seems causeless – why is all this happening? Within a few seconds, though, the explanation becomes clear – the viewer works it out – even as the fact that the scene itself remains level never quite ceases to surprise. In other words, because the CCTV camera was fixed, the original video foregrounds causality precisely by introducing a sort of "gap" between the external forces that rocked the ship and the consequences of that rocking within the ship's restaurant. Demand in his film helps the viewer bridge an equivalent "gap" by providing a hanging lamp in the farther room to the right for which there is no precedent in the original video: as the lamp swings right or left according to the tilt of the ship, it records exactly the degree of the supposed angle of inclination. In fact its movements *precede* the mass movements of the objects, cluing the viewer as to what is about to happen, a "violation" of causality that places even more emphasis on the intentional structure of the film as a whole.

(2) As no one could fail to notice, Demand eliminated from *Pacific Sun* the ten or so crew members and passengers who desperately try and mostly fail to keep their footing in the CCTV video. In an obvious sense, this was simply in accord with his usual practice: there are no persons, ever, in Demand's photographs. But in the case of *Pacific Sun* that absence is overdetermined by the fact that persons such as those thrown about by the storm would inevitably have been perceived as sources of intention in their own right, which would have gone totally against the grain of his project as I have described it. At the same time, removing them involved a significant change in affective tonality: in the original video the men and women who lurch back and forth or, once they fall, are swept along with the furniture are, at least at first, a source of amusement, even laughter; in Demand's terms, they introduce an element of "slapstick" into the proceedings.[18] With all human beings banished, however, and all the original objects replaced by fragile imitations, not to mention the soundtrack accompanying the controlled chaos before our eyes, the mood is quite other, and it is a nice question how exactly to characterize it.

Here it is to the point that Demand by his own admission felt the need to introduce a "hero-object"[19] for which there was no precedent in the video, a yellow plastic mop-trolley (and mop). Actually, I think there is a second "hero" (or "heroine"), a largish

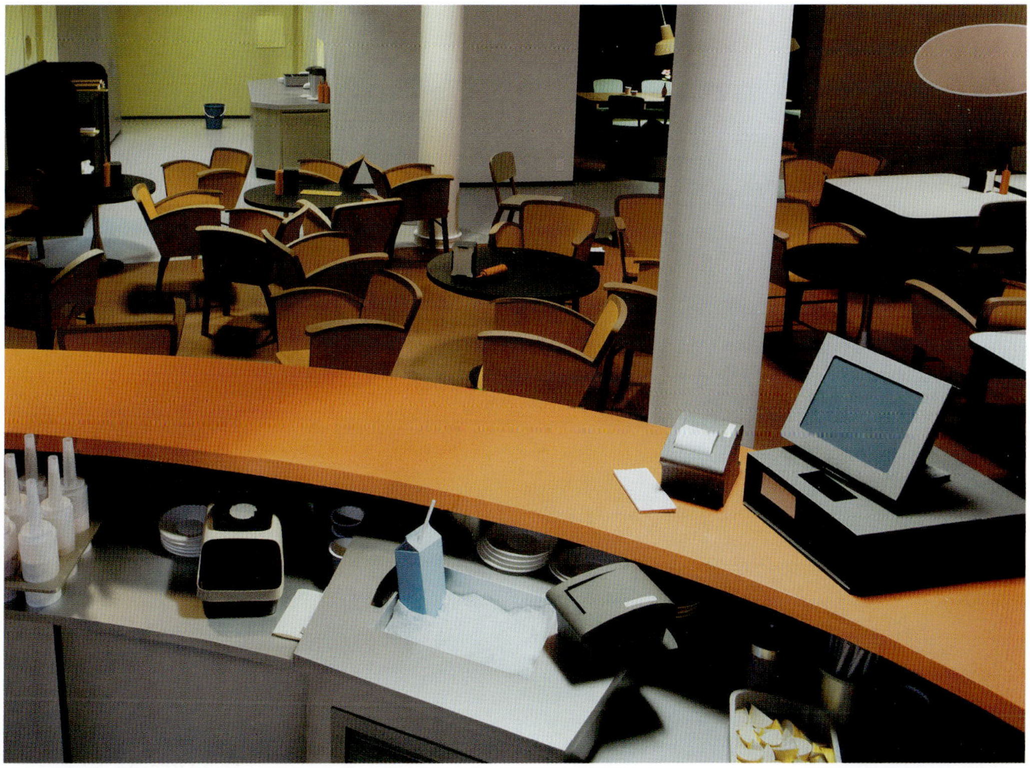

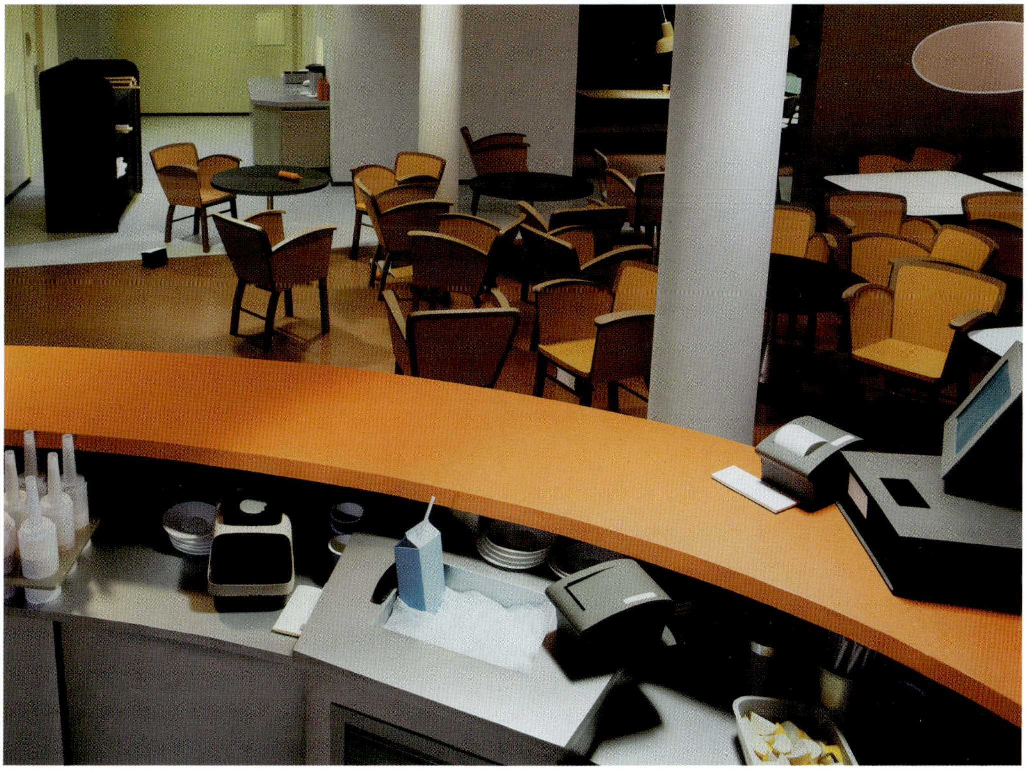

182 and 183 Thomas Demand, *Pacific Sun*, 2012, Video, 2,02 min, stereo (frames 557 and 588).

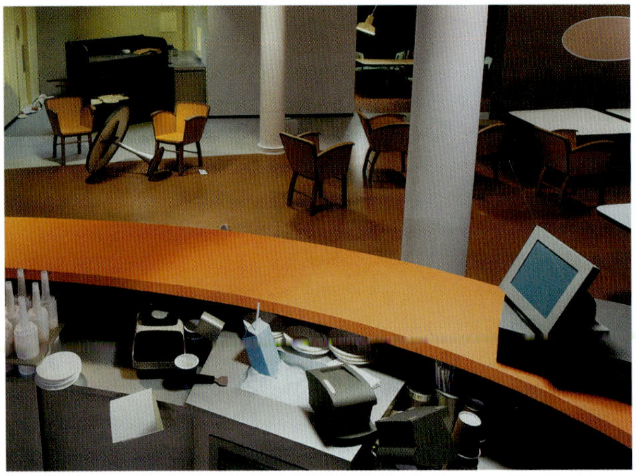

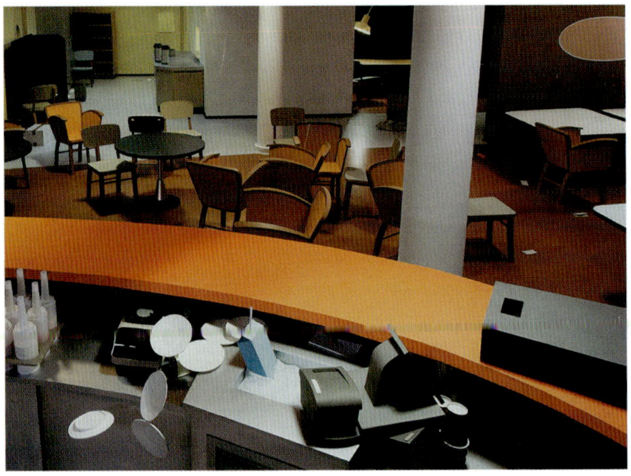

184 and 185 Thomas Demand, *Pacific Sun*, 2012, Video, 2,02 min, stereo (frames 818 and 905).

flowerpot containing a small plant, for which there is a precedent but which figures more importantly in *Pacific Sun* than in the video. Each appears only very briefly: first the mop-trolley rolls from left to right under the impact of swell number four, rotating on its axis as it goes; then it rolls from right to left, still rotating, under the impact of number five – and never returns, though we continue to look for it. (On the first few viewings it is easy to miss in the general commotion, but once it catches our attention we look out for it each time through the film. Even so, sometimes we miss it.) And just as it speeds past the second time, the flowerpot with its plant bursts into view from the right, bangs into a round pillar, bustles diagonally across the floor, and gets knocked over by a chair before exiting front left. All this very fast: we are on the *verge* of slapstick but the flowerpot is gone almost as soon as we take it in. There are other objects that particularly catch our eye, especially the large dark pianolike credenza that ends up covering a lot of ground, but the mop-trolley and flowerpot introduce a note of all but explicit animism, almost of demonic enchantment, that recalls the fictional world of the great German Romantic writer E. T. A. Hoffmann. As does the unexpected proliferation of objects, especially chairs, as the film proceeds: with the fourth, fifth, and sixth swells the object population rushing and tumbling right then left then right again increases almost beyond plausibility. Hoffmann, in turn, is the exemplary figure in Baudelaire's 1855 essay "On the Essence of Laughter," where the latter identifies the higher of two modalities of the comic as what he calls "the absolute comic."[20] The lesser modality is the "significative comic," which always has some worldly meaning and which is epitomized by a man falling on ice or stumbling over a paving-stone (think of

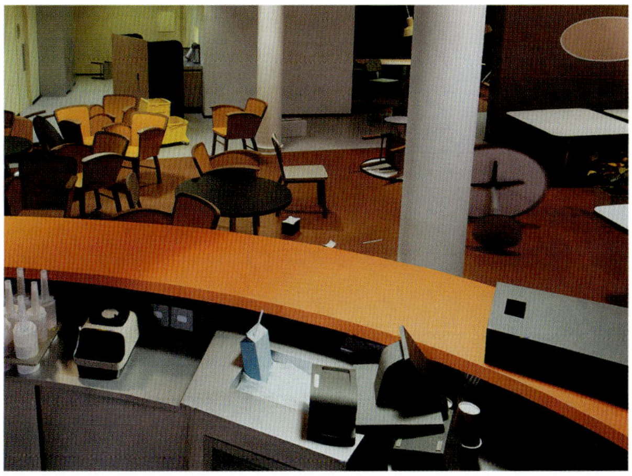

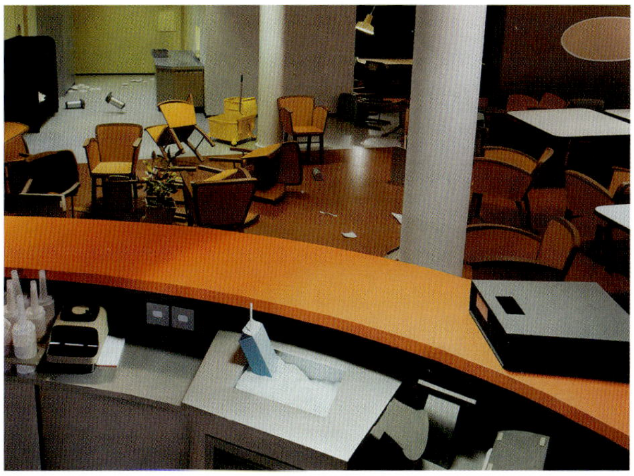

186 and 187 Thomas Demand, *Pacific Sun*, 2012, Video, 2,02 min, stereo (frames 1147 and 1477).

the CCTV video) (152); in contrast, the "absolute comic" is devoid of such a social dimension, coming "much closer to innocent life" in one or another respect (157, translation modified).[21] Maybe this is as near as one can come to capturing the expressive tenor of Demand's brilliant film. "I should perhaps add that one of the most distinctive marks of the absolute comic is that it remains unaware of itself," Baudelaire writes (164) – an antitheatrical claim if ever there was one.

(3) Another basic difference between the original video and *Pacific Sun* concerns the construction of space, by which I mean the way in Demand's film the viewer's attention is divided, indeed torn, between the bar and dishes, milk container, television-like screen, and other small objects in the near foreground; the tables, chairs, columns, and so on in the main room; the continuous but in effect separate space to the left rear, where at the outset the credenza, a large refrigerator, and a bookcase are to be found; and the room still farther back to the right, with a long table, chairs that slide as the ship tilts, and the hanging lamp. This is Demand's version of a similar *dispositif* in works by some of the other artists I have been referring to – to take a classic example, Gordon's *Play Dead; Real Time* (2003) deploys two large translucent screens at right angles to each other on both of which are projected different videos of an elephant in a gallery space standing still, lying down, rising to its feet, taking a few steps forward and back, and so on, the point being that the viewer is made aware from the first that wherever he or she chooses to look, something equally compelling will inevitably be missed. (The screens, moreover, may be looked at from either side, while a third projection runs on

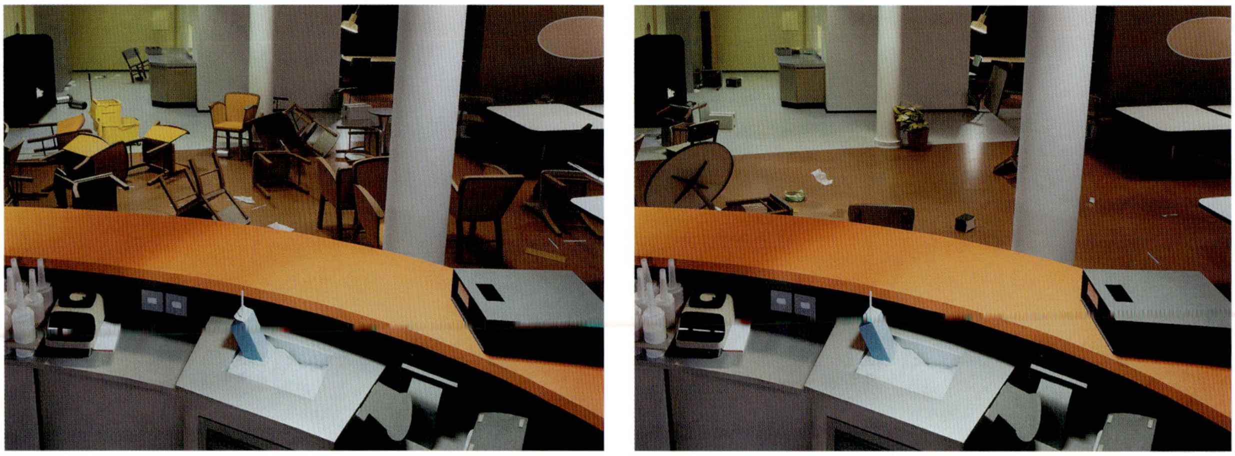

188 and 189 Thomas Demand, *Pacific Sun*, 2012, Video, 2,02 min, stereo (frames 1488 and 1520).

a television monitor set directly on the floor.)[22] In the case of *Play Dead*, however, there is no feeling of having to look quickly: two of the three projections last more than twenty minutes, the third over fourteen minutes, and there is only the elephant to observe – whereas in *Pacific Sun* one's consciousness of having at every instant to decide where to focus is exacerbated, brought to a pitch of near-anxiety, by the brevity of the film, the rapidity of what is happening, and the sheer multiplicity (the increasing multiplicity, up to a point) of the objects and events that compete for one's attention from start to finish.

The inbuilt compensation for this, it turns out, is that *Pacific Sun* is on a loop[23]: when shown, as at the Matthew Marks Gallery in New York in the spring of 2012, or in subsequent exhibitions in Des Moines and Montreal, it played again and again after an interval of not quite fifteen seconds, giving the viewer a new chance to see whatever was missed the first or the first ten or the first hundred times through (in principle, at any rate). This is a structural feature of the film, not an incidental one: viewing *Pacific Sun* involves an acute sense of events happening too fast, too prolifically, and in too many distinct "spaces" for the viewer to take in more than a fraction of them at any given moment, and at the same time an awareness that it will be possible to see those events again, to focus elsewhere, to (for example) lie in wait for the mop-trolley and the flowerpot, or the wanderings of the piano-like credenza, or the fall of this or that object or series of objects (the stack of small dishes in the near foreground), or the uncanny entrance from the right toward the end of the film of a single woman's sandal (a superb detail: the sandal slides into view on its side and is then knocked flat) – not that on the

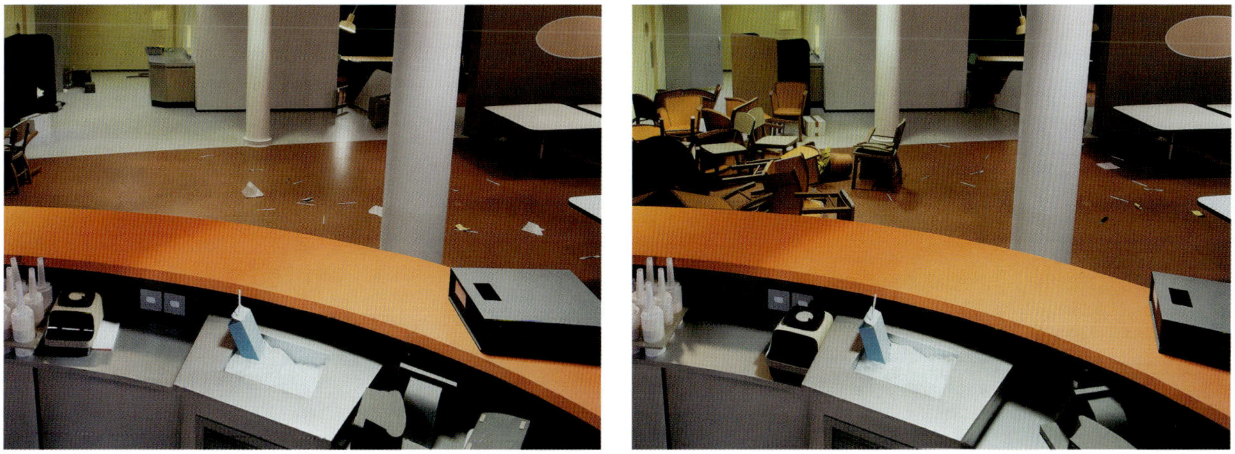

190 and 191 Thomas Demand, *Pacific Sun*, 2012, Video, 2,02 min, stereo (frames 1627 and 1750).

strength of any number of viewings one comes to feel that the work as a whole has been mastered, brought under perceptual and intellectual control. Nor is there a feeling of repetition, exactly: each viewing is too intense, too singular, for the notion of repetition to have any bite. Rather, the effect is not without analogy to Edwards's logic of perpetual destruction/creation, giving rise to a "same" that is also radically new. (As if the loop structure spells out what was already implicit in the stop–motion technology.) Alternatively, I think in this connection of Rilke's "*Once* for each thing, only once. Once and no more. And we, too, / only once" – not as an existential condition *tout court* (literally once, so to speak) but rather as an artistic effect expressive of such a condition, made possible by the loop structure (as in "The Ninth Elegy" it is made possible by the unexpected and gripping reiteration of the word "once," *einmal*). (Onceness as presentness.) All this is in stark contrast with what in "Art and Objecthood" I characterize as Minimalist/Literalist endlessness, going on and on with no end in sight – the endlessness of a purely subjective experience that by its very nature cannot be framed. A final framing or at least closing touch in the last few seconds of *Pacific Sun* is the movement across the floor from left to right of a broken chair leg so as to make contact with, almost to lock into, a broken square-top table resting on an angle, having come free of its base (we see the table's underside). The configuration that results seems oddly "right," as if we have just witnessed the making of an *abstract* sculpture or at least part of one. (I am thinking of the work of Anthony Caro, not that I imagine Demand had him in mind. What matters is the quiet force of this climactic gesture.)

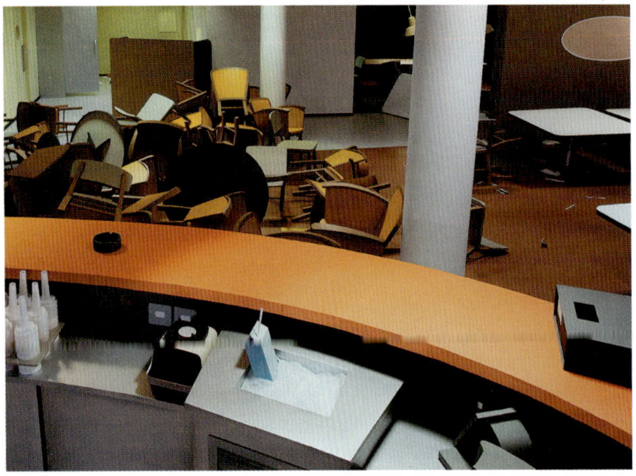

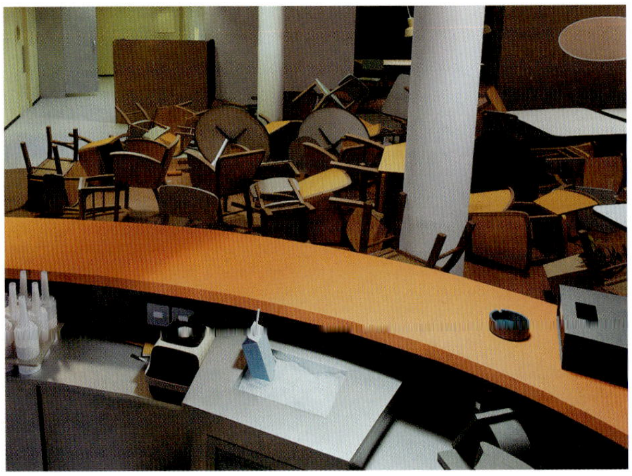

192 and 193 Thomas Demand, *Pacific Sun*, 2012, Video, 2,02 min, stereo (frames 1766 and 1791).

(4) I mentioned earlier that Demand replaced *Pacific Sun*'s original musical soundtrack with one that evokes the sounds that might be made by actual objects such as those in the film sliding back and forth, banging into one another, falling over, dropping onto the floor, and so on. This was a good decision: it may be true that, as Demand earlier remarked in an interview with Daniel Kehlmann, "Obviously the most idiotic solution [to the soundtrack] would be a realistic soundtrack with the chairs making chair noises, because they aren't chairs – just the idea of chairs. It's tricky."[24] At that moment, he seems still to have been thinking of a musical accompaniment. But some relation to "chair noises" and the like proved necessary – as if any musical soundtrack would in the end have remained too remote from what was taking place on the screen to be anything but anodyne, intensity-diluting, in its effect. (As if, too, the imagetrack's inherent musicality would have been obscured by such a soundtrack.) In its present form, the film begins with the sound already at a considerable volume: one's sense is of a kind of hollow rumbling or thrumming (as of a ship's engine?), quickly punctuated by impact noises of various sorts, mainly in a low register, with just a few sharper noises as of objects falling and at one point toward the end a sound like small bits sprinkled on a hard surface as pieces of paper and what appear to be paper straws suddenly enter the scene from the right foreground as if blown by a gust of wind – and is there a background sound like wind as well? – it is impossible to be more precise (I say this after having listened to the track 50 or 60 times). In any case, the effect is simultaneously one of intimate commentary on what is visibly happening and of a palpable distance from it in that the viewer cannot but be aware that the immaculate objects on the screen

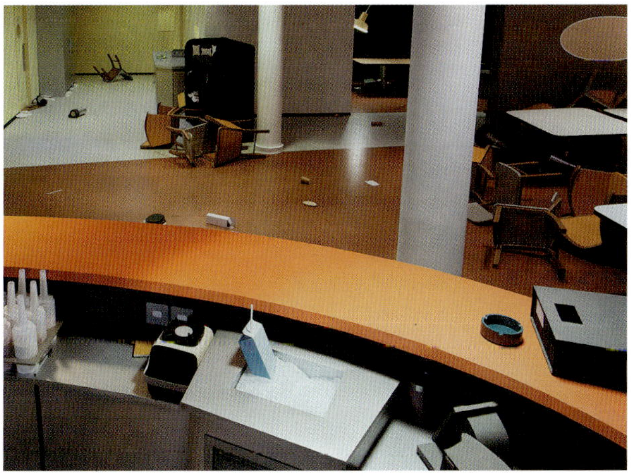
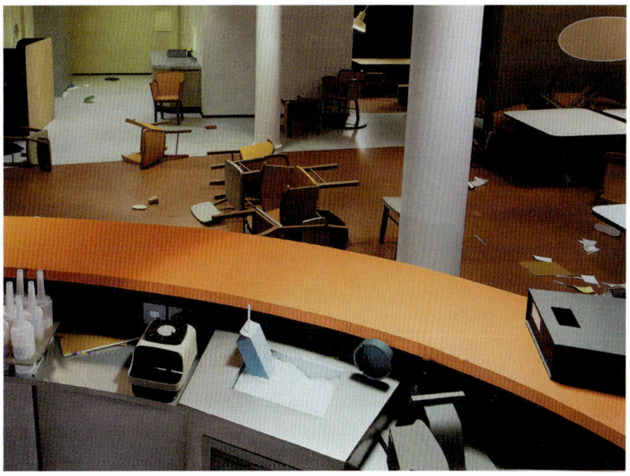

194 and 195 Thomas Demand, *Pacific Sun*, 2012, Video, 2,02 min, stereo (frames 2034 and 2071).

somehow lack the weight or solidity to produce those particular sounds. (And yet the movements of the objects, based on the CCTV video, are predicated on fidelity to the weight and solidity of the original objects as impacted by the external force of the swells. There is a subtle mismatch here that grows more obvious with repeated viewings.) Put the other way round, the soundtrack acknowledges the relative lightness and indeed hollowness, the "idea"-likeness, of Demand's not-quite-simulacra at the same time as it provides a sufficiently plausible "account" of the noises of sliding, toppling, and colliding that the actual objects would have made to lend the stop–motion depiction of those events a farther degree of aesthetic authority than would otherwise be secured.

(5) A few final, perhaps less than fully serious remarks. In a well-known essay, *Shipwreck with Spectator*, the philosopher Hans Blumenberg begins by noting that the ancients considered sea voyages transgressive of natural boundaries, hence likely to be punished. He writes:

> The powers and gods responsible for [the sea] stubbornly withdraw from the sphere of determinable forces. Out of the ocean that lies all around the edge of the habitable world come mythical monsters which are at the farthest remove from the familiar visage of nature and seem to have no knowledge of the world as cosmos. Another feature of this kind of uncanniness is that myth assigns earthquakes – since time immemorial the most frightening of natural occurrences – to the sea god Poseidon's realm. In the half-mythical explanation given by the first of the Ionian natural

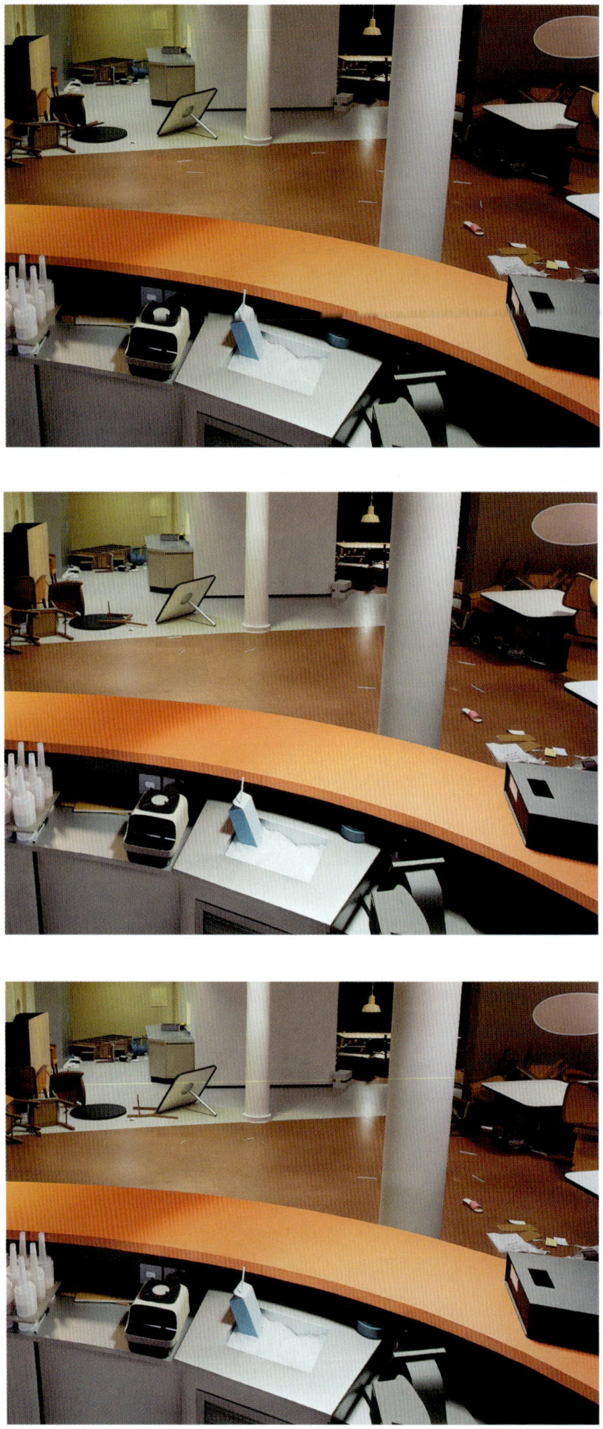

196–8 Thomas Demand, *Pacific Sun*, 2012, Video, 2,02 min, stereo (frames 2425, 2441 and 2465).

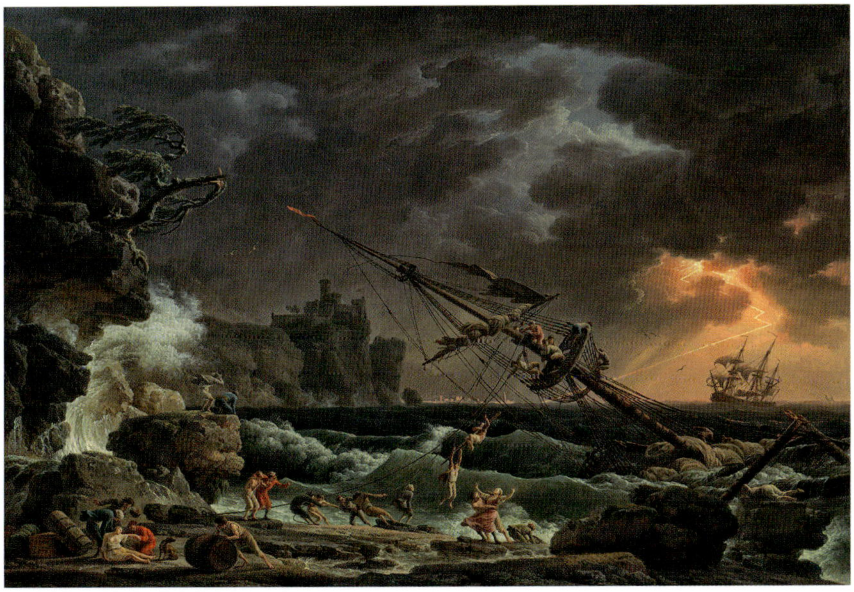

199 Claude-Joseph Vernet, *The Shipwreck*, 1772. Oil on canvas. 113.5 × 162.9 cm. Washington, D.C., National Gallery of Art. Patrons' Permanent Fund and Chester Dale Fund

philosophers, Thales of Miletus, earthquakes are compared with the swaying of a ship on the sea – and not only metaphorically, since for him dry land floats on the world ocean.[25]

Now it turns out that an unforeseen complication encountered in the making of *Pacific Sun* was the frequent occurrence during the night of extremely slight seismic shifts, the sort no one in Los Angeles particularly notices, that required Demand and his team to readjust the positioning of the paper and cardboard chairs and other objects when they arrived at the studio in the morning. Demand himself has alluded in interviews to the "hubris" involved in a project of this nature.[26] Mythically speaking, correcting for earthquakes seems an appropriate price to pay.*

* One last thought, in line with my overarching claim that advanced art today represents the dialectical unfolding of a set of basic issues that first came to the fore in mid- and late eighteenth-century Paris. Among the leading painters of Diderot's time was Claude-Joseph Vernet, one of whose specialities became scenes of storms and shipwreck; it requires only a little historical imagination, so it seems to me, to understand a canvas such as *The Shipwreck* (1772; fig. 199) as a predecessor (a prevision?) of *Pacific Sun*, in a manner of speaking.

NOTES

INTRODUCTION

1 Michael Fried, "Caillebotte's Impressionism," *Representations*, no. 66 (Spring 1999): 1–51; repr. in Norma Broude, ed., *Gustave Caillebotte and the Fashioning of Identity in Impressionist Paris* (New Brunswick, N.J., and London, 2002), 66–116.

2 Michael Fried, "Roger Fry's Formalism," *The Tanner Lectures on Human Values*, vol. 24 (Salt Lake City, Utah, 2004), 1–40.

3 Michael Fried, "David et l'antithéatralité," in Régis Michel, ed., *David contre David*, 2 vols. (Paris, 1993), 1: 199–227.

4 Michael Fried, "Géricault's Romanticism," in Régis Michel, ed., *Géricault*, 2 vols. (Paris, 1996), 2: 641–59.

5 Michael Fried, "Thomas Couture and the Theatricalization of Action in Nineteenth-Century French Painting," *Artforum* 8 (June 1970): 36–46.

6 See, e.g., Michael Fried, "Shape as Form: Frank Stella's Eccentric Polygons," "Morris Louis," "Art and Objecthood," "New Work by Anthony Caro," and "Two Sculptures by Anthony Caro" in idem, *Art and Objecthood: Essays and Reviews* (Chicago and London, 1998; hereafter, *AO*), as well as, in the same volume, "An Introduction to my Art Criticism."

7 Michael Fried, "David/Marat: The *Self-Portrait* of 1794," in Mark Ledbury, ed., *David after David: Essays on the Later Work* (New Haven and London, 2007), 191–203.

8 Michael Fried, "Another Light: Douglas Gordon's *k.364: A Journey by Train*, in *Douglas Gordon*, exh. cat. (Frankfurt, 2011), 106–17.

9 Michael Fried, "Thomas Demand's *Pacific Sun*," in Jeff Fleming, ed., *Thomas Demand: Animations*, exh. cat. (Des Moines and Montreal, 2012), n.p.

10 The full rubric of the symposium, organized by Joachim Küpper, Patrice Veit, Danièle Cohn, and Andreas Kablitz and held on May 17–18, 2013, reads: *Synergies. Französisch-deutscher Kulturaustausch im 19. und 20. Jahrhundert: Malerei, Literatur, Musik, Philosophie und Design. Les échanges culturels franco-allemands au XIXème et au XXème siècle: Peinture, littérature, musique, philosophie, arts décoratifs.*

11 Michael Fried, *Realism, Writing, Disfiguration: On Thomas Eakins and Stephen Crane* (Chicago and London, 1987); idem, *Menzel's Realism: Art and Embodiment in Nineteenth-Century Berlin* (New Haven and London, 2002; hereafter, *MR*).

12 Todd Cronan, *Against Affective Formalism: Matisse, Bergson, Modernism* (Minneapolis, 2014). See also Marnin Young, *Against Impressionism: Later Realism and the Politics of Time* (New Haven and London, forthcoming).

13 Greenberg's brief 1954 essay "Abstract, Representational, and so forth" (in *Art and Culture: Critical Essays* [Boston, 1961], 133–8) shows clearly the limitations of his thought in this regard. Early in the essay he writes:

> No one has yet been able to demonstrate that the representational as such either adds to or

> takes away from the merit of a picture or statue. The presence or absence of a recognizable image has no more to do with value in painting or sculpture than the presence or absence of a libretto has to do with value in music. Taken by itself, no single one of its parts or aspects decides the quality of a work of art as a whole. In painting and sculpture this holds just as true for the aspect of representation as it does for those of scale, color, paint quality, design, etc., etc. (133–4)

Greenberg's basic point is that neither representational nor abstract art is in principle superior to the other. But by way of making the point he deploys a concept of representation that could scarcely be more etiolated, the comparison with a libretto in certain genres of music being particularly feeble – as if the relatively small proportion of serious music involving libretti (operas, oratorios, songs) were equivalent to the great mass of representational art in the Western tradition, to speak only of the latter. Even apart from that, the notion that "the representational as such" can simply be equated with the presence of a recognizable image (equivalent to a libretto!) falls far short of doing justice conceptually to what I will call the enterprise of representational painting and sculpture in the art of the past (think of Giotto at work in the Arena Chapel or Velázquez painting *Las Meninas* or Manet paintbrush in hand before *Olympia* and ask yourself what force the notion of "recognizable image" has in those contexts, or for that matter the notion that representation is a "part or aspect" of what they are producing).

Toward the end of the essay Greenberg imagines connoisseurs of the future possibly finding the Old Masters "wanting in physical presence, in corporeality" in comparison with abstract art. He continues:

> There have been such reversals of taste before. The connoisseurs of the future may be more sensitive than we to the imaginative dimensions and overtones of the literal, and find in the concreteness of color and shape relations more "human interest" than in the extra-pictorial references of old-time illusionist art. They may also interpret the latter in ways quite different from ours. They may consider the illusion of depth and volume to have been aesthetically valuable *primarily* because it enabled and encouraged the artist to organize such infinite subtleties of light and dark, of translucence and transparence, into effectively pictorial entities. They may say that nature was worth imitating because it offered, above all, a wealth of colors and shapes, and of intricacies of color and shape, such as no painter, in isolation with his art, could ever have invented. At the same time, these connoisseurs of the future may be able, in their discourse, to distinguish and name more aspects of quality in the Old Masters, as well as in abstract art, than we can. And in so doing these things they may find much more common ground between the Old Masters and abstract art than we ourselves can recognize. (137–8; emphasis in original)

The intelligence of the passage as a whole is unmistakable but in the second sentence the phrase "extra-pictorial references" – meaning anything to do with subject matter or considerations of action or drama or illustration generally – gives the game away. As if half-aware of this, Greenberg adds one last paragraph to his essay. It reads:

> I do not wish to be understood as saying that a more enlightened connoisseurship will hold that *what*, as distinct from *how*, Rembrandt painted is an indifferent matter. That it was on the noses and foreheads of his portrait subjects, and not on their ears, that he piled the juiciest paint of his last manner has very much to do with the aesthetic results he obtained. But we still cannot say why or how. Actually, my own hope is that a less qualified acceptance of the sheerly abstract or formal factors in pictorial art will open the way to a clearer understanding of the value of illus-

> tration as such – a value which I, too, am convinced is indisputable. Only it is not a value that is realized by, or as, *accretion*. (138, emphasis in original)

That the aged Rembrandt piled his juiciest paint on his portrait subjects' noses and foreheads is, once more, an almost comically impoverished notion of what, as distinct from how, the artist painted. Just as the notion of "illustration as such" seems hopelessly inadequate to the historical and theoretical issues Greenberg imagines himself to be addressing. I think it is fair to say that his thinking about the topic never moved beyond these formulations.

Then there is the following from Greenberg's last recorded interview (with Saul Ostrow) in 1994. At one point Greenberg mentions listening with pleasure to the tenor Luciano Pavarotti singing, adding: "Aesthetic pleasure transcends sensuousness. It's a state of pleasure that is more abstract, though abstract is a misleading word." Ostrow remarks: "Michael Fried tries to build part of his argument against theatricality on just such a distinction. For him, theatricality forces self-consciousness onto the viewer." To which Greenberg replies:

> He's picked up on something that's beneath him. He goes on about the importance of whether the subject is facing you, or whether the subject is absorbed in some activity. I don't think he sees that well anymore. God knows, Pavarotti's theatrical in the best way, without being too show-offy, but an Italian tenor is supposed to be theatrical. And there's Pavarotti doing it without any effort, no effort at all. That's what is of importance. ("The Last Interview," in Robert C. Morgan, ed., *Clement Greenberg: Late Writings* [Minneapolis and London, 2003], 239–40).

What in effect he considers beneath me is nothing less than the entire Diderotian tradition as well as my own writings on the topic (in 1994, *Manet's Modernism, or, The Face of Painting in the 1860s* [Chicago and London, 1996; hereafter, *MM*], was just being completed). No comment seems necessary.

14 My reference to Kant is ultimately indebted to three seminars on the *Critique of Judgment* given by Richard Moran at Johns Hopkins University in the fall of 2005, as well as to numerous conversations with Robert Pippin. See in this general connection Walter Benn Michaels, "Neoliberal Aesthetics: Fried, Rancière and the Form of the Photograph," http://nonsite.org/issue-1/neoliberal-aesthetics-fried-ranciere-and-the-form-of-the-photograph, in which Michaels, taking off from discussions by me of Diderot on Chardin and of Fry's criticism, writes: "The radicalization (or literalization) of the commitment to absorption [as a vehicle of antitheatricality] thus produces an antinomy – the works of art we value are those which seek to produce no effect on the beholder, but without the effort to produce an effect on the beholder (without the effort, as we might say, to make something that can be seen), there would be no works of art." His key example is John Cage's notorious *4′33″*, a piece of which Cage wrote "there are no (intentional) sounds." Michaels continues: " 'The essential meaning of silence,' Cage says is not the absence of sound, but 'the giving up of intention.' That is, the point of *4′33″* is not that the performance should actually be silent but rather that whatever sounds there are should not be controlled by or in any way come from the composer." And this leads, Michaels says, to

> the inevitable primacy of the listener, since whatever sounds s/he happens to hear . . . are the sounds that make up the piece. . . . *4′33″* can thus be understood as an exemplary case of the way in which a radicalized absorption – produced by the commitment to not impose one's intentions on the listener/beholder/reader, to not perform for an audience – becomes indistinguishable from

> an account of the work of art in which it is theatricality that's radicalized – the only thing that matters is the audience's response. The way Cage puts this is to say that for him and other composers "who have accepted the sounds they do not intend," the tendency is toward musical performance as "theatre," which he values because it is the art that most "resembles nature" and which he imagines would in its ideal form be indistinguishable from "everyday life," so you could then "view everyday life as theatre"; art would, in effect, become indistinguishable from nature. The artist who begins with the fiction that his work was not made for the world (not made to be seen, not made to be listened to) ends by collapsing the work into the world – it's whatever you see, whatever you hear.

(In fact, Cage's music is characterized as theatrical in "Art and Objecthood" [*AO*, 164].)

This is acute, as is Michaels's discussion of Barthes's notion of the *punctum*, which in *Why Photography Matters as Art as Never Before* (New Haven and London, 2008; hereafter, *WPM*) I gloss as implicitly antitheatrical on the grounds that according to Barthes himself it can only be a detail (for example) that was never actually seen, and therefore never intended to be photographed, by the Operator, and which Michaels goes on to observe will therefore turn out to be whatever the beholder makes of it. "The *punctum*, in other words," he writes, "functions as an absorptive reproach to the 'artifice' of the photographer, resisting and reproaching his inevitably theatrical attempts to produce a particular effect on the beholder while at the same time (and for the same reason) it transforms the photograph into a work dependent entirely on the beholder – a purely theatrical object. The absorptive demand of indifference to the reader/beholder becomes an insistence on the absolute primacy of the reader/beholder." (My further gloss in *Why Photography Matters* on Barthes's account of the *punctum* is that the theoretical collapse of antitheatricality into its opposite to which Michaels points was in effect the harbinger of a new photographic *practice* [345–6], that of Wall, Bustamante, Ruff, Struth, Gursky, Delahaye, Demand, et al., in none of whose work is there anything like an attempt to "radicalize" or "literalize" absorption or any other artistic means. Or to eliminate the appearance of intention; on the contrary, I characterize one major aspect of their art as an insistence on a certain "to-be-seenness." See in particular the discussion in *WPM* of Wall's *Adrian Walker, Artist, Drawing from a Specimen in a Laboratory in the Dept. of Anatomy at the University of British Columbia, Vancouver* (1992), 37–43; and, with respect to the issue of intention, the discussion of Thomas Demand, 261–81.)

It follows that what Michaels also calls "the internal crisis of absorption – the transformation of the refusal of theatricality into the refusal of intentionality, the refusal, that is, of the effort to produce any effect on the beholder/listener/reader at all" – is one that by his own account took place either in the writings of thinkers (Fry, Barthes) who remained oblivious to their own antitheatrical leanings (and who therefore stumbled blindly into the conundrums summarized above) or in the work of a composer (Cage) whose extreme, which is to say "radicalizing" and "literalizing" aesthetic stance placed him outside the Diderotian current or tradition from the very start. In other words, there is a crucial distinction to be made between the inherently, necessarily dialectical (i.e., non-antinomic) status of antitheatricality as an aesthetic strategy and the (not at all Diderotian; rather, more nearly Kantian) project of avoiding any manifestation of artistic intention, indeed of rejecting intention as such, a project that, as Michaels says, is bound to emphasize the beholder's response in precisely the respects castigated in "Art and Objecthood." (For a recent, helpful summary of Kant's aesthetic thought, see Robert B. Pippin, *After the Beautiful: Hegel and the Philosophy of*

Pictorial Modernism [Chicago and London, 2014], pp. 9–17.)

I am not sure to what extent this puts me in disagreement with the overall thrust of Michaels's argument, but it has seemed important to spell out certain basic differences between what the notion of crisis involves in his article and what it signifies in the present book. (Michaels's views are elaborated in his forthcoming book, *The Beauty of a Social Problem*.) Let me go a step farther and suggest that one way of understanding the crises in the Diderotian current or tradition represented by the art of later David or Géricault, or indeed by that of Daumier, Courbet, Manet, and Caillebotte (to mention no more names, as one might), is that to a large degree that current or tradition consists precisely of successive, interlocked moments of crisis or its equivalent: at every dialectical turn the current or tradition is concerned with its possible – one is tempted to say its inevitable – dissolution. This suggests not only that the current or tradition can best be understood at its moments of crisis, but also that it most fully emerges as such – as a historically developing force – in those moments. (My thanks to Jeremy Melius for inspiring these last sentences.)

It goes without saying that the larger topic of Kant and antitheatricality calls for far more serious treatment than it receives here.

15 In the light of the fact that the last two essays in this book deal with films (one regular film, the other stop-motion), it may be to the point that the 1760s in France saw the thought-invention, or one thought-invention, of movies in Diderot's brilliant account in his *Salon of 1765* of the young Jean-Honoré Fragonard's large history painting, *Corésus et Callirhoé*, one of the most original works of the period. See Michael Fried, *Absorption and Theatricality: Painting and Beholder in the Age of Diderot* (1980; Chicago, 1986), 141–5; hereafter, *AT*.

1 DAVID / MANET

1 In *AT* I show that Diderot's *Salons* also imply what I call a "pastoral" conception of painting, according to which the beholder was to be led to imagine himself or herself within a particular picture (and therefore no longer in front of it), though again the actual outcome of that imagining was that the beholder was stopped and held before the canvas (118–45). The "pastoral" conception applied to landscapes, paintings of ruins, even still lifes – genres that for obvious reasons did not lend themselves to rigorously dramatic treatment. It therefore has no direct relevance to David's art; its fullest "realization" comes later, with the advent of Courbet.

2 I do this in part by reading David's canvas in the light of Diderot's commentary on a famous engraving after a seventeenth-century painting of *Belisarius Receiving Alms* then thought to be by Van Dyck and now attributed to Luciano Borzone. The commentary is found in a characteristically brilliant letter of 1762 to Sophie Volland (*AT*, 147–8).

3 As I note in *AT*, David felt that his knowledge of perspective was deficient and urged his students not to suffer under the same handicap (156). But something more than simple ineptitude is required to explain the awkwardness of the perspective structure in the *Belisarius*, and in any case David's difficulties with perspective may betray an emerging tension between the scenographic as such and the requirements of antitheatricality.

4 Also in *AT* I go on to consider the function of the obelisk in David's composition as well as to compare the *Belisarius* of 1781 with a smaller variant (the work largely of David's student François-Xavier Fabre) of 1785 (158–60). I further remark on how, in the painting of 1781, the two figures conversing behind the soldier and to his right (our left), who seem on the verge of leaving the scene, not only appear oblivious to the principal action but also, by virtue of their truncation by the left-hand framing edge, suggest the unboundedness of the

representation in that direction (a notion consistent with the possibility of rotation).

Finally, there is an analogy between the woman's gesture of drawing her cloak across her face with her left hand so as to conceal herself from viewers within the painting (while in the process leaving the right side of her face exposed to us) and Diderot's discussion of an unnamed Italian painter's treatment of the difficult because intrinsically voyeuristic subject of *Susannah and the Elders* (*AT*, 96–97). Interestingly, the same gesture will recur in one of David's last canvases, the *Fortune Teller* (1824; see fig. 22), to be briefly discussed toward the end of this essay.

Apropos of the *Belisarius*, see also Charles Dempsey, "The Eye of the Needle: Jacques-Louis David's *Bélisaire reconnu par un soldat qui avait servi sous lui, au moment qu'une femme lui fait l'aumône*," in Machtelt Israels and Louis A. Waldman, eds., *Renaissance Studies in Honor of Joseph Connors*, 2 vols. (Cambridge, Mass., 2013), 2: 645–50.

5 Norman Bryson, *Word and Image: French Painting of the Ancien Régime* (Cambridge, 1981), 226.

6 Thomas Crow, *Painters and Public Life in Eighteenth-Century Paris* (New Haven and London, 1985), 240. The quotation from Honour is from his *Neo-Classicism* (Harmondsworth, 1968), 34–6.

7 "If the beholder is in the theater as before a canvas," Diderot writes, "on which the different *tableaux* follow one another by enchantment, why shouldn't the philosopher seated at the foot of Socrates's bed, and who is afraid to see him die, be as pathetic on the stage as are the wife (sic) and daughter of Eudamidas in Poussin's painting?" (Denis Diderot, "De la poésie dramatique," *Oeuvres esthétiques*, ed. Paul Vernière [Paris, 1959], 276; translation mine). ("Si le spectateur est au théâtre comme devant une toile, où des tableaux divers se succéderaient par enchantement, pourquoi le philosophe qui s'assied sur les pieds du lit de Socrate, et craint de le voir mourir, ne serait-il pas aussi pathétique sur la scène, que la femme et la fille d'Eudamidas dans le tableau du Poussin?") For Diderot's scenario for a pantomime (by which he meant a succession of paintable *tableaux*) based on the death of Socrates, see ibid., 272–6. The closeness of the *Socrates* to its probable source in Diderot is also emphasized by Anita Brookner, *Jacques-Louis David* (New York, 1980), 46–7.

8 I do not mean by this to minimize the differences, quite apart from that of size, between Poussin's stoic masterpiece and David's apotheosis of masculine will. As the last phrase suggests, one difference concerns the treatment of gender, a topic I must let pass. Another concerns the extent to which David's painting is felt to depict a single "pregnant" moment in a rapidly unfolding narrative as against the stilled, relatively unvectored temporal modality of the *Eudamidas*. Note, though, how the fact that swearing an oath typically cannot be done in an instant but rather requires at least some continuous engagement over time allowed David to combine an evocation of vectoredness with an effect of duration, just as the nature of that particular action enabled him to represent all three brothers participating in it not just simultaneously but *synchronically*: as if each is felt to belong to exactly the same *phase* of the action as the others.

9 E[tienne]-J[ean] Delécluze, *Louis David, son école et son temps, souvenirs*, new ed. with preface and notes by Jean-Pierre Mouilleseaux (1855; Paris, 1983), 120. "Around the years 1796–1800," Delécluze writes, "when he was entirely preoccupied with rediscovering Greek [artistic] doctrines, David judged his *Horatii* with truly remarkable and severe impartiality. He focused on the difficulty relative to the composition by saying that the latter was theatrical; as for the drawing, he found it small, petty [*petit, mesquin*] (those were his expressions), rendering the anatomical details with excessive care; and finally the color now struck him as inconsistent, destroying the beauty and grandeur of local tones." At the same time, as if

in partial contradiction to his own revisionist views, David is quoted as saying, "After all . . . there is energy in this painting, and the group of the Horatii is something I will never renounce!" (translation mine). Maybe, but the treatment of Romulus and Tatius in the *Sabines* is of an altogether different character. ("[V]ers les années 1796–1800, lorsqu'il était tout préoccupé de retrouver les doctrines grecques, David jugeait ses *Horaces* avec une équité sévère bien remarquable. Il tranchait la difficulté relativement à la composition en disant qu'elle est théâtrale; pour le dessin il le trouvait *petit, mesquin* (ce sont ses expressions), rendant les détails anatomiques avec recherché; et enfin le coloris, comme procédant par *enchantillons de couleur*, et détruisant la beauté et la grandeur du *ton local*. . . . Après tout . . . il y a de l'énergie dans ce tableau, et le groupe des Horaces est une chose que je renierai jamais!")

10 For the text of David's *livret*, including Hersilia's speech, see Daniel and Guy Wildenstein, eds., *Documents complémentaires au catalogue complet de l'oeuvre de Louis David* (Paris, 1973), 148–50.

That what I have described as a dedramatization of action in the *Sabines* was nevertheless perceived in 1799 within a dramatic framework emerges in contemporary responses to the picture. At the same time, David's choice of a moment of relative repose is commented on both by Chaussard (an antitheatrical critic), who writes that "David has seized the moment when the action is suspended naturally by that of Hersilia and the women who thrust themselves with their children between the swords" (P[ierre-Jean] Chaussard, *Sur le tableau des Sabines par David* [Paris, 1800], 4; translation mine) ("David a saisi le moment où l'action est naturellement suspendue par celle d'Hersilie et des femmes qui se precipitent avec leurs enfans entre les glaives"), and by Landon, who observes that "all the personages are in action and the pantomime is organized with such art that there is not a single personage who could not maintain for several instants the attitude in which he [or she] is represented. This point is of the highest importance, it adds to the illusion and soothes the beholder. One feels that repose suits painting much better than a sudden action or a fleeting movement" ([Charles-Paul] Landon, "Réflexions sur ce tableau," Paris, Bibliothèque Nationale, Collection Deloynes, MS. no. 593, 662–3; translation mine) ("tous les personnages sont en action et la pantomime est dirigée avec tant d'art qu'il n'y a pas un seul personnage qui ne peut conserver pendant quelques instans l'attitude où il est représenté. Ce point est de la plus haute importance, il ajoute à l'illusion et soulage le spectateur. On sent que le repos conviens à la peinture bien plus qu'une action subite ou un movement passagère").

Apropos of my association of the temporal modality of the *Sabines* with that of an operatic aria, it is striking that Chaussard draws an analogy between the women and children that David placed in the middle of the battle and "those priestesses of Diane that Gluck lets us hear among the ferocious Scythians, when the melodious laments of those virgins mix with the terrible accents of the bloodthirsty joy exhaled by Thoas and his atrocious horde" (in the opera *Iphigénie en Tauride*; *Sur le tableau des Sabines par David*, 20–21; translation mine) ("ces prêtresses de Diane que Gluck fait entendre au milieu des Scythes farouches, alors que les plaints mélodieuses de ces vierges se mêlent aux accens déchirans de la joie sanguinaire qu'exhalent Thoas et la horde atroce qui le suit").

11 See [François-Pierre-Guillaume] Guizot, "De l'état des beaux-arts en France, et du Salon de 1810," in *Etudes sur les beaux-arts en général* (Paris, 1858), 12–14; and Stendhal, "Salon de 1824," in *Mélanges d'art* [1932; Nendeln/Liechtenstein, 1968), 45–7.

12 Norman Bryson, *Tradition and Desire: From David to Delacroix* (Cambridge, 1984), 94.

13 There is more to be said about the differences in our views. Bryson stages his chapters on

Belisarius and the *Oath of the Horatii* partly in rebuttal of my argument in *AT* (about which he also has favorable things to say). He writes:

> [Fried's approach] confines itself to a definition of the viewing subject narrowly concerned with the issue of the admission and the exclusion of the observer: the viewing subject is variously kept out [of the painting] or ushered in, but either way he remains an agent who simply sees, a viewing substance invited into the sphere of perceptions. Fried's subject is the same subject that is posited in the phenomenological reduction: monadic and self-enclosed, the subject sees the world from the world's centre and in unitary prospect. . . . This leaves (at least) two things out: the presence of the other in vision which makes of *human* visuality (as opposed to the vision of the camera) a divided visuality, divided because the subject is not alone in his perceptual horizon, but surrounded by the visualities of others with which it must interact; and secondly (a corollary of this) the permanent division of visual subjectivity in the visual *sign*. (46; emphasis in original)

But in the first place, the identification of "Fried"s subject" with the "subject . . posited in the phenomenological reduction" does not hold water; the demand that paintings establish the ontological fiction that their dramatis personae are alone in the world precisely implies a subject who is anything but "alone in his perceptual horizon"; one might even say that it is precisely a new awareness of being part of a universal realm of spectatordom that underwrites the Diderotian aesthetic with its attempt to suspend that awareness in the grip of the work. Put slightly differently, *AT* speaks of Diderot as calling for "at one and the same time the creation of a new sort of object [artifact] – the fully realized *tableau* – and the constitution of a new sort of beholder – a new 'subject' – whose innermost nature would consist precisely in the conviction of his absence from the scene of representation" (104) – a hyperbolic aim that is only intelligible as a response to a new consciousness of "the presence of the other in vision," indeed of the existence of others generally. See too my discussion in an appendix in *AT* of Rousseau's *Lettre sur les spectacles*, in which I remark that Diderot and Rousseau each expresses "an extreme distaste for what might be called the theatricality of theater as they know it, together with a suspicion that the corruptness of the theater in their time is only one manifestation of a deeper or more pervasive state of affairs involving the function of beholding and the condition of being beheld" (167).

More broadly, Bryson's commitment to a certain sort of divided subject, when brought to bear on David's paintings of the 1780s and after, produces dubious results. Specifically, Bryson's Lacanian assumption that human visuality is marked by "a decentering gaze, the Gaze of the Other" (58) leads to the repeated claim that figures in David's canvases are crucially involved in "projecting" images of themselves out toward others. "In the case of Belisarius and the child," Bryson writes, "an invisible inner state of want and need can only be relieved by transmitting into the world a certain image that will forcibly enter the vision of others . . . We can say that in the act of begging the essential terms are the hidden (hunger) and the theatrical (the image of pathos); just as in the sister act, charity, the essential terms are the discomfort of *concealment* (of money, of guilt, of sympathy) and a *conspicuous* act which relieves that discomfort (donation)" (59; emphasis in original). Similarly, Bryson states of the *Horatii*: "The image exactly traces the negative consequences of the subject's insertion into language and gender, for the visuality of the males is now dominated by the outward projection of heroically gendered self-imagery, moving forward to meet the description coming from outside, in the oath itself" (71).

As these citations demonstrate (a dozen others would have done as well), the combination of an a priori commitment to an ontology of the divided subject and an essentialist account of human action (acts of charity by definition involve a tension between concealment and conspicuousness) produces readings in which both the *Belisarius* and the *Horatii* (and, as seen, the *Sabines*) emerge as inherently theatrical. Needless to say, I find Bryson's readings of these and other paintings by David unpersuasive in their own terms. But what I want to stress is, first, that my disagreement with Bryson is not based on an *opposite* account of the works in question (it explicitly is not my claim that the *Belisarius* and the *Horatii* conclusively overcome the theatrical); and second, that Bryson's approach, by virtue of its assumption that a certain theatricality (his words for it are Otherness, decentering, splitting, etc.) is inherent in human visuality, prevents him from even considering the possibility that David's paintings may be the product of an antitheatrical *intention* (the heart of my account). He thereby blinds himself to their historical reality.

14 It is also true that according to Antoine Montfort, a young painter who had assisted Géricault during his campaign on the *Raft*, the latter after seeing the *Sabines* and *Leonidas* in David's Cluny studio came back discouraged; in particular the running Spartans at the lower right made him "almost turn his eyes away from his own work" (Antoine Montfort, "Le Manuscrit de Montfort," in *Géricault*, exh. cat. [Paris, 1991], 313); translation mine) ("il détournait presque les yeux de son travail"). A recent book that attempts a revaluation of the "chains" of figures in the Leonidas is Satish Padiyar, *Chains: David, Canova and the Fall of the Public Hero in Postrevolutionary France* (University Park, Penn., 2007). Let me also take this opportunity to cite the extremely interesting discussion of the *Belisarius* and the *Horatii* in John Bender and Michael Marrinan, *The Culture of Diagram* (Stanford, Cal., 2010), pp. 92–151.

15 Delécluze, *Louis David*, 225–7. "Je veux peindre un général et ses soldats se préparant au combat comme de véritables Lacédémoniens, sachant bien qu'ils n'en échapperont pas; les uns absolument calmes, les autres tressant des fleurs pour assister *au banquet qu'ils vont faire chez pluton*. . . . Je veux essayer de mettre de côté ces mouvements, ces expressions de théâtre, auxquels les modernes ont donné le titre de *peinture d'expression*. . . . Mais j'aurai bien de la peine, ajouta David, à faire adopter de semblables idées dans notre temps. On aime les coups de théâtre, at quand on ne peint pas les passions violentes, quand on ne pousse pas l'expression en peinture jusqu'à la *grimace*, on risque de n'être ni compris ni goûté." [Emphasis in original]) For Diderot's contrast in the *Entretiens* and the *Discours* between *tableaux* and *coups de théâtre* see *AT*, 78, 79, 93, 95–6, 207. According to Delécluze, David also found in the art of the ancients, as well as in Italian painting from Giotto to Perugino and Raphael, the inspiration for a system of composition which, instead of "sacrificing everything to dramatic effect," would seek on the contrary to fix the viewer's attention "successively on each personage by virtue of the perfection with which it was treated" (*Louis David*, 220–21; translation mine) ("sacrifiant tout à l'effet dramatique . . . successivement sur chaque personnage par la perfection avec laquelle il serait traité").

16 In *Courbet's Realism* (Chicago, 1990; hereafter, *CR*) I remark that David in 1807 gave Delécluze a drawing of two heads that he had made roughly thirty years before; one head had been copied accurately from the antique while the other, based on the first, had been enlivened in various ways. "I gave it," David remarked, "what the moderns call expression and what today I call grimace" (18; the reference is to Delécluze, *Louis David*, 112; translation mine). Significantly, the suspension of dramatic action in the *Sabines* goes hand in hand with an unmistakable toning down of expression among the principal figures.

17 Philippe Bordes, *Le Serment du Jeu de Paume de Jacques-Louis David: Le Peintre, son milieu et*

son temps de 1789 à 1792, Notes et documents des musées de France 8 (Paris, 1983), 59; translation mine. Bordes's remarks on Diderot are explicitly based on *AT*. Further page references will be in parentheses in the text.

18 See Philippe Bordes, *Jacques-Louis David: Empire to Exile*, exh. cat. (Los Angeles and Williamstown, Mass., 2005), 69 (hereafter Bordes). When the painting was finished, however, Napoleon made a publicized visit to see it in David's Cluny studio; with the defeat of the Empire in the cards, the *Leonidas* could now be seen as rallying the French to fight on against overwhelming odds.

19 Dorothy Johnson, *Jacques-Louis David: Art in Metamorphosis* (Princeton, 1993), ch. 5, 221–72; Bordes; Ledbury, *David after David*. Further references to Johnson will be in parentheses in the text.

20 The only writer I have come across who notes this stability is Bordes, 209. Thomas Crow sees Phaon as having just approached Sappho in *Emulation: Making Artists for Revolutionary France* (New Haven and London, 1995), 265. He adds: "The characters' solicitation of the spectator's regard, insistent without carrying any expressive interest, seems a plea to excuse the insipid and derivative quality of the entire exercise, which he dispatched to Russia with almost surreptitious discretion" (265).

21 Susan Siegfried, "The Artifice of Antiquity: Sappho's Dream," in Ledbury, *David after David*, 95–8.

22 Writing in the Clark symposium volume, Siegfried follows me in noting that the "Anacreonic" works feature outward-facing figures but then adds specifically about the *Sappho, Phaon, and Cupid*, "In the final painting, Phaon exists on the threshold between drama and portraiture, fiction and reality. He is not gratuitiously 'theatrical,' as is often said in deference to Michael Fried's work, since his attitude is anchored in the text [by which she means Ovid's poem, "Sappho to Phaon"]" (ibid., 102). I suggest, first, that Siegfried's adverb "gratuitously" is out of place – that is, notions like theatricality or facingess in no way imply that the actions of a particular figure or group of figures might not be anchored in a supporting text. Second, there is, however, no reason to think that David's painting follows Ovid's poem (in other words, in this case I see no such "anchoring"). And third, the "deference" to my work by previous David scholars that Siegfried wishes to contest has largely escaped my notice. She is referring to Antoine Schnapper's (to my mind perfectly straightforward) remarks in the 1989–90 Louvre catalogue entry for the *Sappho*: "Here the painter systematizes a procedure of portraitists, who have their personages look at the beholder, not at the scene in which they participate; this procedure is the opposite of that described by M. Fried . . . under the name of *absorption*. Already the plague-victim in the *Saint Roch* [a painting of 1780] or Brutus in the painting of 1789 address the beholder, but in this work there are two protagonists, which contributes strongly to the disconcerting impression, not of realism but of reality, provoked by the painting, as in, slightly later, *Cupid and Psyche* in Cleveland" (in Antoine Schnapper, Arlette Sérullas, and Elisabeth Agius-d'Yvoire, eds., *Jacques-Louis David, 1748–1825*, exh. cat. [Paris, 1989], 441). Siegfried also remarks that my thesis "lingers in Bordes" (107; like the aftermath of an illness?), and of course there are Bryson's criticisms cited earlier. But Siegfried need not worry – my arguments in *AT* and related writings have played only a modest role in David studies over the past forty-plus years. (There is a grand total of one passing reference to my work in a footnote in Johnson's monograph.)

23 *MM*, 262–364.

24 On Millet and absorption see ibid., 188–92.

25 Facingness and strikingness are major themes throughout ibid. My account of Manet's art, in particular his response to increasingly problematic status of the depiction of absorption as a resource for ambitious painting, is discussed at length in Robert B. Pippin, *After the Beautiful: Hegel and the Philosophy of Pictorial Mod-*

ernism (Chicago and London, 2014). See also idem, "Authenticity in Painting: Michael Fried's Art History," *Critical Inquiry* 31 (Spring 2005): 575–98.

26 A. de Kératry, *Annuaire de l'école française de peinture ou lettre sur le Salon de 1819* (Paris, 1819), 100–01; cited by Johnson, *Jacques-Louis David*, 250.

27 In this connection, look ahead to David's *Mars Disarmed by Venus and the Graces* (see fig. 21) and note Cupid's gleaming quiver, which in effect replaces the god's genitals covered by the cooing doves.

28 Issa Lampe, "Repainting *Love Leaving Psyche*: David's Memorial to an Empire Past," in Ledbury, *David after David*, 112. Further references to Lampe will be in parentheses in the text.

29 Johnson remarks that "[t]he brutal characterization of the god brings to mind an Amor [Cupid] equally shocking in its realism – Caravaggio's *Amor Vincit Omnia* – a work well-known to David and his contemporaries" (248), which is true as far as it goes. Equally to the point, perhaps, might have been a *Resurrection* painted by Caravaggio for the church of Sant'Anna dei Lombardi in Naples around 1608 and destroyed in an earthquake in 1788 (so David, who visited Naples in 1779, could not have failed to see it). In that painting, according to one early commentator, Christ was depicted "with one foot in the tomb and the other resting outside it" (the commentator is Luigi Scaramuccia; see the interesting discussion of the *Resurrection* in Peter Robb, *M: The Man Who Became Caravaggio* [New York, 1998, 1999], 411–14).

30 In fact Cupid was modeled for by the 17-year-old son of the American diplomat Albert Gallatin; amusingly, the young man in his journal regrets that he and the young model for Psyche are not to pose together (Bordes, 232).

31 E.-F. Miel, *Essai sur les beaux-arts et particulièrement sur le Salon de 1817* (Paris, 1817), 237–8. Cited by Johnson, *Jacques-Louis David*, 248. In fact Johnson compares David's use of the myth of Cupid and Psyche to "the problematic of sexual exploitation raised by Manet's *Olympia* as well as modern psychoanalytic interpretations of the mythology of desire. David understood and demonstrated the essence of the Odalisque theme – male domination over, and imprisonment of, a captive woman who is reduced to a sexual slave and denied an existence independent of her sensuality" (254).

32 See *MM*, 153.

33 See ibid., 172, 525–6 n. 114. Cf. Anne Wagner, "Why Monet Gave Up Figure Painting," *Art Bulletin* 76 (Dec. 1994): 613–29.

34 Thomas Crow, "The Imagination of Exile in David's *Anger of Achilles*," in Ledbury, *David after David*, 132.

35 Claude Lebensztejn, "Histoires belges," in Michel, *David contre David*, 2: 1018.

36 Johnson cites a letter from Mme David to Gros of May 13, 1819: "At this moment [David] is finishing a painting which represents the wrath of Achilles at the moment when Iphigenia is led to her sacrifice. It is composed of four half-length figures; it is harmonious overall. The expressions are of the greatest beauty. The head of Clytemnestra unites fear and hope to a most eminently beautiful degree. The majestic calm of Agamemnon is also of a rare beauty. The resignation of Iphigenia is of an admirable sensibility. In short, our friend makes his exile enjoyable with his cherished painting and I assure you that the paintings he will have executed in Flanders will mark another epoch in his painterly life" (258). Ecole nationale supérieure des beaux-arts, MS. 316, no. 34.

37 This is stressed by Johnson in *Jacques-Louis David*, 11–69 (a chapter entitled "The Eloquent Body: 'Gestes sublimes' and the Formation of a Corporal Aesthetic").

38 See in this connection Ewa Lajer-Burcharth, *Necklines: The Art of Jacques-Louis David after the Terror* (New Haven and London, 1999), 130–235 (a chapter entitled "The Revolution *Glacée*"). Hereafter, Lajer-Burcharth.

39 There are two especially pertinent texts in this regard, Paul Friedland, *Political Actors: Repre-*

sentative Bodies and Theatricality in the Age of the French Revolution (Ithaca, N.Y., and London, 2002); and Susan Maslan, *Revolutionary Acts: Theater, Democracy, and the French Revolution* (Baltimore, 2005). Friedland's book, the work of a historian, is particularly good on the deliberations in the Estates General and the National Assembly as regards the issue of the so-called general will; Maslan's book, the work of a literary scholar, provides a rich and detailed account of the interface between the political arena and actual theatrical productions of the period. (The two studies complement each other.) Apropos of the question of "transparency," the fundamental text remains Jean Starobinski, *Jean-Jacques Rousseau: Transparency and Obstruction*, trans. Arthur Goldhammer (1957, 1971; Chicago and London, 1988).

40 The classic work on the Revolutionary festivals is Mona Ozouf, *Festivals and the French Revolution*, trans. Alan Sheridan (Cambridge, Mass. and London, 1988). But see also Warren Roberts, *Jacques-Louis David and Jean-Louis Prieur, Revolutionary Artists: The Public, the Populace, and Images of the French Revolution* (Albany, N.Y., 2000), ch. 6, "Robespierre, David, and Revolutionary Festivals," 269–311. The previous chapter, "David and the *Tennis Court Oath*," 227–68, is also of interest.

41 Mention of the *Tennis Court Oath* suggests another question: to what extent (if at all) might the dramaturgy of that composition, with its intended inclusion of the beholder in the action of swearing the oath, have prepared the way for the "facing," beholder-acknowledging character of the "Anacreonic" paintings?

42 On these drawings see especially Dorothy Johnson, "Lines of Thought: David's Aporetic Late Drawings," in Ledbury, *David after David*, 153–69. "Aporetic" is her term, a good one. She notes that Pierre-Yves Kairis has shown that four of five figures in one *A Scene of Mourning* are adapted from figures in Lambert Lombard's *Burial of Saint Denis* (ca. 1550), which was in a church in Liège which David could have visited (and evidently did) (163).

43 Interestingly, there is a somewhat analogous development in the late, smudged carpenter's pencil drawings of the great nineteenth-century German painter-draftsman Adolph Menzel, which suggests that we may be dealing here with a psychological – specifically, an old-age – phenomenon as well as a strictly artistic one. It is striking, though, that none of the personages in Menzel's drawings stares out at the viewer, theatricality and related issues never having been among his concerns. See *MR*, 219–29.

2 DAVID / MARAT

1 See T. J. Clark, "Gross David with the Swoln Cheek: An Essay in Self-Portraiture," in Michael S. Roth, ed., *Rediscovering History: Culture, Politics, and the Psyche* (Stanford, Cal., 1994), 243–307 (hereafter, Clark); and Lajer-Burcharth, 33–54. Subsequent references to both will be in parentheses in the text. See also the brief discussion in Bordes, 16, cat. 1.

2 See Delafontaine's brief account of accompanying David to prison and bringing him the mirror in Daniel and Guy Wildenstein, *Documents complémentaires*, 131, no. 1 (hereafter, Wildenstein).

3 Umberto Eco, in a chapter on mirrors, insists that mirrors do not reverse or invert. "A mirror reflects the right side exactly where the right side is," he writes, "and the same with the left side. . . . It is only when we anthropomorphize the virtual image that we are puzzled by right and left – that is, only at this point do we start wondering what right and left would be *if* the virtual image were the real object." See his *Semiotics and the Philosophy of Language* (Bloomington, Ind., 1984), 205–6.

4 Zirka Zaremba Filipczak, *Picturing Art in Antwerp, 1500–1700* (Princeton, N.J., 1987), 202.

5 *MM*, 365–98. See also *CR*, 53–84 and passim.

6 Michael Fried, *The Moment of Caravaggio*,

Andrew W. Mellon Lectures on the Fine Arts (Princeton, N.J., 2010), 7–67 and passim (hereafter, *Moment of Caravaggio*). See also Fried, "Thoughts on Caravaggio," *Critical Inquiry* 24 (Autumn 1997): 13–56.

7 Cf. Lajer-Burcharth, 36: "Both paintings [David's self-portraits of 1791 and 1794] use the same basic format of self-presentation – facing the viewer, with the upright torso shown in three-quarters – and both are distinguished for the artist's air of intense concentration and seriousness, and a certain rigidity in the look and in the pose" (36). This sort of formulation, pretty much standard in the secondary literature, falls short of capturing the internal dynamic of the pose.

8 I proposed this earlier, in a long footnote in *MM*, 601–2 n. 9), but no one seems to have noticed (understandably: long footnotes in long books on other subjects are not the best venues for important announcements). The present essay seeks to make the proposal stick. As Jean-Rémy Mantion has remarked, the title of David's canvas is an open question. "Who or what are we talking about when we say . . . David's *Marat*? How are we to name him, what are we to call him, in order to recall him and the event? *Marat Assassinated*, as the label in Brussels has it? *Marat Expiring*, as Delécluze and Proudhon suggested according to Wildenstein's catalogue? *Marat Dying in his Bathtub*, as it was called by the court in 1889 assembled to authenticate it? *The Death of Marat*, according to an inventory of 1854? Or, as David himself seems to indicate, *Marat at His Last Breath*" ("I have just finished the painting representing Marat at his last breath," October 16, 1793, Wildenstein, 601)? "Enveloppes à Marat David," in *La Mort de Marat*, ed. Jean-Claude Bonnet (Paris, 1986), 206; translation mine. I have chosen the last of these as most probably expressing David's intentions.

On *Marat at His Last Breath* see esp. T.J. Clark, "Painting in the Year Two," *Farewell to an Idea: Episodes from a History of Modernism* (New Haven and London, 1999), 15–53; and William Vaughan and Helen Weston, eds., *David's The Death of Marat*, Masterpieces of Western Painting (Cambridge, 2000).

9 A recent indicator of this is the catalogue of the rich and fascinating exhibition of self-portraits that was held in 2005 at the National Portrait Gallery in London. See Anthony Bond and Joanna Woodall, eds., *Self Portrait: Renaissance to Contemporary*, exh. cat. (London, 2005). The catalogue, a serious production, includes essays by T. J. Clark, Ludmilla Jordanova, and Joseph Leo Koerner in addition to ones by the organizers. But neither in the essays nor the entries to specific works does the issue of mirror-reversal arise in a conceptually sustained form, and in the case of one exceptional work – Sir Joshua Reynolds's *Self-Portrait* of ca. 1747–9 – the fact that it is mirror-reversed goes unremarked. I should add that Koerner shows an acute awareness of issues of mirror-reversal in his discussion of Albrecht Dürer's self-portraits in *The Moment of Self-Portraiture in German Renaissance Art* (Chicago and London, 1993).

10 Lajer-Burcharth, 34–5: "It is as if, to begin with, the artist had problems in making his body image literally *fit* the format he had chosen, for the frame seems to have caught him moving to the left and almost out of the picture: his body seems to be sliding off the armchair – which is itself cropped – and his palette and brush are abruptly cut off as a result. . . . Furthermore, because of the considerable distance that separates the chair from the body, the armchair gains an existence of its own, materializing as a kind of excess – a dark shell of absence behind David's back." Schnapper characterizes the armchair as "somewhat bizarrely drawn" in his catalogue entry on that painting in Schnapper, Sérullaz, and Agius-d'Yvoire, *Jacques-Louis David, 1748–1825*, 304, no. 135; translation mine.

11 Lajer-Burcharth, 43: "The houppelande, a typical garment of the sans-culottes, became the characteristic attire of the radical deputies in Year II. Marat set the fashion for wearing it at the National Convention."

12 Here is Lajer-Burchharth, 39, going on from Clark (the 1791 *Self-Portrait* she refers to is illustrated and briefly discussed toward the end of this essay): "In the 1791 image, David's triple-collar *redingote* participates in producing an elaborate pattern of pleats and *doublures* – a common pictorial trope of inside-outside used in portraiture to suggest the interiority within the body. In 1794, what is striking is not the doubling as such but the disjunction it produces within the torso, as if echoing the physiognomic disarray. It is as if the David of the prison image had *two* bodies: one, rendered in off-whites, emerges from underneath his coat; another is suggested by the coat, an *houppelande*, with the broad and asymmetrical folds of its collar and the giant lapels that seem to have a life of their own, both because of the way they were shaped, with their suggestive, fleshy nooks and crannies, and because of the tactile matter in which they were painted, with the mobile strokes and fingerprints that are still visible on the painterly surface – strokes at once exceeding the task of description and insufficient in securing it."

13 According to Clark, it was I who suggested that the thumb might be seen in that light, in a verbal response to an early draft of his essay presented at Johns Hopkins University (492 n. 70). Clark also says in that note that he is certain that my treatment of the topic of self-portraiture in *Courbet's Realism* influenced his essay in various ways – at least he hopes so. The compliment is hereby returned: the present essay, modest as it is, would be inconceivable without his contribution. Lajer-Burchharth's account (39) of the hands and palette in the *Self-Portrait* seconds Clark.

14 Bordes, 16. Bordes also writes: "In fabricating this assertive image of the artist as practitioner if not as artisan [a reference to the depiction of the brush and palette], David sought to reinvest a reality from which he had been excluded by his imprisonment: no longer the realm of the National Convention nor the political gatherings, but the free urban spaces of social interaction that after Thermidor were emblematic of the release from the Terror, as the street scenes of Louis-Léopold Boilly from the period so eloquently make clear" (2).

15 Cited and discussed by Lajer-Burcharth, 48–54.

16 Wildenstein, no. 674.

17 Jean-Claude Bonnet, *La Naissance du Panthéon: Essai sur le culte des grands hommes* (Paris, 1998), 290–91; translation mine. See also Bonnet, "Les Formes de célébration," in Bonnet, *Mort de Marat*, 101–27, esp. 125–7, and "Les Images négatives," in ibid., 167–84. My thanks to David Bell not only for both references but also for discussing with me the standing of Marat in August–September 1794.

Tom Gretton emphasizes the tension between Marat and the popular movement within the Revolution on the one hand and Robespierre and the Jacobins on the other in 1793 in "Marat, *L'Ami du people*, David: Love and Discipline in the Summer of 1793," in Vaughan and Weston, *David's The Death of Marat*, 34–55. In Gretton's account, however, David is understood as closer to Robespierre than to Marat, and the painting is imagined as "transform[ing] the values Marat embodied into their own opposites" (51). See also Warren Roberts, *Jacques-Louis David and Jean-Louis Prieur*, 288–92. Roberts notes, significantly, that Marat had nominated David for the Convention (289).

18 Bonnet, *Naissance du Panthéon*, 292; translation mine.

19 Ibid., 293; translation mine.

20 Wildenstein, no. 1166.

21 As is emphasized by Lajer-Burcharth, 48–9. But in the light of the *Self-Portrait*'s relation to Marat, does it follow from David's repeated mentions of Robespierre "that it was particularly through Robespierre that David identified – embraced and united himself – with the Revolution" (51)?

22 We owe this information too to Delafontaine. Bordes writes: "Worth noting is that David did not want to keep this work associated with his

close call with the guillotine and his year in prison and that never again would he execute a self-portrait" (16). But it was not simply because of unpleasant associations that David wanted it out of his hands.

23 See the entry on that painting in Schnapper, Sérullaz, and Agius-d'Yvoire, *Jacques-Louis David*, 238, no. 98. I was fortunate to view it again at an exhibition of paintings and drawings by David at the Musée Jacquemart-André. See Musée Jacquemart-André, *Jacques-Louis David, 1748–1825*, exh. cat. (Paris, 2005), 100–01, no. 34.

24 Let me say in closing that I take the present essay to offer an unequivocally affirmative answer to Clark's de Manian question as to whether David's *Self-Portrait* "ends up being *by* someone – and understandable to the extent that this is the case." Clark, 490 n. 56; emphasis in original.

3 GÉRICAULT'S ROMANTICISM

1 Basic modern secondary sources on Géricault include Lorenz E. A. Eitner, *Géricault: His Life and Work* (London, 1983); Germain Bazin, *Théodore Géricault: Etude critique, documents et catalogue raisonné*, 8 vols. (Paris, 1987–97); *Géricault*, exh. cat., curated by Sylvain Laveissière and Régis Michel (Paris, 1991; hereafter, *Géricault* 1991); Régis Michel, ed., *Géricault*, 2 vols. (Paris, 1996), a collection of papers given on the occasion of a 1991 colloque at the Louvre and Musée des Beaux-Arts de Rouen (hereafter, *Géricault* 1996); and *Géricault: La folie d'un monde*, exh. cat., curated by Bruno Chenique and Sylvie Ramond (Lyon, 2006; hereafter, *Géricault* 2006). The catalogue of the 1991 exhibition includes an invaluable detailed chronology of the artist's life, "Géricault: une vie," by Bruno Chenique (261–308); hereafter, Chenique. The still indispensable nineteenth-century study of the painter's life and work is Charles Clément, *Géricault: Etude biographique et critique avec le catalogue raisonné de l'oeuvre du maître*, 3rd ed., 1879, re-ed. Lorenz Eitner (Paris, 1973). But see the extended critique of Clément by Bruno Chenique in *Géricault au coeur de la création romantique: Etudes pour le Radeau de la Méduse*, exh. cat. (Clermont-Ferrand, 2012), esp. 70–87. See also *Tout l'oeuvre peint de Géricault*, documentation by Philippe Grunchec (Paris, 1978) and Germain Bazin, *Théodore Géricault: etude critique, documents et catalogue raisonné*, 7 vols. (Paris, 1987–97).

2 The comment is reported by Géricault's first biographer, Louis Batissier, "Biographie de Géricault," *Revue de XIXe siècle*, Paris, 1842; republished by Pierre Courthion, *Géricault raconté par lui-même et par ses amis* (Vézenas-Geneva, 1947), 35. See Eitner, *Géricault*, 322 n. 10.

3 In this connection see esp. Bruno Chenique, "A l'extrême gauche de Géricault," in *Géricault* 2006, 45–63.

4 For Chenique, the "small success" attributed by Clément to the *Raft* in the Salon of 1819 "is a myth, a pure creation of the history of art. As for the prize that Géricault didn't obtain, its history is much more complex. The prize for history painting was purely and simply canceled. Several artists, Géricault among them, then obtained a gold medal" ("Les Fondations mythologiques du Radeau de la Méduse," in *Géricault au coeur de la création romantique* [129]; translation mine). There is truth in this in the sense that with the *Raft* Géricault established himself as one of the most promising painters in his generation, but it is also true that he appears to have been disappointed in the response to it and of course it was not acquired by the government until after his death, and then owing to persistent appeals by the Director of the Louvre, the Count de Forbin, who finally succeeded in persuading the relevant ministry to provide sufficient funds to purchase it from Géricault's friend Dedreux-Dorcy, who made it available at a low price (Lorenz Eitner, *Géricault's "Raft of the Medusa"* [London and New York, 1972], 67).

5 For information and documents pertaining to the London stay, see Chenique, 288–97, and the letter of April 14, 1821 to Dedreux-Dorcy in "Lettres et documents," ed. Bruno Chenique, *Géricault* 1991, 320.

6 See "Le Manuscrit de Montfort" in *Géricault* 1991, 316. The manuscript, reminiscences of Géricault by the painter Antoine Montfort, was written in the mid-1860s for the use of Clément.

7 In this I am happy to find myself in agreement with Roger Fry, who wrote of Géricault that he "was almost the most gifted artist of the nineteenth century, at least as regards what one may call his physiological equipment" (*Characteristics of French Art* [New York, 1933], 87).

8 Wheelock Whitney, *Géricault in Italy* (New Haven and London, 1997), 201.

9 Eugène Delacroix, *Journal*, ed. Michèle Hannoosh, 2 vols. (Paris, 2009), 2: 1741.

10 The secondary literature on Delacroix is less than inspiring. But see Hannoosh's edition of the *Journal* as well as the following essays by Ralph Ubl (who currently is preparing a book-length study of the artist):

"Eugène Delacroix: Das Detail des Anderen," *Was aus dem Bild fällt: Funktionen des Details*, ed. W. Pichler, E. Futscher, S. Neuner, and R. Ubl (Munich, 2007), 351–72.

"Eugène Delacroix: Von der Freiheit zur ästhetischen Gemeinschaft," *Bild und Gemeinschaft*, ed. B. Fricke, M. Klammer, and S. Neuner (Munich, 2011), 273–313.

"Eugène Delacroix: Mit dem Meer malen," *Das Meer, der Tausch, und die Grenzen der Repräsentation*, ed. H. Baader and G. Wolf (Berlin and Zurich, 2010), 75–99.

"Delacroix' Tiere," *Politische Zoologie*, ed. J. Vogel and A. von der Heiden (Berlin, 2007), 243–57.

"Delacroix' Wärmeräume," *Räume der Romantik*, ed. G. Neumann and I. Mülder-Bach (Freiburg, 2007), 277–306.

"Delacroix's *Jewish Wedding* and the Medium of Painting," *Judaism and Christian Art*, ed. H. Kessler, D. Nirenberg (Philadelphia, 2011), 359–88.

"Entwurf und Leben: Zu Delacroix' Zeichnungen," *Notizen, Skizzen, Gekritzel: Zeichnen und Schreiben als Entwurtsinstrumente*, ed. Karin Krauthausen and Omar Nasim (Zurich, 2010), 189–218.

"Figurationen der Freiheit," *Ästhetische Regime um 1800*, ed. Friedrich Balke, Harun Maye, and Leander Scholz (Munich, 2009), 139–64.

"Tiefe des Lebens, Reflexion der Malerei, Sitten der Tiger: Zu Eugène Delacroix' *Jeune tigre jouant avec sa mère*," *Transgressionen/Animationen: Das Kunstwerk als Lebewesen* (Hamburger Forschungen zur Kunstgeschichte Bd. 4), ed. U. Pfisterer and A. Zimmermann (Berlin, 2005), 183–206.

11 Nothing in the large literature on Ingres matches in penetration Ubl's essay on the *Jewish Wedding*, to name only that impressive text. But there is much that is relevant to my overarching claim in Susan L. Siegfried, *Ingres: Painting Reimagined* (New Haven and London, 2009).

12 *CR*, 40–45; idem, *MM*, 188–92, and passim. Further page references to both books will be in parentheses in the text.

13 In what follows I shall be making use of portions of the first chapter of *CR*, "Approaching Courbet," along with ones in my essay "Géricault's Romanticism" in *Géricault* 1996, 2: 641–59. On Gros's Napoleonic paintings see Robert Herbert, "Baron Gros's Napoleon and Voltaire's Henri IV," in *The Artist and Writer in France: Essays in Honour of Jean Seznec*, ed. Francis Haskell, Anthony Levi, and Robert Shackleton (Oxford, 1974), 52–75; Christopher Prendergast, *Napoleon and History Painting: Antoine-Jean Gros's La Bataille d'Eylau* (Oxford, 1997); Darcy Grimaldo Grigsby, *Extremities: Painting Empire in Post-Revolutionary France* (New Haven and London, 2002), ch. 2, "Plague. Egypt–Syria: Gros's *Bonaparte visiting the Plague Victims of Jaffa*, 1804," 65–103; David O'Brien, *After the Revolution: Antoine-*

Jean Gros. Painting and Propaganda Under Napoleon (University Park, Penn., 2006); and Marnin Young, "Napoleon Disfigured: Injury and Identity in Antoine-Jean Gros's *Battle of Eylau*," *Nineteenth-Century Studies*, forthcoming.

14 The affinity between Géricault and Crane would need to be developed at length. But see the last chapter of John Berryman's brilliant study, *Stephen Crane* (New York, 1950), "The Color of This Soul," 297–325. The least that one can say is that in Crane, too, themes of war, violence, shipwreck (as in "The Open Boat"), and blackness (as in "The Monster") play crucial roles. In addition Berryman notes Crane's passionate interest in horses, culminating in the remark: "Even Crane's conversation shows the obsession: 'Say, when I planted those hoofs of mine on Greek soil . . .' One wonders with pain, at last, just what form he has – animal or man – in his dying words to [his friend Robert] Barr: 'Robert – when you come to the hedge – that we must all go over –' " (324). My own intense interest in Crane is evident in my essay "Stephen Crane's Upturned Faces" in *Realism, Writing, Disfiguration: On Thomas Eakins and Stephen Crane* (Chicago and London, 1987), 91–161.

15 See Régis Michel, "Le Mythe de l'oeuvre," *Géricault* 1991, 36.

16 See Régis Michel, "Le Nom de Géricault ou l'art n'a pas de sexe mais ne parle que de ça," introductory essay to *Géricault* 1996, 1: 1–37. Michel's essay is paginated only every other page; I will designate unnumbered pages "b," following the previous paginated ones. His discussion of the *Chasseur* is on 5–11, the reference to Michelet (specifically to a journal entry of 1840) is on 6b. As its title suggests, Michel's essay is rhetorically extreme but it is also continually insightful – *passionant* is the French term that fits. In the light of my particular concerns I am struck that Michel elsewhere describes Géricault's military figures as often "absorbed to the point of ecstasy in their interior dream" ("Mythe de l'oeuvre," 36; translation mine). On the *Chasseur* project see also Eitner, *Géricault*, 26–36. Michelet's greatest text on the painter belongs to the course of lectures at the Collège de France that he was forced to discontinue in early 1848; see Jules Michelet, *L'Etudiant* (Paris, 1970), 107–15.

17 A sadistic sexual strain glossed in psychoanalytic terms in Géricault's art is a major theme in Michel, "Nom de Géricault"; see esp. its last two sections headed "La Guerre des sexes" and "Le Destin de pulsions," 25b-27. See also Régis Michel, "Géricault ou le coït sadique," in *Posséder et détruire: Stratégies sexuelles dans l'art d'Occident*, exh. cat. (Paris, 2000), 126–43.

18 Géricault quoted by Montfort, cited in *Géricault* 1991, 316.

19 On the Riderless Horses project see esp. Eitner, *Géricault*, 99–135, and Whitney, *Géricault in Italy*, 89–155.

20 As reported by Clément, *Géricault*, 266. At greater length: "He was remarkably well-built, and [Horace] Vernet affirmed that he had never seen a more handsome man; his legs above all were superb: those of the ephebe who holds the horse in the middle of the [Louvre] *Race of the Riderless Horses*, M. Dorcy tells me" (translation mine).

21 See Montfort, "Manuscrit de Montfort," 316.

22 For example, writing in 1810 the young Diderotian art critic (and future politician and historian) Guizot criticized the *Sabines* for subordinating action to posing and warned against the theatricalizing effect of gestures taken from the actor Talma (François-Pierre-Guillaume Guizot, "De l'État des beaux-arts en France, et du Salon de 1810," in *Etudes sur les beaux-arts en général* [Paris, 1852], 13–14, 22–3).

23 On the *Raft*, see, in addition to sources already cited, Eitner, *Géricault's "Raft of the Medusa"*; Grigsby, *Extremities*, 165–235, and *Géricault au coeur de la création romantique*, esp. the texts by Chenique.

24 Charles Paul Landon, *Annales du Musée et de l'école moderne des beaux-arts: Salon de 1819* (Paris, 1820).

25 Delacroix quoted in Chenique, 286; translation

mine ("On a descendu le tableau de *Naufragés* et on le voit de plein pied pour ainsi dire. De sorte qu'on se croit déjà un pied dans l'eau. Il faut l'avoir vu d'assez près, pour en sentir tout le mérite").

26 See *CR*, 85–110, 148–55.

27 See n. 21 above.

28 Eitner, *Géricault*, 73.

29 Eitner also sees a reference to the Ugolino episode from Dante's *Inferno* ("*Raft*", 45–6), and in fact the Ugolino story occurred to other viewers at the time. In her powerful and original chapter on the *Raft* (see n. 23 above), Grigsby focuses on the issue of cannibalism, which she sees the painting as at once thematizing and suppressing. More recently, Chenique writes of the "father" figure with the Napoleonic Legion of Honor on his breast: "Flaunting that now useless medal, symbol of the warlike follies of a despot, this cannibal father, who turns his back on the scene of hope and deliverance, is guilty, like Ugolino, like Brutus, of having devoured the living forces of the nation, symbolized here by the dead son" (*Géricault au coeur de la création romantique*, 177; translation mine).

30 A basic study of the *Brutus* is Robert L. Herbert, *David, Voltaire, "Brutus" and the French Revolution: An Essay in Art and Politics* (London, 1972).

31 Grigsby finds that "the so-called father is the final picture's least successful figure," seeing in its "classical" (Davidian) origins an unsuccessful disguise for its grounding in earlier drawings and sketches of rape and cannibalism (*Extremities*, 214–15). My counter-suggestion (see p. 99, footnote, and fig. 71) is that the "father" alludes beyond the framework of French painting of the late eighteenth and early nineteenth centuries to the ancient sculpture of *Laocoön and His Sons*.

32 Michel writes:

> There are, in the *Raft of the Medusa*, two paintings in one: the scene of hope and the scene of mourning. One is riveted to the distant motif of the rescue ship – the brig *Argus* – of which one does not know with certainty whether it is approaching or sailing further away: the personages there are absorbed in the action (it is a collective narrative with a unitary tendency) and the beholder identifies with their uncertain question (he adheres to their group without any mediation). Michael Fried long ago showed the crucial importance of such narrative phenomena. The other is dominated by the father who clasps his moribund son in a pose analogous to that of Dürer's *Melancholy*. This frontal attitude – almost: the gaze is elsewhere – has for its rhetorical function to implicate the beholder in this work of mourning. Now, the two paintings ignore one another. Indeed they turn their backs on one another. This centrifugal scheme – a major violation of the proprieties – is almost without precedent in the classical tradition, founded on a tireless requirement of centrality (spatial, narrative, psychological). The *Raft of the Medusa*, a monumental work, has an hiatus at its center: it is constructed around a void. And this void is a constant of loss ["un constant d'échec"]. It marks the failure of history painting. Géricault ruins the naïve illusion of a linear narrative which presumes to reproduce the world by giving it a meaning ("Nom de Géricault," 25; translation mine).

Of course, my point all along has been that the *Eudamidas* model installs an hiatus at the very center of the Davidian *tableau*.

33 In *CR* I suggest that the "son" lies behind the foreshortened corpse in Honoré Daumier's large lithograph *Rue Transnonain* of 1834 (37); and in *MM* I claim to find an allusion to the former in the figure of Christ in Manet's *Dead Christ with Angels* of 1864 (92–5), a proposal that seems to have persuaded almost no one since it was first put forward in 1969. Nevertheless, I hold to it still. The "son" is also clearly a term of reference (also of difference) in Delacroix's ambitious early paintings, most obviously the *Bark of Dante* and *Liberty at the Barricades* (1830).

34 Norman Bryson, "Géricault and 'Masculinity'," in Norman Bryson, Michael Ann Holly, and Keith Moxey, eds., *Visual Culture: Images and Interpretations* (Hanover, N.H., 1994), 228–59.

35 The pertinence of Maine de Biran's philosophical writings to the issues at stake in the present essay as well as in "David/Manet" is considerable even as it is also difficult to pin down. The concept of "sensation of effort" plays a decisive role in one of Biran's major texts, *De l'aperception immédiate*, the so-called *Mémoire de Berlin* of 1807. (See the recent edition by Anne Devarieux [Paris, 2005].) Basically, Devarieux explains in a useful Introduction, Biran associates the sense of self with the notion of *effort*, "a relative fact that comprises two terms, 'distinct but not separate,' namely, a force called hyperorganic and the interior resistance of the body itself" (8; translation mine). As she also writes: "Biran never abandons his 'principle of principles,' the primitive fact of effort, the internal feeling of a willed movement, sui generis, unrepresentable (excluding all throwing into relief of the interior man), altogether distinct from a banal sensation of movement because arising from an originary modification which cannot be denied without denying one's own existence. Michel Henry has seen in his philosophy an 'ontological dualism,' with immanent effort as its principle, which comports badly with traditional dualisms and forces one to rethink radically the means of apprehending consciousness [la conscience]" (11; translation mine). See e.g. Michel Henry, *Philosophy and Phenomenology of the Body*, trans. G.J. Etzkorn (The Hague, 1975). Thus Biran:

> [I]l y a un mode individuel, très distinct de toutes les autres espèces de sensations, et que l'on est autorisé à regarder comme *formel* en tant qu'il a son fondement unique dans le sujet de la perception, dans le *moi*, qui n'est peut-étre pleinement constitué qu'en lui et par lui. Ce mode actif est celui que j'appelle *effort*, lequel, s'effectuant librement et suivant certaines conditions que nous verrons à determiner par la suite, comprend dans l'aperception immédiate de la force vivante que le reproduit sans cesse le sentiment corrélatif d'une résistance organique ou matérielle, nécessairement et primitivement perçue hors de la force comme son terme d'application, hors du *moi* comme son objet. (111–12; emphasis in original)

> (There is an individual modality, very distinct from other species of sensation, and which one is authorized to regard as *formal* in that it has its basis solely in the subject of perception, in the *moi*, which perhaps is only fully constituted in and by it. This active modality is the one I call *effort*, which, acting freely and obeying certain conditions which we will determine further on, contains [embraces?] in the immediate apperception of the living force which unceasingly reproduces it the correlative feeling of an organic or material resistance, necessarily and primitively perceived outside the force as its term of application, outside the *moi* as its object" [translation mine].)

A great deal more would need to be said to develop the point adequately, but this should at least be enough to show that the concepts of effort and of the sensation of effort were the focus of sustained phenomenological analysis during the years of David's later production, a body of work in which the evocation of effort is strikingly etiolated, and of Géricault's entire career (Biran, born in 1766, died in 1824), which I am suggesting took place under the sign of titanic physical effort (indeed of a titanic effort to "project" physical effort) from the outset through at least the campaign on the *Raft*, after which the heroic body recedes, in a certain sense.

A further aspect of Biran's thought concerns the role of habit, "habitude," which he understands in a negative sense as always tending to reduce the volitional to the merely habitual or automatic. This calls for special efforts to make the actions in question volitional once more, but of course there is no gainsaying the tendency of habit to undo those efforts sooner or later. On this complex topic see François Azouvi, *Maine de Biran: La science de l'homme* (Paris, 1995), 456–63. Various other difficulties involved in Biran's conception of effort are scrupulously analysed by Azouvi; see esp. 217–52. (The next philosophical development with respect to the concept of habit takes place in Jean-Gaspard-Félix Ravaisson's treatise *De l'habitude* [1838], a text I relate both to Flaubert and to Courbet in *Flaubert's "Gueuloir": On* Madame Bovary *and* Salammbô [New Haven and London, 2012], 63–84.)

Régis Michel with characteristic acuteness draws attention to the affinity between Biran and Géricault several times in "Nom de Géricault" (6b, 10b, 11).

36 In Delacroix's so-called "Cahier autobiographique, 1853–1860," he regrets the loss of Géricault and recalls: "He squandered his youth; he was extreme in everything: he liked only to leap onto horses, and chose the stormiest. I saw him several times at the moment when he mounted a horse: he almost could only do this by surprise; hardly in the saddle, he was swept away by his mount. One day when I was dining with him and his father, he left before dessert to ride to the Bois de Boulogne. He took off like a lightning bolt, having no time to turn around to say good evening, and I sat down to table with the good old man. After ten minutes we heard a loud noise: he returned on the gallop; he was missing one of the tails of his outfit: his horse had brushed him up against something or other, and he had lost this necessary accompaniment" (*Journal*, 2: 1740; translation mine).

37 The French word for "accord" is "unisson," a term that plays a key role in the remarkable discussion in Balzac's short story "Massimilla Doni" (written 1837, published 1839) between two characters, Capraja and the Duke of Cataneo, on the respective merits of two artistic devices, "la roulade" (basically, the arabesque) and "l'unisson." (The art in question is music, but the concepts themselves have much broader implications.) This is not the place for a fuller treatment of this opposition, but see Jean-Pierre Richard's brilliant summary of the exchange in "Corps et décors balzaciens," *Etudes sur le romantisme* (Paris, 1970), 137–38. Richard has more to say about the relevance to Balzac's fiction of both notions, which he understands as lying very near the core of his enterprise (138–9). My own interest in the topic concerns the relevance of Balzac's notion of "unisson" to the accord between men and horses in Géricault's art. And it is given further point by the appearance of an imaginary arabesque toward the end of Balzac's story "Le Colonel Chabert," which I discuss in relation to Géricault in the last part of this essay. For "Massimilla Doni" see Honoré de Balzac, *Le Chef d'oeuvre inconnu, Gambara, Massimilla Doni*, ed. Marc Eigeldinger and Max Milner (Paris, 1981), 157–269.

38 A painting that all but spells this out is the *Portrait of a Carabinier* (ca. 1815) in Rouen, which depicts a cavalryman in a cuirasse gazing directly out of the painting with the dark head of a horse bent and downward-looking just beyond his left shoulder. It is impossible not to see the horse as an "emanation" of the man, or perhaps vice-versa; in any case, the two together make a single psychic "presence."

39 Martin Heidegger, *The Fundamental Concepts of Metaphysics: World, Finitude, Solitude*, trans. William McNeill and Nicholas Walker (Bloomington, Ind., 1995), 185ff. The statement that "the stone is worldless, the animal is poor in world, man is world-forming" first occurs on 185; Heidegger's attempt to elucidate the concept of "world" takes off from the second item in this statement. Further page references will be in parentheses in the text.

40 Cf. my claim in *CR* that Géricault found in the subject of horses in movement "a means of representing actions and expressions that at once relate intimately to human impulses and desires, far surpass human capabilities, and

owing to their nonhuman nature – their animality – escape being perceived as theatrical, as grimace. . . . More broadly, the representation of animals, whether active or in repose, provided Géricault with something like a natural refuge from the theatrical, as if for him the relation of animals to their bodies and to the world precluded the theatricalizing of that relation no matter what. This is to say more than that animals take on an unprecedented expressive burden in Géricault's art, though that is certainly true. It's also to maintain that, in his tragic pictorial universe, animality becomes an ideal of humanness that ultimately lies beyond human reach. (The unattainability and consequent bestializing of that ideal is variously imaged in his oeuvre, most movingly in the *Cattle Market.*)" (24).

41 Eitner suggests ca. 1815 (*Géricault*, 72). Interestingly, he notes that "Géricault did not take this expressive study from life, but based it on a very indifferent print after Carle Vernet" (ibid.).

42 I hesitate to suggest this but just possibly Géricault's feeling for blacks or say for non-Caucasians such as his domestic, the Turk Mustapha, also has something to do with the sense in which at least in European society they were rendered "poor in world." A recollection by Louis-Alexis Jamar (like Montfort, a young painter who assisted Géricault) of the artist's burial is pertinent here. "I remember that at the burial there were three of us, Montfort, Lehoux [another young painter], and me together we wept also I was very moved to hear the words that were pronounced over the tomb. Mustapha, his servant, wasn't far away from us also I remember that Ernest Leroy seeing him weep said pretty stupidly that friends weren't Turks [i.e. that Mustapha had no business being there?] and at such a moment I didn't find those words truly spiritual for a friend of Géricault's" (cited by Chenique, 307–8; translation mine).

43 On the landscapes see Eitner, *Géricault*, 142–5, and Gary Tinterow, *Géricault's Heroic Landscapes: The Times of Day*, repr. from *The Metropolitan Museum of Art Bulletin* (Winter, 1990/91). Tinterow places the *Deluge* around 1818 (57), a dating that goes against the consensus but seems to me to have a lot to recommend it.

44 The basic article remains Margaret Miller, "Géricault's Portraits of the Insane," *Journal of the Warburg and Courtaud Institutes* 4, no. 3/4 (1940–41): 151–63. See also Eitner, *Géricault*, 241–9 (though I find wholly unpersuasive his suggestion that the portraits of monomaniacs show the influence of the British painter Sir Thomas Lawrence); and Michel, "Mythe de l'oeuvre," 244.

45 According to Etienne-Jean Georget, a student of Esquirol and Géricault's exact contemporary, persons afflicted with the illness then known as monomania were described not only as wholly absorbed in one or another obsessive delusion but also as seeking to flee their fellows, either to escape being seen by them or "to entrench themselves all the more securely in their own manner of looking" (*De la folie: Considérations sur cette maladie* . . . [Paris, 1820], 112; translation mine). The lability that this alternative captures goes to the heart of Géricault's vision. The key passage reads: "Dans la lypemanie [a term for depressive monomania invented by Esquirol] ou mélancolie, les aliénés sombres, ennemies du tumulte, absorbés et profondement attentifs à l'idée qui les domine, fuient leurs semblables, tantôt pour se soustraire à leur vue s'ils croyent leur déplaire, ou s'ils craignent d'en devenir victimes, d'autres fois pour chercher un repos qu'ils ne peuvent trouver, ou pour se fortifier à leur aise dans leur manière de voir."

46 Honoré de Balzac, *Le Colonel Chabert*, ed. Stéphane Vachon (Paris, 1994 and 2012). Page references will be in parentheses in the text.

47 "Another quality, very great, very vast, of Delacroix's talent, and which makes him the painter loved by poets, is that he is essentially literary" (Charles Baudelaire, "Exposition Universelle de 1855," *Curiosités esthétiques: L'Art romantique et autres oeuvres critiques*, ed. Henri

Lemaitre (Paris, 1962), 239; translation mine. Cf. in this connection Baudelaire's characterization of Delacroix's singularity in his "Salon of 1846":

> Each of the old masters has his kingdom, his territory – which he is often compelled to share with illustrious rivals. Raphael has form, Rubens and Veronese color, Rubens and Michelangelo the imagination of drawing. A portion of the empire remained, where only Rembrandt had made some excursions, – drama – natural and living drama, terrible and melancholy drama, expressed often by color but always by gesture.
>
> As regards sublime gestures, Delacroix's only rivals are outside his art. Frédérick Lemaître and Macready. (129; translation mine)

The comparison with Rembrandt and the reference to color show that Baudelaire when he speaks of drama has something other in mind than the Davidian tradition, while the reference to Lemaître and Macready, two of the leading actors of the period, suggests that the entire issue of theatricality was something of a dead letter for him.

48 Honoré de Balzac, *Père Goriot*, trans. A.J. Krailsheimer (Oxford and New York, 1991), 9. For the French see Honoré de Balzac, *Le Père Goriot*, ed. Pierre-Georges Castex (Paris, 1981), 18. A superb analysis of Balzac in this regard is Jean-Pierre Richard, "Corps et décors balzaciennes," 89–11. See also Jacques Neefs, "L'intensité dramatique des scènes balzaciennes," in Stéphane Vachon, ed., *Balzac: une poétique du roman* (Montreal, 1996), 143–52.

49 The classic study is Peter Brooks, *The Melodramatic Imagination: Balzac, Henry James, Melodrama, and the Mode of Excess* (New Haven and London, 1976), 1–5, 110–52.

50 Significantly, the second half of the 1820s and early 1830s saw the emergence of the painter Paul Delaroche (b. 1797, so six years younger than Géricault and a near-exact contemporary of Balzac), whose canvases of historical subjects such as the *Children of Edward IV in the Tower* (1830) and *Jane Grey* (1833) were understood by contemporary audiences as referring to the stage by virtue of their emphasis on historically accurate costumes, choice of moment, and manifestly theatrical *mise-en-scène*. See my discussion of Delaroche in *CR* (32–5), in the course of which I emphasize the fact that his work was criticized on those grounds in its own time and indeed that during the 1830s "a liking for the theatrical became identified by a gradually emerging avant-garde as the hallmark of a general debasement of artistic taste, an identification that persisted throughout the rest of the century" (35). Various observations by Gustave Planche are especially telling in this connection (298–9 n. 38). On Delaroche see the masterly study by Stephen Bann, *Paul Delaroche: History Painted* (London, 1997).

51 See the ambitious study by Sheryl Kroen, *Politics and Theater: The Crisis of Legitimacy in Restoration France, 1815–1830* (Berkeley, Cal., and London, 2000). More broadly, there are interesting essays on a range of topics in Jean-Yves Mollier, Martine Reid, and Jean-Claude Yon, eds., *Repenser la restauration* (Malesherbes, 2005).

52 Charles Baudelaire, "Théophile Gautier," *Curiosités esthétiques*, 679.

53 See in this connection the brief discussion of Daumier in *CR*, 35–40.

54 For example, Joseph Brideau in *La Rabouilleuse* admires the poetry of Byron, the painting of Géricault, the music of Rossini; the *Raft of the "Medusa"* is cited favorably early on in *Pierre Grassou*; a painting by Géricault figures in the collection of Pons in *Cousin Pons*; and so on.

55 A term that recurs in the last pages of "Le Colonel Chabert" when Derville, recognizing Chabert in the inmate of Bicêtre by the side of the road, says to Godeschal, "That old man there, my dear, is an entire poem, or, as the romantics say, a drama" (138; translation mine).

56 See in this connection n.37 above.

57 Three further points. Early in the story, after Chabert leaves, the clerks call him back and ask

his name. He tells them Chabert and one asks, mockingly, whether he is the colonel killed at Eylau, and of course Chabert answers, "The same." He departs again, and the clerks engage in a spirited conversation as to whether they have just seen a "spectacle" and, going on from that, about what exactly a "spectacle" *is*:

> "What is a spectacle," Godeschal resumed. "Let's first establish the facts of the case. What am I betting on, gentlemen? a spectacle. What is a spectacle? something that one sees . . ."
>
> "But on that system, would it be enough for you to show us the water flowing under the Pont-Neuf?" cried Simonnin interrupting him.
>
> "That one pays to see," said Godeschal, continuing.
>
> "But one pays to see lots of things that aren't a spectacle. The definition isn't exact," said Desroches.
>
> "But, listen to me!"
>
> "You reason badly, my dear," said Boucard.
>
> "Curtius [the creator of waxworks and teacher of the future Madame Tussaud; his establishments, on the boulevard du Temple and at the Palais Royal, still existed during the Restoration], is that a spectacle?"
>
> "No, responded the master-clerk [Boucard], "that's a cabinet of figures."
>
> "I bet a hundred francs against a sou," countered Godeschal, "that Curtius's cabinet constitutes the ensemble of things on which has devolved the name of spectacle. It applies to something to see at different prices, according to the different places one occupies." (65–6; translation mine)

> (– Qu'est-ce qu'un spectacle? reprit Godeschal. Etablissons d'abord le *point de fait*. Qu'ai-je parié, messieurs? un spectacle. Qu'est-ce qu'un spectacle? une chose qu'on voit . . .
>
> – Mais dans ce système-là, vous vous acquitteriez donc en nous meanant voir l'eau couler sous le Pont-Neuf? s'écria Simonnin en interrompant.
>
> – Qu'on voit pour l'argent, disait Godeschal en continuant.
>
> – Mais on voit pour l'argent bien des choses qui ne sont pas un spectacle. La definition n'est pas exacte, dit Desroches.
>
> – Mais, écoutez-moi donc!
>
> – Vous déraisonnez, mon cher, dit Boucard.
>
> – Curtius, est-il un spectacle?
>
> – Non, répondit le Maître-clear, c'est un cabinet de figures.
>
> – Je parie cent francs contre un sou, reprit Godeschal, que le cabinet de Curtius constitue l'ensemble de choses auquel est dévolu le nom de spectacle. Il comporte une chose à voir à différents prix, suivant les différentes places où l'on veut se mettre . . .)

In other words, the conversation concerns the nature of something like a theatrical production ("spectacle" was Rousseau's term of choice in his *Lettre à d'Alembert*), and I take one implication of Godeschal's position to be that "Le Colonel Chabert" is itself a "spectacle," offering something to be viewed for money, perhaps with the further qualification that the nature of a literary text eliminates the difference between places.

Second, an early review of "Le Colonel Chabert" appeared in the October 20, 1832 issue of the *Journal des femmes*; the author, Mme Alida de Savignac, praises the story highly, concluding with the following statement, the pertinence of which to my argument I take to be self-evident. "I used to believe," she writes, "before reading [*Le Colonel*] *Chabert*, that the genre that consists in imitating in words the works of great painters, and in shaping one's style to the point where a literary work becomes a *tableau*, was worthless. I take it back. The pages I have just read proved to me that in literature there is no bad genre, there are only bad authors" (213; translation mine) ("J'avais cru, jusqu'à la lecture du *Comte Chabert*, que le genre qui constitue à imiter avec la parole les oeuvres de grands peintres, et à travailler son style jusqu'à ce qu'une oeuvre littéraire soit devenue un tableau, ne valait rien. Je m'en retractes. Les quelques pages que je viens de lire m'ont prouvé qu'en literature il n'y a pas de mauvais genre, qu'il n'a y que de mauvais auteurs.")

Third, in a recent article Diana Knight persuasively demonstrates Balzac's engagement with Diderotian issues in an early story, "Une double famille" (1830); Diana Knight, "Absorption and Theatricality: Tableaux of Toil in Balzac's 'Une double famille,'" *Dix-neuf* 17 (July 2013): 104–23.

4 ORIENTATION IN PAINTING

1 Joseph Leo Koerner, *Caspar David Friedrich and the Subject of Landscape* (New Haven and London, 1990), 163; hereafter, Koerner, *Subject*. Koerner continues: "They are the ubiquitous, almost obsessive, signatures of Friedrich's *Erlebniskunst* ['art of experience']," a notion Koerner deploys throughout his important study.

2 Entitled "Synergies," the symposium was held on May 17–18, 2013 in Berlin. My thanks to the organizers, Joachim Küpper and Danièle Cohn, for inviting me to deliver the keynote lecture on a subject of my choosing.

3 On Chardin and absorption see *AT*, 11–16, 44–53. Further references to this book will be in parentheses in the text.

4 For more on Géricault see Ch. 3, "Géricault's Romanticism," above.

5 *CR*. No specific page references seem necessary.

6 I go on to say that my remarks on the concept of the self in Fichte were indebted to a course of lectures on German Idealism taught at Harvard in the spring of 1973 by Professor Dieter Henrich, who remains to this day perhaps the major figure in the renewal of interest in Kant's immediate successors. It was a great stroke of luck for me to be able to attend those lectures. It is also true that my familiarity with the writings of Kant, Fichte, and others at the time I wrote that footnote could not have been more tenuous. Henrich's lectures were much later published as *Between Kant and Hegel: Lectures on German Idealism* (Cambridge, Mass., and London, 2003). I should say, too, that my use of the terms "cognizing" and "cognition" in the present essay are intended in a *loosely* Kantian spirit. There is today lively debate as to the precise meaning of Kant's notion of "Enkenntnis," usually translated as cognition, in relation to "Wissen," or knowledge proper – not a topic that I am qualified to explore, much less resolve.

7 Immanuel Kant, "What does it mean to orient oneself in thinking?," *Religion within the Boundaries of Mere Reason and Other Writings*, trans. and ed. Allen Wood and George di Giovanni (Cambridge, 1998), 4–5; emphasis in original. Further page references will be in parentheses in the text.

8 This painting along with a number of others discussed in this essay was on view in the exhibition "De l'Allemagne 1800–1939 de Friedrich à Beckmann" at the Louvre in spring 2013; the exhibition complemented the symposium mentioned in n. 2. In this connection see the catalogue of the same title, ed. Sébastien Allard and Danièle Cohn (Paris, 2013). Particular thanks to Jennifer Ashton, Jean-Pierre Criqui, Thomas Demand, Walter Benn Michaels, and Robert Pippin, in whose company (mostly separately) I had the pleasure of looking closely at Friedrich's work in Paris, Berlin, and Hamburg during the writing and revising of this essay. Also to Ruth Leys, Leonardo Lisi, Charles Palermo, Ralph Ubl, and David Wellbery for feedback on various drafts.

9 William Vaughan, *Friedrich* (London and New York, 2004), 197–8.

10 Cf. in this connection Kant's treatment in the *Critique of Judgment* (1790) of the "I think" that always, in his view, "precedes the experience which is required to determine the object

of perception" (cited by Eckart Förster, *Kant's Final Synthesis: An Essay on the Opus postumum* [Cambridge, Mass., and London, 2000], 102) as well as his further development of this theme in the so-called *Opus postumum*.

11 *MR*, 84–91. In an endnote to that passage I suggest that Friedrich's art may be illuminated by reference to Kant's "What does it mean to orient oneself in thinking?," specifically to the latter's stress on the felt difference between right and left (275–6). The present essay seeks to make good on those brief remarks.

12 Thus Vaughan, *Friedrich*: "By these means Friedrich separates out the spectator of the picture and the viewer in the picture . . ." (198). I have suggested that this is true only up to a point.

13 This is as good a place as any to mention two fascinating topographical studies by Frank Richter: *Caspar David Friedrich: Das Riesengebirge und die böhmischen Berge* (Dresden, 2012) and *Caspar David Friedrich: Spurensuche in Dresdner Umland und in der Sächsischen Schweiz* (Dresden, 2009). *Morning in the Mountains* is illustrated and briefly discussed in the former, p. 103.

14 The claim to universality is, however, qualified by the fact that there are cultures whose mode of spatial cognition is not relative (keyed to the speaking subject's own body) but absolute (keyed to directions such as north, south, east, west). See Stephen C. Levinson, *Space in Language and Cognition: Explorations in Cognitive Diversity* (Cambridge, 2003). My thanks to Frances Morphy for alerting me to Levinson's important work.

15 Caspar David Friedrich, "Observations on Viewing a Collection of Paintings Largely by Living or Recently Deceased Artists," in Charles Harrison and Paul Wood with Jason Geiger, eds., *Art in Theory 1815–1900: An Anthology of Changing Ideas* (Oxford, 1998), 51.

16 Werner Hofmann, *Caspar David Friedrich*, trans. Mary Whittall (London, 2001), 128.

17 Friedrich, "Observations," 51.

18 Illustrated and discussed in *MR*, 186–98.

19 See Timothy Hutton, "Romantic Landscape Painting and Historical Geology," *Art Bulletin* 66 (Sept. 1984), 459–61. See also idem, *Art and Science in German Landscape Painting 1770–1840* (Oxford, 1996), 176–9.

20 There is obviously room for disagreement here. Koerner, for example, at one point stresses the degree to which Friedrich's many "symmetries, always felt as contingent on our own specific point of view, keep us fixed in place before the picture, so that movement to the side, or into depth, would throw the entire scene into chaos" (*Subject*, 113). I agree that the import of any given configuration in a Friedrich landscape is to fix the viewing subject before the painting, but I understand that effect as having less to do with the strictly ocular implications of a point of view and more with the question of orientation as I have developed it in these pages.

21 There is a larger topic implicit in my references to Kant, namely, the role of bodily experience and subjective feeling in his later thought, leading to the thematization of the feeling of life in the *Critique of Judgment* and, considerably beyond that, his realization in his late writings, the so-called *Opus postumum*, of the crucial role played by "the exhibition of the subject's own bodily forces in the systematization of experience" in "ascertaining the objective validity and real applicability of the pure concepts of the understanding" as those were analyzed in the first *Critique* (Förster, *Kant's Final Synthesis*, 74). Further discussion of these issues is beyond my present competence, but I have found Förster's brilliant book revelatory of their importance. I have also found illuminating Rudolf A. Makkreel, *Imagination and Interpretation in Kant: The Hermeneutical Import of the Critique of Judgment* (Chicago and London, 1990). My thanks to Leonardo Lisi and Robert Pippin for pointing me toward these studies.

22 My reference to symbolic interpretation is above all to the extensive writings of Helmut Börsch-Supan, for example his *Caspar David Friedrich*, trans. Sarah Twohig (1974; enlarged

and revised edition Munich, 1990). Börsch-Supan of course emphasizes the Christian, i.e., Protestant and Lutheran dimension of Friedrich's pictorial imagination, which indeed is incontestable, though it seems highly unlikely that his canvases are as densely and methodically saturated with symbolic equivalents as Börsch-Supan contends. There is also widespread agreement as to the importance to Friedrich's art of the thought of his slightly older contemporary, Friedrich Schleiermacher, as expressed for example in the latter's early *On Religion: Speeches to Its Cultural Despisers* (1799). The pertinence of Schleiermacher to my reading of Friedrich's paintings can be brought out by comparing the terms of that reading with Terry Pinkard's summary of Schleiermacher's views: "'Every intuition,' Schleiermacher insisted, 'is, by its very nature, connected with a feeling,' and 'if a determinate religion is not supposed to begin with a fact, it cannot begin at all; for there must be a basis, and it can only be a subjective one for why something is brought forth and placed in the center.' This 'fact,' however, is a subjective 'sense,' more or less, that 'this is how I *must* stand with regard to the greater scheme of things [emphasis in original]' and that the rest of one's orientation to life emerges out of one's *responsiveness* to that basic 'fact'" (*German Philosophy 1760–1860: The Legacy of Idealism* [Cambridge, 2002], 152; emphasis in original). My thanks to Ralph Ubl for pointing me toward Schleiermacher, who of course owes much to Kant (that transcendental "*must*").

5 CAILLEBOTTE'S IMPRESSIONISM

1 This essay was first drafted as one of two Una's Lectures and in that form was given at the University of California, Berkeley in March 1995. My thanks to Tom Laqueur for the invitation to speak there and to T. J. Clark and the late Richard Wollheim for their comments in a follow-up seminar. Also to Brigid Doherty and Marc Gotlieb for reading an earlier version of this essay in manuscript and making various suggestions that I have used.

The basic sources on which I have relied are J. Kirk T. Varnedoe, Marie Berhaut, Peter Galassi, and Hilarie Faberman, *Gustave Caillebotte: A Retrospective Exhibition*, exh. cat. (Houston and Brooklyn, N.Y., 1976; hereafter, *GC*); Anne Distel, Douglas W. Druick, Gloria Groom, Rodolphe Rapetti, with Julia Sagraves, *Gustave Caillebotte: Urban Impressionist*, exh. cat. (Paris, Chicago, Los Angeles, 1994; hereafter, *UI*); Marie Berhaut, *Caillebotte: Catalogue raisonné des peintures et pastels*, rev. and expanded ed. (Paris, 1994); and *The New Painting: Impressionism 1874–1886*, exh. cat. (Washington, D.C. and San Francisco, 1986; hereafter, *NP*). Page references to the three museum catalogues will be given in parentheses in the text.

Finally, an updated version of the essay as it appeared in *Representations* was published in Norma Broude, ed., *Gustave Caillebotte and the Fashioning of Identity in Impressionist Paris* (New Brunswick, N.J. and London, 2002), along with other essays on the painter by J. Kirk T. Varnedoe, Michael Marrinan, Norma Broude, Tamar Garb, and Douglas Druick (all except Broude's reprinted from elsewhere); hereafter, Broude.

2 See also Kirk Varnedoe, *Gustave Caillebotte* (New Haven and London, 1987), a book based on the 1974 catalogue.

3 See in this connection Robert Rosenblum, "Gustave Caillebotte: The 1970s and 1870s," *Artforum* 15 (March 1977): 46–52, which stresses the affinities between Caillebotte's art and various artistic developments of the 1970s; J. Kirk T. Varnedoe, "Caillebotte: An Evolving Perspective," *GC*, 47, which associates the rise of interest in Caillebotte with the emergence of "a revisionist movement in popular taste and among art historians"; and idem, "Odd Man In: A Brief Historiography of Caillebotte's Changing Roles in the History of Art," *UI*, 13–16, which makes the same point.

4 "Avec un dos, nous voulons que se révèle un tempérament, un âge, un état social . . . Des mains qu'on tient dans les poches pourront êtres éloquents" (Edmond Duranty, *La Nouvelle peinture: A propos du groupe d'artistes qui expose dans les galeries Durand-Ruel* [1876; Caen, 1988], 35); "Du dedans, c'est par la fenêtre que nous communiquons avec le dehors; la fenêtre est encore un cadre qui nous accompagne sans cesse, durant le temps que nous passons au logis, et ce temps est considérable. Le cadre de la fenêtre, selon que nous en sommes loin ou près, que nous nous tenons assis ou debout, découpe le spectacle extérieur de la manière la plus inattendue, la plus changeante, nous procurant l'éternelle variété, l'impromptu qui est une des grandes saveurs de la réalité" (39); both translations mine. Duranty's text is also conveniently available in *NP*, 477–84.

5 Duranty, *La Nouvelle Peinture*, 34. Duranty's criticism figures importantly in *MM*, esp. 259–61.

6 See *AT*, *CR*, and *MM*. Subsequent references to the last two books will appear in parentheses in the text. In general I have tried to minimize such references; in all cases allusions in the present essay to works by Courbet and Manet are based on much fuller discussions in *CR* and *MM*.

7 See Stephen Melville, "Compelling Acts, Haunting Convictions," a review of *CR*, originally in *Art History* (1991), repr. in Stephen Melville, *Seams: Art as a Philosophical Context*, ed. Jeremy Gilbert-Rolfe (Amsterdam, 1996), 190. On these grounds Melville also characterizes the relation of painting to painter in my account of Courbet's art as metonymic rather than (I would prefer to say as well as) metaphoric (191).

8 See the discussion of this point in *MM*, 18–19.

9 This is recognized by Eric Darragon, who writes: "One believes that one sees what this man sees and one immediately recognizes the illusory character of that naïve idea. One only sees, in fact, what he doesn't see and one is only able to identify with him by becoming aware of the optical reality of the scene. A doubling [dédoublement] constructed by the painting. An inaccessible objectivity" (*Caillebotte* [Paris, 1994], 36; translation mine). Cf. also Varnedoe on the painting's "double focus . . . an oscillation of concentration between the depicted seer and what he sees" (*GC*, 89). The *Young Man at His Window* is also discussed by Marrinan, "Caillebotte as a Professional Painter," in Broude, 50–57.

10 See *MM*, ch. 4.

11 Cf. Varnedoe: "There are basically two states of consciousness in Caillebotte's world: either the person is intently absorbed by some activity within arm-span – reading and sewing to cite only the two most recurrent themes – or the person is staring across space at a (usually unseen) distant point. There is no communication between these characters, and rarely (portraits excepted) any communication between them and us. Caillebotte's psychic world is one in which constant internal isolation or self-enclosure is offset only by the loss of self-consciousness through focused activity or reverie" ("Caillebotte: An Evolving Perspective," *GC*, 54). This is acute though of course it does not recognize the larger pictorial and ontological significance of Caillebotte's concern with absorption.

12 See the discussion of this point in *MM*, 186–97 and 259–61. As I make clear there, it is not for nothing that *The New Painting* "singles out Diderot as the theoretical precursor of 'all that the art of the nineteenth century will have wanted to realize'" (260). In *MR*, I argue that Duranty's passionate admiration for Menzel's art as expressed in two posthumously published articles was largely based on what he took to be the absorptive basis of Menzel's practice (part 9, "The French Response to Menzel: Edmond Duranty," 125–39). For those articles see Edmond Duranty, "Adolphe Menzel," *Gazette des Beaux-Arts*, 2e pér., t. 21 [March 1, 1880]: 201–17; ibid., t. 22 [Aug. 1, 1880]: 105–24.

13 "Cette qualité suprême de l'art, la vie, se dégage de cette toile avec une intensité vraiment incroyable." (J.-K. Huysmans, "L'Exposition des Indépendants en 1880," *L'Art moderne/Certains* [Paris, 1975], 107; translation mine). Another canvas by Caillebotte in the same Salon, *Interior, Woman Seated* (1880), is understandably faulted by Huysmans for the excessive diminutiveness of the man reclining on a sofa and reading a book, but he nevetheless praises both that figure and the figure of a woman reading in the near foreground on the grounds that "they occupy themselves, without posing for the gallery, without that attitude of persons whose portraits are being painted" (ibid., 108; translation mine) ("En tous cas, ils s'occupent, sans pose pour la galerie, sans cette attitude des gens dont on prépare le portrait"). See also Huysmans's praise of works by Jean-François Raffaëlli and Fantin-Latour, two consistently absorptive artists, and his intense dislike of theatricality (as for example in the portraits of Emile-Auguste Carolus-Duran).

14 On this score, see the observations of Paul Mantz writing in *Le Temps*, quoted in translation in *NP*, 319.

15 As was recognized at the time by Armand Silvestre, quoted in translation in *NP*, 167.

16 "Tradition has it," Varnedoe writes, "that the occasion for the painting was the reconditioning of floors in the family home. The activity depicted, however, is more familiar in connection with a new building where humidity trapped during construction has caused the floorboards to buckle upwards along their edges. The dark shining surface of the floor does not owe to old wax being removed, but to the water with which the scrapers originally soaked the bare floor to prevent splintering of the wood. The 'stripes' in the floor are dry wood exposed by the first step in the process, the passage of a heavy-duty two-handled plane, the *rabot*, over the buckled edges of the planks. The right-hand worker here holds the *rabot*. The broad light area at lower left is the result of the second step, the overall scraping with a smaller, finer blade, the *racloir*, which is held by the middle worker and cupped in the far hand of the leftmost worker. The hammer between the two men at the right was used to pound down loose nails. The knife-like tool intruding from the lower left edge of the picture is (like the similar blade reached for by the leftmost man) a file, used every few strokes to keep the blade of the *racloir* at peak sharpness. In the back, against the wall, lie the sacks used by each man to carry his equipment" (*GC*, 84). Moreover, in a personal communication Varnedoe kindly confirmed, on the basis of his knowledge of the actual use of their respective tools, that the middle worker should be seen as moving away and the worker on the right as coming toward us. (That the file juts into the picture space from the bottom framing edge would therefore be a further indication of movement into the picture.) My thanks to Varnedoe for his help and to Brigid Doherty for prompting a more precise description of the actions of the middle worker. See also Marrinan, "Caillebotte as a Professonal Painter," in Broude, 21–8.

17 In *MM* I argue that critics such as Duranty found in the work of members of Manet's generation, Legros in particular, a not dissimilar "forcing" of absorption in the interests of what I characterize, basing myself on the writings of Duranty and others, as a pursuit of "strikingness" (see esp. ch. 3). But of course whatever impelled Manet's co-generationists to that course of action could not have been the example of Manet's art, which was contemporary with their own productions. By the same token, I see no reason to speak of Caillebotte's art in terms of strikingness, an ideal I associate mainly with the 1860s.

18 A similar but less diagrammatic work in this vein, one that portrays the protagonist's face but deflects his gaze, is Caillebotte's *Oarsman in a Top Hat* (1877).

19 By far the most searching discussions of Caillebotte's handling of perspective recession, including considerations of its relation to photography, are Varnedoe with Peter Galassi,

"Caillebotte's Space," and Peter Galassi, "Caillebotte's Method," in *UI*, 60–73 and 192–206. The latter essay contains indispensable spatial and compositional analyses of two of Caillebotte's most important works, the *Pont de l'Europe* and *Paris Street; Rainy Day*. See also the entries on individual works in that catalogue.

20 Caillebotte's interest in reflective sheen is already evident in his treatment of the glistening bands on a cloth drape or coverlet in the Courbet-like pastel, *Nude on a Divan* (1873), illustrated in color in Darragon, *Caillebotte*, 18–19, fig. 9.

21 In this connection see both the ecumenical composition of Caillebotte's collection (as reconstituted in *UI*, 322–40) and the accounts of Caillebotte's strategic role in the organization of individual Impressionist exhibitions, especially those of 1877, 1879, 1881 (from which he abstained), and 1882 in *NP*. I might add that a thematics of absorption is combined with one of reflections in Thomas Eakins's interior and rowing pictures of the 1870s (see Michael Fried, *Realism, Writing, Disfiguration: On Thomas Eakins and Stephen Crane* [Chicago and London, 1987], 46–50).

22 See e.g., Maurice Merleau-Ponty, *Phenomenology of Perception*, trans. Colin Smith (London, 1962); and from a different point of view Jonathan Crary, *Techniques of the Observer: On Vision and Modernity in the Nineteenth Century* (Cambridge, Mass., and London, 1990).

23 Another point I owe to Brigid Doherty.

24 In a related painting, the *Floor-Scrapers (Variant)* (1876, private collection), there are only two workers, an older and a younger man, and they are seen from the side and slightly from the rear; the older man, to the right and nearest us, is roughly in the position of the two workers on the right in the painting we have been discussing (like them, he is depicted in the act of scraping or planing the floor), while the young man is seated on the floor adjusting one of his tools. There is thus a closer affinity with the composition of the *Stonebreakers*, but what is particularly striking and leaves no doubt as to Caillebotte's intentions is that his signature at the lower left has the same backward lean that Courbet habitually favored for his.

25 On the unintelligibility of Manet's achievement in his own time see *MM*, ch. 4 and Coda. I argue in that book that the gradual assimilation of Manet's art by critics and others in the 1870s and after took place under the sign of Impressionism, indeed that Manet was for the most part seen as the *chef de file* of the Impressionists despite his refusal to take part in their exhibitions. It therefore testifies to an unusual acuteness on Caillebotte's part that, if I am right, he distinguished *between* Manet and Impressionism and that his reading of Manet's art in terms of facingness made a positive virtue, not to say a formal imperative, out of a feature of that art that in its own time virtually defied comprehension.

26 The most useful pages in Richard Shiff's studies of the rhetoric of Impressionist theory and criticism argue that such a tendency was inbuilt from the start. See Richard Shiff, *Cézanne and the End of Impressionism: A Study of the Theory, Technique, and Critical Evaluation of Modern Art* (Chicago and London, 1984), 3–52, and idem, "The End of Impressionism" (a summary of chs. 1–5 in the book), *NP*, 61–89.

27 See Jules-Antoine Castagnary, "Exposition du Boulevard des Capucines," *Le Siècle* (April 29, 1874). The crucial passage reads: "Ils sont *impressionnistes* en ce sens qu'ils rendent non le paysage, mais la sensation produite par le paysage. Le mot même est passé dans leur langue: ce n'est pas *paysage*, c'est *impression* que s'appelle au catalogue le *Soleil levant* de M. Monet. Par ce côté, ils sortent de la réalité et entrent en plein idéalisme" (cited and discussed by Shiff, *Cézanne and the End of Impressionism*, 3 and Part One, "The End of Impressionism"; emphasis in original). This is not the place for a detailed discussion of Shiff's argument; suffice it to say that he neglects to engage with the writings of other early positive critics of Impressionism such as Armand Sil-

vestre, Ernest Chesneau, and Philippe Burty, and that some of his central claims – for example, that "early observers [of Impressionism] either insisted that the aims of those artists were not unique at all or spoke hardly a word about their aims" (16) – are incorrect. Nevertheless, his insistence that later nineteenth-century commentators (like Castagnary in 1876) saw a strongly subjective component in the work of at least some of the Impressionists, and more broadly that throughout the period in question the terms "impression" and "sensation" were used in ways that hovered between notions of subjectivity and objectivity, has been productive.

28 Cf. Anne Wagner, "Why Monet Gave Up Figure Painting," *Art Bulletin* 76 (Dec. 1994): 613–29, and the further discussion of the question in *MM*, 172 and 525–6 n. 114. See also the brief treatment of the topic in "David / Manet" above (pp. 30–31).

29 Cf. for example Varnedoe and Galassi's observation that in a painting like *Paris Street; Rainy Day* (to be discussed in detail further on) Caillebotte combined a kind of hyper-perspective with a mode of drawing in which "each figure in the scene is conceived from a separate, face-on viewpoint, rather than being distorted to conform to the central spatial system" ("Caillebotte's Space," 68). This has "the effect of partially cancelling the deep space and affirming the flat surface"; as they also put it, Caillebotte was attracted to perspective *both* "as a device not only for evoking space but for heightening its pull" *and* "as a logical system of order in design, to the point of its existing independently of a single viewpoint and in contradiction to spatial plunge." They add: "This bivalence is, moreover, central to Caillebotte's special relevance to the generation that followed him" (69). See also Galassi's analysis of the spatial construction of *Paris Street; Rainy Day* in "Caillebotte's Method" (*GC*, esp. 193–9) as well as the summary statement: "The Janus-head of perspective defines the two poles of Caillebotte's artistic consciousness – two opposing levels of intention, if you will: one, an intense involvement with the scene before him; the other, a detached aesthetic awareness through which that involvement is filtered. The tension between these poles, reflected in his work, is never stable" (204).

30 Cf. the brief discussion of an analogous crossing structure in Whistler's etching *Vauxhall Bridge* (1861) in *MM*, 232.

31 I owe the suggestion that there exists an uncertainty about the degree of the central figure's absorption to T. J. Clark.

32 I stress the close connection between early Impressionism and the rise of a "manifestly judgmental, self-consciously 'aesthetic' mode of seeing and experiencing painting," which I relate to the new conditions of exhibition pioneered by the Impressionists, in *MM*, 413–16. See also Galassi's statement in "Caillebotte's Method" quoted at the close of n. 29 above.

33 Reference to MM, 404–7.

34 On Manet and strikingness see *MM*, ch. 4; cf. also n. 17 above. For an opposed reading of the composition of the Fort Worth *Pont de l'Europe* and its relation to Manet's painting see Julia Sagraves's entry on the former in *UI*, in particular her claim "that the bold X formed by the iron girders . . . functions compositionally like a magnet, drawing viewers to the scene and joining them in the shared activity of looking" and that "unlike Manet's closed-off space [in the *Gare St.-Lazare*], the notably asymmetrical composition of Caillebotte's *Pont de l'Europe* invites the viewer to join in the socializing activity of gazing at the spectacle – both real and painted – of modern, industrial Paris below" (109).

35 On Courbet's persecution (for that is what it amounted to) by the Third Republic and his years in exile (he died in 1877), see e.g. Jack Lindsay, *Gustave Courbet: His Life and Art* (New York, Evanston, San Francisco, London, 1973), chs. 15–18.

36 For a lucid summary of the political situation in the mid-and late 1870s, see Jane Mayo Roos, "Within the 'Zone of Silence': Monet and

Manet in 1878," *Art History* 11 (Sept. 1988): 372–407. My reading of the implicit politics of the *Floor-Scrapers*, as well as of the Geneva *Pont de l'Europe*, has much in common with Roos's analysis of Manet's two paintings of *The Rue de Mosnier with Flags* of 1878 (see esp. 392–4).

37 After a comma the sentence continues: "a gaze that is the very crux of the X-composition and the painting's principal focal point. It is also a relationship realized by the viewer's own gaze," split between that focal point and the head of the worker and between "the two different social groups indicated by them" (Sagraves, "The Street," in *UI*, 97).

38 At the risk of pushing Caillebotte's relation to Courbet too far, the position of the dog at the bottom of the canvas takes advantage of the freedom dogs enjoy in paintings like the *After Dinner at Ornans* and the *Burial at Ornans* to turn up at or near the bottom edge of the picture. As Galassi was the first to note, the dog's boldly vectored movement into the painting reinforces the sense of perspective recession that leads to the *flâneur*'s head and from there towards the worker (*GC*, 199). In general it would be hard to overstate the importance of vectors in Caillebotte's art; when they are deployed so as to reinforce perspectival sightlines, as in the *Pont de l'Europe* and, still to come, the *House-Painters*, the effect is of a virtual corporealization of vision.

39 In this connection Galassi has shown how in the *Pont de l'Europe* the painter "composed a single picture from *two* planes of projection," the first and dominant one centered on the *flâneur* and the second on the worker, with the result that "the picture . . . has two equally valid centers of vision: the viewer is by implication looking in two directions at once" ("Caillebotte's Method," *GC*, 195; emphasis in original). This in itself has no bearing on the question of the precise direction or object of the *flâneur*'s gaze (Galassi speaks of following that gaze "across the picture to the worker at the rail" [196]), but as Galassi explains, the implication carried by the second plane of projection is owing to the artist's decision to "flatten" the near bay of the lattice of girders – to bend it "towards" us – relative to what would have been its angle of recession according to a perspective structure rigorously centered on the head of the *flâneur*. Consequently we are able to see significantly more of the scene beyond and below the bridge than would otherwise be the case, and although the portion of the scene we glimpse cannot be equated with the vista open to the worker, we are nevertheless led in the end to look *past* the figure of the worker, which is what I am claiming the *flâneur* does as well.

40 The relations among the three main figures thus recall the triadic structures of male homosociality brilliantly explored by Eve Kosofsky Sedgwick in *Between Men: English Literature and Male Homosocial Desire* (New York and Guildford, Surrey, 1985) and subsequent writings. Cf. Norma Broude, "Outing Impressionism: Homosexuality and Homosocial Bonding in the Work of Caillebotte and Bazille," in Broude, 117–74.

41 Near the end of "The Street" Sagraves abruptly qualifies her previous remarks. After stressing still further the notion of a leveling of differences between the classes associated with the two men, she writes as if by way of an afterthought: "Nevertheless, while indeed drawn together compositionally, these two social groups do remain distinct in Caillebotte's image. It is a picture of social compromise and coexistence, but not assimilation, as the two principal figures (and the two sorts of middle classes they represent) are separated by a broad section of pavement, made even broader by Caillebotte's compositional manipulations. Moreover, the social difference between the two figures is never in question, as they are given distinct costumes and demeanors" (*UI*, 98). (Her reference in this passage to "the two sorts of middle classes [the two men] represent" alludes to her belief that the figure of the worker is to be understood as a *petit bourgeois*

[97].) I will only note that the notion of "social compromise and coexistence" comes no closer than that of social leveling to my reading of the relations between the two men.

Caillebotte is briefly associated with "classic republican" interests by Philip Nord, *The Republican Moment: Struggles for Democracy in Nineteenth-Century France* (Cambridge, Mass. and London, 1995), 178.

42 Again, I owe this suggestion to Clark (see n. 31).

43 Sagraves goes on to rephrase her claims more positively. After quoting the critic Georges Rivière, who described the house-painters as conscientiously contemplating the work before them and then characterized Caillebotte himself as "a laborer, a bold seeker on whom I think we can base solid hopes," she writes: "It seems possible to understand Caillebotte's house-painters both as urban workers painting the city over again, and as the pictorial counterparts of the Impressionist painters themselves, who in a sense were aiming to do the same" (*UI*, 94).

44 The reader might wish to compare both Sagraves's and my readings of the paintings just discussed with Albert Boime's in *Art and the French Commune: Imagining Paris after War and Revolution* (Princeton, 1995), esp. ch. 4, "The Impressionist Agenda." Boime's study is full of useful observations and hitherto inaccessible images from illustrated newspapers and the like; but his unflagging commitment to the view that "the Impressionists preeminently politicized their creations by reimagining and reconstructing symbolically their partially destroyed country and disrupted social hierarchy" (11) gives rise to interpretations of individual works that I find unpersuasive. Nevertheless, *Art and the French Commune* is an important book.

45 Cf. Varnedoe on the "uncommunicative isolation" of the strollers, "particularly the foreground couple, so close and yet so psychically remote from us as well as from each other," in *GC*, 112.

46 *MM*, 260. I also write that "Duranty's vision [in *The New Painting*] was of a network of spaces which, for all their seeming openness and accessibility, were fundamentally *closed*" (261; emphasis in original).

47 Nor does it seem right to describe the top-hatted man depicted from the rear and cut off by the right-hand framing edge as the viewer's "pictorial surrogate." Presumably Sagraves does so on the basis of the figure's proximity to the picture plane and orientation relative to the scene as a whole. But the figure is much too marginal to bear the weight she assigns to it.

48 Cf. in this connection Sharon Marcus's pathbreaking account of what she calls the interiorization of Paris in the decades after 1850 in *Apartment Stories: The City and the Home in Nineteenth-Century Paris and London* (Berkeley and Los Angeles, 1999), chs. 4 and 5. Marcus writes: "My claim that Paris became interiorized after 1850 challenges the received interpretations of Second Empire Paris as a city of spectacle, *flânerie*, and circulation, a Paris making the transition, as historian Jeanne Gaillard puts it, from an 'introverted' to an 'extroverted city,' a Paris about which the Goncourt brothers famously wrote, 'the interior is going to die. Life threatens to become public.' My purpose is not to dismiss those understandings of the city, but to complicate them by showing that during the Second Empire [and after], the very notion of a public realm based on mobility, exchange, and visual display developed alongside articulations of urban space as a private realm of intromission and seclusion" (139).

49 Cf. the rigorously absorptive thematics and dispersive compositional logic of Edgar Degas's *Portraits in an Office (New Orleans)* (1873), which like the *Young Man at His Window* and *Floor-Scrapers* was shown in the Impressionist exhibition of 1876, as well as the excerpts from contemporary reviews of that picture by Charles Bigot and Marius Chaumelin quoted in translation in *NP*, 171. Degas's painting is

read in political terms – unpersuasively, to my mind – by Boime, *Art and the French Commune*, 55–9, and (in a less ideologically overdetermined manner but with no more regard for the issues central to the present essay) by Marilyn R. Brown, *Degas and the Business of Art: A Cotton Office in New Orleans* (University Park, Penn., 1994). The precise relation of Degas's art to the developments analysed in *MM* and the present essay remains a topic to be explored in the future.

50 Leonardo da Vinci, quoted by Mary Pardo, "Veiling the *Venus of Urbino*," in Rona Goffen, ed., *Titian's "Venus of Urbino"* (Cambridge, New York, and Melbourne, 1997), 118. Pardo continues: "The antithetical pairing of bad weather with sweetness and grace, making one give birth to the other, plays poetically on the double sense of the word *aria*, which denotes air, atmosphere (and by extension weather, climate), as well as the 'look,' the animation, the style of a person." The result is an "effect of aesthetic filtering. With its help, real bodies are transmuted into perfected and magically heightened apparitions, their physical bulk subtly transmuted into a crepuscular glow" (118).

51 Cf. Varnedoe, who notes "the pure magic of the one pearl that shines from the ear of the delicately veiled lady on the right" (*GC*, 111).

52 See Maurice Merleau-Ponty, "Cézanne's Doubt," in *Sense and Non-Sense*, trans. Hubert L. Dreyfus and Patricia Allen Dreyfus (Evanston, Ill., 1964), 14.

53 The point of these remarks is to emphasize the sense of distinct angles of vision, not the idea of temporal sequence (the effect is the same however one scans the painting). Cf. the photograph of a table set with the same crystal-ware as in the *Luncheon* and photographed with a camera with a 24 mm. lens in *GC*, 93, fig. 1a. The rendering of space in the photograph is admittedly comparable to that in the painting, but the photograph itself is not a "normative" one, that is, the effect of the wide-angle lens is to mimic the kind of "lived perspective" I ascribe to the painting. In any case, the segmented spatiality of the painting goes beyond anything in the photograph; this is especially clear in the treatment of the plate, glass, and silver in the immediate foreground.

54 Gloria Groom in her entry on the *Luncheon* notes that initially René was to have been represented reading a book (*UI*, 194), a traditional absorptive motif. Groom's insistence on the painting's evocation of a mood of distance, alienation, and malaise seems overdone, however. On the *Luncheon* see also Marrinan, "Caillebotte as Professional Painter," in Broude, 34–5.

55 Throughout this essay I have been using the English titles given Caillebotte's painting in *UI*, but the latter renders *L'Yerres, effet de pluie* as *The Yerres, Rain*.

56 Nevertheless, commentators have been sufficiently troubled by the absence of raindrops in the latter to suggest that the concentric circles in the water might have been made by bubbles or insects instead of by rain (*UI*, 60). In fact raindrops falling onto the surface of a pond or pool (or even a large puddle) tend not to make splashes but rather to give rise – immediately, as it were – to radiating concentric circles. The point is that Caillebotte saw in that ordinary occurrence the basis for a picture that would encapsulate his vision of painting.

57 Materialism is a central concern of a remarkable chapter entitled "Freud's Cézanne" in Clark's *Farewell to an Idea: Episodes from a History of Modernism* (New Haven and London, 1998), 139–67, as well as of his essay "Phenomenality and Materiality in Cézanne," in Tom Cohen, ed., *Material Events* (Minneapolis, Minn., 2001), 93–113. There is also common ground between my account of Caillebotte's corporeal and materialist Impressionism in this essay and Michel Serres's remarks about and around the art of Pierre Bonnard in the chapter entitled "Voiles" in *Les Cinq Sens: Philosophie des corps mêlés – 1* (Paris, 1985), esp. 27–36. My thanks to Mikkel Bogh for bringing Serres's text to my attention. Finally, I note that there is a rough analogy

between the concentric circles, which express the energy of the initial impact, and the coiled wood-shavings in the *Floor-Scrapers*, which as I have said may be seen as "containing" the labor of the three workmen.

58 See Varnedoe, *Gustave Caillebotte*, 130.

59 For a discussion of *Man at His Bath* and related works as images of "modern masculinity," see Tamar Garb, "Masculinity, Muscularity, and Modernity in Caillebotte's Male Figures," in Terry Smith, ed., *In Visible Touch: Modernism and Masculinity* (Chicago and London, 1997), repr. in Broude, 175–96.

60 See the discussion of this aspect of Caillebotte's still lifes by Douglas Druick in *UI*, 232–53, and by Darragon, *Caillebotte*, 98–103. Druick's essay, "Caillebotte's Still Lifes," is repr. in Broude, 197–224.

61 "There you are again, great magician, with your mute compositions!" ("Vous revoilà donc, grand magicien, avec vos compositions muettes!"), Diderot writes at the beginning of his commentary on Chardin's paintings in the Salon of 1765 (Denis Diderot, *Salons*, ed. Jean Seznec [1765; repr., Oxford, 1979], 2: 111). A thematics of silence is associated with what I call Diderot's "pastoral" conception of painting in *AT*, ch. 3. More recently, James H. Rubin in *Manet's Silence and Poetics of Bouquets* (London, 1994) makes much of the alleged "silence" of Manet's paintings by virtue of what is taken to be their relation to still life and to flower painting in particular. For a brief critique of Rubin's thesis see *MM*, 573 n. 97.

62 As Varnedoe writes in *UI*: "The dozen or so indelibly memorable images [Caillebotte] created between 1875 and 1882 seem more to foretell the devices of later cinema [than to be in any sense novelistic]; and in these important respects – as regards their construction of space, distinctive viewpoints, and assertive compositional architecture – they rival or outstrip the art of his more illustrious colleagues in inventiveness" (J. Kirk T. Varnedoe, "Odd Man In," *UI*, 13). Four mutually related aspects of Caillebotte's art might be stressed in this connection: his preoccupation with effects of movement in time as against those of instantaneousness; his predilection for vectors implying physical or visual (or physico-visual) traversal of the picture space; his construction of representational fields the outer limits of which appear not exactly provisional but somehow fluid, subject to change before our eyes; and his activation of a certain unrepresented "beyond," either off-picture as in the Geneva *Pont de l'Europe* or in the picture's depths, as in the Forth Worth variant. Indeed there is something cinematic in the relation *between* the Geneva and Fort Worth pictures, as there also is, come to think of it, in the relation between the two laundry canvases (taking the presumed study as a close-up of the final work). It may be, too, that what I have described as the emergent desire to represent sensations would find its fullest expression in narrative cinema, especially in those techniques concerned with the specification of point of view. Cf. Gilles Deleuze on the "movement-image" in *Cinema 1: The Movement Image*, trans. Hugh Tomlinson and Barbara Habberjam (Minneapolis, Minn., 1986).

63 *Moment of Caravaggio*, ch. 1, "Boy Bitten by a Lizard," 7–37.

64 I also suggest that certain artists in the Impressionist orbit such as Camille Pissarro and the short-lived Frédéric Bazille retained a commitment to effects of embodiment, in Pissarro's case within the parameters of a thoroughly Impressionist technique. See *MM*, 394–5 (for Pissarro), and 607–8 n. 31 (for Bazille); the latter note also briefly discusses Cézanne and Caillebotte. The embodied aspects of Pissarro's art are further analyzed in Rachael Ziady Delue, "Pissarro, Landscape, Vision, and Tradition," *Art Bulletin* 80 (Dec. 1998): 718–36.

65 Cf. in this connection Caillebotte's *In a Café* (1880), a portraitlike painting of a man standing with his back to a mirror in which we see reflected part of his head and back along with two seated figures playing cards near the opposite wall of the café (on which hangs a

second mirror, with all the spatial ambiguities which that implies). The complexities of this composition, which almost certainly played a role in the conception of Manet's *Bar at the Folies-Bergère*, are acutely analyzed by Varnedoe in *GC*, 145–6.

66 On Manet's *Self-Portrait with a Palette* see *MM*, 395–8. A self-portrait drawing in which the sitter's hand is depicted as if in motion (and is therefore strongly contrasted with the treatment of the sitter's steadily gazing head) is Degas's *Portrait de l'artiste* from ca. 1865 in the Louvre (RF 24232). Degas's drawing is illustrated in *Des mécènes par milliers: Un siècle de dons par les Amis du Louvre*, exh. cat. (Paris, 1997), 345, cat. no. 564.

67 Cf. the similarly tilted canvas, "angled to avoid the glare of the sun," in the photograph by Ker-Xavier Roussel of Cézanne at work on the hill of Les Lauves, 1906, reproduced by Joel Isaacson in "Constable, Duranty, Mallarmé, Impressionism, Plein Air, and Forgetting," *Art Bulletin* 76 (Sept. 1994): 427, fig. 1. The quoted words are Isaacson's.

68 In the light of these aspects of the *Self-Portrait at the Easel* it is tempting to go back and suggest that the partly reflective wooden floor in the *Floor-Scrapers* might be analogized to the reflective surface of the painting-in-progress, just as the actions of the floor-scrapers, which consist simultaneously in the establishment of a plane surface (the refurbished floor) and the violation or exceeding of that surface by the generation of actual-seeming wood-shavings, might be analogized to the making of the painting itself, with its double thematization of modernist flatness and untrammeled illusion. In that connection, too, the file jutting into the picture space at the bottom of the *Floor-Scrapers* recalls various thematizations in Courbet's art of the painter-beholder's brush or palette knife and more broadly of his bodily orientation relative to the canvas on which he is working. I stop short, however, of seeing in the *Floor-Scrapers* a "real allegory" of the process of its production as in my readings in *CR* of the *Wheat Sifters*, *Painter's Studio*, and *Quarry*; see *CR*, ch. 5.

6 FRY'S "FORMALISM"

1 Roger Fry, "Giotto," in *Vision and Design* (orig. 1920; Harmondsworth, Middlesex, 1961), pp. 109–45; the footnote appears on 109. Further page references to articles in *Vision and Design* will be in parentheses in the text, with the designation *V*.

2 See Maurice Denis, "Cézanne" and "Définition du néo-traditionnisme" in *Du Symbolisme au classicisme: Théories*, ed. Olivier Revault d'Allonnes (Paris, 1964), 155–72 and 33–46 respectively. The implied reference to Berenson is noted by Caroline Elam, "Roger Fry and Early Italian Painting," in *Art Made Modern: Roger Fry's Vision of Art*, ed. Christopher Green, exh. cat. (London, 1999), 106 n 96. Berenson says this apropos of Giotto.

3 Fry reflects further on these these issues in "Some Questions in Aesthetics," the first essay in *Transformations* (orig. 1932; Garden City, N.Y., 1956), 1–57, where he essentially arrives at the same conclusion (see my discussion of his analysis in that essay of Rembrandt's *A Schoolboy at His Desk* below). Further page references to *Transformations* will be in parentheses in the text, with the designation *T*. An important late text, "The Double Nature of Painting" (1933), acknowledges the existence of certain rare "composite" works "in which the literary element and the plastic element enter into a very intimate combination, so to speak, a sort of chemical combination [he also speaks of them as "fusing"]" (in *A Roger Fry Reader*, ed. Christopher Reed [Chicago and London, 1996], 387–8), though at the end of the essay it turns out that only two great masters, Giorgione and Rembrandt, come to mind in that connection (391–2). In an even later essay, " 'The Toilet,' by Rembrandt" (on Rembrandt's *Bathsheba* in the Louvre), Fry remarks: "Let us admit that a full understanding

of the picture demands that we should feel both the psychological motive and the plastic one. Yet my own experience shows that one can enjoy intensely the plastic and pictorial appeal of this picture without ever becoming conscious of the psychological situation. When I do, I get another shock of pleasure, but do the two pleasures combine into a single more intense feeling or do they remain separate? That is a question which I have never quite been able to answer" (419). Further page references to items in *A Roger Fry Reader* will be in parentheses in the text, with the designation *R*.

4 See Christopher Baker and Tom Henry, *The National Gallery, Complete Illustrated Catalogue* (London, 2001), 284.

5 Fry's article concludes: "For never was a work more perfectly transparent to the idea, never was an artist's intention more deliberately and precisely recorded" (*V*, 171).

6 Fry continues: "Again the representation merely as representation, will set up a number of feelings and perhaps of critical thoughts dependent upon innumerable associated ideas in the spectator's mind" (*V*, 233).

7 See *AT*.

8 See, however, Ch. 1, n. 1 above, on what I call Diderot's "pastoral" conception of painting, which applied to genres that did not lend themselves to dramatic treatment.

9 But see Todd Cronan, *Against Affective Formalism: Matisse, Bergson, Modernism* (Minneapolis, 2014).

10 French antitheatrical critics whom Fry might have read include Jules-Antoine Castagnary, Ernest Chesneau, Edmond Duranty, Félix Fénéon, and Joris-Karl Huysmans. In the British tradition, antitheatrical attitudes are expressed by the 3rd Earl of Shaftesbury, Sir Joshua Reynolds, and William Hazlitt.

11 In "Line as a Means of Expression in Modern Art" (1918), in *A Roger Fry Reader*, 337. This is said in connection with Henri Gaudier-Brzeska, most of whose drawings are held to "tend to an exuberant and demonstrative effectiveness which reminds one only too much of the assertive and self-conscious calligraphy of the Japanese." Fry goes on: "But everything in Brzeska's career shows that he would have rapidly outgrown this as well as all other mannerisms into which he may have temporarily fallen" (ibid.).

12 See, e.g., the discussion of Poussin in *Characteristics of French Art* (New York, 1933), which includes the remark: "But perhaps, in a sense, the very insipidity and artificiality of Poussin's drama leaves us all the freer to concentrate on his formal harmonies" (28). Further page references will be in parentheses in the text, with the designation *C*. See also the brief remarks on Poussin's *Baptism* (no further reference given) in "The Double Nature of Painting": "Well, we do see the figures in the *Baptism* making emphatic gestures; but these gestures are too conventional, too formal to convince us of the reality of such over-theatrical beings. He hardly arouses in us the idea of the inner life of his characters, but on the other hand what deep feeling emanates from the general *ordonnance* of his forms, what equipoise there is between the two sides of his composition, how well all the directions of the limbs balance and echo one another. What unshakeable unity results from this diversity! . . . No, Poussin never moves us by his frigid demonstrations of antique virtue, but he is one of the great composers of plastic and spatial harmonies" (in *R*, 390).

13 See Fry's account of these developments in "Retrospect" as well as the discussion of the evolution of his thought in Christopher Green, "Into the Twentieth Century: Roger Fry's Project Seen from 2000," in Green, *Art Made Modern*, 13–30; and Elizabeth Prettejohn, "Out of the Nineteenth Century: Roger Fry's Early Art Criticism, 1900–1906," in ibid., 31–44. See also Jacqueline V. Falkenheim, *Roger Fry and the Beginnings of Formalist Art Criticism* (Ann Arbor, Mich., 1980).

14 Roger Fry, review of Wölfflin's *The Art of the Italian Renaissance* in *The Athenaeum*, no. 3974,

26 Dec. 1903: 863. The phrase in quotation marks – "rhetorical rather than truly dramatic" – may come from Wölfflin but I have not been able to find it. (The edition I have used was published in New York and London in 1913.) In any case, Wölfflin in the Introduction to his book draws a sharp contrast between the immensely appealing "*naïveté* of vision and emotion" of the Quattrocento (1) and the more stately and considered character of the art of the High Renaissance, which contemporary viewers, in his account, find difficult to accept. The public, he writes, "feels itself on insecure ground, and cannot tell whether it should accept the gestures and ideas of classic art as genuine. It has had to swallow so much false classicism, that it turns with zest to coarser but purer fare. We have lost faith in the grandiose. We have become weak and distrustful, and everywhere we detect theatrical sentiment and empty declamation" (3).

Fry's remarks on Michelangelo might be compared with Gustave Moreau's observations – which Fry could not have known – to the effect that all of Michelangelo's figures seem to be acting somnambulistically, as if they were asleep or absorbed in another world (or worlds) (*L'Assembleur de rêves: Ecrits complets de Gustave Moreau* [Fontfroide, 1984], 197).

15 Fry, review of Wölfflin. Bellini's Naples *Transfiguration* is discussed by Fry in his early *Giovanni Bellini* (1899; New York, 1995), 34–6.

16 *Letters of Roger Fry*, ed. Denys Sutton, 2 vols. (London, 1972), 2: 497. See also Fry's letter of 20 Feb. 1913 to P. J. Atkins: "The reality of a picture is immensely greater if the spectator is not referred back by illusion to a possible exterior reality (which is stronger and more real), but is held within the reality of the artistic creation by its sheer necessity and intensity of unity. [This notion of the viewer not being referred back to the real world will be important shortly.] As to the things that we find don't matter, they are innumerable if you consider our work from the point of view of imitative likeness, but if we succeeded (I don't say we do for a moment) every line, every tone would matter intensely to the particular unity. Indeed it is essential to us that we should never put in anything which does not matter, anything which does not count in the whole. Because anything that is not functional is actually destroying the rest. You see the whole focus of effort and attention changes fundamentally when once you give up the idea of imitative likeness and aim at the creation of absolutely *necessitated* form" (*Letters*, 1: 364; emphasis in original).

17 See *AT*, 82–92.

18 For Fry on chiaroscuro see e.g. the important previously unpublished lecture of 1908, "Expression and Representation in the Graphic Arts" (*R*, 68–69); the claim in "Post-Impressionism" (1911) that chiaroscuro has always been at odds with linear design and color, hence decorative unity (*R*, 107); his comments on Caravaggio in "The Seicento," where he notes "the relation between certain violent and unusual effects of light and the expression of what we may call melodramatic emotion" (*T*, 141); and on Leonardo in "The Art of Florence" (*V*, 150).

19 At any rate, in works that conform to what I call his "dramatic" conception of painting; his "pastoral" conception, which applies to genres such as landscapes with figures or paintings of ruins, tends to involve effects of temporal dilation (see *AT*, 131–2).

20 This is said apropos of the art of Vanessa Bell in "Independent Gallery: Vanessa Bell and Othon Friesz (1922) in *R*." Cf. Fry on Cézanne: "His work has the baffling mysterious quality of the greatest originators in art. It has that supreme spontaneity as though he had almost made himself the passive, half-conscious instrument of some directing power. So little seems implied at first sight in his apparently accidental collocation of form and color, so much reveals itself gradually to the fascinated gaze" ("The Post Impressionists – II," in *R*, 90). See however Fry on Giotto in 1901:

"Almost every composition [in the Arena chapel] gives one the shock of a discovery at once simple, inevitable, and instantly apprehended, and yet utterly unforeseeable" (*V*, 115). And indeed on Matisse in 1935: "In spite of [the violence of his paradoxes, the brevity of his allusions, the incessant equivoque], in spite of this, Matisse is nearly always legible at a glance. No one is in doubt as to what anything is or exactly where it is in the picture space even though the design is built on the strangest, most unfamiliar appositions, the oddest turns of nature's kaleidoscope" (from *Henri-Matisse*, in *R*, 409).

21 See the discussion of "at-onceness" in "The Case for Abstract Art" (1960) in Clement Greenberg, *The Collected Essays and Criticism*, 4 vols., *Vol. 4: Modernism with a Vengeance, 1957–1969*, ed. John O'Brian (Chicago and London, 1993), 80–81. And the following short exchange from a 1978 interview with James Faure Walker: Walker asks, "your sense of a work's value is instantaneous?" To which Greenberg replies, "It's got to be instantaneous." And a short time later he says, "I look at a Mondrian the way I look at any other kind of picture, for that instantaneous unity" ("Interview with James Faure Walker," Clement Greenberg, *Late Writings*, ed. Robert C. Morgan [Minneapolis, 2003], 163).

22 "Some Questions in Aesthetics," 14.

23 As Richard Shiff remarks in the chapter on Fry in *Cézanne and the End of Impressionism: A Study of the Theory, Technique, and Critical Evaluation of Modern Art* (Chicago and London, 1984), 143–52.

24 "The Post-Impressionists – II," in *R*, 90.

25 "Post Impressionism" (1911), in *R*, 109.

26 Thus Fry writes of Cézanne, "Every word and every gesture [cited in Ambroise Vollard's book on the artist] sticks out with the rugged relief of a character in which everything is due to the compulsion of inner forces, in which nothing has been planed down or smoothed away by external pressure – not that internal pressure was absent but that the inner compulsion – the inevitable bent of Cézanne's temperament, was irresistible" ("Cézanne," in *V* [180]). And a bit further on: "Nothing is less possible to the real artist than pose – he is less capable of it than the ordinary man of business because more than any one else his external activities are determined from within by needs and instincts which he himself barely recognises" (ibid., 182). It is perhaps worth noting in this connection that Fry begins his Giotto essay of 1901 with a discussion of St. Francis and his teaching, which includes the observation that Francis "was actually a poet before his conversion, and his whole life had the pervading unity and rhythm of a perfect work of art" (111). Fry continues: "Not that he was a conscious artist. The whole keynote of the Franciscan teaching was its spontaneity, but his feelings for moral and aesthetic beauty were intimately united" (ibid.). Note, too, that Fry in 1903 had described the dramatic ideal of medieval art as "the presentment of definite personalities acting freely and unconsciously under the impulse of a strong emotional situation" (see above).

27 "Line as a Means of Expression," in *R*, 337. This is said in the course of a brief discussion of works by Nina Hamnett and Edward Wolfe (336–7). Of Matisse Fry later writes: "It is I think from a, perhaps unconscious perception of this necessity [not to lose time . . . upon describing and evoking his volumes because to do so would arrest the sequence of his surface design] that he has developed his deformation of the figure" ("Henri-Matisse," in *R*, 409).

28 "Mr. Walter Sickert's Pictures" (1911) in *R*, 142.

29 "Line as a Means of Expression," 333–5. The passage continues: "Synthesis is of course always made by a jump of the unconscious, but the materials out of which the synthesis is made are given by the conscious mind. Sickert provides his unconscious self with the total vision as detected by his richly experienced and marvellously aware sensibility" (335).

30 "Independent Gallery: Vanessa Bell and Othon Friesz" in *R*, 348.

31 "Henri-Matisse," in *R*, 403.

32 "Rembrandt: An Interpretation," in *R*, 377.

33 In Uccello's art "the simplifications and abstractions imposed upon his observation of nature by the [conscious] desire to construct his whole scene perspectively, really set free in him his [unconscious] power of creating a purely aesthetic organisation of form" (*V*, 154).

34 Fry immediately goes on to compare Rembrandt's wood with Alma Tadema's marble. "The whole point of Alma Tadema's celebrated performances lay in his having given one a rather weak illusion of marble itself. To say 'How like marble!' was precisely all that could be said. It had no other purpose, no further meaning than that, being, in fact, totally inexpressive of anything else. Whereas nothing appears more impertinent before this Rembrandt than to call attention to this likeness, exact though it may be" (*T*, 55).

35 A page before this Fry transcribes notes he had made on another Courbet, a *Baigneuse endormie* he had recently seen at the French Gallery. The notes read: "How nearly Courbet comes to the total transmutation of the theme into plastic values, and by what a curious misunderstanding of the problem he misses complete purity! Here he touches the imagination almost in exact proportion to his absorption in the thing seen. He painted his 'Baigneuse' with a passionate intensity of feeling which carries one entirely away from the actual world, but when he sought the adventitious aid of a poetical *mise-en-scène* and borrowed from literature and the theatre the stereotypes of rocks and overhanging foliage and water, he went near to destroying all sense of illusion. The want of plastic consistency here refers us back, for all their poetical intention, to the actual world" (*T*, 48–9).

36 See the discussions of Chardin's *Un Philosophe occupé de sa lecture* and Greuze's *Un Ecolier qui étudie sa leçon* in *AT*, 11–13 and 16–17.

37 "Rembrandt: An Interpretation," (1927) in *R*, 373; throughout that essay Fry stresses Rembrandt's mastery of drama.

38 See the discussion of Diderot on Chardin's still-lifes in *AT* (82), where I quote Diderot as writing in his *Salon of 1765*: "Choose his site; dispose on this site the objects I am about to indicate to you, and be sure that you will have seen his paintings" (translation mine). ("Choisissez son site; disposez sur ce site les objets comme je vais vous les indiquer, et soyez sûr que vous aurez vu ses tableaux.")

39 As Fry writes in "Expression and Representation in the Graphic Arts" (1908): "[A]ny presentment in which unity was obviously lacking would prevent that sense of finality, that self-contained repose which [is] necessary . . . to pleasurable contemplation. Any apparent lack of unity will at once stir the mind to an undesirable activity, the activity of seeking in the world outside the work of art for the missing and complementary elements" (*R*, 69). And in "Some Questions in Aesthetics": "It will be noticed that the full value of the representational element almost always depends on a reference to something outside the actual work of art, to what is brought in by the title and such knowledge as the title implies to the spectator, whereas plastic values inhere in the work itself" (*T*, 31). And: "We can say, supposing the picture to envisage plastic expression, that the moment anything in it ceases to serve towards the edification of the whole plastic volume, the moment it depends on reference to something outside the picture, it becomes descriptive of some other reality, and becomes part of an actual, and not a spiritual, reality" (*T*, 56).

40 Cf. Clement Greenberg: "Van Gogh was a great artist, Monet's example serves even better than Cézanne's to remind us that he lacked a settled largeness of view. In Monet we find a world of art, with the variety and spaciousness and ease of a *world*; in the short-lived Van Gogh, we find only the glimpse of one" ("The Later Monet," *Art and Culture: Critical Essays* [Boston, 1961], 45; emphasis in original).

41 The by now classic reference here is to Jacques Derrida on framing in "Parergon" in *The Truth in Painting*, trans. Geoff Bennington and Ian

McLeod (Chicago and London, 1987), esp. 37–82. See also the acute remarks on frames by Gertrude Stein in "Pictures," *Lectures in America* (Boston, 1935), 85–7. For example: "And then there is another trouble. A painting is painted as a painting, as an oil painting existing as an oil painting, it may be in or it may be out of its frame, but an oil painting and that is a real bother always will have a tendency to go back to its frame, even if it has never been out of it. That is one of the things that an oil painting any oil painting has a very great tendency to do. And this is a bother sometimes to the painter and sometimes to any one looking at an oil painting" (85). By "trouble" and "bother" Stein means conceptually difficult issues that have never been resolved, in this case the relation of a painting to its frame (Derrida would add, whether it is in a frame or not).

42 Fry cites it under the title *Chez le docteur*.

43 He immediately adds: "A kind of desultory alertness and distraction seems indeed to be the condition for making such rare and enchanting discoveries as Chardin and Corot did" (96–7).

44 Thus in "Mr. Walter Sickert's Pictures at the Stafford Gallery" Fry remarks that "Mr. Sickert has never, it would seem, wanted to do anything but paint. With him his passion is so strong that he is almost indifferent as to what he paints, his care being altogether for the manner of it. I have always had the pleasure of differing from Mr. Sickert's views on art, but [his current exhibition] convinces me that I have never done him justice" (in *R*, 1410. Less ambivalently, in "The Allied Artists" (1913) Fry criticizes two of Sickert's pupils, Mr. Gore and Miss Sands, for "seem[ing] too much preoccupied with *métier* of painting to become definite creators." Even there, though, he adds, "Still, the influence of their conscientious and honest craftsmanship makes itself felt" (in *R*, 152). See also Anna Gruetzner Robins, "Fathers and Sons: Walter Sickert and Roger Fry," in Green, *Art Made Modern*, pp. 45–56.

45 "Dürer and Company" (1913) in *V*, 161.

46 Thus he writes in "Some Questions in Aesthetics": "This habit of putting psychological above spatial values in graphic art comes, of course, only too naturally to men of letters who occupy themselves with plastic art. Diderot's celebrated critiques of the Salons of his day are almost entirely devoted to the psychological aspects of illustration. No wonder that for him Greuze was the greatest of painters" (*T*, 55). See also Fry's remarks about Diderot in "The Double Nature of Painting" in *R*, 383–4, 386–8. The most embarrassing statement of all, given Fry's unacknowledged dependence on Diderot's thought, is "it is hard to reason worse than Diderot when he sets about it" (387).

47 Among the artists Fry's discussion of whom touches on issues of theatricality are the brothers Le Nain, Poussin, Delacroix, Corot, and Degas.

48 *Cézanne: A Study of His Development* (New York, 1927), 41.

49 Ibid., 42.

50 Something similar occurs in Fry's admiring comments on Giorgione's *The Three Philosophers* in Vienna: "First of all we are struck with the amplitude of these forms, by the disposition of these figures both so unexpected and so inevitable in so strange a space. This very disposition induces in us a heightened frame of mind, a state in which we expect some mysterious revelation. This effect, produced by the disposition of forms, prepares us to meet beings far removed from our everyday life, to hope for something unknown and fateful, and Giorgione does not disappoint us. He has created people that appear to come from far away, from out of another world . . ." ("The Double Nature of Painting," 391–2).

51 Fry does provide a formal analysis of the *Christ Appearing to Mary Magdalen* in the last of the broadcasts, "The Meaning of Pictures – Truth and Nature in Art," *The Listener*, Nov. 6, 1929, 617. Not surprisingly, he stresses what he sees as Giotto's perfect meshing of design and drama: "We take in the whole scene at once because of its closely knit unity, because of the subordination of every part to the whole. We

notice first the surprising invention of the great sloping contour of the rocky background which carries everything in its sweep from left to right, bringing everything, as it were, to a focus at the point of greatest dramatic significance, the gesture of Christ's right hand as He repels the Magdalen's touch" (ibid.). And so on, including the following: "You will notice that no movements in the general design bring the sleeping soldiers into question. Giotto expressly subordinates them because of their being so entirely cut off from the drama" (ibid.). Later in the same article he compares Raphael's *Galatea* fresco in the Farnesina, which he admires, with Bouguereau's *Birth of Venus*, which he does not. Specifically, he finds in "poses like that of Galatea . . . the expression of fullness of life, and of un-conscious unpremeditated grace," whereas Bouguereau's figures seem to him to be "posing in a *tableau vivant*, and posing affectedly and badly. No one would take these poses, except to be seen doing so" (618).

52 Thinking about Fry's hostility to identification with figures in a painting has made me realize the importance of the fact that Diderot's aesthetics of the *tableau* was, to say the least, open to effects of identification. It is as if what I have called Fry's radicalization of the concept of the *tableau* meant that the figures in a painting had not only to appear unaware of being beheld but also to be psychologically or say spiritually remote from any imaginable viewer. The combination of a structural unawareness of being beheld with a positive invitation to identification characterizes the movies, a medium one would expect Fry not to value highly. (Having said this, I should acknowledge that for Fry Rembrandt's genius was in part an identificatory one. At any rate, he writes in *Characteristics of French Art*: "When Poussin painted his picture of *The Israelites Gathering Manna*, he did not, as Rembrandt would have done, project himself by an effort of sympathetic imagination into the bodies of men and women dying of hunger . . ." [27–8].)

53 Fry, *Letters*, 2: 688.

54 Ibid., 689.

7 GORDON'S *k.364*

1 This is to say that I shall be discussing the film (or movie) version of *k.364*; there is also a two-screen-plus-mirrors exhibition version, which made its debut at the Gagosian Gallery in London in February 2011. Another incarnation of the latter was on view at the MMK (Museum für Moderne Kunst) in Frankfurt am Main between November 2011 and March 2012.

2 Quoted in Charlotte Higgins, "Tracks of my tears," *The Guardian*, Feb. 9, 2011, 24.

3 See *WPM*, 226–33.

4 See the discussion of that work in Michael Fried, *Four Honest Outlaws: Sala, Ray, Marioni, Gordon* (New Haven and London, 2011), 192–6; hereafter, *FHO*.

5 For a detailed analysis of Sala's *Long Sorrow* see ibid., 32–49.

6 Michael Fried, "Art and Objecthood," in *AO*, 148–72, esp. 166–7. Eventually there will be more to say along these lines, a key early text, I now see, being Gertude Stein's remarkable essay "Plays" from her 1935 *Lectures in America*.

7 Stanley Cavell, "The Avoidance of Love: A Reading of *King Lear*," in *Must We Mean What We Say? A Book of Essays* (New York, 1969), 320–21; emphasis in original. Further page references will be in parentheses in the text.

8 "Douglas Gordon Interviewed by Michael Berkeley," in *Douglas Gordon: k.364, A Journey by Train* (London, Gagosian Gallery, 2011), n.p.

9 My thanks to Dudley Andrew and Mary Ann Doane for directing me to various classic essays on the close-up in film, notably including (suggested by Andrew) Doane's "The Close-Up: Scale and Detail in the Cinema," *differences* 14 (2003): 89–111.

10 Charles Rosen, *The Classical Style: Haydn, Mozart, Beethoven*, expanded ed. (New York

and London, 1997), 211. Further page references will be in parentheses in the text.

11 Ben Luke, "Thinking in Film," *Apollo* 173 (Feb. 2011): 55. In that article, too, Gordon cites Robert Bresson's *Notes on Cinematography*, perhaps *the* classic of antitheatrical film theory (53).

12 Ludwig Wittgenstein, *Culture and Value: A Selection from the Posthumous Remains*, ed. Georg Henrik von Wright, in collaboration with Heikki Nyman, rev. ed. of text Alois Pichler, trans. Peter Winch (Malden, Mass. and Oxford, 1998).

13 Translation mine. Winch's translation reads: "A theme, no less than a face, wears an expression" (Wittgenstein, *Culture and Value*, 59e). But the concept of *wearing* an expression is out of key with Wittgenstein's thought. The German original states: "Ein Thema hat nicht weniger einen Gesichtsausdruck, als ein Gesicht" (59).

14 See Edward Said, "Performance as an Extreme Occasion," *Musical Elaborations*, Wellek Library Lectures (New York, 1991), 1–34. In that chapter Said discusses the career of the pianist Glenn Gould, a performer for whom actual performance before an audience came to seem irredeemably theatrical, not that Gould's post-performing career was devoid of its own brand of manifest theatricality.

15 Quoted by Ben Luke, "A Masterpiece to Make the Spirits Soar," *Evening Standard* (February 15, 2011), 33.

16 My thanks to Emily Anderson, Ruth Leys, Leonardo Lisi, Kate Markoski, Yi-Ping Ong, Itay Fainmesser, Stefan Petrov, and Robert Pippin for helpful discussions of *k.364*.

8 DEMAND'S *PACIFIC SUN*

1 Rainer Maria Rilke, *Duino Elegies*, trans. Edward Snow (New York, 2000), 53.

2 There are several versions of the CCTV video available on YouTube under the rubric "Pacific Sun."

3 Diverse figures for the film's duration and the number of frames it comprises appear in different places. The figures stated here come from a personal communication from Thomas Demand.

4 Kathy Ryan, "A Sneak Peek at Thomas Demand's Storm-Tossed Imagination," *The 6th Floor: Eavesdropping on The Times Magazine* (a New York Times Blog), May 4, 2012. nytimes.com/2012/05/04/a-sneak-peek-at-thomas-demands-storm-tossed-imagination.

5 The evening began with brief comments by Demand, followed by a showing of the film and then a public conversation between Demand, the film-maker Florian Henckel von Donnersmarck, and myself, moderated by Thomas Gaehtgens, Director of the Getty Research Institute. My thanks to Gaehtgens for inviting me take part in the occasion.

6 *WPM*, 261–76. Further page references will be in parentheses in the text.

7 Régis Durand, "Tracings," in *Thomas Demand*, exh. cat. Paris, 2000), 87; cited and discussed in *WPM*, 266.

8 Charles Baudelaire, "Salon of 1846," *Art in Paris 1845–1862: Salons and Other Exhibitions*, trans. Jonathan Mayne (London, 1965), 111, translation modified; cited by Jean-François Chevrier, "The Adventures of the Picture Form in the History of Photography" (1989), trans. Michael Gilson, in *The Last Picture Show: Artists Using Photography, 1960–1982*, exh. cat., curated by Douglas Fogle (Minneapolis, Los Angeles, 2003–04), 114.

9 On *Hinoki* see *FHO*, 91–103.

10 On *Untitled (Tractor)* see ibid., 98–100.

11 I owe to Robert Pippin the thought that Demand's photographs and Ray's *Hinoki* ultimately foreground intentionality as such, rather than the discrete or specific intentions that undeniably went into the making of the works in question. Thus in the case of *Hinoki* each cut or gouge in the wood is very precisely, determinately intended. But what is intended in so intending – the ultimate point of the operation, in my account – is not manifest or

formulable in a determinate way. (Hence my characterization in *WPM* of the intentions behind Demand's constructions in his photographs as inscrutable and opaque.) Put slightly differently, the foregrounding of determinate intentions is only the beginning of a free play, as it were, on or of the intentionality of art itself, which is not at all the same as the normal teleological structure of productive action. With the notion of "free play" (also "intentionality as such," which recalls that of "purposiveness without purpose") we are in the general realm of Kant's third *Critique* and Schiller's *Letters on the Aesthetic Education of Man*, two of the foundational texts of modern aesthetics.

Here I might add that the thematization of intentionality through something like "reenactment" (in the first place, involving the reconstruction of an apartment house in which the first-person protagonist remembers once possibly having lived, complete with other inhabitants trained to perform various remembered pieces of business), governs the plotline of a brilliant recent novel, Tom McCarthy's *Remainder* (New York, 2005). *Remainder* was called to my attention by Walter Benn Michaels, who has more to say about it in his forthcoming book, *The Beauty of a Social Problem*.

12 Fried, "Art and Objecthood," *AO*, 148–72. For Smith's ride see 157–9. Further page references will be in parentheses in the text.

13 See Walter Benn Michaels, *The Shape of the Signifier: 1967 to the End of History* (Princeton and London, 2004), 84–93, 113–14. See also Jennifer Ashton, *From Modernism to Postmodernism: American Poetry and Theory in the Twentieth Century* (Cambridge and New York, 2006), 175. Further page references to the latter will be in parentheses in the text.

14 E.g., in "Introduction (Optional)," *FHO*, 1–27.

15 See Ashton's ch. 5, "Authorial inattention: Donald Davidson's literalism, Jorie Graham's *Materialism*, and cognitive science's embodied minds," 146–76. The text by Edwards quoted by Graham and discussed by Ashton is *The Great Christian Doctrine of Original Sin Defended* (1758). Ashton writes toward the end of her chapter: "In short, what distinguishes the presence of meaning/intention from any succession of effects is, finally, what distinguishes art from objects for Fried and divine from human knowledge for Edwards. Put in terms of the . . . conclusion of 'Art and Objecthood,' 'Presentness is grace'" (175). One of the (to me) startling revelations of Ashton's book is that Gertrude Stein, routinely conscripted to an aesthetics of indeterminacy and more broadly to Post-Modernism *avant la lettre*, should instead be understood as a singularly lucid and uncompromising theorist of modernism.

16 See my essay "Sala with Schiller: World, Form and Play in *Mixed Behaviour*," in *Anri Sala*, exh. cat. (London, 2011), 97–104; and nonsite.org, issue #5, March 18, 2012.

17 For *Long Sorrow* and *After Three Minutes* see *FHO*, 32–66.

18 Demand uses the term "slapstick" in the conversation with Ryan cited in n. 4 as well in the conversation at the Getty cited in n. 5 above.

19 Demand said this in the course of his introductory remarks at the Getty, cited in n. 5 above.

20 Charles Baudelaire, "On the Essence of Laughter," in *The Painter of Modern Life, and Other Essays*, trans. Jonathan Mayne (London, 1964), 157. Further page references will be in parentheses in the text.

21 Baudelaire adds that the "absolute comic . . . presents itself as a *unity* which calls for the intuition to grasp it" (ibid; translation modified, emphasis in original), which seems to place it in an implicitly aesthetic register.

Another German text with analogies to the action of *Pacific Sun*, especially the sense of events flying out of control as emblematized by proliferating objects, is Goethe's "The Sorcerer's Apprentice," a ballad in fourteen stanzas written in 1797. Briefly, an apprentice sorcerer enchants a broom to fetch water for him, but the broom does much too good a job and the young apprentice soon discovers that he has no idea how to stop the flooding that threatens to inundate the entire house. The 1940 Disney film *Fantasia* made "The Sorcerer's Apprentice" the basis of one of eight sequences set to classical music, in this case to a symphonic poem by Paul Dukas. My thanks to Molly Warnock for encouraging me to make the connection.

22 On *Play Dead* see *FHO*, 166–77.

23 As are the projections in *Play Dead*.

24 Demand interviewed by Daniel Kehlmann, *Art Review*, 58 (April 2012), accessible at www.artreview.com/profile/blogs/thomas-demand-daniel-kehlmann.

25 Hans Blumenberg, *Shipwreck with Spectator: Paradigm of a Metaphor for Existence*, trans. Steven Rendell (Cambridge, Mass., and London, 1997), 7–8.

26 Demand interviewed by Kehlmann, cited in n. 24 above. Demand describes the difficulties caused by microtremors in his conversation with Ryan, cited in n. 4 above.

INDEX

Page numbers in *italics* refer to figures.

COPYRIGHT AND PHOTOGRAPH CREDITS

© RMN - Grand Palais/Philipp Bernard/Lille, Palais des Beaux-Arts: 2

Image © The Metropolitan Museum of Art: 4

Statens Museum for Kunst/National Gallery of Denmark, www.smk.dk: 5

© RMN-Grand Palais (musée du Louvre) / René-Gabriel Ojéda : 7

© RMN-Grand Palais (Château de Versailles) / Gérard Blot: 8

Photograph © The State Hermitage Museum /photo by Vladimir Terebenin, Leonard Kheifets, Yuri Molodkovets.: 9

© The Cleveland Museum of Art: 10

Pushkin Museum, Moscow, Russia / Bridgeman Images: 16

© RMN-Grand Palais (musée d'Orsay) / Hervé Lewandowski:17

U. Edelmann–Städel Museum/ARTOTHEK: 18

© RMN-Grand Palais (Château de Versailles) / Peter Willi: 20

Musées royaux des Beaux-Arts de Belgique, Brussels © 2014. Photo Fine Art Images/Heritage Images/Scala, Florence: 21

Photograph courtesy of the Denver Art Museum: 24

Photo © The Cleveland Museum of Art: 25

© RMN-Grand Palais (musée du Louvre) / Gérard Blot: 26, 29

Pinacoteca di Brera, Milan © 2014. Photo Scala, Florence. Courtesy of the Ministero Beni e Att. Culturali: 27

Musées royaux des Beaux-Arts de Belgique, Brussels © 2014. Photo Scala, Florence: 28

Galleria degli Uffizi, Florence © 2014. Photo Scala, Florence. Courtesy of the Ministero Beni e Att. Culturali: 30

Photo © The Walters Art Museum, Baltimore: 32

Louvre, Paris, France / Giraudon / Bridgeman Images: 33, 34, 50, 69, 73

Louvre, Paris, France / Bridgeman Images: 35, 38, 46, 49, 31, 76

© RMN-Grand Palais (musée du Louvre) / Daniel Arnaudet: 36, 51

© RMN-Grand Palais (musée du Louvre) / Hervé Lewandowski: 37

© RMN-Grand Palais (musée du Louvre) /René-Gabriel Ojéda: 39, 53

© RMN-Grand Palais (musée du Louvre) / Michèle Bellot: 40, 45, 54, 58

Photo © RMN-Grand Palais / Philipp Bernard: 41

Musée Fabre, Montpellier, France /Bridgeman Images: 42

Photo © Nationalmuseum, Stockholm:43

Palais des Beaux-Arts, Lille, France / Giraudon / Bridgeman Images: 44

Imaging Department © President and Fellows of Harvard College: 47, 57

© RMN-Grand Palais (musée du Louvre) / Jean-Gilles Berizzi: 48, 55

© RMN-Grand Palais (musée du Louvre) / Gérard Blot / Christian Jean: 52

© RMN-Grand Palais (musée du Louvre) / Franck Raux: 56

Bibliothèque nationale de France: 59, 60, 61, 63, 64, 65, 66, 68, 133

Musée du Louvre, Paris © 2014. White Images/Scala, Florence: 62, 77

Musée des Beaux-Arts, Rouen, France / Giraudon / Bridgeman Images: 67

Musée de la Ville de Paris, Musée du Petit-Palais, France / Giraudon / Bridgeman Images: 70

Museum Pio Clementino, Vatican © 2014. Photo Scala, Florence: 71

Photography by Erik Gould, courtesy of the Museum of Art, Rhode Island School of Design, Providence: 72

Musée des Beaux-Arts, Lyon, France / Bridgeman Images: 74

Museum Folkwang, Essen, West Germany / Bridgeman Images: 86

Copyright-Vermerk: Klassik Stiftung Weimar, Bestand Museen: 85

bpk / Nationalgalerie, Staatliche Museen zu Berlin / Jörg P. Anders: 87, 97, 100, 106

bpk / Hamburger Kunsthalle / Elke Walford: 89, 90, 112, 115

© ARTOTHEK: 91, 92

Photograph © The State Hermitage Museum /photo by Vladimir Terebenin, Leonard Kheifets, Yuri Molodkovets: 94, 99, 103

Staatsgalerie Stuttgart, © Foto: Staatsgalerie Stuttgart: 95

Photo:SIK-ISEA (Philipp Hitz): 96, 104

Pommersches Landesmuseum, Griefswald: 98

bpk / Staatliche Kunstsammlungen Dresden / Jürgen Karpinski: 101

David Hall/ARTOTHEK: 102

bpk / Staatliche Kunstsammlungen Dresden / Elke Estel / Hans-Peter Klut : 105

bpk / Bayerische Staatsgemäldesammlungen: 108, 110, 111, 134

bpk / Nationalgalerie, Staatliche Museen zu Berlin / Leihgabe der DekaBank / Jörg P. Anders: 109

bpk / Museum der bildenden Künste, Leipzig / Bertram Kober (Punctum Leipzig): 113, 114

Private Collection / Bridgeman Images: 117, 118, 120, 122, 130, 132, 143

Musée d'Orsay, Paris, France / Bridgeman Images: 121

Image © The Metropolitan Museum of Art: 123

Courtesy National Gallery of Art, Washington: 128, 181

Petit Palais, Geneva, Switzerland / Bridgeman Images: 129

Photography © The Art Institute of Chicago: 131, 139

Michael Cavanagh and Kevin Montague: 135

Minneapolis Institute of Arts, MN, USA / The John R. Van Derlip Fund / Bridgeman Images: 136

Photograph © 2014 Museum of Fine Arts, Boston. Museum purchase with funds by exchange from an Anonymous gift, Bequest of William A. Coolidge, Juliana Cheney Edwards Collection, and from the Charles H. Bayley Picture and Painting Fund, Edward Jackson Holmes Fund, Fanny P. Mason Fund in memory of Alice Thevin, Arthur Gordon Tompkins Fund, Gift of Mrs Samuel Parkman Oliver- Eliza R. Oliver Fund, Sophie F. Friedman Fund, Robert M. Rosenberg Family Fund, and funds donated in honour of George T. M. Shackelford, Chair, Art of Europe, and Arthur K. Solomon Curator of Modern Art, 1996-2011 2011.31: 137

Foto: © Rheinisches Bildarchiv Köln, rba_c004549: 140

Photo © RMN-Grand Palais (musée d'Orsay)/ Martine Beck-Coppola: 142

© 2014. Digital image, The Museum of Modern Art, New York/Scala, Florence: 145

Alinari Archives-Anderson Archive, Florence: 146

Scrovegni Chapel, Padua © 2014. Photo Scala, Florence: 147, 157

© The National Gallery, London: 148

Vatican, Pinacoteca. © 2014. Photo Scala, Florence: 149

Sistine Chapel, Vatican © 2014. Photo Scala, Florence: 150

Museum Boijmans Van Beuningen, Rotterdam © 2014. Photo Fine Art Image/Heritage Images/Scala, Florence: 151

Courtauld Institute Galleries, London © 2014. DeAgostini Picture Library/Scala, Florence:152

Alinari Archives-Alinari Archive, Florence: 155

© Tate, London 2014: 156

Pinacoteca di Brera, Milan© 2014. Photo Scala, Florence – courtesy of the Ministero Beni e Att. Culturali: 158